Key:
1 Wm Denny & Bros Ltd, Dumbarton Engine Works
2 Wm Denny & Bros Ltd, Leven Shipyard, Dumbarton
3 Scott & Sons Ltd, Bowling Shipyard
4 John Brown & Co (Clydebank) Ltd, Shipyard & Engine Works
5 Barclay Curle & Co Ltd, Elderslie Dry Docks
6 Yarrow & Co Ltd, Scotstoun Shipyard & Engine Works
7 Blythswood Shipbuilding Co Ltd, Scotstoun Shipyard
8 Chas Connell & Co Ltd, Scotstoun Shipyard
9 Barclay Curle & Co Ltd, North British Engine Works
10 Barclay Curle & Co Ltd, Clydeholm Shipyard
11 D. & W. Henderson Meadowside Dry Dock & Repair Quay
12 A. & J. Inglis Ltd, Pointhouse Shipyard
13 David Rowan & Co Ltd, Finnieston Engine Works
14 Harland & Wolff Ltd, Finnieston Engine Works
15 British Polar Engines Ltd, Govan Engine Works
16 Harland & Wolff Ltd, Govan Shipyard

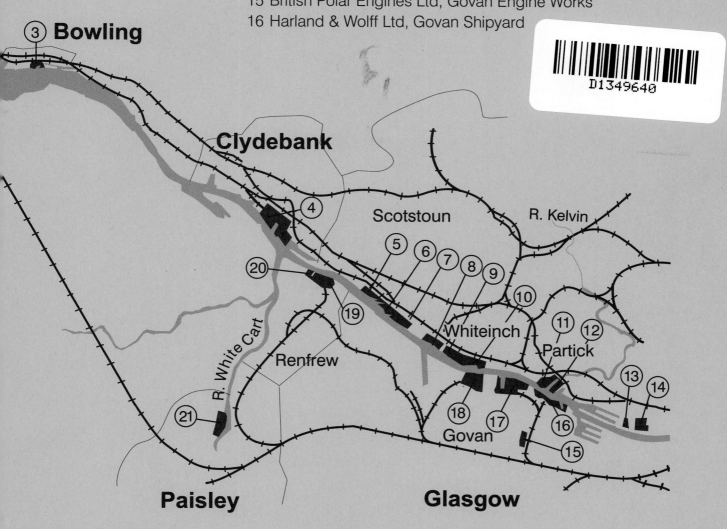

Bowling

Clydebank

Scotstoun

R. Kelvin

Whiteinch

Partick

Renfrew

R. White Cart

Govan

Paisley

Glasgow

0   1   2
Scale miles

IRONFIGHTERS,
OUTFITTERS
and
BOWLER HATTERS

Geo. C. O'Hara

Copyright: First Published 1997
                              ISBN 0 9530821 0 5
                              © Clyard Novella Ltd 1997
                              All rights reserved
                              No part of this publication may be reproduced or
                              stored in any form without the prior permission of
                              the copyright holders.
                              Jacket design from an original idea by E.M. O'Hara

Published by: Clyard Novella Ltd
                              16 Garryhorn
                              Prestwick
                              South Ayrshire
                              Scotland KA9 2HU

Typesetting by: Frances J. Anderson
                              Desk Top Publishing
                              32 Little Road
                              Edinburgh EH16 6SQ

Colour separation and   Arneg Ltd
film output by: 88 Bell Street
                              Glasgow G1 1QL

Printed and bound by: Lothian Print
                              7 New Lairdship Yards
                              Broomhouse Road
                              Edinburgh EH11 3UY

IRONFIGHTERS, OUTFITTERS AND BOWLER HATTERS

Description of photographs portrayed on the cover and frontispiece of this book

COVER CAPTIONS

The set of photographs on the front cover of the book attempts to graphically illustrate the meaning of its title – *Ironfighters, Outfitters and Bowler Hatters*. On the back are a number of views showing scenes of activity associated with some of the former Clydeside shipyards who employed ironfighters, outfitters and bowler hatters.

Front cover top depicts a group of steelworkers setting the night alight, performing some 'ironfighting' inside part of the starboard pontoon of yard no. 1200, e.s.v. IOLAIR 11,019 g.r.t. under construction at the Glen/East yard complex of Scott-Lithgow Ltd during 1980. (Burniston Studios Ltd)

Front cover bottom left depicts an assemblage of steelworkers, outfit workers, lady and gentleman guests in their best 'outfits' about to watch the launch of yard no. 825, m.v. NILI 7851 g.r.t. from the Govan shipyard of the Fairfield SB & Eng Co Ltd on the beautiful day of 11 August 1964. (Burniston Studios Ltd)

Front cover bottom right depicts the impending launch of yard no. 501, m.v. BENARMIN 10,870 g.r.t. from Scotstoun shipyard of Chas Connell & Co Ltd on the 26 April 1963. Addressing the group of workers between the fore poppet launch cradle and the VIP platform is Mr R.E. Butler, shipyard general manager resplendent in his slate grey suit and black 'bowler hat'. (Burniston Studios Ltd)

Back cover top left depicts the first launch about to take place from the then brand new Clydeholm shipyard of Barclay Curle & Co Ltd, Whiteinch, of yard no. 744, m.v. CITY OF SYDNEY 10,551 g.r.t. on 24 May 1960. Note the limosines belonging to management and guests parked near the launch platform.

Back cover top right depicts yard no. 127, m.t. BRITISH GANNET 11,238 g.r.t. entering the filthy water of the River Clyde from the Scotstoun shipyard of the Blythswood Shipbuilding Co Ltd on the hazy day of 5 June 1959.

Back cover centre left depicts the former west yard of John Brown & Co (Clydebank) Ltd, then operating as the Clydebank Division of Upper Clyde Shipbuilders Ltd, on the stormy day of 3 September 1971. Visible on the two berths of the bisected yard are a pair of Clyde class cargo liners, from left to right yard no. 118, m.v. VARDA 11,895 g.r.t. and one of her four sisterships yard no. 119, m.v. ORLI 11,897 g.r.t. (George C. O'Hara)

Back cover centre right depicts the entire waterfront of the Cartsburn Dockyard of Scotts SB & Eng Co Ltd (then part of Scott-Lithgow Ltd) in the autumn of 1977. In the fitting out basin is yard no. 746, dynamically positioned drilling ship PACNORSE 1 10,820 g.r.t., recently launched from the group's Cartsdyke Dockyard. Nearing completion on one of the yard's two main berths is yard no. 738, r.f.a. FORT AUSTIN 16,053 g.r.t. The extensive row of red-brick buildings facing the road comprised the yard offices, and on the other side can be seen part of the company's marine engine works. (Burniston Studios Ltd)

Back cover bottom left depicts part of the extensive Scotstoun waterfront of Yarrow Shipbuilders Ltd in early 1971. Noticeable in the river are a pair of Leander class frigates fitting out, whilst the hull of another is under construction on one of the yard's open berths. The large light grey building is the company's then new covered building hall which was built on the site of the former Blythswood S.B. Co Ltd yard, four of whose former hammerhead cranes can still be seen framing the new facility.

Back cover bottom right depicts a bygone scene once regularly synonymous with the former River Clyde shipbuilding industry. Yard no. 497, m.v. CLAN MACNAB 9428 g.r.t. sails past the famous landmark of Cloch lighthouse, with part of the town of Dunoon, the Holy Loch and the Cowal Hills of Argyll forming the background. She is returning to the Greenock Dockyard Co Ltd, the yard who built her after performing part of her sea trials during April 1961. (Burniston Studios Ltd)

FRONTISPIECE CAPTIONS

Four pictures which illustrate the dynamic shipbuilding activity that formerly existed on the River Clyde in the post-war era. Scenes like these regularly occurred about twice a week up until 1962.

Top view depicts yard no. 677, s.t. BRITISH SAILOR 20,961 g.r.t. under tow by a pair of tugs passing the north bank landmark of Dumbarton Castle, perched on top of Dumbarton Rock. The oil tanker is on route to the Firth of Clyde to begin her sea trials in the spring of 1953. Built and engined by John Brown & Co (Clydebank) Ltd for the Anglo-Iranian Oil Co Ltd, London (later BP Tankers Ltd), she was at the time of launching the largest oil tanker built on the River Clyde. She remained with her original owners until 1972 when she was sold and renamed MARISIRA, being broken up in 1980 under the name of FAGR. The cranes of the then busy Leven shipyard of Wm Denny & Bros Ltd are quite noticeable in the background, as is part of the peak of Ben Lomond 3192 ft, over twenty miles further north in the county of Stirlingshire.

Centre view left depicts yard no. 727, m.v. WINDSOR 7652 g.r.t. immediately after her launching by H.R.H. The Princess Royal on 23 May 1952. Built and engined by Barclay Curle & Co Ltd, this simple yet highly stylish looking vessel was the first of four ships built by the Whiteinch company for the Britain SS Co Ltd, London. Designed by the eminent naval architect Edmund Watts, who was a joint owner of that shipping company, she was sold and renamed JAG KETU in 1963. In 1967 she became the EASTERN LION, as which she was presumably broken up in 1993, after a forty year career. Noticeable in this picture are a number of ships being fitted-out on the Shieldhall side of the river, having recently been launched by Alexr Stephen & Sons Ltd, Linthouse. Moored alongside the wharf of the North British Engine Works on the opposite bank is the s.s. UGANDA 14,430 g.r.t. launched by Barclay Curle earlier that year. This stylish vessel lasted until 1986 when she was renamed TRITON for her tow to the breakers' yard. Throughout the 1950s all of the fitting-out quays and wet basins on Clydeside were occupied with the sight of newly launched ships, or older vessels being repaired or converted.

Centre view right depicts yard no. 505, m.v. HELLENIC TORCH 7510 g.r.t. prior to her launching from the Glen shipyard of Wm Hamilton & Co Ltd, Port Glasgow on 21 August 1956. Note the group of impatient shipwrights in the foreground itching to clear the berth after the launch and lay-down the keel of the next new ship order, some of the frames for which are stored in the foreground. Engined by the Fairfield SB & Eng Co Ltd, for Hellenic Lines Ltd of Piræus, this vessel remained with these owners until 1981, when she was sold and renamed CHALLENGE, as which she was broken up in 1982. (Burniston Studios Ltd)

Bottom view depicts yard no. 783, s.t. NORDIC HAWK 22,920 g.r.t. under tow by a trio of tugs passing the location of Renfrew Ferry on route to the Firth of Clyde to commence her sea trials in the month of January 1959. Built and engined by the Fairfield SB & Eng Co Ltd for Nordic Tankships I/S Copenhagen (Dansk BP), this well-proportioned vessel was the second of a pair of large tankers ordered from the yard by BP, her sister ship was the s.t. BRITISH ENERGY completed a year earlier. She retained her original name until 1970 when she was sold and renamed THIRESSIA VENIZELOS as which she was broken up in 1977. Noticeable up-river from the stern of the ship are a number of vessels under repair or conversion at the Elderslie Docks of Barclay Curle & Co Ltd. This popular river crossing point between the district of Yoker on the north bank and the town of Renfrew on the other side of the river became used less frequently after the opening of the Clyde Tunnel in 1963. The chain operated ferry had always to give way to river shipping, an inconvenience that was then quite common due to the extensive shipbuilding, ship-repairing and commercial maritime activity in the port of Glasgow. The ferry still existed in 1996, bereft of her chains, the car deck covered over, being used as a floating entertainment centre moored up-river at the Broomielaw.

ACKNOWLEDGMENTS

Few Clydeside families existed without either a direct involvement, or indirect awareness of shipbuilding. This ranged from being a major employer of labour, to a source that impinged on their everyday life, usually through noise pollution, or exposure to regular headline stories that exaggerated the magnitude of unrest in the industry. This pervasive acquaintance existed from the last century well into the 1980s.

As a young boy growing up in the Whiteinch district of Glasgow during the 1950s, the author was conscious of the pulsating dynamism generated by a sprawl of adjacent busy shipbuilding companies. Lunch break at primary school was frequently spent viewing various ships being built, usually seen from one of the free ferries that then crossed the River Clyde. Regular launchings of new ships from the open berths of these nearby yards made this recreation more enthralling.

Some years later, acceptance as an apprentice draughtsman into one of these former shipyards realised a boyhood ambition to work in this vibrant industry. The personal change encountered from leaving school to starting work, was leavened by a traditional protective training system that disbursed an inexhaustible supply of technical erudition from a free-tap of experience. Outpouring of information was administered by virtually the whole spectrum of employees from tradesmen to shipyard general manager. The 'two-way street' of training resulting in knowledge was a byway of responsibility discharged with gusto and pride by men towards apprentices in their charge, usually by sight of example that would be repeated to ensure absorption.

Fortunate to have met a wide spectrum of interested, committed, capable men during this short, halcyon period of character building, the author soon became aware of the reality and credulity of the much-used hallmark 'Clyde built'. Whilst a free-flow of explanation was selectively passed to almost any apprentice who sought such information, individual keenness became dampened by the formidable, yet invisible, barriers created by the incomprehensible retention of craft inflexibility. This resistance to change was as indomitable in trades foremen as it was amongst artisans. Realisation of the antiquated attitudes which thralled shipbuilding gradually led to disillusionment of a long term career hewn from such industrial myopia.

The much vaunted collective 'no holds barred' spectral analysis mooted as necessary to modernise, restructure, and recapitalise shipbuilding whilst it was still a major industry, was alas never successfully accomplished. The motley collection of culpable individuals who represented trade unions, yard managements, civil servants and cabinet ministers from both major UK parties, allowed their collective ineptitude coupled with profligate squandering of public money and wanton dereliction of opportunity, to greatly assist the Far East with its current position of domination of world shipbuilding.

The author spent two separate periods of employment in Clyde shipyards, as an apprentice, then a decade later as a project engineer. Further spells were spent in down-river offshore module and rig building yards that had strong shipbuilding histories. This book is an individual objective critique of River Clyde traditional shipbuilding circa 1946–1987. Observations and statistics are based on factual records, gleaned from a diverse array of archive material.

Ironfighters, Outfitters and Bowler Hatters were some of the nicknames bestowed on the three main labour elements of the industry. *Ironfighters* included the collective array of steelwork trades and helpers, *outfitters* comprised the myriad of engineering subcontract and finishing crafts, and *bowler hatters* were the management who supervised all of them. Commentary followed by assertions are formed from a detached personal viewpoint within the middle of the industrial spectrum, that hopefully apportions criticism and compliment without favour. All opinions expressed throughout are entirely those of the writer.

The author is indebted to many ex-workers, from directors, managers, tradesmen and helpers who painstakingly attempted to instill within him some technical, practical and street-wise nous during his time in shipbuilding. Their unflinching perseverance and encouragement is appreciated with grateful thanks. Furthermore, their commitment, contribution and creation of volume shipbuilding in the West of Scotland provided the driving force for this book. This dissertation on such a labour intensive, artistically creative subject as volume shipbuilding, cannot be covered in narrative alone. The 607 photographs that graphically depict the effort and output from shipbuilders of yore, illustrate many of the diverse range of ship types previously built by the shipyards and engine works on Clydeside during the period of this book. This extensive pictorial representation has been possible due to the help and cooperation of those photographers and industrial studios appended below.

Views of all of the former shipyards, engine works and repair docks have been included. Alas, most of their former locations have been transformed into derelict wasteland, domestic housing schemes, or shopping centres, with only a few previous works regenerated for new industrial development. The map on page 355 depicts the actual sites of all of the companies portrayed in the following text.

Additionally, the author wishes to thank the following individuals, companies, custodians of archives and other sources for their time, effort and assistance with research, confirmation, corroboration, compilation or criticism during the protracted preparation phase.

D.B. Adair, Aerofilms, K. Alexander, J.P. Allan, T.M. Allison, Sir A.R. Belch, Ben Line Ltd, BP Archives (c/o University of Warwick), BP Photographic, T. Bryce, Carnegie Library (Ayr), Clyde Shipping Co Ltd, Clydebank Library, E.H. Cole, C.R. Connell, A. Cowne, J. Cox, C.B.I. Statistical Information Office, J. & J. Denholm Ltd, A. Duncan, J. Dobson, Ferguson Shipbuilders Ltd, Jas. Fisher & Sons Ltd, Glasgow District Archives (formerly Strathclyde Regional Archives), Glasgow University Archives, J. Goodall, J. Gospel, T. Gourley, J. Grant, Greenock Telegraph, J. Hall, M. Humphrey, A. Inglis, B. Jones, Kværner-Govan Ltd, Kværner-Kincaid Ltd, M. Kingsley, Dr. Wm. Lind, Sir Wm. Lithgow, Lloyds Register of Shipping (Information Department), H. McGranachan, I. McLullich, G.K. Morgan, S. Morris, L. Palmer, C. Parker, A. Paton, A. Peill, P & O Ltd (Archive & Information Department), I. Ramsay, J. Reid, Dr. J.F. Robb, J. Rorke, K. Roscamp, Safmarine Ltd, A. Sanders, Scottish Maritime Museum, Scottish Record Office, The Shipbuilding and Shipping Record, Prof. A. Slaven, W.A.C. Smith, A.M.M. Stephen, W. Swan, The Scotsman Publications Ltd, N. Thomson, Texaco Overseas Tankships Ltd, M. Tilney, L. Ubee, UIE (Scotland) Ltd, Ulster Folk & Transport Museum, W. Weyndling, R. Whitelaw, M. Willis, Yarrow Shipbuilders Ltd, David Young, Geo. Young Photographers.

With special thanks to:

- Mrs Beatrice O'Hara for thorough deciphering of the vast amount of handwritten text, thence assiduously typing this wordy work, a task that strained, yet nevertheless affirmed the probity of marriage.
- K.T.C. O'Hara for the painstaking compilation and interpolation of the bulk of the statistical matrices.
- J.B. McLeod for rendering his meticulous computer skills to transform the raw narrative into concise compact disc format.
- J.M. McIntosh of Jim McIntosh Photography, Unit #5, Halfway Business Centre, Glasgow G20, for permission to use many pictures from the extensive former Ralston Photographic Collection of industrial archives. Unless noted otherwise, *all* illustrations without credits appended are reproduced by kind permission of Jim McIntosh.
- Norman Burniston for permission to use various pictures from the huge James Hall Collection of Industrial Archives. Norman Burniston can be contacted at Burniston Studios Ltd, Annet Lodge, 14 Shore Road, Skelmorlie, PA17 5DY.

DEDICATION

This book is dedicated to the thousands of workers who were employed in post-war River Clyde shipbuilding and marine engineering, and in particular to the memory of Frank Hunter and Donald MacLennan, both section leaders in the former drawing office of Charles Connell & Co Ltd, Scotstoun, Glasgow. The author is thankful to this pair of august gents for their generous teaching of technical nous, as well as imparting subtle influences on the development of his character. Furthermore, their unique forte for continual wryness of wit, no matter how eminent the company, or serious the situation, combined to create a balance of humour and pathos that has long been admired, but never emulated.

FOOTNOTE: With the passing of time, less and less of the workers who built the impressive total of nearly 2,000 vessels on the River Clyde in the four decades since World War II remain alive. Equally, the expiry of design duration, onset of inflationary running costs, along with developing technology and increasing safety regulations, continually consigns more of these craft to the shipbreakers yards. In the not too distant future, when all those who designed and built such a formidable array of ships have passed away, it will be left to the custodians of museums to try and preserve a few tangible reminders of this once great industry. Furthermore, current prices for scrap, ironically, sometimes value the recoverable metals and materials of these vessels greater than the cost of their construction many years earlier.

George C. O'Hara
Prestwick, South Ayrshire, Scotland
January 1997

FOREWORD

The Clyde isn't just a river it's a way of life. The word resonates with ships and shipbuilding, of a unique culture spawned and shaped by the river and that industry. The Clyde is synonymous with marine engineering and engineering excellence. Clyde built was a guarantee of quality. In literature a chief engineer was invariably a Scot trained somewhere on Clydeside. The tradition extends to outer space. The engineer on Starship Enterprise was—surprise, surprise—called Scotty! The steamship and the hovercraft were pioneered on the Clyde. Post sail shipbuilding came of age on the Clyde. Twenty-five per cent of world shipping was once built on the Clyde.

A ship cannot be built on a conveyor belt. They are built from the ground up. Sections and components are added and assembled. No matter how the process is rationalised, modifications and adaptations remain part of the process. Bits and pieces are joined together to an overall plan and design. Everything is interconnected. The multiplicity of skills must mesh for they're essentially interdependent. The ship is a highly social product. There is collective pride when the overall plan is realised. The launch of a ship was a social event, time for a party. When it sails away there is sadness akin to the departure of a well-loved daughter from the family hearth.

To the men who built her a ship is a she—a lady. They take pride in her beauty. In her purity. She is, they insist, of good stock. I've heard shipyard workers arguing heatedly about which ship from the Clyde was the most beautiful. The exchanges could be heated. Aesthetics, whether the word was ever used, was integral to our shipbuilding concepts. The workers, far from being alienated from the finished product by the often far from congenial conditions of work, actually identified with it to an extent that applied in no other heavy industry. I saw workers in Clydebank weep when the *Queen Elizabeth* had been ravaged by fire and sank in Hong Kong Bay. It's difficult to imagine a car worker weep because a Ford Prefect had been burnt to a frazzle on a motorway.

Shipbuilding communities were often poor but they were communities with a sense of interdependence, a collective sense of responsibility. They closed ranks when times were bad. You have to have a sense of humour to walk into a shipyard at 7.30 on a cold winter's morning when it isn't yet light. In the words of the old Negro blues singer, *you had to laugh to stop from cryin'*. This became the humour of Clydeside. From Tommy Lorne to Billy Connolly.

Shipbuilding, alas, has all but gone from the Clyde. There was nothing natural about this. Nothing inevitable or inexorable about the industry's decline and fall. Like other British manufacturing industries it died of investment starvation between 1900 and 1955 as Britain started exporting capital at the expense of goods. By the 1960s British shipbuilding was in crisis faced with the competition of hi-tech yards from Europe and Asia. There is no viable economic alternative to ships for the mass transportation of cargos across the seas. Ships are still being built but not, by and large, by us.

We need books that remind us of our heritage. Not for nostalgia's sake but so that we may learn from the past, from our wise moves and mistakes, particularly the mistakes. In his book *Ironfighters, Outfitters and Bowler Hatters*, George O'Hara has gone a long way to meeting this need. He deals essentially with the post-war years, years of great achievements and then rapid decline. His research has been immense. In a sense it is a reference book but it's more than that. He seeks to analyse the reasons for decline and does so with passion. He was an apprentice in the yards and became a qualified engineer, with a successful career outside shipbuilding, and yet that remains his first love.

He's produced this book in his spare time in different parts of the world where his work had taken him. He has pride in the Clyde's achievements and anger at those he perceives as having brought this precious tradition to a halt. You might not agree with all his detailed points or emphases, but overall I think his critique is valid. I take from it a certain pride in past glories and a rekindled belief that shipbuilding should have its place on the Clyde of the next century. Why not?

Jimmy Reid

Chapter 1

INTRODUCTION

For decades, the cacophony of men manipulating metal into the contours and contents of steel ships, resonated from the many shipyards and marine engine works that once lined the banks of the River Clyde. These establishments stretched from the industrial hamlet of Govan, in the heart of the city of Glasgow, to the golfing resort of Troon, some seventy miles away on the eastern shore of the Firth of Clyde.

The tenemental skyline of the adjacent conurbations was once profusely interspersed with the lattice structures of over a hundred jibs, derricks and hammerhead cranes. These towered and stooped over open building berths, barely discernible as such between the teeming amount of uprights and staging that were criss-crossed like a giant stockade. This formed the crude scaffold grillage, which provided the far from safe access, bereft of weather protection for those working on the external framing and shell plating of ships under construction.

The magnitude of this infernal clanging is nowadays much diminished as a result of the extensive contraction of volume shipbuilding and marine engineering, arguably the most famous duo in the West of Scotland's distinguished industrial past. Established in a relatively short duration within the second half of the nineteenth century, marine engine manufacture was effectively conceived and developed in the West of Scotland, due to the earlier engineering inventiveness of James Watt of Greenock. Subsequent innovative engineer disciples later improved, redesigned and duly patented better types of steam reciprocating engines. With greater power from higher thermal efficiency these ships created cheaper running costs which stimulated demand for, and later development of, bigger and faster steam ships. It made sound economic sense to locate the shipyards that would build these new vessels adjacent to this centre of marine engineering expertise. In fact, the first batch of shipyards were extensions of engine building companies, indeed the embryonic science of naval architecture was spawned from these advances in marine engineering.

When the use of iron and later steel instead of wood for ships' hulls was eventually appreciated, the County of Lanarkshire, east of Glasgow was hastily exploited as a desirable location for the establishment of iron and steel-making. This area possessed vast resources of indigenous coal, sufficient initial amounts of iron ore to originate a smelting industry, good rail connections to easily transport finished products, and later import quantities of iron and limestone when these became required.

With a plentiful supply of cheap labour, Central Scotland rapidly became a steel-making centre, close enough to the River Clyde to make the establishment of a steel shipbuilding industry a feasible notion. Once ensconced, the industry made extensive profits for yard-owners during its irregular boom years, giving meaningful, though mostly tenuous and parsimonious employment to tens of thousands of workers over the best part of a century. The random engagement of the shipbuilding industry labour force on each successive new ship contract, gave purposeful impetus to the need for the collective representation of workers. The assiduous establishment and gradual ascendancy of trade unions representing virtually every type of employee, created a power base whose strength varied according to whether shipbuilding was in one of its 'boom or bust' cycles.

The formation of similar organisations to represent the interest of the shipbuilding and marine engineering employers, resulted with the concurrent establishment of bosses' cartels, called The Clyde Shipbuilders Association and the Engineering Employers Federation.

Neither of these disparate, contentious faculties representing workers or employers actually created high levels of employment. Each were steeped in a perverse form of mutual esteem, interspersed with reciprocal disdain. They were inextricably linked to either their correlative survival or common destruction, depending on the ideology or dogma of their respective leaders. Such entrenchment of polarised doctrines remained features of shipbuilding, and to a lesser extent marine engineering from their inception, until their contraction and virtual elimination as major industries within the United Kingdom.

Immediately after World War II, the shipyards of Britain shouldered most of the burden of replacing the vast tonnage of shipping lost during the hostilities. This monumental task was borne by an industry practically exhausted as a result of the immense wartime building effort, eked out of tired men, and women, working with outmoded machinery or equipment. Difficulty among British shipbuilding companies in meeting peacetime demand from ship-owners at home and overseas, was further compounded by the protracted enforcement of rationing of essential materials by HM Government. This austerity measure of the late forties through the early fifties affected the supply of steel for shipbuilding, which was limited to one million tons for the entire UK shipbuilding industry.

Some of the major issues and resolutions confronting post-war shipyard managements were to wrest from the diverse array of artisans and helpers the establishment of peacetime wage rates, more flexible practices of operation and other unpalatable facets of non-wartime working conditions. The internecine discourse that emanated from these edicts was to remain synonymous with an industry, whose few excellent, largely unsung achievements were almost always discredited by factious widespread disputes and, arguably, the worst public relations profile in British industry.

Much of this deep rooted enmity between workers and management, was a throwback from the 'not so good old days' of casual labour which were within living memory of more than half the work force employed during the pre-war years of the great depression. The perfunctory safety profile, that saw accidents and fatalities as regular statistics of work within shipbuilding, meant that yard-owners and managers were rarely viewed as altruistic bosses. Regrettably this widely held view of the industries' management compounded the public conception of shipbuilding's perpetually woeful labour relations.

Despite its dreadful PR, shipbuilding was perhaps the most undervalued industry in Britain. This was definitely so in the West of Scotland, where approximately 100,000 mostly skilled men were employed during the early part of this century. Much more than that amount of men and women were employed in the support industries which existed in either essential or service capacities to shipbuilding. Some of these downstream industries employed young journeymen recently trained in their respective crafts from either a shipyard or marine engine works. This lengthy chain of meaningful employment, ranged from miners digging coal to provide fuel for the power stations, that sent electricity to the shipyard substation, steelmakers and founders who formed the plates, sections, pipes and castings, to upholsterers, carpet makers and many others who produced some of the internal ship furnishings.

These products would be carried by trains and lorries to the shipyards, for installation aboard the ships which contained thousands of items as unique and diverse as glass for windows, valves for plumbing, locks for doors, wire ropes for derricks, cables, lights, baths, basins and curtains for inside cabins. In effect the inventory of accoutrements installed in a ship was akin to that required of a small town, with the facilities provided being as varied as propulsion, power generation, fresh water making, food storage, communications, sewage treatment equipment, fire-fighting and cargo handling.

The last peacetime boom years of Clyde shipbuilding from 1946 to 1962 didn't employ the large numbers involved in the early part of the twentieth century. However, it has to be admitted that most of the ships completed during these later years, were built utilising partial fabrication techniques, instead of the single frame, single plate, single pipe, single door, single window, erection methods of the previous epoch. The output during this latter era was prolific and impressive, both in content and complexity. Alas it is unfortunate that the production statistics emanating from this period were always prefaced or eclipsed by peripheral reference to the industry's parallel record of disputes and stoppages.

Nearly 2,000 ships with a total in excess of 12 million gross registered tons were launched between 1946 and 1987, when Scott-Lithgow Ltd launched the semi-submersible drilling rig, *Ocean Alliance* 15,517 g.r.t., thus effectively ending volume shipbuilding on the River Clyde. The year of greatest output was 1955 when 74 ships of 471,556 g.r.t. and eight naval craft totalling 8,292 tons displacement were launched. No mean feat when it is remembered that as each ship was completed some workers were usually made redundant. It was also the transitional era when riveted content was still a significant part of Clyde built ships. Constructed in traditional shipyards, whose owners were wringing the last vestiges of profitability from an industry now so competitive due to world over capacity, that cost (only) became a common, commercially suicidal type of tender. During this era the River Clyde produced between 35–45% of the total UK shipbuilding output, which was at that time the world's leading shipbuilding nation, remaining so up until the mid-1950s. It was also the last decade of autocratic line management, invoked controversially using 'piecework' methods of payment, a system of remuneration whereby workers were paid for completing incremental jobs, within specific aggregate man hour durations.

The once regular and familiar sight of keel plates being laid down on an open building berth, very shortly after the launch of a new vessel, was followed by the rapid lifting into position of asymmetrical frames and bulkheads, precariously tethered to the keel plates by wire strops and guy ropes, prior to riveting or welding together. Erection of these ribs quickly created the fared outline and form of the ship's hull, soon to be swarmed over by an ever increasing number of black trades workers, whose individual skills and combined industry would speedily transform a rust bespeckled steel skeleton, from a featureless empty carcass into a full bodied flared ship's hull in a relatively short number of weeks.

The meaningful evaluation of not only the main companies, but also the coterie of component industries and communities whose well-being depended on steel shipbuilding, certainly escaped the limited academic prowess of the quasi-intelligent economists, theorists and political experts who propounded the demise of the industry from the 1960s onwards. This advocacy of industrial genocide was no doubt based on the antagonistic employment relations, embarrassingly illustrated by inflexible intransigence, exhibited equally by companies and unions towards the future well-being of shipbuilding. The concomitant targets of common interest and commitment to customer requirements, coupled with the inevitable acceptance of ever changing technology, were never achieved during the halcyon days of full order books. When rebuilt, invisibly subsidised and modernised European and Japanese shipyards could produce a similar, sometimes superior, product for less money, on time, every time (or so they expounded). The main support base for Clyde shipbuilding, the shipping companies who constituted the British Merchant Navy, voted with their cheque books and ordered many of their new ships from foreign shipyards.

This departure of customers, prompted some shipping companies to go public in their condemnation of 1960s shipyard management ineptitude that failed to uproot inefficient working practices which resulted in dilatory delivery of new ships. Such inert output soon fuelled the rhetoric of adverse, para-intellectual gurus and industrial voyeurs, who gloated and smirked, as one famous company after another slithered down the slipway into oblivion. Decanting thousands of employees on the scrap-heap, concurrently consigning other support industries, like crane-making, heavy machine tool manufacture, and marine engine building to a feeble short term existence, before they too contributed involuntarily to the de-industrialisation of Scotland. The vacuum created by this decline was never replaced by a promised sunrise of opportunity in new technology industries. Instead the void was filled by the inexorable emigration of skilled personnel, or casual employment of small numbers of workers in furtive, low technology business parks and services, boasting semi-skilled jobs devoid of career opportunities with limited self-fulfilment.

Volume shipbuilding, marine engineering and ship repairing on the upper Clyde had contracted to less than half of its post-war capacity by the formation of Upper Clyde Shipbuilders Ltd in 1968. This was five years before the inauguration and operation of the South Korean mega shipbuilding yards. This reduction had taken place in an era, when those companies that remained, spent significant amounts of their own money in replacing some aspects of status quo shipbuilding techniques, with virtually negligent increases in productivity.

At that time the United Kingdom still had a sizeable merchant fleet. This customer base regularly accounted for more than half of the British shipbuilding industry new order intake, which was then roughly equal to the UK annual output of over one million gross registered tons of new shipping. Finland, Poland and East Germany had not asserted their recondite multi-product shipbuilding prowess on western merchant fleets, constructing only for the then burgeoning USSR naval programme. Clearly markets existed at that time for building the massive ship modernisation projects, that included container ships, large passenger-vehicle ferries and tankers then in demand from ship-owners at home and throughout the world. The abysmal statistic that the upper Clyde built only one container ship, the belated, controversial s.s. *Jervis Bay* 26,876 g.r.t., and no large ferries or tankers during this boom, was testimony that the industry, on this part of the river, had passed its collective best performance. Lower Clyde shipyards existed in a more competitive frame, remaining virtually intact with some seven separate yards completing significant numbers of tankers, bulk carriers, reefers, cargo liners, coasters, small ferries, dredgers, and Royal Navy craft up until the formation of British Shipbuilders Ltd in 1977. Some diversification into the construction of jack-up drilling rigs, and dynamically positioned drill ships, had been successfully undertaken by two Clyde shipyards during the 1960s and early '70s.

The inveterate cultural impasse that pervaded the 'bowler and the bunnet' from the inception of shipbuilding, belied an empathetic bond which transcended this unfortunate chasm. Innate pride was exhibited by all levels of labour in their finished ship product. Towards the end of the industry's last years of volume ship production, vessels were being completed with depressing tardiness, late deliveries that were to execute the final crippling loss-making salvoes which would consign the industry on the River Clyde to the history books. Many ships were late, but they were all accepted by their respective owners (some heavily discounted by penalty clause liens), quality products the like of which will never be constructed again. Built during a period of unbridled inflation throughout the UK, when the inability of a shipbuilder to control his unit labour costs was compounded with erratic crippling increases to the price of every commodity, from metered electricity to steel plates and sections including the absorption of fuel increases on all items transported to the yard.

The following tome mourns the loss of over 80% of *the* industry that epitomised the soul of the West of Scotland. It also attempts to analyse and dissect the companies and trades that tried to wring longevity out of an industrial behemoth which had become enmeshed in internal as well as an international morass of technical, political and economic skulduggery. Flippantly and continually undervalued by successive post-war British Governments, and surprisingly under-appreciated by some of the former owners, directors and employees, their collective lack of foresight, commitment and indomitable resistance to the nascent changes necessary for prolonged competitiveness, contributed as much towards the ignominious decline of the industry as that of over-capacity, cloaked in latent subsidies throughout world shipbuilding.

The anticipated panacea of nationalisation of virtually the whole British shipbuilding industry under the Labour Government in 1977 created the opposite effect. Productive shipyards like Scott-Lithgow on the Lower Clyde were insidiously reduced to loss-making caricatures of their past glory. Practically every former independent shipbuilding or marine engineering company that was conscripted into this misguided act of government interference, was similarly smitten with the spectre of state controlled sloth. Former yard-owners were niggardly recompensed for this coercive act of belated dubious fiscal assistance. Vast amounts of taxpayers' money was spent in a few short years by this inept and inefficient corporation, some of it on a few selective capital expenditure projects, but most was frittered away on lamentable loss making new shipbuilding contracts, with heavy penalties incurred for late delivery. The remainder was written off by the new Conservative administration against depreciating assets and bloated redundancy payments to most of the total UK labour force. Elected in 1979, that government decided arbitrarily that shipbuilding— and indeed UK merchant shipping—were antiquated, life-expired industries, totally incompatible with the 'yuppy' image of service-driven, self-aggrandisement that was to be the hallmark of 1980s Britain.

Alas, the blather of bureaucratic buffoonery masquerading as a frugal emissary for sound husbandry, impugned any rational intervention to assist either shipbuilding or its main patron, the UK merchant shipping industry. The world's second most important island trading nation is now virtually dependent on vessels with 'flags of convenience' to carry its products in ships now built in state-of-the-art, Far Eastern shipbuilding factories, funded, and invisibly amortised by supportive governments, international banks or multinational industrialists, as well as many UK investors.

The rapid cataclysmic evaporation of the British Merchant Navy effectively resulted in the disappearance of the core customer base, which led to the concurrent annihilation of volume shipbuilding throughout the UK within less than a decade. Nevertheless despite considerable attrition of the River Clyde shipbuilding industry, the river still ranks as the major shipbuilding centre of the United Kingdom, albeit with only a handful of warship, merchant and offshore construction yards still in existence.

This book is an attempt at recollecting the final Indian summer of volume shipbuilding on the Clyde, through the '50s to early '60s when two dozen shipyards and eighteen marine engine works had orders for millions of tons of shipping...orders to be completed by the *Ironfighters, Outfitters and Bowler Hatters* of the River Clyde, most of whom have now passed into local folklore. Collectively maligned by the establishment and media, but singly regarded with admiration and bewilderment by those fortunate individuals whom they trained—technical, practical, even commercial aspects of labour for hire—were subtly or coercively imbued with guile swathed in a sense of humour, a formidable combination of traits for inclusion in each young man's tool box for life.

No tradesman from a Clyde shipyard or marine engine works, could ever consider himself truly time-served, if his considerable pragmatic skills were not augmented with a personalised brand of finely honed, spontaneous deprecating West of Scotland wry wit. A number of fortunate souls put this supplementary form of training to good effect, when they left the shipyards to forge successful second careers as thespians, drolls or comic singers of national, or even international, fame. The less famous droves of colleagues spent their working lives not on the stages of the West End, but on the staging of the West of Scotland shipbuilding yards where discovery by an irascible manager was more likely to result in a discourteous rebuke rather than a customary curtsey at the end of a well paid performance.

The following three pictures depict different views showing ostensible aspects of volume shipbuilding on the River Clyde in the 1950s.

An early evening scene at the John Brown & Co (Clydebank) Ltd shipyard in the spring of 1958 showing yard no. 703, s.t. BRITISH DUCHESS 27,585 g.r.t. nearing completion on the world famous no. 4 berth. The intensity of uprights and staging illustrate the necessity for steelworkers and subsequently painters to access the whole surface area of the hull of the ship during construction. The horizontal scaffold grillage in the foreground is the carcass for the launch platform, that will be bedecked with bunting and other ostentatious adornments for the vessel's launch by royalty on 2 June 1958.

The smoke begrimed tenemental sprawl and industrial district of Govan, Glasgow, looking south in 1959. The then busy shipyard of Harland & Wolff Ltd is seen occupying most of the south bank waterfront. Note the Govan vehicular ferry nestling in her recessed berth between the shipyard slipways and plating sheds severed by Water Row, which led down from Govan Cross. Govan Old Parish Church is prominent surrounded by rows of tenements and the west end of the shipyard. Flanking the west side of Govan goods yard are some of the buildings of British Polar Engines Ltd and the adjacent Govan Shafting Co Ltd. In the centre right is Ibrox stadium, home of the famous Glasgow Rangers FC, showing the spartan terracings of the day, far removed from the magnificent football stadium of the 1990s. Commercial shipping can be seen occupying some of the berths in Princes Dock, the man-made inshots upstream from Govan drydocks. Part of the Pointhouse shipyard of A. & J. Inglis Ltd is noticeable on the east bank of the River Kelvin at its confluence with the River Clyde. The vacant ground in the foreground used to be the Meadowside shipyard of D. & W. Henderson & Co Ltd, closed by National Shipbuilding Securities Ltd in 1935.

Yard no. 1571g, m.t. ESKFIELD 18,851 g.r.t. takes shape within a stockade of wooden staging at the Govan shipyard of Harland & Wolff Ltd during the summer of 1959. Single frame, single plate erection methods are still very much in use, made relatively easy to implement due to the extensive array of fixed hammerhead cranes in the yard. The triangular shaped items at the top of the row of port side frames are beam knees that will connect the foc'sle deck frames to the side shell of the ship, either by riveting or welding.

Chapter 2

IRONFIGHTERS

Ironfighter' is a generic colloquialism for any of the steelwork trades, who built the keel, frames, shell, decks, tanks, bulkheads and superstructure of a ship. These trades were also identified by another inverted euphemism the 'Black Squad'. Shipbuilding is unfairly smitten with apocryphal denouncement of these trades being totally responsible for all of that industry's disputes, shortcomings and ultimate decline!

Whilst disappointingly capable of consistent idiosyncratic intransigence abetted with whimsical petulance, when properly motivated, managed, inspired, and most importantly of all, ably rewarded for their efforts, the best steelworkers of the River Clyde shipyards were capable of achieving output and quality comparable to that of tradesmen anywhere. Such superlative performances were the result of coordinated, yet archaic labour intensive craft working practices, harnessed to primitive, exploitive payment by results methods of incentive induced earnings. Crude, though effective in their day, these arrangements for remuneration were the hard won alternatives for the previous anachronistic era of random employment.

Steelwork fabrication was collectively performed, utilising all of the individual trades identified in this chapter. Each had a unique, specialised function that was inextricably linked to the other. All had their roots in either the initial industrial revolution or the subsequent furtive technological pogroms, that thrust coercive change into the manner of fabrication, with respect to its application in steel shipbuilding.

Some yards (though by no means all of the companies) invested in apprentice training schools. This training, diverse and comprehensive, as it was during a tradesman's formative years, invariably, inevitably yet regrettably led to the creation of 'pigeon-holed specialists' at 21 years of age! As much a contradiction of the multi-discipline knowledge gleaned, as it was the endorsement of demarcation, with the disbarment of skill deployment required for the type of ship being constructed.

The parallel between the ship designer, draughtsman, and to a lesser extent the loftsman, who by definition must comprehend all facets of steelwork and certain outfit elements (excepting marine engines, auxiliaries or electrical systems), and the plethora of trades who executed the work depicted on ship drawings, attest to the multiplicity of occupations which have evolved, retaining single facet skills, in a new age of rationalisation and consolidation.

The practice of demarcation which reached its height of public awareness during the 1950s, was established quite deliberately in the last century to recruit, exploit, partially train and isolate poorly educated men into the then expanding captive labour intensive British industries. Virtually the whole of industry was affected by this initial method of basic job evaluation, but UK shipbuilding suffered most.

Restrictive practices were inevitable at the birth and subsequent evolution of engineering technology. As industries developed they identified the need for basic craft functions, which rapidly became the domain of adept artisans, craftsmen and tradesmen. These trades were supplemented, after their establishment, with one more strata of inverse demarcation: the appointment of helpers. This action slotted another tranche of men into a spiral of very limited achievement. Many helpers were adaptable, articulate, dextrous, integritous and hard-working, sometimes knowing as much of the specific job skill as the tradesmen they assisted, yet they were denied tradesman status because they had not learned that craft, boy and man spending five years as an apprentice! Numerous helpers had been former apprentices who had not 'completed their time' when some yards were closed during the pre-war depression years. Those unfortunate men, who never finished their training were therefore deemed unskilled and would only be employed as helpers.

With the inexorable development of less labour intensive processes, companies began to realise that this demarcation dragon that they had quite deliberately created, was becoming a difficult beast to control!

Not only had they to contend with a surfeit of tradesmen, whose once indispensable skills had now evaporated, but a supporting cast of helpers, holders-on and the like, whose loyalty to journeymen and firm would also be put into the melting-pot of industrial attrition.

Demarcation failed to selectively differentiate the inescapable affliction that smote ironfighters and helpers alike…deafness! The steel shipbuilding process encompassed the summation of a number of metal-working methods. From hammering to chipping and grinding, all of these operations exacerbated noise transmission. Due to steel's excellent capacity to resonate the slightest din, the preponderance of box-like compartments that comprise the tanks and holds of a ship, created many echo-chambers that resulted in a veritable discordant crescendo from the start of the shift until the final whistle blew. This ordeal was not discriminate in its effectuation. By the time medical science had appreciated the tribulations caused by steel shipbuilding, the industry had virtually disappeared. Most of the old ironfighters were then too short of hearing to know or understand that their life-long subjection to the dissonant clatter of rivet and caulking guns had resulted in deafness.

Shipbuilding on open slipways lacking basic weather protection contributed as much to casual employment of the bulk of the labour force, as did irregular ordering of new ships. The effect of this lack of investment in beating the elements had a far greater impact on the steelwork trades and helpers, rather than the outfitters or subcontractors who worked within the 'cover' of the hull or superstructure.

After the Second World War, the main method of steelwork assembly was, as it had been since the establishment of steel shipbuilding, riveting. A basic highly labour intensive process of the last century, whereby steel plates and frames were joined together by lapping one over the other, clamping them together using bolts, fitted through some pre-drilled holes, this assembly was later re-drilled, punched or reamed, then the holes were filled by passing through red-hot rivets. The rivet was held in place by a holder-on (*hawdur oan*) on the other side of the plate. The protruding end was then instantly hammered to form the type of head required, usually snap or countersunk in shipbuilding. Hand riveting was carried out by a pair of riveters who hammered the rivet in rapid synchronous tempo, always hitting its head with every blow. The rivet then relied on its metallurgical cooling and contraction to further compress the assembly, which might later be peened or caulked to ensure watertightness. Other less popular shipbuilding methods of riveted construction used joggled and offset plates to create a smoother external hull profile. The fitting of internal backing straps from plate or flat-bar also produced a flush plate hull contour. Irrespective of which method was deployed, the adjoining frames had to be joggled in way of each riveted splice. Post-war riveting was carried out using pneumatic hand-held hammers or guns that required considerable strength to manipulate, and reduced riveter numbers as well, as one man could now perform the function of a pair.

Electric arc welding, having been introduced into most Clyde shipyards from the USA during World War II, was inevitably to become the preferred method for future ship construction. The electric arc welding process utilises a high current to create an arc which melts a steel electrode. Positioning this electrode between two closely abutted steel plates, high current is passed through the electrode holder which instantly melts the electrode or welding rod in a pool of hot molten steel, as well as the adjacent faces of the plates, thus fusing together the assembly. The electrode is coated in flux which diffuses during the welding process, creating a shield of gas that prevents the welded joint from oxidising. It has the following benefits over riveted shipbuilding methods, *viz.* better watertightness, smoother hull form, greater vessel speed, less actual steel used in construction, quicker production process, therefore less time to build a hull, meaning theoretically less man hours per joint, relatively low capital cost of welding plant and welder training. All-in-all an open and shut case for the advancement of technology, and the rapid substitution of riveting by welding.

By the time the shipbuilding industry on the River Clyde had accomplished this transition (well after 1960), the rest of the world had in place alternative excessive shipbuilding capacity, strewn with a profusion of superior manufacturing processes and procedures. These competitors offered many new designs of ship types, most shrouded with subtle construction subsidies. Such inducements would prove an insurmountable aggregate of advantage in the near future.

Riveting was performed by squads of hard, arrogant, self-motivated, stoical men with veritable work ethics who were paid on completion of the strake of rivets installed: vertical, horizontal, diagonal, or radial, etc. Their productive capacity, whilst admirable to watch, was directly proportional to the respective skills and abilities of the shipwrights and platers, whose task it was to prepare, erect and fair the frames and plates that were to be riveted together. Being of such self esteem and the self proclaimed 'Kings of the Iron-fighters', *riveters* did not take easily to the replacement of their hard man's job, with a task performed most admirably by 'wee lassies' in wartime shipyards. This macho–egotistical stance set the first impasse between riveters and companies, who wanted to substitute yesterday's folklore with tomorrow's technology. Thus the period required for the replacement of traditional steelwork assembly became both protracted and discordant.

Clyde shipyards met this reluctance head-on. The obvious palliative was to offer new welder jobs to redundant riveters. Some young riveters were quickly convinced to take this transfer of trade as the welding content of ships inexorably increased. Older riveters were more reluctant to accept this new career. Fewer squads painstakingly persisted to perform the ever-decreasing riveted content that encapsulated each new shipbuilding contract, although the outmoded preference of a handful of ship-owners for the retention of riveting frames to shell plating, strung-out 'the craft' well into the 1960s. The last few gangs of traditional riveters eked their livelihood bargaining their by now specialised services to the remaining shipyards, whose products were fast approaching 100% all welded construction with every new keel laid down on the building berth.

Riveters possessed a sartorial similarity comprising a unique working apparel of oil begrimed, once blue dungarees, sometimes strapped tightly to the legs with leather knee pads, always topped-off with a sweat-stained, dirt encrusted bunnet, usually so discoloured, the initial pattern was long since discernible. Individually dissimilar in physical stature, they were collectively recognisable by muscular bulging forearms of 'Popeye proportions', which supported gnarled, sinewed hands that constantly trembled, due to the nerve shattering pulsation of hammering millions of rivets in a lifetime of toil. Most men were scourged in later life with the numbing debilitation of 'white finger', a colloquialism for colourless skin, with virtually nerveless sensitivity. The final hallmark of genuine Clydeside riveters was the constant puffing on a Woodbine, high nicotine cigarette, which was usually clenched between their teeth. Their lips forced apart, nostrils and mouths gasping noisily, inhaling and exhaling rapidly to enable coercive respiration throughout the physically demanding task of riveting, never made easier by their collective addiction to tobacco.

These proud tradesmen, whose average age by then was nearer 60 than 50, commanded intangible respect from management and workforce alike. Branded Luddites, dinosaurs and yesterday's men by sarcastic sages, kerbside philosophers and assorted disaffected malcontents, such cynicism failed to address the magnificent metronome work ethics riveters possessed. The last riveters clung defiantly to an empathetic bond of unique skills and peerless identity, which united them as close to each other and their dying trade, as their ingenuity at joining together steel plates and frames was inextricably linked to their enviable proficient dexterity.

When the eventual all welded ships were ultimately constructed, the final gangs shuffled out the yard gates for the last time to their local pubs, parks and benches along the River, to muse among their diminishing numbers about, among other things, the final halcyon days of Clyde shipbuilding. Gone by now, alas forgotten by most, their likes will never be born again. These stalwarts, characters to a man, played an indispensable part, and left an indelible mark on their particular era of industrial anthropology.

The riveter's heaters, holder-ons, hole-borers, drillers, reamers, catchers and fire-boys were more enthusiastic at attaining a real trade where and when the opportunity arose. Despite being insultingly called 'dilutees' (a diluted tradesman; not a time served man!) they graciously accepted this rung on the ladder of instant trade identification. This pool of labour, regularly supplemented by school leavers, now formed the nucleus of Clyde shipyard welders…the new breed of 'Kings of the Ironfighters'.

The vociferously self-proclaimed aristocrats of post-war shipbuilding, the *welders*, should have been the single trade who catapulted shipbuilding from the very labour intensive 'manumatic' traditional building methods, into (at least) a semi-automatic fabrication industry whose future and well being could have been established for decades ahead...alas it was not to be!

Disparagingly affirmed as 'dilutees', 'sparkler holders', and 'wee lassies', among many other less complimentary aspersions, by the constantly diminishing number of riveters, whose function they were replacing, it is dreadfully unfortunate, but nevertheless accurate, that no single trade contributed more (either by design or accident) to the dismal reputation...and subsequent demise of Clyde shipbuilding, than the welders!

The technology and benefits of electric arc welding were correctly, although nevertheless prematurely, thrust upon western shipbuilding by the advent of the Second World War. Most of this cataclysmic transformation took place in the USA, where the world's greatest industrial power, bereft of the stranglehold of traditional restrictive practices endemic in the UK, was able to identify, quantify and implement welding as a hyper-productive alternative to riveting, virtually overnight! This replacement was made by companies like Kaiser Shipbuilding, Bethlehem Shipbuilding and Permanente Shipbuilding, whose multi-fabrication and engineering group interests made them aware of the considerable advantages this process had over riveting. Substitution was made easier when the USA entered the war, and many men left industry to join the armed forces. This created the necessity for female labour, and the new 'black-art' of electric arc welding was a skill at which these 'wee lassies' were both adept and productive.

Given the unpleasantness of the manual welding process, especially in confined spaces, these ladies in the USA, Canada and to some extent the UK, did more than their fair share for emancipation during the early 1940s, culminating in the never to be equalled statistic of fabricating and launching liberty ships of 10,000 t.d.w. in *days* rather than *weeks*. Wartime welding inevitably consigned riveting to a statistical component of industrial history.

Such impressive productive outputs were not lost on the managements of Clyde shipyards, although their initial disbelief succoured much boardroom conjecture and astonishment. 'If semi-skilled American lassies can achieve that, we can do better with our skilled men,' resonated the self-proclaiming consensus from directors and managers. Thus the interminable process to replace traditional steelwork construction methods was put in train. Set against the industrial battlefield of autocratic coercion, arbitration and negotiation were as much a suspicious trap to the trade unions, as they were considered anathema to the ostensibly enlightened post-war Clyde shipbuilding management. Welding was the way forward, and welding would replace riveting. Most of the workforce inwardly knew this, but were more than content to stonewall this transition all in good time. Welding was really a wartime expedient, and now that peace had returned, Clyde craftsmen could return to hawking their traditional crafts in the booming busy shipyards, eradicating the female labour that was used very successfully during the hostilities. Perhaps this complacency in the late 1940s was the real reason for the industry's demise two decades later. Shipyards were now inundated with millions of tons of new vessels, valued in tens of millions of pounds, with completions scheduled over many years ahead. The sparse, unprofitable order books of earlier decades were not conducive to invoking the necessary fundamental changes to construction methods. This was illustrated in a 'hire and fire employment profile' that was nothing more than casual exploitation of labour.

The repressive retention of riveted percentages were reluctantly accepted by managers, who were deluded by their own self-satisfaction into disguising gradual welded encroachment as a partially productive, better-cost alternative to total riveting. After all, once all the old riveters retired, fully welded hulls could be achieved without the long drawn out retention of rivet quotas. This painful transition took too long, resulting in an inordinate and disproportionate power base being achieved by welders. Most importantly, it took place whilst Japanese and European shipyards were being totally rebuilt with new equipment, more flexible working agreements and producing new ship designs (especially of big bulk carriers and tankers) that were now the main types in demand worldwide. Competitive tenders, illustrating lower prices with shorter building durations, attested to this former latent threat which had now become a reality.

When Clyde yards finally achieved all-welded construction methods around two decades after the end of World War II, the archetypal welder displayed an irrational, covetous, intransigent and irascible mentality towards his craft, his employers and his future well-being. Quite unique among his artisan contemporaries, he displayed individuality in every facet of his disposition and demeanour starting initially with his acquisition of a French onion salesman beret, as a distinctive symbol that set him apart from the rest of the workforce. This was later replaced by an imitation Casey Jones American engine driver cap which was garishly adorned with polka dots or stripes, worn with the skip to the side, accompanied by a matching kerchief. Atop of his upper torso was a 'Spartacus pig-skin shoulder protection cape' that depicted a transparent conceitedness more in common with a pseudo-dago bull-fighter than a skilled ironfighter. His traditional footwear was 'Hush Puppy' shoes of compatible hue to that of his cape and elbow length leatherette gauntlets, very avant garde, and nothing like the sartorially congruent masses with their dungarees, bunnets, 'jaykitts and tackity bits'! The welder was the most vain and ostentatious tradesman on the Clyde and he made sure everyone knew that. Wearing jeans or denims instead of boiler suits, this substitution of fashion as a beacon of singular trade identity could only be perpetuated by men with more money than sense. Where all steelwork tradesmen had valued the good wearability of stout industrial clothing, well-paid welders frittered away their earnings on distinctive jeans that were rapidly burnt out by weld spatter, and made to measure shirts that had even less durability.

Now nearly outnumbering the other individual steelwork trades, they overtly displayed this newly acquired power, wrought from collective and individual managements by a combination of sheer bloody mindedness, coupled with adept free-market collective bargaining. It is unfortunate, regrettable and lamentable that this hard-won shop floor muscle was not 'welded' to a more ambivalent comprehension of the benefits and disadvantages of this new found potency while volume shipbuilding still existed.

From the inception of welding, continual improvements in terms of increased methods of production, especially those of automatic and semi-automatic processes, allied to improved metallurgical qualities, gave companies who invested in this technology advantage over those that continued to deploy the initial manual metal arc welding techniques of one welder burning one electrode! The 'manual metal arc welding process' when executed under the strictest quality control precepts is a repetitive, boring, suffocating, hot, dehydrating, monotonous operation. Surely any improvement that negated or eliminated all or any of these discomforts would gladly be accepted by the welders...*not so!* Piecework wage rates, which incorporated weightings for all of the above factors (and more), effectively created a 'rod' for yard management's back, which the welders used at any hint of diminishment or evaporation of their status or earning potential.

Managements painstakingly extracted some savings with the gradual establishment of semi-automatic welding machines for shell, deck, bulkhead and virtually all flat plate fabrication, but these economies were restricted by the physical dimensions determined by 60 ton prefabricated units, which then had to be joined together outside on the berth using more welders deploying manual metal arc welding methods. Semi-automatic flux-cored machines were rejected out of hand by the welders for vertical, horizontal or overhead positional welding. This was the 'process' that every overseas yard adopted with significant improvement in fabrication output. Few yards had any success with the introduction of selective semi-automatic welding processes. Enlightened management and ambivalent men were aware of the mutual problems from different sides of the same fence. Semi-automatic welding could deliver higher quality prefabricated output tonnages, consistently and cheaper than the manual process that was accounting for over 75% of the welded fabrication costs, yet only accounted for about 35% of the deposited weld metal in a typical 15,000 t.d.w. cargo ship. 'Pay the welders more, retrain or dispense with the surfeit, and make those remaining implement semi-automatic welding wherever it can be sensibly and justifiably employed.' Alas, this simplistic panacea wasn't the only thorn in the flesh of an industry which was finding that no sooner had it solved yesterday's difficulties than the worldwide opposition would divulge another. Anyway, other trades would balk at any further disparity between 'the rest of the black squad' and the new '*Ironfighters Extraordinaire*', a self-proclaimed genus that manifestly exemplified 'trade union tribalism'!

Protracted, vehement dialogue ensued. Strike followed strike in every yard along the river. The tacit compromise that emanated with minor differences depending on each yard management's respective resolve, was that fabrication shop plate and frame sub-assemblies for hull, deck, bulkhead, tank-top and superstructure would be totally or partially sub-arc welded. That was basically flat plate fabrication work only. All shaped and flared plates, frames, girders, webs, longitudinals, transverses, flanges and brackets remained virtually manual, as well as all vertical, horizontal and overhead berth welds of plates and frames forming splices between units. Given the parameters of tonnage restriction due to crane capacity, such dictates effectively consigned volume hull construction to stagnate at these predetermined levels for at least another decade, by which time more than half the total industry had disappeared, along with it half the men employed…and more than half the welders who advocated this technical retrenchment, and the wholesale repudiation of the flux-cored semi-automatic process.

The collective failure of Clyde shipbuilding to capitalise on the long term potential benefits, both in productivity and working environment from more widespread use of automatic and semi-automatic welding methods, was always lost on the thousands of 'Jimmies' who plied their trade as manual metal arc welders. Contorting their bodies into the irregular nooks and bilges of marine vessels with the flexibility of circus acrobats, such racking and twisting was necessary to achieve both physical access and positional comfort. Inhaling sometimes almost as much diffused flux gas as oxygen, assuming the position of 'arse-up, head down' (face buried in their bucket, or welders screen), they poured volumes of hot weld metal through white hot tongs, held in blistered hands by threadbare baked-hard gloves. Welders had to endure discomfort, pain and in many cases permanent damage to their health to wrest the attractive earnings that were paid for straight piecework during the era of full order books.

Subsequent preliminary investigations by medical experts predicated the harmful effects of prolonged inhalation of welding fumes. The potential dangers of calcium deficiency and gross dehydration attributable to such subjection, was attempted to be neutralised with the free issue of a pint of milk each day. Chidingly resented by fellow workers, this magnanimous gesture was nevertheless graciously accepted by the welders, later to be called a CSA (confined space allowance). The metal crates (later made out of plastic) in which the milk was delivered to the yards were rapidly purloined, to be used by the welders as makeshift seats or step ups to assist ergonomic comfort whilst performing positional welding, both in the fabrication shop and the building berth.

Whilst welders were the main recipients of fume inhalation, the lingering acrid rancidity that permeated fabrication sheds during or after intense welding activity, created a unique pungency which scorched the throat and watered the eyes of all personnel who were subjected to such flux-diffused vapours. The clammy dense blue-grey haze that enveloped the welding shop floor exhibited a rigorous resistance to natural evaporation, and retained a permanent odour redolent of tainted turnip. Interspersed with the diffused searing white lights of welding arcs, the scattered convex trajectories of orange rain spewn from an array of hand-held oxy-acetylene torches created an infernal vulcan surrealism, which hid from discernible view the human effort and industry necessary to produce fabricated steel ship sections. Where the welders' intransigence and inimitable aversion to change led to their inevitable demise, other ironfighters showed a more compromising and forward looking attitude to the ineluctable advance of technology.

Loftsmen balk at their collective synonymity with the 'black squad'. Detached and isolated between the drawing office and the shop floor in that what they do and what they made wasn't part of a ship, they nevertheless are an essential and integral part of the traditional shipbuilding process. Loftsmen are responsible for taking the dimensions, scantlings and details from drawings and plans. Translating this information into templates, battens, ordinates, cutting sketches, profiles, margins and other data, whereby steel plates and sections can be identified, cut, shaped, prepared, rolled, formed, flanged and 'set-out' into the primary elements required for ship construction, including the incorporation of additional surplus for weld shrinkage, overbending and cutting allowances. The summation of skills required for this painstaking job encompass a high threshold of interest, a three-dimensional 'seeing eye', virtually total comprehension of the subsequent fabrication, erection and launching operations, plus diligent dexterity in the art of measurement. All in all a fair spectrum of capability! Not surprisingly these high levels of aptitude were identified as the prime job specification elements required by respective yard managers, chief draughtsmen, fabrication and berth managers, for prospective loftsmen. This senior caucus took a high level of interest in the appointment of the head loftsman, with more than a passing interest in the performance of his underlings. If the loftsman didn't get it right first time, then the downstream trades of platers, welders, caulkers and shipwrights would be involved in either considerable costly time consuming re-work, or scrapping of incorrect fabrications.

A blue collar profession who were part of the shipwright department, loftsmen fared better than their fellow ironfighters with almost a white collar working environment. This 'perk' was not reflected in their collective adoption of office working apparel of collar and tie. Modesty, underwritten by conformity, resulted in nondescript sartorial anonymity. The donning of the traditional ubiquitous Clydeside garb of boilersuit underneath a working jacket, usually on top of a collarless shirt virtually hidden by a woollen faded tartan scarf. Their remaining visible attire was topped by a worn-out, sweat-stained bunnet, with heavy duty boots as the habitual type of footwear.

The wide range of functions carried out by loftsmen, extended from the mundane setting out of the simplest superstructure feature, to the brain-racking traumas of comprehending a stern frame with twin-screw propeller boss, bulbous bow, or a long sheered upper deck with flared fo'c'sle. The loft carried an inordinate responsibility for the good name of the company. Traditional Clyde shipbuilders were aware of this burden from the inception of the industry. The warmest, quietest, driest, brightest, most spacious building in every yard was usually the loft. This was necessary for essential temperature and humidity control, thus ensuring that the timber floor, incorporating the scrieve board on which the hull and deck lines were drawn full size, as well as all the wooden templates and battens, were kept dry and did not rot, warp, shrink or expand due to temperature differentiation. Any solace bestowed on the industrious occupants was a grudged benefit, often grudgingly regurgitated by polemical shipyard managers when annual wage negotiations took place!

Notwithstanding the new skill plateau that was quickly reached by all the steelwork trades, as a result of the wholesale adaptation of welded prefabrication methods, the responsibility for faultless geometry still remained with the loftsmen; whereas the empirical erstwhile method adopted for steel shipbuilding had been single frame—single plate erection sequence—utilising a greater combination of the individual skills of shipwrights, platers and loftsmen. This method was a throwback from the times of wooden shipbuilding, when the keel was set out, true and straight on the declivity slipways. Transverse ribs were erected at right angles to this keel using ropes and guy wires to retain them in temporary position, until the planks that formed the hull were attached longitudinally to these frames. Steel hulls duly replaced those made of wood. Timber frames were substituted with rolled sections, called either zed-angles or bulb angles, which were riveted to the shell or hull plating of the vessel.

This ancestral, laborious method of ship construction allowed the loftsmen the luxury of setting and fairing the steel frames in conjunction with the skills of the shipwrights and platers. The more difficult task of fitting the steel plates, which were, on over 50% of a ship's hull, three-dimensional shaped profiles, was initially undertaken by using the ship's framing as a carcass to provide a solid full-size template for accurate measurement, thus preventing undercutting of the plate's dimensions. This additional skilled operation gave birth to the new steel work trade of *plater*.

The onset of prefabrication with its hoped for reductions in cost and duration, removed the comfort of the loft being able to lift and verify difficult ship-shape profiles from the building berth. After dimensional scrutiny this information was passed to the plater to form the developed profile of such plates in the plating shop. This new method effectively killed-off the need for shipwrights and in so doing elevated the standing in terms of technical competence and practical application of the loftsmen. Fabrication shops were added to every shipyard that now used welded methods of ship construction. Each shipyard had its own quirks to assist unit building techniques. These varied from the wholesale building of ship sections, usually upside down utilising the flatness of the deck, hold or tank-top plating which provided a sound working datum, to staggered splicing of shell or bulkhead plating that used the continuity of frames to provide subsequent location aids for the next adjoining section. This subtle transition of shipbuilding technology was borne totally on the competence of loftsmen assisted by the practical dexterity of platers, whose collective skills could fashion two-dimensional drawings into real fabrications.

The high quality of prefabricated ship sections, repetitively produced with consummate ease by loftsmen along the Clyde, inured shipyard management into another niche of self-induced complacency. This traditional and adaptable method of steelwork development works very well, has worked very well… and will continue to work satisfactorily. A trite maxim that endorsed post-war thinking on most facets of ship construction (as proclaimed by ironfighters and outfitters)…but this edict was being expounded by managements.

Messer-Sicomat A.G. of Greisham, West Germany, revolutionised post-war shipbuilding and all other metal fabrication industries in the same dynamic all conquering inevitable style, as the Lincoln Welding Co of the USA had achieved with electric arc welding earlier this century. The introduction of 'one-tenth scale' profile burning of virtually every plate component, reduced the traditional workload of the template loft overnight. Where the loftsman was previously reliant on his ability to measure correctly, he now had to acquire a draughting dexterity of flawless accuracy that would enable him to make one-tenth full size sketches on special transparent plastic sheets. These sketches would be optically traced by a 'magic-eye' connected to multiple-head burning nozzles, mounted on a cross-rail above a table containing the plates, which would be profile burned to the exact size and shape in a fraction of the time previously taken, using laborious tape and chalk-line marking-off followed by hand-burning.

These machines, including tables, burning-heads operating console and magic-eye were not cheap! They cost tens of thousands of pounds in the late '50s, but if they had cost millions they would still have paid for themselves in a relatively short time. This nascent technology was accepted unilaterally by management, drawing office, planning office, template loft and most of the platers and burners whose erstwhile jobs this new machine replaced. The process was so high-tech and successful in its day, that virtually every shipyard worker (including welders) whose shipyard invested in these machines boasted to their mates about what these Sicomats could do. Here was an example of management investing…and ironfighters responding…if only the Germans hadn't invented the machine first (*sic*).

The natural progression from profile burning was the wholesale use of jigs and fixtures, to assist the set up and fabrication of prefabricated ship units. Used extensively in virtually every UK manufacturing industry except shipbuilding, this technological advantage was never really applied on the Clyde until more than half of the industry had vanished! Traditional shipyard managements weaned on a cocktail of semi-aristocratic arrogance, infused with autocratic self belief, propounded 'If we didn't think of that idea first…its not a good idea!' Such quasi-philosophical technical myopia would have been moderately funny…if they were referring to the inclusion of à la carte menus in the shipyard canteen… (if that yard had a canteen). Unfortunately, selective comprehension of methods and practices deployed in foreign shipyards was exactly the attitude emergent Japanese and European shipyards needed to assert their ever-increasing commercial advantages.

'Why have skilled loftsmen and platers, pay them skilled wage rates, then diminish that skill factor with the use of jigs and fixtures?' This type of inflexible adherence to the 'status quo modus operandi', bemused the militant, less industrious ironfighters, as much as it entrenched the lotsmen in a web of traditional building methods with the emphasis on repetitive dexterity at the expense of productivity! The ship types constructed on the Clyde in the late '60s, when all-welded hull construction methods were commonplace, contained considerable areas of component repetition, eg. parallel shell panels, bulkheads, decks, double bottom units, hopper, wing tanks, web frames of large tankers, and bulk carriers, ideal for the application of simple jigs and fixtures.

Tradition prevailed, there would be no diminution in the considerable skills manifested by the ship's plater, perceived by themselves as *the* quintessential shipbuilder. This complimentary adage is not far from the truth! They were trained to read drawings of varying degrees of information and clarity. Visualise that nomen-clature as a three-dimensional sub-assembly or finished item. Diligently and productively identify the material required, set out that steel, invent the build method, then direct the welder with respect to preliminary tacking of these plates and sections. Systematically building these components into a hull, deck, bulkhead, superstructure or outfit unit, all the time being aware of the accessibility for himself, the welders, outfit trades and painters who also need entry to enable their functions to be performed safely, concurrently or successively.

A very wide spectrum of ability and capability were essential prerequisites of ships' platers. These traits were seldom appreciated by those other than their fellow workmates who would often gaze in dumb amazement as journeymen, old and young, would scrupulously, usually quite rapidly, transform brown bits of steel into shaped and flared metallic works of art. In addition to possession of a strong metal tool-box containing hammers, centre punches, angle squares, protractor and level, the innate or acquired ability to measure meticulously then 'mark-off' flat or shaped steel using a tape or rule, ball of string and block of chalk were the essential hallmarks of a good plater. The range and scope of the plater's skills has been much simplified since the advent of all-welded steel construction methods. Accurate profile burning of plates, coupled with cold bending of section frames that are themselves already prepared for welding, assures a far quicker fabrication cycle than the time taken to 'joggle and offset' plates, or fit backing strips to every riveted joint in that erstwhile laborious building method. Templates, battens and formers prepared by the loftsmen would be handed over to the respective chargehand platers. This interface between the 'brains' and the 'brawn with the brains', was another critical step in the cascade of information and instructions from the drawing office to the building berth, culminating in the accurate rolling of shell plates, flanging or forming of corrugated swedges for bulkheads, masts, casings, superstructure and other sundry components, ready to be assembled and welded into part of the ship under construction.

The main peripheral learning curve associated with welded fabrication technology, which was quickly comprehended as much by trial and error than pre-emptive methodology, was that the excessive heat input actuated by electric arc welding quickly cooled after deposition, resulting in 'shrinkage' in the order of at least one millimetre for each welded joint, butt or splice. This was further compounded by distortion along the free length of components that were not inherently stiff, ie. relatively thin flat plates would distort to a greater extent than either thick plates or steel sections like bulb bars, angles, channels and columns, etc. These problems of dimensional control caused by locked-in stress were summarily identified and solved with the judicious use of oxy-acetylene burning torches applied, either pre- or post-welding, depending on the configuration of unit, or most effectively by welding all flat plates before assembly of subsequent stiffeners, thus minimising distortion and preventing cumulative lateral shrinkage.

These problems and solutions were identified independently in all of the Clyde yards in the late 1950s when wholesale welding was gradually replacing riveting. It did not take long for the 'workspeak' of the day, rhetorically propounded in the pubs and clubs, to travel from yard to yard. It was as effective between tradesmen, as it was between directors, managers, draughtsmen and foremen.

Having mastered the transition from riveted to welded fabrication, as well as overcoming its inherent pitfalls, the last craft/skill hurdle to be cleared before the demise of the industry was the construction of the various types of bigger ships that were now entering the diverse product range, within the volume output of the River Clyde shipyards.

Crane capacities in fabrication shops and berths, of between 35 to 60 tons in most of the yards, limited prefabricated unit size considerably. Such relatively small lift capability created berth and slipway plating activity in more ship units, rather than the optimum construction of whole transverse ship sections, with a continuous uniform splice. Due to the greater scantlings of these larger ships, units within the maximum capacity of cranes sometimes represented smaller sections of these big vessels. This unfortunate under-capacity in craneage meant more platers were attached to berth erection and fairing functions than was originally envisaged at the outset of fabrication shop philosophy, culminating in only partial savings in ship construction activities and durations. No matter what erection methods were deployed, the considerable range of skills, albeit never consistent in every plater, would be needed wherever a new ship was laid down.

Unlike the welders, their 'sartorially trend setting' boilermaker colleagues, the platers' working attire was as traditional as it was indistinctive. Spanning generations, it remained unchanged and synonymous with this skilled trade from the outset of steel shipbuilding, until the introduction of compulsory safety helmets and fire-retardant free-issue cover-alls. Often emulated, seldom eclipsed, other tradesmen somehow didn't seem to possess the jaunty confidence and bearing of the time-served ship's plater. This was regularly apparent to any fellow traveller on public transport, as well as the rest of the shipyard trades. With steel toe-capped boots, best suit 'jaykit' from a few eons ago, worn ostentatiously over their dungarees or boilersuit, supplemented in winter with a 'manky muffler' wrapped round the neck. All year round this apparel was topped off with the mandatory 'who dunnit' firmly planted on his head, at a rakish angle of cockiness. This ubiquitous garb, worn by old and young tradesmen alike, was sported with a uniform pride, and resolute bearing that would have embarrassed members of the Grenadier Guards. So great was the inherent pride in craft, status and demeanour borne by the ship's plater, he felt far from humble in depicting this industrial suavity throughout his whole working day.

The above trades were *the* essential team necessary to build a steel ship in the era of post-war technology. Despite what may be said to the contrary, the active retention of the following 'service trades' to the main 'black squad' illustrate shipbuilding craft unions collective loyalty to historical functions, at the expense of the industry's progression and longevity! *Shipwrights, caulkers, burners,* and an almost endless list of assorted semi-skilled jobs like *cranemen, slingers, helpers, drillers, mates, labourers* and *stagers,* comprise another tranche of labour performing regressive labour intensive functions. These tasks were perpetuated on the back of misplaced atavistic retention of traditional steel shipbuilding practices. Refusal to permit evolutionary attrition and consolidation of such activities illustrated further the extent of the obdurate web of demarcation.

The simplified process of welded prefabricated ship construction effectively rendered obsolete the need for shipwrights and caulkers, whose functions were required for the building of wooden vessels, and were partially essential for the single frame/single plate riveted building methods of previous decades. The considerable artisan power base held by traditional shipbuilding unions throughout the UK, after World War II, was unfortunately squandered on the perpetuation of outdated, outmoded labour intensive methods enshrouded in a total commitment to job retention, whatever the long-term impact this had, not only on these jobs but also on the industry that employed these workers! The withholding of trades, crafts and practices identified by management as long past their respective technological sell-by dates was indubitably a contributory factor in the rapid contraction of shipbuilding as a major industry in Britain.

This anathema to shipyard owners was as incomprehensible to the ship owning customers as it was to the UK public at large. Whether the alternative establishment of a '*shipbuilder*', boy and man, who would specialise in one of the three main skills of developing, making and joining together, at the same time being flexible and adept enough to divert to another discipline, depending on workload, or demand, would have created a practical panacea, will always be conjectural. Whether this postulation of a hyper-flexible attitude, driving a compendium of comprehensive skills would have saved volume shipbuilding, is only one of many hypothetical caveats tossed into the retrospective crystal ball of failure of a once great industry.

Shipwrights remained very much a main stream trade and slotted into the deployment of methods necessary for the erection of fabricated units, setting-out of launch-ways and the very important function of fore-poppet construction and assembly. The fore-poppet is the 'cradle' that supports the bow of a ship before and during launching from the declivity slipways. This 'support frame' is necessary to resist the downward reaction on the bow, created during launching, because of the upward buoyancy force applied to the hull when the aft end of the ship enters the water. Additional activity was found in the outfit of vessels depending on ship type, and to a greater extent the numbers of shipwrights in that particular yard. These activities ranged from fitting of hatch covers (which used to be made of wood), to installation of hardwood planking on accommodation decks, both tasks throwbacks from ship types and building methods of yore, and capable of being performed by a '*shipbuilder/fabricator*'.

Caulkers and burners merged to form a dual trade capable of dressing and burning steel. Caulking of metal joints, an essential element of riveted construction, became obsolete with the advent of all welded methods. Burning and chamfering of plates and sections became the domain of loftsmen and platers with the introduction of one-tenth scale profile burning machines, although hand-burning lingered on for berth fairing and other miscellaneous metal removal necessities like the back-gouging of double-sided welds. Yet these two trades retained an importance disproportionate to their respective necessities in the new era of steelwork fabrication. With the inevitable consolidation of wage rates throughout shipbuilding, perpetuation of these trades was perceived by shipwrights, caulkers and burners as a victory for their identity—after all by now these men were all members of the Amalgamated Society of Boilermakers. In reality, it consigned these tradesmen to under-deployment, isolated them as 'service trades' to the mainstream steelwork fabrication function, and retained levels of overmanning with pigeon-holed specialisation that hamstrung future productivity.

Shipyard managements were prevented at every juncture from achieving anything like 'singularity' among steelwork trades, yet most of the fabrication process was now shared among loftsmen, platers and welders. This resulting 'power-skill' strata created virtual trade elitism as it accentuated divisive craft limitations. Failure by the Boilermakers Union to recognise and implement these multiplicities of skills, functions and practices into, if not a single *shipbuilder*, then a core of multi-specialised fabricator crafts, was a betrayal to thousands of loyal men who may still have eked a living from a shipbuilding industry of partially reduced capacity. With power should come some shred of responsibility, a maxim as apposite to trade unions and management as it should be to parliamentarians! An unfortunate if highly applicable axiom to the erstwhile lumpish leadership of the Boilermaker's Union, when it had many thousands of shipyard worker members. The myopic misconception by that union that Clyde shipyard managements were beckoning the abolition of restrictive practices and the dismantling of demarcation as a profit-motive palliative, was as half-true as it was incredulous. Foreign shipbuilding opposition would not need to be super efficient, they only needed to employ less than the numbers working on the River Clyde and have them performing more productively!

The high profile ideology, yet regressive attitude to craft retention, and blatant mistrust of shipyard management by unions representing their yard working members, merely demeaned the profile of shipbuilding, and in so doing contributed quite considerably to the industry's demise. A profitable, vibrant shipbuilding industry was as necessary to the well-being of the Boilermakers Union as it was to the directors, shareholders and managers who ran the shipyards, and the tens of thousands who worked in service and supply functions of subcontractors. This torpidity towards change allowed volume shipbuilding to contract then disappear still clinging to the remnants of outmoded working practices as ruthless overseas competition and customer preference dictated otherwise.

It is lamentable that the cultural chasm which separated union and management during the years of full order books could not have been bridged with some form of level-headed thinking towards mutual long-term industrial empathy. The drastic loss of membership achieved in three decades of attrition, coupled with the present diminished status within the trades union movement, are but a few of the unfortunate legacies that the stewards, delegates and full-time officials of the Boilermakers Society have bequeathed on all of the trades, who perpetuated the father to son craftsmanship ethos, of the once powerful and revered ironfighters.

The following selection of photographs depict the work of the tradesmen who were ironfighters in some of the former River Clyde shipyards in the post-war era.

Above, left. *Riveters performing deck plate closure on a cargo ship under construction at Lithgows Ltd, Port Glasgow in the late 1940s. These two fortunate workers are performing the 'easier' down-hand operation. In the ship's hold beneath a pair of up-hand 'hawdur oans' will be resisting the hammering actions of these two. The strake of still white countersunk rivet heads gives some idea of the number of rivets made in a relatively short time.* (Glasgow University Archives)

Above, right. *A riveter operates a pneumatic rivet gun to form a snap-head rivet between the bilge-keel and an internal angle frame on a vessel under construction at Lithgows Ltd in the late 1940s. Note the bolts, clamping plates and frames together prior to riveting, and the white snap heads of recently completed riveted connections.* (Glasgow University Archives)

Middle. *Resplendent in 'full pigskin jacket', an apprentice welder kneels to perform a welding operation on the aft part of the funnel of yard no. 505 m.v. BENLEDI 11,758 g.r.t. built by Chas Connell & Co Ltd in 1965. This garment afforded better protection from 'arc spatter' than the crass 'spartacus', sleeveless, yoke-less, virtually protection-less popular Clydeside jib. This young man also sports highly fashionable Hush Puppy shoes, sleeve length gauntlets and a beret that provides good adhesion and sweat absorption for his face screen or 'bucket'.*

Below, left. *Work under way on the upper deck of yard no. 731, t.s.s.s. EMPRESS OF BRITAIN 25,516 g.r.t. at the Fairfield SB & Eng Co Ltd in 1955. Note the deck seams dogged and toggled ready for welding together, and the precarious bits of staging supporting the caulker/burner at the left and plater at the right. The shipwright in the centre seems quite oblivious to the spatter of burning sparks showering down to his right.*

Below, right. *Resting on a timber baulk for comfort, a left-handed welder performs an overhead closing 'butt' on one of the bottom shell transverse plate seams of yard no. 502, m.v. INVENTOR 9171 g.r.t., in the Scotstoun shipyard of Chas Connell & Co Ltd during the summer of 1963.*

Left. *Lithgows Ltd made serious attempts at higher output from their welders, and introduced as much automatic fabrication equipment as they could afford…and their labour force would accept! This January 1962 view inside Kingston fabrication shed shows a welder operating a semi-automatic twin fillet welding machine (with only one head welding). The unit under construction is a bottom shell section with bulb flat longitudinals being welded to the hull plating. Note the strake of pre-drilled holes at the upper bilge location. These will be riveted to the matching side shell panel on the building berth. Ship no. 1137 became the bulk motor carrier CAPE HOWE 19,032 g.r.t. (Burniston Studios Ltd)*

Middle. *A Messer Sicomat profile burning machine cutting apertures in double bottom tank floors (plate frames) in Lithgows Ltd Kingston shipyard during 1960. The control cabin to the left housed the 'magic eye' that traced one-tenth full size the profile of whatever plate that was to be cut by the multi-headed machine. This German designed and built equipment revolutionised most plate burning operations in the late 1950s and became common place in most British shipyards. (Burniston Studios Ltd)*

Below, left. *The stern-frame and rudder-post assembly of yard no. 735, motor bulk carrier CAPE ST VINCENT 12,835 g.r.t. being fabricated into the lower part of the vessel's aft end in the west yard of John Brown & Co (Clydebank) Ltd in early 1966. This unit is being built on its side, with the aft peak bulkhead on the concrete floor raised and levelled on blocks, forming the flat datum from which to set out the asymmetrical frames. The two welders are performing synchronised welding on each side of the joint in order to minimise distortion. Note the gent at the right in the bowler hat (presumably the head foreman plater) talking to the plater on the staging. The stern tube aperture that will be later machined to accept the propeller shaft is also clearly seen. (Glasgow University Archives)*

Below, right. *A group of loftsmen at work in the 'old' loft of Barclay Curle & Co Ltd, Clydeholm shipyard during 1959. Battens and templates can be noted stored in the roof trusses. The wooden floor is called the 'scrieve board' on which a new ship's 'lines' will be drawn then scrieved full size. The loftsman in the left centre is performing this function. Note the abundance of natural light, and the two apprentices being supervised on the table in the corner.*

Above, left. *The west yard fabrication shed of John Brown & Co (Clydebank) Ltd in 1962, showing part of the aft end of yard no. 715, s.t. BRITISH MARINER 43,605 g.r.t. under construction. The unit is being built upside down and the welders are joining deck beams to the under-side of the steering gear flat, which runs parallel with the ship's keel. Note the use of old railway lines to form a flat building datum, and the two maintenance workers perched up on the shed wall stringers.* (BP Photographic)

Above, right. *This picture shows a plater at work in one of the Lithgow shipyards circa late 1950s. He is 'dogging' a 'wedge' between a 'strong-back' or 'toggle' that is tack welded to the plate on which he is kneeling, and the top of a bulb flat which is to be welded to the plate. This labour intensive practice of skilled 'preparation' work was necessary to position the bulb flat for subsequent fillet welding. UK shipyards never managed to replace this type of work with jigs, fixtures and variable manipulators. Plate stiffening and its positioning, tacking and subsequent welding accounted for over 60% of the man hours used in the construction of all hulls!* (Burniston Studios Ltd)

Below. *The antiquated plating shed of Barclay Curle's Clydeholm shipyard, Whiteinch, circa 1959. Machine tools still in use would be more at home in a museum rather than a working shipyard. Yet the good piecework ethics and obvious familiarisation that existed in this dated facility were not to be replaced by higher productivity from the same labour force working in a totally rebuilt shipyard still located at Whiteinch a few years later.*

Top, left. *The aft end of yard no. 1489 t.s.m.v. BARDIC FERRY 2550 g.r.t. prior to her launch at Dumbarton on 5 March 1957, clearly showing the extended keel, with on either side the port and starboard rudders and propellers. Note the extensive amount of rivets used to connect the ship's frames to her shell plating. The headless shipwright on the right gives some idea of scale. Note also the greased fixed launch ways with the aft poppet cradle arrangement underneath the hull below the propeller shafts.*

Top, right. *Almost the entire tranche of ironfighters are depicted in this picture on board yard no. 502, m.v. INVENTOR 9171 g.r.t., then under construction at the Scotstoun shipyard of Chas Connell & Co Ltd in 1963. The plater, wearing his jacket over his coveralls, and welder in the foreground are 'dogging' together two tween-deck units, whilst in the background a group of shipwrights are 'offering-up' some starboard shell panels to their respective deck chocks, assisted by the caulker/burner with the dark glasses and burning torch, waiting on his next instruction. Bunnets and jackets are well in evidence, and the wet (shiny) deck surface indicates the unpleasantness of open-berth working.*

Below. *A picture that sums up the discipline and camaraderie that existed at all levels in Clyde shipbuilding. Ten retired worthies from the former shipyards of the lower reaches perform a game of draughts in the Wellpark, Greenock in the spring of 1958. The customary bunnet, suit, collar and tie worn by most of the group infer they had a trade or semi-skilled working background, whereas the two gents with the soft hats might have been foremen. Such regular games no doubt prompted recollection of the 'good old bad old days' when only a few of these stalwarts might have had the privilege of continuity of employment, working in the inclemency of the exposed Renfrewshire shipyards during the great depression. The absence of grafitti and vandalism relate to an era when life was less hedonistic and selfish, and most youths had apprenticeships. Note the profusion of paper blinds on the windows of the tenements.* (Burniston Studios Ltd)

Chapter 3

OUTFITTERS

The essential difference between outfit tradesmen and ironfighters is that each outfit trade performs a single function, as opposed to those of the comparative black trades who accomplish partial operations of the steelwork fabrication process. Consequently demarcation tends to be less endemic amongst these artisans. Furthermore, being definitively measurable jobs, outfit trades lend themselves to reasonably accurate estimating, rate-fixing and pricing for piecework, measured day output, or wholesale unit subcontracting, usually managed by the small companies who employ such trades. These different trades performed unique types of work, pertaining to each and every type of ship built. The collective skills deployed, by virtue of their respective definitions, afforded a flexibility and marketability away from shipbuilding when contraction and closures of shipyards gathered apace. This simplistic analogy would have been no more than a transfer of employee to new employer, were it not for the fact that much of the indigenous engineering and manufacturing industry of the West of Scotland was, initially, and eventually inextricably linked to that former great provider and customer: *shipbuilding*. Specific skills borne by redundant outfit tradesmen were both marketable and transferable, although many had to adapt, retrain or in the worst cases, de-skill themselves in order to maintain a living. Initially abhorrent aspects, but far preferable to industrious tradesmen than dependence on the state for benefit. Outfit trades comprised two distinct divisions consisting of many different artisans. These were *marine engineers* and other *outfitters*.

Marine engineers comprised fitters, turners, borers, grinders, millwrights, patternmakers, miscellaneous smiths and a plethora of subcontractors from tool-makers to moulders and founders. Virtually all time-served craftsmen but, when employed individually or collectively in a marine engine works, appositely referred to by themselves and contemporaries as…marine engineers. Under 20,000 marine engineers were employed by the eighteen engine works that existed on the River Clyde during the boom post-war years of the 1950s. Essentially *the* traditional heavy mechanical engineering industry, engine building was not adverse to the imposition of advancing technology – after all engineers were the initial innovators! Their existence was dependant on the efficiency of the engines they built, so why shouldn't they impart the benefits of parallel production engineering developments onto their shop floor? In principle this tenet was applied to all of the engine works on the River Clyde. Rolling capital expenditure featured in the annual returns of companies who revealed their accounts. Each new lathe, boring mill, gear-cutter, planer, grinder or drilling machine was tangible evidence to the commitment in new plant and equipment of the private concerns who did not publicise their balance sheets. Every recently installed machine tool assisted with the attainment of the combined aims of greater output at lower unit costs. This superior equipment invariably created higher standards of manufacturing tolerances that were directly reflected in superior workmanship throughout the entire assembly process.

The unfortunate underlying element in this quest for ephemeral efficiency was that each engine built —diesel or steam—was a 'one off'. Economies of investment in new plant were therefore proportional to the ability of that new machine tool to recoup its capital cost against the profit margin on each engine manufactured, at the same time reducing the duration, labour costs, and unit overheads previously borne by the former operations that were now replaced. Fundamentally the more efficacious the engine-builder, the more engines they had to build, in order to remain efficient, profitable…and stay in business.

The labour employed in these marine engine works was hyper-skilled, dedicated, proud, adroit and productive. These men not only built many faultless engines: they also built generations of engineers from raw 'pimple-pocked' school boys! During the boom years of the 1950s, most Clyde engine works encouraged young journeymen engineers to 'go to sea' after completion of their apprenticeships. This policy of 'off-loading' a partial surplus of trained skilled labour satisfied a lot of aspirations and fulfilled many requirements. Some young engineers wanted to join the British Merchant Navy as a free vehicle to see the world. Others wanted to become career, sea-going marine engineers. Others wanted neither! Distraught, rapidly becoming homesick and seasick, they didn't or couldn't remember how or why they were where they were, and returned with piston-firing alacrity to life onshore. Stirred and shaken, these young engineers found the experience memorable, maybe even invaluable, but were convinced in their hasty indomitable resolve that sea-going marine engineering was more than a wee bit different from building engines! Three years spent at sea in the British Merchant Navy was also an acceptable alternative to National Service, permissible by HM Government in lieu of conscription, even if it was purgatory to the pro-tem seamen who were really landsmen at heart!

This circle of instruction and re-investment of trained expertise was one of the many 'invisible national assets' that emanated from the proud traditional industry of marine engineering. The British Merchant Navy, primarily the main recipient of marine engine works products, received a pool of willing, if somewhat immature, partially trained personnel, very familiar with marine engine construction who were an adaptable alternative to the press-gang recruitment methods of yore! This continual supply of enthusiastic hands-on artisans, whose training costs were paid by their previous employer provided a source of skilled, relatively cheap labour that was exploited by shipping companies because of the young engineer's innate inducement to sea-going life. Those tradesmen who returned onshore imparted operating expertise of engines at work, that was disseminated by management and workmates alike. Clyde trained marine engineers who displayed more than average amounts of interest, aptitude, technical awareness, academic fulfilment, through day-release or evening classes, and industrious work ethics, set the bench mark for the unique combination of theoretical/practical capability, becoming the envy of their contemporaries throughout the engineering world.

A parallel training course with a heavier scholastic slant was also offered, and sponsored by most major UK shipping companies who recruited their own engineer apprentices straight from school. These trainees were referred to as cadets. This particular type of marine engineer spent a similar five-year training duration, that was sandwiched between a combination of full-time attendance at a technical college, supplemented with practical experience in the workshops of an engine builder, and regular voyages as a sea-going trainee engineer.

The comprehensive engineering skills exhibited in a marine engine works were much sought after by other manufacturing companies. When workload diminished, or engines and turbines were finished ahead of schedule, it was not uncommon for marine engine builders to subcontract some of their pool of fitters, turners and borers to outside contract site projects. This suited both engine works and the new customer. The former could recoup training costs and deploy his skilled labour force on fill-in, semi-lucrative jobs, while the latter could obtain specific engineering expertise without incurring the expensive training, capital machinery and fixed overhead costs associated with a heavy engineering establishment. Other forms of subcontract fill-in engineering encompassed in-house machining and fitting of a variety of components for many non-marine customers, using machine tools that were never fully utilised building diesel engines, gearboxes and steam turbines. All this diverse activity was taken on to fill a hiatus created between high and low levels of workload. Ably carried out by that multitude of adroit artisans collectively referred to as *marine engine builders* as opposed to sea-going marine engineers who made ships go!

The all embracing skill base that was an inherent and integral facet of each marine engineer's formative training, was lost on young journeymen ironfighters who aspired to become boilermakers or fabricators. A typical training itinerary for a marine engineer consisted of specific durations spent in the tool-room, fitting shop, thence operating all the different lathes or vertical and horizontal boring mills. Additional expertise was gleaned in the gear-cutting shop, heat treatment furnace, heavy machine shop, usually culminating in the engine erection shop and test-bed, occasionally interspersed with short spells in the planning, estimating and maybe even drawing offices. Further education of apprentices was actively encouraged by all companies. This experience in the building of engines, gear-boxes and turbines would be augmented, with regular site experience whence a completed engine would be knocked down, transported by lorry or coaster, then re-erected in the engine-room of the ship for which it was intended, sometimes in component parts weighing 60 to 80 tons if that ship wasn't yet launched, or the complete engine would be lifted on board using the engine works or adjacent quayside heavy fixed craneage.

The one specific shipbuilding task that entailed the marine engineers overlapping with the steelwork trades, was the function of line-boring the stern-frame prior to shipping the stern-tube. The fitting thereafter of the propeller, shaft and gland-packing had to be completed prior to the launching of each new ship in order to ensure total water tightness of the hull. To enable the engineers to finish this operation, the erection and weld-out of the stern-frame, shaft tunnel, aft end framing engine room double bottom, tank top and engine bed-plate needed to be completed first. The critical action of boring-out the stern-frame to accommodate the stern-tube was achieved by sighting the centre line of this hole through the shaft tunnel to line up with the centre line of the engine crank-shaft or gear-box. This skilled operation was performed using a combination of tape rules, templates, slip blocks, verniers, callipers and a piano wire— a taut piece of fine gauge tough steel cable—that provided the discernible datum from engine to propeller. This function was always performed on the declivity building berth. After the shaft axis was established, the boring-out gear was set-up concentric and square to this line, enabling the bore of the stern-frame to be turned true to the required alignment.

Subsequent successful installation of the lignum vitae or white metal lined stern-tube and propeller tail shaft, which rested on shimmed plummer blocks, was dependant on the accuracy of the initial boring of the stern-frame aperture. On ships whose building schedule had slipped for various reasons, it was not uncommon for the engineers to be performing all of the above tasks, whilst subjected to a cascade of welding and burning spatter raining down from a team of ironfighters working overhead. That the above comprehensive engineering expertise should culminate in manufacturing definitions as specific as fitter, turner, grinder, borer and the like, was a product of the need for a productive and flexible manufacturing structure, rather than a plateau of skill development.

Virtually all of these engineers were capable of performing cross-discipline functions, very much as a result of intensive perception of manufacturing principles, learned or instilled during the formative years of technical training. However, the respective monetary weightings attached to every specific task, coupled to unique quality and output requirements of each job, ensured a natural selection process, whereby the top tradesmen were entrusted with the most complex operations and invariably were rewarded accordingly. This group of tradesmen were employed primarily to produce the engine, boiler or turbine components, thousands in number, from bushes and pins to crankshafts and cylinder heads. Castings, forgings, blades, gears, bearings and fabrications were usually made outside the engine works by a further batch of skilled subcontractors. In some cases such procured parts were heat treated, ground, honed or lapped, to finished machine tolerances then delivered to the engine works for acceptance, installation and testing. In other cases, raw material—ferrous, non-ferrous, alloy and synthetic—was delivered to the stockyard or stores, identified, piece-marked then duly despatched to the appropriate machining or fitting centre where it further resembled an engine, gear-box turbine or auxiliary component.

Machining, balancing and finishing crankshafts, making, then trial fitting pistons, rings, cylinder liners, cross-heads, gudgeon-pins into diesel engine housings, was never seen by time-served engineers as just being component sub-assembly! Transforming black billets of steel into bright gleaming parts that resembled objects of impressionist artwork as much as functional elements of marine engines, attested to the tangible empathy that existed between engine designer and hands-on tradesman. Reading shop drawings, setting-up various types of machine tools, working out sequential location, cutting or fitting operations, each time totally aware that inadequate clamping or over-machining could result in scrapping of valuable components, appointed an endemic combination of responsibility and job interest.

This was real shop floor accountability, where the summation of each tradesman's individual skills was the deafening knocking and shuddering vibration of a large bore marine diesel engine developing thousands of man-made shaft horse-power on the engine test bed. A vastly different amplitude and frequency was created by the more complex array of machinery inherent within a steam turbine. Coupled by shafts to herring-bone gear-boxes nestling in a labyrinth of asbestos insulated pipework, fed by boilers and condensers, the constant humming, whirring and hissing of this assembly revealed vibrant audibility as this one-time preferred method of marine propulsion produced measured output torque to its simulated propeller. Less popular combinations of gas turbines or diesel-electric units tended to be specified only by the Royal Navy for use in either frigates or submarines.

Any engineer who worked on the construction of a marine engine or a superheated steam turbine will adjure to the peerlessness of his particular footprint on that machinery. After all if each hull and superstructure was unique, then the engine that propelled that ship through the sea was just as individual. A sound ship comprised a seaworthy hull driven by powerful and reliable engines.

Marine engineers fared better than other shipbuilding trades when engine works closures took place in tandem with the demise of shipyards. In the 1960s, there then existed a number of heavy mechanical engineering companies in the West of Scotland, all with reasonably healthy order books, each employing many thousands of skilled men and women. The finished products of these firms usually bore little resemblance to marine engines. However, the clawing odour created by diluted coolant dripping onto hot bright metal being machined, was redolent of the lingering smells of former riverside heavy machine shops.

Albion, Rootes, Weir Pumps, Euclid, Caterpillar, Babcock & Wilcox, Rolls Royce, Anderson-Mavor, and many others, all with their myriad of respective subcontractors formed part of a 'non-marine' engineering industry, although Weir Pumps and Babcock & Wilcox made many items for marine use. This prospective alternative employment market was successfully penetrated by many able and adaptable engineers made redundant by the closure of Clyde engine works. Sadly now, some of these once famous companies have either disappeared from the map of industrial Scotland, or have contracted to smaller, less labour intensive remnants. They made different products, but the artisanship required for these 'new' industries was soon demonstrated to more than acceptable standards by former marine engineers, arguably among the most important tradesmen required by an island nation.

The collection of mainly 'white' trades who comprised the bulk of the non-marine engineer outfitters, were those who 'finished' the work content required to complete a ship thus enabling issue of a 'certificate of sea-worthiness', distributed after extensive scrutiny by the Board of Trade inspector. This comprehensive listing of tradesmen, many of whom derived part of their livelihood from outwith shipbuilding, were contracted to provide specific adornments, appurtenances, facilities or functions depending on the uniqueness of that particular vessel. The basic 'core' trades of electrician, ship's plumber, blacksmith, joiner, sheet metal worker, rigger and painter were supplemented on a sporadic basis with such pure specialists as upholsterers, glaziers, terrazzo floor tilers, insulators, carpet fitters, refrigeration engineers and vendors' specialist representatives, who would oversee the correct installation, testing and commissioning of the essential and preferential equipment that owners insisted upon being fitted into their new ship.

The total number and mix of core outfit trades employed varied from yard to yard along the River Clyde. All of the shipyards maintained distinct sections within their respective drawing offices. These were usually steelwork, piping, electrical and arrangement, or outfit, which was responsible for the draughting, and sometimes outside manufacture or procurement of all of the additional equipment for each ship.

The electrical drawing office, in the medium to larger-sized shipyards was responsible for all of the electrical work content. This ranged from the design and specification of electric motors, contactor panels, generators, alternators, batteries, invertors, transformers to cables and electric light fittings. Installation of these items would be undertaken by the shipyard electrical department, usually consisting of a nucleus of in-house foremen and some *electricians*, whose numbers would be swelled by subcontract labour depending on the work content, complexity and exigencies of each ship contract.

The medium to smaller-sized shipyards tended to subcontract the electrical work element of each new building or conversion contract that they were awarded. Invariably this type of arrangement was tied up in a form of share holding or part ownership of that electrical subcontractor by some, or all, of the shipyard directors. This example of contract management worked very well. It was an area where specialised rationalisation was identified and implemented, with mutual savings to the shipyard, sometimes with enhanced earning capacity for the subcontract electricians.

The large pool of shipyard or boat electricians tended to move from yard to yard, 'wiring-up' all of the electrical systems on the ships that were being built. Wage rates during the post-war boom years were very consistent, varying only by a few 'old pence' (or coppers) an hour, invariably linked to each shipyard's distinctive piecework bonus scheme. These 'coppers' an hour differentials 'sparked' wage disputes with wildfire profusion, depending on the volume of electrical work available. Invariably motivated by monetary reward, good 'sparks' were conspicuous by their aversion to, and avoidance of 'who does what disputes'! These 'good sparks' built up a reputation for quality and performance, every bit as favourable as their more famous black trade or marine engineering workmates. Trained to standards of technical comprehension and levels of workmanship envied by other industries, many electricians left shipbuilding during this period, disenchanted, disheartened and partly impoverished by the inconsistent earning levels. The electrical skills gleaned in cabling marine equipment was a sound basis for the growing onshore petrochemical plant construction projects that were burgeoning at this time. Former shipyard 'sparkies' initially found these new specifications challenging, but the increased financial rewards soon became very acceptable palliatives for the only drawback…the long hours of toil and exhaustive travelling that this new form of contracting required.

The cargo, utility, ballast, sewage, or fire-fighting pipework that are important and integral parts of a ship are fabricated, installed and tested by the adept, flexible and innovative trade known as *ships' plumbers*. Directed by the piping drawing office, the plumbing shop carried experienced ships' plumbers who were known as 'sketchers'. The responsibility of these men was to translate the information depicted on the respective piping general arrangement drawings into isometric sketches, whereby the ships' plumbers would be able to make lengths of pipe known as spools in the plumbing shop. These spools would either be joined together using unions, flanges, bolts and gaskets, or be welded onto other pipes by a further trade called *plumber/welder*. This combination was arguably the best example of sensible cross-fertilisation of trades, whereby two independent crafts mixed and matched their complimentary skills to produce a multi-discipline, effective and efficient tradesman.

This evolution was not a straightforward transition, and was not achieved in every Clyde Shipyard! Much enmity was expounded by other trades, especially by obdurate and intransigent hull welders who saw this consolidation as an erosion of their rapidly acquired power base. However, it transpired through a long process of bitter demarcation disputes, that the resolve, dexterity and marketability of the plumber/welder was a wee bit more enduring than the furtive, might-crazed selfish ascendancy of the flat-bashing limited prowess of their fellow tradesmen! The intricacy of pipework that was to be fabricated, then installed into the many confined spaces, pipe-passages, double-bottoms and cargo tanks of ships presented a challenging 'obstacle course' for the proficient plumber/welder. Only men with sound work ethics, bereft of claustrophobia, and more than a passing interest in their craft, made the grade. Depending on their intended usage, many of the spools so constructed had to be sent outside the shipyard for hot-dip-galvanising after fabrication but prior to installation in the ship.

Welding instructors throughout the steel fabrication industry propound the easiness for any welder to join together flat-bar stiffeners onto a double-bottom tank girder, compared to performing a 360 degree butt weld at a compound angle on a cargo pipe in a tank or hold. Despite the ostensible flexibility between trades, the complexity and volume of pipework required for each type of ship inevitably created its own level of specialisation. Fabrication shop plumbers, shop welders, plumber-erector-installers, positional welders—with the ability/facility of each tradesman to set up and tack weld as and when required—exemplified the flexibility of this craft. All these tasks had their own 'piecework' weightings and, like all of the jobs in the shipbuilding trade pyramid, only a few men were capable of performing the complex three-dimensional pipe elbow developments, with an equally small number able to weld these assemblies together without incurring defects.

The protean range of pipework in the ship's plumbing department, or the subcontractor's fabrication shop provided an excellent training ground for those individuals with an aggressive 'can-do' attitude. Prior to the accelerated run-down of volume shipbuilding on the River Clyde, some former ships' plumbers were being recruited by the growing petro-chem construction industry. The able and productive tradesmen, who successfully made this transition coped with mastering the different codes, standards and practices of this new industry with the adroitness of their traditional crafts. Few regretted their adaptation of this alternative occupation with its double barrelled cognomen of *pipe-fitter*, a title that attracted higher rates of pay than ship's plumber or any of its multi-skilled derivatives.

Blacksmith, as the sonorous name implies, is a trade which wrought raw unfinished steel into a multitude of products of various shapes, complexities and specific marine applications. Work varied from the making of spiral ornate staircases for passenger liners, ferries and cruise ships, to the forging of stanchions, cleats, sheaves, complicated brackets, hangers and chains used extensively throughout all ship types, but rarely seen or appreciated by those other than a ship's crew. Most marine engine works also employed blacksmiths who made a diverse range of hot-worked shapes to be used in marine engine manufacture. Probably the oldest craft in the history of metal working, the highly specialised workload produced by this trade remained virtually unaffected by the onset of welded fabrication methods and improved techniques of metallurgy. Whilst a very physical, dirty and noisy job, the bulk of the output from the blacksmith's shop was invariably associated with outfit trades, such as ships' plumbers, riggers, shipwrights and marine engineers. Using hydraulic and latterly mechanical presses (or power hammers), '*The Smithy*' was capable of working steel, hot or cold, to obtain the required metal flow, grain structure, ductility, malleability, toughness or hardness and complexity of shape required for each special product.

Not every shipyard possessed a blacksmith's shop. The high overheads of plant and equipment purchase, coupled with the fuel costs (coke) for the furnaces and ovens, and the relatively small product output, meant that only yards with reasonable workloads could sustain this facility. The shipyards with smiddies actively pursued regular subcontract work from smaller shipbuilders. The increased throughput that this created, stabilised workload and continuity of employment, as well as usually covering overheads. 'Outside' subcontract work was pursued, tendered and obtained for: railings, gates and staircases to be installed in hotels, parks and public buildings. Small batches of special components were occasionally made for lorry and railway wagon builders. This reasonably wide range of diverse, non-shipbuilding products was possible when Scotland had a broad spectrum of manufacturing engineering and development work, meaning that under-utilisation of the shipyard smithy and forge, could be channelled to supply the sporadic demands of other busy industries.

Not to be confused with ships' carpenters (latterly known as shipwrights), *joiners* performed the manufacture and fitting of the non-metallic architectural elements within the steel superstructure carcass that had been fabricated by the ironfighters. This work extended from the 'marking-off' of steel accommodation decks to accept the internal wooden or, more recently, plastic laminated bulkheads, already partly constructed in unit form in the joiners shop, to the design and manufacture of most of the furniture required in the cabins, offices, staterooms, lounges, cinemas and other living spaces throughout the ships' accommodation areas.

Arguably the most definitive and quantitative of all the outfit shipbuilding trades, this ease of unique job establishment lent the joiner craft to be readily identified and subsequently packaged into production targets of measurable outputs, commonly and collectively known as 'contract' piecework. This method of incentive payment assured a fixed price, shared among the participating tradesmen and helpers, for a measured amount of joinery work. Once the sum total was suitably accepted by management and joiners' representatives, payment was duly authorised. Basic wages could be drawn against the contract amount each week. The incentive for the joiners was to complete the work-scope as soon as possible…and thence obtain the balance as a completion bonus. This system worked exceptionally well at the Scotstoun shipyard of Charles Connell & Co Limited.

Joiners had a reasonable amount of autonomy in the execution of their work. Bereft of virtually any negative impact due to bad weather, as soon as accommodation spaces were completed by platers, welders, shipwrights, electricians, ships plumbers and painters, joiners would have the internal bulkhead partition battens installed in a handful of shifts. Where necessary, terrazzo, bitumastic or phenolic floor coverings were installed around these upstands, then each accommodation space would resemble a mini furniture store as walls, desks, beds, wardrobes, divans, tables and chairs appeared in their respective woods, laminates and veneers. These were then quickly installed with jigsaw puzzle accuracy, to bewilder fellow shipyard workers, management and owners as to how they were painstakingly located into such small finished spaces! This bamboozlement was all a product of phased installation methods—many bulkheads were incomplete until all furniture and fittings were safely, accurately and securely positioned.

Wood was the primary material used for the manufacture of marine furniture. From the minuscule cabins of tiny coasters to the expansive sumptuous day rooms of high class passenger liners, the finest tropical hardwoods were profusely utilised. Each item made displayed the individual craft skills of the joiners and upholsterers. However the surface finish and ultimate durability of desks, tables, chairs or wardrobes was created by the proficiency of another craft, the *french polishers*.

Unique throughout the entire UK shipbuilding industry, this trade was a harbinger of sexual emancipation in that it employed women and men in virtually equal amounts. The skill of the french polisher was measured by their capability of transforming pallid insipid obeche, stale ochrous teak or inconsistent cinnabaric mahogany into lustrous grain defined durable surfaces that immediately changed not only the appearance of the wood, but also that of the entire cabin. Usually located adjacent to the shipyard joiner's shop, the vaporous aromatic petroleum-based smell that permeated the french polishing department created so many involuntary euphoric highs, as it produced biliousness or long-term ill effects induced from its inadvertent inhalation. Even the wholesale advent of plastic laminated woodchip and veneered plywood for internal ships bulkheads failed to eliminate the need for this highly specialised function. French polishers remained part of the diminishing yet varied inventory of outfit trades so long as ships had cabins.

Another reasonably flexible trade who carried their 'own' welders were the *sheet metal workers*, who relied on the outfit drawing office for the production of arrangement drawings, depicting ventilation trunking, galley, laundry and cold store stainless steel furniture, cupboards and shelving, as well as lots of other miscellaneous lightweight metal items. The flexibility of this trade, like that of the ships' plumbers and electricians was far greater among the subcontract companies who supplied the shipyards than it was within the big yards who had their own in-house sheetmetal working facilities. Basically, sheet metal workers fabricated steel, aluminium and stainless steel up to and including a plate thickness of quarter-inch (6 mm). Above that gauge was generally accepted as being within the scope and capability of platers. The exception tended to be the use of stainless steel, which when used on special applications above quarter-inch was usually still fabricated by sheet metal workers. Hull welders were invariably ill-disposed to successfully perform the inert gas process needed to weld alloys. Furthermore, the sheet metal workshop was specifically equipped to perform such welding, as well as possessing the special cutting and forming machinery also necessary for this type of material.

Sheet metal workshops contained a diverse range of expensive plant and equipment, all tailor-made by specialist machine tool makers to facilitate the different workability of steel, aluminium and stainless steel. 'Use' of these items of machinery was not seen as the right of a given tradesman, consequently sheet metal workers became very adept and productive at the development, setting-out, fabrication, erection and installation of all of the facets of sheet metal fabrication. A large amount of this work, especially the ventilation and air-conditioning trunking, and support steelwork was deemed 'lift, make and fit'. Using freehand sketches, single line diagrams, sometimes arrangements and layouts produced by the outfit drawing office, 'sheetys' would sketch the simplest routing for the required fabrication. This would be approved by the sheet metal shop foreman or manager, be passed to the rate-fixer for pricing, material ordered or obtained from stock, then manufacture would commence. Invariably most of this work could only take place when, the respective cargo holds, plant rooms, galley, laundry, engine casing and other accommodation spaces had been constructed by the steelworkers. This meant that sheet metal workers were always one of the last trades to be allowed unrestricted access to the ship, either prior to launching or immediately the vessel entered the water. The diverse range of products made by sheet metal shops that existed within the larger shipyards was not lost on the business acumen of shipyard managers and directors. Just as the smaller shipyards used subcontract sheet metal work companies, so the larger shipyards subcontracted their specialised equipment and skilled labour to other industries. However, if no such fill-in work materialised then most of the unfortunate souls would be paid off. The sundry scope of skills and techniques gleaned by 'sheetys' with good work ethics produced versatile tradesmen well versed in the full spectrum of light gauge metal fabrication.

The one traditional shipbuilding trade that has been insidiously pushed towards the edge of extinction due to the tumultuous changes in ship design, as much as the attempted modernisation of shipbuilding practices, is the *rigger*. In the days of sail, wooden ships were built by shipwrights and rigged by sailmakers and riggers. Steel hull construction spawned steel-working trades. When these early ships were fitted with reliable steam engines, sails were no longer required, however, masts and derricks required for merchant and naval vessels remained a necessity or aesthetic feature for many decades, up until the advent of shipboard deck cranes in the late 1950s. These cranes were supplied in knock-down kit form, requiring only minor installation and commissioning work to complete...or so the manufacturers advocated! In any case, the rigging or reeving work on these new products was considerably diminished, when compared to that of traditional cargo liners with conventional masts and derricks. These cranes were designed and built with sheaves already installed on the jib, their hoist drums fitted to the cab housing, requiring only the reeving of the lifting wire to complete the rigging content, followed by additional interface with electricians and fitters.

A further technological blow to the rigger's existence was the design, also in the 1950s, of the universal bulk carrier or UBC. The bulk carrier rapidly became the most ubiquitous ship type of the 1960s. Most of the Clyde shipyards belatedly entered the construction market for these vessels. Built for rapid loading and discharge by high capacity dockside cranes, more than 70% of these ships were constructed without any derricks or craneage, and consequently less rigging! The replacement of fixed derricks with higher capacity travelling cranes, negated much of the need for extensive rigging activity during the ship erection sequence on the building berth. Prefabricated units that comprised hull, deck or bulkhead plating with frames and longitudinals already welded in place were constructed with such inherent stiffness that the temporary array of guys and strops previously required for single frame/single plate erection methods were now considered redundant. Whatever assistance was required to pull or push these fabricated sections into place on the berth now became the domain of the shipwrights.

Rigging lofts were usually isolated outbuildings, strewn with rusty shackles, sheaves, wire ropes and hooks. Gradually they degenerated from skill centres for reeving and splicing into dilapidated ram-shackled 'howfs', inhabited by disheartened gnarled old riggers, with very few apprentices. Their total numbers now counted in handfuls, rather than the previous hundreds. Continuity of employment was uncertain for this traditional craft. At least these diminished numbers were ensured a chance of retention, assisting the shipyard maintenance fitters with overhead and berth crane repairs and wire rope change-out, where their rigging expertise allied to their innate comfort for working at elevations was fully utilised. Displaced shipyard riggers adapted to life outside the yards. With their inherent head for heights, many became erectors in the construction industry, others ended up offshore, in the infant UK oil platform construction industry, where the title rigger is somewhat of a misnomer for a 'helper' of the more skilled artisans. The rigging element in that industry is restricted to the provision of lifting assistance with pipes, fabrications and items of equipment, even the reeving of cranes is performed by specialist personnel.

The 'last' outfit trade employed by most of the shipyards was the *painter/red leader* (pronounced *'ridd leedur'*). Traditionally the final trade to get access to completed steelwork, pipework, sheet metalwork or outside procured ships' equipment, the painter was required to transform a rust bespeckled hulk into a pristine shop window product in as short a time as possible, despite the inclemency of West of Scotland weather! By the early 1960s most of the yards had installed in-line shot-blasting and spray-painting booths, a facility that enabled all plates and sections to be cleaned and prime-coated prior to the start of prefabrication. This investment did reduce some of the manual painting activity, however it also created a new problem with the formation of a foul cocktail of noxious odours during welding in pre-painted areas. These objectionable fumes given off by this operation generated such resentment by welders that whatever material benefits this aspect of modernisation achieved, it was seriously deficient in its consideration of matters of environmental health.

Aided by the inimitable dimensional skills of loftsmen and platers, the draught marks, plimsoll lines, hull colour scheme, boot topping, name and port of registry were applied speedily by the painter to a ship hull, sometimes further assisted by the small band of welders who could do sign-writing with their tongs and electrodes! All this hull decoration work had to be done with painstaking accuracy, intimidated by 'piecework' motivated stagers who were trying to strip the staging almost as soon as the painters had finished, in preparation for the impending launching of the new ship. It was not unusual for the painter to be suspended from a makeshift staging, constructed of a couple of planks held by a pair of ropes! When finished, the external colour scheme of the hull, superstructure, hatch covers, masts, derricks or cranes displayed the noticeable skill of the ship's painter.

The 'hidden' work-scope was just as considerable. With the exception of some crude oil tankers, all other types of ship required painting or special coating of their cargo spaces. When the frames, bulkheads, tween-decks, tanks, pipe passages, engine room and miscellaneous areas like deck-houses are taken into account, this hidden work could amount to more than three times that of the ostensible paintwork! These areas were far from accessible. As soon as fabricated units were completed and inspected, they were available for painting or, in many corrosive areas like double-bottom tanks, the application of red lead—a painting process that created heavy vapour fumes, now deemed injurious to health. This was applied manually by brush or roller in confined spaces with, at best, crude air extraction equipment only. At worst, paint as much as you could before you became 'spaced-out' with the fumes, or you got 'carried out' by your mates or gaffer, hopefully after you met your piecework targets!

The remaining band of tradesmen, trades-ladies and specialists who performed the final outfit functions were not usually employed by shipyards. Some trades, like insulators, were utilised quite consistently on the lagging of pipes in engine rooms and accommodation spaces as well as the fitting of insulation material on refrigerated cargo ships. Known throughout the River Clyde as 'white mice', initially because of their white boilersuits, but more appositely because of the adherence of asbestos (dust and paste), the essential components of wet applied insulation. This process was identified some years after the zenith of post-war shipbuilding, as most hazardous and injurious, and has subsequently been banned from wholesale application in UK manufacturing industry. Some insulators and many other former workers who contracted asbestosis, allegedly as a result of working on ships during the '40s, '50s, and '60s, have raised legal actions against former employers.

Terrazzo floor coverers were another group of regular subcontract specialists, required to screed the floors of showers, bathrooms, laundries, galleys, food stores and special cargo spaces. As the name implies, this specialist function was of Italian origin, and all the companies who performed this work remained in the control of Italian families. Scottish labour was employed, and carried out a lot of these flooring contracts, however, access to the marble and ceramic materials imported from Italy ensured this industry was not for transfer of ownership.

Vendor's engineers were required to supervise the installation of virtually every piece of 'bought-out' equipment that carried a warranty. This superfluous function, or so the bulk of the yard engineers thought, was specified by owners and shipbuilders alike, to alleviate any costly liens imposed on the shipbuilders, or delays or damage to cargo, during the vessel guarantee period of up to one year after completion of the builders and owners trials. From engineers who specialised in the operation of refrigerator plant, winches, pumps, deck cranes, air conditioning, hatch covers, to navigation and communication equipment, this group of vendors could always be found fastidiously directing and cajoling shipwrights, engineers, electricians and plumbers to change, modify, adjust, remove, tighten up, etc., prior to and during sea trials.

Neither ironfighters nor outfitters, the shipyard or engine works maintenance crews, were the unsung unfavoured few who made the establishment work. Comprising mechanical fitters, millwrights, electricians, plumbers and handymen, most companies referred to their 'plant department' as a mixed bag of 'hands-on specialists' who knew every bit of shipyard equipment far more intimately than their respective families. They should have, as the main prerequisite to work in the maintenance section, no strong family ties due to the inordinate number of hours worked by these men maintaining essential plant, thus ensuring that production output from the shipyard could be met without disruptions due to breakdowns.

The fairer sex figured most significantly and admirably in the short-term tenure of shipboard specialists. Ladies fitted curtains, upholstered in situ furniture, as well as performing repairs to damaged couches and settees. They also cleaned the accommodation spaces to seaborne four-star hotel standard, and woe betide any slovenly tradesman or helper who deliberately or inadvertently traipsed through their pristine handywork!

When this stage of ship completion was reached, absenteeism among miscreant lothario shipyard tradesmen was redirected from the 'howf' or pub...towards the outfit quay. A crookedly concocted, spurious excuse for their presence on board the ship would be hatched with haste by these scamps and proffered to whoever was in charge. This risible ruse would be cross-examined, possibly approved or more likely refuted by the outfit manager or foreman, summarily denying access to the ship followed by a stern rebuke, and maybe even suspension for a day or two.

If admission was granted, any further prevarication amongst the industrious ladies, old and young, would be embarrassingly met with either a tirade of personal abuse attesting to the young man's laziness, or a more vexing rebuttal from these sirens of shipbuilding, whose susceptibility to flattery was not concordant with their objective of achieving their respective piecework bonuses even if it did make them feel good for a few fleeting moments. Invariably, this action was rounded-off with a collective salvo of monosyllabic prurient calumny, this time directed towards the gullible supervisor who sanctioned the interloper's presence... Right of reply was not considered part of the management's prowess in such indiscreet circumstances. Alas, many a true romance was founded on such a potent combination of inveterate dogged pursuit and rebounding acerbic lampoonery!

The selection of photographs on the following pages illustrate some of the different craftsmen who made up a part of the outfit trades seen working at activities associated with their diverse range of skills.

Bereft of safety harness and working on a precarious staging, a well-dressed painter sporting a Tony Curtis hairstyle with his unspeckled jacket worn over his coveralls, applies the name to yard no. 503 m.v. LETABA 6897 g.r.t. at the Greenock Dockyard Co Ltd during the summer of 1963. Such dangerous working practices have long since been replaced in what remains of the River Clyde shipbuilding industry. (Burniston Studios Ltd)

Right. *A group of skilled marine engine builders (probably fitters) installing a rotor shaft complete with blades into the bottom half of a high pressure steam turbine casing (that already contains the stator blades) at the Finnieston engine works of David Rowan & Co Ltd in 1956. Note the four vertical guides that will accurately locate the rotor shaft concentric with the stator and prevent damage. The whistle in the mouth of the gent at the left is his method of contact with the crane driver above. Part of the low pressure steam turbine for this contract (order no. 1281) can be seen in the background, already fitted with rotor/ stator assembly.*

Middle. *The light machine shop of the former Finnieston marine engine works of Harland & Wolff Ltd circa 1959, when the company still had a reasonable order book. Noticeable in this view are some of the many 'small' parts made on-site that were essential components of a large bore diesel engine, viz pistons and very*

(continued)

large hexagonal nuts and bolts. Noticeable also is the fact that the two centre lathes in the foreground, and the two capstan/turret lathes beyond bear the name 'Lang', a former venerable Scottish manufacturer of heavy machine tools.

Below, right. *Assisted by a group of shipyard workers, including engineers and riggers, the port 2SA 10 cylinder 'Denny-Sulzer' diesel engine is lowered into the engine casing of yard no. 1489, t.s.m.v. BARDIC FERRY 2550 g.r.t. during fitting-out at Dumbarton in the summer of 1957.*

Below, left. *Probably the most exacting and prestigious turning job in an engine works was the individual turning of the journal diameters of a balanced crank shaft. Such an operation is about to be performed by a pair of top class tradesmen resplendent in status discerning dust coats on a six cylinder crankshaft, on a Cravens crankshaft lathe at the Greenock engine works of John G. Kincaid & Co Ltd in 1965.*

Left. *A batch of recently fabricated pipe spools about to be heat-treated or stress-relieved in the pipe shop furnace of Fairfields (Glw) Ltd circa 1967. The furnace is the container-like building in the background. Note the four chain slings attached from its roof to an overhead electric travelling crane which will lift the furnace or oven on top of the firebrick plinth. Heat is induced from gas-fuelled burner nozzles within the furnace.*

Middle. *A crew of blacksmiths and hammermen hot-work a heavy billet of white hot steel in the smithy of David Rowan & Co Ltd Finnieston engine works circa 1956. At this early stage of forging it is difficult to ascertain what the component will be, most likely a connecting-rod for a David Rowan Sulzer or Doxford marine diesel engine. Note the combined expressions of confidence and concentration clearly indicated on the faces of the entire group. The Lithgow owned engine works of David Rowan & Co Ltd were amalgamated with the other group marine engine builders to become Fairfield-Rowan Ltd in the early 1960s, an association that would only last until 1965.*

Below, left. *Joiners, labourers, helpers and electricians at work in the accommodation section of yard no. 741 m.v. TREVAYLOR 6501 g.r.t. shortly after launching from the Clydeholm ship-yard of Barclay Curle & Co Ltd in the spring of 1959.*

Below, right. *The then 'state-of-the-art' joiners shop at Barclay Curle & Co Ltd, Clydeholm shipyard shortly after inauguration in 1960. Dehumidifiers, dust extractors, electric lighting and marked-out passageways in addition to a whole inventory of new machine tools made this facility second to none when pronounced for business. The facility was so good that subcontract work outwith the yard's shipbuilding contracts became a regular source of work. The unique building was still extant in 1996.*

Disorderly housekeeping can be seen on part of the recently launched motor ore carrier DUNADD 10,682 g.r.t. in Lithgows Ltd fitting-out basin, Port Glasgow during 1955. Most of the workers in this scene belong to various outfit trades, with shipwrights presumably being to the fore. Despite the apparent chaos on view, a well-filled metal bucket can be seen behind the forward starboard bridge indicating scrap and rubbish removal did take place! A sole member of management looks conspicuous in his ostentatious attire of bowler hat and knee length mackintosh raincoat, as he chats with the pair of men leaning on the hatch coaming. The portable tower crane was a beneficial concept widely used by Lithgows Ltd to provide low-cost craneage to assist ship construction. (Burniston Studios Ltd)

Wearing paint-speckled coveralls, bunnet and boots, minus his mask and gloves, presumably for the benefit of photographic recognition, a painter sprays a metal coat finish to one of the hopper tank web frames of the bulk ore carrier CAPE HOWE 19,032 g.r.t. then under construction at Lithgows Ltd in 1962. This picture gives some indication of the size of ships' confined spaces. These tanks were located underneath the upper deck on the port and starboard sides running the length of the ship from fore peak to engine room bulkhead. The painter is kneeling on the tank floor that sloped diagonally from the hatch coaming to side shell. The castellated (flanged or swedged) floor plate created high strength and stiffness. These tanks usually carried water ballast or grain cargoes.

Chapter 4

BOWLER HATTERS (MANAGEMENT)

The Bowler Hatters comprised directors, shipyard and engine works general managers, fabrication shop, berth and ship managers, head foremen and, optionally, chief draughtsmen and naval architects—in essence, owners, management and (very) senior staff. Not included were draughtsmen, planners and foremen, staff positions with none of the status and perks of senior management, and nothing like the collective power of the labour force. Yet the triumvirate that was the drawing office, planning, material and cost control department and the respective shop floor foremen, were the nerve centre of every shipyard or engine works.

All of the Clyde shipbuilding companies were established by a handful of individuals who were steeped in the resolute Presbyterian culture that was an immutable product of the Scottish Reformation. This perspective infixed a tabulation of conduct and acumen, borne with regular synonymity, by virtually every upholder of the distinct black circular head apparel. The staunch protestant populace that provided the catchment for nearly every Clyde shipyard manager was a correlation, realised of selective academic demography rather than a statistic of bigotry. Permeated with esoteric associations of brotherhood, the clique that controlled the entire strata of shipbuilding management coincidentally recruited mostly very able employees who just happened to share a similar religious conviction. This fact belied a total sectarian denominator as it secluded the bulk of the entire labour force who, whilst of similar religious belief, were bereft of the selective family or school background that enabled almost automatic pre-selection.

The *directors* projected the image and reputation of the shipyard among ship-owners. They propounded the combined roles of salesman, engineer, designer, accountant, politician, bon viveur, raconteur as well as business man, and delivered the contracts that kept the yard in work. Announcement of these orders was constantly reported with gleeful regularity in the local press, which always emphasised the approximate value of the work and the length of time it would take to complete. Collectively deporting an elan that was surprisingly reminiscent of British cabinet ministers, this debonair disposition created an aloofness redolent of the industrial revolution, not industrial development. Such haughtiness was further exemplified by a few shipyard owners who were gentleman farmers. Not liege lords of a distant feudalism, but agricultural as well as industrial businessmen, whose capacity for enterprise seemingly knew few boundaries.

Individual managers ruled their respective departments with steadfast and unyielding resolve. This policy of uncompromising autocracy was carried out by a cabal of senior and head foremen whose unflinching loyalty was invariably supplanted with a latent streak of perfidy, as much a prerequisite as the boundless comprehension of the nuances of their distinctive crafts. This management structure had worked successfully in Clyde shipyards since their inception. Coupled with deliberately restrictive training regimes, these methods ensured that knowledge, power and financial control remained firmly in the boardroom! The three immediate post-war decades were to put this imperious system of management to the test of compatibility with the insidious social changes that were unfolding in the United Kingdom. Clyde shipyard managements so long used to indomitable superintendence, gradually found their industry wallowing in a morass of subversive political factors and pseudo socio-influences outwith their control!

Post-war trading parameters were different from the 1930s. Shipyard directors, now inundated with orders for many new ships were aware of this. They were also initially cynical and dismissive towards the ability and capability of initially European and, latterly Japanese shipyards to pose threats towards the then dominance of the Clyde as the major shipbuilding area of the world. Despite the standoffish, arrogant public perception of shipyard management, they knew the business of designing and building ships. They also were aware of the need to remain competitive, offering keen costs as well as second to none quality, in terms of state-of-the-art ship and marine engine design. It is more than unfortunate, that these precepts were not similarly endorsed by the bellicose and disaffected trade union activists, whose profound interest in craft retention were not akin to the longevity of a now internationally competitive shipbuilding industry, with most overseas nations then harnessing and utilising the fruits of wartime technology, as well as establishing merchant fleets of their own.

Modernisation of facilities, plant and equipment went hand-in-glove with modernisation of working practices as well as the eradication of antiquated attitudes to employment of labour. These latter tenets were a malediction to the development and consolidation of a truly modern industry. That the potentially formidable combinations of intellect, business acumen and customer confidence displayed by managements could not be fused arbitrarily with the work ethos, innate pride and craftsmanship of yore into a cohesive, technology-based industry of the future, were some of the main reasons for the failure of Scottish shipbuilding.

Most shipyard directors were products of a hereditary system. Weaned on privileged private education, totally enshrouded in the technical, commercial and aloof social precepts of the day, wholly class and background based, such elitism had worked successfully for many British companies since the inception of industrial development. This method produced articulate, erudite and sagacious businessmen. It also created a caucus of clones, with clipped staccato enunciated, very non-Scottish dialects. Such alien accents, coupled with bombastic dialogue was used extensively and deliberately to great advantage throughout all negotiations. It disarmed, infuriated and in most cases totally bamboozled the loquacious but strategy bereft shop stewards and delegates, who usually had to reconvene amongst each other to decipher and delineate what they thought had been said within such turgid verbosity! 'Confusion being the harbinger of self doubt.' Tactics used, such as bluff and bluster, only succeeded in widening the industrial relations chasm that was symptomatic of shipbuilding. Nevertheless, despite continued trade union ascendancy, overall company control remained in the boardroom...

Of the 24 shipyards and 18 marine engine works that existed on the River Clyde after World War II, more than half were owned by the descendants of the families who founded them. Of the other half, most of the active directors were descendants of shipbuilding or marine engineering 'career families'. Very few 'craft' shipbuilders from the shop floor or draughtsmen from the drawing office aspired to director level, the most famous exception being Mr John Rannie, formerly of John Brown & Co, (Clydebank) Ltd. Respected and revered by his workforce, contemporaries, customers and competitors, he was an excellent ambassador for his company, shipbuilding and Scottish engineering prowess, representing the epitome of Scottish shipbuilding and marine engineering accomplishment. Later, successful examples of similar career-based ascendancy were Sir Ross Belch, formerly of Lithgows Ltd, and Sir Robert Easton of Yarrow Shipbuilders Ltd.

Such elitism was not totally nepotistic! Whilst fathers and grandfathers painstakingly manipulated, wheedled, coerced and ultimately ensured continuity of the lineage, they also insisted that their heirs would have more than a smattering of the comprehension of the shipbuilding business. This varied from 'farming-out' the offspring as privileged, itinerant apprentices in competitive friendly yards, to enrolment in sandwich graduate courses at university or technical college. Perpetuation of the family business was not so simple as sitting in the boardroom, consuming coffee, puffing cigars and discharging instructions, just because you were the boss's son.

Reciprocity of confidence between shipyard directors and ship owning customers was a fundamental concordat of the immediate post-war era, when Clyde shipyards possessed bountiful order books. Implicit trust existed between yard and ship-owner that the ships would be built to the usual impeccable standard and delivered on time, with the invoiced cost 'fixed' as agreed at the time of signing the contract. These three elements provided distinctive targets for foreign shipbuilders to initially identify, and ultimately surpass. Directors persisted with fixed price contracts during this era when total costs were controllable. This practice continued up until the inflation ravaged early '70s, when it would have been easier to win a lottery than predict the final price of a new ship.

The 'furtive fifties' was to be the last Indian summer, not only for Clyde shipbuilding, but for the Victorian class-ridden cliques that persisted in administering management by confrontation and coercion. Debatable tenets that were eclipsing their sell-by dates, as insidiously as the retention of outdated labour intensive working practices were being avidly advocated by misguided misinformed trade union zealots!

The conceited quick to criticise, slow to compliment pretentious style of mock encouragement that suffused Clydeside managements, was an odious gesture of industrial genealogy used to substitute inspiration by intimidation. This offhandedness was deliberately plied as one of the many psychological assertions wielded by bosses in their constant paranoia that familiarity bred contempt. Such lowbrow fervour served to prolong the impression of a passé plutocracy lacking the objective deference required to coalesce their fast waning industry, now beset by uncontrolled global expansion and spurred by the resolve of many nations to eclipse the previous British dominance of the world shipbuilding market. As international competition intensified, somehow Clydeside management still found the need for the perpetuation of an imperious genus of control. This purblind act of status retention remained with Clyde shipbuilding from the embers of private ownership until the fiasco of nationalisation.

If commonality in apparel was symptomatic of all the manual shipyard workers, then the sartorial unaptness of the shipyard general manager was as much an ostentatious symbol of incongruity with his industrial surroundings, as it was the uniform of authority and respect. Whether by accident or design, or the economies of bulk purchase…every *shipyard general manager's* attire comprised the obligatory black bowler hat, dark suit, white shirt, collar and tie, stout brogues, garishly complemented with tan coloured suede kid gloves. If uniform maketh the man, then Clydeside shipyard managers made the above uniform totally synonymous with that position. From the coaster building slipways of the Ardrossan Dockyard to the 1000 ft berths of John Brown's at Clydebank, including every other yard up or down-river, the shipyard general manager was the one position everybody knew, even if they didn't know him!

Interviewed by the yard directors prior to appointment, the specification for this exalted job was as meticulous and uncompromising as that of any ocean-going vessel. Requiring a strong backbone, no-nonsense every day vernacular, ably substituted on launch days with impeccable enunciation, wit and charm to be feted on the entertaining of ship-owners, their wives, guests and offspring, these chameleon traits could and would be interspersed with converse powers of audibility and deafness that would astound director and yard worker alike.

Invariably of a unique practical and technical background, their pre-computer era cerebrum could calculate percentages of farthings quicker than the local bookmaker. Called everything from a gentleman, by those workers about to retire, to the human fruit of an illicit paramour, by those unfortunate enough to incur his wrath, more factual, fictional and slanderous after-work tales were extolled about these, sometimes venerable men, than any other shipyard worthy! The similarity in dress, dialogue and deviousness between each individual yard manager usually bore witness to the all pervading power and steadfast standards of man-management proclaimed by the Shipbuilding Employers Federation, as well as a smattering of rhetoric and discipline imbued from a brief tenure in one of Her Majesty's armed services. The collective tone of the company was administered and portrayed via the demeanour of the general manager. It would not do if some liberal socio reformer infiltrated this hallowed position, took exception to the diktat of his board of directors, and allowed a surreptitious attrition of power to wane from the shareholders to the shop floor! This was never likely to happen during the felicitous post-war years of bulging order books that supported control of the industry by a handful of families and corporations.

The unflinching loyalty exhibited by general managers towards their respective companies was never in question, yet this absolute style of management was now evincing its own ignominious and protracted demise. Post-war Britain was a different place from the depressed, hungry, deprived thirties. Aspirations for career advancement spurred by more enlightened education were prevalent among many workers. Aversion and antipathy towards martinet methods of management had taken root and were pervading. Such dissent merely entrenched established conservative managements who considered confrontation as an essential canon of control. Indomitable, inflexible resolve as displayed by the archetypal general manager would continue to be the vanguard of policy…for as long as the industry lasted. It is unfortunate that this immutable obduracy, so trenchantly mooted by managers was by now being emulated vituperatively by the equally stubborn, but a lot more intransigent, stewards, delegates and leadership of the Boilermakers Society, and other representatives of the shipbuilding trade unions.

Conciliation took place eventually, with combinations of compromise and appeasement painstakingly reached. Labour relations settled down, orders were eventually completed, but the close of the friction-fraught fifties was the end of an era, and the beginning of the end. Union power, long fought after, seemed to spawn a hustling, oblivious self-destructive urge to wreak that power with sheer bravado, whatever the consequences. It appeared compelled to invert the existing system of structure, to substitute the dogma of the dolt or the disaffected delegate for the rationale of management ethos, in turn contributing towards the contraction of the shipbuilding industry. This philosophical battlefield was to harbour the final most perplexing issues with which the last great traditional shipyard general managers were to wrestle.

The second string of managers had more definitive terms of reference than the distended multi-functional portfolio bestowed on the general manager. Categorised into such mundane titles as *ship*, *berth*, *fabrication* and *outfit managers*, these line responsibilities required all of the grit and profanity necessary to become general manager of a shipyard, however, much greater in-depth technical comprehension was needed for these tasks than the all embracing 'King of the Bing' rationale displayed with such mellifluous aggrandisement by the GM. Performing very complex linkman roles from arbiter to salesman, liaising between the drawing office, classification society, owner's representative, Board of Trade, senior foremen, subcontractors and shop stewards et al., these jobs encompassed virtually the full spectrum of communication within a shipyard's activity inventory. Among the more indifferent functions was the regular writing of scripts outlining progress (or regress) for the general managers 'weekly meeting'. This entailed the infusion of boring statistics with acerbic witticisms, alas mostly lost in a cacophonous farrago of bedlam, as these initially orderly get togethers usually degenerated into semi-slanderous invectives of wrath, mirth and lampoonery!

This weekly ritual of supposed disorder was far from disorderly. Chaired by the GM the ensuing melee was the essential element of the script. Having rapidly gleaned the salient facts, figures, statistics and apologies for absence, some 'raw meat' in the form of inference, or mendacity would be tossed into the ensemble by the irascible general manager. The irate, incensed, offended quorum would invariably take the bait, vehemently remonstrate with each other, inadvertently disgorging further half-truths and accusations, duly sating the palate of the chairman. Whereupon, with objectives clearly achieved and with timing and training akin to that of a graduate thespian of the Royal Scottish Academy of Dramatic Art, he would interrupt the gathering on cue with stilted authoritative vernacular and summarily bring the meeting to order, followed shortly by the announcement of 'meeting now closed'.

Acrimony, ire and frustration was vented profusely by each member present. Then, like a shoal of spent salmon gawping disdainfully at each other, lacking of any further outbursts, heads bowed in partial embarrassment, they would slither out in ones and twos to resume their individual responsibilities. This system of devolved accountability with minimum overlap, worked reasonably well within the labour intensive post-war era, when 'piecework' methods of induced earnings for all hourly paid workers held sway. This basic incentive system of payment by result was identified and constantly monitored by 'rate-fixers' and 'counters'; a new tranche of staff specifically recruited and now wallowing in the mantle 'poachers turned gamekeepers'.

Each line or function manager had either his own team of rate-fixers, or was given targets with prices already set, for the construction or outfit of the respective parts of the ship, for which he was responsible.

Tasks to be undertaken varied in magnitude and complexity, from cold-frame bending of bulb bar hull frames in the fabrication department to the erection and weld-out of a heavy lift 'Stülcken' mast and derrick on board a ship on the declivity building berth.

The specific and specialist knowledge required for the particular 'under' manager functions were not totally lost on the GM and board of directors. This was reflected in quite a range of practical, technical and academic experience, with impressive attendant formal qualifications spread across the shipyard management organigram, which usually identified the outfit manager as the most comprehensively certificated manager in the yard, on a par with the naval architect. The minimum qualification for this position was a Board of Trade Chief Engineer's ticket in steam and diesel, whereby he could assume control of the ship's engines and equipment whilst fitting-out, or, most especially when overseeing the builders' trials when the ship was proving her worth, with virtually all systems working concurrently.

Berth and fabrication shop managers did not require such formal qualifications. Recruited from the diverse backgrounds of draughtsman, plater, engineer, shipwright, welder and sometimes even caulker, sound practical knowledge of the company's fabrication and erection procedures, allied to an awareness of the 'ship construction plan', with respective man-hour estimates for all trades concerned, were the specific precepts for these jobs. Notwithstanding, singular strength of character, confidence, brinkmanship and acerbic verbosity, required to riposte with indolent tradesmen, semi-intelligent foremen and sometimes seditious shop stewards. Achievement of production schedules was the main requirement for second-string managers. Failure to deliver on time, within or below budget, invariably resulted in a public buttock-punting, embellished with a derisory tirade impugning total incompetence, delivered in monosyllabic vernacular by the GM. Successful attainment or betterment seldom was rewarded with anything like a mild plaudit, more likely silent contempt or a muted snide reference to 'not bad'…but 'must try harder'. Such was the inspirational patois of the GM's stimulating sarcastic drollery.

Yard owners, directors and most managers invariably insisted on being addressed with the aloof, sham British patrician sobriquet of 'mister' prior to any discourse. This was as much an attempt at perpetuating an imposed 'chasm of class' between themselves and their employees, as it was a feigned act of arrogance trying to veil the slithering status of their once great industry. A similar, yet more voluntary delineation of reverence existed between all the boys who were employed after their 15th birthday, and their immediate superiors whether they were foremen or tradesmen. Such was the respect shown by these lads towards their seniors, however, many found it quite difficult later in life to address these gentlemen by anything other than this courteous precedence.

Not all of the shipbuilding trades possessed the position *head foreman*—an elitist, but nevertheless partly functional title credited to ostensibly the 'best' foremen within the number of foremen who supervised that particular craft. Traditionally these titles were only bestowed on the mainstream craft trades of plater, shipwright and riveter. This reason was virtually self-explanatory, given that these trades numbered many hundreds of men in each of the medium to large-sized shipyards. With a foreman to tradesman ratio of anything up to 1:20, it wasn't long before the general manager and directors reckoned that a wee bit of order, more control and maybe better long-term achievement, could be realised by appointing a head foreman, usually but not always from within the company.

The title 'best'…was always correct! In the structure strictured personnel pyramid that comprised the labour force of a traditional Clydeside shipyard, different men bore traits, nuances, talent and ethics that varied in complexity and content from man to man. All shipyards operated unique but similar types of incentive payment schemes of varying intricacy. This produced a great leveller in terms of aptitude within a regime that quite deliberately disbarred all men from all skills. This ability-selection process ensured the men with the best capability, work ethics and ambition, typically aspired to create the best workers, and maybe the best foremen…but not automatically the 'best' head foremen. With hundreds of men in each craft being supervised by their kith and kin, there existed a considerable chasm between this excessive number of artisans and senior management via the position of foremen. This isolation was identified many decades ago, and was bridged with the appointment of head foremen amongst the critical core crafts. Principles of specific craft competence and productive excellence were identified as desirable, but not essential prerequisites for these hallowed positions. Much more important, and surreptitiously brought to the general manager's attention prior to appointment, were the mixed-bag of nefarious traits and oblique chicanery more akin to the job specification of James Bond or an aspirant of the KGB. These were:

- Resolute fealty, martinet discipline and above-average technical and commercial awareness of the shipbuilding process
- A mental capacity for remembering the faces and names of each of the men in their departments
- Possession of a network of cliques and spies, who knew the trade union activists and sleepers.
- Personal details about the families of the tradesmen within their charge
- Membership of an esoteric fraternal, extra-curricular social club, with a penchant for geometry, dressing up and communicating in riddles.

Notwithstanding this formidable list of caveats, head foremen required compassion, fitness, and the not inconsiderable talent for chastising indolent or miscreant tradesmen and apprentices. Total knowledge of the entire shipyard layout was also necessary, as much for the furtive sporadic establishment of illicit dens and 'howfs' where supine work-shy employees might refrain from honest toil, as well as the whereabouts of all other operating departments.

Appointment to this exalted position was usually bestowed upon men in their late '40s or early '50s, and seen as the pinnacle of that man's career. Promoted to this title were always foremen with many years of successful supervision behind them, supplemented with considerable knowledge of the shipyard methods and practices. Seldom were these positions filled by outsiders. The only exceptions to this rule were when the directors appointed an interloper general manager. This new man then needed to surround himself with his band of loyal lieutenants. Such moves were usually frowned upon by the directors, however, if the new GM earned his bacon and delivered the goods, this success would enable him to recruit his outsiders, to circumvent the boards aversion to hiring strangers. Head foremen, once appointed, remained incumbent until their retirement—subtle recognition by management for their respective contributions towards the discipline and order of the yard during their tenure.

Arguably the cornerstone of the shipbuilding industry were the trades *foremen* who were always recruited from the ranks of thousands of artisans who worked in the yards. Kept at arms length by management, sometimes reviled by refractory trade union activists, they were admired and criticised in unequal amounts. Regularly charged with subliminal expectations, which when duly achieved were passively assuaged, they were isolated and outcast until the next crisis required their inspirational prowess. This helter-skelter of direction by disruption was all part of abstruse company ploys to wreak commitment from a collection of individuals who never really felt a true part of management but, when they became gaffers, were no longer one of the men.

This apparent loneliness was the spur that made a good foreman. Specifically recruited by head foremen and sometimes managers, the painstaking selection process encompassed many aspects. From the necessary technical 'on the job skill', through a comprehension of rate-fixing and piecework practices, to the essential strength of character needed to deliver in good Clydeside parlance, 'I've asked you nicely, now I'm telling you …!' and mean every word that was said. Such centre-stage gamesmanship provided the 'theatre', which was viewed from opposite sides by managers and tradesmen alike; a 'lonely' workplace where routine instructions could rapidly degenerate into vehement confrontations, requiring the intervention of one or two other supervisors to mitigate the embarrassment. Or, after a brief altercation expounding forceful rhetoric, asserting authority over impudence, wring wry internal elation, creating an instantly respected reputation and high profile on the shop floor. Such profane thespian behaviour usually resulted in a nickname that would stick to that foreman until he retired. Less assertive foremen failing to climb this primary hurdle of asseveration would be found more subversive tasks, like 'internal policemen' or foremen without portfolios—a Clydeside euphemism for management lackey or covert detective. Unable to effect line supervision, reluctant to resume shop-floor identity, these neo-technical peripherals remained part of shipyard management's unorthodox but effective information gathering techniques, being treated as industrial lepers throughout their working lives.

Respect was either earned...or commanded! Most shipyard foremen were introduced to management with a firm covered handshake from the head foreman or general manager and a perfunctory welcome, appended with 'remember son, familiarity breeds contempt! And don't ever forget it!' This exposition, like virtually all of the yardspeak psychology or kidology, worked in an era when motivational influence was frequently replaced with bellicose browbeating and was symptomatic of one of the worst aspects of British man-management! The foremen who earned the respect of the labour force and the management deployed the duality of carrot and stick with instinctive and equitable application. They were the cornerstone of an industry who were inwardly aware of the need for high cost technical innovation, but complacently content to linger with outdated labour intensive craft practices. These loyal disciplined reynards turned foxhounds dutifully administered control by autarchy rather than by the subtlety of management, such were the collective edicts under which they were employed.

The wearing of protective helmets in shipyards became mandatory under an amendment to UK safety legislation in 1974. Long overdue in terms of forceable enactment, this instruction in working attire resulted in virtual elimination of routine head injuries. It also provided a specious token of rank or trade when applied with a colour scheme depicting seniority. Somehow a throwback to the bowler hat era was insidiously revived by Trafalgar House Offshore Ltd, the new owners of Scott-Lithgow's yards who retained black to be the most senior colour, other companies throughout the UK shipbuilding industry preferred white. When viewed from a high enough vantage point, such profuse use of coloured helmets prompted witty reference to their many owners being akin to the spilled contents of a tube of 'smarties'.

The *drawing office* was far from a single identity, and the designers and draughtsmen who worked there numbered many hundreds, of which only a few were capable of producing detail drawings of more than one discipline. These fortunate individuals, soon realised the lucrative marketability of this varied drafting ability, and, if promotion to section leader, assistant, or chief draughtsman didn't beckon, then the well-paid drawing boards of subcontract drawing offices were a far more rewarding, if somewhat uncertain source, of enhanced remuneration. Drawing offices were subdivided into types: ship, engine and electrical. Depending on the size of the company, a *chief draughtsman* in a ship drawing office was usually responsible for the production of hull and superstructure drawings depicting steelwork, outfit and piping work contents —this could mean supervising up to 100 draughtsmen. Overseeing the entire output of the drawing office, this exalted position attracted quite differing impressions of job specification. These varied from a total technical awareness of the DO workload, that was implemented via the auspices of trusty conscientious section leaders to a formal, fusty detached stance steeped in a standoffish bearing that quite deliberately isolated the 'chief' from his workforce. Such disparate attitudes tended to be steeped in the accrued traditionalism of shipbuilding, beholding esoterism as a laudable bastion, which repelled the outpouring of knowledge. Regrettably the lack of regular contact with personnel stifled the necessary free-flow of information required to ensure the constant evolution of technical progress, in short, part of the raison d'être of a drawing office. Not all Clyde yards persisted with such myopic obstinacy. However, during the days of volume shipbuilding enough companies encouraged or allowed such arrogant elitism to exist that apprentices and junior draughtsmen thought such behaviour was prevalent throughout shipbuilding and UK manufacturing industry!

Engine works drawing offices had their own chief, who was of a mechanical/marine engineering background and was in charge of the design, detail and procurement of steam turbines, boilers, gear-boxes, diesel engines, alternators and generators, as well as engine room piping and ventilation systems. These offices also worked the same system of assistant chiefs and section leaders, with total numbers of draughtsmen usually about half that of shipyard DOs. Electrical design and detail was usually carried out by either the main shipyard electrical drawing office, led by its own chief draughtsman, or in the case of yards without such a section, by highly specialised capable subcontractors like James Scott or James Kilpatrick, who had extensive marine design and construction expertise, and were more than capable of designing, pricing, installing, testing and commissioning total electrical and instrumentation systems for any type of nautical contract.

The ship drawing office was the vehicle for the prolific output of shop drawings that were translated from calculations and designs created by the *naval architect* and his ship designers, formally qualified to degree standard, most of whom were usually professional engineers, sometimes of more than one institute. The naval architects and designers were the 'brains' of the shipyard. Usually joining the company at 16 or 17 years of age with a bundle of good Scottish Education Department 'Highers', they were immediately enrolled as student apprentices studying naval architecture at either Glasgow University, or 'The Tech', latterly given varsity status in 1964, and now known as Strathclyde University. Called sandwich courses, this type of training comprised full-time studies, alternating between spells in the shipyard design, drawing or planning offices during the university holidays. This facility was only available to the academically gifted, who invariably fulfilled the expectations of the companies who sponsored them.

Ship designers were responsible for translating owners' rudimentary vessel specifications that outlined type and volume of cargo to be carried, maximum operating draft, and preference of propulsion machinery, into a hull form depicting all major scantlings from which stability, displacement and speed calculations could be compiled. This fundamental information enabled accurate tenders to be produced, it also assisted prospective customers to formulate the final contract design specification that would control the standard of ship constructed. After completion of a new vessel, verification of deadweight tonnage and contract speed would be regarded with similar importance as the mandatory inclining experiment witnessed and certified by a Board of Trade surveyor. Successful performance of this test resulted in the formal issue of the 'Trim and Stability' booklet, that would remain on board for the life of the ship.

Apprentice draughtsmen sat an entrance examination on or about their sixteenth birthday, with successful applicants usually commencing their apprenticeships immediately after the annual trades' holidays in the month of July. The draughtsman's training period, like all the other shipyard trades was of five years duration, incorporating spells in most of the shipyard or engine works departments. Structured quite deliberately to foster total awareness of the constituent methods, practices and procedures of manu-facturing, this enabled the young man to comprehend the shop floor 'jargon' which he would ultimately append to his future drawings.

During the 1950s the Clyde shipyards and engine works began to allow all of their apprentices the facility of paid day-release to enable further education studies at their nearest technical college. In the case of apprentice draughtsmen, the full five-year training period could be spent including day-release, sometimes supplemented with evening classes that were used as extra tutorial, or comprised additional courses for endorsement of the National Certificate curriculum. It was not uncommon for apprentice draughtsmen and the occasional academically gifted craft apprentices to be tutored by section leaders, designers or even their chief draughtsman at night school. This vocational, supplementary training was accepted by most of the young men who had more than a modicum of aspiration towards career advancement. Unfortunately, many teenagers seemingly content in the then popular belief that continuous employment existed at the end of their training, desisted from this studious pursuit, preferring to spend evenings dancing, working unlimited amounts of overtime or indulging in sports or other interests rather than studying. This lack of commitment to academic pursuits, invariably led to poor examination results, the net effect of which was the suspension of day-release facilities. Quite simply, companies investing in paid leave for the training of their future tradesmen expected annual success in examinations, as a precursor to continuation of these privileges.

The draughtsmen and engineers who pursued part-time parallel careers as night school lecturers, displayed a humbling as well as gratifying aspect of post-war collective educational advancement. Their commitment was responsible for imparting the significance and importance of academic studies combined with a sound on-the-job knowledge. These night school teachers were not total altruists, spending two and a half hours per night, plus travelling, plus marking homework free gratis. The extra money then earned was certainly useful. During the 1950s, the hourly rate paid to these part-timers was greater than that to be earned in a shipyard or engine works drawing office! A few well-qualified 'draffies' found the status and security of teaching a temptation unable to resist. After being enticed or poached by a local education authority, they completed their wage earning careers as full-time teachers or lecturers in colleges of Central Scotland. Alas the once endless stream of apprentices that regularly enlisted each year for further education diminished with the contraction of shipbuilding and marine engineering, resulting in the parallel reduction of a great many courses and decrease in teacher opportunities as well.

The remaining groups of management were the bundles of 'cushy numbers' created in hope, profusion, expectation and despair by post-war management, finally cognisant that their traditional labour intensive industry must establish itself in the hyper-competitive, no holds barred, semi-automatic and invisibly subsidised world of international shipbuilding. The creation, or categorisation of titles such as planner, work study engineer, material controller, et al. was an ostensible and sincere attempt at collectively divesting shipbuilding of its archaic traditional reputation of a 'hold-all' for craft retention, directed by imperious industrial time lords.

Unfortunately, the realisation of such potentially far reaching changes sent ripples upwards and inwards as well as downwards and outwards. In essence, the newly identified universal beast called progress, masquerading as the science of 'production engineering', had to do battle with traditionalism from the shop-floor to the boardroom. Even the most Luddite trade union activist knew in his heart of hearts (though his head would never admit it) that the unavoidable consequence of technological investment was the inevitable 'de-skilling' of most of the traditional shipbuilding crafts. The corollary for the boardroom and senior management was that new technology meant an infusion of highly qualified innovative engineers and managers…who inevitably would have to convert the status quo into at least an equal competitor or, at best, the international market leader. Alas, achievement of the latter remained the rhetoric of the industrial somnambulist!

This cataclysmic option, which might have saved some of the industry, was fudged to the point of a neutered compromise. The directors read the script, they liked the theory, they invested in some of the hardware, but they failed to implement the total transition necessary to achieve longevity—prevented as much by their own lack of dogged foresight as the stone-walling intransigence and non-cooperation of the workforce, abetted by overdue frugal financial assistance from Government.

Titles for the team members responsible for this hoped-for transformation, were created with the flippancy and exactitude of desperation, associated with the last throw of the dice in a crap game. The fortunate souls, who were allocated such meaningful, but regrettably meaningless job titles as motion time measurement engineers, production controllers, progress chasers, material controllers, planners et al., merely duped themselves, their workmates, and ultimately connived in the downfall of the industry.

Swanning about the shipyard dressed in duffle coats, with clipboards and stop watches, they rapidly became aware that this once great industry, was in fact possessed with an all pervading 'death wish' for its own destruction. Talk was easy, but substitution, replacement and eradication of practices and jobs on the altar of progress was another matter, with much of the labour force averse to wholesale change. Too profane, shorn of the introvertive humility and self-analysis required to identify their collective shortcomings, too complacent to realise that overseas competition in the form of apparently cheaper prices, quicker deliveries, with comparable and sometimes better quality meant starvation of orders. The hoped-for saviour that in-house industrial engineering activities would provide never materialised. However, the glaring need for effective planners was recognised rapidly and without question. It was generally accepted that planned ships were easier to build than those that evolved in the foremen's office.

The tradesmen who opted for these second chance careers were to be admired rather than pitied. Everyone who worked in a shipyard or engine works, from tradesman to labourer, engineer to designer, knew or thought they knew how to cure the ills and ails of the company, and now here was a better-paid opportunity to practice what they'd always preached, or so they hoped. Hostility was encountered from the outset. Proposed de-skilling and redeployment were met with inevitable and irrational Clydeside logic…walk out strikes!

Planners, or more to the point planning, always existed in shipbuilding since the inception of the industry. Alas, the function was cloaked within the remit of either the general manager, head foreman or drawing office, or a combination of all three. Every ship built was laid out to a plan which, although it was not called such, was an inherent element of the craft skills and limited technology of the day. Shop drawings were drafted sequentially for the keel, main framing, bulkheads, decks hull plating to superstructure, with material purchased, identified and erected systematically for these specific functions. This sound method of ship construction worked successfully for virtually a century without much, if any, improvement. The advent of electric arc welding enabled fabrication of ship pieces or units to be utilised as an improved method of shipbuilding.

Harnessing the skills of experienced tradesmen, retraining these individuals in the application of planning technology, unleashed a boundless panorama of potential improvement to the extant methods of shipbuilding. Ranging from increased unit size depending on craneage availability to the systematic outfit of prefabricated units with pipes, valves, cables or ventilation ducts fitted at the earliest possible stage, all brought handsome reductions in the ship construction duration cycle.

Abstract subsystems, like PERT (Programme Evaluation and Review Technique) or CPA (Critical Path Analysis), were universally accepted by the shipyards who averted the first round of closures in the early 1960s. Application of these invisible tools rendered further assistance to the elemental analysis of traditional shipbuilding techniques, and by the early 1970s planning offices were firmly established as 'bona-fide' parts of the companies. Further successful wholesale dedication to the benefits of method planning technology were lost in the combined attrition of volume shipbuilding as a vibrant developing industry. Limited investment expenditure by under-capitalised companies with the retention of previous manning levels, perpetuated labour intensive skills that inhibited increased productivity. The infusion of planning as part of an all embracing function, assisted the retention of the handful of shipyards that survived the virtual annihilation of the industry on the River Clyde.

The final pair of technical management appointees were the two disciplines of estimator and rate-fixer. These were traditional and fundamental control elements in the design and construction of steel hulled ships. Essentially if the estimated, usually fixed-price, tender wasn't correct, the contract wasn't won, and if you didn't build it within budget, and on time, then the shipyard lost money! The estimator was responsible for the pricing of the raw materials, engines, pumps, equipment and finishings which were identified in the contract building specification. Actual purchase orders were then processed and expedited by the yard's buying department. Many of the these subcontracts for long-lead items like engines or generators had cost adjustment factors to take into account such elements as foreign exchange rates, inflation and design changes, depending on where or when these items were bought. The shipyard controlled fabrication and outfit areas were also within the domain of the estimator. Theoretically the estimating department priced the job, plus profit, for all of these areas. Cost control functions monitored what actual amounts were incurred in performing these works. If the actual cost was below the theoretical estimate then that job was profitable. If it was greater loss was incurred, however, if the contract was over budget and excessively overdue when delivered, then the summation of gross financial loss, compounded with penalty payments, and total loss of face among customers became the harbingers of bankruptcy and evaporation of markets!

Estimators were usually recruited from experienced draughtsmen or designers. They were the single staff job with the potential for enhanced earnings due to the need to complete bids by a specified date, thus justifying continuous overtime. Their work took account of some, if not all, of the imponderables associated with cost escalation. Various formulae were available, based on empirical data that went a long way to identifying areas for potential cost growth. When the estimate was finished it would be passed to the naval architect, general manager and board of directors for scrutiny and discreet final adjustment. Confidentiality enshrouded the bid document, as it was known prior to becoming a contract. It was not uncommon for the considerable commercial and technical nous of the above senior triumvirate to modify, mostly upwards, the tender price prior to submission.

Rate-fixers like estimators were in a relatively privileged position who were recruited from loyal and experienced, discreet tradesmen of above the ordinary level of practical comprehension. The rate-fixing department covered all the trades in the shipyard or marine engine works. In the era of 'contract piecework' when prices were identified and agreed for a dollop of measured work, rate-fixers were the key to the success of this system. The basis for these incremental unit costs were the elements of the estimate that pertained to these targets. If the job was done too quickly for the allotted price, both tradesman and company gained. If the converse occurred, then the company and tradesman lost...this invariably led to instant disagreement, usually culminating in an instant walkout, followed by a review of the rates. The rate-fixer's task was to try and achieve a balance that addressed the former and avoided the latter. Rate-fixers performed a high profile, thankless task and were always the first men to be sought out in the pubs, social clubs or football terracing by irate belligerent tradesmen who saw themselves as becoming benefactors to the yard owners, due to the incompetence of the rate-fixer! It's no understatement that the department was always kept busy during the time of piecework.

The new types of supertankers and bulk carriers in demand in the 1960s with their inherently larger scantlings taxed the capacity of the shipyard cranes handling these heavier units. It also required the reassessment, reappraisal and extrapolation of established fabrication rates and norms which were duly addressed. In the immediate post-war era with minimal annual inflation, rate-fixing was, like estimating, a definitive science. Rampant inflation of the mid to late sixties put paid to such definition. The subsequent decade of the '70s was to reduce rate-fixing and estimating to the haphazard rationale of a tombola caller...*think of a number!* The setting-up of measured day work at this time consolidated and eradicated many of the established vagaries of rate-fixing, as well as replacing piecework as the customary method of payment.

Traditional drawing offices throughout the whole of the UK manufacturing industry found out very quickly that shop drawings rapidly produced on tracing paper by adept draughtsmen, soon crumpled and ultimately disintegrated with constant use for reference or photographic reproduction of shop floor working prints. The immediate effect of this was that working prints from paper drawings, which were essentially instructions of manufacture, soon became illegible, unreadable and really unusable for tradesmen to work from. Time wasted by skilled tradesmen traipsing off to the DO every half hour because they could not interpret drawings was frowned upon by all levels of management, and did nothing to sustain or enhance shop floor output.

The immediate solution to this problem was the establishment of a drawing office subsidiary staffed by *tracers*, whose task it was to obtain 'first-off' prints of the main used plans, and trace these drawings on to linen sheets which would then become the master drawing, then capable of extensive usage without sustaining the damage incurred by tracing paper. However, many shipyard drawing offices followed the tradition of producing 'cloth and ink' original drawings made by their draughtsmen. Tracers were ladies, young and not so young, initially recruited straight from school, and introduced into the tracing section of the DO. Some were daughters, girlfriends and wives of the company's managers, foremen and draughtsmen.

Drawing offices with adjacent tracing sections maintained exemplary standards of decorum. Spontaneous chauvinistic rhetorical excursions by draughtsmen, with inane prattling about football, politics or fictional paramours would be embarrassingly dismissed with silent contempt coupled with scornful stares by the nearby tracers. Honoured, and privileged to possess a reasonably well paid job, the feminine superiority of a bygone era was regularly asserted quite subtly and cogently by the females who were employed in such mixed gender establishment drawing offices.

Drawing office adornment and seemliness were not the main function of tracers. Trained throughout shipbuilding and marine engineering industries to more than acceptable standards of draughtsmanship and neatness, alas the responsibility for the accuracy of the traced print reverted to the originator of the actual drawing, the DO checker or section leader. Whilst the technical comprehension of many details remained beyond the knowledge of these bonny lassies, the differentiation in line definition, between the thinner dimension, and the thicker actual component was seldom if ever missed by an experienced tracer. The inexorable combined wheels of attrition, inversely entrained with advancing technology in the shape of durable translucent plastic drawing sheets, unfortunately consigned this fair art to the same industrial museum as riveting and other time-expired working practices in less than a decade. CAD (Computer Aided Drafting) has further replaced the need for the fair art of tracing…as well as the functions of many former draughtsmen.

The indispensable mercantile departments of accounts, buying and wages completed the management team. Of no specific singularity to shipbuilding, those sections which were always cheeseparingly staffed, possessed uniqueness of operations that were usually implied by the will and character of the senior management and directors. This was certainly so of the buying and accounts departments where on some contracts, notably passenger liners, warships and ferries, the value of externally purchased items were in excess of the costs directly controlled by the shipyards, sometimes in the order of two to four times as much. It was no wonder that many suppliers and subcontractors to the major Clyde shipyards, were subjected to the same ruthless bargaining by head buyers, as yard stewards and delegates were similarly harangued by general managers during negotiations on wages and conditions.

Fundamental to the existence and commercial success of the shipyard, astute buying with deferred durations for subsequent payment ensured healthy cash flow and positive cost control, as well as creating considerable employment for many thousands of workers in a diverse range of industries. It also provided a ruthless training ground that gave the fortunate few who held these key jobs, a level of skill that was recognised and recompensed outwith shipbuilding when the industry disappeared.

This very brief selection of photographs under the chapter on Bowler Hatters, reflects as much the modesty of some of that esteemed group of individuals, as well as the paucity of archive material depicting them at work in the former West of Scotland shipbuilding industry.

The shipyard drawing office of Lithgows Ltd, Port Glasgow, in 1960 showing an industrious assemblage of designers and draughtsmen. Various DO sections were responsible for the preparation of shipbuilding data, including design, steelwork, outfit, piping and electrical drawings. Plans tended to be drafted on long lengths of either tracing paper or linen before the advent of plastic sheets, hence the need for long flat drawing boards. This office was very typical of the layout and facilities in most Clyde shipyards, and like every other could quickly produce shop drawings and order steel and other materials not long after a ship contract was awarded.

Above. *Some of the bowler hatted management of Wm Hamilton & Co Ltd observe the successful launching of yard no. 504, m.v. HELLENIC GLORY 7510 g.r.t. for Hellenic Lines Ltd, Piræus, on 29 December 1955. Engined by the Fairfield SB & Eng Co Ltd, the vessel has been taken in tow by a pair of tugs, fore and aft, for the journey up-river to Govan where her propulsion machinery will be installed.* (Burniston Studios Ltd)

Below, left. *Sir Charles Connell, DL, MA, venerable Chairman and Managing Director of Charles Connell & Co Ltd, with Ben Line Ltd's lady sponsor at the launch of yard no. 512 the cargo motor liner BENSTAC 12,011 g.r.t. on 20 November 1967. This event was the last launch of the Connell dynasty at their Scotstoun yard. In the spring of 1968, the company became the Scotstoun division of UCS Ltd. Sir Charles passed away in 1972.* (Burniston Studios Ltd)

Chapter 5

POST-WAR ATTRITION

The UK Government and populace were always aware of the superhuman efforts made by British shipyards and engine works towards construction of naval and merchant shipping during World War II. A common propaganda slogan of that time, 'Every rivet is a bullet', reflected this national awareness. The country-wide feeling of relief at the allies victory in that war was not to earn any respite for Clyde shipyards. The material appreciation of six years of arduous endeavours was rewarded with a profuse order book of profitable new shipbuilding and ship repair contracts from 1946 onwards. This victory bounty was to become a Trojan Horse hiding the many carry forward facets of industrial anthropology, synonymous with this great West of Scotland industrial twosome. The huge post-war demand for new vessels to replace the vast amount of shipping lost to axis and allied action was further augmented with a new order in world trade. This upsurge in peacetime commerce created the need for virtually every class of marine vessel from tugs, dredgers and ferries to cargo/passenger liners and oil tankers, types of vessels built to familiar specifications and designs that did not require any extensive research to transform an enquiry into a new building order, providing the price and delivery were acceptable to the ship-owners.

Talk of terminal decline in these heady, yet austere post-war years was prematurely exaggerated and far from accurate. The UK replaced the USA as the world's major shipbuilder, and would remain so for a few more years. The River Clyde with its then total of 24 shipbuilding yards and 18 marine engine works was the market leader in terms of product range, price, quality…and initially delivery. A total of nearly 60,000 people were directly employed in the Clydeside industry during this era. Living in cramped, tenemental property mostly built during the last century with minimal sanitary facilities, many of these buildings were owned by the shipyards. Some of the districts of Dumbarton, Clydebank, Scotstoun, Whiteinch, Partick, Govan, Port Glasgow and Greenock possessed residential areas that abutted against stockyards, sheds or offices. The post-war upsurge in orders for new ships acted as a spur for the improvement of many of these dwelling places. New housing developments called 'schemes' resulted in vast expenditure by local authorities constructing thousands of replacement homes. Bereft of new ideas, capped by Government parsimony, housing departments utilised the omnipresent tenement as the well-proven 'blue-print' for these estates. Initially accepted by workers and their families as superior to their previous homes, at least because of separate bedrooms and a bathroom, the 'schemes' were not long-term successes. Hastily conceived, and built, shorn of the amenities of the long-established district communities they were supplementing, many workers duly left the 'schemes' after fairly short terms of their accepted tenancy. The small number of itinerant shipyard workers who followed work throughout the UK resided in sub-standard accommodation called 'models', also provided by local authorities. These flea-ridden dormitories lasted as long as the volume shipbuilding industry they were built to serve, and were well known local landmarks in most of the Clydeside shipbuilding districts.

Inundated with collateral from bulging order books, these shipbuilding companies embarked (slowly at first) on replacing worn-out life expired plant and equipment. In between this investment was the not to be forgotten task of completing ships, hardly the background against which to examine and hopefully eradicate or replace outmoded working practices, as well as satisfy customers whilst competing with a growing number of international shipbuilders. In the space of less than a decade, UK shipbuilding, arguably one of the more sensitive industries to the world trade barometer, had gone from no more than ticking over in the 1930s to flat out working in the 1940s. The casual 'hire and fire' tenets of employment, driven by the laws of supply and demand, could never be construed as having a stabilising effect on good industrial relations. Memories were long, long enough amongst the bulk of the pre-war labour force to doubt the new security and longevity of employment being expounded by shipyard owners and managers alike.

This unfortunate mistrust between management and men varied in intensity and magnitude from shipyard to shipyard. Nevertheless, that facet of suspicion remained permanently associated with shipbuilding, becoming another significant element of contention which prevented total updating of the industry. The widespread cynicism that enshrouded shipyard workers' feelings towards their employers was further fuelled by eclectic manipulation of piecework weightings brought about by the advent of fabrication. Where the building berth or slipway had previously been the main area for man-hour liquidation, construction of ship sections in covered sheds changed this ratio considerably. When management adjusted the enhanced berth allowances downwards to reflect the supposedly better working environment, this precipitated the dispute riven post-war period.

Modernisation began as soon as the supply industries like machine tool building, crane making and others could provide shop floor capacity and space for these orders. Thus was set in train a remarkable oft maligned era in British industrial history, when shipbuilders wrestled with the concurrent problems of winning and completing orders, designing, funding and implementing extensive expensive shipyard modernisation projects and the interminable, only partially solved problem of improvements in working conditions and practices.

During this time the UK Governments of initially Labour, followed by Conservative then Labour again, completely undervalued the total contribution by shipbuilding and marine engineering to the well-being of the British economy. Here were well-established industries with a good financially sound customer base, employing directly many tens of thousands of mainly skilled men and indirectly responsible for employing figures many times greater, being chided by economists, political advisers and other assorted voyeuristic ne'er do wells. Those critics deemed quite arbitrarily that this smokestack, metal bashing dinosaur be consigned to the scrapheap of history, presumably because of its bad 'public relations'. This indifference was given further impetus by latent political charity that inclined the UK towards gradual divestment of its considerable global industrial impact, mainly in the form of contraction of the British merchant fleet.

Established UK investment houses ensured that the guilt-ridden surrender of traditional heavy industries, and with it the fast diminishing returns that these former profit sources yielded, would not haemorrhage their future invisible incomes. Directed by the United States Marshall Plan of huge financial and technical support for the regeneration of the industries of vanquished Germany, Japan and most of the other European countries devastated by the war, this programme was created overwhelmingly as a tangible sop towards the perceived American paranoia at the spread of worldwide communism. The trickle of British overseas investment which had earlier this century and last, supported the growth and exploitation of Empire and Commonwealth countries, was now transferred towards the rebirth of the two axis states who had plunged almost the entire world into six years of war.

Such voluntary British contraction assisted the governments of these two countries, and a host of emerging nations, whose post-war development programmes included the establishment and expansion of shipbuilding, marine engineering and support manufacturing, the rapid success of which progressively consigned the UK industry to interminable decline. Surreptitiously bolstered by subsidies disguised in the form of capital building grants, below market rate credit facilities for both purchase of plant and the contract price of the actual ships, these countries' desire and commitment to the founding of permanent shipbuilding industries were initially dismissed by the UK competition. This was due to the then seemingly endless worldwide growth potential of the market for new ships, coupled with the myopic complacent self-belief, shared by shipbuilding directors and workers alike, that 'Clyde built was best…and would never be surpassed… anywhere…anytime!'

Apart from the hidden subsidies meted out to these rebuilt or nascent shipbuilding industries, they also possessed the considerable advantage of comparing and improving upon what was then 'modus operandi' in UK shipbuilding. This would be seen in lesser amounts of tradesmen required to perform steelwork sub-assembly, consequently producing far higher fabrication tonnage output, with a more coordinated 'module' approach to the complicated fabric of fitting-out and subcontract activities. Labour rates were also less than those in the UK.

What created this post-war boom was the worldwide need for stability and expansion of trade. Britain then possessed the largest merchant navy in the world, comprising many established shipping companies run by third and fourth generation ship-owners. In the 1940s these companies were intensely loyal to the UK shipbuilding industry, associations going back many decades resulted in yards receiving orders for ships, with prices to be agreed later. However, the widespread workload now common in all shipyards, upset this tradition. When could the owner get his vessel? The relentless demand for new vessels just drove UK new building prices upwards, providing an attractive basis for foreign countries to invest in the industry.

The Norwegian merchant navy, very aware of the immense contribution in terms of effort and sacrifice shown by the UK towards that country's liberation during World War II, inundated Clyde (and other British) shipyards with orders for every type of ship from whale catchers to cargo liners and oil tankers. Greece was another country whose merchant navy supported UK shipbuilding during this time.

The healthy multi-product order book of the Clyde shipbuilding industry remained buoyant from 1945 up until around 1960, when the dark clouds of competition foreshadowed the impending end of the final Indian summer of volume shipbuilding on this famous river. Throughout this period the combined yearly output ranged between 60 to 100 ships with an annual average over 400,000 gross registered tons. This represented between £40–£50 million total annual turnover which varied regularly depending on the complexity and added-value of specific ship types, notably ferries, large passenger liners and warships.

During this 15-year spell many across the board methods, with practices good and bad, pervaded the industry, which was quite remarkable considering that only three 'groups' existed during this time. Lithgows controlled their East and Kingston shipyards in Port Glasgow, as well as Fairfields and David Rowan in Glasgow, William Hamilton's Glen yard also in Port Glasgow, and a number of other small subcontractors... Harland & Wolff Limited owned their traditional yard at Govan along with the small Pointhouse shipyard of A. & J. Inglis Ltd across the river at the confluence of the River Kelvin as well as the Meadowside ship repair yard of D. & W. Henderson Ltd. The last 'group' was the belated amalgamation of William Simons & Co Ltd and Lobnitz & Co to form Simons-Lobnitz Ltd at Renfrew in 1959. Despite the collective status attached to the above locations, each yard assumed total autonomy for virtually everything from tendering to procurement and annual levels of investment. This situation of self-control was repeated in the other existing shipyards the length and breadth of the river.

What helped to make this collective control among so many different trading companies possible, were two elements:

1. The Clyde Shipbuilders Employers Association, and
2. Piecework methods of payment for all hourly paid employees except staff.

The powerful Shipbuilding Employers Federation, comprising all of the shipbuilding, marine engineering and ship repair firms, established parity of wage rates within coppers of each member company. Provision existed for local yard negotiated incentives, usually in the form of 'contract packages'. Those pretexts served and performed very well during the post-war period and helped to maintain wage levels within what the industry could afford.

This collective capitalist power base was well appreciated and persistently resented by the labour forces, trade unions and Labour politicians who despised this all-powerful cartel. Paradoxically, this titular clique, along with a productive, though not very remunerative payment by results system, created the twin driving forces that contributed to the post-war success of Clyde shipbuilding. Such authority would be displaced, as seditious moves were afoot to initially undermine and ultimately remove the old order from the boardrooms along the River Clyde.

Piecework, whereby the artisan was paid for what he produced, was a throwback from the inception of the industrial revolution, and worked very well as far as the bosses were concerned. The weightings were always loaded in favour of the firms. Not many, if any, shipyard hourly paid employees achieved the status of home ownership during a lifetime of body and soul breaking toil building ships, engines and profits for shareholders during the times of full employment. Any doltish rate-fixer who inadvertently over-calculated a tradesman's rate would be summarily dismissed by his nefarious shipyard manager. The subsequent consternation usually resulted in a management-induced dispute, not for the reinstatement of the miscreant rate-fixer, but for the renegotiation (downwards) of the generous rate.

This method of payment certainly had some benefits. It was an accurate tool whereby management could predict, using simple arithmetic computation, how long and how much it would cost to perform certain works, and was the cornerstone of fixed price contracts. It failed to transcend the social changes that were taking place not only in the UK but throughout the free world during the post-war era. Essentially it was 'The Tool' that controlled the labour force, and it prompted bad stewardship of workmen's finances. Based on a feast or famine planning rationale, it encouraged good work ethics but fostered profligate disbursement of men's wages. Such squandering, when bonuses were paid out, usually resulted in buoyant trade for the adjacent hostelries, rather than a bounty for the worker's family. The immediate solace from 'the hops and the cratur' is best comprehended from the physical and mental relief, then financial satisfaction that completion of a job engendered. All of the shipbuilding and marine engineering jobs were hard tasks, performed by resolute men. Not many managed to achieve top class trades status and temperance in a working lifetime. Those who did were either mocked…or deified. If a more enlightened management and more conciliatory labour force had exploited the benefits and eliminated the disadvantages of this system, then the subsequent industry would have had a less tenuous future.

This period was pockmarked with destabilising counter productive disputes and interminable bickering, official unofficial, many of them quite irrational and incomprehensible, not only to the public who viewed the Industrial Relations profile of this era with disbelief, but by the many tradesmen and helpers, who perceived the inverse power now held by the workforce (unions) as directly proportional to a full and healthy order book and lack of competition from other (foreign) shipbuilders. A shop-floor power base that contemptuously contradicted trade union responsibility would ultimately be evaporated as a future consequence of these disputes. This open and shut logic was not lost on ship-owners during this time. Norwegian ship-owners, most of whom were and still remain successful international shipping companies, invoked penalty clauses for late delivery of ships and stopped repeat orders forthwith in the late 1950s. Other less prominent Norwegian and British ship-owners followed suit. A major overseas customer, established over many years was lost without trace very quickly. Many individual Norwegian captains part-owned and sailed their ships. Norway's merchant marine was very appreciative of Clyde designs. They paid on the nose upon successful completion and, most significantly, constantly reinvested in new tonnages, being actively behind the bulk carrier revolution of the late '50s and '60s. This loss of market was an embarrassment and reduction in income that was to contribute towards the inexorable decline of shipbuilding in the next decade. Despite late deliveries, when months worth of cargo carrying revenue would be lost to competitors, the ships built during this time were arguably the most comprehensive in regard to types constructed. They were also the most stylish in terms of appearance, were mechanically reliable, of exceptional sea-worthiness, and duly became comparators for foreign builders to copy. Norway was indeed only one of many customers, the disaffected activists bleated, believing their own bigoted, self defamatory diatribe. This rhetoric of destruction confounded the hard-won workers' power base that was now being squandered in a miasma of irrational militancy. Norway's departure was followed by Greek, Liberian, Panamanian and Commonwealth owners, until the only regular clients left were the fast contracting British merchant and Royal Navies, along with a handful of foreign ship-owners who remained loyal, some through joint ventures with shipbuilders like Charles Connell and Lithgows Ltd, with the ships usually being managed by J. & J. Denholm Ltd, of Glasgow. Such irascible behaviour deliberately lost Clyde shipyards a sizeable percentage of the worldwide market for new ship products, which at the same time directed these ex-customers towards the burgeoning European and Japanese yards.

This watershed of once significant industrial activity was taking place in parallel with the nascence of skill technique, and exhibition of the sport that provided escape careers for some lucky shipyard apprentices, but mostly pleasure and hours of arbitrary discourse for the workers—football. In the spring of 1960, Real Madrid played Eintracht Frankfurt in the European Cup Final at Hampden Park, Glasgow, watched by over 120,000 mostly Scots supporters, many of them shipyard workers. In arguably the finest, cleanest exhibition of the 'Ba' gemme' ever seen in the UK, thousands of 'Jimmys' (management and men) discussed in dismissive yet appreciative guttural West of Scotland dialect, 'This is how football should be played.' No room for apologetic substitution here, Glasgow Rangers had been beaten home and away in the semi-final of this competition by the defeated Eintracht Frankfurt, and this team were humiliated by Real Madrid 7–3! If only these same football 'converts' had been similarly ambivalent and analytical towards their 'bread and butter industry', when it still existed anything like a major employer, then maybe the industrial detritus that scars the River Clyde today would be replaced with a larger vibrant remnant shipbuilding and marine engineering industry. The spectre of demarcation and other working practice trivia that haunted shipbuilding received more coverage in the National press, and had more of an impact on the lunchtime agenda of shop stewards and union officials than it ever had on the significant diminishment of volume shipbuilding on the River Clyde.

If the powerful Clyde Shipbuilders Association had grasped the nettle and consolidated the steelwork trades into, say, erectors (comprising loftsmen, plater and shipwright) and fabricators (comprising welder, caulker and burner) with helpers being selected into the above groups, then the archaic specific trades' identification that continued to persist could have been eradicated. To achieve the above objectives would have required a number of major costly concessions, with only the slightest hint of any tangible return in productive value. Flexibility could not be achieved without extensive retraining with, most unpleasantly of all, considerable redundancy. Not all artisans were either capable or interested in such disruption, or skills enhancement, a dreadful but nevertheless endemic trait amongst a large tranche of the West of Scotland populace. Such fundamental change would not come cheap, and might create an even stronger power base for the Boilermakers Union. If such flexibility and trade structure simplicity had been achieved during the era of full order books, then it could be assumed future generations of shipyard workers would have achieved more comprehensive marketable trades skills, with greater earning potential and a future less fraught with uncertainty. Charles Connell & Co Ltd achieved singular eradication of boilermaker demarcation with a local 'Restriction of Working Practices' agreement that cost an extra 1/– (5p) per hour in 1966. Still coupled to that yard's unique contract piecework system, this pact ran for over two strike-free years up until the company's incorporation into Upper Clyde Shipbuilders Ltd.

Alas any panacea that would have perhaps prolonged the competitiveness of shipbuilding was considered too revolutionary for both sides. The easier option of maintaining the 'status quo' prevailed. An oft reiterated 'minute' at management and union meetings alike, this latter phrase (not the malaprop hostelry in Paisley Road West, Glasgow or the UK rock group) really endorsed and exemplified the opposite but similar conservatism displayed by both sides of the shipbuilding industry. Demarcation therefore became a euphemism and inverted maxim for a very real throwback from shipbuilding's labour intensive past…'overmanning'. Interchangeability between specific trades was perhaps as irrational and illogical as inferring or insinuating that accountants and economists would make good 'models'…because they also work with figures! Thus this profligate and seemingly insoluble element of a once productive industry was to become one of a flock of albatrosses that would hang around its neck and accompany it into a state of partial oblivion.

Extensive shipyard modernisation projects of differing complexity, magnitude and cost were embarked upon during this time frame. Underwritten by initially profitable and seemingly endless supply of orders for new building work, these schemes provided millions of pounds worth of contracts for the specialist suppliers of cranes, burning, rolling, forming and welding machines as well as buildings and other facilities. Once completed, the new output from this collective modernisation failed to impress the managements and shareholders who had argued for such investment. Sad disparaging statistics like this emanated from virtually all of the boardrooms along the Clyde. Anticipated gains in productivity, helped by the replacement of shacks with sheds, derricks with cranes, labour intensive preparation machines with panel lines and riveting with welding, had not been effectively realised!

The trite, vacuous, sometimes bellicose rhetoric expounded by trades union officials, stewards and labour forces pertaining to the long overdue replacement of antiquated plant and equipment, had failed abysmally to address the need and will required to endorse such investment in the new technology of the day, with the proven work ethics of the past. A similar analogy exists between the above average sportsman who achieves about 75–80% of the desired standard with not a lot of real effort, but is surprised at the superhuman efforts required to achieve the next 20–25% improvement!

Despite such shortcomings from 1945 to 1960, Clyde shipyards still managed to produce over 30% of the United Kingdom's shipbuilding annual total of over 1,000,000 g.r.t. All the yards on the river built a truly mixed bag of ship types, each constructed using traditional methods with virtually no use of production engineering techniques. Consistent output was attained quite specifically by 'the sweat of the brow and the strength of the sinew', with a smattering of traditional ruthless 'man-management ethos' thrown in for good measure. Such conditions that created this impressive plateau of performance could no longer be sustained in the face of a diminishing UK customer base, and hyper-capitalised production engineering driven overseas shipbuilding industries.

The zenith of the post-war boom was achieved on the back of a system that frowned on tax incentives to private companies. It saw the confrontational idiom of Draconian management and intransigent protectionist trade unions as being a coercive, diametrically opposed driving force, with some mystical aura that actually worked together! While the rest of the world's shipbuilding industries were, if not getting it right first time, they were certainly not doing it along the same lines as the atavistic Clydesiders.

Yet in 1960, 24 shipyards and 18 marine engine builders still existed, albeit with reduced orders from a market that still had faith in this indigenous industry…but for how long? Two long discussed projects that were hopefully to underpin the long term future of shipbuilding and ship repairing on the River Clyde were approved during this time. Although the Employers Federation was in the forefront of labour rate and working condition stability, concordant joint working ventures between the individual companies who made up this perfidious caucus were virtually non-existent until now.

Drydocks with facilities for ships of 40,000 t.d.w. and 100,000 t.d.w. capacities, respectively, were authorised and duly constructed at Elderslie, Glasgow and Inchgreen, Greenock. Managed by groups containing most of the then shipbuilding companies, alas they were not commercial successes. The River Clyde never boasted an inclination or aptitude for volume ship repairing. The niggardly amount of work in this category emanated from the handful of traditional shipping companies like The Blue Funnel Line, City Line and Clan Line, who regularly used the port of Glasgow. The hoped for increase in this limited scope of repair work resulting from the provision of two new drydocks was marketing naïvety. Anyway, the existing shipbuilding industry needed these facilities and the new docks would eliminate the need for the larger Clyde built vessels to sail to Southampton or Belfast. The larger dock also anticipated regular dry-docking, repair work and tank cleaning of the supertankers that had recently started carrying crude oil from the Middle East to the deep water ocean terminal at Finnart on nearby Loch Long.

The initial shock, followed by crass indifference displayed by the public, government and the remaining shipbuilding companies towards the announcement of liquidation and closure of Denny's of Dumbarton in 1963 set the tone of apathy that was to enshroud the subsequent demise of volume shipbuilding on the River Clyde. Here was a family company, renowned throughout the world for innovation and quality, synonymous with all of their marine products. A firm, whose multi-product repertoire invariably included the construction of a cross channel or coastal ferry, along with general cargo ships, was considered up to its closure the most capable and experienced designer and builder of these types of vessels, many of which still remain in service four and five decades after their completion. Denny's foresaw development of ferries as a market of vast potential growth (a fact that was borne out a few years later), so much so that they spent considerable amounts of their own money on designing and producing a prototype passenger carrying hovercraft. Unfortunately, its high development costs, coupled with no bona-fide customer base, invariably contributed to the liquidation of the shipyard. The company's departure was a sad loss, not only to the Clyde but also to the shipbuilding capability of the UK, and the town of Dumbarton, so long synonymous with the name of Denny, has never recovered from the loss of its last shipyard and engine works.

When the boom in large passenger/car/vehicle ferry demand occurred in the late 1960s, stimulated by the vision of some British ferry operators, the 'design and build' challenge for these ships was met not by the UK but by German, French, Dutch, Belgian and Scandinavian shipyards, a number of which employed a handful of redundant British designers and tradesmen. This recent lack of empathy between the main customer base, the British Merchant Navy, and the shipyards that used to build virtually all of their ships, was another significant factor that contributed towards the accelerating demise in volume shipbuilding on the Clyde and the UK.

A year earlier in the winter of 1962, further bad news had beckoned with the announcement that the Clyde's most famous dredger/tug/hopper/specialist craft builder, Simons-Lobnitz Ltd would cease ship construction at their two Renfrew yards on completion of existing orders. Future new shipbuilding contracts would be undertaken by Alexander Stephen & Sons Ltd at Linthouse, who had now acquired all of their 'Si-Lo' designs. This body blow of the loss of a core, highly specialised element of the River Clyde's varied multi-product capability, was ostensibly softened by the promise at the time of the announcement that the larger, more modern Linthouse facility would be more able to satisfy this specialist niche, and at the same time safeguard the 3,000 jobs that existed there between the shipyard and the marine engine works. Most of the Simons-Lobnitz labour force did not transfer to Linthouse, which perhaps contributed to the initial difficulties Stephens encountered in building a wide range of craft, with very unique construction methods, not akin to the volume conventional hull piecework throughput, that was a hallmark of Stephens of Linthouse in its heyday.

The Simons-Lobnitz and Denny failures were followed in 1963 by the not unexpected announcement that A. & J. Inglis at Pointhouse on the River Kelvin, and Harland & Wolff, Govan, both of whom had launched their last ship in 1962 and were operating on a care and maintenance basis, would officially close that autumn. The attrition that pervaded the run down of these two venerable and at one time very productive shipyards meant that by the time of formal closure only a handful of men were made redundant. The few thousands employed at these yards during the 1950s had either retired, or found other employment in what was still perceived as a large collection of adjacent shipbuilding and engineering works along the River Clyde. These closures were announced by the Harland & Wolff parent company in Belfast, who had taken the decision that all future group shipbuilding activities would be concentrated in Northern Ireland. This policy had already been tacitly established with the earlier cessation of marine engine building at Harland & Wolff's Finnieston engine works, so ending many years of ship and engine building association between the Northern Ireland firm and its Scottish subsidiaries.

The launch of the m.v. *Freetown* 7689 g.r.t., for the Elder Dempster Line at the Glen shipyard of William Hamilton & Co Ltd, of Port Glasgow in September 1963 was preceded by the announcement that this old yard with more than 90 years of shipbuilding expertise would cease to exist. This specific contraction was more akin to rationalisation, as the company was part of the adjoining Lithgows Limited. The release of the Glen yard real estate to the parent group enabled most of the acreage to be put to good use a few years later when the old berths became part of the site of the modernised Glen/East complex of Scott-Lithgow Limited, which built some large bulk carriers and VLCCs.

Further closure announcements continued early in 1964 with the news that the Norcross Group, owners of the Blythswood Shipbuilding Co Ltd, would stop shipbuilding at its Scotstoun yard after delivery of the lighthouse tender *Fingal* 1342 g.r.t., launched the previous year. This once prolific yard had found a paucity of profitable shipbuilding contracts in the early 1960s. Its aggressive and determined management had dabbled with diversification to keep what it saw as a loyal, skilful and hard working labour force employed. This survival instinct resulted in a number of contracts for the 'jumbo-ising' (lengthening) of various small oil tankers of about 8–10,000 t.d.w. into 16–20,000 t.d.w., retaining the original aft end of the hull, accommodation and propulsion machinery. The work entailed building a new enlarged midships and fore-body, cutting off the old fore-end, welding the new forward and old aft sections together, to create a much larger vessel at a fraction of the cost of a new ship. The International Oil Company, Regent/Texaco/Caltex, who had been very good customers of the Blythswood, supported this work and at one time it looked like a Clyde shipyard would steal a march on the German, Dutch and Swedish shipyards who were the main promotors of this type of conversion. Unfortunately this did not occur. The jumbo-ising work did not create much activity for outfit trades, only steelworkers. The Blythswood management addressed this shortfall by undertaking the construction of portable wooden prefab houses for Glasgow Corporation Housing Department. The productive capacity and good piecework rate-fixing that existed at Scotstoun led to these contracts being completed on time to the satisfaction of the housing department, and the new tenants! However, the Norcross Group had now taken the view that shipbuilding and house building were not part of their future corporate strategy, and the Blythswood shipyard duly closed.

1965 saw what was thought the last launch from the Paisley shipyard of Fleming & Ferguson Ltd. Providentially, the unique design and build reputation, built up over many years by this specialist builder of dredgers, tugs, mining pontoons, lighters and other one-off crafts, was recognised and subsequently milched by the American Marine and Machinery Co Inc, who bought the yard and presided over the construction of some two ships at the River Cart shipyard until they announced total closure of the facility in 1968. The Paisley yard was still implementing very small unit construction methods at the time of their demise. The unusual product range that they manufactured could neither justify nor sustain the capital expenditure in burning, forming, welding, machining or fabrication equipment and processes, that were needed to defray the rising building costs then symptomatic of 1960s British industry, not only shipbuilding. With the passing of one more yard down the slipway to oblivion, the West of Scotland lost yet another bundle of skilled artisans as well as a design knowledge and expertise that might be spirited abroad, lost forever to future generations, however, a few years later, an independent design company called Seadrec Ltd became established in Paisley. They resurrected many of the Fleming & Ferguson designs and partly redressed this deficiency by designing specialist craft for construction throughout the world. The occasional dredger was latterly built by the more conventional shipbuilders, however volume construction of this nautical niche has now virtually ended on the River Clyde.

Also towards the end of 1965, the Fairfield Shipbuilding and Engineering Co Ltd and associated Fairfield-Rowan Ltd marine engine works announced their failure, despite an enviable but unprofitable order book. This event was the watershed for the future of Clyde shipbuilding. The Labour Government of the day assumed the standpoint that enough was enough, and intervened under the auspices of George Brown, the Industry Minister. After a brief period under receivership, Fairfields (Glw) Ltd was resurrected in early 1966 with an influx of some new and apparently talented managers. Amidst a brouhaha of public debate, the phoenix company set off to resuscitate Clyde shipbuilding, underwritten by an influx of state money and a prospective agenda for productivity improvements.

This insidious attrition of the shipbuilding industry was not lost on the profusion of 'Jimmys' who relied on its existence for their livelihood. Fairfields ability to maintain a healthy order book, for virtually any kind of ship, merchant and naval, had meant there was always employment at its Govan yard. This workload created an artificial cushion for labour fortunate enough to be employed there, with some having been previously displaced by the closures of those nearby yards depicted earlier. This realisation that the 'grim reaper' of contraction was looking them squarely in the face no doubt instilled a conciliatory compliance between management and men which pervaded the brief Fairfields (Glw) Ltd experiment.

'The Fairfields (Glw) Ltd experiment' was meant to last five years. Concurrent with this analysis emerged the long awaited publishing of the Geddes report on British shipbuilding under the effective chairmanship of A.R.M. Geddes, a successful UK industrialist. This report, which was the result of the findings of the Shipbuilding Inquiry Committee, advocated the establishment of group shipbuilding centres throughout the UK in basically geographical locations, ie. Tyne, Wear, Tees, East of Scotland, Barrow/Mersey, Belfast (already established), and for the West of Scotland…upper and lower Clyde shipbuilding companies. The report was a belated yet well intentioned attempt by the Harold Wilson administration at recognising the insidious shrinkage of UK shipbuilding, set against a growing world market for new ships. Fiscal response to the need for help was however a decade too late to arrest further eradication of British shipbuilding capacity. Nevertheless, a brutal realisation then existed in most Clyde boardrooms that this was not a report over which to prevaricate.

The irrefutable logic of some of its proposed nostrums was alas lost in a sea of socialist euphoria. The Labour Government's ideological solutions to the continuing problems of a staple industry's inexorable contraction were naïve, profligate and totally one-sided, and wrongly assumed the dadaistic stance of employment at all cost. The industry's evolvement, technically and commercially, was founded fairly or unfairly on the success (albeit now diminished) between companies contending with each other for orders, won in the open market place, invariably and inevitably a product of price, delivery and rival innovative designs, all related to what the customer wanted and what he would afford.

This ruthless competition which is the ethos of business, existed at a more diffused level between the tradesmen who worked in many cases boy and man in these companies. This was so in Fairfields (Glw) Ltd where given the chance to compete and survive, an 'esprit de corps' emerged, apparently not witnessed in post-war UK shipyards. Whilst flexibility between trades never really became established, slightly higher levels of output per man shift were briefly attained. This notable improvement in productivity was not lost on the Cardiff-based Reardon Smith Shipping Co who, having taken delivery of two bulk carriers within weeks of each other, ordered a follow-on series of ships from this yard.

Fairfields (Glw) Ltd existed from early 1966 until the spring of 1968 whence it became the Govan Division of Upper Clyde Shipbuilders Ltd. During this period when Britain was attempting to enter a more enlightened era in industrial relations, some progress was made in developing management and labour force accord. The management team at Fairfields (Glw) Ltd made conscious efforts towards dismantling the barriers of industrial aristocracy. To their credit, most of the conveners, stewards and labour force reciprocated, but the experiment never lasted its intended duration. Investment in hardware, infrastructure, method improvements and techniques were perfunctory. The shipyard, like most other UK establishments, never capitalised on semi-automatic large unit fabrication or modular outfitting and continued to deploy labour intensive techniques throughout all shipbuilding functions. The purported benefits and supposed ground work that emanated from Fairfields (Glw) Ltd would soon be lost in that medley of managerial mediocrity which would presage the demise of volume Clyde shipbuilding, the creation of Upper Clyde Shipbuilders Ltd.

A year after the establishment of Fairfields (Glw) Ltd, another world-renowned shipyard ignominiously slithered out of existence in 1967. Barclay Curle & Co Ltd of Glasgow had been established at its Clydeholm shipyard in Whiteinch since 1855 and built hundreds of liners, troop ships, cargo tramps and oil tankers over these years. It had an excellent record for quality, painstakingly achieved over many years using the traditional single frame/single plate shipbuilding techniques synonymous with riveted construction. This success was rewarded in the late 1950s with a multi-million pound investment programme which created a brand new shipyard built on open ground between the existing berths at Whiteinch and the adjacent North British Marine Engine Works at Scotstoun East.

The completed Clydeholm facility was the envy of all other Glasgow shipyards. With thousands of square feet of covered preparation and fabrication shops, a pair of state-of-the-art 60-ton travelling hammerhead cranes and brand new joinery, plumbing and electrical workshops, the yard should have had an assured future. This was not the case. Having invested so much money, the Newcastle parent company, Swan Hunter & Whigham Richardson Ltd, surprisingly didn't demonstrate the will to make the facility perform! The modernised Clydeholm shipyard struggled to build two medium-sized cargo liners in any one year. It had an exemplary labour force, but failed to match the next door Charles Connell shipyard for output and consistency. The Geddes report endorsed or coerced the Swan Hunter Group's decision to rid itself of the Clydeholm facility (but not the adjacent North British Engine Works and nearby Elderslie Drydocks). Clydeholm shipyard was offered to the embryonic management team that was shaping UCS, but the internecine dialogue that imbued the formation of that company, resulted in the abandonment of the most modern shipbuilding facility in Glasgow! The 60-ton travelling hammerhead cranes were dismantled and re-erected at Swan Hunter's Tyneside shipyards, along with some of the profile burning and welding machinery, but the buildings and site were allowed to deteriorate. After a brief occupancy by some transient sunrise industries, who never filled the breach left by the departure of shipbuilding, the site became a small industrial estate.

In the spring of 1968 the then Labour Government pronounced Upper Clyde Shipbuilders Ltd would be responsible for shipbuilding in the Glasgow area. Apparently not a knee-jerk reaction to the interminable decline that was engulfing UK shipbuilding, but ostensibly a cohesive multi-site facility for ship production of all types. Utilising the considerable designer and craftsman skills from all of the five yards within the group, and strengthening the extensive customer portfolio that had been built up over the years, this company would consolidate, expand and set the industrial bench mark not only for shipbuilding but for UK industry!

Reality was to prove a wee bit different from rhetoric! Implementing the dictate of the recently published Geddes report on British shipbuilding, the government forced the merger of the five remaining shipyards that existed from Clydebank to Govan into Upper Clyde Shipbuilders Ltd. They were:

- John Brown & Co (Clydebank) Ltd, Clydebank.
- Yarrows Ltd, Scotstoun, Glasgow
- Charles Connell & Co Ltd, Scotstoun, Glasgow
- Fairfields (Glasgow) Ltd, Govan, Glasgow
- Alexander Stephen & Sons Ltd, Linthouse, Glasgow

The marine engine works of Alexander Stephen would remain within the ownership of that company, although operating at a much reduced capacity. The Clydebank engine works of John Brown Engineering Limited had already been hived off from the shipyard in 1966. This meant the new group would only build ships. Marine engines would be supplied by other companies, however propulsion machinery installation would be performed by UCS labour. At its formation, the total work force of the group numbered nearly 14,000 people.

With corporate headquarters in plush offices at Cadogan Street, in the centre of Glasgow, the company was led by Mr Anthony Hepper, a captain of industry with no specific shipbuilding experience, this shortfall was made up later by appointing as his deputy Mr Ken Douglas formerly of Austin & Pickersgill Ltd, Sunderland. Douglas was not new to shipbuilding, having been instrumental in the design, marketing and series production of the most successful peacetime cargo ship type ever constructed in a UK shipyard, the S.D.14, over a hundred of which were completed from their two north-east shipyards and nearly as many again were built under licence by various shipyards throughout the world. This much vaunted acronym is variously reported as standing for standard design, shelter-deck or the dubiously esoteric connotation of first and last letters of the city of its birth, Sunderland. In any case, whatever the real derivation of this 'mackem' conundrum (that prefaced the ship's capacity of 14,000 t.d.w.), it will remain synonymous with the cultural and practical shipbuilding skills of Wearsiders long after the eradication of that industry which spawned its title. Douglas came to Glasgow armed with productive knowledge of efficacious volume shipbuilding and a high market profile, essential to fuse UCS into a cohesive Scottish competitor of Austin & Pickersgill Limited, et al.

The first task of this arranged marriage was the announcement of the closure of one of the constituent companies. The group of five would be reduced to four, with the immediate closure of the Linthouse shipbuilding yard of Alexander Stephen & Co Ltd. The two remaining vessels currently under construction for Port Line Ltd would be completed, along with the Royal Navy Leander class frigate *HMS Hermione*, thereafter shipbuilding would cease at this famous location. The extensive facilities would then be utilised for the construction and pre-assembly of units for the four remaining shipbuilding divisions, to be shipped by barge up or down-river.

When the *Port Caroline* 12,398 g.r.t., finally entered the Clyde (already several months late), workers not only of Stephens but from all the group yards, winced at the vast open berth space formerly occupied by up to five ships at any one time during the earlier busier times of shipbuilding at Linthouse. Another world famous company noted for the design and construction of warships, ferries, oil tankers, liners, and latterly dredgers, had launched its last ship! The diversification into dredger building filled a gap in the order book, albeit at the expense of Simons-Lobnitz Ltd, but it was an expensive fill-in. Stephens were in the forefront of training and skill development, building virtually any kind of conventional ship. These skills were deployed in the construction of seven dredgers at Linthouse in the 1960s, but the complexity of the new product was contributing to a lengthy construction time-scale which cost the company money. This poor productivity on a much smaller order book did not portend well for the inclusion of Linthouse within UCS, and, despite larger and superior facilities than that of Connells at Scotstoun, Stephens closed and Connells became the Scotstoun Division of UCS. This initial decision was to set the tone of irrational, spontaneous inconsistency, and latterly infighting that was to permeate UCS throughout its short and controversial life. With a new Board of Directors, the bulk of whom were recruited from sources outwith shipbuilding, these men came from companies that essentially ran themselves. Process, service and consumer supply industries, which were capital intensive requiring little of the street-wise prescience, commercial sagacity, man management motivational prowess and customer awareness that this once great, now almost totally demoralised shipbuilding industry was craving!

A hotch-potch of individuals, they were more concerned with their public profile rather than the establishment and future well being of the company. Devoid of leadership, denuded of drive, and displaying a factious lack of harmony, they were constantly assailed by dissatisfied ship-owners. Virtually from the outset, appeasement and climb down became their hallmark and that of UCS. Bereft of any strong production engineering gist, they discarded the experience and long standing customer contacts of Browns, Connells and Stephens, as well as the debatable partial 'success' of Fairfields (Glw) Ltd. This new board was transparent from the outset to the many skilled workers, foremen and managers, who saw Tony Wedgewood Benn's genuine and sincere attempts at shipbuilding longevity, about to be squandered in a short space of time when the reputation of shipbuilding on the upper reaches of the River Clyde would plummet to the nadir of public disparagement and lampoonery.

Either by accident or design, the first actions of this phoenix board were to establish and recognise an unbelievable preponderance of full-time, part-time, some-time and every-time trade union delegates, stewards, conveners and others, purportedly representing the combined labour force. In reality, this grossly overmanned cabal of self-seeking orators had more in common with the 'clone of clowns' at the helm of the rudderless UCS board than ever they had in common with the work force.

Driven by the industrial philosophy of the Geddes report, and the will of the then government to wrest control of this fundamental industry from the handfuls of families and private companies who controlled shipbuilding, UCS was formed as the precursor of future Labour Government dogma and policy. Such statecraft was always a thinly veiled idealism that was exhumed or interred depending on its controversiality, to be propounded depending on the zealotry of whoever was making party policy. The Shipbuilding Industry Board became the government department responsible for the financial structure of Upper Clyde Shipbuilders Ltd.

It became an unfortunate statistic of modern day British industrial history that Tony Benn did not recruit, coerce, cajole and create the right team to implement fundamental changes to a major industry. At the inception of UCS in 1968 a number of significant facts bode well for the future of volume shipbuilding, *viz.* Britain still had a significant highly capitalised modern merchant navy, comprising many long-established shipping lines. These go-ahead companies were then embarking on extensive modernisation schemes for container ships, ro-ro ferries and VLCCs (very large crude carriers). This meant that probably the most important aspect necessary for the well being of the phoenix company, an expanding market, was already in existence!

From the outset, UCS was unfortunately seen as an employment agency perpetuating craft skills at the taxpayers' expense, rather than an industry employing people, performing profitable work, constantly developing and selling its products in the market place. Customer contact, customer awareness, customer satisfaction were anathema to the whole team. The irresolute timidity of those who directed UCS failed abysmally to address such market place necessities or essential new ship developments. With major contracts already under way at its three merchant yards for three of the major UK shipping companies, UCS displayed a self-destruct policy of customer alienation that was to spell doom to the company, and subsequently unfairly tarnish the whole UK shipbuilding industry.

The Clydebank Division, formerly John Brown & Co (Clydebank) Ltd, was in the throes of completing *Queen Elizabeth 2* 65,863 g.r.t., for Cunard Line Ltd, a magnificent vessel, the like of which will never be built again. Running late, with cost over-runs numbering many millions of pounds, this loss-making contract would most likely have presaged the closure of the world-renowned shipyard. The new board led by Mr A. Hepper adopted a bellicose confrontational stance with Cunard. Sir Basil Smallpiece, chairman of the ship-owners, reciprocated. The ensuing 'bunfight' resulted in four years of coordinated craftsmanship being despatched down the tubes of rhetorical mudslinging. Cunard received their ship for much less than the cost to build, and the newly formed Clydebank Division obtained a derisory reputation it did not wholly deserve…and lost its oldest customer, who would now continue to order its new vessels over the next two decades from foreign shipyards!

Govan Division, formerly Fairfields (Glw) Ltd, had a mixed bag of work including a County class destroyer for the Royal Navy, two survey ships for the US Navy, some Cardiff class bulk carriers, and a vessel type that should have created much bread and butter work for the next two decades—the steam turbine containership *Jervis Bay* 26,876 g.r.t., for Overseas Containers Ltd (OCL), a recently formed consortium of leading UK liner companies, established by P & O, Blue Funnel Line, British and Commonwealth and Furness Whithy, all major players in the world shipping scene. Part of a six ship order, with the other five ships being ordered in West Germany, Fairfields were slow in receiving the main steelwork scantling drawings from Germany, and commercially remiss at not imploring OCL to redress that situation. The late delivery of these drawings, coupled with insufficient heavy lifting capacity of berth craneage to make any significant impact on a tight building schedule, led by a befuddled management and indifferent work force, most of whom wanted to see the Fairfields (Glw) Ltd experiment run its course, meant that the Govan yard had nothing but trouble throughout the execution of this prestigious contract. The unfortunate *Jervis Bay* was over a year late when handed over to her owners. The then chairman of P & O Group vowed vociferously she would be the last ship built for them on the River Clyde. This major customer, whose constituent shipping lines had supported UK shipyards for over 100 years now denigrated UCS and took its considerable custom elsewhere. In the post-war period between 1946 to 1987, P & O and their group subsidiaries took delivery of 155 ships (including liners, tankers, bulk carriers and ferries) totalling 1,258,781 g.r.t. from no fewer than 16 River Clyde shipyards, making this long established and venerable shipping line the largest customer not only of the River Clyde, but of the entire UK shipbuilding industry.

Scotstoun Division, formerly Charles Connell & Co Ltd, were a medium-sized family run shipyard previously profitably prefabricating over 300 tons per week from a labour force of less than 1,000 men (mainly steelworkers). The shipyard, under the able leadership of Sir Charles Connell and his son, also called Charles, was run fairly efficiently. Both astute businessmen as well as shipbuilders, they formed joint ventures with some UK and Scandinavian ship-owners, becoming part owners of many 'no frills', well-designed, reliably constructed cargo tramps, tankers and special vessels like reefers and lumber carriers which were built at the Scotstoun yard. Recently completed were a batch of 'state-of-the-art' fast cargo liners for the Ben Line Ltd, of Edinburgh, with two further vessels still to be constructed for this company. The unique incentive payment scheme at Scotstoun had worked well in the past, but the recent departure to the Furness Shipbuilding Co Ltd, on the River Tees, of Mr R.E. Butler, yard general manager, his assistant, D. Ellis and a handful of head foremen, made a considerable impact on the future continuation of impressive steelwork and outfit production figures. Despite this, the Connell family had arguably the best customer contacts amongst the remaining shipbuilders of the upper Clyde, however, the Connell tenure on the board of UCS became short-lived. The long term contact and respect of the Ben Line for Clyde-built truisms was one of the first casualties. Here was another major UK shipping company now in the market for a pair of large container ships about to go abroad for the first time this century, quite disillusioned with the customer indifference now being shown by UCS. The crass client pre-selection practice displayed by the board of directors of the new group set in train another stage of self destruction, by arrogantly choosing what they thought was a suitable customer profile, from an ever diminishing circle of ship-owners.

Yarrows Limited were an average-sized shipyard building warships, logistic and other highly specialised vessels exclusively for the Royal Navy and some Commonwealth governments. The knee-jerk inclusion of such a unique company within UCS was repudiated from the outset by Sir Eric Yarrow and his executives. Their persistent objection to the inclusion of the company with its unique customer profile, led successfully to its extraction from UCS in 1970.

The abject disappointment of UCS in virtually every facet of its commercial, technical and public profile save its short-term significant contribution to employment in Scotland, was a fiasco that need not have happened, and a watershed of opportunity squandered. The emulsified hegemony of the board, with its attendant failure to consolidate, innovate and invest in the last vestiges of a major industry, now in transitional contraction, yet still with a future, was a renouncement with few parallels in post-war Britain.

The three shipyards that constituted the merchant shipbuilding identity of UCS, all had considerable expertise in ship construction of a wide range of varied vessel types with a customer base that should have proved a springboard for future market penetration. The healthy complimentary competition that had existed beforehand between what became the Clydebank, Scotstoun and Govan Divisions was observed by their respective managements, labour forces and union representatives as a benchmark for the perpetuation of factional discord, rather than the ingredients for a harmonious industrial super company. The limited craneage of all three yards was embarrassingly exposed by the fact that the recently closed Clydeholm facility of Barclay Curle (offered to the group for a song by its Tyneside owners) was having its heavy travelling cranes dismantled and re-erected in the North-east of England. Craneage throughout UCS was therefore pitched at late 1950s capacity thus hindering any increased efficiency of fabrication and erection techniques.

The buoyant shipping market in 1968 was for large scantling VLCCs, first generation container ships and ro-ro ferries and cruise liners. New types of vessels that required a considerable investment in design capability, and new building technology, two aspects of company strategy that were lost on the board members of UCS. Furthermore, the shipping companies that were the sponsors of these new investment programmes were previously satisfied customers of the former shipyard owners, *viz.* BP Tankers Ltd, Shell Tankers Ltd, British Railways Board (cross channel ferries), Ben Line, British & Commonwealth, P & O Group, Alred Holt, as well as a host of Norwegian, Greek and Commonwealth ship-owners. The capricious refusal to invest in the necessary new shipyard hardware at the same time touting these established clients, set the tone of mediocrity that was to become synonymous with UCS throughout its brief existence.

Unwilling and unable to compete in these upmarket niches, the design and build of handy size low technology bulk-carriers and the unsuccessful Clyde class cargo liner duly became the stock portfolio of the group. The basis for the Clyde class cargo liner was derived from the international success of the S.D.14, and was Ken Douglas's brainchild. A total of only seven Clyde class vessels were built by the group: two at Scotstoun and five at Clydebank. UCS were unable to match the 'off the shelf' specification, price and delivery of Austin and Pickersgill's S.D.14, with the Clyde class ships taking as long to complete as specialised cargo liners or heavier scantling bulk carriers. Be that as it may, the passage of time provided a quirky affirmation of Mr Douglas's faith in the Clyde class ships that he and his sales executives found difficult to sell in anything like the hoped for numbers. By 1996, all seven Clyde class vessels were still in existence albeit trading under different names and owners, clearly fulfilling meaningful if limited functions throughout the shipping world, performing the roles for which they were built over two decades earlier.

Clydebank, a yard with acres of space for development should have been further modernised to build either VLCCs or large container ships. Unfortunately, it struggled manfully deploying traditional labour intensive craft methods to produce a mixed bag of jack-up drilling rigs, one cruise ship, one railway ferry, a batch of bulk carriers and Clyde class cargo liners, during its tenure within UCS. The former John Brown shipyard, for years the leading British shipbuilder, long starved of state-of-the-art investment and in need of a revolution in working practices, was reduced to that of an old soldier marking time on the parade ground, waiting impending retiral.

Scotstoun Division's transformation from a bustling builder of three or four ships under the Connell family to two vessels a year with a larger labour force under UCS, was the antithesis of the previous owner's shipbuilding expertise, and a soul destroying portent of catastrophe ahead for the many good men who worked there.

Govan Division possessed the most modern facilities within the group, a legacy from the partial investment programmes of the previous Lithgow group nearly 15 years earlier. This meant the yard was best placed technically (though not geographically) to achieve some attempt at profitable ship production. Bereft of any extensive jigs, fixtures or semi-automated panel fabrication lines for steelwork, it was also minus any attempts at modular construction for outfit disciplines of pipework, joinerwork, electrical or mechanical pre-installation. The facility was rooted in the modus operandi of the previous decade.

The visionless parameters of UCS management complacently accepted the predisposed levels, standards and methods of shipbuilding, inherited from the demoralised employees of its erstwhile constituent companies. It was even unsuccessful with the most rudimentary negotiation of higher wages in return for guaranteed increased output, to be achieved at less cost than previously ascribed from a workforce now assured better continuity of employment. The infant board of directors eschewed from dismantling the over manned labour levels inherited from all of the constituent yards. In fact the situation was exacerbated by the inclusion of many workers from Stephens of Linthouse, who were dispersed throughout the other four 'ship launching' divisions. The retention of Linthouse as a common steelwork fabrication centre provided the only tangible hardware facility inherent within the 'group'.

The Luddite myopia engendered by the respective labour forces towards the former constituent identities prior to the formation of UCS, created a collective power base and latent respectability disguised as concordance, an unfortunate euphemism for the inability of the management to structure the company efficiently from board room to shop floor. This contrasted quite conspicuously with the craven parochialism towards the retention and perpetuation of single, labour intensive crafts, displayed by the trade unions, despite their dishonest rhetoric to the contrary. 'Investment in new plant and machinery' became a caveat effectively gainsaid by the sacrosanct attitude to job retention. Govan Division tried the introduction of 'Gravi-max'—simple to operate, semi-automatic high deposition, welding machines that afforded one welder to achieve the previous output of six men! This process in use in Scandinavia for many years was rejected out of hand on Clydeside. One man works one machine! So much for investment in new methods!

Such immutable intransigence to the inexorable development of fabrication technology had previously been identified by the former shipyard owners, but met with very limited acceptance by most of the boilermakers.

Such all pervading self-destruct attitudes were symptomatic of an opportunity that should have been the precursor for the consolidation and retention of volume shipbuilding. This bellicose rejection merely served to supply the ammunition for opposition MPs who saw this exercise in State intervention being reduced to a short-term employment exercise, jealously decried by other manufacturing industries within the UK which, given the financial support meted to UCS, maybe could have achieved more from their committed managements and enlightened labour forces. With its easy option market research, and customer selectivity, the company surprisingly won sufficient orders to retain short term employment throughout its divisions at a cost of only partial recovery of overheads.

Stagnant productivity figures with the highest labour rates for shipbuilding work in the UK, only served to accelerate the day of reckoning, and in June 1971, a receiver was duly appointed to wind up the group. Thus the brief existence of what should have been the shop window for partial worker involvement and total commitment to the shipbuilding industry on upper Clydeside, ignominiously ended as an abject failure. The reactive, acquiescent, smug and bridled management never bridged the culture chasm inherited from the previous owners, nor did they implement any meaningful development of the traditional shipbuilding crafts. This deficiency was perhaps the worse advert for the inactive effect of state control, which was made worse by the increase in trades union power due to the group's formation.

Unfortunately for the employees of UCS a change of government had taken place since the inception of the company barely more than three years earlier. Mr John Davies, the new Secretary of State of Trade and Industry was less than sympathetic to the existence and perpetuation of the failed 'idealogue' that was UCS. With predictable British political antipathy and aversion to any scheme concocted by the opposition, the new Conservative Government advised by faceless bureaucrats in grey suits, intended to slay the socialist behemoth that was UCS, decanting thousands of shipyard and ancillary workers on the invisible burden of the state sponsored dole queue, with immediate and uncompromising effect, or so they thought!

Totally underestimating the attachment, support, feeling and sympathy towards the labour force of UCS, not only from the denizens of Clydeside and Scotland, but throughout the UK and parts of Europe and afar, thus began a public battle of wills between Mr Davies, the Prime Minister Edward Heath, and the collective labour force of UCS, now represented and ably led by a pair of charismatic and colloquially astute Clydesiders, Jim Airlie and Jimmy Reid. As conspicuous by their centre stage commitment to the retention of shipbuilding on the upper Clyde, as the inept former board of directors and executives were by their instant departure from the ensuing fray, Reid and Airlie indubitably provided the driving force for the successful retention of merchant shipbuilding on the upper Clyde. Their succinct incisive Glaswegian rhetoric, entrapped, coerced and ultimately convinced Messrs Davies, Heath and the then UK cabinet into a political climbdown over total closure. The government announced an official investigation would take place by the consultants, Hill Samuel, through their associates H.B. Maynard into the retention and potential viability of merchant shipbuilding in the Glasgow area. It was unfortunate that the belated energy commitment and enthusiasm generated by the UCS sit-in, had not been identified and harnessed by the company after its formation three years earlier.

The official receiver, Mr Robert Courtney-Smith, oversaw the completion of the existing ship contracts under construction at the Govan, Scotstoun and Clydebank yards. The expertise and versatility of craft produced by the former John Brown yard resulted in an interest to purchase that facility by the American jack-up drilling rig builder, Messrs Marathon Le Tourneau Shipbuilding Company. Discussions followed apace and the yard was purchased for rig building in 1972. The last merchant ship built at Clydebank, the *m.v. Alisa* 11,897 g.r.t., a Clyde class cargo liner, was towed up-river immediately after her launching to the former basin of Harland & Wolff Ltd at Govan, where she was completed under the auspices of the receiver.

The H.B. Maynard report subsequently recommended retention of merchant shipbuilding at Govan and Scotstoun. In 1972 HM Government sanctioned the formation of Govan Shipbuilders Ltd, with Scotstoun Marine Ltd a wholly owned subsidiary. The Glasgow businessman, Mr Ian Stenhouse, had been greatly impressed by the UCS sit-in and was convinced of the need to retain such a vital industry in Scotland, this resulted in his appointment as chairman of the latest phoenix of the former Fairfield yard. His untimely death a few months later deprived the new company of a high profile Scotsman, whose promised contribution to the continuation of shipbuilding was sadly never realised.

Concurrent with the contention that engulfed the formation and short term existence of UCS, Yarrows Ltd continued to develop their Scotstoun facility, and in so doing absorbed some ex-UCS employees to meet their growing workload of naval work. Down-river the still productive Lithgows Ltd (already incorporating Ferguson Bros in 1961), Greenock Dockyard, Scotts SB & Eng Co Ltd, James Lamont and George Brown shipyards continued their respective shipbuilding activities. John G. Kincaid & Co Ltd, recently re-equipped with an influx of new machine tools, was emerging as the pre-eminent large bore marine engine builder in the UK.

On the recommendation of the Geddes Report, Lithgows Ltd, Kingston and East yards merged with the Cartsburn and Cartsdyke shipyards of Scotts SB & Eng Co Ltd (the former Greenock Dockyard having since amalgamated in 1966) to form Scott-Lithgow Ltd in 1969. A formidable shipbuilding group with six reasonably modern shipbuilding yards, the marine engine works of Scotts in Greenock and a large drydock, the new firm also had access to a host of companies controlled by Lithgows Ltd, who provided specialised outfitting expertise. The initial success of this kindred super-yard was derived from the collective technical expertise, commercial sagacity and very strong customer support base painstakingly built up over many years by the Lithgow and Scott dynasties. This was supplemented by their hand-picked executives, ably led by A.R. Belch who knew and respected shipbuilding as an industry of immeasurable benefits to the conurbation of Port Glasgow, Greenock and Gourock.

The adjacent independent James Lamont shipyard in Port Glasgow and repair docks in Greenock, continued under private ownership to build and repair coasters and ferries until it closed in 1979. George Brown & Co (Marine) Ltd had an intermittent but varied post-war shipbuilding record. After the firm stopped shipbuilding, they persisted to design, market and build marine equipment in the shape of winches, derricks, hatches and doors under the name Cargospeed Ltd until 1983.

Scott-Lithgow virtually achieved all of the directives set out by the Labour Government sponsored Geddes dissertation. The new company accomplished a smooth transition to cohesive group identity, being bereft of the internecine bickering, position juggling and publicity posturing profile, endemic within UCS on the upper reaches of the same river. This harmonious association was based on deep rooted career commitment to shipbuilding, displayed by the executive management and labour force of the new company. The list of customers of the constituent shipyards read like a 'who's who' of shipping not only of the UK, but Norwegian, Indian and other famous overseas ship-owners. Actively pursuing as diverse a marine workload as their respective technical and production departments could handle, successful diversification into the market for offshore dynamically positioned drill ships endorsed the capability of the group's work force. This innovative diversification would in time provide the ultimate downfall of volume shipbuilding on the lower reaches of the River Clyde. In less than a decade of Scott-Lithgow Ltd, orders were obtained and completed for a mixed bag of ship types, both merchant and naval, amounting to several hundred million pounds. The company also entered the hyper-competitive world market for VLCCs and large bulk carriers. Between 1969 and 1976, the group built a total of 84 ships aggregating some 1,316,431 g.r.t.

When the then Labour Government totally nationalised virtually the entire UK shipbuilding industry, forming British Shipbuilders Ltd on 1 July 1977, as a consequence of the Aircraft and Shipbuilding Industries Act 1976, they substituted yet again ideology for assistance and inspiration. Perceived over-capacity within the British shipbuilding industry had been systematically reduced almost annually since

1960. This attrition had left the total UK labour force at 87,000 workers in July 1977 when the industry was taken over by the state. About 25% of that total were employed on the Clyde.

By the late 1970s what was needed was a cohesive UK maritime strategy that:

(a)   Recognised the retention of merchant and Royal navies

(b)   Rendered 'assistance' to the major UK ship-owners who were experiencing retrenchment among their members

(c)   Identified a 'core' shipbuilding and marine engineering capability, based commercially on the above two caveats.

Coordination of these admonitions was regrettably beyond the aptitude and resolve of either Labour or Conservative administrations. The indomitable legislation that blindly nationalised the shrinking and financially precarious remnants of the UK mainland shipbuilding industry, replaced a totem pole of withering competitive private company culture, with a haphazard collection of preserved identities that soon levelled out to form an impassive corporation of under achievement. The formation of this conglomeration was thwarted by prefacing technical and economic planning with the inhibitions of political dogma and the inertia of state bureaucracy. Its cumbersome structure denuded conventional commercial drive, creating a less capable company than the locally managed autonomous geographical groups, which had emanated from the Geddes Report less than a decade earlier.

In the mid-1970s, the total annual capacity of mainland UK shipbuilding stood at over 1,000,000 g.r.t. of shipping, which was roughly equivalent to the yearly order intake necessary to keep the industry busy, and was achieved from the combined output of over thirty different yards scattered throughout Scotland and England. This figure, which had remained constant against a background of selective regional closures, now represented less than 4% of the world annual shipbuilding aggregate, whereas 30 years earlier it had been over 50%. The types of shipyards absorbed by nationalisation fell into four distinct categories *(excluding ship repair yards, and marine engine works)*.

1.   Large, reasonably modern yards that built big tankers and bulk carriers. These companies were Swan Hunter on Tyneside and Teesside, and Scott-Lithgow on Clydeside.

2.   Medium, reasonably modern yards that built cargo liners, products tankers and small bulk carriers. These companies were located on the rivers Clyde, Tyne, Wear, Tees, Mersey, and more than half of them were controlled by the Swan Hunter and Scott-Lithgow groups.

3.   Relatively modern warship building companies located on the rivers Clyde, Tyne and Mersey, as well as at Barrow and Southampton.

4.   Small, mostly traditional shipyards that built specialised craft, dredgers, ferries, trawlers, coasters and tugs. These companies were scattered throughout Scotland and England from Aberdeen to Lowestoft, and Goole to Troon.

With very few exceptions, most of these companies had suffered significant reduction in their order intake prior to nationalisation. Alas, the saviour that was to be state ownership failed abysmally to provide anything like the workload necessary to sustain meaningful activity at all of the companies swept within its possession. The enervated performance of British Shipbuilders Ltd at obtaining new orders rapidly led to work starvation, followed by significant announcements of closures within two years of the company's formation. This immediate act of attrition prevented any meaningful group harmony in the form of standard ship product rationalisation, or the hoped-for invoking of better national levels of productivity.

Thus within three years, the panacea of national ownership that was anticipated in the shape of state control, had quickly been replaced by the spectre of extensive contraction. With BSL now under the ownership and stewardship of a 'free market' government, misguided public control was replaced with the phased annihilation of mainland UK shipbuilding and marine engineering. This new 'proprietorship' showed scant regard for the national importance of these strategic industries, or the invisible benefit contributed both to the exchequer and the economy, by the myriad of their supply companies.

At the time of nationalisation the worldwide tanker fleet had just completed an unparalleled bout of expansion of mainly VLCCs powered by large bore marine diesel engines, in part precipitated by the closure of the Suez Canal after the 1973 Arab-Israeli war. A similar increase affected the market for dry bulk carrier tonnage, container ships and products tankers. Most of these vessels were built in Japanese shipyards which launched an incredible total of *946* vessels totalling 17,987,322 g.r.t. in 1975! Consequently, replacement orders for these types of ships would not be so abundant in the years to come, and what orders that were available would be very difficult to prevent from being built in Japan, or the fast emerging mega yards of South Korea.

Cargo liners were quickly being replaced by container ships on virtually every traditional shipping route, forcing the bulk of the established British shipping companies into enforced mergers, diversification or disappearance. This combination of ship type obsolescence and customer departure concurred with the formation of British Shipbuilders Ltd and bode ill for the existence and viability of the new company. British shipyards had virtually invented the cargo liner in all of its numerous derivations, and UK shipping companies were the principal owners of this type of ship throughout the world. A shipping market bereft of such traditional products, previously owned by familiar customers was not a friendly environment for a recently nationalised industry in which to compete and survive. The high value international growth markets for cruise ships, large fast ferries, chemical tankers, offshore rigs, specialist craft and large container ships became the competitive arena into which British Shipbuilders Ltd had to contend. The anticipated synergy of group identity that was envisaged by the architects of state control, was replaced very quickly by 'a dog eat dog' contest for survival by the few firms that evaded the first rounds of closure. Subsequent order intake in the short life of British Shipbuilders Ltd was a pitiful acquisition of loss making contracts, spread thin and far throughout the non-warship building shipyards of the group. This diminishing workload of unprofitable work drove the infant corporation out of existence in less than a decade.

The company's lack of corporate strategy was a smoke screen that disguised deficiencies in competitive state-of-the-art innovative ship designs, which had been the hallmarks of most of its former constituent companies, albeit trading in a less ferocious marketplace than the mid-1980s. Benevolently conceived by its political paymasters, it was a misguided act of industrial philanthropy reactively cast in virtual isolation against the ruthless subsidy enveloped international shipbuilding market. Its lamentable performance and lame duck stigma did not succour any favours from replacement politicians of limited tolerance, with even lesser comprehension of the complexities and benefits of a national shipbuilding industry.

Within a relatively short span of time, Scott-Lithgow Ltd found long-term customers being redirected to other BSL group yards. The reduction in workload that this created had a detrimental effect on productivity at the lower Clyde firm. Scott-Lithgow was later designated as one of two BSL yards to become the group's 'Offshore Division', which thrust the yard into front line competition with the rest of the world's hi-tech offshore fabricators, with disastrous effects. The previous Scott-Lithgow management had seen offshore work as complimentary to traditional shipbuilding, thus providing a balanced workload during the cyclic nature of the ship replacement market. Total dependence on a highly risky and specialised element of the marine market, meant extensive investment in training, design capability and state-of-the-art production processes. Such subjection of company dependence on the fickle whims of oil companies meant 'putting all your eggs in one basket', an act of singular customer reliance, that was not a tenet of the former Scott and Lithgow lineage. The inflexible edict stood. Scott-Lithgow Ltd would build offshore vessels along with Cammell Laird & Co Ltd of Birkenhead within the umbrella of British Shipbuilders Ltd, but without the shake-out of traditionalism and minus any infusion of state aid. The unhappy coercion of Scott-Lithgow Ltd into BSL's offshore division barely lasted more than four years. By 1984, having launched its last ships in 1979, 1981 and 1982 respectively from its lower Clyde yards, and then working on its third semi-submersible vessel contract for a consortium of Britoil, Odeco and Ben Line, the whole Renfrewshire waterfront was sold to Trafalgar House Investments Ltd for a peppercorn amount. Nearly three kilometres of waterfront, sheds, docks, slipways and a marine engine works were returned to the UK private sector for less than its value as real estate, yet for a greater sum than was paid in compensation to the former Scott and Lithgow families at nationalisation in 1977.

Trafalgar House partly completed the dynamically positioned drilling rig *Ocean Alliance* 15,517 g.r.t., in 1989, which upon completion was owned by BP. The new owners brought in some dribs and drabs of offshore work which trickled through what remained of the former Glen/East and Kingston yards. Cartsburn and Cartsdyke facilities were duly closed and razed to the ground, along with Scotts former engine works. Nationalisation dealt similar blows to other shipbuilding yards on the River Clyde, closing Scotts of Bowling and Scotstoun Marine within less than two years of enforced vestment.

Govan Shipbuilders Ltd, the third phoenix of the former Fairfield SB & Eng Co Ltd, defied closure, survived cut-back after cut-back and even a protracted period in the 1980s without building any new ships. The main recipient of taxpayers' money over a decade earlier, the facility was capable of quality volume ship production, but was now so far up-river as to make retention of commercial shipbuilding in the City of Glasgow a dubious issue. Kværner of Norway bought the whole shipyard from the final embers of BSL in 1988, and immediately set about investment in new ship types, new building facilities, new methods of training and working practices. This commitment to shipbuilding in Glasgow was affirmed by the concurrent announcement of over £100m worth of new ship orders.

The small shipyards at Troon and Port Glasgow survived the imposed debacle of nationalisation, both returning to the private sector in 1986 and 1988, respectively. Yarrow Shipbuilders Ltd became part of the GEC-Marconi Group in 1985 and have invested considerably in their extensive Scotstoun site.

UIE Shipbuilding (Scotland) Ltd are the current owners of the former John Brown shipyard at Clydebank, continuing the proud tradition of innovative marine technology synonymous with the men of that town, now directed towards the wants and needs of the offshore oil and gas industry.

Thus in the period from 1987 onwards, the shipbuilding, marine and offshore engineering capability of the River Clyde drastically shrunk to four shipyards, two offshore yards, and two very small remnants of former marine engine builders (now only making spare parts). The captious conjecture surrounding the acrimonious formation of British Shipbuilders Ltd, its deficient failure with fiasco after fiasco, comprehensively underwritten by British taxpayers, serves as testimony to the inflexibility and inability of governments to solve major industrial problems by either benign intervention or spiteful political refraction.

The befuddled altruistic dictum of the UK state shipbuilding corporation was enmeshed in a mire of social well-being, oblivious to the slightest whim of commercial reality. Socialist government antipathy towards established, but loss-making capitalist entrepreneurs was substituted with the reciprocation of civil service careerists, whose managerial ineptitude brought belated inverted credence to the former leadership of UCS. Subsequent Conservative Government disdain towards the profligate use of the public purse to offset loss-making contracts 'bought by BSL' to retain shipbuilding within the UK, only resulted in the same public purse being used to pay thousands of ex-workers...to do nothing! If only pragmatism had ensured at the outset of shipbuilding's ills, nearly a generation beforehand! Perhaps part-nationalisation or acquisition of the shipbuilding and marine engineering real estate on behalf of the nation, later leased (at reasonable rents) to the former owners, might have created a balanced level of ownership, stewardship and commitment by all of those formerly connected with the industry!

Meaningful, ongoing involvement with the British merchant navy was necessary to establish market needs or shipping joint ventures as well as emphasising strategic importance. This opportunity for united development was squandered on the unstable altar of ambiguous political chimera. Ensuing enmeshing of the UK within the European Union means the likelihood of such hyperbole now remains no more than a pipedream. The combined factors of cut-throat competition, over-capacity, stagnant design capability, diminishing markets, ageing inflexible labour force, rampant inflation, and stale management all accelerated by high invisible costs, drove UK shipbuilding to the commercial abyss.

Rising wages in the post-war era was only one of the elements that contributed towards the decline of River Clyde shipbuilding. Inexorably pushed upwards with each national and local round of bargaining, somehow the collective volume shipbuilding industry retained some semblance over what it could afford. It constantly compared the costs it incurred in producing each new ship, with those that its future order intake could absorb. This simplistic analogy rode precariously astride the stumbling horse of diminishing productivity, fettered to the dated yet effective carrot and stick incentive scheme called 'piecework'. Where neo-despotic yard owners had invoked frugality within each annual increase in trades' wage rates, their profligate, thriftless successors who superintended a disastrous state intervention omitted to identify, address and implement an equable payments by results method of remuneration.

Alas, the wholesale use of the public purse in pursuit of the secured liquidity of British Shipbuilders Ltd, which traded for less than one decade, resulted in the subsequent amortisation of plant and equipment, subsidy on loss-making contracts, dissolution of constituent companies, and redundancy payments to many tens of thousands of workers, amounting to over £2 billion, with the British shipbuilding industry decimated as the end result. A fraction of that money well spent would have ensured a greater shipbuilding, marine engineering and shipping industry than is currently associated with the UK.

This group of pictures illustrate a selection of scenes depicting some of the previous narrative of the Post-war Attrition chapter.

Page 71. *The Glasgow districts of Linthouse, in the fore ground, and Whiteinch and Scotstoun on the north side of the River Clyde in 1948, clearly illustrating occupation of every available shipyard berth with many new vessels under construction. In the Alexr Stephen & Sons Ltd shipyard on the south bank the vessel in the middle berth nearing launching is the t.s.m.v. CUMBERLAND 11,281 g.r.t. flanked by the t.s.m.v. GOLFITO 8470 g.r.t. to the right, and a pair of French vessels, the t.s.m.v. FORT RICHEPANSE 5038 g.r.t. and t.s.m.v. FORT DAUPHIN 5038 g.r.t. to the left. On the other up-river berth is the s.s. DORSET 10,108 g.r.t. On the opposite bank in the Clydeholm shipyard of Barclay Curle & Co Ltd, the vessel fourth from the right is the m.v. CARPENTARIA 7268 g.r.t., flanked by her sistership, from left to right, m.v. COROMANDEL 7065 g.r.t., m.v. CANNANORE 7065 g.r.t., m.v. CHANDPARA 7274 g.r.t. and a further sistership, m.v. CHANTALA 7556 g.r.t. on the isolated berth of the former Jordanvale yard. Down-river, m.v. DARA 5030 g.r.t. is fitting-out at the North British Marine Engine Works wharf. Beyond, the Scotstoun shipyard of Chas Connell & Co Ltd is also full with m.v. CORINALDO 8378 g.r.t. nearing launching. Moored down-river at Stephens fitting-out basin is m.v. KAITOKE 3551 g.r.t. recently launched at Linthouse, with a further two vessels moored at Shieldhall riverside quay. In the bottom left hand side can be seen the Clyde Navigation Trust Whiteinch vehicular ferry laden with vehicles either about to arrive or leave from the Linthouse bank of the river. The white pall of smoke from the chimneys in the Scotstoun district is from the former foundry of G.M. Hay Ltd which closed in the early 1960s.* (Aerofilms)

Previous page, above. *The East yard of John Brown & Co (Clydebank) Ltd viewed from the air looking north in the winter of 1959, when the shipyard still clung to the boast of being Britain's most famous shipyard. Noticeable beyond the fitting-out berth are the extensive marine engine works which had recently received many new machine tools. Being towed down-river to commence her trials is s.t. BRITISH QUEEN 32,431 g.r.t. launched by HRH The Queen Mother earlier that year. On the building berths of the East yard are, from left to right, s.t. DERBY 31,791 g.r.t., t.s.s.s. TRANSVAAL CASTLE 32,697 g.r.t. and HMS HAMPSHIRE 6200 tons displacement, the first County class destroyer built on the Clyde. In the fitting-out basin is m.v. CLAN MACINDOE 7395 g.r.t. launched by the shipyard earlier that year.* (BP Photographic)

Previous page, below. *Tangible evidence of the considerable financial investment by Lithgows Ltd in their Kingston shipyard in the summer of 1965. Looking south, yard no. 1156, the motor bulk carrier JERSEY BRIDGE 22,593 g.r.t. is seen nearing completion on one of the new berths now served by a pair of 60-ton electric travelling hammerhead cranes, supplied by Sir Wm Arroll & Co Ltd, Glasgow. Running north-south is the new covered prefabrication hall, with the plate and section preparation sheds and steel stockyard to the south. In the new fitting-out basin is the m.v. RUKMAVATI 2729 g.r.t. recently launched by the nearby group shipyard of Ferguson Bros (Port Glasgow) Ltd. The nearness of the A8 road can be seen forming the south boundary of the shipyard. Most of the tenements facing the shipyard were demolished when the new course of the road was constructed a few years later.* (Aerofilms)

The Govan shipyard of the Fairfield SB & Eng Co Ltd looking north in early summer 1964, a few weeks before the yard's annual fair holidays. On the four building berths are, from left to right, motor bulk carrier CLUDEN 22,341 g.r.t., t.s.m.v. NILI 7851 g.r.t., motor bulk carrier AUSTRALIAN CITY 18,621 g.r.t. and HMS FIFE 6200 tons displacement, all of which were launched that year. The shipyard's new fabrication and preparation sheds can be seen running almost the entire length of the yard. The huge Fairfield-Rowan Ltd marine engine works dominate most of the road frontage of the site, and the fitting-out basin is currently being dredged by vessels of the Clyde Navigation Trust. Commercial shipping is moored alongside Meadowside Granary quay on the north side of the river, and the tenements of the suburb of Partick are smoke-free on this summer's day.

Three views which illustrate the location and initial marine activity that accompanied the inauguration of the new Firth of Clyde Dry Dock at Inchgreen, Greenock in 1964.

Left. The honour of being the first newly built ship to berth at the new Firth of Clyde Dry Dock at Inchgreen, Greenock was achieved by m.v. AUSTRALIAN CITY 18,621 g.r.t., launched by Fairfield SB Co Ltd on 14 July 1964 (broken up as the MIRANDA in 1986). She is seen here in the winter of the same year located in the new dry dock with plenty of room to spare. Staging is already in place to allow painters to touch-up her bottom shell plating. Two of the new level-luffing electric travelling cranes built by Butters Bros Ltd, Glasgow, are providing lifting assistance. The first ship to use the new dock was the cruise ship m.v. DEVONIA 12,795 g.r.t. which was damaged whilst in the port of Greenock and needed to be dry-docked immediately for urgent repairs. (Burniston Studios Ltd)

Below. Two generations of River Clyde shipbuilding are evident in this 1965 picture of the Inchgreen dry dock, Greenock. q.s.s.s. QUEEN ELIZABETH 83,673 g.r.t. completed by John Brown & Co (Clydebank) Ltd in 1940 for the Cunard SS Co Ltd, Liverpool, provides tangible evidence that the new drydock could handle the biggest ships then in service. The second Queen had returned to the river of her birthplace for a multi-million pound refit to enable her to exploit the then infant cruise market. This exemplary example of the skills of the West of Scotland shipbuilding and marine engineering industry was later sold to Mr C.Y. Tung, a Hong Kong ship-owner. Renamed SEAWISE UNIVERSITY she caught fire and sank off Kowloon in January 1972. Removal of her scrap hulk took until 1975. (Burniston Studios Ltd)

Above. *A significant coup for the new Firth of Clyde drydock company was the berthing of s.t. BRITISH ADMIRAL 61,768 g.r.t. launched by HM the Queen at Vickers shipyard, Barrow-in-Furness on 17 March 1965. This oil tanker was the first 100,000 t.d.w. ship built in the UK, and it was hoped she would lead to future regular work from England and overseas for the Inchgreen drydock. She is seen neatly tucked in the dry dock prior to handover to BP Tankers Ltd in the summer of 1965. (Burniston Studios Ltd)*

Middle. *Mr C.R. Connell, centre left, and Sam Barr, centre right, yard convenor, sign the annual working agreement for all hourly paid employees at the Scotstoun shipyard during 1967, surrounded by a group of other trade union representatives. The enlightened management and pragmatic workforce at the Scotstoun shipyard always saw conciliation to be much superior to confrontation. Loss of the family ownership of the yard was gradually followed by gross over-manning and pitiable productivity that resulted in the yard's closure in 1980.*

Below left. *The Scotstoun shipyard of Chas Connell & Co Ltd in the autumn of 1967, the last calendar year of ownership by the descendants of the firm's founder. On berth no. 2 is yard no. 512, m.v. BENSTAC 12,011 g.r.t., a derivative of m.v. BENDEARG 12,140 g.r.t. built for the same owners some three years earlier. On berth no. 1, some double bottom units for yard no. 511, s.s. BENCRUACHAN 12,092 g.r.t., also on order for the Ben Line Ltd, Edinburgh, can be seen. By the following April this once efficient yard had been consumed by the coercive merger that created Upper Clyde Shipbuilders Ltd, becoming the Scotstoun Division of UCS Ltd.*

Above. *Yard no. 701, m.v. PORT CAROLINE 12,398 g.r.t. makes a sad sight as it is taken in tow immediately after launching from the Linthouse shipyard of Upper Clyde Shipbuilders Ltd on 16 April 1968. Bearing the distinction of being the last ship built by the former shipyard of Alexr Stephen & Sons Ltd, this view is even more depressing in that the Whiteinch shipyard of Barclay Curle & Co Ltd has already completed its last ship and is in the throes of systematic asset stripping by its parent company. The lattice structures on the fore and aft end of PORT CAROLINE are additional temporary tower cranes fitted to assist lifting of materials for the fitting-out period at Shieldhall wharf which only had a fixed crane. The other vessel partly visible in this view, launched at the same time from the down-river Scotstoun Division of UCS Ltd (formerly Chas Connell & Co Ltd) is yard no. 511, s.s. BENCRUACHAN 12,092 g.r.t. Both tugs on view belong to the Clyde Shipping Co Ltd of Glasgow.*

Right. *Jimmy Reid (centre) clutching a copy of the Glasgow Herald newspaper, addresses a mass meeting of workers at the Clydebank Division shipyard during the UCS work-in on 24 September 1971. In addition to representation from the news and television media, the platform is shared with Jimmy Airlie (extreme right), Jimmy Clougherty, with glasses, and Sammy Gilmour, both behind Jimmy Reid, all active members of the UCS Work-in committee. The eloquent dogged persistence, and guileful charismatic leadership displayed by Messrs Reid and Airlie were among the main reasons in forcing the Heath government to perform a u-turn and rescue merchant shipbuilding on the upper Clyde the following year. (The Scotsman Publications Ltd)*

Chapter 6

THE SHIPBUILDING AND
MARINE ENGINEERING COMPANIES

After the end of World War II, 23 shipbuilding companies, some with their own marine engine building facilities and attendant ship repair subsidiaries, existed on the River Clyde. Less than 25% of these firms were public limited concerns which in the verity of post-war Britain was a bit of a misnomer. The half dozen or so public shipbuilding corporations were all parts of conglomerates, controlled by few wealthy individuals and families who realised replacement of wartime shipping losses, allied to the encouragement and virtually incessant development in global trade, made shipbuilding and marine engineering very profitable areas of investment during this austere era.

These facts were immutably borne out by the coyness in the publication of balance sheets, a matter transacted in the strictest confidence between yard owners, directors, shareholders and HM Government revenue collection department. Nevertheless, this redoubtable control, wreaked by a handful of individuals, their offspring, colleagues and affluent fraternal toadies, drove a thriving, if somewhat technically suspect industry in terms of post-war working practices, through a decade and a half of reasonably profitable ship construction, amassing some quite impressive output statistics in the process.

These companies were archetypal of Scottish and indeed UK manufacturing industry. The owners were mostly the direct descendants of the firm's founders, a laudable if somewhat nepotistic precept that fared and prospered with varying degrees of success. Commercial and technical acumen had been kept within closely guarded trading circles, tenets that had acquitted successful business projection throughout the former British Empire. Unfortunately, this conservatism would not stand the test of inexorable overseas post-war expansion and ruthless competition from countries who had no such class-based right to ownership of major industries, or any fear or respect for the antediluvian British order and the nascent power of UK trade unions.

The British establishment regularly acknowledged the important contribution of private shipbuilding and marine engineering companies to the national economy. This was evinced by the fact that in the post-war period, over 30% of some of these firms on Clydeside had members of their boards of directors knighted. Similar recognition also extended to the labour force with many workers receiving subordinate honours in the biannual issue of awards by Her Majesty the Queen.

Three quarters of these firms were totally Scottish. The remainder were part of major UK groups that allowed a certain amount of autonomy in the every day trading portfolio. Such local self-determination was later extirpated following the illogical nationalisation of the remains of the industry in 1977. This act saw regional control of all persisting shipbuilding companies gravitate to the inert decision-making headquarters of British Shipbuilders Ltd (BSL) in London.

Post-war shipyard labour forces were inadvertently swollen by the return to employment of many thousands of former ex-servicemen, basically replacing jobs previously performed quite successfully by women during hostilities. This extra labour was absorbed by bulging order books, and did not really have any significant effect on the cost of new ships, as labour rates were very low, productivity fairly good and the then market was captive, with whatever extant shipbuilding competition milching the same customers. The Trojan Horse that this magnanimous gesture hid was levels of overmanning which would prove crippling to the real need for greater competitiveness and higher productivity in later years. That such market dominance, when nearly 15% of the world's new shipping total was built on the River Clyde, could plummet to virtual oblivion, now reflected in a slough of industrial dereliction along the river four decades later, became the epilogue for this brief post-war history of the shipyards of Clydeside.

This period from 1946 until 1987 saw the total output from Clyde shipyards amount to 1,901 vessels aggregating over 12 million gross registered tons. From small barges to the pride of the Clyde, the 65,863 g.r.t. *Queen Elizabeth 2* (QE2), the varied range comprised many types of merchant, naval and specialised craft. The combined industries of shipbuilding and marine engineering employed around 60,000 workers during this era, nearly 10% of this total were apprentices in various stages of trade development. Something like four times that amount worked in support, service and subcontract industries, not all of these firms were located in Scotland.

Each ship built on the river was a unique product, the hallmark of the firm that built her, the embodiment of the total skills of the tradesmen who crafted her, constructed to last—as long as her owners could afford to run her. The post-war Indian summer of volume shipbuilding on the River Clyde had past its zenith when the oil crisis brought about by the Arab/Israeli war of 1967 seriously affected the running costs of merchant navies. Thus another oblique dimension of swinging operating economies needed by ship-owners, forced the necessity for elemental rethinking in ship types, sizes and profitability.

This chapter looks specifically at the Clydeside shipyards that existed during the above era in virtually every town along the river, or Glasgow suburb that possessed a waterfront. These traditional, long established family firms operated a collective system of labour recruitment, almost feudal in its relationship between owners and workers. Yet this archaic method of employment, acrimonious and vitriolic during the frequent post-war era of sporadic trades' disputes, nurtured an intangible bond of inverted loyalty between both sides that has remained beyond the existence of the shipyards. River Clyde journeymen will always refer with wry nostalgia to the shipyard or engine works where they were trained. With a twinkle in a glazed eye, they'll raise a chuckle or scorn, and wilfully recollect the autocratic despots, or patient pseudo-paternal artisans who helped to forge the skills which were implanted during their formative years of development. Such proficiency was indelibly embedded within their character, and became overlaid with sufficient adaptability, with which to earn a living outside of shipbuilding or marine engineering.

The preferential treatment shown by employers towards existing employees urged fathers to speak for sons, nephews or neighbours' offspring to become tea-boys, thence apprentices prior to these firms annual intake of trainees. This assistance with recruitment policy was usually prompted by that man's respect for the company he was employed by, and the future opportunities thorough training might realise. Workers within shipbuilding and marine engineering did not harbour the same emotional affliction towards their industry as coalminers bore towards theirs. Generations of families spent their entire working career in the employment of the same firm, no doubt due to the one-time provision of regular work within a short travelling distance from their homes. There was always widespread sincere good feelings towards a workmate's son or nephew who did well at night school, completed his apprenticeship and went on to further his career, unfailingly boasting of the thorough training imparted by those responsible for his technical and practical tutelage.

Locations of former yards and engine works are depicted on the map of the river (page 355 and end-paper). For ease of reference, companies are listed in the same clockwise identification. The following narrative outlines the nature, size and product range of these former Clyde companies.

▌ WM DENNY & BROS LTD 1865–1963

The name Wm Denny had been synonymous with shipbuilding in Dumbarton since 1818. The company possessed a medium-sized shipbuilding yard that nestled on the East bank of the River Leven on part of the isthmus between Dumbarton Rock and the River Clyde, where over a thousand workers were employed in the busy full order book era of the early 1950s. It also owned its own marine engine works about half a mile further up the River Leven, on the same bank occupying a limited site with its own dredged quayside and attendant heavy craneage. It employed only half as many workers as the shipyard. Here, marine diesel engines were built under licence from Sulzer Bros of Switzerland, along with steam turbines which were designed in-house, tested in situ, then loaded on to Denny's small cargo barge to be towed downstream by their tug, the *Second Snark*, to the Leven shipyard. There they were transhipped, using a set of shear legs, either on to the outfit basin quayside or into the engine casing of a ship already fitting out. The company also had another product in the shape of ship's stabilisers, which were designed, patented and manufactured under a joint venture with Brown Bros of Edinburgh. Many ferries, liners and naval vessels built throughout the world were fitted as standard with these 'Denny-Brown' items of necessity for passenger comfort or operational reasons.

The Denny family, direct descendants of the firm's founder, continued to run the above works throughout its entire existence as a private limited company, bereft of any group involvement. World renowned for their expertise in the science of naval architecture, the Dumbarton firm possessed the first full-sized experimental ship model test tank, which was used extensively on a contract basis by many other Clyde shipyards, as well as many others throughout the UK, and remained in use long after the closure of the shipyard being acquired by the English shipbuilders, Vickers Ltd

With strong customer ties to a large number of long-established British shipping companies and overseas governments, the post-war era saw 100 ships, river steamers and barges totalling 278,021 g.r.t. being built at Dumbarton for many different owners, 44% of which were for export, and one frigate of 2300 tons displacement for the Royal Navy. Of these vessels 46 were ferries, the final designs of which were futuristic, squat, very stable craft with parallel sides and high 'block coefficients' (cb), that predated by nearly two decades the large unoriginal types produced with monotonous regularity in German, French and Scandinavian shipyards. The largest ship built at the Leven yard during this period was the *s.s. Cape Wrath*, a semi-bulk carrier of 10,905 g.r.t. for the Lyle Shipping Co Ltd of Glasgow, launched on 25 April 1960. Other notable post-war ship completions were five handsome and distinctive cargo liners for Bowater Paper Corporation and six then state-of-the-art passenger, vehicular/rail ferries for different UK and overseas owners.

Over £1.5 million was spent on selective shipyard modernisation schemes in the mid-1950s, resulting in less but larger building berths, and an enviable but limited capacity-covered fabrication facility. The go-ahead disposition of the last board of directors was inadvertently a factor towards the subsequent demise of the firm, spending many hundreds of thousands of pounds on the design, research and development of a novel type of side wall hovercraft, purportedly capable of replacing the many ferries that were Denny's long-established hallmark over decades of successful shipbuilding activity. The prototype hovercraft was duly completed and ran partially successful sea-trials with shop window sojourns on the River Thames, but alas resulted in no firm building orders from prospective ferry operators, government bodies or navies, resulting in a considerable financial loss to the company. A few Denny designed hovercraft later operated quite successfully in the Far East on the short crossing between Hong Kong and Kowloon.

Concurrent with this visionary development activity, no new shipbuilding orders were obtained, and in 1962 committed to the retention of their company and the employment of the rump of their labour force, the board of directors sanctioned the construction of a 'speculative new shipbuilding order' for a cargo motorship to be designed, built and engined at Dumbarton, the first and only such venture on the River Clyde since the 1930s. This altruistic act of blind faith was to prove the beginning of the end for the Dumbarton company. Midway through the construction of the speculative new building, during the summer of 1963, the board of Wm Denny & Bros Ltd announced their impending liquidation which was a dreadfully unhappy time for the town of Dumbarton. Shipbuilding resumed at Dumbarton later that year when Alex. Stephen & Sons Ltd acquired yard number 1504 from the Denny receiver, and subsequently launched the *m.v. Melbrook* 11,075 g.r.t. on 27 February 1964, towing her up-river to Linthouse where she was duly completed. Also included in this purchase by Stephens was the goodwill of the renowned Denny name. The engine for this vessel was completed and installed by the Tyneside firm of Hawthorn Leslie (Eng) Ltd.

The Leven shipyard assets were later disposed of by the liquidator, with the two relatively new 25-ton electric mono-tower travelling cranes being bought for the new Elderslie drydock of Barclay Curle & Co Ltd. The cranes were uprated by their original makers, Butters Bros Ltd of Glasgow, and graced the Scotstoun skyline for much longer than they had been used at Dumbarton, but alas infrequent use led to one of the pair being dismantled in 1996. The liquidator was able to meet all the company's creditors, and to pay the shareholders 28/- for each £1 share.

The Leven site was used briefly by the Foster Wheeler Power Products Company for the construction of offshore modules for the UK North Sea oil industry in the 1970s, and completed many units that were installed in the first generation of fixed offshore platforms. UIE (Shipbuilding) Scotland Ltd repeated this tenancy a decade later, also building some prefabricated units at the site. However, by the mid-1990s most of the area of the former shipyard was now occupied by a supermarket and car park.

The photograph below, and those immediately after the list of ships built by Wm Denny & Bros Ltd between 1946 and 1963, illustrate the location of the former Leven shipyard, followed by a few scenes of shipbuilding activity and some of the different vessels built by the company in the decade before its closure.

This 1959 picture of Dumbarton looking east towards the Kilpatrick Hills shows the full extent of the Wm Denny shipyard on the east bank of the River Leven. The new preparation and prefabrication sheds are prominent in the left centre. The company had recently realigned its berths, retaining four out of six for shipbuilding with the two end berths only used for storage. In the fitting-out basin at the foot of Dumbarton Rock is the frigate HMS JAGUAR 2300 tons displacement with the BR cross channel ferry t.s.s.s. MAID OF KENT 4413 g.r.t. moored on the opposite quayside. Under construction from right to left are bottom shell plating of m.v. PHILLIS BOWATER 4083 g.r.t., a newsprint carrier, s.s. CAPE SABLE 10,660 g.r.t., a semi-bulk carrier, empty berth under preparation, and m.v. NORNA 580 g.r.t., a small fishery protection cruiser. The large building in the centre right was owned by the Blackburn Aircraft Co, with the town's gas works, the factory of Babcock and Wilcox Ltd, and the bonded warehouse complex at Dumbuck beyond. The large building at the bottom left hand corner is the distillery of Hiram Walker Ltd, which was built on the site of the former Archibald McMillan & Son shipyard after its closure by National Shipbuilding Securities Ltd in 1930.

List of ships built by Wm DENNY & BROS Ltd, Dumbarton, between 1946 and closure in 1963

YEAR	NAME	TYPE	COUNTRY OF REGISTRATION	DISPL/ G.R.T.	TOTAL OUTPUT
1946	ASHBURTON	m. Cargo	Britain	5005	
	PRINCESS VICTORIA	m. Ferry	Britain	2649	
	FALAISE	s. Ferry	Britain	3710	11364
1947	ORMARA	s. Cargo	Britain	5417	
	FARRINGFORD	m.e.p. Ferry	Britain	489	
	WINCHESTER	m. Cargo	Britain	1149	
	LOCH SEAFORTH	m. Ferry	Britain	1126	
	MINGYI	s. Ferry	Burma	500	
	MAHA	s. Ferry	Burma	500	
	MINDON	s. Ferry	Burma	500	
	MINNAN	s. Ferry	Burma	500	
	YOMA	s. Cargo	Britain	5809	
	INNISFALLEN	m. Ferry	Eire	3741	19731
1948	BRADING	m. Ferry	Britain	837	
	SOUTHSEA	m. Ferry	Britain	837	
	ROYAL SOVEREIGN	m. Ferry	Britain	1851	
	LAIRDS MOOR	m. Cargo	Britain	990	
	FULTALA	s. Cargo	Britain	4589	
	MAID OF ORLEANS	s. Ferry	Britain	3777	
	TEAL	s.p. Ferry	India	460	
	TERN	s.p. Ferry	India	460	
	IRANI	s.p. Ferry	India	460	
	MAZBI	s.p. Ferry	India	460	14721
1949	LAIRDS BEN	m. Cargo	Britain	995	
	QUEEN OF THE CHANNEL	m. Ferry	Britain	1472	
	MARY QUEEN OF SCOTS	m.p. Ferry	Britain	230	
	SANDRA	m. Ferry	India	190	
	SELA	m. Ferry	India	190	
	LALI	m. Ferry	India	190	
	MEKLA	m. Ferry	India	190	
	GHAZI	s.p. Ferry	India	630	
	MARTABAN	s. Cargo	Britain	5740	
	BRIGHTON	s. Ferry	Britain	2875	
	OLINDA	s. Cargo	Britain	5424	
	—	n.p. Barge	Nigeria	200	
	—	n.p. Barge	Nigeria	200	
	—	n.p. Barge	Nigeria	200	
	—	n.p. Barge	Nigeria	200	
	—	n.p. Barge	Nigeria	200	19126
1950	ABERDARE	s.p. Cargo	Nigeria	349	
	QUORRA	s.p. Cargo	Nigeria	349	
	JAMES PINNOCK	s.p. Cargo	Nigeria	349	
	EASTERN QUEEN	s. Cargo/ Pass	Hong Kong	8644	
	TRENCHARD	s.p. Cargo	Nigeria	842	
	ORDIA	s. Cargo	Britain	5449	
	CITY OF KARACHI	s. Cargo	Britain	7320	
	ROYAL IRIS	m.e. Ferry	Britain	1234	
	RICHARD LANDER	m.p. Ferry	Britain	280	
	SOSHI	s. Tug	Pakistan	352	
	SURJA	s. Tug	Pakistan	352	
	BRISHA	s. Tug	Pakistan	352	25872
1951	SHANKLIN	m. Ferry	Britain	833	
	GENERAL LECLERC	m.p. Ferry	Britain	273	
	TOFUA	m. Ref/C/P	Britain	5299	
	BRENDA	m. Fish Pr	Britain (RN)	380	
	NORMANNIA	s. Ferry	Britain	3543	
	LORD WARDEN	s. Ferry	Britain	3333	13661

YEAR	NAME	TYPE	COUNTRY OF REGISTRATION	DISPL/ G.R.T.	TOTAL OUTPUT
1952 •	CITY OF WINCHESTER	s. Ref/ Cargo	Britain	10594	
	FENERBAHÇE	m. Ferry	Turkey	994	
	DOLMABAHÇE	m. Ferry	Turkey	994	
	AL MIRRIEKH	m. Ferry	Sudan	680	
	—	n.p. Barge	Sudan	220	
	—	n.p. Barge	Sudan	220	
	—	n.p. Barge	Sudan	220	
	—	n.p. Barge	Sudan	220	
	AL ZAHRA	m. Ferry	Sudan	600	
	MARKLAND	s. Cargo	Britain	6037	20779
1953	GEORG	s. Cargo	Liberia	9149	
	NICKY	s. Cargo	Liberia	9188	
	SANGANEB	m. Barge	Sudan	108	
•	ARRAN	m. Ferry	Britain	568	
	COTOPAXI	s. Cargo	Britain	8559	27572
1954	POLI	s. Cargo	Greece	9188	
	KENTUNG	m. Cargo	Britain	5558	
•	MARGARET BOWATER	s. Cargo	Britain	6581	
	FREYA	m. Fish Pr	Britain (RN)	274	21601
1955 •	CLAYMORE	m. Ferry	Britain	1024	
	AL THORAYA	m. Ferry	Sudan	600	
	AL NIGM EL GUTBI	m. Ferry	Sudan	600	
	SARAH BOWATER	s. Cargo	Britain	6471	
•	EASTERN ARGOSY	s. Ref/C/P	Hong Kong	6907	
	SIR WILLIAM WALLACE	m. Ferry	Britain	227	15879
1956	DUKE OF ROTHESAY	s. Ferry	Britain	4780	
	VALETTA	s. Cargo	Norway	9367	14147
1957 •	BARDIC FERRY	m. Ferry	Britain	2550	
	JAGUAR	s. Frigate	Britain (RN)	2300 displ	
•	KOOLAMA	m. Ref/C/P	Australia	3777	8627
1958 •	NICOLAS BOWATER	s. Cargo	Britain	7136	
	IONIC FERRY	m. Ferry	Britain	2557	
•	GLADYS BOWATER	m. Cargo	Britain	4045	
•	MAID OF KENT	s. Ferry	Britain	4413	18151
1959 •	NORNA	m. Fish Pr	Britain (RN)	580	
	CAPE SABLE	s. Cargo/B	Britain	10660	
•	PHYLLIS BOWATER	m. Cargo	Britain	4083	15323
1960 •	CAPE WRATH	s. Cargo/B	Britain	10905	
	CITY OF ST. ALBANS	m. Cargo	Britain	4976	
	CITY OF LICHFIELD	m. Cargo	Britain	4976	20857
1961 •	CALEDONIAN PRINCESS	s. Ferry	Britain	3630	
•	ARAMOANA	m.e. Ferry	N. Zealand	4160	7790
1962 •	CITY OF GLOUCESTER	m. Cargo	Britain	4961	4961
1963	MARY FISHER	m. Yacht Hull	Britain	159	159
1964 •	MELBROOK	m. Cargo	Britain	*11075	excluded

44% export	1 vessel total	=	2,300 tons displ.
56% Britain	100 vessels total	=	278,021 g.r.t.

*Speculative new building: completed by Alex. Stephen & Sons Ltd, Linthouse

• Indicates vessel depicted in subsequent photographic section.

For explanation of abbreviations see Glossary on page 345.

Above. *Yard no. 1478, s.s. EASTERN ARGOSY 6907 g.r.t. is positioned in the fitting-out quay of Wm Denny & Bros Ltd immediately after launching on 30 September 1955. The tripod structure in the foreground is Denny's shear legs that will lift the boilers and turbines into the vessel, after they are towed down-river from Denny's engine works. In the background work has commenced on the modernisation of the shipyard with the installation of two new 25-ton mono-tower electric travelling cranes. Various keels of new ships just laid down can be discerned on the berths between the forest of uprights and staging.*

Below, left. *Yard no. 1478, s.s. EASTERN ARGOSY under construction at William Denny's Dumbarton shipyard during 1955. Single frame/single plate erection techniques are still evident despite the recent installation of a pair of 25-ton mono-tower electric travelling cranes on separate tracks. Note the partly visible ornate fabricated bow crest at the top of the vessel's stem bar and soft nose.*

Right. *Launch of yard no. 1504 m.v. MELBROOK on 27 February 1964 from the Dumbarton shipyard of Wm Denny & Bros Ltd. Started as a speculative new building by the Denny board, this ship was duly given a Linthouse yard number (685) by Alexr Stephen & Sons who completed her at Linthouse. Her Denny-Sulzer engine, also built 'on spec', was finished by Hawthorn-Leslie (Eng) Ltd, Newcastle. After launching she was towed up-river to Stephens fitting-out quay where she was completed.*

s.s. CITY OF WINCHESTER 10,594 g.r.t. *launched in 1952 for Ellerman Lines Ltd, London. Engined by Wm Denny & Bros Ltd, she was the largest ship built at Dumbarton for these owners. She was sold and renamed BENVANNOCH in 1970 and retained that identity until being broken up in 1975. She is seen passing Greenock on route to her trials in the Firth of Clyde. (Burniston Studios Ltd)*

t.s.m.v. ARRAN 568 g.r.t. *launched in 1953 for the Caledonian Steam Packet Co Ltd, Glasgow. Engined by British Polar Engines Ltd, this first generation passenger car ferry stimulated tourism and commercial trade between the towns on the Firth of Clyde. She is seen on her maiden voyage on 11 January 1954. Refitted in 1972 she was sold in 1981 as a floating restaurant in Dublin and was scrapped in 1993. (Burniston Studios Ltd)*

s.s. MARGARET BOWATER 6581 g.r.t. *launched in 1954 for the Bowater Steamship Co Ltd, London. Engined by Wm Denny & Bros Ltd, this distinctive cargo liner was the second of six ships built by the Dumbarton firm for Bowater's paper trade. Sold and renamed JOHN W. HILL in 1968, she was broken up in 1971 as the GRAND STATE. Note the elegant Bowater logo aft of the bow crest.*

t.s.m.v. CLAYMORE 1024 g.r.t. *launched in 1955 for David MacBrayne Ltd, Glasgow. Engined by Wm Denny & Bros Ltd, this distinctive ship plied the West coast of Scotland for over two decades. Performing a life-line between many Hebridean Islands and the port of Oban, she had a good record of sea-keeping in stormy weather. She was sold and renamed CITY OF ANDROS in 1976 and was still in existence in 1996 as the CITY OF HYDRA. Note the distinctive MacBrayne bow crest of a kilted Highlander holding aloft a claymore.*

t.s.m.v. BARDIC FERRY 2550 g.r.t. *built and engined by Wm Denny & Bros Ltd is towed out from the Dumbarton fitting-out basin to commence sea trials in 1957. This Denny designed ferry for the Atlantic Steam Navigation Co Ltd, London was the first of four such vessels constructed on the River Clyde. Denny's built one more and the Ailsa SB Co Ltd of Troon two in the early 1960s. After a long successful working career she was sold and renamed NASIM II in 1976, being broken up under that name in 1989. Part of the bow of the frigate HMS JAGUAR can be seen on the right hand side, with both of her gun turrets stored on the other quayside.*

m.v. KOOLAMA 3777 g.r.t. *launched in 1957 for the Government of Western Australia, Freemantle. Engined by British Polar Engines Ltd, this distinctive small passenger cargo liner was sold and renamed GRAIN TRADER in 1974, being broken up in 1979 as EASTERN PEACE. Very little exhaust is being emitted from her engines as she speeds through the silky waters of the Firth of Clyde.*

s.s. NICOLAS BOWATER 7136 g.r.t. *launched in 1958 for the Bowater Steamship Co Ltd, London. Engined by Wm Denny & Bros Ltd, this vessel was the largest of the series of six built for Bowaters. The handsome, well-proportioned lines and derrick posts made the ship a very pleasing 1950s cargo liner. Sold and renamed VALL COMET in 1971 she retained that name until being broken up in 1978. Her distinctive funnel top cowling was an attractive feature that was designed to reduce down draught of engine exhaust onto the decks.*

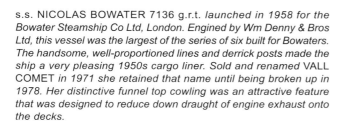

m.v. GLADYS BOWATER 4045 g.r.t. *launched in 1958 for the Bowater Steamship Co Ltd, London. Engined by Wm Denny & Bros Ltd, this vessel transported newsprint from Canada to the UK until she was sold and renamed GIGI in 1972. Later renamed LAMYAA, she retained that name until being broken up in 1985. She is seen passing the seafront at Skelmorlie whilst performing various sea trials prior to handover.*

t.s.s.s. MAID OF KENT 4413 g.r.t. *launched in 1958 for the British Railways Board, Dover. Engined by Wm Denny & Bros Ltd, this stylish pre-box boat passenger and car ferry regularly plied between Dover and Calaise for many years until her expensive steam turbines, coupled with restricted carrying capacity, rendered her too expensive to run. She was sold in 1981 and was broken up in 1982. Her square side and large block coefficient gave her good stability and she clearly exemplified the individuality of a Denny design.*

The small motor *fishery protection cruiser NORNA 580 g.r.t. launched in 1959 for the UK Government, Department of Agriculture, Fisheries and Food, Leith. Engined by British Polar Engines Ltd, this vessel was still in existence in 1996 under the overseas name of* ISPRINSEN. *She bore the distinction of being the last naval vessel built by the famous Dumbarton shipyard.*

m.v. PHYLLIS BOWATER 4083 g.r.t. *launched in 1959 for the Bowater Steamship Co Ltd, London. Engined by Wm Denny & Bros Ltd, she was sold and renamed* CHARLOTTE *in 1978. She underwent further changes of name and was still in existence in 1996 as the* NAZ K, *bearing the distinction of being the longest serving cargo vessel built by the shipyard, clearly attesting to the truism of 'Clyde built'.*

s.s. CAPE WRATH 10,905 g.r.t. *launched in 1960 for Lyle Shipping Co Ltd, Glasgow. Engined by Wm Denny & Bros Ltd, this vessel was the largest ship built at the Dumbarton shipyard. Sold and renamed* STEPHANIE *in 1966, she sank off South Africa in stormy seas during July 1980 under the name of* ATHLOS. *Note the throng of shipyard workers huddled together on the poop deck.*

t.s.s.s. CALEDONIAN PRINCESS 3630 g.r.t. *launched in 1961 for the Caledonian Steam Packet Co Ltd, Stranraer. Engined by Wm Denny & Bros Ltd, this ferry's success on the Stranraer-Larne route established that crossing as the main UK-Ireland bridgehead. The ship's limited passenger and vehicle carrying capacity, coupled with her expensive to run steam turbines, led to her premature replacement by larger ferries. In 1996 she was a static nightclub in Glasgow called the TUXEDO PRINCESS. Note her squat but well proportioned lines which gave her a larger impression of size.*

t.s.d.e. rail ferry ARAMOANA 4160 g.r.t. *launched in 1961 for New Zealand Government Railways, Wellington. Engined by English-Electric Ltd of Rugby, this handsome ferry transported railway wagons and passengers between the North and South Islands of New Zealand for many years. She was sold to Saudi Arabia in 1985 for further use as a pilgrim ship and, renamed NAJD II, she was broken up in 1994 as the NIAXCO III after being used as a static floating accommodation vessel to house construction workers.*

m.v. CITY OF GLOUCESTER 4961 g.r.t. *launched in 1962 for Ellerman Lines Ltd, London. Engined by Wm Denny & Bros Ltd, this small cargo liner was the last in a series of three built for these long standing customers. Sold and renamed SUERTE in 1979 she was broken up in 1985. The conventional three island style of this vessel was somewhat dated compared with the other post-war vessels designed and built by the Dumbarton firm.*

Undergoing sea trials on the Gareloch in early 1963, Denny's unique design of hovercraft no. D2.002 resplendent with Saltire and Union Jack flags under the port side of her bridge. The hovercraft later went on further trials on the River Thames, but this speculative singular attempt at Scottish marine engineering innovation failed to save the Dumbarton firm from liquidation that later year.

▌ SCOTT & SONS (BOWLING) LTD 1851–1980

Originally constituted as Scott & McGill, this small family run concern was located at the hamlet of Bowling, on the north bank of the River Clyde near the western end of the Forth and Clyde canal. The limited shipbuilding facility was snuggly situated between the eastern end of the Esso oil storage terminal at Dunglass, and the western side of Bowling harbour basin. The northern boundary was created by the Glasgow to Dumbarton railway line, a private siding once used as the main method for conveyance of steel and other materials into the site. The three sides of the landward perimeter of the site were so tight that the only road access into the yard was via a level-crossing over the railway controlled by a signal box at nearby Bowling station.

It employed nearly 200 workers building and repairing tugs, coasters, trawlers, ferries and high speed craft up to a length of 60 metres for the UK and overseas markets. In the post-war period the yard was able to regularly employ fully its two repair slips of 500-ton and 1000-ton capacity along with the three building berths. Acquired by Scotts SB & Eng Co Ltd of Greenock in 1965, it latterly became part of the Scott-Lithgow Group and maintained a reasonable workload of varying profitability until the formation of British Shipbuilders Ltd in 1977.

The purchase of the company by the larger Clyde shipbuilder with the same name did not stifle the creativity and flair of the yard. Within its brief term of ownership by Scotts SB & Eng Co Ltd, and hitherto by Scott-Lithgow Ltd, it produced a mixed batch of attractive and functional merchant and naval vessels that exemplified the originality and talent of the smallest shipyard on the river. During this latter period orders were obtained and successfully completed for the largest vessels built at Bowling. All three ships were built for UK owners and reflected the wider customer base that became available to the yard within membership of the go-ahead lower Clyde shipbuilding and marine engineering group.

The infant nationalised conglomerate, having inherited a host of small specialised shipbuilding companies that were scattered throughout Scotland and England, implemented its first stage of rationalisation immediately after the change of government in 1979 and identified the Bowling yard as surplus to requirements. This extirpation of capacity was implemented despite the shipyard having produced a profit of £1.25m from building five Mexican fast patrol vessels between 1974/75. The run-down towards closure was swift and surprisingly did not result in prolonged construction durations of the yard's last orders.

The final new-building contract to be completed by the company in 1980, was for four Voith Schneider twin propeller tugs for use at Milford Haven and Grangemouth, the company having built the first single propelled Voith Schneider tractor tug in Scotland in 1958. The shipyard completed 77 small craft, mainly tugs and coasters, amounting to 28,150 g.r.t. and five fishery protection craft amounting to 650 tons displacement from 1946 up until formal closure in 1980, of which 32% of the total were for export. The customer base was diverse, with regular orders being undertaken for overseas ship-owners as well as many long standing UK clients. The largest vessel completed during this period was the *m.v. Pinewood* 1599 g.r.t., a coaster launched in 1977 for British ship-owners. The site was later acquired by SB Offshore Ltd and used for a few years performing minor fabrication work for the UK offshore oil and gas industry. The yard was still in use in 1996, repairing small craft by some of the displaced employees of the Robert Adams boat-building yard at Gourock, however, by then the pair of aged and limited capacity berth cranes and most of the former shipyard buildings had long since been dismantled.

List of ships built by SCOTT & SONS (BOWLING) Ltd under all ownerships between 1946 and closure in 1979

YEAR	NAME	TYPE		COUNTRY OF REGISTRATION	DISPL/ G.R.T.	TOTAL OUTPUT
1946	NIRUMAND	s.	Tug	Britain	307	
	TANUMAND	s.	Tug	Britain	307	614
1947	VOORTREKKER	m.	Cargo¹	S. Africa	940	
	BALSA	s.	Cargo¹	Britain	405	
	EBONY	s.	Cargo¹	Britain	405	1750
1948	TABAS	s.	Tug	Britain	209	
	HAMMAL	s.	Tug	Britain	363	
	TAFTAN	s.	Tug	Britain	209	
	HALIF	s.	Tug	Britain	209	
	HIDAYAH	s.	Tug	Britain	209	1199
1949	TANB	s.	Tug	Britain	209	
	TAFT	s.	Tug	Britain	209	
	MERINO	m.	Cargo¹	N. Zealand	549	967
1950	HAIL	s.	Tug	Britain	462	
	CALM	m.	Cargo¹	N. Zealand	789	
	FIRUZMAND	s.	Tug	Britain	462	1713
1951	EL SUAKIN	s.	Tug	Sudan	162	
	–	n.p.	Barge	Sudan	100	262
1952	LADY MCGOWAN	m.	Cargo¹	Britain	690	
	GLENSHIRA	m.	Cargo²	Britain	153	
	OAK	m.	Cargo¹	Britain	709	1552
1953	–	n.p.	Barge	Sudan	200	
	–	n.p.	Barge	Sudan	200	
	CAEDMON CROSS	m.	Tug	Britain	132	532
1954	HAZIM	s.	Tug	Iraq	462	
	–	n.p.	Barge	Sudan	200	
	–	n.p.	Barge	Sudan	200	
	–	n.p.	Barge	Sudan	105	967
1955	SHERIFA	s.	Tug	Sudan	297	
	GOLDEN CROSS	m.	Tug	Britain	132	
	INGLEBY CROSS	m.	Tug	Britain	132	
	–	n.p.	Barge	Sudan	120	
	–	n.p.	Barge	Sudan	120	801
1956	NORTH BEACH	s.	Tug	Britain	220	
	NORTH QUAY	s.	Tug	Britain	219	
	–	n.p.	Barge	Sudan	120	
•	PIBROCH	m.	Cargo²	Britain	157	716
1957	FIERY CROSS	m.	Tug	Britain	192	
	HASHIM	s.	Tug	Iraq	462	654
1958	HUTTON CROSS	m.	Tug	Britain	105	
	DELAVAR	m.	Tug	Britain	357	
	NORTH BUOY	s.	Tug	Britain	219	
	ZERANG	m.	Tug	Britain	357	1038
1959	NORTH WALL	s.	Tug	Britain	219	
	KONGONI	m.	Tug	Kenya	193	
	ERIMUS CROSS	m.	Tug	Britain	192	604
1960	STORM	m.	Cargo¹	N. Zealand	931	
	ESSO JERSEY	m.	Oil Tanker	Britain	313	1244

YEAR	NAME	TYPE		COUNTRY OF REGISTRATION	DISPL/ G.R.T.	TOTAL OUTPUT
1961	STRONGBOW	m.	Tug	Britain	225	
	DALMAH	m.	Tug	Britain	371	596
1962 •	HILAL	m.	Tug	Britain	393	393
1963	OLIVE	m.	Cargo¹	Britain	791	791
1964	HADI	m.	Tug	Britain	411	
•	VOORSPELER	m.	Cargo¹	S. Africa	854	1265
1965†	GLENFYNE	m.	Cargo²	Britain	200	200
1966	SAINT RONAN	m.	Cargo¹	Britain	433	
	GLENCLOY	m.	Cargo²	Britain	200	633
1967 •	SAINT WILLIAM	m.	Cargo¹	Britain	781	
	FORTH	m.	Tug	Britain	184	965
1968	CHIEFTAN	m.	Tug	Britain	205	
	14TH OCTOBER	m.	Tug	Aden	208	413
1969†	FLYING SCOUT	m.	Tug	Britain	290	290
1970	WESTONDYKE	m.	Cargo¹	Britain	696	696
1971 •	FENDYKE	m.	Cargo¹	Britain	696	696
1972	SAINT BEDAN	m.	Cargo¹	Britain	1251	
•	GRAMPIAN MONARCH	m.	Trawler	Britain	480	1731
1973 •	NORSE	m.	Factory Trawler	Britain	1448	1448
1974	M.D. CORDOVA	m.	Fish Pr	Mexico	130 displ	
	J.M. IZAZAGA	m.	Fish Pr	Mexico	130 displ	
	GRAMPIAN GLEN	m.	Trawler	Britain	127	387
1975	GRAMPIAN HILL	m.	Trawler	Britain	120	
	LEON GUZMAN	m.	Fish Pr	Mexico	130 displ	
	FELIX ROMERO	m.	Fish Pr	Mexico	130 displ	
	PASTOR ROUAIX	m.	Fish Pr	Mexico	130 displ	
	GREATHAM CROSS	m.	Tug	Britain	193	703
1976	SKELTON CROSS	m.	Tug	Britain	193	193
1977† •	PINEWOOD	m.	Cargo¹	Britain	1599	1599
1978	SHANNON WILLOW	m.	Ferry	Eire	360	
	HOLMGARTH	m.	Tug	Britain	204	564
1979	HALLGARTH	m.	Tug	Britain	204	
	CARRON	m.	Tug	Britain	210	
	LAGGAN	m.	Tug	Britain	210	624

32% export	5 vessels total	=	650	tons displ.
68% Britain	77 vessels total	=	28,150	g.r.t.

Notes

† Acquired by Scotts S.B. & Eng. Co Ltd — 1965
† Became part of Scott-Lithgow Ltd — 1969
† Became part of British Shipubilders Ltd — 1977
¹(coaster), ²(puffer)
• Indicates vessel depicted in subsequent photographic section.
For explanation of abbreviations see Glossary on page 345.

The following batch of photographs illustrate the location and a few scenes of shipbuilding activity at the former Scott & Sons (Bowling) Ltd shipyard. Also included are a few pictures of some of the different ship types built by the small firm in the two decades before closure.

A riverside view of Scotts Bowling shipyard in 1967, showing most of the facility to good effect. On the berth beneath the Scotch derrick is the diesel tug FORTH 184 g.r.t. for service in Grangemouth. Beyond is a small coaster undergoing repairs on the slipway. Moored in the foreground is the puffer PIBROCH 157 g.r.t. built by the yard for Scottish Malt Distillers in 1957. The two large buildings are the preparation and prefabrication sheds, and the drawing office is to the right. The watch house was in use by the Clyde Navigation Trust when Bowling harbour was still operating. This location was the western extremity of the former Forth and Clyde canal.

Yard no. 443, motor stern trawler GRAMPIAN MONARCH 480 g.r.t. prior to launching from the small shipyard of Scott & Sons (Bowling) 1969 Ltd on 29 August 1972. Built for Geo Craig & Son of Aberdeen, this type of vessel was a first for the yard. A total of three more trawlers were built by the company before it closed in 1980. This trawler was still in existence in 1996 as the FORTUNE ENDEAVOUR. Noticeable above the launch platform is the cambered outline of the nearby Erskine Bridge.

Keel laying at the small shipyard of Scott & Sons (Bowling) Ltd in 1964. Yard no. 431 later became the motor coaster VOORSPELER 854 g.r.t. built for South African owners. The prefabricated unit on the left is the stern section of HADI, the second of a pair of diesel engined fire-fighting tugs built for Kuwait. Noticeable in this view are frames, plates and sections all with extensive strakes of holes for riveted construction, still obviously in use by the small shipyard at that time.

Launched in 1962, HILAL 393 g.r.t. was a diesel engined fire-fighting tug built for the Kuwait Oil Co Ltd, London. Engined by Crossley Bros Ltd of Manchester, this powerful vessel was so successful she was followed by a larger sistership from the yard for the same owners in 1964. HILAL was sold and renamed TAREK in 1989, still being in existence under that name in 1996. Noticeable along the vessel's side are strakes of rivets used to connect the ship's frames to the shell plating.

m.v. VOORSPELER 854 g.r.t. launched in 1964 for African Coasters (Pty) Ltd, Durban. Engined by British Polar Engines Ltd, this distinctive looking coaster traded for many years between the major South African ports. She was sold and renamed SAGAR in 1981 and was broken up under that name in 1986. This coaster is quite unique in that her machinery is not located at the aft end of the vessel, which limits the cargo carrying capacity of her no. 3 hold.

motor coaster SAINT WILLIAM 781 g.r.t. *launched in 1967 for J. & A. Gardner & Co Ltd, Glasgow. Engined by Chantier de l'Atlantique France, this handsome coaster was the second of three built for these owners at the Bowling shipyard. She was later sold and renamed SULTANA I in 1984. In 1996 she was still trading as JOELLA.*

motor coaster FENDYKE 696 g.r.t. *launched in 1971. She was the second of a pair of sisterships built by the yard for Klondyke Shipping Co Ltd, Hull. Engined by Lister Blackstone Ltd, Stamford, she was later sold and renamed CLAFEN in 1982. In 1996 she was still in existence as VAUBAN.*

motor fish factory stern trawler NORSE 1448 g.r.t. *launched in 1973 for British United Trawlers Ltd, Hull. Engined by Lister Blackstone Ltd, Stamford, this vessel was the only large factory trawler ever built at Bowling. She was later sold and renamed OSPREY in 1984. She sunk off Cape Chidley after striking ice in June 1990, under the name of NORTHERN OSPREY. Note the crosstree mast arrangement at the vessel's aft end which lifted the engine room exhaust gases to a common vent above the working deck of the trawler.*

m.v. PINEWOOD 1599 g.r.t. *launched in 1977 for Cawood Fuels Ltd, Belfast. Engined by Mirlees-Blackstone Ltd, this functional-looking coaster was the largest vessel built by the small Bowling shipyard. She was later sold, modified and renamed REDTHORN and was still in existence in 1996.*

JOHN BROWN & CO LTD (CLYDEBANK) LTD	1899–1968
CLYDEBANK DIVISION OF UPPER CLYDE SHIPBUILDERS LTD	1968–1971
MARATHON SHIPBUILDING CO (UK) LTD	1972–1980
UIE SHIPBUILDING (SCOTLAND) LTD	1980–

The extensive shipbuilding complex in the town of Clydebank on the north bank of the River Clyde contained the site of arguably the most famous traditional shipyard in the world! Actually comprising two sites, the East and West yards, divided by a dredged fitting out dock, this massive facility also enclosed a vast marine engine works within the same perimeter. The location of the yards, opposite the confluence of the River Cart, provided plenty of deep water into which could be launched the largest types of ships imaginable. This claim was no boast, for up until the advent of supertankers in the mid 1960s the Clydebank company had the enviable reputation of building the biggest and best ships on this planet, known affectionately as the 'two queens'.

Owned and run by the John Brown Group of Sheffield, but registered in London, shipbuilding and marine engineering was a high profile, profitable element of this group's business up until the mid 1960s. The multiplicity of ship types and marine engineering contracts then obtained, usually at fixed prices with minimum cost escalation clauses, gradually led to serious financial haemorrhaging of, initially, the shipyard and, latterly, the parent groups assets. Partly modernised in stages in the 1950s with the limited funds that were available, the West yard ended up as the superior fabrication facility, with two enlarged berths now served by new crane tracks each complete with 60-ton travelling hammerhead cranes fed by the output from a new adjacent covered prefabrication shed. This hardware enabled the simultaneous construction of two vessels, usually supertankers up to 1000 ft long. Considerable shipbuilding activity took place throughout the post-war period, and between 1946 and 1986 the Clydebank shipyard in its four distinctive guises built a total of 115 vessels, of which 25 were large oil tankers, 21 jack-up drilling rigs, 33 cargo liners, six ferries, 14 large passenger liners, seven bulk carriers, seven warships, one barge and one Royal yacht, with totals of 29,190 tons displacement for the naval ships and 1,468,852 g.r.t. for all other craft. Greatest annual output during this period was achieved in 1955, when six ships of 81,838 g.r.t. were launched. A formidable total, with each vessel then built using very traditional methods of shipbuilding. The largest, and most famous ship built by the yard during this period was the *Queen Elizabeth 2* 65,863 g.r.t., launched by HM The Queen on 20 September 1967. Twenty-nine per cent of the vessels built during this period were for export.

The more traditional East yard, with four building berths all served by an array of fixed hammerhead cranes, also constructed oil tankers as well as warships, large passenger liners, ferries and refrigerated cargo ships. This imposing variety of ship types with different scantlings and lack of scope for repetition of fabrication techniques, had a significant impact on production methods at the shipyard.

In common with about half a dozen other Clyde shipyards, John Brown dabbled with the use of aluminium as a lighter alternative to steel in the construction of superstructures for ships. The Clydebank company were in the forefront of implementing the different technology necessary to weld aluminium. In conjunction with their supplier of the metal, the shipyard successfully embarked on extensive retraining of welders to acquire the necessary levels of aptitude for this substitute material.

The customer base during the traditional shipbuilding era of John Brown & Co (Clydebank) Ltd tended to be the elite, well-established constituent companies of the British Merchant Navy, with BP Tankers, British and Commonwealth, Cunard and the P & O Group being the most consistent clients. Export orders tended to be a small percentage of yard output, with the most prestigious post-war contract being the passenger liner *m.v. Kungsholm* 26,678 g.r.t., for the Swedish America Line, which was duly completed in 1966. This excellent vessel was subsequently bought by the P & O Group, no stranger to the quality of ships built at Clydebank. She was renamed *Sea Princess*, extensively modified and duly had one of her two funnels removed. Seven different types of warships were built for the Royal Navy between 1950 and 1966, and one frigate for the Indian Navy.

Becoming the Clydebank Division of Upper Clyde Shipbuilders Ltd in 1968, the shipyard duly completed the hyper-loss-making contract *Queen Elizabeth 2* during this era, as well as an assortment of merchant vessels and two self-propelled jack-up drilling rigs. This period saw the shipyard move significantly downmarket with the main product range now being Clyde class cargo ships, a batch of different size bulk carriers, as well as jack-up drilling rigs. Virtually no investment whatsoever in terms of plant, equipment or training techniques took place throughout this phase. The previous skills, and initiative for large passenger liner construction was now surrendered to overseas shipbuilders, notably the new market leaders in Finland, Germany, France and Italy, who are now the world's major builder of large passenger vessels. The inability of the Clydebank shipyard to outfit the QE2, either within time or within budget, was the single most significant reason to abandon passenger ship construction, although two smaller passenger vessels were built there under the aegis of UCS.

The Clydebank shipyard became a specialist jack-up rig building establishment in 1972, when Marathon Shipbuilding Co (UK) Ltd acquired the facilities from the liquidator of UCS. This American company recognised the rig building capability of the Clydebank labour force which had been successfully building jack-up rigs since 1964. Between 1973 and 1979 these new owners completed nine medium-sized jack-up drilling rigs and one small barge, totalling 43,768 g.r.t. The astute business acumen of Wayne Harbin, the president of the new yard proprietors, acknowledged that the Clydebank shipyard had rightly been perceived as the UK's major jack-up rig building specialists, having constructed a total of six such craft under its two ownerships up to the collapse of UCS. This venture into the market for oil and gas exploration craft truly established the yard with the most diverse marine product range of any shipyard in Britain, if not the entire world. This diversification would ensure its future survival at the expense of traditional shipbuilding.

Subsequently bought by the French offshore construction fabrication concern UIE in 1980, the Clydebank yard completed a further six jack-up drilling and exploration rigs totalling 38,065 g.r.t., of which *Mr Mac* at 12,460 g.r.t. was the largest of its type in the world when launched in 1986. The present owners have since diversified into the construction of fixed platform hardware for the UK offshore oil and gas industry. Considerable experience has been gained with complimentary approbation received from all clients for whom jackets and topside modules were built for some of the major installations in the North Sea, albeit utilising only a fraction of the labour force previously employed in volume shipbuilding.

The Clydebank facility employed about 5,000 workers in the heady days of full order books which included the concurrent construction of large tankers and passenger liners during the 1950s. The adjacent marine engine works employed almost 2,000 during the same period. In addition to the completion of marine diesel engines, built under licence to the designs of Sulzer and Doxford, steam turbines, gear-boxes and boilers were designed in-house to be installed in John Brown and other UK shipbuilding contracts. Additional orders were undertaken for the design and manufacture of various turbines and diesel auxiliaries for power stations in Britain and overseas throughout the world.

The marine engine building establishment was always looked upon as a very separate entity within the parent group, and was duly hived off from the shipyard in 1966 when the traditional marine engineering product range was replaced with the manufacture of industrial gas turbines under licence from General Electric of the USA. The transition from marine engine building to that of gas turbines was a smooth and successful changeover, with the new company now calling itself John Brown Engineering Ltd (JBE). The adept and adroit Clydebank labour force rapidly forged a commendable reputation among its new customers for quality, reliability and prompt delivery of these new high value products. Becoming every bit as prestigious as the former marine engines they built in the past, JBE gas turbines have been supplied to nearly every country in the world, proving both dependable and efficient wherever they run. This success later brought the company within the ownership of the Trafalgar House conglomerate, which itself was later acquired by the Kværner Group of Norway in the mid 1990s.

The new engineering company tried to diversify further by entering into the then burgeoning industry of module construction for the UK oil industry, setting up an associate company called JBE Offshore Limited in 1974, located at the firm's former Whitecrook works and Rothesay Dock, both in Clydebank. Trying to satisfy the then growing need for these new products, the offshoot company recruited mainly traditional shipbuilding labour, and set about the construction of four contracts for different multi-national oil companies. In this highly competitive and demanding market, the venture was not a success and the operation was wound up early in 1978. The management of the yard seriously underestimated the complexity of standards of this new industry, as well as overestimating the flexibility and willingness of a large amount of the labour force to commit themselves to the longevity of a new fabrication industry. The module construction pad at Rothesay Dock has lain semi-derelict since the last order sailed away in the same year, and the Whitecrook fabrication facility has been occupied intermittently by a few small industrial concerns.

List of ships built by JOHN BROWN & Co (CLYDEBANK) Ltd and their successors between 1946 and 1986

YEAR	NAME		TYPE	COUNTRY OF REGISTRATION	DISPL/ G.R.T.	TOTAL OUTPUT	YEAR	NAME		TYPE	COUNTRY OF REGISTRATION	DISPL/ G.R.T.	TOTAL OUTPUT
1946	PORT WELLINGTON	m.	Ref/Cargo	Britain	10585		1955	LYNX	s.	Frigate	Britain (RN)	2300 displ	
	NORFOLK	m.	Ref/C/P	Britain	11272			NORTHUMBERLAND	m.	Ref/C/P	Britain	10335	
	ARNHEM	s.	Ferry	Britain	5008		•	STANVAC AUSTRALIA	s.	Oil Tanker	Britain	17297	
	MEDIA	s.	Ref/C/P	Britain	13345	40210		WHANGAROA	m.	Ref/Cargo	Britain	8701	
1947	HAPARANGI	m.	Ref/C/P	Britain	11281			ALVEGA	s.	Oil Tanker	Panama	21258	
	SUFFOLK FERRY	m.	Train Ferry	Britain	3134			CARINTHIA	s.	Passenger	Britain	21947	81838
	PÁTRIA	s.	Ref/C/P	Portugal	13196		1956 •	SALSETTE	m.	Ref/Cargo	Britain	8202	
	CARONIA	s.	Passenger	Britain	34172			WHARANUI	m.	Ref/Cargo	Britain	8701	
	IMPÉRIO	s.	Ref/C/P	Portugal	13186	74969		SALMARA	m.	Ref/Cargo	Britain	8202	
1948	CITY OF OXFORD	s.	Cargo	Britain	7593			BRITISH INDUSTRY	s.	Oil Tanker	Britain	21083	
	SUSSEX	m.	Ref/C/P	Britain	11272			ESSEX FERRY	m.	Train Ferry	Britain	3242	
	CITY OF BIRMINGHAM	s.	Cargo	Britain	7599	26464	•	SYLVANIA	s.	Passenger	Britain	21989	71419
1949	HINAKURA	m.	Ref/C/P	Britain	11272		1957	BRAMAPUTRA	s.	Frigate	India	2300 displ	
	RANGITANE	m.	Passenger	Britain	21867			BRITISH TRADER	s.	Oil Tanker	Britain	21019	
	VIKLAND	m.	Oil Tanker	Panama	12803			EDGEWATER	s.	Oil Tanker	Liberia	12732	
	VIKFOSS	m.	Oil Tanker	Panama	12803			SCOTTISH PTARMIGAN	m.	Oil Tanker	Britain	12685	
•	NOTTINGHAM	m.	Ref/C/P	Britain	6689	65434	•	OTAIO	m.	Ref/C/P	Britain	13314	62050
1950	AMSTERDAM	s.	Ferry	Britain	5092		1958 •	BRITISH DUCHESS	s.	Oil Tanker	Britain	27585	
	DIAMOND	s.	Destroyer	Britain (RN)	2830 displ		•	LINCOLN	s.	Oil Tanker	Britain	12780	
	OTTAWA	m.	Oil Tanker	Panama	13070		•	BRITISH JUDGE	s.	Oil Tanker	Britain	27585	67950
	ADELAIDE STAR	m.	Ref/Cargo	Britain	12037		1959	YARMOUTH	s.	Frigate	Britain(RN)	2150 displ	
	SINGAPORE	s.	Ref/C/P	Britain	9236		•	CLAN MACINDOE	m.	Cargo	Britain	7395	
	RUAHINE	m.	Ref/C/P	Britain	17851	60116	•	BRITISH QUEEN	s.	Oil Tanker	Britain	32431	41976
1951	NORFOLK FERRY	m.	Train Ferry	Britain	3157		1960	DERBY	s.	Oil Tanker	Britain	31791	
	KIPAWA	m.	Oil Tanker	Panama	12891			KENT	s.	Oil Tanker	Britain	31791	63582
	CLYDEWATER	m.	Oil Tanker	Panama	12703		1961 •	TRANSVAAL CASTLE	s.	Passenger	Britain	32697	
	CLAN MACINTOSH	m.	Cargo	Britain	6487			HAMPSHIRE	cosag.	Destroyer	Britain(RN)	6200 displ	
	ALMAK	m.	Oil Tanker	Panama	12618			CLAN MACNAIR	m.	Cargo	Britain	9338	48235
	CLAN MACINTYRE	m.	Cargo	Britain	6488	54344	1962 •	BRITISH HUSSAR	s.	Oil Tanker	Britain	32341	
1952	ALGOL	m.	Oil Tanker	Panama	12618			SOMERSET	m.	Ref/Cargo	Britain	10027	
	WELLINGTON STAR	m.	Ref/Cargo	Britain	12539			AURORA	s.	Frigate	Britain(RN)	2350 displ	44718
	SUNDA	s.	Ref/C/P	Britain	9235		1963 •	BRITISH MARINER	s.	Oil Tanker	Britain	43605	
	OTAKI	m.	Ref/C/P	Britain	10934		•	CENTAUR	m.	Ref/C/P	Britain	8262	51867
•	BRITISH SAILOR	s.	Oil Tanker	Britain	20961	66287	1964 •	INTREPID	s.	Assault Ship	Britain(RN)	11060 displ	
1953 •	BRITANNIA	s.	Royal Yacht	Britain (RN)	5769			VENNACHER	m.	Bulk Carrier	Britain	18615	29675
•	ARCADIA	s.	Passenger	Britain	29664		1965 •	BRITISH CONFIDENCE	s.	Oil Tanker	Britain	38119	
	ESSEX	m.	Ref/C/P	Britain	10936	46369	•	KUNGSHOLM	m.	Passenger	Sweden	26678	
1954	SAXONIA	s.	Passenger	Britain	21637			NORTH STAR	n.p.	J Drill Rig	Panama	3500	
	EAST RIVER	s.	Oil Tanker	Liberia	12698			CONSTELLATION	n.p.	J Drill Rig	Britain	3600	71897
	BRITISH SOLDIER	s.	Oil Tanker	Britain	21082								
•	IVERNIA	s.	Passenger	Britain	21717	77134							

YEAR	NAME		TYPE	COUNTRY OF REGISTRATION	DISPL/ G.R.T.	TOTAL OUTPUT
1966•	CAPE ST. VINCENT	m.	Bulk Carrier	Britain	12835	
	ORION	n.p.	J Drill Rig	Britain	3600	
•	GLENFINLAS	m.	Ref/Cargo	Britain	12094	28529
1967	GULFTIDE	n.p.	J Drill Rig	USA	3618	
•	QUEEN ELIZABETH 2	s.	Passenger	Britain	65863	69481
1968†	VOLNAY	m.	Bulk Carrier	Britain	22189	22189
1969•	VANCOUVER FOREST	m.	Bulk Carrier	Britain	17660	
•	OFFSHORE MERCURY	m.e.	Self-prop. J Drill Rig	Britain	5519	
	KYOTO FOREST	m.	Bulk Carrier	Britain	17670	40849
1970•	BLENHEIM	m.	Passenger	Britain	10427	
•	VICTORIA CITY	m.	Bulk Carrier	Britain	16639	
•	TEMPLE HALL	m.	Bulk Carrier	Britain	13544	40610
1971†•	OCEAN TIDE	m.e.	Self-prop. J Drill Rig	Britain	5567	
	SAMJOHN PIONEER	m.	Cargo	Liberia	11506	
	SAMJOHN GOVERNOR	m.	Cargo	Liberia	11506	
	VARDA	m.	Cargo	Britain	11895	40474
1972†•	ARAHANGA	m.	Ferry	N. Zealand	3893	
	ORLI	m.	Cargo	Britain	11897	
•	ALISA	m.	Cargo	Britain	11897	27687
1973	PENROD 64	n.p.	J Drill Rig	USA	5451	5451
1974	KEY VICTORIA	n.p.	J Drill Rig	Liberia	3885	3885
1975	AL ITTIHAD	n.p.	J Drill Rig	Panama	2577	
	KEY GIBRALTAR	n.p.	J Drill Rig	Panama	3885	
	PENROD 65	n.p.	J Drill Rig	USA	5555	12017

YEAR	NAME		TYPE	COUNTRY OF REGISTRATION	DISPL/ G.R.T.	TOTAL OUTPUT
1976	PENROD 67	n.p.	J Drill Rig	USA	5555	
	AL GHALLAN	n.p.	J Drill Rig	Abu Dhabi	2408	
	ASNE	n.p.	Barge	Britain	403	8366
1977	*None*		*None*	*None*	–	–
1978	PENROD 80	n.p.	J Drill Rig	USA	7250	7250
1979	PENROD 81	n.p.	J Drill Rig	USA	6799	6799
1980†	BLACK DOG	n.p.	J Drill Rig	Liberia	4426	4426
1981	UXMAL	n.p.	J Drill Rig	Panama	4426	
•	CHICHEN ITZA	n.p.	J Drill Rig	Panama	4426	8852
1982	MORECAMBE FLAME	n.p.	J Drill Rig	Britain	6047	
	BAY DRILLER	n.p.	J Drill Rig	Britain	6136	12183
1983	*None*		*None*	*None*	–	–
1984	*None*		*None*	*None*	–	–
1985	*None*		*None*	*None*	–	–
1986	MISTER MAC	n.p.	J Drill Rig	Britain	12460	12460

29% export	7 vessels total	=	29,190 tons displ.
71% Britain	108 vessels total	=	1,468,852 g.r.t.

Notes

† Became Clydebank Division of Upper Clyde Shipbuilders Ltd 1968–71
† Became " " " (in Receivership) " 1971–72
† Became Marathon Shipbuilding Co (UK) Ltd 1972–80
† Became UIE Shipbuilding (Scotland) Ltd 1980–

• Indicates vessel depicted in subsequent photographic section or another chapter of the book.

For explanation of abbreviations see Glossary on page 345.

The following photographs illustrate the location of extensive shipyard and adjoining engine works of John Brown & Co (Clydebank) Ltd, along with a few scenes of diverse shipbuilding activity. Also included are a selection of some of the vessels built by the shipyard in three of its four post-war guises.

Previous page. *An aerial view of the John Brown & Co (Clydebank) Ltd shipyard and engine works in early 1966, showing the entire establishment stretching over 1 km in length along the north bank of the River Clyde. Under construction from left to right are yard no. 737, self-propelled jack-up drilling rig ORION 3600 g.r.t. and yard no. 735, motor bulk carrier CAPE ST VINCENT 12,835 g.r.t., both being built in the west yard, with yard no. 723, HMS INTREPID 11,060 tons displacement fitting-out in the wet basin. In the east yard on berth no. 4 is yard no. 736, t.s.s.s. QUEEN ELIZABETH 2 65,863 g.r.t., berth no. 3 is empty, berth no. 2 holds yard no. 731, m.v. GLENFINLAS 12,094 g.r.t., and berth no. 1 is also empty. The self-contained aspect of the west and east yards is quite apparent, with both separated by the large wet basin, and each has its own stockyards, plating, fabrication and various outfit sheds. The large marine engine works run from west to east for virtually the entire north perimeter of the site. The unredeveloped town of Clydebank is clearly visible with some tenements abutting the engine works. In the middle of the picture, can be seen the Forth and Clyde Canal which meanders through the town from west to east and forms the southern boundary of the then extant Singer Sewing Machine factory. Rothesay Dock is the inshot to the right, showing the dust covered buildings and quayside of the former Clyde Cement works. The entire north side of Rothesay Dock was the site of the short-lived JBE Offshore Ltd module construction yard.* (Aerofilms)

Above. *Yard no. 703, s.t. BRITISH DUCHESS 27,585 g.r.t. under construction on berth no. 4 at the east yard of John Brown & Co (Clydebank) Ltd in April 1958. Note the shipyard's internal railway system used to transport small prefabricated units from the assembly sheds to the building berth, and the swarm of workers on the main deck. The confluence of the River Cart and the River Clyde is clearly seen in this view which shows the benefits of virtually unrestricted launching from the same berth that built all three Queens for the Cunard Line Ltd.* (BP Photographic)

Below. *The prefabricated bulbous bow (weighing about 25 tons) of yard no. 720, t.s.s.s. TRANSVAAL CASTLE 32,697 g.r.t. being lifted into location in the east yard of John Brown & Co (Clydebank) Ltd in 1960. The hand-shaped plates, flared frames and accurate fit-up are all shown to good effect. The plater or shipwright at the left-hand side gives this unit some idea of scale.* (Courtesy Scottish Record Office)

Above. *Yard no. 715,* s.t. BRITISH MARINER *43,605 g.r.t. prior to launching from the west yard of John Brown & Co (Clydebank) Ltd on 23 April 1963. This steam turbine supertanker of 75,000 t.d.w. measured 815 ft long ∞ 113 ft wide, which made her the largest post-war ship built on Clydeside at that time, and was the biggest oil tanker ever constructed by the Clydebank shipyard. As a steam turbine vessel she had a relatively brief career with the BP Tanker Co Ltd, being broken up in 1975 at Kaohsiung, Taiwan in 1975.* (BP Photographic)

Below. *Yard no. 736 occupies almost the entire length of berth no. 4 in the east yard of John Brown & Co (Clydebank) Ltd in early September 1967. Only painting of her aft end, removal of staging, uprights and hundreds of temporary supports under her hull need to be complete prior to launching on the 20th of the same month, when her name will be revealed …* t.s.s.s. QUEEN ELIZABETH 2. *Note in the centre foreground the triangular legs, hull and heli-deck of the recently launched non-propelled jack-up drill rig* GULFTIDE *3618 g.r.t.*

98

Left. *Yard no. 743, self-propelled jack-up drill rig OFFSHORE MERCURY 5547 g.r.t. one month prior to launching from the Clydebank Division of UCS Ltd on 24 April 1969. The former yard owners John Brown & Co (Clydebank) Ltd showed sound technical and commercial vision in the early 1960s by entering the offshore oil and gas drilling rig construction market. A total of 21 such craft were built by the yard under four separate regimes of ownership between 1964 and 1986. Note the hull of the timber carrier KYOTO FOREST 17,670 g.r.t. under construction on the adjacent berth.* (Courtesy Scottish Record Office)

Middle. *m.v. NOTTINGHAM 6689 g.r.t. launched in 1949 for the Federal Steam Navigation Co Ltd, London. Engined by John Brown & Co (Clydebank) Ltd, this vessel was the third of nine ships built for these owners at Clydebank since 1946 (three of which were oil tankers). She remained within the P & O Group until being broken up under her original name in 1971.*

Below. The Royal Yacht, t.s.s.s. BRITANNIA 5769 g.r.t. *launched in 1953 for HM Queen Elizabeth II. Engined by John Brown & Co (Clydebank) Ltd, this stylish and functional symbol of the United Kingdom and the Royal Family is probably the second most famous ship constructed by her builders in the post-war era, although it was only Her Majesty's namesake, launched in September 1967, which created that juxtaposition. She is seen still thronging with many shipyard workers whilst performing her sea trials in the Firth of Clyde. Faced with impending redundancy before the end of the 1990s, this exemplary symbol of Clyde built flair, skill and artistry deserves a better fate than being reduced to scrap in some Third World shipbreaking yard.* (Burniston Studios Ltd)

t.s.s.s. ARCADIA 29,664 g.r.t. *launched in 1953 for the P & O Steam Navigation Co, London. Engined by John Brown & Co (Clydebank) Ltd, this large passenger liner was built for the UK-Australia route and carried many British families to the Antipodes, and some that returned. Extensively refitted in 1970 for cruising, she had a short career in this market and was broken up in 1979.* (P & O Library Archive)

t.s.s.s. IVERNIA 21,717 g.r.t. *launched in 1954 for the Cunard SS Co Ltd, Liverpool. Engined by John Brown & Co (Clydebank) Ltd, she is seen undergoing sea trials off Glen Sannox, Isle of Arran. She was remodelled for cruising by Cunard in 1962 and renamed FRANCONIA with the work being done by her original builders. Sold and renamed FEDOR SHALYAPIN in 1973 she was still in existence under that name in 1996.* (Courtesy Scottish Record Office)

s.t. STANVAC AUSTRALIA 17,297 g.r.t. *launched in 1955 for the Esso Petroleum Co Ltd, London. Engined by John Brown & Co (Clydebank) Ltd, this vessel was the first of only two ships built by River Clyde shipyards for the world's largest oil company in the post-war period (the other was the m.t. ESSO JERSEY 313 g.r.t. built by Scotts of Bowling in 1960). Renamed ESSO AUSTRALIA in 1963, she was broken up in 1978 as the PETROLA 22.* (Burniston Studios Ltd)

m.v. SALSETTE 8202 g.r.t. *launched in 1956 for the P & O Steam Navigation Co, London. Engined by John Brown & Co (Clydebank) Ltd, this distinctive cargo liner was the third of four 'S' class vessels built at Clydebank in the early 1950s for P & O. Used throughout her life on the UK-Far East route, she was transferred within the Group to a sister company, then sold and renamed UNITED VISCOUNT in 1977. She was broken up under that name in 1979.* (P & O Library Archive)

t.s.s.s. SYLVANIA 21,989 g.r.t. *launched in 1956 for the Cunard SS Co Ltd, Liverpool. Engined by John Brown & Co (Clydebank) Ltd, she is seen passing the site of the former Wm Beardmore shipyard at Dalmuir on route to the Firth of Clyde and her rigorous sea trials. After her career with Cunard she was sold and renamed FAIRWIND in 1968. She has undergone various refits and modernisations with further changes of name. In 1996 she was still in existence as the ALBATROSS. (Burniston Studios Ltd)*

t.s.m.v. OTAIO 13,314 g.r.t. *launched in 1957 for the New Zealand Shipping Co Ltd, London. Engined by John Brown & Co (Clydebank) Ltd, this very traditional ref/cargo liner with passenger accommodation and training facilities for 70 cadets was built for the UK-New Zealand trade. She was sold and renamed EASTERN ACADEMY in 1976, being broken up under that name in 1982. (P & O Library Archive)*

s.t. LINCOLN 12,780 g.r.t. *launched in 1958 for the Federal Steam Navigation Co Ltd, London. Engined by John Brown & Co (Clydebank) Ltd, this vessel was the first of three tankers built at the yard for these owners. After a brief period under the owning P & O Group's Trident Tankers' colours, she was sold and renamed AMPHION in 1965. She was broken up in 1978 as the PHILLIPS NEW JERSEY. (P & O Library Archive)*

s.t. BRITISH JUDGE 27,585 g.r.t. *launched in 1958 for the Tanker Charter Co Ltd, London (BP). Engined by John Brown & Co (Clydebank) Ltd, this fine looking steam turbine tanker lasted within the BP fleet until 1975, when she was broken up. (BP Photographic)*

m.v. CLAN MACINDOE 7395 g.r.t. *launched in 1959 for Neptune Shipping Co Ltd, Glasgow (Clan Line). Engined by John Brown & Co (Clydebank) Ltd, this vessel traded between the UK-Africa-India, until her retiral from Clan Line in 1979 when she was sold and renamed GULF HERON. She became a constructive total loss in 1990 when she was extensively damaged by shelling in the Gulf port of Basra. (Courtesy Scottish Record Office)*

s.t. BRITISH QUEEN 32,431 g.r.t. *launched in 1959 for the Tanker Charter Co Ltd, London (BP). Engined by John Brown & Co (Clydebank) Ltd, she is seen at BP's Finnart Ocean Terminal on Loch Long, an inlet of the Firth of Clyde. This handsome vessel set a new benchmark for tanker looks and comfort, her short working career ended in 1975 when she was broken up under her original name.*

t.s.s.s. TRANSVAAL CASTLE 32,697 g.r.t. *launched in 1961 for the Union-Castle Mail SS Co Ltd, London. Engined by John Brown & Co (Clydebank) Ltd, this handsome fast passenger liner exemplified the shipbuilding and marine engineering skills of John Brown & Co and their many workers and subcontractors. Sold and renamed S.A. VAAL in 1966, she continued to sail between the UK and South Africa until 1977 when she was resold and converted to a cruise ship, then renamed FESTIVALE. She was still in existence in 1996 as the ISLAND BREEZE. (Courtesy Scottish Record Office)*

s.t. BRITISH HUSSAR 32,341 g.r.t. *launched in 1962 for the BP Tanker Co Ltd, London. Engined by John Brown & Co (Clydebank) Ltd, this well-proportioned conventional oil tanker is seen undergoing speed trials in the Firth of Clyde. She was broken up under her original name in 1976. (BP Photographic)*

t.s.m.v. CENTAUR 8262 g.r.t. *launched in 1963 for the Blue Funnel Line Ltd, Liverpool. Engined by Burmeister & Wain of Copenhagen, this distinctive 20 knot passenger/cargo/ livestock carrier was built for the Alfred Holt 'feeder' service between Australia and Singapore. She is seen nearing completion in the Clydebank fitting-out basin with the plethora of cranes in the east yard as a backdrop. After service in the Far East she was chartered to run between St Helena and the Falklands, being finally sold and renamed HAI DA in 1985, and was still in existence in 1996 under that name. (Courtesy Scottish Record Office)*

HMS INTREPID 11,060 tons displacement L11, *launched in 1964 for the Royal Navy. Engined by John Brown & Co (Clydebank) Ltd, this amphibious assault vessel was the last warship built by the Clydebank shipyard. An essential component of the UK MoD fleet, she and her sistership* HMS FEARLESS *(built by Harland & Wolff Ltd, Belfast) were both still in existence in 1996, albeit in standby capacity.*

s.t. BRITISH CONFIDENCE 38,119 g.r.t. *launched in 1965 for the BP Tanker Co Ltd, London. Engined by John Brown & Co (Clydebank) Ltd, this ship was the tenth vessel built for BP at Clydebank since 1946. She was also the last oil tanker built by the shipyard and was broken up after a relatively short career in 1976. Note her very pronounced radiused sheerstrake running parallel with the side shell. This aspect of naval architecture was very popular in the 1960s.* (BP Photographic)

t.s.m.v. KUNGSHOLM 26,678 g.r.t. *launched in 1965 for A/B Svenska Amerika Linien, Gothenberg. Engined by A/B Gotaverken, Gothenberg, she is seen nearing completion in the Clydebank fitting-out basin alongside HMS INTREPID. In the west yard can be seen yard no. 735, the bulk carrier CAPE ST VINCENT on berth no. 5. KUNGSHOLM had a relatively short career with her original owners, being sold to P & O in 1979 and renamed SEA PRINCESS. She has been extensively modified over the years and now has only one funnel. Despite this 'hybridity' she still retains her classic John Brown 'lines', and is the second most famous post-war passenger liner built by the yard. She was still in existence in 1996 as the VICTORIA having been renamed by P & O in 1995. (Courtesy Scottish Record Office)*

motor bulk carrier CAPE ST VINCENT 12,835 g.r.t. *launched in 1966 for Lyle Shipping Co Ltd, Glasgow. Engined by John Brown & Co (Clydebank) Ltd, this small bulk carrier was a stretched version of the CAPE RODNEY, built down-river by Lithgows Ltd in 1965. She was sold and renamed CORNISH WASA in 1972, undergoing further name changes until being broken up as JEZERA following a major fire on board in 1984. (Courtesy Scottish Record Office)*

m.v. GLENFINLAS 12,094 g.r.t. *launched in 1966 for the Glen Line Ltd, London. Engined by Burmeister & Wain of Copenhagen, this Glenalmond class 21-knot cargo liner is seen fitting-out in the wet basin at Clydebank during December 1966. Noticeable is the ship's Stülcken heavy lift mast between Nos 3 and 4 holds. On berth no. 4 to the left of the fitting-out basin can be seen yard no. 736 under construction, later to be named QUEEN ELIZABETH 2 when launched on 20 September 1967. GLENFINLAS was sold and renamed KWEICHOW in 1978, being broken up as SAUDI KAWTHER in 1984. (Glasgow University Archives)*

This November 1968 view taken at Princes Pier, Greenock, shows a watershed in the West of Scotland shipbuilding industry. In failing light, t.s.s.s. QUEEN ELIZABETH 2 65,863 g.r.t. is gingerly manoeuvred down-river by what seems to be half the River Clyde tug boat fleet. Thronging the quayside are many people witnessing this proud, yet melancholy event, some of whom were workers who helped to build her. The 1960s style and selection of chrome-trimmed motor cars date this photograph more so than the dateless lines and symbol of craftsmanship that is about to undergo her controversial sea trials. (Burniston Studios Ltd)

Left. motor bulk carrier VANCOUVER FOREST 17,660 g.r.t. *launched in 1969 for Chas Connell & Co Ltd, Glasgow. Engined by Barclay Curle & Co Ltd, this well-proportioned bulk carrier was built to transport timber from Canada and the USA to Great Britain and reflected the ship-owning prowess of the Connell family after the nationalisation of their Scotstoun shipyard. She was sold and renamed SHARK BAY in 1981, being broken up in 1987 as the BEAUFORT ISLAND.* (Courtesy Scottish Record Office)

t.s.m.v. BLENHEIM 10,427 g.r.t. *launched in 1970 for Fred Olsen Lines Ltd, London. Engined by Crossley Pielstick Ltd, Manchester, she was built for use between the UK and Europe, then was sold and renamed SCANDINAVIAN SEA in 1982. After a fire on board in 1984 she was declared a constructive total loss. However, she was subsequently completely refurbished in 1986 and renamed DISCOVERY 1. After another serious engine room fire off Florida in May 1996, she was deemed too seriously damaged for further repair and was consigned to be broken up.* (Courtesy Scottish Record Office)

motor bulk carrier VICTORIA CITY 16,639 g.r.t. *launched in 1970 for the Reardon Smith Line Ltd, Bideford. Engined by J.G. Kincaid & Co Ltd, this ship was the only vessel built at Clydebank for these owners, all others (12) were built at Govan. Sold and renamed SINGA SWAN in 1983, she was broken up in 1996 under the name MONOLIMA.* (Courtesy Scottish Record Office)

motor bulk carrier TEMPLE HALL 13,544 g.r.t. *launched in 1970 for Lambert Bros (Shipping) Ltd, London. Engined by English Electric Diesels Ltd, Newton-le-Willows, this vessel was the second of two built by UCS Ltd, her sistership TEMPLE BAR was built at the Govan Division.* TEMPLE HALL *was sold and renamed SEAWAY SANDPIPER in 1978. She was later converted to a pipe-burying vessel and renamed SANDPIPER in 1990, and as such she was still in existence in 1996.* (Courtesy Scottish Record Office)

self-elevating, self-propelled, 4-leg jack-up drilling rig OCEAN TIDE 5567 g.r.t. *launched by UCS Ltd, Clydebank Division in 1971 for Ocean Drilling & Exploration Co Ltd, London. Engined by ALCO/Caterpillar, she is seen at the tail of the bank, off Greenock, preparing for leg lowering and jack-up trials. This rig was specifically constructed for exploration drilling work in the North Sea where she performed very successfully for many years. She was sold and renamed BENNEVIS in 1992 and was still in existence in 1996. (Courtesy Scottish Record Office)*

motor rail ferry ARAHANGA 3893 g.r.t. *launched in 1972 for the Government of New Zealand Railways, Wellington. Engined by Crossley Premier Engines Ltd, Manchester, she is seen being towed down-river for dry docking and preliminary sea trials in 1973. Completed by the UCS liquidator many months late, she has in true Clydebank tradition proved an excellent vessel and was still in existence under her original name in 1996. Note the mass of shipyard personnel on board. (Courtesy Scottish Record Office)*

m.v. ALISA 11,897 g.r.t. *launched in 1972 for Haverton Shipping Ltd, London. Engined by G. Clark/NEM Ltd, Sunderland, this vessel (yard no. 120) was the last ship built at the Clydebank Division of UCS Ltd, as the yard was then known. The seventh Clyde class cargo liner, five of which were built at Clydebank, she was sold and renamed GOLD ALISA in 1980 and was still in existence in 1996 as the KOSI BAY. (Courtesy Scottish Record Office)*

self-elevating, 3-leg jack-up drilling rig CHICHEN-ITZA 4426 g.r.t. *launched by UIE Shipbuilding (Scotland) Ltd in 1981 for Permago, Panama (for initial use offshore Mexico). She is seen being manoeuvred at the tail of the bank, off Greenock, by a fleet of tugs, prior to performing lowering of her legs then jacking-up her hull. This vessel did not have propulsion machinery and therefore had to be towed to each location. She was sold and renamed GLOMAR ADRIATIC X in 1994, and was still in existence under that name in 1996. (Courtesy Scottish Record Office)*

YARROW & CO LTD	1906-1966
YARROW (SHIPBUILDERS) LTD	1966-1968
YARROWS LTD (DIVISION OF UPPER CLYDE SHIPBUILDERS LTD)	1968-1970
YARROWS LTD	1970-1977
YARROWS LTD (DIVISION OF BRITISH SHIPBUILDERS LTD)	1977-1985
YARROW SHIPBUILDERS LTD	1985-

Yarrow & Co Ltd became a public company from 1925, being controlled and managed by the direct descendants of the company's founder. Like the adjacent Blythswood shipyard, they were a relatively new company to Clydeside, transferring their works and senior expertise from their origins at Poplar, London on the River Thames to Scotstoun, Glasgow between 1906 and 1908.

The firm merged from World War II with an impressive record for the design and construction of warships mainly destroyers, and successfully extended this long standing association with the Royal Navy. The peacetime workload consisted of building many naval vessels alongside a mixed order book of many small specialised crafts for overseas countries, this varied output continued up until the late 1960s.

The Scotstoun shipyard and engine works were considered medium-sized when compared with the larger yards up and down-river, but had a far from medium-sized reputation for innovation in the fields of warship design or marine and mechanical engineering. This versatility in technical accomplishment had been conspicuous during the 1920s, when Yarrows imaginatively and successfully adapted the Scotstoun company's extensive marine boilermaking expertise towards the design and production of steam raising plant for power stations, uniquely named land boilers. This departure in product range was borne out of a then reduced shipbuilding workload. Thus, Yarrow Land Boilers Limited developed into an autonomous parallel manufacturing activity located in Scotstoun at the right time to supply the increasing demand for new power station construction, especially for England and abroad.

Advanced engineering development was to become synonymous with the name of Yarrows. The post-war surge in technology created both a need and a market niche for the skills, traditions and drive of the company and its workforce. Invited by the Admiralty to participate with the English Electric company into research of marine power equipment in 1946, this successful accord was to lay the foundations for future harmonious long-term association between these two firms.

The in-depth analysis and conclusions gleaned from this early post-war sojourn resulted in the formation of YARD (Yarrow Admiralty Research Department) which covered the multi-functional activities of, initially, state-of-the-art warship engine design. Success in this field was later expanded outwith the defence industry resulting in YARD being established as the UK's most prestigious design and analysis consultants. Projects in industries as diverse as oil and gas development, power generation, merchant and naval shipbuilding for many customers in the UK and overseas were subsequently undertaken by the firm.

Probably the first major success of YARD was the conception of COSAG, combined steam and gas turbines, for application in Royal Navy warships. This system proved both reliable and successful in the propulsion of frigates and other surface vessels. Much other research was undertaken in the field of advanced marine engineering, with studies and concepts completed for various types of nuclear powered vessels, both merchant and naval.

Becoming an entity in their own right since 1969, YARD was a wholly-owned subsidiary company. This reflected in the occupancy of an impressive suite of offices near the heart of Glasgow, whilst only a few miles away from the Scotstoun shipyard. This isolated autonomy illustrates the stand-alone success and development of this offshoot of the traditional design office, humorously referred to as the home of boffins and bean counters. YARD was later taken over by a consortium of British Aerospace and SEMA, a French firm and is now known as BAESEMA.

Development of surface warships after the war rapidly eliminated the need for battleships, cruisers and destroyers. The first two classes were never constructed by the Scotstoun shipbuilder. Destroyers, however,

Previous page, bottom. *Yard no. 2165, twin-screw motor vessel RMS VICTORIA 1570 g.r.t. 'bolt-assembled' at Yarrows Scotstoun shipyard in the summer of 1959. The ship was taken to this stage when every single part was marked and colour-coded, port side red, starboard side green. Then she was dismantled and crated for shipment to Kisumu, Lake Victoria, Kenya. In East Africa she was re-erected on a slipway on Lake Victoria and launched for the first time less than a year later, being handed over in the summer of 1961. This operation was successfully performed with local Kenyan labour supervised by a handful of Yarrow engineers and tradesmen. She was still in service in 1996.*

Above. *An aerial view of the enlarged Yarrow's shipyard at Scotstoun in 1971 looking north. From left to right the covered fitting-out dock adjoins the two remaining open building berths recently modernised with the provision of a 40-ton electric travelling crane. The brand new covered building hall is conveniently located between four remaining fixed hammerhead cranes that used to belong to the former Blythswood SB Co. Ltd. Ships visible are from left to right: F16, HMS DIOMEDE, fitting-out; F72, HMS ARIADNE, on the building berth; F421, HMNZS CANTERBURY, also fitting-out. All three vessels are broad beam versions of the Leander class frigate, ten of which were built by Yarrows over a twelve-year period. Note the rows of commercial vehicles recently completed by Albion Motors Ltd, and the Glasgow suburb of Scotstoun and Knightswood beyond.*

Below. *HMS ARROW 3100 tons displacement, F173, a Type 21 class frigate being taken in tow immediately after launching at Yarrow's Scotstoun shipyard on 5 February 1974. In the distance moored alongside one of the quays at Elderslie is the Iranian support ship HENGAM 2600 g.r.t. launched the previous year. The Type 21 design was not considered a superior vessel to the Leander class it was meant to replace, and all ships of this class spent very brief periods with the Royal Navy.*

Above. HTMS MAKUT RAJAKUMARN 1650 tons displacement *launched in 1971 for the Royal Thai Navy. Engined by Rolls-Royce Ltd and Crossley Pielstick Ltd, this unique frigate is seen on one of the building berths within Yarrows covered building hall. On the adjacent berth the first of a pair of modified Leander class frigates,* PFG CONDELL 2566 tons displacement *is under construction for the Chilean Navy.*

Middle & below. *Two views of Type 21 frigates being fitted-out at Yarrow's Scotstoun shipyard in the summer of 1976. F184 is* HMS ARDENT 3,100 tons displacement *and F185 is* HMS AVENGER 3100 tons displacement. *Both vessels had very short careers with the Royal Navy.* ARDENT *was bombed and sunk with considerable loss of life during the Falklands War in May 1982.* AVENGER *was sold to the Pakistan Navy in September 1994 and was still extant in 1996 as the* TIPPU SULTAN. (E.H. Cole)

Overleaf, upper. *Virtually the entire Scotstoun waterfront of Yarrow Shipbuilders Ltd is seen in this early 1980s view of the site looking north-west. Down-river the former Elderslie ship-repair facilities of Barclay Curle & Co. Ltd have been converted for the fitting out of warships. In the centre foreground the erstwhile pair of open building berths have been down-graded to a storage area for prefabricated units. Only one former Blythswood hammerhead crane remains, and the new module shop adjoining the covered building hall*

(continued)

attests to further expensive investment by the company in this extensive shipbuilding facility. Beyond the shipyard the sprawling Glasgow suburb of Knightswood stretches into the distance where the familiar extinct volcano of Dumgoyne at the west end of the Campsie Fells is just visible on the right hand horizon. (Courtesy Yarrow Shipbuilders Ltd)

Left. motor open screw ferry NAN FUNG 40 g.r.t. *launched in 1952 for the Hong Kong and Yaumati Ferry Co., Hong Kong. She was the first of six similar vessels assembled at Scotstoun, then dismantled and re-erected and launched in Hong Kong. She is seen performing satisfactory sea trials in the Far East after her 'second building'.* (Courtesy Yarrow Shipbuilders Ltd)

t.s.m.v. MAID OF ASHTON 508 g.r.t. *launched in 1953 for the Caledonian Steam Packet Co. Ltd, Glasgow. Engined by British Polar Engines Ltd, this little ferry was one of four sister ships built on the Clyde, which were well patronised by Scottish families in the 1950s and '60s. She was laid up in 1972 then later sold and renamed HISPANIOLA 2, when she had her propulsion machinery removed. After this she was towed to London and moored at Victoria embankment where she became a floating restaurant, a role she still performed in 1996.* (Burniston Studios Ltd)

diesel-electric paddle tug DIRECTOR 472 tons displacement *launched in 1956 for the Royal Navy. Engined by Paxman Diesels Ltd, Colchester, this vessel was the first of seven sisterships built on the Clyde to Yarrows design. Using the combination of diesel engines, electric motors, gear-boxes and paddlewheels, these tugs possessed excellent control and manoeuvrability when berthing the Royal Navy's large aircraft carriers. Alas the demise of these big ships put paid to the paddle tugs' careers, and DIRECTOR was broken up in 1980 after being placed in reserve in 1969.*

motor twin-screw tunnel vessel HMNS VALIANT 400 g.r.t. *launched in 1957 for His Excellency the Governor of Nigeria. Engined by Ruston & Hornsby Lincoln, this well finished vessel with a draught of only 4 ft 3 in. (over 1.2 metres) was specifically designed to navigate the shallow creeks and back waters that exist in Nigeria, and was typical of the unique craft designed and built by Yarrows in the 1950s. She became the Nigerian Presidential yacht after independence.*

SAS PRESIDENT PRETORIUS 2315 tons displacement, F145, *modified Whitby class frigate designed and built for the Navy of the Republic of South Africa and launched in 1962. Engined by English Electric Ltd, Rugby, this vessel was one of a three-ship order for anti-submarine frigates for patrolling the waters around South Africa, all built on the Clyde. She remained in service until 1990 when she was sold for demolition. (Courtesy Yarrow Shipbuilders Ltd)*

Below, left. HMS NAIAD 2350 tons displacement, F39 *launched in 1963 for the Royal Navy. Engined by English Electric Ltd with boilers by Babcock & Wilcox Ltd, this vessel was the second Leander class frigate built at Scotstoun. After a long career and a number of refits she was sunk as a target in 1990. (Courtesy Yarrow Shipbuilders Ltd)*

Below, right. t.s.m.v. UHURU 2200 g.r.t. *seen shortly after being launched on Lake Victoria, Kenya in 1964. Built along with her sistership UMODJA for the East African Railways and Harbour Board, both rail ferries were bolt-assembled at Yarrow's Scotstoun shipyard, then dismantled, transported and re-erected on Lake Victoria, and were still in service in 1996. (Courtesy Yarrow Shipbuilders Ltd)*

Right. HMS HECATE 2700 tons displacement, A137 *launched in 1965 was the second of three oceanograhic survey ships designed and built for the Royal Navy. Engined by Paxman Ventura Ltd, Colchester, this vessel almost saw three decades of service with the Royal Navy before being broken up in India in 1994.* (Courtesy Yarrow Shipbuilders Ltd)

Middle. motor stern trawler CORIOLANUS 1650 g.r.t. *launched in 1966 for Wilemace Ltd, Hull. Engined by Mirrlees National Ltd, Stockport, this factory freezer vessel was the last of a four-ship order completed by Yarrows in between warship construction schedules. Sold and renamed ACHAIOS in 1981, she was still in existence in 1996 as* STRATOS S.

Below. Royal Malaysian frigate K.D. RAHMAT, F24, 1290 tons displacement *launched in 1967 for the Royal Malaysian Navy. Her 'codag' (combined diesel and gas turbine) propulsion machinery was provided by Crossley Pielstick and Bristol-Siddeley, respectively. This custom-built warship exemplified Yarrow's design and build capability, and was still in front line service with the Royal Malaysian Navy in 1996.*

HMNZS CANTERBURY, F421, 2500 tons displacement *broad-beam Leander class frigate launched in 1970 for the Royal New Zealand Navy. Engined by English Electric Ltd, Rugby, this 'export' version only had minor differences from her Royal Navy sisterships. Unlike the UK, New Zealand's navy retain their warships much longer, and HMNZS CANTERBURY was still extant in 1996. Noticeable from the vessel's main mast is the Yarrow company flag, still flying before hand-over to her owners.* (Courtesy Yarrow Shipbuilders Ltd)

HMS APOLLO, F70, 2500 tons displacement *broad-beam Leander class frigate launched for the Royal Navy in 1970. Engined by English Electric Ltd (GEC). This vessel was the second last of a total of 26 Leander class frigates built for the Royal Navy, seven of which were built by Yarrows. She was sold to Pakistan in 1988, renamed ZULFIQUAR and was still extant in 1996.* (Courtesy Yarrow Shipbuilders Ltd)

Iranian support ship LAVAN 2540 g.r.t. *launched in 1979 for the Iranian Navy. Engined by Paxman Ventura Diesels Ltd, Colchester, this twin-screw logistics vessel was the fourth and last of a series designed and built by Yarrows for Iran, and clearly demonstrated the versatile marine engineering capability of the Scotstoun shipbuilders.* (Courtesy Yarrow Shipbuilders Ltd)

Above. HMS BRAVE 4200 tons displacement, F94 *(Batch 2) Type 22 Broadsword class frigate launched for the Royal Navy in 1983. Engined by Rolls-Royce (Olympus and Tyne) gas turbines, this highly armed 'cogag' warship is seen performing speed trials in the Firth of Clyde. The 'honeycomb' effect of combined transverse and longitudinal framing is seen on the ship's hull, further accentuated by good high penetration welding. This vessel was still in service with the Royal Navy in 1996, although some of her sisterships had been sold overseas.* (Courtesy Yarrow Shipbuilders Ltd)

Middle. HMS CORNWALL 4200 tons displacement, F99 *(Batch 3) Type 22 Broadsword class frigate launched for the Royal Navy in 1985. Engined by Rolls-Royce Ltd with a combination of two Spey and two Tyne gas turbines, this configuration is referred to as 'cogag' (combined gas and gas). Subsequent vessels in this class have been designated names of dukes, similar to* CORNWALL. (Courtesy Yarrow Shipbuilders Ltd)

Below. HMS NORFOLK 4200 tons displacement, F230, *Type 23 frigate, designed and built for the Royal Navy by Yarrow Shipbuilders Ltd, was launched in 1987. Her 'codlag' (combined diesel-electric and gas turbine) propulsion machinery was provided by Rolls-Royce Ltd. This state-of-the-art warship and her constantly increasing number of sisterships will remain the backbone of the Royal Navy Surface Fleet well into the next century.* (Courtesy Yarrow Shipbuilders Ltd)

THE BLYTHSWOOD SHIPBUILDING CO LTD 1919-1964

This relatively new shipbuilding concern was founded in 1919 by relatives of the McMillan and Bremner families who had shipyards in the towns of Dumbarton and Port Glasgow. Established after the end of World War I, the yard was set up to help meet the demand for replacement lost merchant ship tonnage, necessary after the Great War. The infant Scotstoun company rapidly gained an enviable record for the design and construction of oil tankers, building many for the major shipping companies who transported crude and petroleum products. Marine engine building and installation was never undertaken by the yard.

Subsequently acquired by the Norcros financial holding group, 'The Blythswood' returned healthy profits to its shareholders when the UK industry was the market leader in world shipbuilding between 1946 until the end of the 1950s. During this period the company was frugally managed, and employed W.A. Livsey, an archetypal shipyard general manager, who was apprehensively revered by his labour force and admiringly respected by his customers.

Possessing a relatively small compact shipbuilding facility, it was boxed in between the north bank of the River Clyde, Yarrow's shipyard to the west, Harland & Wolff's 'gunworks' on the east and the Glasgow industrial thoroughfare called South Street. The Blythswood yard made the best of its limited site area and restricted river frontage. The company latterly possessed three skewed building berths served by a total of seven fixed hammerhead cranes of very limited lifting capacity. Some novel and productive methods of ship construction were developed by the firm who frequently undertook the simultaneous construction of two ships at the same time on its 120 ft wide no. 2 slipway. This feat was often mocked by more prestigious shipbuilders but was never successfully emulated. On launch day the vessel entering the water would slide past about two-thirds of the width of the other ship occupying the remainder of the same berth. This visionary tactic enabled the Blythswood to reduce total building time on at least two of its contracts by maximising the concurrent use of its berths. Other aspects of the company's unique shipbuilding prowess, like leaving off the installation of deck plating until completion of tank or hold internal steelwork, created quite unsafe working conditions that did not attract many complimentary plaudits, and unfortunately resulted in a high accident profile.

With a labour force that peaked about 1000 men during the 1950s, the Blythswood achieved a regular and considerable output of about three medium-sized ships per annum from 1946 until 1959 when repeat orders began to dry up. The company completed 48 vessels between 1946 and the launch of its last ship in 1963. This total included 33 oil tankers, as well as the extensive enlargements of three existing ships, and amounted to 490,835 g.r.t., with 42% of this output for overseas owners. This was a truly impressive performance from a company that spent a minimal amount in capital expenditure for plant modernisation. Furthermore, its final futuristic looking contracts all contained considerable amounts of riveting, which were as much a compliment to the flair of the yard's design office and the industry and craft of its artisans, as it was a sad reflection on the lack of investment in novel fabrication capacity. Whilst renovation was discussed by the shipyard's discerning management and the parent group, the combination of the large cost involved, the limited area that the yard occupied and an unfortunate number of cancelled contracts, precipitated the premature demise of the Blythswood SB Co Ltd.

Hull, deck and bulkhead units were prefabricated in a small shed that existed from the company's inception. Weights of these pieces were of the order of 15-20 tons maximum. These were transported by tractor and trailers from the shed to the building berths where they were lifted into place by a combination of fixed hammerhead cranes, guy ropes, strops, sheaves, pulleys and winches. Ship construction on the berth was, like in all other UK yards, performed in the open with no permanent weather protection. The steelwork erection methods employed by the company placed a heavy emphasis on timely berth completion work, which were a number of labour intensive functions at which the shipyard excelled. This was no doubt due to sensible monetary weightings apportioned against achievable targets of measured amounts of work performed by skilled and motivated employees. The company's individuality was further demonstrated by the wearing of fedora hats instead of bowlers by most of its management. This vagary from traditional shipyard apparel perhaps reflected the newness of the company as much as a disregard for non-functional elite sartorial conformity.

The yard's main product was the oil tanker, which by definition is a hull containing many steel boxes, with pipes, pumps, and some accommodation. These vessels were constructed as a steelwork/piping fabrication project which started with the laying of the keel, and saw the steelworkers and plumbers effectively finished at the launch date.

Blythswood-built vessels were usually engined by some of the marine engine building specialists on the River Clyde, notably David Rowan, J.G. Kincaid, Barclay Curle or Scotts. Each newly launched hull was immediately towed up or downstream to Finnieston, Whiteinch or Greenock where these engineers installed the engines and auxiliaries, whilst the Blythswood joiners, and other subcontractors concurrently fitted out the vessel. As the shipyard had no fitting-out quay or basin, those trades employed in completing each ship invariably had to travel from the yard to wherever the vessel was moored.

This method and system worked very well for the Scotstoun shipyard. Their ships, sensibly designed with minimal trimmings, were well received by their respective owners. Many of the vessels built by the Blythswood were subsequently resold, generating handsome profits for their owners after initial use. No matter how good Blythswood tankers were, other builders were quoting lower prices with slightly shorter building durations quoted against the same specification. The traditional labour-intensive craft assembly method perfected from an art to a science by the Scotstoun company had had its day, and 'The Blythswood' ceased as a builder of fine, basic ships with the completion of the lighthouse tender *m.v. Fingal* 1342 g.r.t. (yard no. 140), launched on 8 August 1963. This outcome was reached after the submission of many unsuccessful tenders for various new building and conversion contracts.

The largest vessel constructed at Scotstoun was the Hong Kong registered steam turbine tanker, *Hamilton Sleigh* 18,772 g.r.t. launched on 7 November 1960, some eight months after her keel was laid (and subsequently lengthened by Barclay Curle six years later). The occasion of her launch was saddened by the announcement of a number of revoked orders that bode ill for the future of the shipyard. Greatest annual output was achieved in 1955, when the shipyard launched three oil tankers, aggregating 42,921 g.r.t.—no mean feat considering that up to 40% of these ships hulls were riveted! The last batch of tankers built by the shipyard were handsome, stylish vessels with pronounced sheer lines, rounded superstructures, raked masts and three-dimensionally tapered funnels, belying the legend of plain vessels built by a no frills traditional shipbuilder. Long after the closure of the yard, when less and less Blythswood built ships existed in service, those remaining vessels brought about favourable comparison with the value engineered, straight sheered vertical superstructure and transome sterned craft that were then being built.

The Blythswood site was subsequently acquired by the neighbouring Yarrow's, and became the location of two covered building berths and a module assembly hall used exclusively for warship construction. The new owners retained most of the array of long-jib fixed hammerhead cranes for many years after the completion of the enclosed shipbuilding facility, perhaps as some tangible monument to the good name of the former company. The original office block front remained intact in 1996, shorn of the distinctive carved masonry that depicted the former company title.

The following group of photographs after the list of ships built by the Blythswood SB Co Ltd, illustrate the location of the former company, as well as showing a few scenes of shipbuilding activity at this one time vibrant shipyard. The supplementary batch of pictures depict most of the ships built by the company in its last decade of operation.

List of ships built by the BLYTHSWOOD SHIPBUILDING Co Ltd, Scotstoun, between 1946 and closure in 1964

YEAR	NAME		TYPE	COUNTRY OF REGISTRATION	G.R.T.	TOTAL G.R.T.	YEAR	NAME		TYPE	COUNTRY OF REGISTRATION	G.R.T.	TOTAL G.R.T.
1946	NEOTHAUMA	m.	Oil Tanker	Britain	8229		1955 •	HERMES	m.	Oil Tanker	Norway	11065	
	NERITOPSIS	m.	Oil Tanker	Britain	8231			NAREK	s.	Oil Tanker	Britain	13646	
	MANCHESTER REGIMENT	s.	Cargo	Britain	7638	24098		• NORTH MONARCH	s.	Oil Tanker	Liberia	18210	42921
1947	LANGLEESCOT	m.	Cargo	Britain	6869		1956	ATLANTIC KNIGHT	s.	Oil Tanker	Liberia	14839	
	PACIFIC FORTUNE	s.	Ref/Cargo	Britain	9400	16269		MERCHANT ROYAL	m.	Cargo	Britain	9722	
1948	BRITISH CHIVALRY	m.	Oil Tanker	Britain	11217			NORTH EMPRESS	m.	Cargo	Greece	10904	35465
	LINCOLN ELLSWORTH	m.	Oil Tanker	Norway	2483		1957 •	GRECIAN EMBLEM	m.	Cargo	Greece	9761	
	BRITISH PROGRESS	m.	Oil Tanker	Britain	8573			• SAGAMORE	m.	Ore Carrier	Britain	10792	
	BRITISH PRUDENCE	m.	Oil Tanker	Britain	8577	30854		• EDENMORE	m.	Ore Carrier	Britain	10792	31345
1949	HAMLET	m.	Oil Tanker	Norway	10259		1958 •	NORTH COUNTESS	m.	Cargo	Greece	10662	
	REGENT LEOPARD	m.	Oil Tanker	Britain	8439			• NORTH LORD	m.	Oil Tanker	Greece	12390	23052
	HULDRA	s.	Oil Tanker	Norway	2485		1959 •	REGENT EAGLE	m.	Oil Tanker	Britain	12834	
	LANCING	m.	Oil Tanker	Norway	12303	33486		• BRITISH GANNET	m.	Oil Tanker	Britain	11238	
1950	LANGLEECLYDE	m.	Cargo	Britain	6642			• PEARLEAF	m.	Oil Tanker	Britain	12353	36425
	MANCHESTER MERCHANT	s.	Cargo	Britain	7651		1960 •	TEXACO OSLO	m.	Oil Tanker	Norway	12884	
	REGENT CARIBOU	m.	Oil Tanker	Britain	12072	26365		• HAMILTON SLEIGH	s.	Oil Tanker	Hong Kong	18772	31656
1951	BRITISH PIONEER	m.	Oil Tanker	Britain	8651		1961 •	TEXACO LONDON*	s.	Oil Tanker	Liberia	14396	14396
	REGENT SPRINGBOK	m.	Oil Tanker	Britain	12175		1962	TEXACO BRISTOL*	s.e.	Oil Tanker	Panama	10496	
	CEARA	m.	Oil Tanker	Brazil	11237	32063		• LAKE WINNIPEG*	s.e.	Bulk Carrier (great laker)	Canada	18660	29156
1952	NORTH KING	m.	Oil Tanker	Liberia	12191		1963 •	FINGAL	m.	Lighthouse Tender	Britain	1342	1342
	EDDYCLIFF	s.	Oil Tanker	Britain (RN)	2173								
	HAROLD SLEIGH	m.	Oil Tanker	Britain	8555	22919								
1953	NICOLAS	m.	Oil Tanker	Liberia	12395			42% export					
	BORDER KEEP	m.	Oil Tanker	Britain	11321			58% Britain		**48 vessels total = 490,835 g.r.t.**			
	HERTHA	s.	Oil Tanker	Norway	2588	26304								
1954	REGENT ROYAL	m.	Oil Tanker	Britain	10024								
	BRITISH CHANCELLOR	m.	Oil Tanker	Britain	11356								
	BRITISH MINSTREL	m.	Oil Tanker	Britain	11339	32719								

*These three contracts involved extensive lengthening of existing vessels, also known as 'jumbo-ising'.

• Indicates vessel depicted in subsequent photographic section.

For explanation of abbreviations see Glossary on page 345.

Yard no. 131, s.t. HAMILTON SLEIGH 18,772 g.r.t. glides into the inky waters of the River Clyde from the Blythswood SB Co Ltd on the crisp, clear day of 7 November 1960. The extensive array of fixed hammerhead cranes then in use by the yard are seen to good effect. Part of the new forebody for the shipyard's first 'jumbo-ising' contract, s.t. TEXACO LONDON 14,396 g.r.t. can also be seen beneath the crane and set of uprights at the right hand side. Although this vessel shows Nassan, Bahamas as her port of registration, this was later changed to Hong Kong.

Above. *This panorama of Scotstoun in 1959 looking south-west shows the entire Blythswood Shipbuilding Co. Ltd to good effect. On the stocks are the* motor tankers PEARLEAF 12,353 g.r.t. *to the left and* TEXACO OSLO 12,884 g.r.t. *to the right at different stages of construction. Note the extensive amount of plates lying in the stockyard, an indication of the firm's busy order book at that time. Down-river the adjacent Yarrow shipyard also displays considerable new shipbuilding activity. Beyond are two cargo liners being repaired by Barclay Curle & Co. Ltd at Elderslie with one of the vessels in drydock. Part of the Albion lorry works occupies the immediate foreground and Scotstoun west goods yard shows a fair number of railway wagons laden with steel for north bank shipyards. The town of Renfrew is situated beyond the chimney of Braehead power station. This site is still associated with shipbuilding in the 1990s. Yarrows have acquired the entire Blythswood location, although Albion Motors have contracted considerably and now only occupy the large buildings on the left hand side which were the former Harland & Wolff Ltd gun works. No trace of former railway activity now exists, and the site of Braehead power station is being developed as another ubiquitous retail shopping centre.*

Next page, top. *The launch of yard no. 112,* s.t. NORTH MONARCH 18,210 g.r.t. *draws gasps of amazement from shipyard managers, ship-owners and fur-coated guests on the launch platform as she enters the murky River Clyde on 1 December 1955 with inches to spare between her port side and the row of uprights. At her time of launching this ship took the Blythswood to a best post-war annual output of three tankers totalling 42,921 g.r.t. This was a formidable total for the Scotstoun shipbuilder, that saw the company achieve its highest output on the River Clyde that year.*

Next page, bottom. *Keel plates and engine room double bottom sections are laid out between showers on one of the berths at Blythswood shipyard, Scotstoun, during 1956. This steelwork is the first vestiges of yard no. 120,* m.v. GRECIAN EMBLEM 9761 g.r.t., *a cargo motor liner for Greek owners. Note the very basic supports holding the bottom shell plating in place before the erection of transverse floors, longitudinals and tank top.*

Above. motor ore carrier SAGAMORE 10,792 g.r.t. *immediately after her launching at Blythswood shipyard, Scotstoun, on 12 September 1957. All of the tugs in this picture are owned by the Clyde Shipping Co. Ltd.* FLYING DUCK 176 g.r.t. *and* FLYING DRAKE 177 g.r.t. *were virtually brand new, having been completed up-river by A. & J. Inglis Ltd of Pointhouse in 1956 and 1957, respectively.* SAGAMORE *had a reasonably long existence, after being sold and renamed* CAPETAN ALBERTO *in 1975 she was broken up in 1992.*

Below. *Considerable berth activity at Blythswood shipyard, Scotstoun, in 1958 with from left to right yard no. 124,* NORTH LORD 12,390 g.r.t., *yard no. 126,* REGENT EAGLE 12,834 g.r.t., *and yard no. 127,* BRITISH GANNET 11,238 g.r.t., *all motor tankers at early stages of construction. This picture illustrates the traditional erection methods, bereft of any weather protection at the yard. The long building on the right is part of Harland & Wolff's Scotstoun factory, always known as the gun-works.*

Shipyard workers at the Blythswood Shipbuilding Co. Ltd express pride and indifference in almost equal amounts as yard no. 126 m.t. REGENT EAGLE 12,834 g.r.t. *is about to be launched from the Scotstoun yard on 24 February 1959. Kilted pipers add strong Scottish musical tones to the event at one o'clock if the yard's clock is correct. Typical Clydeside attire of the era is evident in jaykits, bunnets, dungarees and takkity bits worn by nearly all, and the occasional beret indicating the presence of a welder.*

Two medium-sized motor tankers under construction at the Blythswood shipyard late in 1959. On the left is yard no. 125, m.t. PEARLEAF 12,353 g.r.t., *a few weeks away from being launched. Squeezed alongside her is yard no. 129, m.t. TEXACO OSLO 12,884 g.r.t. Both ships were engined by David Rowan & Co. Ltd of Glasgow. The Blythswood method of erecting bottom shell, bulkheads, web frames and shell plating first is clearly shown in this picture. This method whereby the deck plating was left off for as long as possible allowed crane access into the ship's cargo tanks to install pipes and valves. It also created a very hazardous working environment until the deck plating was connected.*

Above. *Launch of yard no. 129, m.t. TEXACO OSLO 12,884 g.r.t. for Texaco Norway A/S from the Blythswood shipyard, Scotstoun on 12 April 1960. The vessel on the extreme right, yard no. 131, s.t. HAMILTON SLEIGH 18,772 g.r.t. was the last tanker new-building order completed by the Scotstoun shipbuilders. The lattice structure towering up in the centre is a new fixed hammerhead crane.*

Below, right. *The 600 ft plus new mid-ship and forebody section for the* t.e. great laker LAKE WINNIPEG *being positioned against the ship's original stern section in one of the Clyde Navigation Trust drydocks at Govan in 1962. This was the third and last such conversion undertaken by the Blythswood Shipbuilding Co. Ltd, perhaps a fitting affirmation of the company's attempts to survive by diversification. Note the port and starboard wing and hopper tanks which run the entire length of the vessel from the engine room bulkhead to the fore peak.*

Below. *The new forebody of the lengthened T2 tanker, TEXACO LONDON, prior to launching from the Blythswood shipyard in 1961. Apart from the aft section, this conversion re-used the existing 1940s midship accommodation, which was lifted onto the new unit by the Clyde Navigation Trust Finnieston crane. It was located in the gap forward of the elevated walkway on the upper deck which stops at the forward launch flag.*

Top. m.t. HERMES 11,065 g.r.t. *launched in 1955 for Bruusgaard Kiösteruds Skibs A/S of Drammen, Norway. Engined by David Rowan & Co. Ltd, this tanker was among the last traditional straight funnel ships built by Blythswood, before futuristic styling took over the later ship products from the yard. Sold and renamed* PEMEX *in 1965 she was broken up in 1982 as the* LAZARO CARDENAS.

Middle. s.t. NORTH MONARCH 18,210 g.r.t. *launched in 1955 for Compania Naviera Petrolera SA of Liberia. Engined by David Rowan & Co. Ltd of Glasgow, this stylish tanker endorsed the Scotstoun yard's reputation of achieving good looks within functional ship design. She had a twenty-year life span before being broken up in 1975.*

Left. m.v. GRECIAN EMBLEM 9761 g.r.t. *launched in 1957 for Olinares Compania Naviera SA, Andros, Greece. Engined by Scotts SB & Eng. Co. of Greenock, this conventional tramp remained with her original owners until 1974 when she was sold and renamed* CRETE SEA. *She was broken up in 1977 as the* HONG CHUN.

Right. motor ore carrier EDENMORE 10,792 g.r.t. *launched in 1957 for Furness Withy & Co. Ltd, London. Engined by David Rowan & Co. Ltd, the ship is depicted discharging a cargo of imported iron ore at General Terminus Quay, Glasgow in 1958, probably after her maiden voyage. Sold and renamed WELCOME in 1975 she was broken up in 1984. This site is not far from the river crossing known as the Kingston bridge, which gives some indication of how far up-river this former iron-ore import quay was situated.*

Below. m.v. NORTH COUNTESS 10,662 g.r.t. *launched in 1958 for Panconquista Cia. Nav. SA of Greece. Engined by Hawthorn Leslie (Eng.) Ltd of Newcastle, this attractive looking tramp was the last dry cargo vessel built by Blythswood. Sold and renamed ATHENA in 1979 she was broken up in 1984. This vessel had limited accommodation for a small number of passengers.*

m.t. NORTH LORD 12,390 g.r.t. *launched in 1958 for Priam Cia. Nav., Piræus, Greece. Engined by David Rowan & Co. Ltd, Glasgow, this stylish tanker is seen forming an impressive bow wave at her loaded draft during trials in the Firth of Clyde. Her entire career was spent under her original name, being broken up in 1978.*

Four excellent examples of individually designed and crafted Blythswood product tankers.

m.t. REGENT EAGLE 12,834 g.r.t. launched in 1959 for the Regent Petroleum Co. Ltd, London. Engined by David Rowan & Co. Ltd, this tanker carried the Blythswood hallmark of good lines and artistic superstructure. She was renamed TEXACO GLOUCESTER in 1969, being later sold and further renamed before being broken up in 1984.

m.t. BRITISH GANNET 11,238 g.r.t. launched in 1959 for Clyde Charter Co. Ltd (BP). Engined by J.G. Kincaid & Co. Ltd, Greenock, this handsome Bird class products tanker was the sixth ship built for BP by Blythswood since 1946. Sold and renamed HANJIANG in 1976, she was broken up under that name in 1983. (BP Photographic)

m.t. PEARLEAF 12,353 g.r.t. launched in 1959 for John I. Jacobs & Partners Ltd, London. Engined by David Rowan & Co. Ltd, this stylish tanker went on long-term charter to the UK Ministry of Defence immediately after completion. Sold and renamed NEJMAT EL PETROL XIX in 1986, she was broken up in 1993, which was an exceptionally long career for an oil tanker, no doubt a reflection on the combined efforts of her builders and the maintenance rigours of the MoD.

m.t. TEXACO OSLO 12,884 g.r.t. launched in 1960 for Texaco Norway A/S, Oslo, engined by David Rowan & Co. Ltd of Glasgow. She was broken up in 1987, retaining her original name throughout her entire career. The shipbuilder's data plate can be clearly seen as the brass rectangle half way up the forward navigating bridge structure.

s.t. HAMILTON SLEIGH 18,772 g.r.t. *launched in 1960 for the Dominion Navigation Co. Ltd, Hong Kong. Engined with steam turbines supplied by David Rowan & Co. Ltd, this handsome oil tanker was subsequently lengthened by Barclay Curle & Co. Ltd at their Elderslie drydock in 1966. Later sold and renamed EVANGELIA in 1973, she was broken up under that name in 1979.*

t.e. oil tanker TEXACO LONDON 14,396 g.r.t., *lengthened by the Blythswood shipyard for Texaco (Panama) Inc. Although registered in Liberia she is pictured after her completion of sea trials at the tail of the bank in 1961. Renamed TEXACO COCLE in 1971, she was broken up in 1987—this made her aft end and engines (built in the USA as the ESSO UTICAM, 1944) over 40 years old! The raked fo'csle and new funnel enhance the vessel's traditional appearance.*

t.e. great laker LAKE WINNIPEG 18,660 g.r.t. *was converted from the World War II T2 tanker TABLE ROCK by Blythswood shipyard in 1962. Only the original stern unit containing her accommodation and turbine electric generators were retained for the construction of this hybrid. She was altered on behalf of Carryore Ltd, Halifax, Nova Scotia, and had a lengthy and successful additional career before being broken up in 1985.*

Yard no. 140, t.s.m.v. FINGAL 1342 g.r.t. *launched in 1963 for the Commissioners of the Northern Lighthouses, Leith, was the last ship built by the Blythswood Shipbuilding Co. Ltd. Engined by British Polar Engines Ltd, she was decommissioned in 1995, but was still in existence in 1996 under her original name. This final product of the Blythswood SB Co Ltd contained an extensive percentage of riveting in her construction.*

▌ **CHARLES CONNELL & CO LTD**	**1861–1968**	
▌ **SCOTSTOUN DIVISION OF UPPER CLYDE SHIPBUILDERS LTD**	**1968–1972**	
▌ **SCOTSTOUN MARINE LTD**	**1973–1977**	
▌ **SCOTSTOUN MARINE LTD (DIVISION OF BRITISH SHIPBUILDERS LTD)**	**1977–1980**	

The family-owned and managed Scotstoun shipyard of Charles Connell & Co Ltd set many commercial and technical precepts that were taken for granted in their day, but are now propounded as glib, highly original rhetorical nostrums of the new generation of industrial voyeurs who permeate contemporary British industry and commerce.

Under the able stewardship of Sir Charles Connell, third generation of the founding family, the medium-sized shipyard completed some 62 ships totalling 604,194 g.r.t. between 1946 and the takeover of the company into Upper Clyde Shipbuilders Ltd in early 1968. This impressive record equated to approximately three medium-sized ships launched and duly completed each calendar year. A formid-able statistic given that the labour force during this period remained quite stable at less than 1000 employees.

With a sound 'business plan' inherited from the founders of the company, the Scotstoun concern had the science of market research identified, categorised and implemented long before it became a garrulous buzz word expounded by pseudo sages and other propounders of sound bit soliloquy. Investing in the downstream activity of ship owning, this gave the Connell family the constant awareness of the needs and nuances of the shipping industry. The further income that this venture generated was usually reinvested in new vessels, designed and built in their Scotstoun shipyard, all with long-term charters before they were completed. Many of Connell's shared ships were part-owned and wholly-managed by the famous Glasgow shipping company of J. & J. Denholm Ltd. With such a sound market for their ships, Charles Connell & Co Ltd was a busy and productive shipbuilding concern, which provided continuous employment with regular overtime for its workforce throughout the post-war boom years.

A formal apprentice training school was a resource that was always missing within the Connell regime of yard ownership. A dubious deficiency, as the profound instruction and limitless encouragement rendered to keen apprentices was reciprocated after these trainees asserted their genuine interest in shipbuilding. Fostering a partly nepotistic attitude to personnel recruitment, somehow the 'firm but fair' regime of mild autocracy, prevalent throughout all departments within the yard, produced a system of labour control that seldom bred contempt from familiarity.

Aware of the need for extensive investment in the replacement and modernisation of existing facilities, the company spent almost £2 million of its own money during the late 1950s rationalising and upgrading the Scotstoun shipyard, which had undergone gradual transition throughout its century of existence. By the end of that decade the company had in place a fully covered fabrication shed that extended almost the full east-west length of the shipyard. This facility was always highly utilised, and clearly demonstrated the owner's commitment to all welded ship construction. Located on a parcel of land with near square proportions on the north bank of the River Clyde, in the parish of Scotstoun, the yard had sufficient real estate with which to perform a successful specific type of shipbuilding.

The five building berths were reduced to three in the late 1950s, with the largest one capable of building tankers or bulk carriers up to almost 100,000 t.d.w. Unfortunately, this facility never constructed such leviathans! The civil engineering work was virtually complete, but the extra additional extensive craneage that would have been necessary to create such ships was beyond the purse of the company, even during the era of profitable shipbuilding orders. Retaining a unique method of contract 'piecework' for all hourly paid trades, consistent productivity and frugal cost control resulted in the yard processing about 15,000 tons of fabricated steelwork annually. This meant that the basic type of cargo liner for which the company was famous, could be modified and priced to suit various ship-owner's specific needs. Forty-four such ships were successfully built by the shipyard during this period.

The transition to the design and construction of bulk carriers was an expensive lesson for the firm. Poor steelwork material take off by the estimating office underquantified the tonnage of plate and section required for hull scantlings. This produced a far greater intensity of preparation, erection and welding man hour expenditure which meant most of these types of ships were built for a much greater cost than the price of the estimate. Round about 1963, the yard settled down to use a two-berth shipbuilding system utilising the two travelling hammerhead cranes on the same track. When combined to perform tandem lifting, this method enabled ship sections up to 80 tons to be erected. The Connell commitment to maximise the benefits of fabrication often saw this technique practised on heavy ship sections.

In addition to building vessels for shipping companies which were part owned by Connells, the other main customer during the entire post-war period was the Ben Line Ltd of Edinburgh, for whom the shipyard built 19 cargo liners of 201,778 g.r.t. which was approximately 25% of the yard's total output up until its closure. These vessels were built in a series of four ships at a time supplemented with three other one-off liners. The later types of fast cargo liners were among the finest looking ships ever to fly the red duster of the British Merchant Navy, setting standards of excellence in naval architecture that were emulated throughout the international shipping world. These fine vessels were faulted only by their medium cargo carrying capacity, which became unprofitable as fuel costs escalated in the 1970s. Other notable customers during this time were the P & O Group who took delivery of 10 ships, and various Norwegian owners who purchased a total of 15 ships. The Scotstoun yard also had the distinction of being the first shipyard on Clydeside to construct a vessel with a Stülcken heavy lift derrick, which was installed on the *m.v. Inventor* 9171 g.r.t., launched on 21 August 1963 for Harrison Line Ltd of Liverpool. The largest ship built at Scotstoun was the British motor bulk carrier *Stonepool* 27,049 g.r.t., launched on 6 April 1966. The firm's greatest annual output of 39,008 g.r.t. occurred in that same year, although the Connell family and most of the former employees consider the five ships totalling 34,052 g.r.t. achieved in 1962, when two ships actually shared the same berth at the same time, was their most formidable annual production statistic!

The shipyard became the Scotstoun Division of Upper Clyde Shipbuilders in 1968, and duly completed only seven ships of 97,760 g.r.t. in four years within this group. Overmanned with an influx of redundant workers from closed yards, the UCS experience was an unhappy one for the Scotstoun yard, with tardy deliveries, poor productivity, and constant cost overruns, instilling a lethargy in the facility from which it was never to recover. The facility later became Scotstoun Marine Ltd, a wholly-owned subsidiary of Govan Shipbuilders in 1973, after over one year in receivership from UCS. The yard saw extensive capital expenditure during this period with new craneage, fabrication facilities and a fitting-out quay installed and commissioned, in the run up to full UK shipbuilding nationalisation in 1977. The millions spent on the yard during this era produced little permanent gain in terms of greater output or reduced building costs, despite the largest annual tonnage being achieved within this regime, with three Kuwait class cargo liners totalling 46,419 g.r.t. being launched in 1976. During the final existence of the yard, then operating as Scotstoun Marine Ltd, 18 ships totalling 184,450 g.r.t. were built (two of which were constructed for Charles Connell, son of the previous owner). The final vessel completed at Scotstoun was the *m.v. Warka* 2992 g.r.t., the last of seven mini bulk carriers, which were part of the financially suicidal deal concocted by British Shipbuilders Ltd and the government of Poland. Aimed at creating an artificial market for British built ships and employment for UK shipbuilders, this contentious order achieved the former but contributed to the antithesis of the latter. After closure of the yard, the shipbuilding facilities were quickly decommissioned, and either transferred up-river to the Govan parent company, or were sold off or scrapped in the early 1980s. The layout of sheds, a legacy of the Connell ownership and investment of yore, were still standing in 1996, then in use as a steel stockyard. Only the reinforced concrete travelling crane tracks adjacent to the large piled sloping building berth and the belatedly installed fitting quay identifies the site as a former bustling shipyard. Between 1946 and the final closure of the yard in 1980, 89 vessels totalling 915,198 g.r.t. were completed under its four different identities, 33% of this amount was for export.

List of ships built by CHAS CONNELL & Co Ltd, Scotstoun, and their successors between 1946 and closure in 1980

YEAR	NAME		TYPE	COUNTRY OF REGISTRATION	G.R.T.	TOTAL G.R.T.
1946	KALLADA	m.	Cargo	Britain	6612	
	MOUNTPARK	s.	Cargo	Britain	6722	
	WELLPARK	s.	Cargo	Britain	6722	
	MARJATA	m.	Cargo	Britain	6656	
	MUTLAH	m.	Cargo	Britain	6647	33359
1947	PURNEA	m.	Cargo	Brtiain	5340	
	BENMACDHUI	m.	Cargo	Britain	7847	
	FACTOR	m.	Cargo	Britain	6533	
	BENVENUE	s.	Cargo	Britain	7846	27566
1948•	CORINALDO	m.	Ref/Cargo	Britain	8378	
	BENCLEUCH	s.	Cargo	Britain	7868	16246
1949	CARRONPARK	m.	Cargo	Britain	5328	
	CORONA	m.	Cargo	Norway	5136	
	BENALDER	s.	Cargo	Britain	7877	
	TAMESIS	m.	Ref/Cargo	Norway	6749	25090
1950	GANGES	m.	Cargo	Britain	6724	
	BETWA	m.	Cargo	Britain	6722	
	TARTAR	m.	Oil Tanker	Norway	11103	24549
1951	LYLEPARK	m.	Cargo	Britain	5269	
	HORNBLOWER	m.	Oil Tanker	Norway	11102	
	CASTOR	m.	Oil Tanker	Norway	11107	27548
1952	TALISMAN	m.	Ref/Cargo	Norway	6785	
	BENREOCH	s.	Cargo	Britain	10142	16927
1953	NORSCOT	m.	Oil Tanker	Britain	12709	
	TURCOMAN	m.	Oil Tanker	Norway	12552	25261
1954•	TIBETAN	m.	Oil Tanker	Norway	12608	
	INDUS	m.	Cargo	Britain	7049	
	BENVRACKIE	s.	Cargo	Britain	10302	29959
1955	FERNSTAR	m.	Oil Tanker	Norway	12719	
•	FERNMOOR	m.	Ref/Cargo	Norway	7082	
•	SCOTSTOUN	m.	Oil Tanker	Britain	12723	32524
1956•	BENDORAN	s.	Cargo	Britain	10355	
•	GLENPARK	m.	Cargo	Britain	8097	
	TEMERAIRE	m.	Ref/Cargo	Norway	6017	24469
1957	BENLOMOND	s.	Cargo	Britain	10325	
•	TURANDOT	m.	Ref/Cargo	Norway	6018	16343
1958•	FERNHAVEN	m.	Oil Tanker	Norway	12689	
•	FERNSTATE	m.	Ref/Cargo	Norway	6759	
•	BENLOYAL	s.	Ref/Cargo	Britain	11463	30911
1959	BROOMPARK	m.	Cargo	Britain	8084	
•	TIJUCA	m.	Ref/Cargo	Norway	5999	
	CRAIGALLIAN	m.	Ore Carrier	Britain	7088	21171
1960	CRINAN	m.	Ore Carrier	Britain	7086	
•	FOYLE	s.	Oil Tanker	Britain	24549	31635
1961	BENGLOE	s.	Ref/Cargo	Britain	11282	
•	ERNE	s.	Oil Tanker	Britain	14244	25526
1962•	SAINT AIDAN	m.	Cargo[1]	Britain	973	
•	TUSKAR	m.	Ref/Cargo	Britain	1598	
	BENVALLA	m.	Ref/Cargo	Britain	11391	
•	JUMNA	m.	Cargo	Britain	10051	
•	KOHINUR	m.	Cargo	Britain	10039	34052

YEAR	NAME		TYPE	COUNTRY OF REGISTRATION	G.R.T.	TOTAL G.R.T.
1963•	BENARMIN	m.	Ref/Cargo	Britain	10870	
•	INVENTOR	m.	Ref/Cargo	Britain	9171	
•	SCOTSTOUN	m.	Cargo	Britain	11457	31498
1964	BENDEARG	m.	Cargo	Britain	12140	
•	ROMANDIE	m.	Bulk Carrier	Switzerland	21449	33589
1965•	BENLEDI	m.	Ref/Cargo	Britain	11758	
	MOUNTPARK	m.	Bulk Carrier	Britain	21833	33591
1966•	STONEPOOL	m.	Bulk Carrier	Britain	27049	
•	BENWYVIS	m.	Ref/Cargo	Britain	11959	39008
1967•	BENALBANACH	m.	Ref/Cargo	Britain	11466	
•	BENSTAC	m.	Ref/Cargo	Britain	12011	23477
1968†	BENCRUACHAN	s.	Ref/Cargo	Britain	12092	
	CONON FOREST	m.	Bulk Carrier	Britain	17659	29751
1969	SCOTSPARK	m.	Bulk Carrier	Britain	16793	16793
1970•	BENLAWERS	m.	Ref/Cargo	Britain	12784	
•	CITY OF LONDON	m.	Cargo	Britain	9793	
•	SIG RAGNE	m.	Cargo	Britain	11857	34434
1971†	GLENPARK	m.	Bulk Carrier	Britain	16782	16782
1972	VANCOUVER ISLAND	m.	Bulk Carrier	Britain	16782	
	HILLA	m.	Cargo	Britain	11897	28689
1973†	HARFLEET	m.	Bulk Carrier	Britain	16715	
•	HARFLEUR	m.	Bulk Carrier	Britain	16715	33430
1974	NORSE HERALD	m.	Bulk Carrier	Britain	16682	
•	LOCH LOMOND	m.	Ref/Cargo	Britain	10397	27079
1975	LOCH MAREE	m.	Ref/Cargo	Britain	10397	10397
1976	IBN ABDOUN	m.	Cargo	Kuwait	15516	
	IBN AL HAITHAM	m.	Cargo	Kuwait	15516	
	IBN HAZM	m.	Cargo	Kuwait	15387	46419
1977†	IBN ZUHR	m.	Cargo	Kuwait	15387	
•	ARAFAT	m.	Cargo	Kuwait	15387	30774
1978	AL MUHARRAQ	m.	Cargo	Kuwait	15387	
•	GNIEZNO II	m.	Bulk Carrier	Poland	2995	
	SIERADZ	m.	Bulk Carrier	Poland	2996	21378
1979	WYSZKOW	m.	Bulk Carrier	Poland	2997	
	CHORZOW	m.	Bulk Carrier	Poland	2996	
	LOMZA	m.	Bulk Carrier	Poland	2996	
	WIELVN	m.	Bulk Carrier	Poland	2992	
	WARKA	m.	Bulk Carrier	Poland	2992	14973

33% export
67% Britain   **89 vessels total = 915,198 g.r.t.**

Notes
† Became Scotstoun Division of Upper Clyde Shipbuilders Ltd   1968–71
† Became   "   "   "   (in Receivership)   "   1971–72
† Became Scotstoun Marine Ltd   1973–80
† Became Scotstoun Marine Ltd (Division of B.S. Ltd)   1977–80

[1]coaster

• Indicates vessel depicted in subsequent photographic section.
For explanation of abbreviations see Glossary on page 345.

The following collection of photographs illustrates the location of the former Scotstoun shipbuilding yard of Charles Connell & Co Ltd, as well as portraying a few scenes of shipbuilding activity. The additional bunch of pictures reveal some of the ships built by the shipyard in its three post-war guises.

Two views of the former Scotstoun shipyard of Chas Connell & Co. Ltd on the 10 October 1960.

Top illustration shows yard no. 496, s.t. FOYLE 24,549 g.r.t., the largest vessel yet built by the company, occupying most of the company's new lengthened and piled no. 1 building berth.

Bottom picture shows the tanker sliding into the River Clyde later the same day. Built for the Charter Shipping Co. Ltd (a division of the P & O Group), this vessel bore the colours of James Nourse Ltd, who were long standing customers of Connells. Engined by Barclay Curle & Co. Ltd, she was launched with her boilers, turbines and gear boxes already installed. Renamed MEGNA in 1965 she was transferred within P & O to the new offshoot called Trident Tankers Ltd, and was broken up in 1978. (Burniston Studios Ltd)

Above. Yard no. 501, m.v. BENARMIN 10,870 g.r.t. *prior to launching from the Scotstoun shipbuilding yard of Chas Connell & Co. Ltd on 26 April 1963. This ship was the fourth of a quartet of fast cargo liners (one steam, three motor) all capable of 20 knots, designed and built by Connells for the Ben Line Ltd. Only BENARMIN was engined by Barclay Curle & Co. Ltd. Her three sisterships were supplied with machinery built by David Rowan & Co. Ltd, also of Glasgow. She was later sold and renamed YONG CHUN in 1972 remaining so up until 1990. (Burniston Studios Ltd)*

Left. Ship no. 505, m.v. BENLEDI 11,758 g.r.t. *was the first vessel built by Chas Connell & Co. Ltd that had a bulbous bow. The fine lines and flared artistry of this futuristic cargo liner clearly illustrate the skill and workmanship of the former Scotstoun shipyard. Note the extensive 'fore poppet' that protects and supports the bow during launching, which is about to take place on 18 February 1965.*

Next page, upper. Yard no. 508, *motor bulk carrier STONEPOOL 27,049 g.r.t. occupies almost the whole length of berth no. 1 at the Scotstoun shipyard of Chas Connell & Co. Ltd shortly before her launch in early April 1966. Built for Ropner Shipping Co. Ltd of Hartlepool, this vessel was the largest ever built at the Scotstoun yard. She was launched with her engines already installed by Barclay Curle & Co. Ltd. This twin funnelled bulk carrier remained with her original owners throughout her entire working life, being broken up in 1986 as STONEPOOL. (Burniston Studios Ltd)*

Previous page, lower. *Yard no. 514, m.v. BENLAWERS 12,784 g.r.t. under construction at the Scotstoun Division of UCS Ltd in September 1969. The box-like holds of this semi-container vessel are seen to good effect before the erection of decks and bulkheads. Scotstoun Division of UCS retained the Connell practice of commencing work in the ship's engine room as soon as possible to reduce overall build duration.*

Right. *m.v. CORINALDO 8378 g.r.t. launched in 1948 for the Donaldson Line Ltd of Glasgow. Engined by Barclay Curle & Co. Ltd, this ship was built for the North Atlantic trade between the UK, Canada and USA. Sold and renamed NINGPO in 1967 she was broken up in 1980.*

Below. *m.t. TIBETAN 12,608 g.r.t. launched in 1954 for Wilh. Wilhelmsen of Tönsberg, Norway. Engined by Barclay Curle & Co. Ltd, this squat vessel was the third and last oil tanker built for these owners by Chas Connell & Co. Ltd. Sold and renamed NORTHERN SHELL in 1964 she was broken up in 1976. The Roseneath peninsula and the hills of Argyll beyond make a very attractive back-drop as the vessel idles between performing sea trials in the Clyde estuary. (Burniston Studios Ltd)*

Bottom. *m.v. FERNMOOR 7082 g.r.t. launched in 1955 for A/S Glittre (Fearnley & Eger) of Oslo. Engined by Barclay Curle & Co. Ltd, this traditional ref/cargo liner sports cowl neck vents atop of her derrick posts between hatches 2 and 3 and 4 and 5. Sold and renamed KOTA TIMUR in 1975 she retained that name until being broken up in 1982. (Burniston Studios Ltd)*

m.t. SCOTSTOUN 12,723 g.r.t. launched in 1955 for Falkland Shipowners Ltd (J. & J. Denholm Ltd), Glasgow. Engined by Barclay Curle & Co. Ltd, she was sold and renamed NORTH EARL in 1962 and retained that name until being broken up in 1977. (Burniston Studios Ltd)

s.s. BENDORAN 10,355 g.r.t. launched in 1956 for Ben Line Steamers Ltd, Leith. Engined by David Rowan & Co. Ltd, this vessel was the third of the four ship Benreoch class all built by Connells in the 1950s for the same owners. Lacking the style, flair and speed of the later Ben Line ships, this series all lasted with their original owners well into the 1970s. She was broken up in 1977 and is seen in revenue earning service in the 1960s. (E.H. Cole)

m.v. GLENPARK 8097 g.r.t. launched in 1956 for J. & J. Denholm (Mgt) Ltd. Engined by Barclay Curle & Co. Ltd, she possessed a very distinctive profile with her 'back combed' funnel which was a brief fad of 1950s naval architecture. Sold and renamed DINOS M in 1969, she came to an unfortunate end in her twentieth year, when she became stranded in fog and later sank off the Goto Islands in April 1976 as the GOLDEN LEADER. (Courtesy J. & J. Denholm Ltd)

m.v. TURANDOT 6018 g.r.t. launched in 1957 for Wilh. Wilhelmsen of Tönsberg, Norway. Engined by Barclay Curle & Co. Ltd, this handsome conventional ref/cargo liner was the second in a batch of three sister ships built by Connells for this major Norwegian ship-owner, and was the seventh of eight post-war vessels built at Scotstoun for these owners. She was sold and renamed BANGLAR PREETI in 1976 before being broken up in 1983. (Burniston Studios Ltd)

m.t. FERNHAVEN 12,689 g.r.t. *launched in 1958 for A/S Glittre (Fearnley & Eger) of Oslo. Engined by Barclay Curle & Co. Ltd, this was a very traditional looking tanker from the artistic Connell shipyard, whose flair for good looking cargo liners was never applied to other vessels. Compared to the oil tankers built by the nearby Blythswood shipyard, this vessel looked at least one decade older. Sold and renamed POLLUCE in 1967, she retained that name until being broken up in 1982. (Burniston Studios Ltd)*

m.v. FERNSTATE 6759 g.r.t. *launched in 1958 for A/S Marina (Fearnley & Eger) of Oslo. Engined by Barclay Curle & Co. Ltd, this typical 'Connell design' of ref/cargo liner was the last ship built at Scotstoun for these owners and the fourth launched between 1955 and 1958. Sold and renamed CERAM SEA in 1976 she retained that name until being broken up in 1985. (Burniston Studios Ltd)*

s.s. BENLOYAL 11,463 g.r.t. *launched in 1958 for Ben Line Steamers Ltd, Leith. Engined by David Rowan & Co. Ltd, this distinctive fast cargo liner was the first 20 knot vessel in the British merchant navy. Followed by three sisterships she emphasised Connells excellent design and build capability and set standards that only other UK and overseas companies could emulate. She was broken up in 1979. The heavy fuel oil being burned by her boilers creates a plume of smoke, more in keeping with a coal burning engine of the last century than a relatively modern steam turbine. (Burniston Studios Ltd)*

m.v. TIJUCA 5999 g.r.t. *launched in 1959 for Wilh. Wilhelmsen of Tönsberg, Norway. Engined by Barclay Curle & Co. Ltd, this stylish yet very traditional ref/cargo liner was the eighth vessel built by Connells for Wilhelmsens, as well as being the last of a total of fifteen ships built for Norway by these builders in the post-war period. She differed from her two previous sisterships with the substitution of a single mast in place of a pair of derrick posts between Nos 2 and 3 holds. All three ships carried a maximum of twelve passengers. She remained with Wilhelmsens for almost twenty years before being sold and renamed UZMA in 1977, as which she was broken up in 1979. (Burniston Studios Ltd)*

s.t. ERNE 14,244 g.r.t. *launched in 1961 for James Nourse Ltd, London. Engined by Barclay Curle & Co. Ltd, this vessel was transferred within the P & O Group to the newly formed Trident Tankers in 1963 when the flamboyant Nourse Line funnel colours were replaced by an all over black stack with a large white trident. She spent her entire life with the same name, being broken up in 1984.* (Burniston Studios Ltd)

m.v. SAINT AIDAN 973 g.r.t. *launched in 1962 for J. & A. Gardiner & Co. Ltd of Glasgow. Engined by the English Electric Co. Ltd of Newton-le-Willows, Lancashire, this coaster for the UK trade was the smallest ship ever built by Charles Connell & Co. Ltd during the post-war period. Sold and renamed in 1980 she was still trading as SAN ANDRES in 1996.* (Burniston Studios Ltd)

m.v. TUSKAR 1598 g.r.t. *launched in 1962 for the Clyde Shipping Co. Ltd, Glasgow. Engined by Nydqvist & Holm A/B of Trollhättan, Sweden, this distinctive vessel was built primarily for the transport of livestock and other perishable cargoes between the UK and Ireland. By 1968 when most of this traffic was lost to juggernauts on ferries, she was sold and renamed BRIONI which she retained until being broken up in 1988. She is seen in revenue earning service on a very misty River Mersey shortly after being handed over.* (Courtesy Clyde Shipping Co. Ltd)

m.v. JUMNA 10,051 g.r.t. *launched in 1962 for James Nourse Ltd of London. Engined by Barclay Curle & Co. Ltd, this was the eighth vessel built by Connells for James Nourse since 1946, and the eleventh for P & O Group. She was transferred within the Hain-Nourse Division of P & O and was renamed STRATHNAVER in 1977. She was sold and renamed SINGAPORE PROGRESS in 1979 before being broken up in 1985.* (Burniston Studios Ltd)

m.v. KOHINUR 10,039 g.r.t. *launched in 1962 for the New Zealand Shipping Coy Ltd, London (although ordered by the Asiatic Steam Navigation Co. Ltd, another P & O Group company). Engined by Barclay Curle & Co. Ltd, she was the last vessel built by Connells for the P & O Group, an association that lasted for a century. She was renamed STRATHNAIRN within the P & O Group in 1977 and lasted until 1986 when she was broken up as ANTILLA. Note the tradesmen working on the radar mast as the vessel performs her speed trials. (Burniston Studios Ltd)*

m.v. INVENTOR 9171 g.r.t. *launched in 1963 for the Harrison Line of Liverpool. Engined by Sulzer Bros of Winterthur, Switzerland, this unique ship had the distinction of being the first vessel built on the River Clyde with a Stülcken heavy lift derrick seen between the Nos 2 and 3 cargo holds. She saw service between the UK, Africa and India for almost two decades. After sale to Singapore owners in 1981 she was broken up at Kaohsiung in 1985. (Burniston Studios Ltd)*

m.v. SCOTSTOUN 11,457 g.r.t. *launched in 1963 for Falkland Shipowners Ltd (J. & J. Denholm Ltd), Glasgow. Engined by J.G. Kincaid & Co. Ltd, this functional low-cost cargo vessel was virtually identical to the m.v. BENDEARG which was the next ship built at Scotstoun. Sold and renamed BORDATXOA in 1972 she was broken up in 1985 as the JAY BABA (Burniston Studios Ltd)*

motor bulk carrier ROMANDIE 21,449 g.r.t. *launched in 1964 for Suisse-Atlantique Soc. D'Arm. Mar. SA of Basle, Switzerland. Engined by Barclay Curle & Co. Ltd, this ship was the first bulk carrier built by Chas Connell & Co. Ltd. She was sold and renamed DELFI in 1984 being broken up a year later under that name. (Burniston Studios Ltd)*

This page depicts four elegant and well-proportioned fast cargo liners designed and built by Connells for their most loyal post-war customer, Ben Line Ltd of Edinburgh.

Above. m.v. BENLEDI 11,758 g.r.t. *launched in 1965 for Ben Line Steamers Ltd. Engined by Barclay Curle & Co. Ltd, this vessel was the pinnacle of achievement between Connells and the Ben Line. With a service speed of 21.5 knots, triple hatches at holds 3 and 4, this ship effectively started the containerisation trend, as the tween decks at these holds created rectangular cargo stowage space between the two longitudinal bulkheads. She was sold and renamed DA NOLI in 1972, and had further name changes before being broken up in 1987 as TINA.* (Burniston Studios Ltd)

Above. m.v. BENWYVIS 11,959 g.r.t. *launched in 1966 for Ben Line Steamers Ltd. Engined by Barclay Curle & Co. Ltd, this vessel was the second of the Benledi class. She was sold by Ben Line Ltd to Italian owners in 1972 and renamed DA RECCO, being broken up in Italy in 1979, which was a very short life for such a modern vessel.* (Burniston Studios Ltd)

Right. m.v. BENALBANACH 11,466 g.r.t. *launched in 1967 for Ben Line Steamers Ltd. Engined by Barclay Curle & Co. Ltd, this handsome fast cargo liner had a very short career with Ben Line, becoming a victim to the twin rages of high fuel costs and containerisation. She was sold to Italian owners in 1972 and renamed DA VERRAZANO, being broken up in 1988 as GLINT. Note the three transverse hatches at holds 3 and 4, which was a feature of the four sisterships of the Benledi class.*

m.v. BENSTAC 12,011 g.r.t. *launched in 1967 for Ben Line Steamers Ltd. Engined by Barclay Curle & Co. Ltd, this vessel was a derivative of the earlier Connell built BENDEARG launched in 1964. As yard no. 512, BENSTAC was the last shipbuilding contract completed by Chas Connell & Co. Ltd. Two further Connell orders for the Ben Line were completed by Upper Clyde Shipbuilders Ltd, Scotstoun Division: BENCRUACHAN launched in 1968, and BENLAWERS launched in 1970. BENSTAC was sold and renamed JOHN P in 1982 and sank off Brazil under that name in April 1985.* (Burniston Studios Ltd)

m.v. BENLAWERS 12,784 g.r.t. *launched in 1970 by the Scotstoun Division of Upper Clyde Shipbuilders Ltd for Ben Line Steamers Ltd. Engined by Barclay Curle & Co. Ltd, this fast cargo liner (21.5 knots) had a relatively short career with Ben Line being sold and renamed GLOBE EXPRESS in 1978. She was later resold and converted to the livestock carrier UNICEB, as which she sank in the Indian Ocean during September 1996 whilst in transit from Freemantle to Aqaba with a cargo of 67,488 live sheep. They were all lost with the ship after a fire broke out in her engine room and gradually engulfed the entire vessel.* (Glasgow University Archives)

m.v. CITY OF LONDON 9793 g.r.t. *launched in 1970 for Ellerman Lines Ltd, London. Engined by Barclay Curle & Co. Ltd, this ship was one of three sisters, the other two built by Robb-Caledon Ltd at Dundee. Arguably amongst the most well proportioned ships built by UCS Ltd at Scotstoun, this 18 knot liner was sold to Greek owners in 1981 and tramped for a few years before being broken up in 1988 as SEA LORD.* (Courtesy Dr William Lind)

m.v. SIG RAGNE 11,857 g.r.t. *launched in 1970 for J. & J. Denholm (Mgt) Ltd, Glasgow. Engined by G. Clark/NEM Ltd, this ship was the first 'Clyde class' of handy-sized semi-container/cargo liner built by UCS Ltd at their Scotstoun Division. Only seven ships were built to this design, two at Scotstoun and five at Clydebank. The concept and hull form was later modified to create the 'Kuwait class' of cargo liner built by Govan Shipbuilders at Govan and Scotstoun in the late '70s. Sold and renamed AGIOS NIKOLAS in 1979 she was later resold with many changes of name, being still in existence (along with her other six sisterships) in 1996 as the LADY ANAIS. Despite their tardy construction schedule these 'Clyde class' cargo liners have proved able and durable competitors to the ubiquitous SD14s.* (Glasgow University Archives)

motor bulk carrier HARFLEUR 16,715 g.r.t. *launched in 1973 by Scotstoun Marine Ltd for J. & C. Harrison Ltd, London. Engined by Harland & Wolff Ltd, Belfast, this Cardiff class bulk carrier was the second of a pair built for these British owners during the early years of Scotstoun Marine Ltd, a wholly owned subsidiary of Govan Shipbuilders Ltd. Subsequently sold and renamed, this vessel was still trading in 1996 as the* ARHON. (Glasgow University Archives)

m.v. LOCH LOMOND 10,397 g.r.t. *launched in 1974 for joint ownership by Chas Connell & Co. Ltd and J. & J. Denholm Ltd (Glenfar Shipping Co. Ltd). Engined by J.G. Kincaid & Co. Ltd, this fully refrigerated cargo liner was one of a pair ordered by the family of the previous owners of the Scotstoun Marine shipyard. Their faith in the future of the now nationalised yard with this order gave some breathing space during which time the fate of the company was being discussed. Sold and renamed* AL ZAHRA *in 1981, subsequently resold and renamed she was still trading in 1996 as the* PACIFIC KORU. (Courtesy Dr William Lind)

m.v. ARAFAT 15,387 g.r.t. *launched in 1977 for the United Arab Shipping Co. Ltd, Kuwait. Engined by J.G. Kincaid & Co. Ltd, this was the fifth of six similar vessels built for these owners by Scotstoun Marine Ltd between 1976 and 1978. This ship was still trading as* ARAFAT *in 1996. The Stülcken derrick on most of these vessels enabled the regular transport of heavy equipment from Europe, the USA and Japan to the countries in the Persian Gulf.* (Glasgow University Archives)

m.v. GNIEZNO II 2995 g.r.t. *launched in 1978 for Polska Zegluga Movska (Polish Steamship Coy). Engined by Zgoda Zaklady Uvzadzen Technicznych, this mini bulk carrier was the first of seven similar vessels built by Scotstoun Marine Ltd in the late 1970s for the above owners. A total of thirteen similar ships were built by the River Clyde shipyards of British Shipbuilders Ltd: three at Govan, two at Fergusons and one at Ailsa—all with minor cargo-handling modifications.* GNIEZNO II *was still trading in 1996.* (Glasgow University Archives)

BARCLAY CURLE & CO LTD	**1855-1967 end of shipbuilding**
	1974 end of ship repairing
	1982 end of engine building

This Company possessed five different work sites in Glasgow which were managed since 1912 by three separate divisions of the owning Newcastle marine conglomerate of Swan Hunter and Whigham Richardson Ltd. The English parent company were very supportive in terms of allocation of work and authorisation of working capital, with which to finance modernisation schemes at their Scottish subsidiaries whilst the industry was booming, and healthy returns were made on such investment.

Comprising the Clydeholm Shipyard with the adjoining North British Marine Engine Works, this combined site was one kilometre long and formed a narrow rectangle between the north bank of the River Clyde and South Street being further bordered by the access to the Whiteinch ferry to the east, and the Charles Connell shipyard to the west. Further down-river at Elderslie, the company owned three drydocks, mould loft, plating, fabrication, machining and outfit sheds with a waterfront of quays, all served by electric travelling cranes of limited but adequate lifting capacity. This extensive ship repair facility was the largest non-naval site in Scotland.

Assured captive markets existed for the initial drydock surveys prior to handover, of most newly completed ships, which in the post-war boom era were being completed at a rate of more than one per week from all of the then operating shipyards on the River Clyde. This niche was extensively supplemented by the passing trade in mainly conventional cargo liners that regularly used the port of Glasgow, needing routine as well as essential maintenance, modification or marine survey work. A further repair facility existed at Whitefield Road in Govan. Utilising the three adjacent graving docks which were owned by the Clyde Navigation Trust, this section of the company handled minor deck and machinery repairs as well as tank, boiler and hull cleaning work. Both locations employed a total of over 1000 workers for nearly three decades.

The firm invested in a new 680 ft long ∞ 95 ft wide graving dock at Elderslie in the early 1960s. Unfortunately this facility was never fully utilised for extensive marine conversion work. The site gradually became a victim of its isolated geography, as much as it was of the decline in its traditional markets, and the contraction of shipbuilding on the upper reaches of the river. The Newcastle parent group retained their Clydeside ship repair facilities for as long as they could see some financial return, however, by the early 1970s, activity and profit were ghosts of the former industry. The extensive Elderslie complex was sold in 1974 to the then expanding adjacent Yarrow concern who continued to drydock the new vessels of Govan Shipbuilders Ltd. Although the graving docks at Govan were used for a few more years by the independent Clyde Dock Engineering Co Ltd, commercial ship repairing effectively ceased on the River Clyde when this company closed in the early 1980s.

The Clydeholm shipyard at Whiteinch was the most enigmatic establishment on the River Clyde. Bereft of substantial post-war capital expenditure on anything other than welding transformers and rectifiers, it managed to cope successfully with a varied output of two to four ships a year from four open building berths, irrespective of the ship types constructed. In the period between 1946 and 1967, 51 ships were built at the Clydeholm yard, amounting to 513,065 g.r.t., of which only 19% were for export. This total comprised 38 cargo liners, seven oil tankers, one large troop carrier, two large passenger liners, two bulk carriers and one dredger. The most valuable regular customer of the company was the P & O Group, especially the British Indian Steam Navigation Co Ltd, who took delivery of 25 ships during this time.

Between 1946 and 1960, traditional single frame, single plate erection techniques supplemented with very minor unit fabrications including Isherwood tanker sections were assembled in corrugated iron huts. These components were transported by trailer or lorry to beneath the array of fixed hammerhead cranes astride the building berths, where they were lifted on to the respective ship being built. This was akin to the very basic empirical method of proven traditional shipbuilding deployed throughout the UK at this time.

The good work rate, high quality of ship delivered, reasonable labour relations and profitability of Clydeholm was rewarded in kind by the Newcastle Board, in the form of authorisation of a multi-million pound investment in a completely new shipyard to be built on vacant ground between berth no. 4 and the North British Marine Engine Works. The new shipyard was approved in the late 1950s, was designed and supervised by the Glasgow civil engineering company of Babtie, Shaw & Morton Ltd, and effectively pronounced open with the launch of the cargo motor ship, *City of Sidney* 10,551 g.r.t., for Ellerman Lines on 24 May 1960. Whilst the new yard was being hewn out of the derelict adjacent ground, that had been the former Jordan Vale shipyard, shipbuilding work continued apace on the existing traditional berths. The modernised concern comprised two berths of 700 and 800 ft long, each with four then state-of-the-art electric travelling hammerhead cranes designed and built by Sir Wm Arrol & Co Ltd. The heaviest pair were capable of lifting 60 tons each and 100 tons total using tandem lift facilities. The brand new stockyard, preparation, plating and fabrication facilities were augmented with separate buildings for joinery, electrical and plumbing work with a custom built template loft, all of which were south facing with excellent natural lighting, as well as a good dry working environment. Worker's canteen, separate offices and stores, with some of these utilising the space created beneath the new reinforced concrete berths and crane tracks, were all improvements to the accepted norm of poor working conditions and lack of amenities. The whole project cost in excess of £3 million when completed and was the envy of the entire shipbuilding workforce on the upper Clyde. One vessel was completed from the traditional building berths after the inauguration of the new facility, thereafter after all ships completed at Clydeholm were launched from the new slipways.

The euphoria surrounding the very public proclamation of this new resource was not endorsed by an influx of orders from the parent group. Theoretically capable of building three to four medium-sized cargo liners per calendar year, the new yard struggled to build two. For five years the shipyard only launched one vessel per annum, although one of these was a motor supertanker of 38,996 g.r.t. for the P & O Group, called the *Opawa*, launched on 13 July 1964. This was the largest vessel ever built at Clydeholm. The on-site drawing office closed in 1965 and the shipyard reverted to single shift working. The total number of employees dwindled to around 500. What management that remained were either incapable of motivating the labour force or, as was generally perceived at the time, were under surreptitious instruction to run the facility down. Existing on a contract at a time basis, with shop drawings prepared on Tyneside by the parent group, the labour force remarkably continued their long tradition of loyalty to the firm and completed all contracts on or about their required delivery dates, with no public utterances from ship-owners about defective or tardy new ships.

By the time the Norwegian motor bulk carrier *Hamlet* 29,256 g.r.t. was launched on the beautiful autumn day of 8 September 1967, the formal announcement of cessation of shipbuilding at Clydeholm had been made public. The bamboozlement surrounding the considerable investment in the yard, lack of will on the part of the parent company, and attrition of workload was the subject of much recondite conjecture amongst not only the workers of Barclay Curle but also other shipyard employees along Clydeside. That ostensibly the most modern yard on the upper reaches of the Clyde should be abandoned, when the other extant shipbuilders were in dire need of further investment, remained a controversial and inexplicable caveat of UK capitalism. Aware of this outcry the Newcastle owners offered the yard to the designate embryo board of UCS but this was rejected, either in terms of over valuation, no justification for the capacity, or the equally implausible hyperbole...the new shipyard was a white elephant! This last comment was always vehemently refuted by the Barclay Curle labour force, yet the abysmal final output statistics from the facility always invited such criticism.

Shortly after sail away of the last ship, systematic dismantling of the yard commenced, with the parent company the net beneficiary through the acquisition of selective items of the modern plant. Some of the former outfit buildings still existed in 1996, being used by a host of small business enterprises in what is now called the Clydeholm industrial estate. A further nostalgic connection with the sites shipbuilding past is the naming of streets within the complex after some former famous ships built by Barclay Curle & Co Ltd.

The first British marine diesel engine built and successful installed in a motor ship was achieved by Barclay Curle & Co Ltd prior to the start of the first world war. Built to the design of the Danish engineers Burmeister & Wain of Copenhagen, this was the precursor of over half a century's output from the Whiteinch plant, which was later called The North British Engine Works. The association with Burmeister & Wain did not last too long. By the end of World War II, Barclay Curle were firmly established as one the many UK licensed builders of the engine designs of Wm Doxford & Sons (Eng) Ltd of Sunderland. Towards the end of the 1950s, this specific licenceship was augmented with one for the products of Sulzer Bros of Switzerland, which later became the preferred engine type to build at Whiteinch. Occasional steam turbine contracts were also undertaken at the works.

At Kelvinhaugh Street, Finnieston, Barclay Curle built large water-tube boilers under licence to Foster Wheeler, Babcock & Wilcox and Yarrow. These works also performed hot forging of boiler ends and combustion chambers as well as manufacture of hydraulic couplings, high pressure storage vessels and the fabrication of ancillary marine engine equipment including funnels, ventilation trunking, silencers and pipework.

Output increased at both locations to meet the demand from the Clydeholm shipyard as well as that of the adjoining Charles Connell & Co Ltd, who had more than 70% of their motor ships engined by Barclay Curle. This was a mutually acceptable agreement for both firms. The Scotstoun shipbuilder did not possess an outfit quayside, therefore their newly launched ships could be moored alongside the North British Engine wharf, beneath Barclay Curle's 150-ton fixed hammerhead crane, where engines and auxiliaries would be installed, concurrent with the completion of the remaining fitting-out work. Other customers also made use of these facilities.

The quality of the finished marine engine product built at Whiteinch was 'second to none'! This ubiquitous plaudit, also frequently bestowed on virtually every other Clydeside marine engine builder, was tarnished only latterly by the teething troubles encountered on the prototype design of steam turbines which were installed in the QE2, built by John Brown & Co (Clydebank) Ltd to a design of PAMETRADA of Wallsend, England.

The North British Marine Engine Works evaded the closure of the adjoining Clydeholm shipyard in 1967, continuing to supply the latest design of Sulzer marine engines to its parent company in Newcastle, as well as Scotstoun Marine Limited, and a few other UK shipbuilders. It survived as a marine engine building entity to be included in the formation of British Shipbuilders in 1977 and persisted to supply a reduced volume of engines to an ever decreasing number of UK shipbuilders.

When engine building ceased in 1982, the works retained full use of the machinery and erection bays then used for the construction of missile launching units for installation in warships on order at shipyards throughout Britain for the Royal Navy. Shortly after engine building terminated, the North British design office produced plans for a 'constant speed generator' to be included in a marine engine driven by swash plate control and an epicyclic gear-box. This refinement would supply electric power to a ship whilst in transit, diesel auxiliary power only being needed when the vessel was still in port. Unfortunately for Barclay Curle, Sulzer Bros used this highly innovative Clyde designed idea which is now fitted as standard to their engine types.

British Shipbuilders Ltd finally relinquished ownership and involvement with the works in 1985. The facility was sold off, much of the machine tools were resold and part of the site became the subject of a management buyout. A few fractions of the facility are presently occupied by a number of small independent trading companies. Virtually the entire site is still dominated by the large former engine erecting shed, its adjoining buildings and stockyard. The location continues to be referred to as the North British engine works, the riverside front of which still bore the name Barclay Curle & Co Ltd in 1996. Part of the drawing office was briefly occupied by the European office of The American Bureau of Shipping.

List of ships built by BARCLAY CURLE & Co Ltd, Whiteinch, between 1946 and closure in 1967

YEAR	NAME		TYPE	COUNTRY OF REGISTRATION	G.R.T.	TOTAL G.R.T.
1946 •	EUCADIA	m.	Cargo/Pass	Britain	7142	
	LANDAURA	m.	Cargo	Britain	7289	
	DUMRA	m.	Ref/C/P	Britain	4867	
•	SANGOLA	m.	Ref/C/P	Britain	8647	27945
1947	CITY OF JOHANNESBURG	m.	Cargo	Britain	8207	
	SOUDAN	m.	Ref/C/P	Britain	9080	
	DARA	m.	Ref/C/P	Britain	5030	22317
1948	SOMALI	m.	Ref/C/P	Britain	9080	
	CARPENTARIA	m.	Ref/Cargo	Britain	7268	
	CANNANORE	m.	Ref/Cargo	Britain	7065	
	COROMANDEL	m.	Ref/Cargo	Britain	7065	30478
1949	BRAESIDE	m.	Ref/Cargo	Britain	5867	
	CHANDPARA	m.	Ref/Cargo	Britain	7274	
	CHANTALA	m.	Ref/Cargo	Britain	7556	20697
1950	DARESSA	m.	Ref/C/P	Britain	5180	
	SANTHIA	m.	Ref/C/P	Britain	8908	
	KENYA	s.	Passenger	Britain	14464	28552
1951	POLARBRIS	m.	Oil Tanker	Norway	12551	
	CHAKDARA	m.	Ref/Cargo	Britain	7132	
	MALEKULA	m.	Ref/Cargo	Britain	3786	23469
1952 •	UGANDA	s.	Passenger	Britain	14430	
•	WINDSOR	m.	Cargo	Britain	7652	
	CHINKOA	m.	Ref/Cargo	Britain	7102	
	POLARTANK	m.	Oil Tanker	Norway	12651	41835
1953	NUDDEA	s.	Ref/Cargo	Britain	8596	
	ARAFURA	s.	Ref/Cargo	Britain	8775	17371
1954	SOLSTEN	m.	Oil Tanker	Norway	10251	
•	POLARPRINS	m.	Oil Tanker	Norway	12453	22704
1955 •	CITY OF COLOMBO	m.	Cargo	Britain	7739	
•	NEVASA	s.	Troopship	Britain	20527	28266

YEAR	NAME		TYPE	COUNTRY OF REGISTRATION	G.R.T.	TOTAL G.R.T.
1956	NARDANA	s.	Ref/Cargo	Britain	8511	
•	WOODARRA	s.	Cargo	Britain	8753	17264
1957	WAROONGA	s.	Cargo	Britain	8753	
	WEYBRIDGE	m.	Cargo	Britain	9221	17974
1958 •	WIMBLEDON	m.	Cargo	Britain	9223	
•	HURRICANE	m.	Oil Tanker	Norway	12909	22132
1959	TREVAYLOR	m.	Cargo	Britain	6501	6501
1960 •	ATHELQUEEN	m.	Oil Tanker	Britain	13040	
•	CITY OF SYDNEY	m.	Ref/Cargo	Britain	10551	
•	WILLESDEN	m.	Cargo	Britain	8556	32147
1961	HOPECREST	m.	Cargo	Britain	7610	
•	CITY OF CANBERRA	m.	Ref/Cargo	Britain	10543	18153
1962	HOPEPEAK	m.	Cargo	Britain	7457	7457
1963 •	HOPECRAG	m.	Cargo	Britain	7308	
•	CITY OF ADELAIDE	m.	Ref/Cargo	Britain	10551	17819
1964 •	OPAWA	m.	Oil Tanker	Britain	38996	38996
1965 •	NAKWA RIVER	m.	Cargo	Ghana	7447	
•	PORT BURNIE	m.	Ref/Cargo	Britain	8374	15821
1966 •	NEEDWOOD	m.	Suction Dredger	Britain	1567	
	VITKOVICE	m.	Bulk Carrier	Czecho-slovakia	24344	25911
1967 •	HAMLET	m.	Bulk Carrier	Norway	29256	29256

19% export
81% Britain   51 vessels total = 513,065 g.r.t.

• Indicates vessel depicted in subsequent photographic section or another chapter of the book.

For explanation of abbreviations see Glossary on page 345.

The following set of photographs illustrates the locations of the former Barclay Curle & Co. Ltd Clydeholm shipyard, North British marine engine works and repair docks at Elderslie and Govan, as well as depicting construction activity at these places. Appended to this are trials photographs of some of the different types of merchant vessels built by the company in its last two decades of operation.

The recently extended and piled fitting-out quay complete with new 15-ton travelling hammerhead crane of Barclay Curle & Co Ltd, in the spring of 1960. The large set of buildings on the right belongs to the North British marine engine works, part of the same company. The massive 150-ton fixed hammerhead crane was used to install engines and boilers into new ships moored underneath. Note the pair of intrepid riggers dressing the foremast of m.t. ATHELQUEEN 13,040 g.r.t. launched by the same yard on 13 January that year. In the distance, some of the cranes of the Scotstoun shipyard of Charles Connell & Co Ltd can be seen. The pronounced knuckle on the new quayside in the foreground was designed to prevent large vessels built in the no. 6 berth at the Clydeholm shipyard from damaging the port side of their hull when they were launched, then skewed into the River Clyde by the action of drag chains.

The Barclay Curle Clydeholm shipyard during the height of extensive redevelopment circa 1959 looking north-west. This photograph shows from the bottom right, yard no. 743 m.t. ATHELQUEEN 13,040 g.r.t. on berth no. 2, yard no. 746 m.v. WILLESDEN 8556 g.r.t. on berth no. 4, and bottom shell plating of yard no. 744 m.v. CITY OF SYDNEY on berth no. 5. Civil engineering work is well under way throughout the yard. Noticeable are the new outfit trades building, steel stockyard, fabrication shed and erection of the first 60-ton crane on one of the two new crane tracks. The temporary sheds on berth no. 1 were the then main locations for small unit sub-assemblies. The hotch-potch layout of the old yard is in stark contrast to the new facility. Adjoining the Clydeholm shipyard is the North British Engine Works and fitting-out quay, with the m.v. BROOMPARK 8084 g.r.t. recently launched by the adjacent Scotstoun shipyard of Charles Connell & Co Ltd moored alongside. This neighbouring shipyard is also undergoing modernisation with extension of their fabrication shed, large berth and erection of new 60-ton crane underway. On the south side of the river, the Alexander Stephen shipyard has under construction from left to right: m.t. BRITISH CURLEW 11,157 g.r.t., m.v. CHATHAM 3563 g.r.t., s.t. MOBIL ACME 12,755 g.r.t. and HMS LOWESTOFT 2150 tons displacement. In the bottom right hand corner one of the CNT vehicular ferries chugs from Whiteinch to Linthouse. Noticeable in this view of the west end of Glasgow is the omission of the number of high rise flats built in the early 1960s.

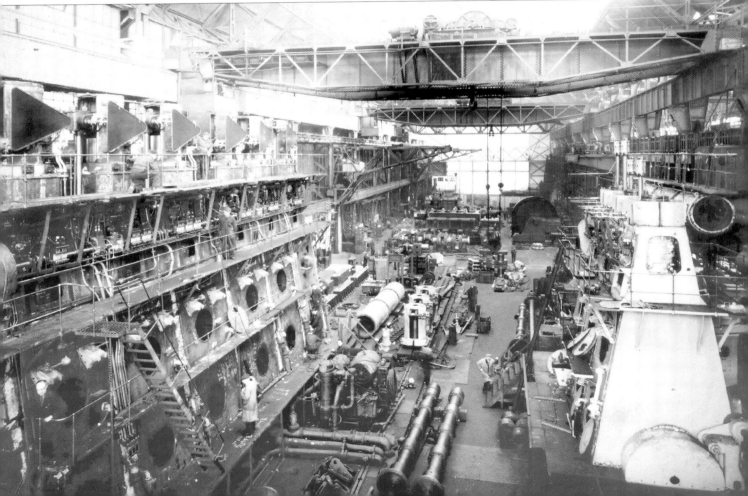

Previous page, top. *Bowler hats, homburgs, fedoras, fur coats and a veritable cornucopia of outfits not redolent of shipbuilding attire are present in great numbers at the Clydeholm shipyard of Barclay Curle & Co Ltd on 30 November 1955. Included in the illustrious list of guests is the then Lord Provost of Glasgow at the occasion of at the launch of the steam turbine troopship NEVASA 20,527 g.r.t. for the British India Steam Navigation Co Ltd, London. The bottle of champagne is carefully being held (to prevent premature breakage) by the gent in the overcoat and bunnet to the left of the platform.*

Previous page, bottom. *An impressive array of diesel engines and various components in the engine erecting hall of Barclay Curle & Co Ltd, North British Marine Engine Works, Whiteinch, during 1960. Various personnel give some idea of scale not only to the large engines, but also the miscellaneous parts.*

Next page, top. *The three Clyde Navigation Trust dry docks at Govan looking west circa 1959. None of the vessels in dock were built on the River Clyde, but all are undergoing repair or survey by Barclay Curle & Co Ltd. In the left background can be seen the forest of cranes that was the Govan shipyard of Harland & Wolff Ltd, with the recently launched m.v. BANKURA 6793 g.r.t. fitting out. An Anchor Line 'T' class motor ship is berthed at Yorkhill Quay on the north bank of the river. In the centre distance can be seen the derricks of A. & J. Inglis Ltd Pointhouse yard on the east bank of the River Kelvin. A CNT passenger ferry plies between Yorkhill and Govan in the middle of the river. This location is no longer associated with ship-repairing or shipbuilding, however this site is continually considered as a possible site for some type of maritime heritage centre that might regale Glasgow's glorious association with these former major industries.*

Next page, bottom. *Bridge and wheelhouse unit for ship no. 744 m.v. CITY OF SYDNEY 10,551 g.r.t. is comfortably lifted into place by one of the 60-ton travelling hammerhead cranes recently installed at Barclay Curle & Co Ltd, Clydeholm shipyard early in 1960. Both of the giant cranes were dismantled and re-erected in the North-east of England in sister companies of Swan Hunter & Wigham Richardson Ltd, after the Whiteinch yard closed in 1967. Noticeable in this view are the wide roadways from the prefabrication shed to the building berths that made transport of large prefabricated units relatively easy.*

Below. *The Elderslie dry dock and repair quay facility of Barclay Curle & Co Ltd looking north, circa 1959, showing the two existing dry docks and adjacent repair quays. The oil tanker in the centre dock is the recently completed m.t. HURRICANE 12,909 g.r.t. launched in 1958 from the sister Clydeholm shipyard undergoing some work on her hull prior to commencement of sea trials. A plume of smoke can be seen from a steam locomotive shunting at the busy railway yard at Scotstoun West.*

Above. Ship no. 744 m.v. CITY OF SYDNEY 10,551 g.r.t. *prior to launching from the modernised berth no. 5 of the Clydeholm shipyard of Barclay Curle & Co Ltd on 24 May 1960. Yard workers, guests and motor cars are much in evidence in this photograph, which should have heralded a renaissance of Clyde shipbuilding. On the left hand side on berth no. 4 is the carcass of* ship no. 746, m.v. WILLESDEN 8556 g.r.t. *still being built using traditional single-frame and plate erection methods. Beyond is the double-bottom of* ship no. 745 m.v. HOPECREST 7610 g.r.t. *on berth no. 6, whilst leaving the North British Engine Works quay is the recently completed yard no. 743 m.t. ATHELQUEEN 13,040 g.r.t. departing to commence sea trials.*

Below. *Steelwork prefabrication activity at the Clydeholm shipyard of Barclay Curle & Co Ltd during late 1960. Noticeable under construction are superstructure sections left centre, and an aft-end unit all for ship no. 745 m.v. HOPECREST 7610 g.r.t., which was launched in 1961. The spacious well-lit fabrication shop with two tiers of overhead electric travelling cranes was a vast improvement on the yard's previous temporary sheds.*

Above. *The new 680 ft long ∞ 95 ft wide drydock under construction at Elderslie for Barclay Curle & Co Ltd during 1965. Re-erection of the pair of Butters mono-tower electric travelling cranes from the former Wm Denny & Bros shipyard are noticeable on either side of the dock. The two existing Elderslie dry docks are currently in use by the* m.v. HINDUSTAN *built in West Germany and an unidentified liner.*

Previous page, top. *Yard no. 750, m.v. CITY OF ADELAIDE 10,511 g.r.t. immediately after her launch from the modernised Clydeholm shipyard of Barclay Curle & Co Ltd on 22 August 1963. This refrigerated cargo liner was the third of a series built for Ellerman Lines Ltd in the early 1960s by the Whiteinch company. Unfortunately, she was the last ship built for these owners by Barclay Curle & Co Ltd, an association which had lasted many decades and saw five ships built at Whiteinch in the post-war period.*

Previous page, bottom. *Yard no. 751, m.t. OPAWA 38,996 g.r.t. prior to launching from the Clydeholm shipyard of Barclay Curle & Co Ltd on 17 July 1964. At her time of launching this supertanker was the largest ship built in the City of Glasgow. Constructed for the newly formed Trident Tankers Ltd, a subsidiary of the P & O Group, she was engined by J.G. Kincaid & Co Ltd, Greenock. Originally ordered from the Newcastle parent firm of Swan Hunter & Wigham Richardson Ltd, she was transferred to Scotland because her owners wanted a quick delivery! She remained within P & O until 1974 when she was sold and renamed ANANGEL FRIENDSHIP, being broken up under that name in 1984. Note the double-bottom units for yard no. 752, m.v. NAKWA RIVER 7447 g.r.t. stretching almost the entire length of the adjacent no. 5 berth.*

Next page, top. *A new forward-mid-ship section built up-river at the Clydeholm shipyard is floated into position against the cut-off aft section of the s.t. HAMILTON SLEIGH in the largest Elderslie dry dock during 1966. All of the work for this lengthening contract was undertaken by Barclay Curle & Co Ltd. Note the difference between the original hull's riveted plates and the all-welded new ship section. The bow section of the vessel can be seen in the background.*

Next page, bottom, left. *The entire bow section of yard no. 2023, the twin screw suction dredger NEEDWOOD 1567 g.r.t. is lowered onto the berth at Barclay Curle & Co Ltd, Clydeholm shipyard in 1966. On the adjacent berth, yard no. 2020, the bulk carrier VITKOVICE is under construction for Czechoslovakian owners. The paint burn on the vessel's shell plating indicates good penetration of welds joining the transverse frames and bulk-heads. This dredger has out-lasted all other vessels built at the Clydeholm shipyard.*

Next page, bottom, right. *The last ship built by Barclay Curle & Co Ltd, yard no. 2027 (Swan Hunter Group number) m.v. HAMLET 29,256 g.r.t. prior to launching in September 1967. The faired and shaped bulbous bow clearly depicts the skill and artistry of the Clydeholm platers, loftsmen, shipwrights and welders who built this fine, yet final bulk carrier.*

m.v. EUCADIA 7142 g.r.t. *launched in 1946 for the Anchor Line Ltd, Glasgow. Engined by Barclay Curle & Co Ltd, this vessel was the last of three Clyde-built sister ships (Lithgows Ltd constructed the other two). With their limited passenger accommodation for 12, all three ships were used between the UK and North America, as well as to India. EUCADIA was sold and renamed IONIAN in 1963. She ran aground and broke up at Ras Beirut in November 1964 as the MACEDON.*

t.s.m.v. SANGOLA 8647 g.r.t. *launched in 1946 for the British India Steam Navigation Co Ltd, London. Engined by Barclay Curle & Co Ltd, this traditional passenger/cargo liner was a novel type of immediate post-war vessel in that she possessed a pair of diesel engines. She was broken up in Japan in 1963. (P & O Library Archive)*

m.v. WINDSOR 7652 g.r.t. *launched in 1952 for the Britain Steam Ship Co Ltd, London. Engined by Barclay Curle & Co Ltd, this handsome and futuristic motor ship without either foc'sle or poop decks was the first of four distinctive vessels built for these owners by Barclay Curle & Co Ltd between 1952 and 1960. She is shown leaving the North British Engine works wharf prior to trials in 1952. Sold and renamed JAG KETU in 1963, she later became the EASTERN LION in 1967 and remained in existence until 1991.*

m.t. POLARPRINS 12,453 g.r.t. *launched in 1954 for Melsom & Melsom A/S of Larvik Norway. Engined by Barclay Curle & Co Ltd, this well proportioned oil tanker was the third vessel built at Clydeholm in the early 1950s for these Norwegian owners. She was sold and renamed KAVO AETOS in 1968, retaining that name until being broken up in 1974.*

m.v. CITY OF COLOMBO 7739 g.r.t. *launched in 1955 for Ellerman Lines Ltd, London. Engined by Barclay Curle & Co Ltd, this conventional 'three island' cargo liner was sold to the Ben Line in 1977 and renamed BENMOHR, as which she was broken up at Kaohsiung in 1979.*

t.s.s.s. NEVASA 20,527 g.r.t. *launched in 1955 for the British India Steam Navigation Co Ltd, London. Engined by Barclay Curle & Co Ltd, she was built as a troop-ship for charter to HM Government. She later became well known as an educational cruise ship, ferrying many British schoolchildren round Europe on special charters until withdrawn in the mid 1970s. She was broken up in 1975.*

s.s. WOODARRA 8753 g.r.t. *launched in 1956 for the British India Steam Navigation Co Ltd, London. Engined by Barclay Curle & Co Ltd, this traditional looking cargo liner was the second last of a total of 71 vessels built by Barclay Curle & Co Ltd for the British India Steam Navigation Co Ltd over nearly a century. She was sold and renamed BENALBANACH in 1974, then broken up as that in 1978.*

m.v. WIMBLEDON 9223 g.r.t. *launched in 1958 for the Britain Steam Ship Co Ltd, London. Engined by Barclay Curle & Co Ltd, this distinctive motor vessel became the PORT WIMBLEDON very shortly after her completion in 1960. However, she reverted to WIMBLEDON in 1965. She was resold in 1967 and renamed SWAT, as which she was broken up in 1982. Along with her sister ship, WEYBRIDGE 9221 g.r.t., also built for the same owners by Barclay Curle & Co Ltd in 1957, this pair were arguably the most original looking ships built on the Clyde in the post-war era.*

m.t. HURRICANE 12,909 g.r.t. *launched in 1958 for Tönsberg Rederi A/S of Norway. Engined by the Wallsend Slipway & Eng Co Ltd, this conventional oil tanker possesses a stylish funnel that seems out of character with the ship's vertical superstructure. Sold and renamed PRIMA in 1970, she retained that name until being broken up in 1976.*

m.t. ATHELQUEEN 13,040 g.r.t. *launched in 1960 for the Athel Line Ltd, Liverpool. Engined by Barclay Curle & Co Ltd, this very traditional looking vessel belied the more modern styles of other tankers then being built by River Clyde shipyards. Sold and renamed ANCO QUEEN in 1971, she underwent further changes of ownership before being broken up in 1981 as SANIKA.*

m.v. WILLESDEN 8556 g.r.t. *launched in 1960 for the Britain Steam Ship Co Ltd, London. Engined by Barclay Curle & Co Ltd, this sleek motor vessel was the last ship built at Clydeholm for these owners. Sold and renamed GEORGI SAVA RAKOVSKI in 1962, she retained that name until being broken up in 1984.*

Below. m.v. HOPECRAG 7308 g.r.t. *launched in 1963 for Hopemount Shipping Co Ltd, Newcastle and engined by Barclay Curle & Co Ltd. This vessel was the last in a series of three built at Clydeholm for these owners. Bearing uncanny resemblance to the layout, lines and style of the 'Austin & Pickersgill SD14', which she and her sisters predated by a number of years, the comparison ends when it is noted the Clydeside yard built its three sister ships in three years, whereas its Wearside competitor built its design at the rate of nearly one a month! Sold and renamed ELENI E.F. in 1971, she was broken up in 1985 as the BLUE BAY.*

Above. m.v. CITY OF CANBERRA 10,543 g.r.t. *launched in 1961 for Ellerman Lines Ltd, London. Engined by Barclay Curle & Co Ltd, this vessel became a victim of containerisation of her traditional UK-Australia route which resulted in her sale to Singapore owners who renamed her TASGOLD before selling her for scrap in 1980.*

m.v. NAKWA RIVER 7447 g.r.t. *launched in 1965 for the Black Star Line Ltd, Takoradi, Ghana and engined by the Wallsend Slipway & Eng Co Ltd. This handsome cargo motor ship was the only one of a series ordered from Swan Hunter & Wigham Richardson Ltd to be built on Clydeside, all others were built on the Tyne, and all traded between the UK and West Africa. She retained her original name up until being broken up in 1984. Noticeable in the background is the mountain of Goat Fell and Glen Sannox, Isle of Arran.*

m.v. PORT BURNIE 8374 g.r.t. *launched in 1965 for Port Line Ltd, London and engined by The Wallsend Slipway & Eng Co Ltd, Newcastle. This attractive refrigerated cargo liner was sold and renamed ANGELIKI in 1972, being broken up in 1993 as the SKOPELOS. Port Line Ltd claimed to be the 'only' major British shipping line who had all their ships built in British shipyards.*

t.s. suction dredger/sand carrier NEEDWOOD 1567 g.r.t. *launched in 1966 for France, Fenwick Hoveringham (Dredging) Ltd, London. Engined by Caterpillar Diesels Ltd, Peoria, Illinois, USA, this was the first and only dredger built by Barclay Curle & Co Ltd. Sold and renamed STONE MARSHALL in 1973 she was sub-sequently resold, renamed and in 1996 was still in existence as the SEAL SANDS. This made her the longest lasting ship to be built by Barclay Curle. The large number of personnel on board are owners and builders' representatives.*

The lengthened s.t. HAMILTON SLEIGH 22,119 g.r.t. *undergoing builders' trials on the Firth of Clyde in 1966. The new prefabricated mid-ship section is noticeable forward of the bridge accommodation, where the longitudinal shell plating strake is offset either side of the new section. This lengthening work was carried out between Clydeholm and Elderslie facilities and prolonged the life of this tanker until 1979 when she was broken up as the EVANGELIA. This lengthening work also resulted in extensive modification of the vessel's attractive funnel.*

motor bulk carrier HAMLET 29,256 g.r.t. *launched in 1967 for Bruusgaard, Kïosterud Skibs A/S, Drammen, Norway. Engined by Harland & Wolff Ltd, Belfast, this well proportioned bulk carrier was the last ship built at Barclay Curle & Co Ltd, Clydeholm shipyard. This vessel was the second Clyde built ship to bear the same name (a tanker from the Blythswood SB Co Ltd in 1949 was also built for these owners). Sold and renamed MEDIOLANUM in 1972, she was broken up in 1984 as IRENES RHAPSODY.*

A. & J. INGLIS LTD   1847-1962

Located on the east side of the River Kelvin at its confluence with the River Clyde, the Pointhouse shipbuilding yard of A. & J. Inglis Ltd occupied a narrow strip of land that limited the size of vessels which could be built there. It was hemmed in between the 'Iron Bridge', a former footbridge that was appended to the structure carrying the Glasgow north bank suburban railway line over the River Kelvin, and Ferry Road which used to be the north embarkation point for the long abandoned Govan vehicular and passenger ferries. The yard was sold by its founder Dr John Inglis to Harland & Wolff Ltd of Belfast in 1919 with a pre-condition that both of his sons were employed as directors for as long as they wished to do so.

The minuscule Partick shipyard regularly turned out a mixed bag of barges, coasters, dredgers, tenders and tugs frequently interspersed with the occasional small specialised passenger ferry or small cargo liner. A successful product from the small shipyard, which would be reprehensibly abhorred today, was a series of 17 whale catcher ships built for British and Norwegian owners between 1948 and 1953. Some of these vessels were fitted with steam reciprocating engines, steering gear, stern-frame, shafting and propellers purloined from redundant former Royal Navy Flower class corvettes, which were winched up the 'Pointhouse Slip', and broken up in situ by the shipyard employees. Thirteen of these vessels were for United Whalers (UK) Ltd, who had ordered the whale factory ship *Ballena* from the parent company's Belfast shipyard and needed a complement of catchers.

Probably the most famous vessels built by A. & J. Inglis Ltd were the paddle steamers *Waverley* 632 g.r.t. and *Maid of the Loch* 555 g.r.t. The latter vessel was bolt assembled in kit form on one of the Pointhouse slipways, marked and colour coded (red for port, green for starboard), dismantled, then transported in small sections by road or rail to Balloch where the units were re-erected on British Railways repair slipway. This adaptable manufacturing technique was then possible due to the combination of riveting and bolting construction methods which were still very much in use in 1953. The completed ship was launched into Loch Lomond where she plied for many years before dwindling patronage led to her being mothballed in 1981. After many years of neglect during which she became a vandal prone hulk and nearly sank, she was bought by the former Dumbarton District Council in 1992. She is now under protracted restoration under the aegis of the Loch Lomond Steamship Company, supported by some enthusiastic volunteers and a few like-minded Scottish companies. Prior to the completion of the *Maid of the Loch*, the paddle steamer *Waverley* had been launched by the yard in 1946, although her fame was not to come to hand until the late 1970s when she became the world's last ocean going paddle steamer. She has since seen many voyages from various ports and seaside resorts throughout the UK, latterly being berthed in the City of Glasgow, where she still performs 'trips doon the watter'.

The small shipyard, whilst visibly in possession of antiquated shipbuilding hardware, regularly produced fine looking vessels that saw reliable service for their owners throughout the world. In addition to shipbuilding, the company undertook ongoing repair work on coasters and pleasure steamers that regularly plied the Firth of Clyde and UK inshore waters. These tasks were usually carried out on the patented winch operated slipway, which was a large carriage running on four rails set into a declivity berth with keel and bilge blocks mounted on its top. This system slowly enabled ships to be pulled out of the water for extensive hull examination and subsequent renovation. It was extensively upgraded in 1952 and remained in use for the next decade. Hoisting of material was performed by a few fixed Scotch derricks, with limited lifting capacity, that were located alongside the berths. Their restricted ability created only minor encumbrances, as the small types of ship constructed at Pointhouse did not generate the raising of heavy constituent components. The yard retained a set of 80-ton 'shear legs' similar to those in existence at a handful of other West of Scotland shipyards. This robust tripod-like machine helped to create a site of industrial antiquity that belied the modernity of the ships built at Pointhouse in the post-war era. This dated Edwardian lifting equipment was regularly used to assist the installation of boilers and machinery into the craft that Inglis built. Most of these engines of the steam reciprocating type were built in the yard's engine works located two miles east of the Pointhouse site at Anderston. The company also had a small boiler works which was situated north of the Iron Bridge and was latterly used as a fabrication shop. The more modern craft built by the yard tended to use diesels that were built by other UK specialist engine builders.

The shipyard fell foul of the non-Irish policy of retrenchment conjured by its parent company at the same time as its sister group repair yard of D. & W. Henderson Ltd, on the opposite bank of the River Kelvin, was also being abandoned. Both facilities stopped shipbuilding and ship repair work in 1962, respectively. The last ship built at Pointhouse was the self-propelled motor hopper barge *Aigburth* 1037 g.r.t. (yard no.1645P) built for British Transport Docks Liverpool. Despite her mundane role she was graced with a handsome futuristic profile of integrated superstructure, funnel and mast, and viewed from the waterline looked more like a coaster than a spoil vessel.

In the period from 1946 until 1962, the shipyard built 60 vessels of 33,897 g.r.t. comprising 26% for export. It employed at its peak over 600 workers during the zenith of concurrent shipbuilding and ship repairing activities of the early '50s. The largest vessel built at the yard during this period was the *m.v. Soochow* 3154 g.r.t., a refrigerated cargo passenger vessel built under subcontract from Scotts of Greenock and launched on 23 April 1947 for the China Navigation Co Ltd of London. After closure the site lay abandoned and derelict for a number of years until the buildings, cranes and shear legs were demolished to be replaced with a warehouse. The ends of the berths, slipway and part of the quayside are still discernible as relics of a former shipyard, but the River Kelvin is nowadays silted up and it is almost possible to walk from what was Inglis' yard to Hendersons' drydock across an alluvial sandbank at low tide.

List of ships built by A. & J. INGLIS Ltd, Pointhouse, between 1946 and closure in 1962

YEAR	NAME	TYPE	COUNTRY OF REGISTRATION	G.R.T.	TOTAL G.R.T.	YEAR	NAME	TYPE	COUNTRY OF REGISTRATION	G.R.T.	TOTAL G.R.T.
1946	EMPIRE TEDMUIR	s. Oil Tanker	Britain (RN)	891		1952	BUSEN 5	s. Whale Cat	Norway	588	588
	EMPIRE TEDRITA	s. Oil Tanker	Britain (RN)	891		1953 •	MAID OF ARGYLL	m. Ferry	Britain	508	
	LINSWE	m. Tug	Burma	20		•	MAID OF THE LOCH	s. Passenger	Britain	555	
	LINWET	m. Tug	Burma	20			MAID OF SKELMORLIE	m. Ferry	Britain	508	
	–	n.p. Launch	Burma	20		•	SETTER IX	m. Whale Cat	Britain	754	2325
	LINYON	m. Tug	Burma	20		1954 •	BALLYLUMFORD	s. Cargo²	Britain	1242	
	LINNO	m. Tug	Burma	20			BRAYFORD	m. SD Boat	Britain (RN)	110	
	–	n.p. Launch	Burma	20			YC 327	n.p. Lighter (barge)	Britain (RN)	561	
	LINDA	m. Tug	Burma	20			BRYANSFORD	m. SD Boat	Britain (RN)	110	2023
	LIMPYA	m. Tug	Burma	20		1955	ULSTER PREMIER	m. Cargo¹	Britain	979	
•	WAVERLEY	s.p. Passenger	Britain	693	2655		CONFIANCE	m. Tug	Britain (RN)	642	1621
1947	SOOCHOW	m. Ref/C/P	Britain	3154		1956 •	CONFIDENT	m. Tug	Britain (RN)	642	
	–	n.p. Light Vessel	Britain	100		•	LAPPE	m. Oil Tanker (tender)	Britain	165	
	–	n.p. Light Vessel	Britain	100			FLYING DUCK	m. Tug	Britain	176	
	PELORUS	m. Pilot Tender	Britain	443			FLYING DRAKE	m. Tug	Britain	177	1160
	PENLEE	m. Pilot Tender	Britain	443	4240	1957	ACCORD	m. Tug	Britain (RN)	642	
1948	GRANUAILE	s. L. Tender2	Britain	1101		•	FLYING DIPPER	m. Tug	Britain	274	916
	SETTER I	s. Whale Cat	Britain	599		1958	WAKEFIELD	m. Cargo¹	Britain	1113	
	SETTER II	s. Whale Cat	Britain	599			ADVICE	m. Tug	Britain (RN)	639	
	SETTER III	s. Whale Cat	Britain	586	2885	•	LEEDS	m. Cargo¹	Britain	1113	2865
1949	SETTER IV	s. Whale Cat	Britain	586		1959	YORK	m. Ref/Cargo¹	Britain	1095	1095
	SETTER V	s. Whale Cat	Britain	586		1960	CLYDE	m. Tug (launch)	Britain	65	65
	SETTER VI	s. Whale Cat	Britain	586		1961 •	CRESSINGTON	m. Grab HD	Britain	1431	1431
	ERNST LARSEN	s. Whale Cat	Britain	598		1962 •	AIGBURTH	m. H Barge	Britain	1037	1037
	NATALIA r/n ARNT. KARLSEN	s. Whale Cat	South Africa	598							
	AFRIKANA II	s. Res. Trawler	South Africa	882	3836						
1950	CARNARVON	s. Whale Cat	Australia	598			26% export				
	KVINT	s. Whale Cat	Britain	591	1189		74% Britain	60 vessels total = 33,897 g.r.t.			
1951	SIMBA	s. Tug	Kenya	359							
	SETTER VII	s. Whale Cat	Britain	588							
	NYATI	s. Tug	Kenya	359							
	SETTER VIII	s. Whale Cat	Britain	588							
	STAR XI	s. Whale Cat	Norway	588							
	J.K. HANSEN	s. Whale Cat	Britain	742							
	ANDERS ARVESEN	s. Whale Cat	Britain	742	3966						

¹coaster, ²collier

• Indicates vessel depicted in subsequent photographic section.

For explanation of abbreviations see Glossary on page 345.

This small set of pictures on this and the following pages show a few limited views of the former Pointhouse shipyard of A. & J. Inglis Ltd. Also included are a number of mainly trials photographs of some of the diverse range of vessels built by this adept shipbuilder in its last decade of existence.

Above. *This 1951 view of the River Kelvin looking south shows the river badly polluted and blocked by commercial shipping. On the right hand side is the ship repair quay of D. & W. Henderson Ltd, Partick, with two Lithgow built tramps belonging to Lyle Shipping moored together, both under modification. On the Pointhouse bank, two new whale catchers are being fitted-out beneath the A. & J. Inglis Ltd shear legs. In the distance are the cranes (and Ibrox Park look-alike plating shed and loft) of the Harland & Wolff Ltd Govan shipyard. All three companies were owned by Harland & Wolff Ltd of Belfast, and all firms closed between 1962 and 1963.*

Left. *t.s.m.v. MAID OF ARGYLL 508 g.r.t. seen on the famous 'Pointhouse Slip' shortly before hand-over to the Caledonian Steam Packet Co Ltd in 1953. Engined by British Polar Engines Ltd, this small ferry was built for cruising the waters of the Firth of Clyde. Noticeable in this photograph are the Inglis shear legs and the iron bridge in the left background. Sold and renamed CITY OF PIRAEUS in 1974, this efficient little ferry was still in existence in 1996 as the CITY OF CORFU. (Burniston Studios Ltd)*

Next page, top. *The Pointhouse shipbuilding yard of A. & J. Inglis Ltd assumes a surreal eeriness on the fog-enshrouded afternoon of 2 December 1958. About to be launched into the murky River Kelvin is yard no. 1624p, m.v. LEEDS 1113 g.r.t., the second of three motor coasters built at the yard for Associated Humber Lines Ltd of Goole. Typical Clydeside working garb is seen to good effect as worn by the group of workers in the foreground. (Burniston Studios Ltd)*

paddle steamer WAVERLEY 693 g.r.t. *launched in 1946 for the Caledonian Steam Packet Co Ltd, Glasgow. Engined by Rankin & Blackmore Ltd of Greenock, this ship bears the distinction of being the last ocean going paddle steamer in the world. After a change of ownership in the 1970s, an extensive refit and change of funnel livery, WAVERLEY still plied the waters of the River Clyde and the UK on a regular basis during 1996.* (Burniston Studios Ltd)

paddle steamer MAID OF THE LOCH 555 g.r.t. *launched in 1953 for the Caledonian Steam Packet Co Ltd, Glasgow. Engined by Rankin & Blackmore Ltd of Greenock, this handsome vessel is seen undergoing trials on the beautiful Loch Lomond where she still resides, moored in a partially dilapidated condition at Balloch Pier in 1996. The interest in renovating this excellent example of the combined talents of Scottish naval architecture and marine engineering, may one day see this elegant vessel return to regular trips on the waters of this famous Scottish loch.* (Burniston Studios Ltd)

m.v. SETTER IX 750 g.r.t. *launched in 1953 for United Whalers Ltd (Hector Whaling Ltd), London. Engined by Nat. Gas & Oil Eng Co Ltd of Ashton under Lyne, this vessel was the last whale catcher built on the River Clyde and had a short career sailing under the UK flag before being sold to Kyokuyo Hogei KK of Japan in 1960. Renamed KYO MARU No. 17, her bloody career lasted well into the 1970s before world pressure to stop whaling apparently reduced the size of the Japanese whaling fleet. Overcoats and soft hats are very popular with the entourage of shipyard and owner's personnel on board for sea trials. (Burniston Studios Ltd)*

s.s. BALLYLUMFORD 1242 g.r.t. *launched in 1954 for John Kelly Ltd, Belfast. Engined by Aitchison, Blair Ltd, Clydebank, this coasting collier was built to transport coal from British mainland ports to Northern Ireland. She remained in service with her original owners throughout her entire working life, being broken up in 1971. (Courtesy World Ship Society)*

Yard no. 1530P, the twin screw motor tug CONFIDENT 642 g.r.t. immediately after launching into the River Kelvin from the Pointhouse shipyard of A. & J. Inglis Ltd on 17 January 1956. This vessel was the second in a series of four built by the yard for the Admiralty between 1955 and 1958. Her naval career was ended in August 1986 when she was disposed of by the Admiralty as a target! Noticeable in the background on the south side of the River Clyde is part of the plating shed with template loft above that formed a large part of Harland & Wolff's former Govan shipyard. (Burniston Studios Ltd)

t.s.m.t. LAPPE 165 g.r.t. *launched in 1956 for the Petroleum Marketing Co (West Indies) Ltd and engined by Ruston & Hornsby of Lincoln. This small tanker for use in the tropics with its open wheelhouse is shown undergoing trials off the Roseneath peninsula with personnel from her builders aptly dressed for the Scottish climate. She foundered and sank off Sierra Leone in June 1976. (Burniston Studios Ltd)*

motor tug FLYING DIPPER 274 g.r.t. *launched in 1957 for Clyde Shipping Co Ltd, Glasgow. Engined by British Polar Engines Ltd, this vessel was the third, last and largest ship built by A. & J. Inglis for these owners in the post-war period. Sold and renamed PAMELA JOY in 1977, she was declared a constructive total loss in 1978 after a serious fire on board. Tugs along with the sides of quays and harbours are the main users of worn-out tyres from heavy commercial vehicles, and this new vessel has adorned both her port and starboard sides with a number of such secondhand items.*

m.v. LEEDS 1113 g.r.t. *launched in 1958 for Associated British Humber Lines Ltd of Goole. Engined by Ruston & Hornsby of Lincoln, this well proportioned coaster was the second of three similar ships built for these owners by A. & J. Inglis Ltd. She was sold and renamed GULF SEA in 1972 and broken up in 1990. The vessel's single bipod mast gave her a very stylish yet functional appearance which partly accounted for her career lasting over thirty years.* (Burniston Studios Ltd)

twin screw motor grab hopper dredger CRESSINGTON 1431 g.r.t. *launched in 1961 for the British Transport Docks Board, Liverpool. Engined by Crossley Bros Ltd of Manchester, this distinctive dredger had its signal mast located aft of the bridge superstructure, an unusual but nevertheless attractive feature of the vessel. Sold and renamed W.D. CRESSINGTON in 1971, she was broken up in 1986 as the STAD WESP. Noticeable during the ship's sea trials in the choppy Firth of Clyde is the missing jib and grab equipment of the forward deck mounted crane.* (Burniston Studios Ltd)

motor hopper barge AIGBURTH 1037 g.r.t. *launched in 1962 for British Transport Commission, Port of Liverpool. Engined by Crossley Bros Ltd of Manchester, this handsome self-propelled hopper barge (yard no. 1645P) was the last vessel built at the Pointhouse shipyard of A. & J. Inglis Ltd and was still in existence in 1996 as the BANJAARD.* (Burniston Studios Ltd)

HARLAND & WOLFF LIMITED   1912-1963

In 1946 the Harland & Wolff organisation was among the largest shipbuilding, marine and heavy engineering concerns in Scotland, employing a peak labour force of over 6000 workers at four major establishments in Glasgow, which were:

- Finnieston Marine Engine Works, known locally as 'The Diesel'
- Govan Shipbuilding Yard
- Govan Foundry, better known as 'The Glass House'
- Scotstoun 'Gun Works' which latterly built turbines for hydroelectric power stations.

Throughout the 1950s all the above works saw a regular intake of orders for the different products that each separate entity produced.

The Govan shipyard had the dubious distinction of being sited farthest away from the open sea than any other establishment on the River Clyde. Comprising six berths of varying lengths from 200–600 ft in length, these were unique in that each slipway had its own mini dockgates which, when closed, allowed continuous working at the aft end of a ship under construction, irrespective of the state of the tide. Formerly the location of three small separate shipyards, these were procured by Harland & Wolff Ltd of Belfast in 1912, and were quickly consolidated to become their Govan yard. The location previously bore the names of Robert Napier and William Beardmore, respectively. The former was generally considered as the father of iron shipbuilding on the River Clyde, the latter regarded as one of the many successful archetypal Scottish industrial magnates of the nineteenth century.

The berths were served by a total of 16 fixed hammerhead cranes, some of which were 15 tons capacity. A plating shed with template loft above was located west of the berths. This building was separated from the main shipyard by Water Row, the very short road which lead from Govan Cross to the southern embarkation point for the Govan Ferry. This unique edifice, constructed of terracotta brickwork, bore an uncanny resemblance to the exterior facade of Ibrox park football stadium, home of Glasgow Rangers FC.

Within the confines of the main yard there existed a further plating shed, a covered prefabrication shop that was built in the early 1950s, miscellaneous outfit trades buildings, the drawing office, further adjacent workshops, and a fitting out basin served by 2 x 30 tons capacity, level luffing travelling cranes. It was a compact shipbuilding facility that regularly produced three to four cargo ships, or oil tankers each year from a total labour force of about 2,000 workers. Post-war investment was minimal, and like virtually every other UK shipbuilding concern, was aimed specifically at replacing riveted methods of steelwork construction, with the technique of welding—hence the purchase of the new fabrication shed, some welding plant and very little other items of hardware.

Despite this niggardly application of funds to the improvement of facilities and working environment, the Govan shipyard had an excellent reputation for quality and delivery. Strikes occurring at the yard during the 1950s were symptomatic of the national malaise that then pervaded the industry. When settlement of such disputes was reached, the rapid return to work and the convivial atmosphere that mysteriously permeated the berths, sheds and outfit quays, contradicted the dank and gloomy aura that pervaded the buildings of the yard. The average age of the yard labour force always tended to be high as most men just could not afford to retire. Somehow this maturity resulted in a compliant acquiescence and tolerance of the spartan working conditions throughout the site. The summation of individual and collective craft skills were the hallmark of the shipyard, and this was manifestly endorsed in the fine range of ships built there since 1946.

Seldom if ever sharing the limelight with either its parent Belfast shipyard or the more famous publicity prone Clydeside shipbuilders, the Govan facility produced 54 ships totalling 504,481 g.r.t. from 1946 until 1962, including some 12 oil tankers for British Petroleum, 32% of this total was for export. Many of these vessels constructed were part of a series of two or more and all but one were motor ships engined by either

Harland & Wolff Ltd in Glasgow or Belfast. The most handsome batch, indeed arguably among the finest looking cargo liners ever produced anywhere in the world, were the five 'B' class motor ships built for the British India Steam Navigation Co Ltd by the yard between 1959 and 1961. With sloping sheer lines, raked superstructure, futuristic deck cranes, angled integral radar mast and funnel, these vessels had more in common with the profile of a yacht than that of a cargo liner. These ships had been designed by the renowned London firm of naval architects, Burness Corlett & Partners Ltd. The largest ship built at the yard was the British motor tanker *Eskfield* 18,851 g.r.t. launched on 21 May 1959.

Maximum yearly production during this period was achieved at the yard in 1960, with the launching of two of these 'B' class cargo liners *Barpeta* 6736 g.r.t. and *Bamora* 6744 g.r.t., the ore carrier *Daghestan* 11,204 g.r.t., and the medium-sized oil tanker *Norsk Drott* 18,483 g.r.t., creating a total annual output of 43,167 g.r.t. A formidable statistic for a 'labour-intensive relic of shipbuilding obsolescence' that was still making regular profits for its Irish parent company even on its last contracts! 1961 saw the yearly total drop to three vessels including two handsome Bird class motor tankers for BP, and by 1962 the last orders were being processed through the yard. The launch of the Norwegian motor bulk carrier *Belisland* 10,862 g.r.t. (yard no. 1650G) on 26 September 1962, became the final such event at this traditional shipyard. By then the labour force had been whittled down to a few hundred men, only some of whom were retained on a 'care and maintenance' basis for a further 12 months, by which time the formal announcement of closure had been made by the Belfast parent company. Dismantling the berth craneage and some of the sheds commenced in 1964. The ship repair division of Alex Stephen & Sons Ltd acquired the fabrication shop, outfit basin and quayside cranes, where that company performed refit activities up until the mid 1970's.

Most of the site is now occupied by local authority housing, suggesting little ostensible association with shipbuilding. The outlines of the six berths are still discernible, framed by new brickwork, supporting walkways and handrailing along the side of the river bank. The fitting-out basin remains as an artificial inshot of the River Clyde, now bereft of the travelling cranes that once straddled each quay. One of the outfit sheds still remains, and sees frequent use as an industrial theatre, where various plays depicting the mythos of Scotland have been successfully performed in recent years.

The Harland & Wolff diesel engine works at Lancefield Street, Finnieston, were less than a mile from the centre of Glasgow and evolved during an era that failed to discriminate between the proximity of industrial buildings and domestic dwelling places, which were built adjacent to each other. The only partial differentiation tended to be the number of windows in the houses, each lot of chimneys seemed to spew out the same amount of fumes! The works were locked in on three sides by a combination of small private companies and rows of that ubiquitous smoke begrimed Glasgow edifice, 'the tenement'.

The works had a standard gauge railway system, which was laid as a tramway along Lancefield Street and connected to the British Railways network at Stobcross Quay. Raw material in the shape of billets, forgings, castings, fabrications and components were transported along this route, with the completed diesel engines, depending on their size, being chugged out on special wagons hauled by steam pug locomotives. These trundled their load and positioned it underneath the Finnieston crane, adjacent to Stobcross Quay. This was owned by the Clyde Navigation Trust, whose personnel assisted with the subsequent installation of the machinery into the engine casings of newly launched ships moored alongside. During the 1940s and '50s it was not uncommon for recently launched vessels resplendent in pristine paintwork to be moored two abreast up to six at a time, awaiting marine engine installation by the engineers of either Harland & Wolff or David Rowan & Co Ltd, another marine engine builder of nearby Elliot Street, also in the district of Finnieston. This renowned company was part of the Lithgow Group and was amalgamated with the engine works of the Fairfield SB & Eng Co Ltd to form Fairfield-Rowan Ltd in the early 1960s.

The Harland & Wolff engine works built large bore, slow and medium speed marine diesel engines, under licence to designs patented by the Danish company of Burmeister & Wain of Copenhagen. Employing well over 1000 workers throughout the 1950s, the labour force strove to meet the demand of the Group's Govan shipyard, and other UK shipbuilders. The workload profile was very similar to the shipyard on the other side of the river, working regular, incessant overtime when the order books were full. With routine annual intakes of apprentices up until 1960, the company, like most others, had a perceived stability about continuity of employment. Despite part of the customer base being outwith its parent group, the 'Diesel' was inextricably linked to the existence, output and longevity of the Govan shipyard. The attrition in numbers of workers employed at Finnieston was a subtle, if ostentatious, barometer to the future workload of the plant. The 'Diesel' didn't even build the engines for the last two vessels built at Harland & Wolff's Govan shipyard, these were built by the parent company in Belfast. It was therefore no surprise when closure of the engine works was announced in the early '60s.

Some valuable items of specialised plant and machine tools, were transferred to the owning company in Belfast. Others were surreptitiously sold abroad to competitors or to local scrap dealers, and a highly skilled and motivated labour force was dispersed to man the 'sunrise' car plant at Linwood, or what other Clydeside industry that was then recruiting tradesmen. The site remained an empty shell for a number of years before being purchased and levelled on behalf of the Mirror group of newspapers, where it became the location for the printing and publishing of the 'Scottish Daily Record' and 'Sunday Mail'.

The 'Glass House' at Govan and 'Gun Works' at Scotstoun lingered on for a few more years as manufacturing facilities. The former, a foundry specialising in marine component manufacture, was razed to the ground in 1965, the latter continued to build equipment for hydroelectric power stations up until 1967, when the site was acquired by British Leyland/Albion Motors Ltd. The large buildings remained under these owners and their successors, where vehicle components were still being manufactured in 1996. The west wall of the 'Gun Works' bore the name Harland & Wolff Limited in huge black letters well into the 1990s, and remained the only tangible reminder of a once famous company that was thought to be as permanent a fixture on Clydeside as was the rain on a Monday morning.

List of ships built by HARLAND & WOLFF Ltd, Govan, between 1946 and closure in 1963

YEAR	NAME	TYPE	COUNTRY OF REGISTRATION	G.R.T.	TOTAL G.R.T.
1946	EMPIRE EDGEHILL	s. Oil Tanker	Britain (RN)	8159	
	BRITISH KNIGHT	m. Oil Tanker	Britain	8629	
	LA HAGUE	m. Ref/Cargo	France	4310	
	MORBIHAN	m. Ref/Cargo	France	4450	25548
1947	LA HEVE	m. Ref/Cargo	France	4310	
	• IMPERIAL STAR	m. Ref/Cargo	Britain	13181	
	MELBOURNE STAR	m. Ref/Cargo	Britain	13179	
	• BRITISH RANGER	m. Oil Tanker	Britain	8574	39244
1948	LIPARUS	m. Oil Tanker	Britain	6473	
	• BRITISH MARINER	m. Oil Tanker	Britain	8580	
	BRITISH WORKMAN	m. Oil Tanker	Britain	8575	23628
1949	CAZADOR	m. Oil Tanker	Argentina	6441	
	AMARNA	m. Cargo/Pass	Britain	3422	
	BRITISH CAPTAIN	m. Oil Tanker	Britain	8700	
	BRITISH COMMANDER	m. Oil Tanker	Britain	8655	27218
1950	BRITISH CONSUL	m. Oil Tanker	Britain	8655	
	BRATSBERG	m. Oil Tanker	Norway	8255	
	• BINTA	m. Oil Tanker	Norway	8162	25072
1951	• BOLLSTA	m. Oil Tanker	Norway	16405	
	ILIADE	m. Oil Tanker	France	12801	
	EBRO	m. Ref/C/P¹	Britain	7785	36991
1952	ESSEQUIBO	m. Ref/C/P	Britain	7785	
	CLYDEFIELD	m. Oil Tanker	Britain	11163	
	BLANDFORD	m. Oil Tanker	Britain	12514	31462
1953	• BRITTA	m. Oil tanker	Norway	12757	
	• PORT MONTREAL	m. Ref/C/P	Britain	7179	
	• BRITISH GUNNER	m. Oil Tanker	Britain	10076	30012
1954	BRITISH SERGEANT	m. Oil Tanker	Britain	10073	
	BELFAST	m. Oil Tanker	Norway	12744	
	WESTERN PRINCE	m. Cargo	Britain	7917	30734

YEAR	NAME	TYPE	COUNTRY OF REGISTRATION	G.R.T.	TOTAL G.R.T.
1955	TRIASTER	m. Ref/C/P	Britain	9994	
	• ESCALANTE	m. Ref/C/P	Britain	7791	
	SOUTHERN PRINCE	m. Cargo	Britain	7917	25702
1956	ROWANMORE	m. Cargo	Britain	8495	
	• TUSCANY	m. Ref/Cargo	Britain	7455	
	ALBANY	m. Ref/Cargo	Britain	7299	23249
1957	AFGHANISTAN	m. Ore Carrier	Britain	11188	
	THESSALY	m. Ref/Cargo	Britain	7299	
	• ALARIC	m. Cargo	Britain	6692	25179
1958	IRON AGE	m. Ore Carrier	Britain	11188	
	• TRI-ELLIS	m. Ref/C/P	Britain	11761	
	• BULIMBA	m. Ref/Cargo	Britain	6796	29745
1959	BANKURA	m. Ref/Cargo	Britain	6793	
	• ESKFIELD	m. Oil Tanker	Britain	18851	
	BRITISH GULL	m. Oil Tanker	Britain	11156	36800
1960	BARPETA	m. Ref/Cargo	Britain	6736	
	• DAGHESTAN	m. Ore Carrier	Britain	11204	
	BAMORA	m. Ref/Cargo	Britain	6744	
	• NORSK DROTT	m. Oil Tanker	Norway	18483	43167
1961	BOMBALA	m. Ref/Cargo	Britain	6744	
	BRITISH OSPREY	m. Oil Tanker	Britain	11132	
	• BRITISH MERLIN	m. Oil Tanker	Britain	11132	29008
1962	• RINGWOOD	m. Bulk Carrier	Norway	10860	
	• BELISLAND	m. Bulk Carrier	Norway	10862	21722

32% export
68% Britain   54 vessels total = 504,481 g.r.t.

• Indicates vessel depicted in subsequent photographic section.
For explanation of abbreviations see Glossary on page 345.

The group of photographs on the next pages show the previous locations of Harland & Wolff's long closed and dismantled Govan shipyard and Finnieston marine engine works. Following on from these views are a number of pictures of ships on trials that were built by this erstwhile shipyard, and engined by either its Glasgow or Belfast engine works.

This 1959 photograph of Govan looking west shows the area in the last throes of the post-war shipbuilding boom. In the bottom foreground are the ends of the three graving docks owned by the former Clyde Navigation Trust. Immediately above is the Govan shipyard of Harland & Wolff Ltd. In the fitting-out basin is yard no. 1610g, the cargo liner BANKURA 6793 g.r.t. *recently launched for the British India Steam Navigation Co Ltd, and a destroyer under modification that was not built at Govan. The first berth contains the keel and stern-frame of yard no. 1642g, the* motor ore-carrier DAGHESTAN 11,204 g.r.t. *Next berth holds yard no. 1571g, the* motor tanker ESKFIELD 18,851 g.r.t., *a few weeks away from launching. Beyond is yard no. 1589g, the* motor oil tanker BRITISH GULL 11,156 g.r.t. *under construction, with yard no. 1611g, the third 'B' class motor* ship BARPETA 6736 g.r.t. *on the adjacent berth.*

Between the fitting-out quay and the berths the triangular shaped buildings house the new preparation sheds with the adjoining new fabrication facilities built in the mid-1950s. Left of these are plumbing, electrical, joinery and training departments. In the middle of the picture running the full length of the berths is the covered stockyard and plating sheds. The white roofed building which is severed from the main yard by the short thoroughfare to Govan Ferry is the template loft and a further plating shop. Left of the yard is Govan Road, with tenement dwelling houses in profusion. Further down river the yards of Fairfield and Stephen can be seen on the south bank of the river. Most of the former Harland & Wolff shipyard is today consumed by a housing development. Only the deserted fitting-out basin and the two sheds running parallel with Govan Road remain as tangible evidence of this former busy centre of shipbuilding. These two sheds have recently been used as a theatrical venue for plays with strong Scottish interest.

On the opposite side of the river part of the buildings belonging to the former group company of A. & J. Inglis Ltd can be seen at the end of Ferry Road where the Govan vehicular ferry is berthed, east of the conflluence of the River Kelvin with the Clyde.

Left. *Perhaps the most appositely named ship ever built in the Govan district of Glasgow was m.t. BRITISH RANGER 8574 g.r.t. launched on 11 December 1947 for the Anglo Iranian Oil Co Ltd, London, later known as the BP Tanker Co Ltd. With the Harland & Wolff shipyard launch platform adorned with flags of the nearby Glasgow Rangers FC Supporters Club, this vessel evoked a synonymous pride in the many craftsmen who built her, and supported the more famous local football club. She was renamed CLYDE RANGER in 1957 and ended her association with the West of Scotland in 1963 when she was broken up down river at Faslane.* (Ulster Folk & Transport Museum)

Below. *m.t. BRITISH MARINER 8580 g.r.t. prior to launching from the Govan shipyard of Harland & Wolff Ltd on 16 September 1948. Note the extensive amount of riveting on the hull plating and the frame to shell plating also. This vessel remained with BP Tankers until being broken up in 1962, and was a sister ship of* BRITISH RANGER. *The wire strops draped from the vessel's port side are connected to a nest of drag chains laid on the building berth, which will arrest the ship's travel when she is launched into the river.*

Above. *Yard no. 1419g, m.t. BOLLSTA 16,405 g.r.t. prior to launching from the Govan shipyard of Harland & Wolff Ltd on 5 May 1951. At her time of construction this vessel was the largest oil tanker built on the River Clyde. On the adjacent berth, yard no. 1435g, m.t. ILIADE 12,801 g.r.t., a much smaller oil tanker for French owners, is seen at an early stage of construction. The famous Govan cofferdams are seen to good effect in this view. The buildings on the left were shortly demolished to make way for the new prefabrication shed seen below.* (Ulster Folk & Transport Museum)

Below. *Work under way on the erection of the new fabrication shed at the Govan shipyard of Harland & Wolff Ltd in the early 1950s. Note the rows of asymmetrical frames recently erected and tethered on the berths at the right hand side. This building saw less than a decade of use before the yard was abandoned by its parent company, although the shed was used thereafter by the ship repairing division of Alex Stephen & Sons Ltd into the 1970s.*

Yard no. 1463g, m.t. BRITTA 12,757 g.r.t. shortly before launching on 12 May 1953 at the Govan shipyard of Harland & Wolff Ltd. This vessel ended her days in Bulgaria as the VIT where she was converted for harbour use only in 1983. Virtually all of this tanker's hull has been constructed by riveting. Note the group of shipwrights under the fore end in front of the white painted fore poppet.

This view over some of the six open slipways of the Govan shipyard of Harland & Wolff Ltd shows three ships at various stages of construction. At the right hand side is the bow of yard no. 1545g, m.v. TUSCANY 7455 g.r.t. about to be launched that day (21 June 1956) for Royal Mail Lines Ltd, London. In the centre foreground most of the keel has been laid for yard no. 1567g the motor ore carrier AFGHANISTAN 11,188 g.r.t. whilst almost fully framed is the carcass of yard no. 1559g, m.v. ALBANY 7299 g.r.t., the second of three sister ships for Royal Mail Lines Ltd. The reasonable berth coverage that some of the yard's fixed hammerhead cranes provided is seen in this view. Also noticeable in the left distance (on the other side of Water Row) is the yard's other plating shed with full length template/mould loft above. In the foreground are stowed a number of fixed and sliding launchways. Note the group of apprentices leaning on a trestle on the right hand side.

Two excellent launch-day photographs at the former Govan shipyard of Harland & Wolff Ltd.

The top picture taken on 15 May 1958 shows the ceremonial bottle of champagne being broken on the lower bow of yard no. 1581g, m.v. TRI-ELLIS 11,761 g.r.t. The launch platform personnel consists mainly of old men and old women sporting bowler hats and fur coats as tokens of their status and affluence. On the ground to the right, mothers, sons and shipyard craftsmen who built this ship, view this once common ritual with pride and delight. Note the parallel rows of snap head rivets that connect the vessel's internal frames to the shell plating which is welded together. (Ulster Folk and Transport Museum)

The picture on the left depicts yard no. 1649g, the motor bulk carrier RINGWOOD 10,860 g.r.t., the penultimate vessel built by the yard, entering the River Clyde on 31 May 1962, minus her starboard forward derrick post. The drag chains have not yet been tugged by the ship to arrest her travel in the water. Quite noticeable in this view are four of the sixteen hammerhead cranes that existed in the yard, as well as two grillages of timber uprights from which staging was nailed to provide working platforms for steelworkers and painters. Built for Ringdals Rederi A/S of Oslo, this vessel remained in existence until 1986 when she was broken up as ATAMAS. (Ulster Folk and Transport Museum)

This 1959 photograph of Central Glasgow depicts the location of Harland & Wolff's Finnieston diesel engine works on the north bank of the river, centre foreground. To the extreme left is the Elliot Street marine engine works of David Rowan & Co Ltd. Tenements, schools and shops abutt these plants and other small factories. In the centre right the coal fire smoke haze partly disguises the desirable areas of the west end of the city. Glasgow University tower is in the left far centre, with barely discernable beyond the Campsie Fells and the extinct volcanic cusp of Dumgoyne. This scene nowadays is pock-marked with high-rise flats and urban clearways feeding the Kingston Bridge that carries the M8 through Glasgow.

Below. t.s.m.v. IMPERIAL STAR 13,181 g.r.t. *launched in 1947 for the Blue Star Line Ltd, London. Engined by Harland & Wolff Ltd, Glasgow, this fully refrigerated vessel was the first of a pair of sisterships built at Govan for these owners. She spent her entire life in the trade between the UK, Australia and New Zealand until she was broken up under her original name in 1971. Blue Star Line ships had the most distinctive and germane funnel markings of the entire British merchant navy.*

m.t. BINTA 8162 g.r.t. *launched in 1950 for A/S Bisca of Bergen, Norway. Engined by Harland & Wolff Ltd, Glasgow, this ship was converted into an ore carrier and renamed WENNY by her original owners in 1961. The vessel capsized and sank off Norway in heavy seas during July 1969, with the loss of nine of her crew.*

m.t. BOLLSTA 16,405 g.r.t. *launched in 1951 for A/S Granger Rolf, Oslo (Fred Olsen & Co Ltd). Engined by Harland & Wolff Ltd, Glasgow, this strikingly good looking motor tanker, suitably enhanced by the painting of her hull dove grey, was at her time of building the largest oil tanker constructed on the River Clyde. Sold, renamed and converted to a bulk carrier as DONA MARIA in 1964 she retained that identity until being broken up in 1979.* (Ulster Folk & Transport Museum)

m.v. PORT MONTREAL 7179 g.r.t. *launched in 1953 for Port Line Ltd, London. Engined by Harland & Wolff Ltd, Glasgow, this handsome refrigerated motor vessel with space for a limited amount of passengers traded between the UK, Australia and New Zealand until cheap air travel and containerisation rendered her obsolete. Sold and renamed PUERTO PRINCESA in 1972, she was broken up in 1979.*

m.t. BRITISH GUNNER 10,076 g.r.t. *launched in 1953 for the Anglo Iranian Oil Co Ltd, later known as the BP Tanker Co Ltd, London. Engined by Harland & Wolff Ltd, Glasgow, she was transferred within the BP Group and became CLYDE GUNNER in 1961. She remained within BP for her entire life, reverting to BRITISH GUNNER in 1964, under which name she was broken up in 1972.* (BP Photographic)

m.v. ESCALANTE 7791 g.r.t. *launched in 1955 for Royal Mail Lines Ltd, London. Engined by Harland & Wolff Ltd, Glasgow, this vessel was the third of six ships of similar cargo carrying capacity built by the Govan yard for these owners in the 1950s. She was sold and renamed MANES P in 1970, but unfortunately sank on her first voyage under that name near St Johns, Newfoundland in February of that year.* (Ulster Folk & Transport Museum)

m.v. ALARIC 6692 g.r.t. *launched in 1957 for Shaw Savill & Albion Co Ltd, Southampton. Engined by Harland & Wolff Ltd, Glasgow, this traditional looking British cargo liner plied between the UK and Australia until she was sold and renamed IRAN NIRU in 1972, being later broken up as that in 1977.*

m.v. TRI-ELLIS 11,761 g.r.t. *launched in 1958 for the British Phosphate Commissioners, London. Engined by Harland & Wolff Ltd, Glasgow, this stylish ref/cargo/passenger vessel was built to transport phosphate from the tiny Pacific island of Nauru and remained in service performing that function up until 1974 when she was sold and renamed TRYPHENA. She was broken up in 1980 under the name of MAN TAT.* (Ulster Folk & Transport Museum)

m.v. BULIMBA 6796 g.r.t. *launched in 1958 for the British India Steam Navigation Co Ltd, London. Engined by Harland & Wolff Ltd, Glasgow, this ship was the first in a series of five built by the Govan yard for these owners. The combination of balanced rake and sheer created a futuristic yet undated styling that made the sisters prime candidates for the title of 'finest looking cargo liner' built on the River Clyde. She was sold and renamed BUNGA KENANGA in 1971 and later became a total loss when she ran ashore off Kori Creek, Pakistan in July 1979 as the SEASPRITE. One of her sister ships, m.v. BAMORA 6744 g.r.t., was still in existence in 1996 as the YANG ZI JIANG 3, making her the last Govan-built Harland & Wolff ship still extant.*

m.t. ESKFIELD 18,851 g.r.t. *launched in 1959 for the Northern Petroleum Tank SS Coy Ltd, Newcastle. Engined by Harland & Wolff Ltd, Glasgow, this squat looking tanker bore the distinction of being the largest ship built at the Govan yard. She was jumbo-ised by Harland & Wolff Ltd, Belfast in 1965, then sold and renamed TORERO in 1968. In 1977 she was broken up as APOLLONIAN VICTORY.* (Ulster Folk & Transport Museum)

motor ore carrier DAGHESTAN 11,204 g.r.t. *launched in 1960 for the Hindustan SS Coy Ltd (Common Brothers Ltd) of Newcastle. Engined by Harland & Wolff Ltd, Glasgow, this vessel was the last of a trio built at Govan to import iron ore to new terminals for the UK steel industry at Glasgow, Port Talbot, Tyne Dock, Redcar and Immingham. She plied this trade until sold to Singapore owners in 1976. After further change of name she was broken up in 1987 as the* MERCURY.

m.t. NORSK DROTT 18,483 g.r.t. *launched for Mil Tankrederi A/S of Oslo in 1960. Engined by Harland & Wolff Ltd, Glasgow, this vessel is shown on charter to BP shortly after her completion. She was renamed* GALAXIAS *in 1968 and later broken up in 1983 as the* MIDAS TOUCH. *This vessel was almost identical to the m.t.* ESKFIELD 18,851 g.r.t. *launched by the same yard a year earlier.*

m.t. BRITISH MERLIN 11,132 g.r.t. *launched for the BP Tanker Co Ltd, London in 1961. Engined by Harland & Wolff Ltd of Glasgow, this handsome tanker was the last of a trio built for these owners at Govan. The builder's house flag is clearly seen on the signal mast as the vessel undergoes trials in the Firth of Clyde. Sold and renamed* LSCO BASILAN *in 1977 she sank off the Philippines in November 1983 as the* PNOC BASILAN. (BP Photographic)

m.v. BELISLAND 10,862 g.r.t. *launched on 26 September 1962 for Christen Smith Shipping Co of Oslo (Belships Co Ltd, Skibs A/S) was the last ship built by the Govan shipyard of Harland & Wolff Ltd. Engined by Harland & Wolff Ltd of Belfast, this vessel was unusual in her owner's fleet as she was not a heavy lift ship. She was sold and renamed* ATHENOULA *in 1970, receiving various other names until being broken up in 1991 as the* SEA SUCCESS.

▌ BRITISH POLAR ENGINES LTD   1927–

This small marine engine builder was founded in 1927 as Fiat British Auxiliaries, and became British Polar Engines Ltd in 1938 when the company reached an agreement with Atlas Diesel of Sweden to manufacture their 'Polar' range of engines under licence.

Located in the Govan district of Glasgow, the works occupied a rectangular site located between Helen Street and the adjacent railway sidings of Govan goods and mineral depot. Employing nearly 1000 workers at the height of post-war engine building activity, the company specialised in the design and manufacture of medium-speed diesel engines for installation in small ships and ferries. Occasionally units were supplied as prime movers in diesel-electric power generator combinations for industrial use. This market for 'land sets' was never more than 10% of the output of the firm.

With a healthy order book stretching for almost four decades after World War II and an established customer base throughout the world, the company was acquired by the Associated British Engineering Group in 1955, and built several hundred engines under this ownership.

The relentless contraction of the UK shipbuilding industry virtually disintegrated the market for marine engines by the end of the 1970's. Operating on a manufacturing and sales licence from Nohab AB of Sweden the small company avoided being absorbed into British Shipbuilders Ltd in 1977.

Engine building ceased around the time that the licence agreement with Nohab ended in 1989. The company continued in the field of manufacturing of engineering components and spare parts for the many Polar engines already in use throughout the world. This market is supplemented with repair work for the Ministry of Defence on the Admiralty Standard Range 1 (ASR1) engines. British Polar Engines Ltd built a total of 64 such machines between 1950 and 1970. Many were installed in the successful Oberon class of diesel electric submarine which saw service with the Royal Navy, as well as those of a few overseas countries.

The current premises were later additions to the original site which was sold, then partly demolished shortly after engine manufacture ended. Some machine tools were rehoused in the new building. The company has been trading profitably for the past ten years or so, and rightfully claims the title of the last engine builder in the Glasgow district of Govan, locus of marine engineering on the upper Clyde well over a century earlier.

An 8-cylinder M48M 3040 BHP Nohab-Polar marine diesel engine viewed from the output shaft gearbox end in the former Govan works of British Polar Engines Ltd in 1948. This engine was one of a pair supplied to the former East of Scotland shipyards of Hall Russell & Co. Ltd and the Burntisland SB Co. Ltd. Each was installed in a motor collier built by these yards for the Central Electricity Generating Board. Both ships carried coal from the ports on the east coast of Scotland and the North of England to various power stations on the River Thames. The David Brown gear-box, made in Huddersfield, Yorkshire, reduced the speed of the engine output shaft from 300 rpm to about 100 rpm which was the speed of the ship's propeller. The engine weighed about 160 tonnes and measured 12 metres long ∞ 5 metres wide ∞ 4 metres high. (Courtesy British Polar Engines Ltd)

	FAIRFIELD SHIPBUILDING & ENGINEERING CO LTD	1886–1965
	FAIRFIELDS (GLASGOW) LTD	1966–1968
	GOVAN DIVISION OF UPPER CLYDE SHIPBUILDERS LTD	1968–1972
	GOVAN SHIPBUILDERS LTD	1973–1977
	GOVAN SHIPBUILDERS LTD (DIVISION OF BRITISH SHIPBUILDERS LTD)	1977–1988
	KVÆRNER GOVAN LTD	1988–

The Fairfield Shipbuilding & Engineering Co Ltd became part of the Lithgow group in 1935 and remained within that successful shipbuilding and marine engineering conglomerate for 30 years. In common with other Clyde warship builders at the end of the war, Fairfield took some time to disengage from their naval contracts and the shipyard's first post-war merchant ship was not launched until 1946.

Located on the south bank of the River Clyde, between Govan Old Parish Church to the east, and Holmfauldhead Road to the West, this extensive industrial site was divided by a dredged and piled fitting out basin. This created a natural division between what at one time were two shipyards. However, the western unit that once built submarines was closed by National Shipbuilding Securities Ltd during the great depression between the wars and has lain derelict ever since except for the building of an apprentice training school and shipyard workers' car park in the 1960s.

The Govan Road that runs parallel with the River Clyde created the southern perimeter of the Fairfield Shipyard and Engine Works. Contained within this large complex was an extensive marine engine building facility, capable of manufacturing and testing steam turbines, boilers, and gear-boxes, all designed by the engine works drawing office, as well as large bore marine diesels built under licence from Sulzer Bros of Switzerland and Stork of Holland. The engine works were located on the east side of the fitting out basin. The engine erecting shop and test bed were virtually beneath the 150-ton fixed hammerhead crane that was built specifically to install engines, boilers and auxiliaries into new ships berthed in the fitting out basin.

Obtaining orders for a wide spectrum of ship types, the yard achieved a notable first with the successful completion of the *m.v. Bomi Hills* 17,853 g.r.t., the world's then largest ore/oil combination carrier for Norwegian ship-owners in 1951. This ship was the precursor of the later generation of OBO (ore/bulk/oil) carriers which became off the peg designs offered as standard from Japanese shipyards in the 1970's. Achieving a consistent output of between two to four ships a year, the company became the upmarket specialist yard within the Lithgow parent group. A further four combination carriers were built for the same Norwegian owners between 1951 and 1956. The prestigious passenger liner *s.s. Empress of Britain* 25,516 g.r.t. was completed in 1956 for the Canadian Pacific Steamship Co Ltd, and in between many fast refrigerated cargo liners, ferries, warships and oil tankers were built for UK and overseas ship-owners. The yard launched its first dry bulk carrier *m.v. Australian City* 18,621 g.r.t. on 14 July 1964.

Disruption to the ongoing shipbuilding programme lasted for many years throughout the 1950s, as the shipyard virtually rebuilt all of its berths, in so doing reducing the total number to four, all served with brand new electric mono-tower travelling cranes, designed and built by the Glasgow crane makers, Butters Bros Ltd of Kinning Park. When this phase of modernisation and refurbishment was complete at the end of the decade, the upgraded facilities were very good in terms of steelwork fabrication equipment, but lacked really heavy lift capability, as the new cranes could only lift 40 tons. This deficiency was redressed in 1962 with the purchase of an 80-ton level-luffing travelling crane, designed and built by Babcock & Wilcox Ltd of Dalmuir. Employing nearly 3000 workers in the shipyard, the company was generally regarded as Glasgow's largest shipbuilder, although their annual returns of total new ships launched were always much less than the parent Lithgow yards in Port Glasgow, or John Browns at Clydebank.

The adjoining marine engine works incorporated in the early 1960s the long established Lithgow group company David Rowan & Co Ltd of Finnieston, Glasgow, designers and builders of steam turbines as well as manufacturers of large bore marine diesels, built under licence from Sulzer Bros and Wm Doxford. This rationalisation of engine building capacity initially had a minimal effect on employment at the David Rowan engine works. Both concerns had reasonable order books at the time of the amalgamation. Part of Rowan's more modern plant was transferred to Govan, along with some of the labour force, and the new group title became Fairfield-Rowan Ltd, building many diesel engines and steam turbines in what was to be its short existence. The most notable engine order was the supply of a Fairfield-Rowan-Sulzer of 20,700 S.H.P. for installation in the Norwegian motor tanker *Thorshammer* 34,485 g.r.t., the then largest vessel built by the parent group's recently modernised Kingston shipyard in Port Glasgow, and among the largest motor tankers in the world when launched on 20 June 1963.

The combined order book of the shipyard and engine works during the early 1960s comprised a pot pourri of ship types, the largest repeat order received being for nine small passenger ferries for service in Istanbul, Turkey. Seven of these ships were launched in 1961. Their engines were of a steam reciprocating type similar to those supplied to the same owners some forty years earlier, and specified as mandatory in the new ferries because of the proven reliability of the design and quality of former workmanship.

The varied workload which created much employment did not augur well for profitability, and the Govan shipyard and engine works were put in the hands of the receiver towards the end of 1965. Despite concerted efforts for the total retention of the combined facilities, led most forcefully and with tremendous dignity by Messrs Jamieson and Airlie, the conveners of the engine works, the Fairfield-Rowan plant never reopened. Its assets comprising of the finest array of machine tools on the upper Clyde, were taken over by the Sheffield company T.W. Ward Ltd, who gradually denuded the site. Included in this divestment was probably the best gear-cutting equipment in Scotland. The shipyard became known as Fairfields (Glasgow) Ltd in 1966 after a highly publicised rescue operation led mainly by Lord George Brown, the Trade and Industry Minister for the then Labour Government.

The phoenix that was 'the Fairfields Experiment' became the most contentious, resurrected company ever to be formed in the UK shipbuilding industry. Its inwardly generated public profile proclaimed much rhetoric, but produced scant results and flattered to deceive. Only three merchant vessels aggregating 92,335 g.r.t. and one guided missile destroyer of 6200 tons displacement were launched in two calendar years! One success the company did achieve was convincing the UK ship-owners Reardon-Smith Ltd, of the suitability of the Fairfields designed medium sized standard bulk carrier, which resulted in that Govan ship type later being called the 'Cardiff class'. The shipyard built a total of 12 vessels for the Welsh firm during the ensuing years. The poor output from Govan during this evanescent phase was smoke-screened by its mesmeric management, veiled in a mishmash of new working practices which were apparently being laid down in all departments. Unfortunately, the company did not have sufficient length of time to prove or disprove such optimistic supposition. Vociferous proclamations of industrial 'derring do' were never matched by significant increases in productivity, or the eradication of labour intensive craft practices. The brief existence of Fairfields (Glasgow) Ltd resulted in the dispersal of most of the managerial gurus who unfortunately were denied the five year period to prove the worth of their allegorical nostrums.

The Fairfield yard became the Govan Division of Upper Clyde Shipbuilders Ltd in 1968, and the labour force increased to almost 4000 workers in a short space of time, acquiring many of the men who had recently been decanted from other yards in the area that had just closed. Fifteen vessels of some 208,649 g.r.t. were launched and completed before the liquidation of UCS in the summer of 1971. The yard clearly had the greatest output of that ill conceived state-created organisation, however after two major changes of management in five years, the famous Govan shipyard had barely improved on the performances of the former Lithgow group.

Emerging as a third phoenix, under the moniker Govan Shipbuilders Ltd at the end of 1972, after a well supported public campaign to retain UCS, the new company was very fortunate in that a precondition of its survival was the infusion of large amounts of Government aid, aimed specifically at finally completing the modernisation of the facility which was started by the previous Lithgow Group owners some two decades earlier, as well as providing sufficient working capital to allow protracted trading in the international shipbuilding market.

Spending some tens of millions of pounds on the purchase and installation of new plant and equipment, and making quite tangible efforts at justifying this investment, including extensive use of module outfitting techniques, the company designed and marketed two standard off-the-peg ship designs. These were the Kuwait class, a derivative of the former Clyde class cargo liner and the proven Cardiff class of bulk carrier. The remotivated labour force responded to this combination of new plant and influx of orders, and the shipyard launched six Cardiff class bulk carriers for an assortment of owners in 1976. Amounting to 98,868 g.r.t., this total was the best ever achieved by the shipyard under any form of previous ownership—alas concurrent profitability did not match this considerable annual output. It is most unlikely that this impressive performance of volume ship production will ever be repeated!

Remaining Govan Shipbuilders Ltd up to and into the British Shipbuilders Ltd conglomerate in 1977, the BSL experience was even less successful than all the various post-war guises of the shipyard. Struggling to complete some of the infamous Polish/British Government ship order, the yard inherited part of this agreement for three ships, from the then dispute riven Swan Hunter division of BSL on Tyneside. The firm duly finished the bulk of this ridiculous job-creating contract, which was a political palliative that subsequently created more shipbuilding and ship-owning problems than it ever managed to solve, and which alienated many struggling, long-established British ship-owners from doing business with this infant organisation of dogma induced nationalised ineptitude. Completion of the Polish order saw the modernised yard struggle from contract to contract, decanting much of its established labour force in the process. The total number of employees was in the order of just over 1000 when it was acquired by the Norwegian Kværner Group in 1988. The go-ahead disposition of the new owners, changed its main product range from dry bulk carriers, to chemical and liquid gas tankers. They authorised the building of additional specialised module and sub-assembly prefabrication shops within the Govan yard to assist this transition, and up to 1996 have completed a diverse range of vessels since acquiring the facility.

Between 1946 and 1986, the shipyard under all its different forms of ownership completed a total of 139 vessels comprising seven naval ships of 32,170 total tons displacement, and 132 other craft of 1,895,641 g.r.t., 54% of which were for export. The largest ship built during this period was the motor bulk carrier *Pacific Patriot* 38,409 g.r.t. launched in early 1982 for Furness Whithy Ltd of Liverpool.

List of ships built by the FAIRFIELD SHIPBUILDING & ENG Co Ltd, Govan, and its successors between 1946 and closure in 1987

YEAR	NAME	TYPE	COUNTRY OF REGISTRATION	DISPL/ G.R.T.	TOTAL OUTPUT	YEAR	NAME	TYPE	COUNTRY OF REGISTRATION	DISPL/ G.R.T.	TOTAL OUTPUT
1946	BEAVERCOVE	s.e. Ref/Cargo	Britain	9824	9824	1952	ENDURO	m. Ore/Oil C	Norway	17818	
1947	CALEDONIA	m. Passenger	Britain	11255			ATLANTIC BARON	s. Oil Tanker	Liberia	12696	
	CARDIFF QUEEN	s.p. Ferry	Britain	765			SIRA	s. Cargo	Norway	9539	40053
	WARWICKSHIRE	s. Ref/Cargo	Britain	8917	20937	1953	ATLANTIC BARONESS	s. Oil Tanker	Liberia	12712	
1948	PRINCESS MARGUERITE	s.e. Ferry	Canada	5911			SIMOA	s. Cargo	Norway	9517	
	PRINCESS PATRICIA	s.e. Ferry	Canada	5911			TABOGA	m. Oil Tanker	Liberia	11913	34142
	RUPERTSLAND	m. Ref/Cargo	Canada	754		1954	CHATEAUGAY	s. Ore/Oil C	Norway	18019	
	DORIC	m. Ref/Cargo	Britain	10674	23250		SJOA	s. Cargo	Norway	9506	
1949	CASLON	s. Cargo	Britain	5684			MOISIE BAY	s. Ore/Oil C	Norway	17999	
	LEICESTERSHIRE	s. Ref/Cargo	Britain	8922		•	SOUTH AFRICAN MERCHANT	s. Cargo	South Africa	9866	55390
	ENGLISH STAR	m. Ref/Cargo	Britain	10174	24780	1955	CHICHESTER	s. Frigate	Britain (RN)	2170 displ	
1950	SCOTTISH STAR	m. Ref/Cargo	Britain	10174		•	EMPRESS OF BRITAIN	s. Passenger	Britain	25516	
	PRINCESS OF NANAIMO	s.e. Ferry	Canada	6787		•	OXFORDSHIRE	s. Troop-ship	Britain	20586	48272
	DELIGHT	s. Destroyer	Britain (RN)	2830 displ	19791	1956	FREE STATE	s. Ore/Oil C	Norway	19614	
1951	CIUDAD DE MEDELLIN	m. Ref/Cargo	Colombia	4219		•	CUYAHOGA	s. Ore/Oil C	Norway	19600	39214
	CIUDAD DE BARQUISIMETO	m. Ref/Cargo	Colombia	4219		1957 •	QUEENSLAND STAR	m. Ref/Cargo	Britain	10657	
	BRITISH REALM	s. Oil Tanker	Britain	18557		•	IRISH HAWTHORN	s. Oil Tanker	Eire	12168	
	BOMI HILLS	m. Ore/Oil C[1]	Norway	17853	44843	•	BRITISH ENERGY	s. Oil Tanker	Britain	23124	45949

YEAR	NAME	TYPE	COUNTRY OF REGISTRATION	DISPL/ G.R.T.	TOTAL OUTPUT
1958 •	NORDIC HAWK	s. Oil Tanker	Denmark	22920	
	SHROPSHIRE	m. Cargo	Britain	7244	30164
1959	IRISH BLACKTHORN	s. Oil Tanker	Eire	12168	
	LINCOLN	s. Frigate	Britain (RN)	2170 displ	
•	SHELL ARAMARE	s. Oil Tanker	Venezuela	23524	37862
1960	YORKSHIRE	m. Cargo	Britain	7218	
	SHELL NAIGUATA	s. Oil Tanker	Venezuela	23524	
•	ALERT	m.e. Cable-layer	Britain	6413	
	KUZGUNCUK	s. Ferry	Turkey	781	
	KANLICA	s. Ferry	Turkey	781	38717
1961	PENDIK	s. Ferry	Turkey	781	
	A. KAVAGI	s. Ferry	Turkey	781	
	ATAKOY	s. Ferry	Turkey	781	
	INKILAP	s. Ferry	Turkey	781	
	HARBIYE	s. Ferry	Turkey	781	
•	LEECLIFFE HALL	s. Bulk Carrier (great laker)	Canada	18071	
	IHSAN KALMAZ	s. Ferry	Turkey	781	
•	TURAN EMEKSIZ	s. Ferry	Turkey	781	23538
1962 •	GLENOGLE	m. Ref/Cargo	Britain	11918	
•	GLENFALLOCH	m. Ref/Cargo	Britain	11918	
•	BRITISH GUARDSMAN	s. Oil Tanker	Britain	32287	56123
1963 •	LANCASHIRE	m. Cargo	Britain	9210	
•	SIR LANCELOT	m. Logistic/ support	Britain (RN)	6390	15600
1964 •	FIFE	cosag. Destroyer	Britain (RN)	6200 displ	
•	AUSTRALIAN CITY	m. Bulk Carrier	Britain	18621	
•	NILI	m. Ferry	Israel	7851	
	CLUDEN	m. Bulk Carrier	Hong Kong	22341	55013
1965	EASTERN CITY	m. Bulk Carrier	Britain	18620	
•	WAHINE	s.e. Ferry	N. Zealand	9110	
•	DUHALLOW	m. Bulk Carrier	Britain	25503	53233
1966† •	BRITISH COMMODORE	m. Oil Tanker	Britain	38288	38288
1967	ATLANTIC CITY	m. Bulk Carrier	Britain	27029	
•	INDIAN CITY	m. Bulk Carrier	Britain	27018	
•	ANTRIM	cosag. Destroyer	Britain (RN)	6200 displ	60247
1968† •	WELSH CITY	m. Cargo	Britain	10790	
•	CHAUVENET	m. Survey Ship	United States	6300 displ	
	HARKNESS	m. Survey Ship	United States	6300 displ	23390
1969 •	JERVIS BAY	s. Cont. Ship[2]	Britain	26876	
	CORNISH CITY	m. Cargo	Britain	10799	
	VANCOUVER CITY	m. Bulk Carrier	Britain	17644	
•	PACIFIQUE	m. Hopper/SD[3]	Britain	7349	62668
1970	PRINCE RUPERT CITY	m. Bulk Carrier	Britain	16639	
	TEMPLE BAR	m. Bulk Carrier	Britain	13545	
	FRESNO CITY	m. Bulk Carrier	Britain	16639	46823
1971†	DELTA BAY	m. Hopper/SD	Britain	7986	
	NORSE PILOT	m. Bulk Carrier	Britain	17187	
	NORSE MARSHALL	m. Bulk Carrier	Britain	17187	
	NEW WESTMINSTER CITY	m. Bulk Carrier	Britain	16704	
•	TACOMA CITY	m. Bulk Carrier	Britain	16704	75768
1972	PORT ALBERNI CITY	m. Bulk Carrier	Britain	16694	
•	GUANABARA	m. Hopper/SD	Brazil	4989	
	IRISH PINE	m. Bulk Carrier	Eire	16704	
	IRISH MAPLE	m. Bulk Carrier	Eire	16704	55091
1973† •	IRISH OAK	m. Bulk Carrier	Eire	16704	
	IRISH LARCH	m. Bulk Carrier	Eire	16704	
	GOLDEN ANNE	m. Bulk Carrier	Hong Kong	16628	
	GOLDEN ORIOLE	m. Bulk Carrier	Hong Kong	16628	
	NORSE TRADER	m. Bulk Carrier	Britain	16600	83264
1974 •	AL MUBARAKIAH	m. Cargo	Kuwait	15920	
	AL SALIMIAH	m. Cargo	Kuwait	15920	

YEAR	NAME	TYPE	COUNTRY OF REGISTRATION	DISPL/ G.R.T.	TOTAL OUTPUT
1974	IBN BATTOTAH	m. Cargo	Kuwait	15920	
	IBN RUSHD	m. Cargo	Kuwait	15919	63679
1975	IBN HAYYAN	m. Cargo	Kuwait	15919	
	IBN TUFAIL	m. Cargo	Kuwait	15919	
•	CAMARA	m. Bulk Carrier	Denmark	16821	
	CINCHONA	m. Bulk Carrier	Denmark	16821	
	CAPE ORTEGAL	m. Bulk Carrier	Britain	16646	82126
1976	CAPE RODNEY	m. Bulk Carrier	Britain	16646	
	BARON NAPIER	m. Bulk Carrier	Britain	16646	
•	BARON PENTLAND	m. Bulk Carrier	Britain	16844	
	DONA HORTENCIA II	m. Bulk Carrier	Philippines	16244	
	DON SALVADORE III	m. Bulk Carrier	Philippines	16244	
	DONA MAGDELENA	m. Bulk Carrier	Philippines	16244	98868
1977†	DONA PAZ	m. Bulk Carrier	Philippines	16244	
	IBN SINA	m. Cargo	Kuwait	15387	
	IBN JUBAYR	m. Cargo	Kuwait	15387	
	IBN BAJJAH	m. Cargo	Kuwait	15387	
	AL YAMAMAH	m. Cargo	Kuwait	15387	77792
1978	HIJAZ	m. Cargo	Kuwait	15387	
	AL RAYAAN	m. Cargo	Kuwait	15387	
	SALAH ALDEEN	m. Cargo	Kuwait	15387	
	BOLESLANWIEC	m. Bulk Carrier	Poland	3000	
•	KOPALNIA JASTRZEBIE	m. Bulk Carrier	Poland	11004	
	MALBORK II	m. Bulk Carrier	Poland	2996	63161
1979	KOPALNIA SIEMIANOWICE	m. Bulk Carrier	Poland	10998	
	MIELEC	m. Bulk Carrier	Poland	2994	
	KOPALNIA SIERZA	m. Bulk Carrier	Poland	10997	
	KOPALNIA MIECHOWICE	m. Bulk Carrier	Poland	10998	35987
1980	LORD BYRON	m. Bulk Carrier	Britain	16421	16421
1981	LORD JELICO	m. Bulk Carrier	Britain	16421	
	PACIFIC PEACE	m. Bulk Carrier	Britain	38408	54829
1982 •	PACIFIC PATRIOT	m. Bulk Carrier	Britain	38409	
	SIR JOHN FISHER	m. Bulk Carrier	Britain	37811	
	EL CONQUEROR	m. Bulk Carrier	Philippines	19244	95464
1983 •	SELKIRK SETTLER	m. Bulk Carrier	Canada	21547	
	CANADA MARQUIS	m. (great	Canada	21548	
	SASKATCHEWAN PIONEER	m. laker)	Canada	21548	
	LAKNES	m. Bulk Carrier	Britain	25956	90599
1984 •	LOFTNES	m. Bulk Carrier	Britain	25956	25956
1985	SIR CHARLES PARSONS	m. Bulk Carrier (Collier)	Britain	14201	
	LORD CITRINE		Britain	14201	
	LORD HINTON		Britain	15500	43902
1986 •	NORSEA	m. Ferry	Britain	16793	16793
1987	*None*	*None*	*None*	–	–

54% export   7 vessels total =   32,170 tons displacement
46% Britain   132 vessels total = 1,895,641 g.r.t.

Notes

†	Became Fairfields (Glasgow) Ltd	1966–68
†	Became Govan Division of Upper Clyde Shipbuilders Ltd	1968–71
†	Became " " " " (in Receivership)	1971–73
†	Became Govan Shipbuilders Ltd	1973–77
†	Became " " " (Division of BSL)	1977–88
†	Became Kværner Govan Ltd	1988–

1987 is considered by the author to be the year when volume shipbuilding effectively ceased on the River Clyde. Therefore ships subsequently built by Kværner Govan Ltd are omitted from this table.

• Indicates vessel depicted in subsequent photographic section or another chapter of the book.

For explanation of abbreviations see Glossary on page 345.

The assortment of pictures on this and the following pages illustrates the location of the Govan shipyard of the former Fairfield SB & Eng Co Ltd and its enclosed Fairfield-Rowan Ltd, marine engine works. Also included are a further selection of some of the different types of ships built and engined by the yard in six of its seven post-war guises.

Above. *The Fairfield S.B. & Eng. Co. Ltd, Govan, Glasgow in 1959 looking east and up-river. In the fitting-out basin are from bottom left to right, HMS BLAKE, a Tiger Class cruiser that was launched by Fairfield in 1945, but was not completed until 1961. Next to her is HMS LINCOLN 2170 tons displacement, a Salisbury Class frigate launched on 6th April 1959, and on the other side of the basin, s.t. IRISH BLACKTHORN 12,168 g.r.t., launched earlier the same year. The four berths contain from bottom upwards: first sections of c.s. ALERT 6413 g.r.t., s.t. SHELL NAIGUATA 23,524 g.r.t., s.t. SHELL ARAMARE 23,524 g.r.t. and m.v. YORKSHIRE 7218 g.r.t. The new fabrication sheds are under construction with the steel stockyard to their right faced by the template loft and drawing office. The shipyard engine works, later called Fairfield-Rowan Ltd, occupy the arrangement of large buildings to the right centre, with the sheet metal and joiner shops to its left and plumbing department in the bottom right. Further up-river can be seen Harland & Wolff's shipyard with Princes Dock to the right and Queen's Dock and Yorkhill Quay on the north bank of the river. Downstream the location of the small Pointhouse shipyard of A. & J. Inglis Ltd can be seen on the east bank of the River Kelvin with m.v. YORK under construction. The west bank of the River Kelvin contains the Meadowside ship repair yard of D. & W. Henderson Ltd with the adjacent vacant ground the site of their former shipyard that was closed by National Shipbuilding Securities Ltd in 1935.*

Next page, top. *Yard no. 731, s.s. EMPRESS OF BRITAIN 25,516 g.r.t. nears the stage of her launching at the Govan shipyard of Fairfield SB & Eng Co Ltd in June 1955. Built for Canadian Pacific Steamships Ltd, this ship was the most prestigious vessel built at the yard since 1946. On the adjacent berth work is well under way on Yard no. 775, the troopship s.s. OXFORDSHIRE 20,586 g.r.t. Noticeable on separate tracks are a pair of brand new 40-ton mono-tower electric travelling cranes built by Butters Bros Ltd of Glasgow. These cranes will replace the fixed hammerhead cranes also shown. The unidentified Caledonian Steam Packet Co vessel is heading up-river to the Broomielaw to pick up passengers for a trip 'doon the watter'. (Burniston Studios Ltd)*

Page 186, bottom. *An impressive scene of ironfighting activity seen through the reeky blue-grey haze created by diffused welding flux inside the prefabrication shed of Fairfields (Glw) Ltd in 1967. Virtually all available floor space is occupied by unit and sub-assembly construction. The 'T'-shaped structure in the foreground is part of a transverse watertight bulkhead. Other items being built include shell panels, a pair of hopper ballast tanks and web frames, all components of a Cardiff class bulk carrier.*

Left. *Yard no. 812, m.v. GLENOGLE 11,918 g.r.t. is manouvered into the fitting-out basin of the Fairfield SB & Eng Co Ltd immediately after her launching on 3 May 1962. The first of a pair of 20 knot cargo liners built by the yard for Glen Line Ltd, her fine lines and unique Alfred Holt style of naval architecture are clearly seen, as is her faired bulbous bow, the first one built by Fairfield's. Note the down-river shipyards of Alexander Stephen & Sons Ltd to the left, with* s.t. BRITISH BOMBARDIER 32,351 g.r.t. *on the stocks. On the north bank of the river can be seen the Clydeholm shipyard of Barclay Curle & Co Ltd. Civil engineering activity in the centre left is in association with construction of the Clyde Tunnel on part of the site of the old 'Fairfield' submarine building yard.* (Burniston Studios Ltd)

Launching of HMS FIFE 6200 tons displacement, D20, at the Govan shipyard of Fairfield SB & Eng Co Ltd on 9 July 1964. The fifth of eight County Class destroyers built for the Royal Navy, she was the first of a pair built by the yard, being followed by HMS ANTRIM three years later. Considered well proportioned, futuristic and heavily armed in their day, all of this class have either been sold abroad or broken up. HMS FIFE was sold to Chile in 1987, renamed BLANCO ENCALADA and was still in existence in 1996. (Burniston Studios Ltd)

Two of the then four berths of the Fairfield SB & Eng Co Ltd in June 1962 showing the recently installed 80-ton Babcock & Wilcox Ltd level luffing electric travelling crane. Nearing completion on berth no. 3 is yard no. 813, m.v. GLENFALLOCH 11,918 g.r.t., whilst on berth no. 2 is yard no. 796, s.t. BRITISH GUARDSMAN 32,287 g.r.t., a long deferred order for the BP Tanker Co Ltd. This view clearly shows the tanker's starboard oil cargo tanks including the extensive internal stiffening of transverse and longitudinal bulkheads. The Fairfield yard was among the first on the Clyde to replace traditional staging and uprights with 'quick-fit' scaffolding. This is clearly shown on both ships under construction.

s.s. SOUTH AFRICAN MERCHANT 9866 g.r.t. *launched in 1954 for the South African Marine Corporation Ltd (SAFMARINE), Cape Town. Engined by the Fairfield SB & Eng Co Ltd, this traditional looking cargo liner underwent a change of name to S.A. MERCHANT in 1966, retaining that name until being broken up in 1977. She had originally been part of a four-ship order for Skibs A/S Orenor of Oslo, but transferred ownership to SAFMARINE whilst under construction as yard no. 761. Note the vessel's spare propeller stowed forward of the poop deck house.*

t.s.s.s. EMPRESS OF BRITAIN 25,516 g.r.t. *launched in 1955 for Canadian Pacific Steamships Ltd, London. Engined by the Fairfield SB & Eng Co Ltd, this ship was at her time of construction arguably the finest looking post-war passenger liner built on the Clyde, or indeed the rest of the world. With a traditional profile, topped with a large tapered funnel, four sets of derrick posts, and all of her decks, except the boat deck, totally enclosed, she set standards of naval architecture that became the norm for future shipbuilders throughout the world. She was generally considered the best-looking product ever built by the Govan yard. She was sold, converted and renamed QUEEN ANNA MARIA in 1964, by which time her original transatlantic passenger market had been replaced by rapid air travel. In 1996 she was still in existence as the cruise ship OLYMPIC.*

t.s.s.s. OXFORDSHIRE 20,586 g.r.t. *launched in 1955 for the Bibby Line Ltd, Liverpool. Engined by the Fairfield SB & Eng Co Ltd, this vessel was the last purpose-built British troopship, as well as being the largest. Her very short trooping career ended in 1962. After a brief period during which she was laid up in the River Fal, she was initially chartered, then later sold and renamed FAIRSTAR after being extensively converted in Holland and Northern Ireland during 1963 and 1964. She was acquired by P & O in 1988, but retained her name of FAIRSTAR, continuing to cruise from Australia as she had since her conversion, and was still in existence in 1996.*

steam ore/oil carrier CUYAHOGA 19,600 g.r.t. *launched in 1956 for Skibs A/S Orenor, Oslo, Norway. Engined by Fairfield SB & Eng Co Ltd, this ship was the last of a nine-ship order for these owners completed at Govan in the 1950s. This design of first generation OBO was a world's first for Fairfield. Sold and renamed* SANTOS *in 1972, she was subsequently resold and converted to a pipe-lay vessel and was still in existence in 1996 as* DB OCEAN BUILDER. *She is seen in the Firth of Clyde performing sea trials prior to hand-over, with the hills of Arran in the background.*

t.s.m.v. QUEENSLAND STAR 10,657 g.r.t. *launched in 1957 for Blue Star Line Ltd, London. Engined by Fairfield SB & Eng Co Ltd, this refrigerated cargo liner was the last of only nine vessels built for this major UK ship-owner by Clyde shipyards since 1946. She was briefly renamed* BRASILIA STAR *by the same owners before being broken up in 1980. This distinctive vessel had an unusually long foc'sle deck that extended over all but one of her forward holds.*

s.t. IRISH HAWTHORN 12,168 g.r.t. *launched in 1957 for Irish Shipping Ltd, Dublin. Engined by Fairfield SB & Eng Co Ltd, this ship was the first of a pair of medium-sized tankers built for these owners at Govan. Sold and renamed* ESPERIS *in 1965, she was later sold and renamed* GLOBAL UNITY *in 1973, and broken up in 1979.*

s.t. BRITISH ENERGY 23,124 g.r.t. *launched in 1957 for The Tanker Charter Co Ltd, London (BP Tankers). Engined by the Fairfield SB & Eng Co Ltd, this traditional yet stylish and modern looking tanker was the only ship from a batch of ten sisters built on the Clyde. Six were ordered in Italy, and the other three on the Tyne. She remained with BP all her life and was broken up in 1975. Her plume of oily smoke gives some hint of animation to her sedate movement through the Firth of Clyde.*

s.t. SHELL ARAMARE 23,524 g.r.t. *launched in 1959 for Compania Shell de Venezuela Ltd, Maracaibo. Engined by the Fairfield SB & Eng Co Ltd, this attractive tanker had a long life for a steam turbine ship. Sold and renamed ARAMARE in 1976, she was broken up in 1981. Her smooth and rounded superstructure was typical of all of the large oil tankers built for Shell throughout Europe at that time.*

t.s.d.e. cable ship ALERT 6413 g.r.t. *launched in 1960 for HM Postmaster General, London. Engined by Mirrlees Bickerton & Day Ltd, Stockport, this innovative specialist cable-laying ship revolutionised international undersea cable installation for over thirty years. She was sold and renamed AL in 1995, as which she was broken up in the same year. Noticeable at the fore and aft ends of the vessel are the giant roller fairleads which control the laying of undersea cable.*

s.s. LEECLIFFE HALL 18,071 g.r.t. *launched in 1961 for the Hall Corporation of Canada, Montreal, Quebec. Engined by the Fairfield SB & Eng Co Ltd, this "Great Laker" type of specialised bulk carrier was at 729' 8" long, among the largest of that type of vessel in North America. Her short career was terminated in September 1964 when she was struck by a Greek motor vessel in the St Lawrence River. Carrying a cargo of iron ore, LEECLIFFE HALL sank rapidly with the loss of several lives. Note how far forward her navigation bridge is located to afford maximum visibility.*

t.s.s.s. TURAN EMEKSIZ 781 g.r.t. *launched in 1961 for Sehir Hatlari Isletmesi, Istanbul. Engined by Fairfield SB & Eng Co Ltd, this vessel was the last in a nine-ship repeat order from these owners for passenger service in the Bosphorous Strait. Designed with steam reciprocating engines similar to the ships they were replacing, the whole fleet gave sterling service as stop-start ferries. TURAN EMEKSIZ was still in existence in 1996, along with some of her sisterships.*

m.v. GLENFALLOCH 11,918 g.r.t. *launched in 1962 for Glen Line Ltd, London. Engined by Sulzer Bros Ltd, Winterthur, Switzerland, this vessel was the second of a pair built for these owners by Fairfield. She was sold and renamed* QING HE CHENG *in 1978 and was still in existence with that new name in 1996.*

s.t. BRITISH GUARDSMAN 32,287 g.r.t. *launched in 1962 for the BP Tanker Co Ltd, London. Engined by Fairfield-Rowan Ltd, this tanker was the first all-aft vessel built by Fairfield. She remained with BP for her relatively short working life and was broken up under her original name in 1976. (BP Photographic)*

m.v. LANCASHIRE 9210 g.r.t. *launched in 1963 for the Bibby Line Ltd, Liverpool. Engined by Fairfield-Rowan Ltd, this ship was the sixth and last vessel built by the yard for these owners since 1946. Sold and renamed* SAFINA-E-HAIDER *in 1970, she was broken up at the age of thirty in 1993 under that name. Note how the top of her derrick posts incorporate cowlings that ventilate the holds below.*

twin screw motor logistic landing ship SIR LANCELOT 6390 g.r.t. *launched in 1963 for the UK Ministry of Defence. Engined by Wm Denny & Bros Ltd, Dumbarton, this innovative vessel became the prototype for a series of six ships. A further two were built by Alexander Stephen & Sons Ltd and three by Hawthorn-Leslie (SB) Ltd. After a long career with the MoD she was sold to the Government of Singapore in 1989. Converted and renamed* LOWLAND LANCER *she was still in existence in 1996. The outline of her large forward doors, which enable the loading of tanks and military vehicles, can be clearly seen just behind the bow wake.*

t.s.m.v. NILI 7851 g.r.t. *launched in 1964 for Kavim Shipping Co Ltd of Haifa, Israel. Engined by Sulzer Bros, Winterthur, Switzerland, this handsome passenger-car ferry was among the largest of this type of ferry when commissioned. She was sold and renamed ARION in 1975. Suffering an explosion and fire on board approaching Haifi in December 1981, she was beached then later declared a total constructive loss in 1982 when she was scrapped.*

t.s.t.e. ferry WAHINE 9110 g.r.t. *launched in 1965 for the Union SS Co of New Zealand Ltd, Wellington. Engined by Fairfield-Rowan Ltd and AEI Ltd, Rugby, this good looking ferry was the largest built in the UK when completed. Her very short career came to an unfortunate end in April 1968 when she foundered in a hurricane whilst entering Wellington Harbour with the loss of 51 lives. She subsequently broke into three sections and it took many years before all traces of the wreck was removed.* (P & O Library Archive)

motor bulk carrier DUHALLOW 25,503 g.r.t. *launched in 1965 for Hain-Nourse Ltd, London. Engined by J.G. Kincaid & Co Ltd, this vessel had a brief career within the P & O Group before being sold and renamed JANA VIJAY in 1974. She was broken up in 1985. The amalgamation of the Hain and Nourse shipping companies within the rationalization of the owning P & O Group was one of the many contractions of the British merchant navy, that saw loyal UK ship-owners disappear at the same rate as the shipyards who had built their ships.*

m.t. BRITISH COMMODORE 38,288 g.r.t. *launched in 1966 for the BP Tanker Co Ltd, London. Engined by Harland & Wolff Ltd, Belfast, this ship bore the distinction of being the largest vessel built by the Govan yard, a record that stood until 1981. After nearly two decades of service with BP she was sold for scrap and was broken up in 1982. Note the water in front of the ship raised by the force of her large submerged bulbous bow.*

motor bulk carrier INDIAN CITY 27,018 g.r.t. *launched in 1967 for the Reardon Smith Line Ltd, Bideford. Engined by Clark-NEM Ltd, Sunderland, this ship lasted a decade with her original owners before being sold and renamed* EASTPORT *in 1977. She was broken up in 1987 under her last name* ALKMINI.

HMS ANTRIM 6200 tons displacement, D18, *a County class guided missile destroyer, was launched for the Royal Navy in 1967 and commissioned in 1970. Engined by the combined efforts of Harland & Wolff Ltd, AEI Ltd and Rolls-Royce Ltd, this vessel was the third and last destroyer of her class built on the River Clyde, the other five sister ships being built in either England or Northern Ireland. She was sold to Chile in 1986, renamed* COCHRANE *and was still in existence in 1996.*

m.v. WELSH CITY 10,790 g.r.t. *launched in 1968 for the Reardon Smith Line Ltd, Bideford. Engined by Ruston & Hornsby Ltd, Lincoln, she was sold and renamed* JADE STAR *in 1977. Her lengthy career ended in 1992 when she was broken up as the* LONG PHU. *This impressive photograph shows over two metres of water being ploughed over her bulbous bow as she powers through her speed trials in the Firth of Clyde.*

United States naval survey ship CHAUVENET 6300 tons displacement *launched in 1968 for the United States Navy. Engined by ALCO Diesels (American Locomotive Company), this vessel was the first of a pair built by Fairfields (Glw) Ltd as part of a long overdue trade-off with the USA in respect of excessive one-way spending by Great Britain on American military hardware. She and her sister had reasonably long careers with the US Navy, both lasting in front line service until the 1990s.* CHAUVENET *was decommissioned in 1993, however in 1996 she was transferred to the United States Department of Transport and renamed* TEXAS CLIPPER II. (Glasgow University Archives)

s.s. JERVIS BAY 26,876 g.r.t. *launched in 1969 for Overseas Containers Ltd, London (Shaw Savill & Albion Co Ltd owned and managed her). Engined by Stal Laval Turbine Co, Finspong Sweden, this vessel was the first large containership built on the River Clyde. Her brief career ended in 1983 when she was sold for scrap. She ran aground at Bilbao in 1984 on tow to the Far East and was later broken-up on site.*

twin screw trailling motor suction hopper dredger PACIFIQUE 7349 g.r.t. *launched in 1969 for the DOS Dredging Co Ltd, London. Engined by NV Smit & Bolnes, Holland, this ship was the first of three dredgers built at the Govan yard of UCS Ltd in the late '60s, early '70s. A very successful and reliable vessel she was based on proven design work carried out by many ex-Simons-Lobnitz Ltd engineers and draughtsmen, and still in existence in 1996.* (Glasgow University Archives)

motor bulk carrier TACOMA CITY 16,704 g.r.t. *launched in 1971 for Reardon Smith Navigation Co Ltd, Cardiff. Engined by Harland & Wolff Ltd, Belfast this ship was the fifth in a series of six ordered from the Govan Division of UCS Ltd, and is shown in revenue earning service adorned with some reference to 'support' for one of Glasgow's famous football clubs! Sold and renamed BOUGAINVILLE in 1985, she underwent further changes of ownership and name, being still in existence in 1996 as GOKAR.* (Courtesy The World Ship Society)

twin screw motor hopper suction dredger GUANABARA 4989 g.r.t. *launched in 1972 for the Brazilian Government, Port of Rio de Janeiro. Engined by Vickers Ltd, Barrow-in-Furness, this ship was completed under the auspices of the UCS liquidator and marked a successful diversion by the Govan shipyard into the building of dredgers. This vessel was the last of three orders taken on by UCS Ltd and showed the diverse capability of the Govan division to continue the yard's long tradition of marine innovation. Renamed ESTADO DA GUANABARA, she was still in existence in 1996.* (Courtesy Dr William Lind)

motor bulk carrier IRISH OAK 16,704 g.r.t. *launched in 1973 for Irish Shipping Ltd, Dublin. Engined by J.G. Kincaid & Co Ltd, this vessel was the third of four ships built for these owners during the transition from liquidation of UCS Ltd to Govan Shipbuilders Ltd in the early 1970s. Sold and renamed ALEV in 1982 she was subsequently resold and was still in existence in 1996 as* TAHIR KIRAN. (Glasgow University Archives)

m.v. AL MUBARAKIAH 15,920 g.r.t. *launched in 1974 for the United Arab Shipping Co Ltd, Kuwait. Engined by J.G. Kincaid & Co Ltd, this distinctive vessel was the precursor of the successful Kuwait class of cargo liner. A total of thirteen were built at Govan and a further six at Scotstoun Marine Ltd. Derived from the UCS Ltd Clyde class design of the 1960s, this vessel and most of her sister ships were still trading for their original owners under their initial names in 1996. Apart from being the first new order obtained by Govan Shipbuilders Ltd, this ship was the first built by the yard that possessed a Stülcken heavy lift derrick.* (Courtesy Kværner Govan Ltd)

motor bulk carrier CAMARA 16,821 g.r.t. *launched in 1975 for the East Asiatic Co Ltd, Copenhagen. Engined by Harland & Wolff Ltd, Belfast, this vessel was the first of a pair built by Govan Shipbuilders Ltd for these owners. Sold and renamed ELFIDORUS in 1981 she was still in existence in 1996 as the YUN FENG LING. This vessel and her sistership were modified Cardiff class bulk carriers, with an extra deck for improved accommodation facilities as specified by the East Asiatic Co Ltd.* (Courtesy Dr William Lind)

motor bulk carrier BARON PENTLAND 16,844 g.r.t. *launched in 1976 for Baron Pentland Shipping Co Ltd, Ardrossan (Scottish Ship Management Ltd). Engined by Harland & Wolff Ltd, Belfast, she was the last of a four-ship order completed by Govan Shipbuilders Ltd for the above group. Sold and renamed EVANGELOS L in 1983, she was still in existence in 1996 as the HUA ZHEN. She is seen in pristine ex-yard condition viewed from the deck of the Erskine Bridge bound for her sea trials in the Firth of Clyde.* (Glasgow University Archives)

motor bulk carrier KOPALNIA JASTRZEBIE 11,004 g.r.t. *launched in 1978 for the Polish Steamship Co. Engined by Stocznia Gdanska im Lenina, Gdansk, this vessel was the second of seven ships built by Govan Shipbuilders Ltd for the UK/Poland owned Polish Steamship Co. Renamed WIGRY she was still in existence in 1996. As well as her main engines, most of the other outfit components for these vessels were supplied from Poland.* (Glasgow University Archives)

motor bulk carrier PACIFIC PATRIOT 38,409 g.r.t. *launched in 1982 for Furness Withy & Co Ltd, Liverpool. Engined by Clark-Kincaid Ltd, this bulk carrier was the largest ship built by the Govan yard. She was sold and renamed D. FRANCISCO DE ALMEIDA in 1986, being renamed again in 1989 MASSIMILIANO, as which she was still in existence in 1996. Note the size of her huge bulbous bow, one-third of which is above the waterline.* (Courtesy Kværner-Govan Ltd)

motor bulk carrier (great laker) SELKIRK SETTLER 21,547 g.r.t. *launched in 1983 for Misener Shipping Ltd of Saint Catherines, Ontario. Engined by Clark-Hawthorn Ltd, Wallsend, she was the first of three sister ships built at Govan for these owners. She was sold and renamed FEDERAL ST LOUIS in 1991, and was still in existence in 1996 as FEDERAL FRASER. She is seen in revenue earning service in Canada not long after her completion* (Courtesy The World Ship Society)

motor bulk carrier LOFTNES 25,956 g.r.t. *launched in 1984 for Jebsens (UK) Ltd, London. Engined by Clark-Hawthorn Ltd, Wallsend, this bulk carrier was the second of a pair built by Govan Shipbuilders Ltd for these owners. Sold and renamed WANI RIVER in 1987, she was still in existence in 1996 as the CHINA PROGRESS.* (Courtesy Kværner-Govan Ltd)

t.s.m.v. NORSEA 16,793 g.r.t. *launched in 1986 for North Sea Ferries Ltd, Hull (a Division of P & O). Engined by Oy Wartsila AB Turku, Finland, this prestigious order for the largest ferry built in Britain kept Govan Shipbuilders Ltd in existence during the final years of that company prior to the yard's takeover by Kværner Group Ltd in 1986. NORSEA was still successfully plying the North Sea in 1996.* (Courtesy Kværner-Govan Ltd)

| ALEXANDER STEPHEN & SONS   1750–1899 (1968–1982)
| ALEXANDER STEPHEN & SONS LTD   1899–1968

The name 'Stephen of Linthouse' had been synonymous with shipbuilding since 1870 when the company moved to that site from Aberdeen. Ownership of the shipbuilding establishment remained throughout its existence with the direct descendants of the firm's founder. In the post-war period the company set standards of ship and engine design, coupled with levels of in-house employee training that became the norm for excellence in the shipbuilding and marine engineering industries. Located on the South bank of the River Clyde between the districts of Govan and Shieldhall in what is called Linthouse, the yard was a local landmark for generations.

Emerging from World War II with an exemplary record for naval and merchant ship construction, the Linthouse company spent the first decade of peace time constructing cargo liners. More than 60% of these vessels were fully refrigerated ships, necessary to carry the food produce that was in great demand worldwide throughout this period of growth in global trade. For nearly two decades at least one ship was built every year for one of the associated companies of the P & O Group. This largest UK shipping conglomerate took delivery of 33 vessels from the yard between 1946 and 1964 amounting to 38% of Stephen's post-war output. Seven ships were built for the Elders & Fyffes Group during the same time. These fast distinctive looking 'banana boats' were equipped with luxurious accommodation for a small number of affluent passengers who could afford the return trip between the UK and the West Indies prior to the age of regular low cost flying.

Embarking on phased modernisation as soon as hostilities ceased, the Linthouse yard was the only one at that time on the River Clyde whose building berths were all served by electric mono-tower travelling cranes, no fixed derricks, or hammerheads. The berths were realigned in the early 1950s and a further three mono-tower travelling cranes, this time of 35 tons capacity installed. This investment created nine such cranes serving five berths, a formidable total of available craneage, albeit without any weather protection. Building a relatively consistent yet diverse product range, output varied from two to five ships a year, this fluctuation being proportional to the size and complexity of each vessel, further compounded by the frustrations of internecine trades disputes, that irascible, self-destructive malaise of the post-war shipbuilding industry. Two handsome medium-sized passenger liners, the *m.v. Aureol* 14,083 g.r.t. and the *s.s. Olympia* 17,362 g.r.t., were built in the early 1950s, but the staple diet of new ship construction was cargo liners with the occasional frigate every two to three years. The Suez crisis of 1956 translated into a mini-boom in new shipbuilding orders, and the Linthouse company duly resumed oil tanker construction, obtaining contracts for two ships for The Mobil Oil Co Ltd, and three for British Petroleum Tankers Ltd.

The diminishing order book that existed in the highly competitive international shipbuilding market of the early 1960s, prompted the board of directors to buy the recently merged and highly respected Renfrew dredger building company, Simons-Lobnitz Ltd in 1962. The intention of this acquisition was to construct the established 'Si-Lo' designs of dredgers at Linthouse in the ensuing years. One year later and after prolonged negotiations, an order was announced from the USSR for three self-propelled trailing suction dredgers which were completed a few years later. All of these three sisterships were still operating with their original owners in 1996!

The supertanker *British Bombardier* 32,351 g.r.t. was the largest vessel ever built at Linthouse, when she was launched on 18 May 1962. A total of seven dredgers were built at the shipyard after the much publicised acquisition of Simons-Lobnitz Ltd. The company completed the *m.v. Melbrook* 11,075 g.r.t. in 1964 for part of the P & O Group. This vessel had been started as a speculative new building order by the former Dumbarton shipyard of Wm Denny & Bros Ltd two years earlier. Two Leander class frigates and two assault/landing ships for the Royal Navy became the last warships built by the company. One of these assault ships, *Sir Galahad* 4473 g.r.t., suffered the unfortunate fate to be extensively bombed during the

Falklands war in 1982. Despite considerable loss of life, the ship remarkably did not sink, although it was later scuttled by the Royal Navy then marked as a war grave.

Five fast refrigerated cargo liners were built during the final years of shipbuilding activity by the firm, three for Shaw Savill & Albion Ltd and two for Port Line Ltd. The *m.v. Port Caroline* 12,398 g.r.t. (yard no. 701), launched on 16 April 1968, became the last ship built at Linthouse. The year previously, five different ships were launched from the shipyard, however, profitability on new shipbuilding orders was now a relic of history. This regrettable, yet foreseeable trend, resulted in no new contracts being obtained thereafter.

Between 1946 and 1968 the company built a total of 89 ships comprising nine warships of 18,050 tons displacement and 80 other craft of 585,490 g.r.t., 34% of which were for export. Greatest annual output was achieved in 1962 with the launching of four ships of 47,979 g.r.t. Nevertheless, the 1956 statistic of seven ships totalling 31,789 g.r.t. launched from five berths effected at the height of the strike strewn '50s, was probably the yard's best peace time output accomplishment. A further two craft were constructed under the auspices of Alexander Stephen & Sons after the Linthouse yard was absorbed into UCS. These were a bucket dredger and a tin dredger, and both were despatched in knock-down kit form for assembly overseas.

The shipyard was acquired by Upper Clyde Shipbuilders Ltd in 1968 and subsequently ceased as a shipbuilding entity. During the brief existence of that group, the Linthouse facility was used as a design, preparation and prefabrication centre, as well as the initial location of the new company's headquarters. Many hull units were successfully built at Linthouse throughout this short period, for insertion within ships constructed by the other yards in UCS. The former Alexander Stephen house flag was taken as the logo and emblem of UCS, a light blue Maltese cross on a white background, it was a renowned symbol of successful long-term shipbuilding association. Unfortunately its erstwhile connection with this state-sponsored safety net lasted less than four years.

The adjoining marine engine works designed and built steam turbines, gear-boxes and boilers, marine diesel engines were also built to the patents of Sulzer Bros of Switzerland. These were installed in virtually every motor ship built at the Linthouse complex. The engine works occupied approximately one-third of the total shipyard acreage being located within the perimeter of the Linthouse facility. A short fitting out quay was sited down-river from the western most building berth and was served by a 115-ton fixed derrick crane.

Escaping the fate of the shipyard, at the formation of UCS in 1968, the engine works remained as Alexander Stephen & Sons Ltd and diversified, continuing to exist thereafter for a few years as a versatile fabrication and machining facility. Bereft of the former main product range of marine engines and steam turbines, the future existence of the engineering facility now depended on the production, under licence, of ships' stabilisers as its main item, augmented with some subcontract work on behalf of JBE Ltd of Clydebank. The new workload was erratic and constantly shrouded the long term future of the engine works with uncertainty. Within less than a decade of the cessation of engine building, the remnant associations of ship repairing and downstream marine engineering activities also succumbed to closure. The former engine erection shop was dismantled piece-small, and after safe keeping for a number of years it was subsequently reassembled at Irvine, North Ayrshire, where it forms the main premises of the Scottish Maritime Museum.

The site of both the shipyard and engine works were gradually vandalised by industrial predators, as much as by bored and wanton teenagers! In 1996, half the location was occupied by the high-tech defence contractor Barr & Stroud Limited, who make optical range finders for the Ministry of Defence, thus continuing a tradition of customer continuity, albeit through a different type of product. Also at this time the red brick edifice that had been the company administration and drawing office, still stood in isolation as the last perceptible element of the shipyard.

The name Stephen of Linthouse is now only a memory in the industrial lore of Clydeside. Many former shipbuilders and engineers, ever diminishing with the passage of time, still remain proud, if somewhat disillusioned, to have been trained by this former industrial icon of a company. Imbued with its standards and precepts of technical excellence, alas they are no longer either in its employment or likely to be working in shipbuilding or marine engineering.

List of ships built by ALEXR. STEPHEN & SONS Ltd, Linthouse, between 1946 and closure in 1968

YEAR	NAME	TYPE	COUNTRY OF REGISTRATION	DISPL/ G.R.T.	TOTAL OUTPUT
1946	SOMERSET	s. Ref/C/P	Britain	9943	
	MATINA	s. Ref/C/P	Britain	6801	
	KOMATA	m. Cargo	N. Zealand	3543	
	KAMPALA	s. Ref/C/P	Britain	10304	30591
1947	KOROMIKO	m. Cargo	N. Zealand	3552	
	HUNTINGDON	s. Ref/C/P	Britain	11281	14833
1948	KAITOKE	m. Ref/Cargo	N. Zealand	3551	
	KARANJA	s. Ref/C/P	Britain	10294	
•	CUMBERLAND	m. Ref/C/P	Britain	11281	
•	GOLFITO	s. Ref/C/P	Britain	8740	
	FORT RICHEPANSE	m. Ref/C/P	France	5038	38904
1949 •	FORT DAUPHIN	m. Ref/C/P	France	5038	
	DORSET	s. Ref/C/P	Britain	10108	
•	RIO BERMEJO	m. Ref/Cargo	Argentina	7143	22289
1950	KAWAROA	m. Cargo	N. Zealand	3532	
	DUNEDIN STAR	s. Ref/Cargo	Britain	7344	
	CITY OF BEDFORD	s. Ref/Cargo	Britain	7341	
	DEFENDER	s. Destroyer	Britain (RN)	2830 displ	
	CITY OF SINGAPORE	s. Ref/Cargo	Britain	7338	28385
1951 •	AUREOL	s. Passenger	Britain	14083	
	CORNWALL	m. Ref/Cargo	Britain	7583	
	SURREY	m. Ref/Cargo	Britain	8227	29893
1952	KURUTAI	m. Cargo	N. Zealand	3528	
	KOWHAI	m. Cargo	N. Zealand	3528	
	MIDDLESEX	m. Ref/Cargo	Britain	8284	
	ENTON	m. Cargo	Britain	6443	21783
1953	WAIMEA	m. Ref/Cargo	N. Zealand	3657	
•	OLYMPIA	s. Passenger	Liberia	17362	
	PATONGA	s. Ref/C/P	Britain	10071	31090
1954	WHAKATANE	m. Ref/Cargo	Britain	8726	
	BALLARAT	s. Cargo	Britain	8792	
	BENDIGO	s. Cargo	Britain	8782	
	IRMA	m. Cargo	Norway	4431	
•	FERNVALLEY	m. Ref/Cargo	Norway	4504	35235
1955	MURRAY	s. Frigate	Britain (RN)	1180 displ	
•	PRINCESS OF VANCOUVER	m. Ferry	Canada	5554	
	CASTILIAN	s. Cargo	Britain	3803	
	KAWERAU	m. Cargo	N. Zealand	3698	
	CITY OF NEWCASTLE	m. Cargo	Britain	7727	21962
1956	KAIMIRO	m. Cargo	N. Zealand	3722	
	CAMITO	s. Ref/C/P	Britain	8687	
	PALLISER	s. Frigate	Britain (RN)	1180 displ	
	KAITUNA	m. Cargo	N. Zealand	3722	
	CRUX	m. Ref/Cargo	Norway	4429	
	KORANUI	m. Cargo	N. Zealand	3722	
	DONEGAL	m. Cargo	Britain	6327	31789
1957	CHANGUINOLA	s. Ref/C/P	Britain	6283	
	KORAKI	m. Cargo	N. Zealand	3790	
•	CHIRRIPO	s. Ref/C/P	Britain	6283	
•	CHICANOA	s. Ref/C/P	Britain	6283	22639
1958	KATEA	m. Cargo	N. Zealand	3790	
•	WAIKARE	m. Ref/Cargo	N. Zealand	3839	
•	KIRPAN	s. Frigate	India	1180 displ	
•	BRITISH FULMAR	m. Oil Tanker	Britain	11169	22639
1959	RISDON	m. Cargo	Tasmania	4125	
•	CITY OF MELBOURNE	m. Ref/Cargo	Britain	9914	
•	MOBILE ACME	s. Oil Tanker	Britain	12755	
	CHATHAM	m. Ref/Cargo	Britain	3563	30357
1960	BRITISH CURLEW	m. Oil Tanker	Britain	11157	
•	MOBILE APEX	s. Oil Tanker	Britain	12755	
	LOWESTOFT	s. Frigate	Britain (RN)	2150 displ	
	CHUSCAL	s. Ref/C/P	Britain	6282	
•	IBERIC	m. Ref/C/P	Britain	11248	43592
1961	DUMURRA	m. Ref/Cargo	Britain	6160	
•	PIAKO	m. Ref/Cargo	Britain	9986	
	PRESIDENT STEYN	s. Frigate	South Africa	2380 displ	18526
1962	ANTRIM	m. Cargo	Britain	6461	
•	BRITISH BOMBARDIER	s. Oil Tanker	Britain	32351	
	ZULU	s. Frigate	Britain (RN)	2300 displ	
•	MARKHOR	m. Ref/Cargo	Britain	6867	47979
1963	MAHOUT	m. Ref/Cargo	Britain	6867	
•	AVALON	s. Ferry	Britain	6584	
	SKITTER NESS	m.e. Suction HD	Britain	1577	15028
1964 ** •	MELBROOK	m. Cargo	Britain	11075	
	ZEALANDIC	m. Ref/Cargo	Britain	7946	
•	PHOEBE	s. Frigate	Britain (RN)	2350 displ	21371
1965	NASSAU BAY	n.p. Cutter SD	Britain	1125	
•	SEVERODVINSKI	m.e. Suction HD	USSR	1972	
	BANGKA 1	n.p. Cutter SD	Indonesia	4620	
	ONEGSKI	m.e. Suction HD	USSR	1972	9689
1966	ARABATSKI	m.e. Suction HD	USSR	1972	
•	SIR GALAHAD	m. Logistic/ Support	Britain (RN)	4473	
•	MAJESTIC	m. Ref/Cargo	Britain	12591	19036
1967 •	RIBBOK	m.e. Suction HD	South Africa	4594	
	SIR GERAINT	m. Logistic/ Support	Britain (RN)	4473	
	HERMIONE	s. Frigate	Britain (RN)	2500 displ	
	BRITANNIC	m. Ref/Cargo	Britain	12228	
•	PORT CHALMERS	m. Ref/Cargo	Britain	12398	36193
1968 •	PORT CAROLINE	m. Ref/Cargo	Britain	12398	12398

34% export	9 vessels total	= 18,050 tons displacement
66% Britain	80 vessels total	= 585,490 g.r.t.

*Completed by Alexr Stephen & Sons Ltd after speculative new building by Wm Denny & Bros Ltd.

• Indicates vessel depicted in subsequent photographic section.

For explanation of abbreviations see Glossary on page 345.

The collection of pictures on the following pages illustrate the location of the former Linthouse shipyard and engine works of Alexander Stephen & Sons Ltd. The further batch portrays a selection of the diverse range of warships, merchant vessels and specialist craft built by the company in the two decades before closure.

The two photographs on the this page show the location of the Glasgow shipbuilding and marine engineering interests of Alexander Stephen & Sons Ltd. **Above**. This aerial view of the Linthouse shipyard and engine works is looking north over the River Clyde on a murky day in April 1962. Dominating the photograph is yard no. 672, the supertanker s.t. BRITISH BOMBARDIER 32,351 g.r.t. whose launch had been delayed by a lengthy tug boatman's strike. At this time the Stephen shipyard was at the end of a fairly busy order book and its future workload would comprise building various dredgers alongside warships and merchant vessels. Construction activity associated with the new Clyde Tunnel can be seen on the right hand side, and the Barclay Curle Clydeholm shipyard is barely discernable through the mist on the north bank of the river at Whiteinch.

Previous page, lower. The same vessel, s.t. supertanker BRITISH BOMBARDIER 32,351 g.r.t., *immediately after launching at Linthouse on 18 May 1962. Built for the BP Tanker Co Ltd, London, she was also engined by Stephens and was the largest vessel ever built at Linthouse. Unfortunately, she was not followed by any repeat orders and had a short working life, being broken up in 1976. In the background on the berths are, from right to left, yard no. 678, m.v. MARKHOR 6867 g.r.t. and the Tribal class frigate, HMS ZULU 2300 tons displacement, F.124.*

This page, upper. *The erection shop of the former Linthouse engine works of Alexr Stephen & Sons Ltd, circa 1955, when the company's order book stretched many years into the future. In the distance the main frames, bedplate and columns of a Stephen-Sulzer six-cylinder diesel engine can be seen. In the centre foreground a pair of engine crankshafts rest on timber dunnage. The scale of these components is brought into light with the posing of the fitter adjacent to the nearest crankshaft.*

This page, lower. *Yard no. 658, s.s. CHIRRIPO 6283 g.r.t. immediately after launching at Linthouse on 26 September 1957. Built for Elders & Fyffes Ltd, this fully refrigerated 'banana boat' was the fourth of seven fast reefers constructed totally by Stephens. Note the shell doors and stiffened plating in the way of the cargo holds to allow easy transfer of fruit without using cranes or derricks. In the left foreground is the cast stern-frame of m.v. WIMBLEDON 9223 g.r.t. being built at the Clydeholm shipyard of Barclay Curle & Co Ltd. CHIRRIPO was broken up in 1974 as the MARDINA EXPORTER.*

Yard no. 667, s.t. MOBIL ACME 12,755 g.r.t. *enters the River Clyde from Stephen's Linthouse shipyard on 3 November 1959. Built for Mobil Tankships Ltd of London and engined by Alexr Stephen & Sons Ltd, this vessel's sister yard no. 668, s.t.* MOBIL APEX *can be seen under construction on the adjacent berth. On the extreme left hand berth, yard no. 670, another oil tanker m.t.* BRITISH CURLEW 11,157 g.r.t. *is also nearing launching. Across the river the Clydeholm shipyard of Barclay Curle has the oil tanker m.t.* ATHELQUEEN *under con-struction.* MOBIL ACME *was broken up in 1976. Down river commercial shipping can be seen berthed at Shieldhall wharf and King George V dock beyond.*

Right. *Yard no. 680, t.s.s.s.* AVALON 6584 g.r.t. *enters the River Clyde on 7 May 1963. Built for the British Railways Board Harwich-Hook of Holland passenger service, she was later modified in 1974 as a car ferry. Engined by Alexr Stephen & Sons Ltd, she was renamed* VALON *in 1980 and broken up as that in 1981. Note the aperture at the fore end for her bow thruster and the main deck throng of yard workers enjoying their 'slide into the Clyde'.*

Next page, upper. *Yard no. 686, the diesel-electric self-propelled trailing hopper suction dredger* SEVERODVINSKI 1972 g.r.t. *is manouvered by a pair of Steel & Bennie tugs after her launch on 14 September 1965. The first of three such vessels built for the former USSR by Stephen's, all dredgers were engined by Mirrlees National Ltd of Stockport, and all three were still in service with Northern Shipping Company of Archangel in 1996. The Barclay Curle name is minus a letter 'A' but was still involved in shipbuilding on this grey September day.*

Next page, lower. *The Linthouse shipyard of Alexr Stephen & Sons Ltd in September 1967 showing yard no. 700 under construction. This ship, later named m.v.* PORT CHALMERS 12,398 g.r.t., *was the penultimate vessel built by this esteemed company. The extensive total of nine electric mono-tower travelling cranes are seen to good effect in this view. Alas nearly three decades after this picture was taken, only part of the crane track plinths now exist from this former birthplace of hundreds of fine ships.*

t.s.m.v. CUMBERLAND 11,281 g.r.t. launched in 1948 for the Federal Steam Navigation Co Ltd, London. Engined by Alexr Stephen & Sons Ltd, this fast ref/cargo/passenger vessel was the third of seven ships built at Linthouse for these owners since 1946. She retained her original name and spent her entire career under Federal Steam Navigation until being broken up in 1977.

t.s.s.s. GOLFITO 8740 g.r.t. launched in 1948 for Elders & Fyffes Ltd, Glasgow. Engined by Alexr Stephen & Sons Ltd, this traditional looking passenger cargo liner plied the route from the UK to the West Indies where her main cargo was the speedy return of fruit, mainly bananas, to Britain. She remained in that trade until 1972 when she was broken up at Faslane on the Clyde.

t.s.m.v. FORT DAUPHIN 5038 g.r.t. launched in 1949 for Cie Générale Transatlantique (The French Line), Le Harve. Engined by Alexr Stephen & Sons Ltd, this distinctive looking vessel was the second of a pair of fast sisterships built by Stephens for these owners. She was sold and renamed MARBELLA in 1968, being broken up as GOLFO ARANCI in 1985—well into her fourth decade! Her twin propellers are thrashing well as she speeds through her trials in the Firth of Clyde.

m.v. RIO BERMEJO 7143 g.r.t. launched in 1949 for Empresa Lineas Maritimas Argentinas of Buenos Aires. Engined by Alexr Stephen & Sons Ltd, this refrigerated cargo liner was built to export frozen meat from Argentina to Europe, and performed up until 1980 when she was laid up. She was later reported as being broken in 1982 after a career lasting over thirty years.

t.s.s.s. AUREOL 14,083 g.r.t. *launched in 1951 for Elder Dempster Lines Ltd, Liverpool. Engined by Alexr Stephen & Sons Ltd, this conventional yet attractive and well-proportioned passenger liner was the flagship of the ED fleet and remained so up until she was sold in 1974 and renamed MARIANNA VI. Latterly used as an accommodation ship at the Port of Jeddah, she was still in service in 1996.*

t.s.s.s. OLYMPIA 17,362 g.r.t. *launched in 1953 for Transatlantic Shipping Corporation, Monrovia (The Greek Line). Engined by Alexr Stephen & Sons Ltd, she had the distinction of being the last passenger liner built by the Linthouse yard. Designed to look stylish and futuristic in her day, she is the epitome of her builder's flair and workmanship. Sold and renamed CARIBE in 1982, she was still in existence in 1996 as the REGAL EMPRESS.* (Burniston Studios Ltd)

m.v. FERNVALLEY 4504 g.r.t. *launched in 1954 for Fearnley & Eger of Oslo. Engined by Alexr Stephen & Sons Ltd, this refrigerated cargo liner was sold and renamed CALLIPE L in 1963, retaining that name until being broken up in 1980. Her styling was very typical of a number of vessels built at Linthouse in the post-war period.*

t.s. diesel rail ferry PRINCESS OF VANCOUVER 5554 g.r.t. *launched in 1955 for the Canadian Pacific Railway Co, Victoria, British Columbia. Engined by the National Gas & Oil Engine Co of Ashton-under-Lyne and built for service in the Puget Sound & Straits of Georgia Service, this very North American styled ferry gave sterling Clyde-built reliability for over 30 years to her original owners. Sold and renamed VANCOUVER ISLAND PRICESS in 1987, she was still in existence in the People's Republic of China in 1996 as the NAN HAI MING ZHU.*

s.s. CHICANOA 6283 g.r.t. *launched in 1957 for Elders & Fyffes Ltd, Glasgow. Engined by Alexr Stephen & Sons Ltd, this attractive looking fast reefer also carried passengers as well as bananas in an age before high speed, low-cost air travel rendered such luxury obsolete. The stiffened shell plating in way of the side doors is seen to good effect. This strengthening feature was necessary to compensate for these apertures which assisted with the speedy loading and unloading of her light but perishable cargo. She was sold and renamed ORICA in 1970, being broken up in 1974 as the MARDINA IMPORTER. CHICANOA was the sixth of seven ships built for these owners by Alexr Stephen in the post-war period.*

m.v. WAIKARE 3839 g.r.t. *launched in 1958 for the Union SS Co of New Zealand Ltd, Aukland. Engined by Alexr Stephen & Sons Ltd, she was the last of fifteen refrigerated cargo liners built for these owners (part of the P & O Group) by Stephens since 1946. Sold and renamed MALDIVE SAILOR in 1975, she sank off Cape Cormorin in June 1977 after being in a collision with a Japanese oil tanker.*

Indian Navy frigate KIRPAN 1180 tons displacement, F.144 *was launched at Linthouse in 1958. A Blackwood class frigate similar to ships of that class in the Royal Navy, she was also engined by Stephens who built a total of three such warships. KIRPAN remained in service up until the mid-1980s.*

m.t. BRITISH FULMAR 11,169 g.r.t. *launched in 1958 for the Clyde Charter Co Ltd (BP Tankers). Engined by Alexr Stephen & Sons Ltd, this handsome products tanker was the first Bird class vessel launched on the Clyde, being followed by a total of another nine sisterships from five other builders. Sold and renamed ZHUJIANG in 1976, she later collided and sank off Hong Kong in October 1983 as the DA QING 236. She is seen proudly displaying her builder's house flag against a surrealist background of the island of Arran whilst undergoing sea trials prior to handover. (BP Photographic)* m.v. CITY OF MELBOURNE 9914 g.r.t. *launched in 1959 for Ellerman Lines Ltd, London. Engined by Alexr Stephen & Sons Ltd, this was the fourth and last ship built at Linthouse for these owners since 1946. After the Australian trade for which she was constructed rapidly became containerised, she was renamed CITY OF CAPE TOWN and traded between the UK and South Africa, before being sold then broken up in 1979.*

s.t. MOBIL APEX 12,755 g.r.t. *launched in 1960 for Mobil Tankships Ltd, London. Engined by Alexr Stephen & Sons Ltd, this ship was the second of a pair of sisterships built by the yard for Mobil. Sold and renamed POLLO after a fire on board in 1968, she later underwent various name changes and physical conversion to become the IZARRA, as which she was deleted from Lloyds Register in 1995 presumably now broken up.*

m.v. IBERIC 11,248 g.r.t. *launched in 1960 for Shaw Savill & Albion Co Ltd, Southampton. Engined by Harland & Wolff Ltd, Belfast, this refrigerated cargo/passenger liner was the only one of a series of four built on the Clyde, her sisters being built at Belfast, Birkenhead and Newcastle. Far from being the most attractive ship built at Linthouse she was a functional vessel that was sold and renamed DEASADO in 1976. Later renamed again, the liner was broken up in 1983 as the SAN GEORGE.*

m.v. PIAKO 9986 g.r.t. *launched in 1961 for the New Zealand Shipping Co Ltd, London. Engined by Alexr Stephen & Sons Ltd, this was a very traditional, fully refrigerated cargo liner, and was the thirty-first of thirty-three vessels built for the P & O Group at Linthouse since 1946. Sold and renamed REEFER QUEEN in 1979, she was broken up in 1984. She was virtually identical to the m.v. SOMERSET 10,027 g.r.t. built by John Brown & Co (Clydebank) Ltd in 1962 for the associated company Federal Steam Navigation Co Ltd.*

s.t. BRITISH BOMBARDIER 32,351 g.r.t. *launched in 1962 for the BP Tanker Co Ltd, London. Engined by Alexr Stephen & Sons Ltd, this stylish supertanker was the largest vessel built by the Linthouse shipyard. She is seen discharging her first cargo of Middle-East crude oil at the BP terminal at Finnart on Loch Long, Dunbartonshire in 1963. Her short career only lasted until 1976 when she was broken up under her original name. The natural deep water of this loch provided a good haven for large tankers. The facility was later used to briefly export North Sea crude oil before the inauguration of the BP terminal at Dalmeny on the Firth of Forth.*

m.v. MARKHOR 6867 g.r.t. *launched in 1962 for Thos & Jno Brocklebank Ltd of Liverpool. Engined by Alexr Stephen & Sons Ltd, this attractive cargo liner was the first of a pair of vessels built by the yard for these owners. They were also the first diesel powered ships for Brocklebank Line in forty years. Sold and renamed KARA UNICORN in 1982, she was broken up in 1984.*

m.v. MELBROOK 11,075 g.r.t. *launched in 1964 at the Leven shipyard of the former Dumbarton shipbuilders Wm Denny & Bros Ltd by Alexr Stephen & Sons Ltd. The vessel was begun as a speculative new ship order by Dennys. Stephens completed her and sold the ship to the P & O Group company Duff, Herbert & Mitchell Ltd, London. She was engined by Hawthorn Leslie (Eng) Ltd of Newcastle who completed the original Denny-Sulzer diesel. Sold and renamed EXMOOR in 1972, she was broken up in 1986 as ANTHI-MARINA. The vessel bore one of the Denny hallmarks of lattice bracing between the top of her derrick posts which enhanced the ship's appearance.*

HMS PHOEBE 2350 tons displacement, F42, *a Leander class frigate, was launched for the Royal Navy in 1964 and commissioned in 1966. Engined by Alexr Stephen & Sons Ltd, this ship was the first of two Leander class frigates built at Linthouse in the 1960s. She was refitted in 1977, and her naval career ended in 1990 when she was broken up. Despite their sleek appearance these warships always looked far less armed than the ships they were replacing.*

twin-screw motor logistic landing ship SIR GALAHAD 4473 g.r.t. *launched in 1966 for the MoD. Engined by Mirrlees National Ltd, Stockport, she was the first of two such craft built at Linthouse. Her brief yet successful career was ended in 1982 during the Falklands War when she was extensively bombed, set ablaze, yet did not sink although many casualties were sustained. She was later scuttled and marked as a war grave by the Royal Navy. Her Linthouse built sister, SIR GERAINT 4,473 g.r.t., was still in front line service in 1996.*

m.v. MAJESTIC 12,591 g.r.t. *launched in 1966 for Shaw Savill & Albion Co Ltd, Southampton. Engined by Alexr Stephen & Sons Ltd, this fully refrigerated general cargo/heavy lift vessel was the second of a three-ship order for these owners. Sold and renamed N.Z. AORANGI in 1974, she was later sold and renamed MYKONOS V, as which she was broken up in 1995.*

t.s.d.e. hopper suction dredger RIBBOK 4594 g.r.t. *launched in 1967 for South African Railways & Harbours, Durban. Engined by English Electric Ltd, Newton-le-Willows, this vessel was a 1960 'stylisation' of a proven Simons-Lobnitz 'Si-Lo' design and successfully worked in South Africa for over 20 years, being broken up under her original name in 1990. Despite her stylish superstructure and integrated mast and funnel, the vessel has a very traditional and unflared bow.*

m.v. PORT CAROLINE 12,398 g.r.t. *launched in 1968 for Port Line Limited, London. Engined by Geo. Clark, Sunderland, this attractive refrigerated cargo liner was a fitting tribute 'last ship' from the Linthouse shipyard of Alexr Stephen & Sons Ltd, although she was completed by the phoenix company that was Upper Clyde Shipbuilders Ltd. She is sporting the Stephen house flag which was taken by UCS Ltd at take-over as their logo. It is clearly visible on the starboard side of her signal mast whilst on trials. This ship and her sister PORT CHALMERS were the largest reefers in the world when built. Renamed MATRA in 1982 within the Cunard/Port Line/ Brocklebank Group, she was sold in 1983, renamed GOLDEN DOLPHIN and broken up as that in 1985.*

4582 g.r.t., a twin-screw self-propelled hopper suction dredger for the port of Calcutta launched on 16 February 1961. Maintaining the same overseas sales thrust of its two former constituent companies, the Simons-Lobnitz Ltd export ratio in its brief existence was a credible 54%.

T.W. Ward Ltd bought virtually the whole site after closure and gradually disposed of the extensive amount of plant and machinery. Both sets of slipways have been filled in and all cranes dismantled. Only the dredged fitting-out quay at the Lobnitz site and the buildings of their former engine works attest to a location of former shipbuilding and marine engineering activity.

List of ships built by Wm. SIMONS & Co Ltd, Renfrew, between 1946 and formation of SIMONS-LOBNITZ Ltd in 1959

YEAR	NAME	TYPE		COUNTRY OF REGISTRATION	DISPL/ G.R.T.	TOTAL OUTPUT	YEAR	NAME	TYPE		COUNTRY OF REGISTRATION	DISPL/ G.R.T.	TOTAL OUTPUT
1946	EMPIRE MARSHLAND	s.	Hopper Barge	Britain (RN)	683		1953 •	BONTEBOK	s.	Suction HD	South Africa	3318	3318
	EMPIRE FORAGER	s.	Suction HD	Britain (RN)	2588		1954	HOPPER NO. 25	s.	H Barge	Britain	941	
	EMPIRE WOODLAND	s.	Hopper Barge	Britain (RN)	683			HOPPER NO. 26		H Barge	Britain	941	
	EMPIRE TESSA	s.	Tug	Britain (RN)	302			R.B. WATERSTON	s.	Tug	South Africa	704	
	EMPIRE NORA...	s.	Tug	Nigeria	302			AXFORD	m.	SD Boat	Britain (RN)	120	
	r/n BARMAN THAUNKHOK	s.	Cutter SD	Burma	646	5204		YANTLET	m.	Salvage Tug	Britain	471	3177
1947	SIR GODFREY ARMSTRONG	s.	Suction HD	India	963		1955	BECKFORD	m.	SD Boat	Britain (RN)	120 displ	120
	OYO	s.	Suction HD	Nigeria	3942	4905	1956	T.I.C. NO. 26	m.	H Barge	Britain	477	
1948	RECLAIM	s.	Deep Diving Vessel	Britain (RN)	1257	1257		T.I.C. NO. 27		H barge	Britain	477	954
1949	M.O.P.228C	m.e.	Suction HD	Argentina	3437		1957 •	BHAGIRATHI	s.	Suction HD	India	4697	4697
	IBADAN	s.	Suction HD	Nigeria	2886		1958 •	GRIPER	m.e.p.	Tug	Britain (RN)	472 displ	
	JALENGI	s.	Suction HD	India	4451	10774		GRINDER	m.e.p.	Tug	Britain (RN)	472 displ	944
1950	M.O.P.227C	m.e.	Suction HD	Argentina	2749	2749	1959 •	FAIRTRY II	m.e.	Stern FT	Britain	2857	
1951	NADIA	s.	Buoy Lifting Vessel	India	1255	1255	•	LAYMOOR	s.	Boom DV	Britain (RN)	750 displ	
1952	SANDCHIME	s.	Grab HD	Britain	190	190		FAIRTRY III	m.e.	Stern FT	Britain	2857	6464

30% export   4 vessels total = 1,814 tons displacement
60% Britain   26 vessels total = 44,194 g.r.t.

• Indicates vessel depicted in subsequent photographic section.
For explanation of abbreviations see Glossary on page 345.

List of ships built by LOBNITZ & Co. Ltd., Renfrew, between 1946 and formation of SIMONS-LOBNITZ Ltd. in 1959

YEAR	NAME	TYPE		COUNTRY OF REGISTRATION	G.R.T.	TOTAL G.R.T.	YEAR	NAME	TYPE		COUNTRY OF REGISTRATION	G.R.T.	TOTAL G.R.T.
1946	BIRCHOL	s.	Oil Tanker	Britain (RN)	1440		1952	YZER	n.p.	Bucket D	Belgium	728	
	ROWANOL	s.	Oil Tanker	Britain (RN)	1440		•	TITAN	s.	Crane Ship	Britain	665	1393
	VERA BARTON	n.p.	Bucket D	Britain	180		1953	EDDYCREEK	s.	Oil Tanker	Britain (RN)	2224	
•	OAKOL	s.	Oil Tanker	Britain (RN)	1440			KINGROAD	m.	H Barge	Britain	1045	
	H.A.M. III	n.p.	Bucket D	South Africa	574			EDDYFIRTH	s.	Oil Tanker	Britain (RN)	2222	5491
	TEAKOL	s.	Oil Tanker	Britain (RN)	1440		1954	EDWARD CRUSE	s.	Sludge Car	Britain	1818	
	—	n.p.	Crane Pnt	Unknown	130			SKOTTEN	n.p.	Dipper D	Norway	350	
	—	n.p.	Crane Pnt	Unknown	130			T.C.C. DREDGER NO. 11	n.p.	Bucket D	Britain	508	
	—	n.p.	Rockcutter	Unknown	130	6904		THANLAWADDY	n.p.	Suction D	Burma	250	2926
1947	MEDITERRANEE	n.p.	Bucket D	France	960		1955	ATLAS	s.	Crane Ship	Britain	1137	
	FLANDRE	n.p.	Bucket D	France	960		•	SHIELDHALL	s.	Sludge Car	Britain	1792	
	LABORIEUSE	n.p.	Bucket D	France	960	2880		DOKHTAWADDY	n.p.	Suction D	Burma	250	
1948	KALA NAG	n.p.	Dipper D	France	1050			SITTAUNG	n.p.	Suction D	Burma	250	
	RIBBLE	s.	Suction HD	Britain	1287			WILTON	m.	Tug	Britain	208	
	ASTLAND	s.	Suction HD	Britain	1287		•	OTAGO	s.	Salvage Tug	N. Zealand	502	4139
	CALDER	s.	Suction HD	Britain	618		1956	AMANFUL	n.p.	Rock Cutter	Ghana	301	
	MERSEY NO. 14	m.e.	Grab HD	Britain	459	4701		MERSEY NO. 40	m.	H Barge	Britain	1968	2269
1949	CAMPECHE	s.	Suction HD	Mexico	1833		1957	PERA I	n.p.	Dipper D	Finland	376	
	SAVICK	s.	Suction HD	Britain	618			MERSEY NO. 42	m.	H Barge	Britain	637	
	HAFFAR	s.	Suction HD	Britain	1180		•	ROBERT WEIR	s.	Suction HD	Britain	1030	2043
	SIR FON	m.	H Barge	Britain	814	4445	1958 •	KENLEY	m.	Tug	Britain	246	
1950	SPRINGWOOD	m.	H Barge	Britain	814		•	DENDER	m.	Suction D	Belgium	1100	
	JEAN MANTELET	m.	Pilot Tender	Egypt	625			HEORTENESSE	m.	Suction HD	Britain	604	1950
	T.C.C. HOPPER NO. 5	s.	H Barge	Britain	751		1959	CARDON	m.e.	Tug	Venezuela	324	
	T.C.C. HOPPER NO. 6	s.	H Barge	Britain	751		•	STOREGUT	n.p.	Dipper D	Norway	400	
	MAGADI NO. 3	n.p.	Grab D	Kenya	170	3111		SAMSON	m.e.	Crane Ship	Britain	974	1698
1951	T.C.C. DREDGER NO. 1	s.	Suction HD	Britain	1206			44% export					
	A.D. MACKENZIE	n.p.	Bucket D	Australia	646	1852		56% Britain	54 vessels total = 45,802 g.r.t.					

List of ships built by SIMONS-LOBNITZ Ltd, Renfrew, between 1960 and closure of both yards in 1963

YEAR	NAME	TYPE	COUNTRY OF REGISTRATION	DISPL/ G.R.T.	TOTAL OUTPUT
1960 •	PERAKI	s. Suction HD	N. Zealand	1896	
	LAYBURN	s. Boom DV	Britain (RN)	750 displ	
•	TRINITY SAND	m. Grab HD	Britain	1252	3898
1961 •	CHURNI	s. Suction HD	India	4582	
•	J.H.W.D. ENTERPRISE	n.p. Suction Dredger	Britain	1000	
	W.H. ORBELL	m. Bucket HD	N. Zealand	1240	
	BLEASDALE	m. Suction HD	Britain	1029	7851
1962	THAUNG NAING YAY	m. Suction HD	Burma	1234	
	HOPPER NO. 27	m. H Barge	Britain	981	
	HOPPER NO. 28	m. H Barge	Britain	981	
	KHOFO	n.p. Suction D	Egypt	2700	5896

YEAR	NAME	TYPE	COUNTRY OF REGISTRATION	DISPL/ G.R.T.	TOTAL OUTPUT
1963 •	SEVA	s. Survey Tug	India	1351	
•	CROFTON	m.e. Suction HD	Britain	1062	
•	HOPPER BARGE NO. 2	m. H Barge	India	1200	
	HOPPER BARGE NO. 3	m. H Barge	India	1200	4813

54% export	1 vessel total	=	750 tons displacement
46% Britain	14 vessels total	=	21,708 g.r.t.

• Indicates vessel depicted in subsequent photographic section.

For explanation of abbreviations see Glossary on page 345.

The following batch of photographs illustrates shipbuilding activity at the locations of the former Renfrew shipyards and engine works of Wm Simons & Co Ltd, Lobnitz & Co Ltd, and the short-lived amalgamation of Simons-Lobnitz Ltd. Also included are a batch of trials pictures depicting some of the many ship types built by these distinctive builders during their last decade of operation.

Yard no. 805, twin-screw steam hopper suction dredger BHAGIRATHI 4697 g.r.t. shortly before launching from the Wm Simons & Co Ltd shipyard in the summer of 1957. Note the extensive use of riveting on her shell plating seams, as well as her hull framing. Keel blocks and a strake of bottom shell plating for yard no. 803, HMS GRIPER 472 tons displacement, a diesel-electric paddle tug for the Royal Navy, have recently been laid out on the adjacent berth. The bipod structure on the right was a light weight set of shear legs (or A frame) used between two berths for the lifting of materials. (Glasgow University Archives)

Page 212. *The Renfrew shipyard of Simons-Lobnitz Ltd viewed from the east in the summer of 1961. The former Wm Simons yard occupies the area in the centre foreground, bounded by Renfrew Wharf railway station and the roadway, known as Meadowside Street, with the erstwhile Lobnitz yard beyond. The ex-Simons berths are currently empty, however work is under way in preparation for the next vessels to be built. The buildings in the centre foreground are the engine works to the left, with the plating and welding shops nearest the river. The two groups of buildings in the ex-Lobnitz yard are the plating, preparation and fabrication sheds on the right, with the compact yet extensive engine works on the left. Two vessels are under construction on the berths and in the fitting-out basin the non-propelled suction dredger J.H.W.D. ENTERPRISE 1000 g.r.t. nears completion. Rothesay Dock and its huge marshalling yard, which was later acquired and briefly occupied in the 1970s by the JBE Offshore Ltd module building yard, can be seen on the north bank. Note the proud emblazonment of Simons-Lobnitz Ltd on the east side of the office building wall.*

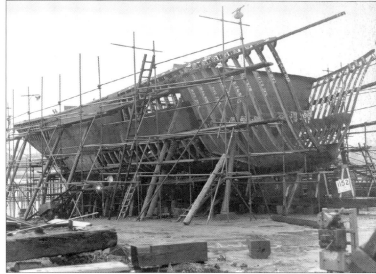

Above. *Yard no. 1152, motor tug KENLEY 246 g.r.t. under construction on one of the berths at Lobnitz & Co Ltd, Renfrew shipyard in early 1958. The traditional single-frame carcass erection sequence is governed by the high amount of rivetting on this tug. Note the pre-drilled bulb angle frames at the forward starboard side. These holes will be used as templates for the riveting of the shell plating after it is erected onto the bulb angle frames. (Glasgow University Archives)*

Left. *The Renfrew fitting-out basin of Lobnitz & Co Ltd in 1959 showing the 'excavator like bucket' of non-propelled dipper dredger STOREGUT 400 g.r.t. and the port side of twin-screw motor hopper dredger HEORTNESSE 604 g.r.t. The riveted box structure to the extreme left is part of one of the legs of Lobnitz's shear legs that was used to install boilers and engines into recently launched craft. (Glasgow University Archives)*

Yard no. 812, twin-screw steam suction hopper dredger CHURNI 4582 g.r.t. is towed out of the Simons-Lobnitz Ltd fitting-out basin to begin her sea trials in the spring of 1961. The full order book of the recently merged yard is evinced in this view that shows a further three dredgers under construction. Note the large amount of proud workers inspecting the port side of CHURNI as she is skewed into the river by a pair of tugs. On the opposite side of the river the Clydebank shipyard of John Brown & Co Ltd can be seen beyond the cranes of Rothesay dock, where an unidentified bulk carrier is moored. The attractive colour scheme of this vessel which was the largest built by Simons-Lobnitz Ltd will soon be discoloured when she starts dredging in India. (Glasgow University Archives)

Part of the Renfrew shipyard of Simons-Lobnitz Ltd in 1962 showing yard no. 1168, twin-screw steam tug SEVA 1351 g.r.t. under construction. Note the crude 'A' frames necessary to assist with rigging loads that were outwith the radii of the shipyard's fixed hammerhead cranes. The Renfrew ferry can barely be seen beyond the right-hand crane making its chain driven passage to Yoker on the other bank of the River Clyde. Yoker power station was then still in existence generating electricity from Scottish mined coal. Note the course of part of the yard's internal railway system which is cased in concrete to perform the dual function of use as a roadway. (Glasgow University Archives)

Left. twin-screw steam suction hopper dredger BONTEBOK 3318 g.r.t. *launched in 1953 for the Republic of South Africa Railways and Harbours Administration, Durban. Engined by Wm Simons & Co Ltd, Renfrew, this large dredger is being manouvered down-river to begin her sea trials. She remained in service under her original name with the same owners until she was broken up in 1986.* (Glasgow University Archives)

Below. HMS GRIPER 472 tons displacement, *a diesel-electric paddle tug, was the first of a pair launched by the yard for the Royal Navy in 1959. Engined by Paxman Diesels Ltd, Colchester, she was broken up in 1980.* (Glasgow University Archives)

Above. twin-screw steam suction hopper dredger BHAGIRATHI 4697 g.r.t. *launched in 1957 for the Commissioners of the Port of Calcutta. Engined by Wm Simons & Co Ltd, this vessel bore the distinction of being the largest ship ever built by the Renfrew shipyard. She had a thirty year lifespan under her original name and was broken up in 1987.* (Glasgow University Archives)

Below. HMS LAYMOOR 750 tons displacement, P-190, *a boom defence vessel, was launched for the Royal Navy in 1959. Engined by Wm Simons & Co Ltd, she was decommissioned in 1984 and towed from Gibraltar to be used as a target whence she was sunk.* (Glasgow University Archives)

Above. diesel-electric stern factory trawler FAIRTRY II 2857 g.r.t. *launched in 1959 for Christian Salvesen & Co Ltd, Leith. Engined by Ruston & Hornsby of Lincoln, this ship was the first such vessel to be designed and built on the River Clyde. Wm Simons also built her sistership in the same year. Predating Eastern Bloc copy-cat ships by a number of years, the relatively small capacity of this vessel led to her early demise in 1972 when she was sold, modified and renamed VICKERS VOYAGER. She was broken up at Troon in 1984 as the BRITISH VOYAGER. Male and female guests throng her decks as she performs her trials in the Firth of Clyde.* (Glasgow University Archives)

s.t. OAKOL 1440 g.r.t. *launched in 1946 for the Admiralty. Engined by Lobnitz & Co Ltd, this vessel was the third in a series of four built at Renfrew for the Royal Navy. She was decommissioned in 1969, thence hulked at Bruges in Belgium.* (Glasgow University Archives)

Above, right. twin-screw steam sludge carrier SHIELDHALL 1792 g.r.t. *launched in 1955 for Glasgow Corporation. Engined by Lobnitz & Co Ltd, this unique vessel was built with lounge and dining facilities to enable usually old-age pensioners to be taken on board, whilst the ship plied the River Clyde discharging her cargo off Garroch Head, south of the Isle of Bute. She was sold and converted in 1991 and was still in existence in 1996 under her original name as a ferry/exhibition ship.*

Above, left. twin-screw steam powered crane ship TITAN 665 g.r.t. *launched in 1952 for the Mersey Docks & Harbour Board, Liverpool. Engined by Lobnitz & Co Ltd, this vessel was an excellent example of the marine and mechanical engineering prowess of her builders. The diesel-electric crane was designed and built by Cowans Sheldon Ltd of Carlisle. She was sold to Greek owners in 1973, and later deleted from Lloyds Register, presumably broken up.* (Glasgow University Archives)

Middle. twin-screw steam salvage tug OTAGO 502 g.r.t. *launched in 1955 for Otago Harbour Board, New Zealand. Engined by Lobnitz & Co Ltd, she was sold and renamed DASHER I in 1981. She was deleted from Lloyds Register in 1992, presumably having been broken up.*

Right, lower. steam suction hopper dredger ROBERT WEIR 1030 g.r.t. *launched in 1957 for the County Borough of Preston, Lancashire. Engined by Lobnitz & Co Ltd, this vessel was still in existence under her original name in 1996.* (Burniston Studios Ltd)

An impressive photograph showing functional trials prior to vessel handover from builders to owners of motor tug KENLEY 246 g.r.t. launched in 1958 for J.P. Knight Ltd, Rochester, Kent. Engined by British Polar Engines Ltd, she is seen testing her water cannons during her trials in the Firth of Clyde. She retained her original name until being broken up in 1984. (Burniston Studios Ltd)

diesel-electric suction dredger DENDER 1100 g.r.t. launched in 1958 for Societe Generale de Dragage, Antwerp, Belgium. Engined by C.D. Holmes & Co Ltd, Hull, this vessel was the second of only two craft built on the Clyde for Belgium, and both were constructed by Lobnitz & Co Ltd. She remained with her original name and owners until being broken up in 1984. (Burniston Studios Ltd)

non-propelled diesel-electric dipper dredger STOREGUT 400 g.r.t. launched in 1959 for Kystdirectorat A/S, Oslo. This vessel, based on a land excavator, was the second of a pair designed and built at Renfrew to help with modernisation of many of Norway's harbours. She was deleted from the DNV Register in 1961, and is presumably now broken up. (Burniston Studios Ltd)

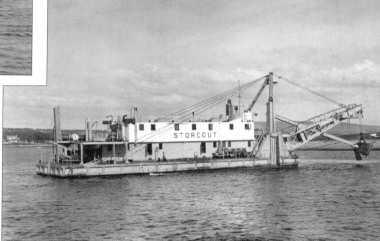

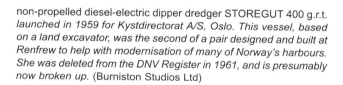

twin-screw steam suction hopper dredger PERAKI 1896 g.r.t. launched in 1960 for Lyttleton Harbour Board, New Zealand. Engined by Simons-Lobnitz Ltd, this unconventional looking vessel's performance belied her ungainly looks, as she was still in existence in 1996 under her original name. (Burniston Studios Ltd)

motor grab hopper dredger TRINITY SAND 1252 g.r.t. launched in 1960 for the British Transport Docks Board, Grimsby. Engined by Ruston & Hornsby Ltd, Lincoln, this functional dredger was still in existence under her original name in 1996. The three grab cranes on her deck were built by Priestman Bros Ltd, Hull. (Burniston Studios Ltd)

twin-screw steam suction hopper dredger CHURNI 4582 g.r.t. *launched in 1961 for the Commissioners of the Port of Calcutta. Engined by Simons-Lobnitz Ltd, the vessel's pristine paintwork is stained by the slurry that has been washed over her decks while performing dredging trials in the Firth of Clyde. This vessel was still in existence under her original name and ownership in 1996.* (Glasgow University Archives)

Above. twin-screw steam survey/salvage tug SEVA 1351 g.r.t. *launched in 1963 for the Commissioners of the Port of Calcutta. Engined by Simons-Lobnitz Ltd, this distinctive and multifunctional vessel was still in existence under her original name and ownership in 1996.* (Burniston Studios Ltd)

Left. twin-screw diesel-electric trailing suction hopper dredger CROFTON 1062 g.r.t. *launched in 1963 for Blyth Harbour Commissioners, Northumberland. Engined by AEI Ltd, Rugby, this stylish dredger was still in existence under her original name in 1996.* (Glasgow University Archives)

twin-screw motor hopper barge HOPPER BARGE No. 2 1200 g.r.t. *launched in 1963 for the Commissioners of the Port of Calcutta. Engined by MAN Augsburg, West Germany, this vessel was the penultimate ship built by Simons-Lobnitz Ltd at Renfrew. She was converted to a survey ship in 1975 and renamed GAVESHANI and as such she was still in existence in 1996. Note the awnings above the winches below the forward mast, considered as 'tropicalising' to provide some form of protection from the heat of the sun for operatives.* (Burniston Studios Ltd)

▌ FLEMING & FERGUSON LTD   1878-1969

The former McIntyre shipyard in Paisley was taken over in 1878 by Fleming & Ferguson Ltd. Renamed Phoenix shipbuilding yard it was situated on the west bank of the Cart, half a mile from the centre of the town. The company was an adaptable concern that built coasters, dredgers, tugs and hopper barges, etc. up to 310 ft long. Their engine works on the same site built steam propulsion machinery for some of their new construction, and all dredging equipment was also designed and built there.

Occupying a site within the harbour that deemed the town of Paisley a seagoing port until its abandonment in 1967, the Phoenix shipyard also saw some passing trade in minor repairs to coasters and puffers, which plied this industrial backwater. With regular ship and barge-borne traffic to and from the large Babcock and Wilcox engineering works down-river at Renfrew, the River Cart was then a reasonably busy shipping tributary of the larger River Clyde. Such frequent use by commercial shipping nevertheless resulted in ongoing dredging of the narrow channel, as well as maintaining a free passage for marine activity to and from the Phoenix shipyard.

Complex nodes, brackets, buckets or other complicated ironmongery that formed the main working parts of a dredger were redesigned for welding throughout the post-war era. Such adaptation managed to phase out part of the previous dependency on the combined skills and unique expertise of blacksmiths, founders, riveters and patternmakers, although these trades remained on the company's payroll inventory as hot-forming, casting, forging and heat treatment were still needed to make various components, work-harden the teeth, bearings and journals that were key elements of the dredgers moving parts.

Employing around 600 men in total, the company regularly produced between two to three specialist craft each year, usually at least one of those vessels was for overseas owners. With limited capacity fixed cranes and derricks, the method of construction was, the traditional laying out of the keel, rib frames, girders, stringers, pillars and columns, followed by the systematic installation of some small items of machinery, with final shell, deck and bulkhead plating completing the hull prior to launching.

Bereft of capital investment, and in possession of a dwindling order book the yard went into receivership in 1965. It was rescued that year by the American Marine and Machinery Co Inc who were attracted by the company's excellent reputation in their specialist field and strong customer base. They promised to revive the fortunes of Paisley's last shipyard, but unfortunately the take-over was too late to make any significant impact on the yards non-profitability. Isolated some three miles up-river from the main shipping activity, in need of many millions spent on improving the shipyard, the hoped for investment required to modernise the facility never materialised. The labour force dwindled to around 200 workers and the small yard closed in 1968.

The following vessels were constructed under the auspices of the new owners, in addition to a number of small work boats for British Waterways Ltd, which were built in kit form and despatched in boxes on the back of lorries. They were:

- two small standard cutter-suction dredgers for Sri Lanka built in knock-down kit form that left the yard in packing cases throughout 1966
- two self-propelled hopper barges for Calcutta Port Commissioners, the last of which, *Hopper Barge No. 5* was launched on 27 May 1968 and completed later that year. This order was transferred from the Blyth Dry Docks & Shipbuilding Co Ltd in the north east of England, after that company went into liquidation
- one non-propelled cutter-suction dredger that was a 'speculative new building'. This small vessel remained on the slipway after the Paisley yard was wound up. Called *Bled*, she was duly completed and commissioned by the Renfrew boat builders Hugh McLean & Sons Ltd, being eventually sold to Yugoslav owners.

Between 1946 and 1969, the shipyard built 48 ships of 41,848 g.r.t. the largest of which were a pair of identical self-propelled suction hopper dredgers for the Argentine in 1948, each of 2749 g.r.t. Both ships plus a bucket dredger also launched that year produced the yard's largest annual output of 6498 g.r.t. The export ratio of 72% of their entire post-war production gave the small Paisley shipyard the highest percentage of overseas custom among the rest of the West of Scotland shipbuilders. Probably the most famous of many fine ships built at the Phoenix yard during this period was the *John Biscoe*, a diesel-electric survey ship of 1584 g.r.t. for the British Antarctic Survey delivered in 1956, and specially designed and strengthened for navigation through ice.

The site is now occupied by a trading estate called Phoenix Park. The ends of the former slipways are still visible from the opposite side of the River Cart at all states of the tide. Some of the yard's former dredger designs have been resurrected, modified and marketed by the nearby Seadrec company and their associates.

List of ships built by FLEMING & FERGUSON Ltd, Paisley, between 1946 and closure in 1969

YEAR	NAME	TYPE	COUNTRY OF REGISTRATION	G.R.T.	TOTAL G.R.T.
1946	TAFF	n.p. Bucket D	Britain	607	
	MANDOVI	s. Suction HD	Portugal	604	
	GRETTIR	s. Bucket D	Iceland	286	1497
1947	CABOT STRAIT	s. Ref/C/P	Canada	2045	
	ABERTAWE	s. Bucket D	Britain	653	
	SPRINGDALE	s. Ref/C/P	Canada	1138	
	BAR HAVEN	s. Ref/C/P	Canada	1138	4974
1948	M.O.P. 225.C.51	m.e. Suction HD	Argentina	2749	
	D.6	n.p. Bucket D	Uruguay	1000	
	M.O.P.226.C.52	m.e. Suction HD	Argentina	2749	6498
1949	COCUR	s. Bucket D	Britain	588	
	SIR JAMES MITCHELL	s. Suction HD	Australia	1233	1821
1950	P.S.I. G.H.	n.p. H Barge	Trinidad	245	
	P.S.II. G.H.	n.p. H Barge	Trinidad	245	
	–	m.e. Dipper D	Thailand	150	
	–	m.e. Dipper D	Thailand	150	790
1951	ST. MARTIN #8	s. Grab HD	Britain (RN)	450	
	ST. GILES #6	s. Grab HD	Britain (RN)	550	
	B.D.I.	n.p. Bucket D	Britain	150	1150
1952	RELUME	s. Lt Tender	Britain	1516	
	RENFREW FERRY	m.e. Ferry (chain)	Britain	170	
	RIO PARDO	n.p. Cutter SD	Brazil	217	
	SALWEEN	s. Suction HD	Burma	750	2653
1953	ENGR. ANTONIO PRADEL	n.p. Cutter SD	Brazil	639	
	GROPER	s. Bucket D	Australia	738	
	ENGR. JORGE PORTO	n.p. Dipper D	Brazil	175	1552
1954	CESSNOCK	s. Bucket D	Britain	723	
	MEE PYA	s. Buoy/Lt T	Burma	856	
	PYIDAWAYE	s. Pass/Cargo	Burma	2217	3796
1955 •	PYIDAWNYUNT	s. Pass/Cargo	Burma	2217	
	RIO IBICUI	n.p. Dipper D	Brazil	175	2392
1956 •	JOHN BISCOE	m.e. Survey Ship	Britain	1584	
	BREMANG NO. 4	n.p. Gold D	Gold Coast	500	
	D.H.T. NO. 7	n.p. Hopper B	Britain	268	2352
1957	L.A. 2	n.p. Crane Pnt	N. Zealand	204	
	AUCKLANDER	s. Tug	N. Zealand	454	658
1958 •	SOUTRA	m. Cargo	Britain	1334	
	NGAMOTU	s. Grab SHD	N. Zealand	923	2257
1959	None	None None	–	–	–
1960 •	AJOY	s. Bucket D	India	1066	1066
1961	LONG REACH	s. Grab HD	Britain	1972	
	• CLEE NESS	m. Drag SHD	Britain	1436	3408
1962	None	None None	–	–	
1963 •	VEDRA	n.p. Bucket D	Britain	326	
	• ANUSANDHANI	m. Res Vessel	India	671	997
1964 •	FATEH	s. Bucket D	Pakistan	997	997
1965	IZHAR	s. Bucket D	Pakistan	997	997
1966	None	None None	–	–	
1967 •	HOPPER BARGE NO. 4	m. Hopper B	India	859	859
1968	HOPPER BARGE NO. 5	m. Hopper B	India	859	859
1969	BLED	n.p. Cutter SD	Yugoslavia	275	275

72% export
28% Britain   **48 vessels total = 41,848 g.r.t.**

• Indicates vessel depicted in subsequent photographic section.

For explanation of abbreviations see Glossary on page 345.

The following small group of photographs illustrate part of the location of the former Phoenix shipyard and engine works of Fleming & Ferguson Ltd, Paisley. Also depicted are a few berth scenes and a handful of trials photographs showing some of the craft built by this specialised shipbuilder during the decade prior to closure.

YARD N° 795
TWIN SCREW BUCKET DREDGER
FOR
CALCUTTA PORT COMMISSIONERS
BUILT BY FLEMING & FERGUSON L™
PAISLEY   SCOTLAND

Above. *Almost the whole spectrum of shipyard employees amassed for an impromptu photograph within the Phoenix shipyard of Fleming & Ferguson Ltd, Paisley on 13 May 1960. The occasion was the launch of yard no. 795,* the steam powered bucket dredger AJOY 1066 g.r.t. *for use in the Port of Calcutta. Noticeable in the foreground are a bunch of blacksmiths, whilst a pair of bowler-hatted managers discuss the forthcoming launch with the photographers standing next to what appears to be a stylish yet dated Vauxhall estate car in the background.*

Left. *Steam reciprocating propulsion machinery under construction in the Paisley engine works of Fleming & Ferguson Ltd during 1960, for installation in the* twin screw bucket dredger AJOY. *The only indication of scale in this picture is the wooden ladder between both engines.*

Previous page, upper. *Yard no. 778, the diesel-electric ice-breaking survey ship* JOHN BISCOE 1584 g.r.t. *is given a rousing send-off at the occasion of her launch into the River Cart from the Phoenix shipyard, Paisley on the beautiful day of 11 June 1956. On the adjacent berth, steelwork has been erected for the non-propelled gold dredger* BREMANG No. 4, *a 'hull only subcontract' undertaken by the yard for use in Ghana (formerly known as the Gold Coast).*

Previous page, lower. *Reasonable activity at the Phoenix shipyard of Fleming & Ferguson Ltd in the summer of 1958. Alongside the fitting-out quay beneath the yard's shearlegs, yard no. 788, m.v.* SOUTRA 1334 g.r.t., *a coaster for Christian Salvesen of Leith nears completion. On the adjacent berth, yard no. 789,* NGAMOTU 923 g.r.t., *a twin-screw grab and suction hopper dredger for New Zealand progresses towards launching. Part of Paisley and its small harbour can be seen in the background. Note how higgledy-piggledy the scaffolding around the dredger has been assembled.*

YARD N° 799
SINGLE-SCREW-RESEARCH-VESSEL
FOR
CALCUTTA PORT-COMMISSIONERS
BUILT BY FLEMING & FERGUSON LTD
PAISLEY   SCOTLAND

Previous page, upper, left. *Yard no. 795, AJOY 1066 g.r.t., a twin-screw self-propelled bucket dredger for the Commissioners of the Port of Calcutta slides into the murky River Cart on the pouring wet day of 13 May 1960. Note the bunch of yard workers huddled on the fore end in their 1950s fashioned wet weather wear.*

Previous page, upper, right. *Yard no. 797, CLEE NESS 1436 g.r.t., a diesel twin-screw drag suction hopper dredger, prior to launching for the British Transport Docks Board, Hull, on 28 September 1961. This vessel was sold and renamed UCO I in 1988 and still retained that name in 1996. Note the extensive use of rivetting of the vessel's frames to the side shell plating.*

Previous page, lower. *Yard no. 799, the single-screw diesel research vessel ANUSANDHANI 671 g.r.t. prior to launching for the Calcutta Port Commissioners on 27 March 1963. Note the builders' flag and bunting draped on the vessel's aft mast, also the starboard bilge keel plate protruding diagonally from the ship's hull, and the fabricated protection casing around the propeller.*

This page, right, upper. *s.s. PYIDAWNYUNT 2217 g.r.t. launched in 1955 for the Five Star Line Ltd of Rangoon, Burma. Engined by Fleming & Ferguson Ltd, this ship was the second of a pair of cargo passenger vessels built for these owners by the Paisley yard. Her career came to an end in July 1979 when she was damaged by fire whilst under repair in a Singapore shipyard, being later declared a constructive total loss, thence broken up.*

Previous page, middle. The diesel-electric survey ship JOHN BISCOE 1584 g.r.t. *launched in 1956 for the British Antarctic Survey, Port Stanley, Falkland Islands. Engined by the Nat. Gas & Oil Engine Co Ltd, Ashton-under-Lyne, the newly completed ship is towed down the River Cart on a hazy day in 1956, heading for the Firth of Clyde and performance of sea trials. The lead tug,* FLYING MERLIN *was built by the Port Glasgow shipyard of Ferguson Brothers (Port Glasgow) Ltd in 1951.* d.e.s.s. JOHN BISCOE *was sold and renamed* FAYZA EXPRESS *in 1992 and was still in existence in 1996.*

Upper. twin-screw steam bucket dredger FATEH 997 g.r.t. *launched in 1964 for Karachi Port Trust, Pakistan. Engined by Fleming & Ferguson Ltd, this traditional dredger with a well-proportioned funnel, and her sistership* IZHAR *launched in 1965, were still in service in 1996 with their original owners. The elegant styling of this ship and her sister* IZHAR 997 g.r.t. *must make them the best looking bucket dredgers ever built on the River Clyde.*

Previous page, lower. non-propelled bucket dredger VEDRA 326 g.r.t. *launched in 1963 for the River Wear Port Commissioners, Sunderland. She is seen performing dredging trials at the mouth of the River Cart with the Clydebank shipyard of John Brown & Co Ltd in the background. This vessel dredged the River Wear for as long as Sunderland had a shipbuilding industry. However, after the closure of the last River Wear shipyard,* VEDRA *was sold to Panama in 1991 but was later deleted from Lloyds Register, presumably broken up.*

Lower. twin-screw diesel-electric hopper barge HOPPER BARGE No. 4 *launched for Calcutta Port Commissioners in 1967. Engined by MAN of Nurnberg, this vessel was the penultimate ship built by Fleming & Ferguson Ltd at the Phoenix shipyard, Paisley, and was still in service in 1996. The ship's superstructure with raked side screens and integrated funnel and mast reflects the styling of 1960s Scottish naval architecture.*

JAS LAMONT & CO LTD   1919–1979

This small concern was the youngest of the group of post-war Clyde shipbuilding companies although the firm's origins date back to 1870. The business began trading as ship repairers at Dock Breast, Greenock where they leased the East India drydock. This location became their permanent base during the First World War. They acquired the Castle yard, east of Newark Castle in Port Glasgow from its previous owners in 1929. Although this site was a fully integrated shipyard comprising three berths and a hauling-up slip, Lamont's continued to concentrate on ship repairing at this time. By 1932 a second repair slip had been added which, combined with the tidal basin and adjacent wharfage, was sufficient for the company's needs up until the Second World War. Like every other Clyde shipbuilding, marine engineering and repair company their record for output during the hostilities was very impressive.

After the war Lamont's re-opened the Castle yard for commercial shipbuilding and by the summer of 1946 the three building berths had been realigned to take vessels up to 320 ft long. The yard was re-equipped with secondhand plant and machinery which was all that could be obtained at the time. Included in this investment were a pair of 10-ton fixed mono-tower berth cranes with extremely long jibs, whose radius of lifting capacity was sufficiently great to cover virtually the entire lengths of all building berths. The first contract for six small river craft for shipment to Rangoon to replace craft lost by the Irrawaddy flotilla, was followed by the motor coaster *Tejo* 1149 g.r.t. The company continued to incorporate shipbuilding and repairing during the post-war period. Such high dependency on marine repair work created a pragmatic approach to working practices which led to regular extemporary assessment throughout the whole gamut of engineering and fabrication.

New shipbuilding contracts for this small company therefore became a complimentary activity, where if a tender was successful and capacity existed, the new ship construction work was undertaken. This statistic is evinced in the fact that on four individual years no new ships were constructed by Lamonts.

From 1946 until the cessation of shipbuilding, with the launch of the sludge carrier *Divis II* 823 g.r.t. in 1978, a total of 73 ships comprising five fishery protection craft of 650 tons displacement and 68 other vessels of 51,361 g.r.t. were built by the company, 36% of which were for export. The vast product range consisted of coasters, tugs, small ferries, dredgers and sludge carriers. The most notable recent contract was part of a 21 ship order, shared between Scotts of Bowling and Ailsa of Troon for the building of five fishery protection vessels for the Mexican Government in the mid-'70s. The largest ship built by the yard was the sludge carrier *Garroch Head* 2808 g.r.t. for the Clyde River Purification Board in 1977.

After total closure of the Castle yard in 1981, some of the equipment was transferred to the Dock Breast facility with the remainder sold or scrapped. Part of the Port Glasgow site was consumed by the course of the new A8 road. This resulted in the demolition of all the yard's buildings and cranes. What remained of the riverside part of the shipyard was extensively landscaped. The ends of the former repair slips and part of their crane tracks are still discernible at low tide. Ship repairing lingered on at the original Greenock location for a few more years, however the inexorable contraction of the UK coastal shipping trade reduced this workload to such an extent that the firm were no longer able to continue in business. By the end of that decade another renowned small Scottish shipyard had disappeared.

List of ships built by JAMES LAMONT & Co Ltd, Port Glasgow, between 1946 and closure in 1979

YEAR	NAME	TYPE		COUNTRY OF REGISTRATION	DISPL/ G.R.T.	TOTAL OUTPUT
1946	*None*	*None*	*None*	–	–	
1947	YANAUNG	n.p.	Barge	Burma	125	
	YANWAY	n.p.	Barge	Burma	125	
	YAW	n.p.	Barge	Burma	125	
	YADU	n.p.	Barge	Burma	125	
	YAWYIN	n.p.	Barge	Burma	125	
	YAMONA	n.p.	Barge	Burma	125	750
1948	TEJO	s.	Cargo[1]	Norway	1149	
	POLARFART	m.	Fishing Ves	Norway	428	
	DOURO	s.	Cargo[1]	Norway	1150	2727
1949	KNUT JARL	m.	Cargo[1]	Norway	1026	
	YEWDALE	m.	Cargo[1]	Britain	987	
	EYSTIEN JARL	m.	Cargo[1]	Norway	1013	
	THERON	m.	Ref/Cargo	Canada	849	3875
1950 •	BENIN	s.	Cargo	Britain	2483	2483
1951	EILEAN DUBH	m.	Ferry	Britain	64	64
1952	YEWGLEN	m.	Cargo[1]	Britain	1018	
	ARDGLEN	m.	Cargo[1]	Britain	1044	2062
1953	BALLYMONEY	s.	Cargo[1]	Britain	1342	
	THETA	m.	Ref/Cargo[1]	Canada	500	
	WOONA	s.	Tug	Australia	297	2139
1954	BALLYMENA	s.	Cargo[1]	Britain	1356	
•	NILPENA	m.	Cargo[1]	Australia	1468	
	NOONGAH	m.	Cargo[1]	Australia	1465	4289
1955	SAINT BLANE	m.	Cargo[1]	Britain	680	
	YEWMOUNT	m.	Cargo[1]	Britain	1031	1711
1956 •	SQUALL	m.	Cargo[1]	N. Zealand	817	
	FIDRA	m.	Cargo[1]	Britain	1333	
	YEWHILL	m.	Cargo[1]	Britain	1089	3239
1957	ARDGARRY	m.	Cargo[1]	Britain	1074	
	WRESTLER	m.	Tug	Britain	248	
	CAMPAIGNER	m.	Tug	Britain	248	
•	YEWFOREST	m.	Cargo[1]	Britain	1097	
•	ROYAL DAFFODIL II	m.	Ferry	Britain	609	3276
1958	DARLINGTON	m.	Cargo[1]	Britain	963	
	HARROGATE	m.	Cargo[1]	Britain	963	1926
1959	SELBY	m.	Cargo[1]	Britain	963	
	TOLSTA	m.	Cargo[1]	Britain	1323	2286
1960 •	LAKSA	m.	Cargo[1]	Britain	1323	1323
1961	PUKEKO	m.	Cargo[1]	N. Zealand	1020	1020
1962	*None*	*None*	*None*	–	–	
1963	SIR JOSEPH BAZALGETTE	m.	Sludge Carrier	Britain	2258	2258

YEAR	NAME	TYPE		COUNTRY OF REGISTRATION	DISPL/ G.R.T.	TOTAL OUTPUT
1964 •	VANGUARD	m.	Tug	Britain	224	
•	SIR JOSEPH RAWLINSON	m.	Sludge Carrier	Britain	2258	
	ARDGARVEL	m.	Cargo[1]	Britain	1121	3603
1965	PORTREE	m.	Ferry	Britain	65	65
1966	BROADFORD	m.	Ferry	Britain	64	
	B.C. LAMEY	m.	Tug	Britain	225	289
1967	ALFRED LAMEY	m.	Tug	Britain	225	
•	FLYING FALCON	m.	Tug	Britain	213	
	JAMES LAMEY	m.	Tug	Britain	219	657
1968	NDOVU	m.	Tug	Kenya	297	297
1969	NGAMIA	m.	Tug	Kenya	298	
	WARRIOR	m.	Tug	Britain	272	570
1970 •	DALMARNOCK	m.	Sludge Car	Britain	2266	2266
1971	LADY VERA	m.	Tug	Britain	263	
	CHALLENGER	s.	Res Vessel	Britain	988	1251
1972	REVOLUCION	n.p.	Cutter/SD	Cuba	994	
	KILBRANNAN	m.	Ferry	Britain	65	
	MORVERN	m.	Ferry	Britain	64	1123
1973	BURERNISH	m.	Ferry	Britain	71	
	RHUM	m.	Ferry	Britain	90	
	COLL	m.	Ferry	Britain	69	
	JUPITER	m.	Ferry	Britain	849	1079
1974 •	JUNO	m.	Ferry	Britain	895	
	EIGG	m.	Ferry	Britain	69	964
1975	JOSE MARIA MATA	m.	Fish Pr	Mexico	130 displ	
	CANNA	m.	Ferry	Britain	69	
	J.M.D.C. VELAZCO	m.	Fish Pr	Mexico	130 displ	
	LUIS MANUEL ROJAS	m.	Fish Pr	Mexico	130 displ	459
1976	RAASAY	m.	Ferry	Britain	69	
	ESTEBAN B. CALDERON	m.	Fish Pr	Mexico	130 displ	
•	JOSE N. MACIAS	m.	Fish Pr	Mexico	130 displ	329
1977	GARROCH HEAD	m.	Sludge Car	Britain	2808	2808
1978 •	DIVIS II	m.	Sludge Car	Britain	823	823

36% export	5 vessels total	=	650 tons displacement
64% Britain	68 vessels total	=	51,361 g.r.t.

[1]coaster

• Indicates vessel depicted in subsequent photographic section.

For explanation of abbreviations see Glossary on page 345.

The collection of pictures on the following pages illustrates the location of the former Castle shipyard of Jas Lamont & Co Ltd in Port Glasgow. Also included are a number of trials photographs of some of the ships built by the company in its last two decades of operation.

Above. *A 1965 view looking south of the Castle shipyard of Jas Lamont & Co. Ltd in Port Glasgow. In the fitting-out basin lies yard no. 400, motor sludge carrier* SIR JOSEPH RAWLINSON 2258 g.r.t. *launched on 26 March 1964. Newark Castle is the ornate building in the bottom right corner, with the slipways and winch houses of the firm's repair yard to the extreme left. A small puffer occupies a cradle on one of these ways. Note the nearness of the tenements, school and church to the yard. The entire site of the former Castle shipyard has now been consumed by the course of the new Glasgow-Greenock A8 road, which runs parallel between the railway line and the River Clyde.* (Aerofilms)

Next page, upper. *Launch of yard no. 401, motor tug* VANGUARD 224 g.r.t. *for Steel & Bennie Ltd of Glasgow on the hazy day of 26 February 1964. Newark Castle is prominent in the left background and the adjacent shipyard of Ferguson Bros (Port Glasgow) Ltd has the small non-propelled bucket dredger* MSC IRWELL 312 g.r.t. *under construction on one of its slipways. Note the strakes of rivets on* VANGUARD's *hull.* (Burniston Studios Ltd)

Next page, lower. *This August 1970 view of the Jas Lamont Castle shipyard in Port Glasgow shows yard no. 412, the motor sludge carrier* DALMARNOCK 2266 g.r.t. *a few weeks away from launching. On the adjacent berth the first prefabricated sections of yard no. 414, the motor tug* LADY VERA 263 g.r.t., *have recently been assembled. Virtually all traces of Lamont's small shipyard and repair slipway have now been removed from this part of Port Glasgow. This photograph clearly shows the impressive jib lengths of the small shipyard's pair of 10-ton fixed mono-tower berth cranes.* (Burniston Studios Ltd)

s.s. BENIN 2483 g.r.t. *launched in 1950 for Elder Dempster Lines Ltd, Liverpool. Engined by Rankin & Blackmore Ltd, Greenock, this large coaster was built to navigate many West African rivers and shallow draft ports, obtaining cargoes for trans-shipment onto ocean-going liners. Sold and renamed YORKWOOD in 1960, she was later resold and renamed. She sank off La Corunna, Spain in July 1969 as the AGIA IRENE.* (Burniston Studios Ltd)

m.v. NILPENA 1468 g.r.t. *launched in 1954 for the Australian Coastal Shipping Commission, Melbourne. Engined by British Polar Engines Ltd, this vessel was the first of a pair of sisterships built by Lamonts for coastal trading around Australia. Sold and renamed SIMANGGANG in 1971 she became a total loss in June 1985 when she sank off the Andaman Islands as the RUSLI.* (Burniston Studios Ltd)

m.v. SQUALL 817 g.r.t. *launched in 1956 for the Canterbury Steam Shipping Co. Ltd, Lyttleton, New Zealand (a P & O subsidiary). Engined by British Polar Engines Ltd, this coaster was built for trading in New Zealand waters. Sold and renamed KING TIGER in 1973 she was broken up in 1985 as the GOLDEN SUMMER. Note her robust set of fenders that extend for almost the entire length of her hull.* (Burniston Studios Ltd)

m.v. YEWFOREST 1097 g.r.t. *launched in 1957 for John Stewart & Co. Shipping Ltd of Glasgow. Engined by Klöckner-Humboldt-Deutz AG of Cologne. This functional coaster was the last of five vessels built by Lamonts for these Scottish ship-owners. She was sold and renamed MARY M in 1974, being broken up in 1987 as LOKMA 1. Note the pair of brass builders' plates on each side of the ship's forward superstructure.* (Burniston Studios Ltd)

t.s.m.v. ROYAL DAFFODIL II 609 g.r.t. *launched in 1957 for the Mayor of the County Borough of Wallasey, Liverpool. Engined by Crossley Bros Ltd, Manchester, this distinctive and functional passenger ferry plied the Mersey Estuary before being sold and renamed ROYAL DAFFODIL in 1968. She was later resold, modified and renamed, and was still in existence in 1996 as the AGIA KYRIAKI.* (Burniston Studios Ltd)

m.v. LAKSA 1323 g.r.t. *launched in 1960 for the South Georgia Co. Ltd, Leith (managers Christian Salvesen & Co. Ltd). Engined by Mirrelees, Bickerton & Day of Stockport, this coaster plied the cold waters of the South Atlantic throughout most of its life and was the last of three sisterships built by Lamonts for these owners. Subsequently sold and renamed, she was still in service in 1996 as the NOURA I.* (Burniston Studios Ltd)

motor tug FLYING FALCON 213 g.r.t. *launched in 1967 for the Clyde Shipping Co. Ltd, Glasgow. Engined by British Polar Engines Ltd, Glasgow, this tug was built for service in the Clyde ports. Sadly the contraction of merchant shipping on the Scottish west coast, concurrent with the demise of shipbuilding has greatly reduced the need for such vessels today. As a result she was sold off and renamed many times, however, she was still in service in 1996 as the BOUKOU L.* (Burniston Studios Ltd)

m.v. DALMARNOCK 2266 g.r.t. *launched in 1970 for Glasgow Corporation (River Clyde Purification Board). Engined by British Polar Engines Ltd, Glasgow, this discreet yet functional sludge carrier and her sistership, GARROCH HEAD 2,808 g.r.t., also built by Lamonts have the unenviable reputation of being the only vessels (apart from ferries) to sail the River Clyde on a daily basis in the late 1990s.* (Burniston Studios Ltd)

m.v. JUNO 895 g.r.t. *launched in 1974 for Caledonian-MacBrayne Ltd, Glasgow (Gourock-Dunoon Service). Engined by Mirrlees-Blackstone Ltd, Stockport, this passenger and vehicle roll-on/roll-off ferry was the second of a pair built for these owner's busiest Firth of Clyde route by Jas Lamont & Co. Ltd. Both vessels and a further sistership built by the Ailsa yard at Troon have proved reliable, stable and effective. All were still in service in 1996 under their original names.* (Burniston Studios Ltd)

High speed acceptance trials of the Mexican fishery protection craft JOSE NATIVIDAD MACIAS 210 tons displacement P.20 launched in 1976. Engined by Paxman Ventura Ltd, Colchester, this vessel was the last of five similar craft which were part of the only new 'naval' shipbuilding order undertaken by Lamonts in the post-war era. Note the builder's house flag above the funnel. (Burniston Studios Ltd)

m.v. DIVIS II 823 g.r.t. *launched in 1978 for the Department of Environment for Northern Ireland (Belfast Corporation). Engined by Mirrlees-Blackstone Ltd, Stamford, this handsome looking sludge carrier was the final vessel built by Jas Lamont & Co. Ltd and was still in service in 1996. The ship's integrated mast and funnel with raked side screens pre-date her otherwise value engineered 1970s styling.* (Burniston Studios Ltd)

FERGUSON BROTHERS LTD	1903–1914
FERGUSON BROTHERS (PORT GLASGOW) LTD	1914–1969
FERGUSON BROTHERS (PORT GLASGOW) 1969 LTD	1969–1981
FERGUSON AILSA LTD	1981–1986
APPLEDORE FERGUSON SHIPBUILDERS LTD	1986–1989
FERGUSON (KVÆRNER GOVAN) LTD	1989–1991
FERGUSON SHIPBUILDERS LTD	1991–

The small Newark, Port Glasgow shipyard of Ferguson Brothers Ltd became part of the Lithgow group in 1963, within which it remained a separate entity dedicated to the design and construction of specialist craft, small ferries, coasters and tugs for the UK and overseas markets. Prior to the takeover the manufacture of triple expansion steam engines for Ferguson-built ships effectively ceased at the yard's small engine works.

The name Ferguson Brothers had been established in 1903, when the four Ferguson brothers broke away from their Fleming & Ferguson Shipyard at Paisley. The yard was located to the west of Newark Castle on a somewhat restricted site which limited the length of ships built to around 100 metres.

Under the auspices of the Lithgow Group and latterly Scott-Lithgow Ltd, the company's reputation flourished. The basic product range remained tugs and dredgers interspersed with the occasional ferry, research vessel or lighthouse tender. Eight large ocean going trawlers were also built over a ten year period. Surprisingly, the firm did not become much involved in the new and expanding market for supply ships for the North Sea oil developments, building only five such vessels up to 1986. The annual output varied from three to five ships each year and the maximum labour force peaked at around 700.

The yard was nationalised into British Shipbuilders Ltd in 1977. It was later coerced into an arranged marriage with the newly modernised Ailsa shipyard at Troon in 1981, an association which achieved nothing tangible for either of these heretofore reasonably successful firms. The Ferguson-Ailsa Ltd association was terminated in 1986, and immediately followed by a new joint venture with Appledore Shipbuilders Ltd of Bideford, North Devon, also a member of BSL. This new amalgamation was even less successful than the previous constrained agreement. Both companies built very similar types of ships in a highly competitive market. Their separate successful track records were proportional to their aggressive individuality, definitely not the equitable ingredients for arbitrary work sharing within a nationalised industry.

The last ships built under the auspices of British Shipbuilders Ltd were two car ferries for Caledonian MacBrayne Ltd, *Isle of Mull* and *Lord of the Isles*, delivered in 1988 and 1989, respectively. The former vessel was extensively modified on the River Tees prior to her acceptance, with the insertion of a new midship section, necessary to rectify a serious design deficiency. All the additional costs incurred in this operation were incurred by BSL, including civil engineering alterations to Scottish west-coast piers and quays necessary to accommodate the lengthened ferry.

In 1989 the yard was sold to Clark-Kincaid, and became part of the HLD group. Kværner-Govan, major shareholders in HLD later sold the yard to Ferguson Marine plc in 1991. Renamed Ferguson Shipbuilders Ltd, this new company under the ownership of Sir A.R. Belch, Sir Ian Denholm, W. Scott, G. Parham and R. Parkinson quickly revitalised the second remaining merchant shipyard in Scotland.

Restructured, and in possession of state-of-the-art CADCAM (computer-aided design and computer-aided manufacturing), the company entered the forefront of naval architecture technology. The preparation and fabrication shops have recently been rebuilt and re-equipped, and the three open berths can construct three vessels simultaneously each up to over 100 metres long. Despite possessing only two limited capacity fixed berth cranes, the shipyard has an exemplary record for achievement of scheduled launch dates.

In addition to investment in practical hardware, perhaps the most novel aspects of this shipbuilding renaissance have been the return to annual profits on timely completion of successful contracts, and a high proportion of share ownership by the present labour force. Alas the high profile profitability that this new enterprise engendered, also created a company that was now desirable for predatory take–over, unheard of in merchant shipbuilding on the River Clyde for over three decades! The shipyard was acquired by the Holland House electrical contracting group of Glasgow in late 1995. The recent proprietors immediately obtained valuable and prestigious orders for various specialised new building contracts and seem intent on improving the record of the previous enlightened owners, hinting towards possible further modernisation and extension of the facility.

Between 1946 and 1987 the Port Glasgow shipyard built a total of 111 vessels comprising one naval tug of 472 tons displacement and 100 other craft of 122,443 g.r.t., of which 34% were for export. Greatest annual output was achieved in 1979 with the launching of three ships totalling 6970 g.r.t. The largest vessel completed by the yard during this period was the passenger/car ferry *Isle of Mull* 4719 g.r.t. launched in 1987 for Caledonian Macbrayne Ltd.

The group of photographs on the following pages illustrate the location of the Newark shipbuilding yard of Ferguson Shipbuilders Ltd. Also included are a number of launch and trials pictures depicting some of the various specialised ships built by this company under its five post-war identities.

List of ships built by FERGUSON BROTHERS (PORT GLASGOW) Ltd, and their successors between 1946 and 1987

YEAR	NAME	TYPE	COUNTRY OF REGISTRATION	DISPL/ G.R.T.	TOTAL OUTPUT	YEAR	NAME	TYPE	COUNTRY OF REGISTRATION	DISPL/ G.R.T.	TOTAL OUTPUT
1946	EMPIRE SORCERER	s. Suction HD	Britain (RN)	2594		1958	CAMEL NO. 7	n.p. Wreck-LL	Britain	600	
	EMPIRE HARTLAND	s. Hopper B	Britain (RN)	683			MENSAH SARBAH	s. Tug	Ghana	216	
	LALI	m. Tug	Iran	145			FAVOURITE	m.e.p. Tug	Britain (RN)	472 displ	
	MANCUNIUM	m. Sludge Car	Britain	1390	4812		DANIE HUGO	s. Tug	South Africa	812	2100
1947	SALVOR	s. Salvage Tug	Britain	671		1959	SIR EMMANUEL QUIST	s. Tug	Ghana	216	
	ARGUS	s. Lt Tender	Britain	1981			F.C. STURROCK	s. Tug	South Africa	812	
	AMRADO	s. Tug	Ghana	201			MAKOURIA	m. Ferry	British Guiana	561	
	SIR GORDON II	s. Tug	Ghana	201	3054		BIRD OF PARADISE	m. Ferry	Trinidad	1268	2857
1948	MERSEY NO. 26	m.e. Grab HD	Britain	1363		1960 •	FARAHMAND	m. Tug	Britain	362	
	MERSEY NO. 27	m.e. Grab HD	Britain	1363	2726		SCARLET IBIS	m. Ferry	Trinidad	1268	
1949	ABEILLE NO. XI	s. Tug	France	389			J.R. MORE	s. Tug	South Africa	805	2435
	MERSEY ENGINEER	s. Bucket D	Britain	749		1961	MERSEY COMPASS	m.e. Grab HD	Britain	2083	
	KVART	s. Whale Cat	Norway	594			ARZANAH	m. Tug	Britain	359	2442
	ABEILLE NO. XII	s. Tug	France	389	2121	1962	ST. GILES	m. Trawler	Britain	658	
1950	F.T. BATES	s. Tug	South Africa	787			FLYING FOAM	m. Tug	Britain	184	
	FARAHMAND	s. Tug	Britain	450			FLYING SPRAY	m. Tug	Britain	184	
	A.M. CAMPBELL	s. Tug	South Africa	787	2024		NUTTAL 3	n.p. Barge	Britain	175	
1951	J.P. WEBB	s. Hopper B	Australia	950			FLYING MIST	m. Tug	Britain	184	1385
	FLYING BUZZARD	s. Tug	Britain	261		1963 •	BLYTHSWOOD	m.e. Bucket D	Britain	786	786
	FLYING MERLIN	s. Tug	Britain	261		1964 •	M.S.C. IRWELL	n.p. Bucket D	Britain	312	
	FLYING PETREL	s. Tug	Britain	278	1750		ST. FINBARR	m. S Trawler	Britain	1139	1451
1952	ANADRIAN	s. Grab HD	Malta	291		1965 •	RUKMAVATI	m. Cargo	India	2729	
•	G.P. 2	n.p. Drilling B	Venezuela	1409	1700		STEENBOK	n.p. Bucket D	South Africa	737	
1953	WYUNA	m.e. Pilot Tender	Australia	1304		•	WILDEBEES	m. Hopper B	South Africa	776	4242
	EVENLODE	n.p. Bucket D	Britain	540	1844	1966 •	ELAND	m. Hopper B	South Africa	776	
1954	LENNOX II	s. Grab HD	Britain	795			BAGLAN	m.e. Suction HD	Britain	1889	
	CHAMPION	s. Tug	Aden	410			ABBOTSGRANGE	m.e. Suction HD	Britain	1864	4529
	J.P. WEBB	s. Hopper B	Australia	967	2172	1967	LAVERNOCK	m.e. Suction HD	Britain	1864	
1955	LAGA II	m. Hopper B	Britain	693			ST. JASON	m. S Trawler	Britain	1288	
•	LOCH ARD	m. Cargo[1]	Britain	611			ST. JEROME	m. S Trawler	Britain	1288	4440
	BERTHA	s. Tug	Nigeria	330		1968 •	SOUND OF ISLAY	m. Ferry	Britain	280	
•	SEDIA	m. Tug	Britain	287	1921	•	PERCY DAWSON	m. Sludge Car	Britain	1525	
1956	POWIS	m. Ferry	British Guiana	299		•	ST. JASPER	m. S Trawler	Britain	1286	3091
	AROLDO BASTOS	s. Oil Tanker	Brazil	1199		1969†	ABERAVON	m. Grab HD	Britain	2156	
•	PAVO	m. Crane/SB	Venezuela	441	1939	•	CIROLANA	m.e. Fish. Res.	Britain	1731	3887
1957 •	MERSEY NO. 41	m.e. Grab HD	Britain	1364							
	CAMEL NO. 6	n.p. Wreck-LL	Britain	600	1964						

YEAR	NAME	TYPE	COUNTRY OF REGISTRATION	DISPL/ G.R.T.	TOTAL OUTPUT
1970 •	GRANUAILE	m. Lt Tender	Eire	2003	
	MARINEX V	m. Suction D	Britain	2825	
	–	n.p. Barge	Britain	307	5135
1971 •	SCOTIA	m.e. Fish. Res.	Britain	1521	
	GILBERT J. FOWLER	m. Sludge Car.	Britain	2548	
	BRASILIA	n.p. Bucket D	Brazil	885	4954
1972	CONSORTIUM I	m. Sludge Car.	Britain	2549	
	ST. BENEDICT	m. S Trawler	Britain	1454	4003
1973	CAMBRAE	m. Suction D	Britain	3896	
	GOTH	m. S Trawler	Britain	1448	
	ROMAN	m. S Trawler	Britain	1448	6792
1974 •	SAND WEAVER	m. Suction D/ Sand Carrier	Britain	3366	3366
1975	SEAFORTH JARL	m. Supply Boat	Britain	1376	
•	SEAFORTH HIGHLANDER	m. Supply Boat	Britain	1376	2752
1976	GARDYLOO	m. Sludge Car	Britain	1952	
	M.S.C. INCE	n.p. Bucket D	Britain	427	
	THAMES	m. Sludge Car	Britain	2663	5042
1977 •	CLARKNES	m. Cargo	Britain	2351	2351
1978 •	LADY CHILEL JAWARA	m. Ferry	Gambia	702	
	M.S.C. NO. 51	n.p. Barge	Britain	340	
	M.S.C. NO. 52	n.p. Barge	Britain	340	
	M.S.C. NO. 53	n.p. Barge	Britain	340	1722
1979 •	MLAWA	m. Bulk Carrier	Poland	2996	
	AURICULA	m. Trials/Sonar Tender	Britain (RN)	982	
	ZGORZELEC	m. Bulk Carrier	Poland	2992	6970

YEAR	NAME	TYPE	COUNTRY OF REGISTRATION	DISPL/ G.R.T.	TOTAL OUTPUT
1980	SULISKER	m. Fish Pr	Britain (RN)	1177	
	DONALD REDFORD	m. Grab/HD	Britain	595	1772
1981 †	FLYING PHANTOM	m. Tug	Britain	347	347
1982 •	VIGILANT	m. Fish Pr	Britain (RN)	1192	
•	STAR CAPELLA	m. Supply Boat	Britain	1599	2791
1983	TIRRICK	m. Tug	Britain	482	
	SHALDER	m. Tug	Britain	482	
•	ISLE OF ARRAN	m. Ferry	Britain	3296	4260
1984	MWOKOZI	m. Tug	Kenya	672	
	FARU	m. Tug	Kenya	361	1033
1985	M.V.A.	m. Hopper B	Britain	770	
	FORT RESOLUTION	m. Supply Boat	Britain	1232	2002
1986 †	FORT RELIANCE	m. Supply Boat	Britain	1232	1232
1987 •	ISLE OF MULL	m. Ferry	Britain	4719	4719

34% export	1 vessel total =	472 tons displacement
76% Britain	110 vessels total =	122,443 g.r.t.

Notes

† Became Ferguson Brothers (1969) Ltd — 1969–81

† Became Ferguson Ailsa Ltd (Division of British Shipbuilders Ltd) 1981–86

† Became Appledore Ferguson Shipbuilders Ltd — 1986–89

† Became Ferguson (Kværner Govan) Ltd — 1989–91

† Became Ferguson Shipbuilders Ltd — 1991–

*1987 is considered by the author to be the year when volume shipubilding effectively ceased on the River Clyde. Therefore ships subsequently built by Appledore-Ferguson Shipbuilders Ltd and their successors are omitted from this table.

¹coaster; • Indicates vessel depicted in subsequent photographic section. For explanation of abbreviations see Glossary on page 345.

m.v. LOCH ARD 611 g.r.t. *being launched almost complete for David MacBrayne Ltd., Glasgow, on 23 May 1955. Engined by British Polar Engines Ltd, this stylish coaster plied the waters of the West of Scotland until being sold and renamed HOLBURN in 1971. She had a further lengthy career under that name before being broken up in 1985. (Burniston Studios Ltd)*

The main gate of the Newark shipyard of Ferguson Brothers (Port Glasgow) Ltd frames a handful of shipyard workers on 24 April 1968. On one of the berths is yard no. 451, the twin-screw motor sludge carrier PERCY DAWSON 1525 g.r.t., *about to be launched later that day for North-West Water, Manchester. This vessel was renamed HAWESWATER in 1988 and was still in existence in 1996 under that name. (Burniston Studios Ltd)*

G.P.2, 1409 g.r.t. *non-propelled drilling barge launched in 1952 for Compania Shell da Venezuela, Maracaibo, about to be towed to South America by the Dutch ocean-going tug RODE ZEE. This specialised floating structure pre-dated the West of Scotland offshore oil and gas construction industry by nearly a decade and a half! Unfortunately her seven sister craft, identical to the Ferguson Brothers design, were built in Holland. G.P.2 was deleted from Lloyds Register in 1970, presumably broken-up. (Burniston Studios Ltd)*

Previous page. *The Ferguson Brothers (Port Glasgow) Ltd, shipyard in the summer of 1965, showing under construction a prestigious three-ship order for South Africa. From left to right are: yard no. 443, a non-propelled bucket dredger later named STEENBOK 737 g.r.t.; yard no. 444, the hopper barge WILDBEES; and yard no. 445, the hopper barge ELAND, both 776 g.r.t. All three vessels were completed and delivered the next year. The compact layout of the small yard is quite evident, with the construction of a handful of new sheds the only apparent investment by the parent Lithgow Group. In the left foreground is Newark Castle which separates the adjoining shipyard of Jas. Lamont & Co. Ltd. Whilst Fergusons still exist as a shipyard, most of the adjacent industry has been eliminated. The re-aligned course of the new dual carriageway A8 road now runs between the railway and the southern perimeter of the shipyard, seriously restricting any further lengthening of the building berths. The six storey building on the right and the adjoining lower level industrial structures were the premises of the famous Gourock Ropework Co Ltd, a company that was born before the industrial revolution. The shell of this now closed factory is a listed building waiting for financial assistance to complete renovation. (Aerofilms)* t.s. motor tug SEDIA 287 g.r.t. *launched in 1955 for Shell (Eastern) Ltd, London. Engined by Crossley Bros. Ltd, Manchester, this traditional looking tug had a thirty-year life under her original name and owners before being broken-up in 1985. Contrast the group of shipyard workers huddled aft of the main mast with the pair of yard managers on the port bridge. Note the manually operated water canons forward and aft of the tug's funnel.* (Burniston Studios Ltd)

motor tug/crane-salvage vessel PAVO, 441 g.r.t. *launched in 1956 for Compania Shell de Venezuela Ltd, Maracaibo. Engined by the National Gas & Oil Engine Co Ltd, Ashton-under-Lyne, this salvage tug saw service in South America until 1965 when she was sold and renamed BEAVER, retaining that name until being broken up in 1977.* (Burniston Studios Ltd)

Above. t.s. motor hopper/grab dredger MERSEY No. 41, 1364 g.r.t. *launched in 1957 for Mersey Docks & Harbour Board, Liverpool. Engined by Ruston & Hornsby Lincoln, this versatile vessel performed positional dredging work in Liverpool's docks. Equipped with three Priestman electric grab cranes and a sizeable hopper hold, this manoeuvrable vessel dredged the Port of Liverpool, and then transported the spoil out to sea where it was discharged through the ship's bottom hopper doors. She was broken up in 1989 under her original name.* (Burniston Studios Ltd)

Left. motor firefloat and salvage tug FARAHMAND 362 g.r.t. *launched in 1960 for the B.P. Tanker Co Ltd, London. Engined by Crossley Bros Ltd, Manchester, this vessel is seen performing fire water monitor tests during her trials in the Firth of Clyde. She was still in existence in 1996 as the ARASHI, having been sold and renamed as GULF SPAN 10 in the previous year. Note the shipbuilders' plate, probably brass, set in the wood panelling of the wheelhouse front.* (Burniston Studios Ltd)

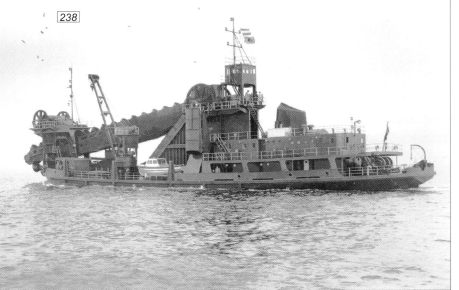

t.s.d.e. bucket dredger BLYTHSWOOD 786 g.r.t. *launched in 1963 for the Clyde Navigation Trust, Glasgow. Engined by W.H. Allen Sons & Co Ltd, Bedford, this vessel was the last dredger built for the CNT to operate in the Port of Glasgow and the River Clyde. Her long career ran parallel with the gradual disappearance of volume shipbuilding on the river, and the virtual elimination of the City of Glasgow as a port for ocean-going ships. She was broken-up in 1994 still under her original name.* (Burniston Studios Ltd)

non-propelled diesel-electric bucket dredger M.S.C. IRWELL 312 g.r.t. *launched in 1964 for the Manchester Ship Canal Company, Manchester. Engaged in year round dredging activity throughout the entire length of the Manchester Ship Canal, this vessel remained with her original owners until 1989 when she was sold. Unfortunately, she capsized and sank in the Irish Sea later that year when on tow to her new owners.* (Burniston Studios Ltd)

m.v. RUKMAVATI 2729 g.r.t. *launched in 1965 for the Scindia Steam Navigation Co Ltd of Bombay. Engined by M.A.N. of Hamburg, this well-proportioned cargo vessel was the only ship built by Fergusons for Indian owners in the post-war period. Sold and renamed AL SHARMEEN in 1980 she was broken up under than name in 1986.* (Burniston Studios Ltd)

motor hopper barge ELAND 776 g.r.t. *launched in 1966 for the Railways & Harbours Administration, Durban. Engined by Ruston & Hornsby, Lincoln, this hopper barge was the last of a three-ship order that Ferguson's completed for South Africa. Note the shipyard cleaning lady taking a stroll on the port side deck whilst the vessel undergoes sea trials. ELAND was deleted from Lloyds Register in 1992, presumably broken up.* (Burniston Studios Ltd)

twin-screw motor ferry SOUND OF ISLAY 280 g.r.t. *launched in 1968 for Western Ferries Ltd, Campbeltown, Scotland. Engined by Bergius-Kelvin Ltd, Glasgow, this small and stylish passenger-car ferry was built for Scottish coastal service and was owned by one of the companies within the Lithgow Group, who owned the Port Glasgow shipyard. This ship was still in existence in 1996 under her original name.* (Burniston Studios Ltd)

motor trawler ST. JASPER 1286 g.r.t. *launched in 1968 for T. Hamling & Co Ltd, Hull. Engined by British Polar Engines Ltd, this stern trawler/freezer was converted to an offshore safety/standby vessel in 1985 and renamed* SEABOARD INTEGRITY. *She was still in existence in 1996 as the* HORNBECK INTEGRITY. (Burniston Studios Ltd)

diesel-electric fishery research vessel CIROLANA 1731 g.r.t. *launched in 1969 for the UK Ministry of Agriculture, Fisheries & Food Department, Grimsby. Engined by W.H. Allen, Sons & Co Ltd, Bedford, this distinctive vessel was still in existence under her original name in 1996.* (Burniston Studios Ltd)

twin-screw motor buoy and lighthouse tender GRANUAILE 2003 g.r.t. *launched in 1970 for the Commissioners of Irish Lights, Dublin. Engined by W.H. Allen Sons & Co Ltd, Bedford, this stylish and highly functional vessel was built to maintain all buoys and lighthouses around the coast of Eire, and was still in existence performing her original role in 1996.* (Burniston Studios Ltd)

twin-screw diesel-electric fishery patrol and survey vessel SCOTIA 1521 g.r.t. *launched in 1971 for the UK Ministry of Agriculture, Fisheries & Food Department, Leith. Engined by British Polar Engines Ltd, this floating laboratory was still in existence under her original name in 1996.* (Burniston Studios Ltd)

motor dredger/sand carrier SAND WEAVER 3366 g.r.t. *launched in 1974 for South Coast Shipping Co Ltd, Southampton. Engined by Lister-Blackstone Marine Ltd, Dursley, this specialised craft was the largest ship built by the Port Glasgow shipyard at her time of launching, and was still in existence under her original name in 1996.* (Burniston Studios Ltd)

twin screw motor tug/offshore supply ship SEAFORTH HIGHLANDER 1376 g.r.t. *launched in 1975 for Seaforth Maritime Ltd, Aberdeen. Engined by British Polar Engines Ltd, this vessel was the second, first generation supply boat built by the yard for service in the North Sea oil and gas fields. Sold and renamed ISOLA GIALLA in 1988 she was still in existence in 1996 as PACIFIC CHEETAH.* (Burniston Studios Ltd)

m.v. CLARKNES 2351 g.r.t. *launched in 1977 for H. Clarkson & Co Ltd, London (Jebsens UK Ltd). Engined by W.H. Allen, Sons & Co Ltd, Bedford, this attractive looking ship was sold and renamed FRIBOURG in 1983, and was still in existence in 1996 as the VECTIS FALCON. Note her enclosed lifeboats, a safety feature that many British shipping companies were slow to adapt.* (Burniston Studios Ltd)

twin screw motor ferry LADY CHILEL JAWARA 702 g.r.t. *launched in 1978 for the Government of the Republic of Gambia, Banjul. Engined by GEC Diesels Ltd/Kelvin Marine Division, Glasgow, this attractive looking vessel was so well styled and proportioned that she looked much larger than her modest dimensions. She had a tragically short career as she sank off the coast of Gambia in December 1984 with the loss of four lives.* (Burniston Studios Ltd)

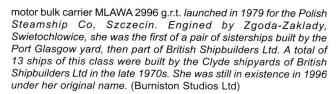

motor bulk carrier MLAWA 2996 g.r.t. *launched in 1979 for the Polish Steamship Co, Szczecin. Engined by Zgoda-Zaklady, Swietochlowice, she was the first of a pair of sisterships built by the Port Glasgow yard, then part of British Shipbuilders Ltd. A total of 13 ships of this class were built by the Clyde shipyards of British Shipbuilders Ltd in the late 1970s. She was still in existence in 1996 under her original name.* (Burniston Studios Ltd)

t.s.m.v. VIGILANT 1192 g.r.t., *a fishery protection vessel launched in 1982 for the UK Ministry of Agriculture, Fisheries & Food, Leith. Engined by Ruston Diesels Ltd, Newton-le-Willows, Lancashire, this vessel was built to patrol the UK Continental Shelf fishing grounds and was still in service performing that role in 1996.* (Burniston Studios Ltd)

twin-screw diesel offshore supply ship STAR CAPELLA 1599 g.r.t. *launched in 1982 for Star Offshore Marine Service Ltd, Aberdeen. Engined by British Polar Engines Ltd, she and her Troon built sistership STAR VEGA are among the most successful British built supply ships ever to have worked in the North Sea oil and gas fields. Both vessels were still in existence in 1996 as* STIRLING CAPELLA *and* STIRLING VEGA, *respectively.* (Courtesy Ferguson Shipbuilders Ltd)

t.s.m.v. ro-ro ferry ISLE OF ARRAN 3296 g.r.t. *launched in 1983 for Caledonian MacBrayne Ltd, Glasgow. Engined by Mirrlees Blackstone (Stockport) Ltd, this vessel, with a pair of slab-sided yet functional funnels, was designed and built for the daily passage between Ardrossan and Brodick, Isle of Arran. She was still performing that role under her original name in 1996.* (Courtesy Ferguson Shipbuilders Ltd)

t.s.m.v. ISLE OF MULL 4719 g.r.t. *launched in 1987 for Caledonian MacBrayne Ltd, Glasgow. Engined by Mirrlees Blackstone (Stockport) Ltd, this futuristic looking ro-ro ferry was at the time of her completion the largest ship built by the Port Glasgow shipyard (then under the moniker Appledore-Ferguson Shipbuilders Ltd). The vessel was unfortunately seriously under-designed by her builders, a fault that was expensively rectified with the insertion of a whole new mid-ship section, work that was carried out the following year on the River Tees. In 1996 the modified ship was still in year round daily service, plying successfully from Oban to Craignure, on the Isle of Mull.* (Burniston Studios Ltd)

▌WM HAMILTON & CO LTD   1871–1963

The Glen shipyard of Wm Hamilton & Co Ltd was located in Port Glasgow between the adjoining East yard and the adjacent Kingston shipyard of Lithgows Ltd. A medium-sized establishment, it had been acquired by Lithgows Ltd in association with the Liverpool ship-owners, Cunard-Brocklebank in 1919.

Hamiltons employed around 1000 workers during the boom years of the 1950s producing a steady stream of cargo liners from a traditional shipyard of the time. They specialised in general and refrigerated cargo liners interspersed with oil tankers. Their principal customer was the part-owner of the shipyard, Cunard-Brocklebank who in the period from 1946 had 18 cargo liners built there for their joint fleets. Hain S.S. Coy Ltd of London and Thorvald Brøvig A/S of Farsund, Norway, were among the other regular major clients during this time taking delivery of eight and four vessels, respectively.

The yard was equipped with three building berths served by six 15 ton capacity fixed electric mono-tower cranes. Productivity was very good from limited facilities being directly proportional to the diligence of the labour force working a well measured incentive piecework scheme. Fabrication methods and sequence of unit erection became tailored to suit the ever increasing content of welding in each new ship under construction, however, the limited capacity of both shop and berth craneage constrained the building of heavy sub-assemblies. This resulted in the establishment of optimum sizes of prefabricated units that could be comfortably handled by the shipyard.

As was the case with all Lithgow owned subsidiaries, the retention of the Wm Hamilton name and house flag confirmed the individualism of the company throughout its entire existence. This was ably evinced in the distinctiveness of each ship built in the Glen yard. The reduction in output from the shipyard in its latter years of existence reflected a combination of reduced order intake, as well as the Clydeside failure to increase steelwork production following the replacement of riveting by welding.

As a division of the then expanding Lithgow Group, it was therefore with some disbelief that the employees heard the parent company intended to close the Glen yard in 1963 after delivery of the *m.v. Treneglos* 9976 g.r.t. (yard no. 527) for the Hain S.S. Co Ltd, the last order fulfilled by Wm Hamilton & Co Ltd, although Lithgows Ltd built one further ship there, the *m.v. Freetown* 7689 g.r.t. (Lithgows yard no. 1149) for Elder Dempster Lines Ltd, in the same year. This unhappy event in the history of Lower Clyde shipbuilding was not the disaster first feared, because most of the Hamilton workforce by that time numbering some three hundred was absorbed by the other Lithgow yards including the new Firth of Clyde drydock company. This gesture of industrial altruism ensured that the renowned workmanship of these remaining employees was not floated down the river with the sailing away of the yard's last ship orders.

The Glen shipyard of Wm Hamilton & Co Ltd built 57 ships between 1946 and 1963, comprising 37 cargo liners, 19 oil tankers and one self-loading bulk carrier for the Great Lakes trade. Total tonnage of ships built during this period amounted to 454,974 g.r.t., with 44% of these vessels built for export, various Norwegian ship-owners being the biggest customers taking 15 ships of 144,423 g.r.t. The largest vessel built at the yard during this period was the motor tanker *Sagona* 11,860 g.r.t., launched for Norwegian owners on 19 June 1958. Greatest annual output was achieved in 1951 when three oil tankers and one cargo liner amounting to 38,675 g.r.t. were launched. The yard subsequently launched five vessels in 1954 but with a slightly smaller total g.r.t.

Part of the preparation and fabrication facilities were retained for some years after 1964 to serve the requirements of the other Lithgow Group yards with some of the berth cranes being re-erected in the Kingston shipyard. However, by the end of that decade, most of the old Hamilton yard and part of the Lithgow East yard were demolished, and replaced with a new large shipbuilding complex erected by the recently formed Scott-Lithgow group. Bearing the old Glen yard name, this modern facility was built specifically to construct large oil tankers, bulk carriers and offshore vessels, and remained in use longer than any of the other Scott-Lithgow shipbuilding yards. The site was acquired by Clydeport Authority a few years after its abandonment by Trafalgar House Investments Ltd in 1992.

WM SIMONS & CO LTD   1810–1959

Located on the south bank of the River Clyde at the northern extremity of the town of Renfrew, the two adjacent independent specialist shipbuilders, Wm Simons & Co Ltd and Lobnitz & Co Ltd, existed in amicable competition up to 1959, when they belatedly amalgamated to become Simons-Lobnitz Ltd.

William Simons had started shipbuilding at Greenock in 1810. He later moved to Canada, back to Greenock, then Whiteinch before finally settling at Renfrew in the 1850s where the company remained for over a century. Originally the firm built small cargo vessels and river steamers under the able leadership of the son of the firm's founder, also called William. A new partnership with Andrew Brown created a visionary team that identified the need to design and build specialist craft, then in demand, to construct harbours throughout the developing world.

After Wm Simons's retiral in 1886 the Brown family and their descendants capably ran the combined shipyard and engine works for over 70 years thereafter. The company developed a wide range of vessels that were suitable to be customised for temperate or tropical climates, with propelling, dredging and ancillary machinery also built at Renfrew in their small engine works. Technical innovation was the firm's hallmark throughout its existence, however, latterly the company's commercial and financial structure did not create the same efficacy. It was therefore not surprising that this blatant business deficiency encouraged G. & J. Weir Ltd of Cathcart, Glasgow to buy the company for £1 million in 1956. In addition to the acquisition of a regular customer for its pumps, the small Renfrew yard and engine works provided extra fabrication capacity to manufacture sea-water desalination plants that were then a growth area of Weir's overseas markets.

Shipbuilding throughout the post-war era remained rooted to very traditional construction techniques, whereby the setting out of the keel and frames was followed by the installation of bulkheads, decks and shell plating. Welding content increased towards the end of the 1950's, but the firm's excellent efforts at improving dredging designs were never equalled, with a comparable approach to the production engineering of these craft, no doubt a consequence of the specialist nature of each vessel.

Output during this period varied from three large dredgers totalling 10,774 g.r.t. launched in 1949 to nothing entering the water in 1955. The shipyard built a total of 30 vessels comprising four naval ships of 1814 tons displacement and 20 other craft of 44,194 g.r.t. between 1946 and 1959, the year of the non-hostile merger with the adjacent Lobnitz & Co Ltd. The largest craft built during this time was the *Bhaghirathi* 4697 g.r.t., a twin-screw self-propelled hopper suction dredger launched on 26 September 1957 for use in the port of Calcutta. Thirty per cent of all craft built during this period were for export.

LOBNITZ & CO LTD   1895–1959

Lobnitz & Co Ltd was founded in 1895 by Henry Lobnitz, a Danish engineer, although the firm's origins date back to 1847. Throughout its existence the small shipyard was renowned for the design and construction of dredgers, hoppers, and other specialised marine craft as well as various small vessels for the Admiralty.

The company emerged from the end of the war with an enviable record for the adaptation of welding to the building of small warships. The company also fabricated many parts of the 'Mulberry floating harbour', that assisted the landing of allied forces and their equipment in France in 1944. This experience gave the shipyard a head start to the routine application of welding as a future alternative to riveting. The firm became a public company in 1945, when the premises were considerably updated and modernised to allow extensive prefabrication of ship units. Visible capital expenditure resulted in a reduction in the total number of building berths from five to three, with the previous array of fixed derricks replaced by two new 20-ton level-luffing electric travelling cranes, whose concrete tracks terminated near a new fabrication shed. This commitment to welding resulted in the provision of a 'school' where welders were trained in the application and appreciation of this science. The vision and technical assessment of this modernisation was originated by Mr H.H. Hagan, the yard's director of shipbuilding.

The order book remained varied and buoyant until the mid-1950s comprising dredgers, oil tankers, crane ships, hoppers and tugs. Maximum annual output during this period was achieved in 1947, with the launching of nine different craft totalling 6904 g.r.t. The largest ship built since 1946 was the coastal oil tanker *Eddycreek* 2224 g.r.t., launched for the Admiralty on 10 September 1959. Between 1946 and 1959, Lobnitz & Co Ltd built 54 vessels of 45,802 g.r.t., of which 44% were for export.

The adjacent engine works manufactured all of the specialised dredging machinery as well as the steam reciprocating engines for some of the ships built by the yard. Reasonably modern, and with greater capacity than that needed to support the shipyard, this division performed specialised construction projects outwith the shipbuilding portfolio of the company, as well as building engines and auxiliaries for other UK shipbuilders.

The established universal market for specialised ships was later eroded by traditional shipbuilders throughout the world, who sought diversification from cyclical merchant ship construction periods of boom and burst. The company was taken over by Hedmex Investments Ltd in 1957, and a year later the new owners approached G. & J. Weir Ltd suggesting a beneficial merger with the adjacent Wm Simons yard. Initially, Weirs declined. However, after protracted reconsideration they duly took over the yard in 1959, immediately forming Simons-Lobnitz Ltd.

| SIMONS-LOBNITZ LTD   1959–1963

The new owners proceeded to merge the two companies and obtain some benefits therefrom. The order book was quickly improved, albeit with some of the contracts taken at unremunerative prices to utilise the total capacity of the amalgamated facilities. The new identity was avidly accepted by the bulk of the labour force of under 2000, who regarded the company as a justifiable, long overdue combination of unique skills that bode well for longevity of employment and the future of specialised Clyde shipbuilding!

Annual trading results highlighted serious heavy losses from these 'bought' contracts, despite the facility working virtually at peak production. Less than two years after its formation, the Weir group parent company announced the yards would close, with the activities taken over by Alexander Stephen & Sons Ltd. The new owner acquired all patents, designs and spare parts contracts, as well as the name 'Si-Lo', which they would append to their future dredger orders built up-river at Linthouse.

Only a handful of the Simons-Lobnitz employees were transferred to Stephens. Shipbuilding in the town of Renfrew ended after more than a century, with the launch of *Hopper Barge No. 3* 1200 g.r.t. (yard no. 1177), supervised by personnel from Alexander Stephen & Sons Ltd, on 27 December 1963.

The loss of this fine traditional and competent company, if somewhat antiquated in its building methods, was glibly addressed by the synthetic sages of the day, as the start of the overdue and inevitable 'attrition of peripheral unsustainable Scottish shipbuilding'. This apocryphal denouncement was offset at the time with the pledge that the good name, goodwill and previous international market dominance would continue at Linthouse under the aegis of the more modern and better capitalised Alexander Stephen & Sons Ltd. Little did they know this closure was the beginning of the end of volume shipbuilding in Scotland. The unfortunate disillusioned and discarded labour force, who uncharacteristically resorted to strikes and go-slows during the run-down, were flippantly assured of instant re-employment at the nearby Rootes car factory in Linwood where retraining in semi-skilled assembly work beckoned future long-term employment. Alas, with the closure of the firm, nearly two hundred years of pioneering first principle practical dredger building experience was irrationally discarded with the temperate contempt for the contents of a bottle of champagne at the launch of a new ship.

During its brief three years' existence, Simons-Lobnitz Ltd built a total of 15 vessels comprising one naval ship of 750 tons displacement and 14 other craft of 21,708 g.r.t., the largest of which was the *Churni*

List of ships built by WILLIAM HAMILTON & Co Ltd, Port Glasgow, between 1946 and closure in 1963

YEAR	NAME	TYPE	COUNTRY OF REGISTRATION	G.R.T.	TOTAL G.R.T.
1946	MAIDAN	s. Ref/Cargo	Britain	8566	
	MAHRONDA	s. Ref/Cargo	Britain	8537	
	AGAMEMNON	m. Cargo	Holland	2515	19618
1947	HELICON	m. Ref/Cargo	Holland	2515	
	OBERON	m. Ref/Cargo	Holland	2515	
	EL HIND r/n	m. Cargo/Pass	India	8521	
	JAL-AZAD				
	POSEIDON	m. Ref/Cargo	Holland	2515	16066
1948	MAHSEER	s. Ref/Cargo	Britain	8961	
	CIS. BRØVIG	m. Oil Tanker	Norway	8996	17957
1949	BERGLJOT	m. Oil Tanker	Norway	8996	
	MATRA	s. Ref/Cargo	Britain	8954	
	NORDBO	m. Oil Tanker	Norway	9064	
	TREGLISSON	s. Cargo	Britain	5975	32989
1950 •	ERLING BORTHEN	m. Oil Tanker	Norway	9074	
	MANAAR	s. Ref/Cargo	Britain	8996	
	AJANA	m. Cargo	Britain	5627	
	DEA.BRØVIG	m. Oil Tanker	Norway	10917	34614
1951	KATARINA	m. Oil Tanker	Norway	9013	
	G.C. BRØVIG	m. Oil Tanker	Norway	10917	
	HOLMGAR	m. Oil Tanker	Norway	8997	
	MAIPURA	s. Ref/Cargo	Britain	9748	38675
1952	PARA	m. Oil Tanker	Brazil	11218	
	TREMAYNE	m. Cargo	Britain	5608	
	BRIS	m. Oil Tanker	Norway	9061	25887
1953 •	PAVIA	m. Ref/Cargo	Britain	3411	
	ALVA BAY	m. Oil Tanker	Britain	11340	
•	MASKELIA	s. Ref/Cargo	Britain	7350	22101
1954	PACIFIC STAR	m. Oil Tanker	Britain	11218	
	TREMORVAH	m. Cargo	Britain	5605	
	LYCIA	m. Ref/Cargo	Britain	3534	
	BRITISH OFFICER	m. Oil Tanker	Britain	11362	
	PHRYGIA	m. Ref/Cargo	Britain	3534	35253

YEAR	NAME	TYPE	COUNTRY OF REGISTRATION	G.R.T.	TOTAL G.R.T.
1955 •	GEROLDA	m. Oil Tanker	Norway	11430	
	MATURATA	s. Cargo	Britain	7365	
	TOBIAS U. BORTHEN	m. Oil Tanker	Norway	9041	
	HELLENIC GLORY	m. Ref/Cargo	Greece	7510	35036
1956 •	NORDNES	m. Oil Tanker	Norway	11470	
•	HELLENIC TORCH	m. Ref/Cargo	Greece	7510	
	MASIRAH	s. Ref/Cargo	Britain	8733	27713
1957	MELITI	m. Oil Tanker	Liberia	11691	
	MAKRANA	s. Ref/Cargo	Britain	8764	
	TREMEADOW	m. Cargo	Britain	6504	26959
1958 •	SAGONA	m. Oil Tanker	Norway	11860	
	MAWANA	s. Ref/Cargo	Britain	8744	
	MANGLA	s. Ref/Cargo	Britain	8805	29409
1959	TRECARRELL	m. Cargo	Britain	6499	
	TRECARNE	m. Cargo	Britain	6499	
	MATHURA	s. Ref/Cargo	Britain	8782	
	ANDANIA	s. Ref/Cargo	Britain	7004	28784
1960 •	ALAUNIA	s. Ref/Cargo	Britain	7004	
	TREVALGAN	m. Cargo	Britain	6706	13710
1961 •	NORDHOLM	m. Cargo	Norway	7187	
•	BRITISH KESTREL	m. Oil Tanker	Britain	11171	18358
1962 •	HALLFAX	m. Bulk Carrier (great laker)	Canada	5780	
•	BENTE BRØVIG	m. Cargo	Norway	8400	14180
1963 •	TRENEGLOS	m. Cargo	Britain	9976	
•	FREETOWN	m. Ref/Cargo	Britain	7689	17665

44% export
56% Britain   **57 vessels total = 454,974 g.r.t.**

• Indicates vessel depicted in subsequent photographic section or another chapter of the book.

For explanation of abbreviations see Glossary on page 345.

The following group of photographs illustrate the location of the former Glen shipyard of Wm Hamilton & Co Ltd, in the town of Port Glasgow. Also portrayed are a selection of merchant vessels undergoing sea-trials in the Firth of Clyde that were built by the shipyard in its final decade of operation.

Previous page, upper. *A panoramic view of the Port Glasgow waterfront on 28 March 1963. Yard no. 527,* m.v. TRENEGLOS *9976 g.r.t. has just been launched from the Glen yard of Wm Hamilton & Co Ltd and is being taken in tow by a pair of tugs. From the left, the Kingston shipyard of Lithgows Ltd has yard no. 1150, the Norwegian* motor tanker THORSHAMMER *34,485 g.r.t. under construction. In the Glen yard,* m.v. FREETOWN *7689 g.r.t. (the last ship built by the company) with Lithgows yard no. 1149 can be seen on one of the berths. Two of her identical 'F' class sisterships,* FULANI *and* FIAN, *occupy a pair of berths on the adjoining Lithgows Ltd East yard. Most of the tenemental houses adjacent to these former shipyards have been demolished to make way for the new alignment of the A8 dual carriageway road.*

Previous page, lower. *This 1958 photograph shows the tank top of a double bottom unit for* ship no. 518, m.v. TRECARRELL *6499 g.r.t. being lifted in one of the sheds of Wm Hamilton's Glen shipyard. The flanged angles attached to the double bottom frames (floors) indicate rivetting is the method used to connect these members to the ship's bottom shell plating.* (Burniston Studios Ltd)

Yard no. 527, m.v. TRENEGLOS *9976 g.r.t. is viewed with a touch of melancholy by four Wm Hamilton apprentices a few minutes prior to her launching on 28 March 1963. This was the penultimate ship launched by the shipyard, the final vessel built there was* m.v. FREETOWN, *a Lithgow order for Elder Dempster Lines that was launched on 19 September 1963. The six mono-tower electric cranes that existed in the Glen yard were fixed to the ground, however despite this restriction the large jibs on each crane enabled virtually complete coverage of any ship built in the shipyard.* (Burniston Studios Ltd)

The Clydeside town of Port Glasgow looking west and down-river in 1964 with shipyard expansion and contraction in evidence. At the bottom of this picture Lithgows East yard boasts a new prefabrication shed and two oil tankers under construction for BP Tankers Ltd, m.t. BRITISH FERN 13,252 g.r.t. *being further complete than her sistership* m.t. BRITISH HOLLY 13,271 g.r.t. *Above the East yard the berths of Wm Hamilton's Glen yard lie empty, with their six fixed mono-tower cranes pointing idly towards the sky, having launched its last ship in the previous year. The totally rebuilt Lithgows Kingston shipyard contains two supertankers for P & O,* m.t. ORAMA 38,982 g.r.t. *in the fitting-out basin, and* m.t. ORISSA 39,035 g.r.t. *on the berth. Beyond lies the town of Greenock on the boundary of which the new Firth of Clyde drydock nears completion. This view ably demonstrates the prime deep-water shipbuilding facility that existed between the three shipyards mentioned above. It also shows how constrained the complex was for further development to the south due to the main A8 road, the Glasgow-Gourock railway line and rapidly rising terrain that was developed with tenemental housing. Three decades after this picture was taken this location had virtually severed its lengthy association with shipbuilding. Only occasional use of the Inchgreen drydock and part of the former Kingston shipyard for marine modifications, as well as the nearby Ferguson Shipbuilders Ltd facility, attest to a diminished contact with the industry that made the town of Port Glasgow world famous. (Aerofilms Ltd)*

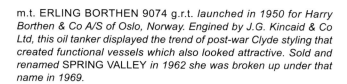

m.t. ERLING BORTHEN 9074 g.r.t. *launched in 1950 for Harry Borthen & Co A/S of Oslo, Norway. Engined by J.G. Kincaid & Co Ltd, this oil tanker displayed the trend of post-war Clyde styling that created functional vessels which also looked attractive. Sold and renamed* SPRING VALLEY *in 1962 she was broken up under that name in 1969.*

m.v. PAVIA 3411 g.r.t. *launched in 1953 for the Cunard SS Coy Ltd, Liverpool. Engined by David Rowan & Co Ltd, this vessel was the first of three sisterships built by Hamiltons for these owners. These ships bore the distinction of being the smallest in the mighty Cunard fleet. Sold and renamed* TOULA *in 1965 she was broken up under that name in 1974.* (Burniston Studios Ltd)

s.s. MASKELIYA 7350 g.r.t. *launched in 1953 for Thos & Jno Brocklebank Ltd, Liverpool. Engined by David Rowan & Co Ltd, this vessel was one of 13 similar ref/cargo liners built by Wm Hamilton & Co Ltd for this line since 1946, an association which reflected that shipping company's part-ownership of the Glen shipyard. The bipod masts, pronounced yet gentle sheer lines and rounded funnel enhance the looks of this liner which was sold and renamed* OCEAN JOY *in 1969 before being broken up in 1972.* (Burniston Studios Ltd)

m.t. GEROLDA 11,430 g.r.t. *launched in 1955 for A/S Gerrards Rederi of Kristiansand, Norway. Engined by the Fairfield SB & Eng Co Ltd, some of her rigging is adorned with bunting presumably to signify acceptance by her owners. Sold and renamed* PANOCEAN *in 1963 she was broken up in 1974 as the* MANA. (Burniston Studios Ltd)

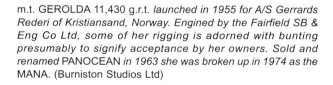

m.t. NORDNES 11,470 g.r.t. *was launched in 1956 for H. Kuhnles Rederi A/S of Bergen, Norway. Engined by J.G. Kincaid & Co Ltd, this vessel was the second of three ships built for these owners by Wm Hamilton since 1946. Sold and renamed* PEMEX *in 1965, she was broken up in 1981 as* ABELARDO L RODRIGUEZ. (Burniston Studios Ltd)

m.t. SAGONA 11,860 g.r.t. *launched in 1958 for A/S Sagona of Kristiansand, Norway. Engined by J.G. Kincaid & Co Ltd, this tanker bore the distinction of being the largest ship constructed by Wm Hamilton & Co Ltd. Sold and renamed STOLT SAGONA in 1967 she had various other names before being broken up as SPETSAI in 1983.* (Burniston Studios Ltd)

s.s. ALAUNIA 7004 g.r.t. *launched in 1960 for the Cunard SS Co Ltd, Liverpool. Engined by David Rowan & Co Ltd, this ship and her sister vessel ANDANIA, also built by Wm Hamilton, plied the North Atlantic between the UK and USA before being transferred within the Cunard-Brocklebank Group. Renamed MALANCHA in 1969, she was broken up in 1993 as the HONG QI 108.* (Burniston Studios Ltd)

m.v. NORDHOLM 7187 g.r.t. *launched in 1961 for H. Kuhnles Rederi A/S of Bergen, Norway. Engined by J.G. Kincaid & Co Ltd, this futuristic looking ship was designed with bridge, accommodation and machinery located aft, as well as a combination of deck cranes and a bipod derrick. She was sold and renamed DJATIPRANA in 1967 and retained that name until being broken up in 1983.* (Burniston Studios Ltd)

m.t. BRITISH KESTREL 11,171 g.r.t. *launched in 1961 for the BP Tanker Co Ltd, London. Engined by J.G. Kincaid & Co Ltd, this vessel remained within the BP fleet until 1976 when she was sold and renamed SUNJIANG, retaining that name until being broken up in 1983. All of the Bird class products tankers built by six yards on the Clyde had minor variations in masts, side screens and accommodation. However, this vessel differed quite noticeably from the others with her taller funnel, which altered her appearance considerably.* (BP Photographic)

t.s.m.v. (great laker) HALLFAX 5780 g.r.t. *launched in 1962 for the Hall Corporation of Canada, Montreal. Engined by Nydqvist & Holm A/B of Trollhätten, Sweden, this vessel was built for service in the Great Lakes of Canada and the USA. She was equipped with a huge boom mounted conveyor to assist with the loading and unloading of bulk cargoes. Sold and renamed COALER 1 in 1981, she retained that name until being broken up in 1990.* (Burniston Studios Ltd)

m.v. BENTE BRØVIG 8400 g.r.t. *launched in 1962 for Th. Brøvig of Farsund, Norway. Engined by J.G. Kincaid & Co Ltd, this ship was similar to the m.v. NORDHOLM built by the yard a year earlier in that machinery and accommodation were located aft, a trend that was gathering popularity among ship-owners in the early 1960s. Sold and renamed JALATARANG in 1969 she retained that name until being broken up in 1985.* (Burniston Studios Ltd)

m.v. TRENEGLOS 9976 g.r.t. *launched in 1963 for the Hain SS Co Ltd, London (a division of P & O). Engined by Fairfield-Rowan Ltd, this functional cargo liner was the eighth ship built by Hamiltons for these owners since 1946. She was renamed STRATHTRUIM within the P & O Group in 1974 before being sold and renamed SIAM BAY in 1979 thence broken up in 1985 as DOMAN.* (P & O Library Archive)

m.v. FREETOWN 7689 g.r.t. *launched in 1963 for Elder Dempster Lines Ltd Liverpool. Engined by Fairfield-Rowan Ltd, Glasgow, this ship was the final vessel built by Wm Hamilton & Co Ltd and was designed for the liner route between the UK and West Africa. She was the fifth of six 'F' class vessels all constructed on the lower Clyde for these owners. Sold and renamed PANSEPTOS in 1978 she was broken up in 1982 as CHERRY RUBY.*

LITHGOWS LTD	1918-1969	(Kingston & East Shipyards)
SCOTT-LITHGOW LTD	1969-1977	(Kingston & East Shipyards)
SCOTT-LITHGOW LTD	1977-1984	(Division of British Shipbuilders Ltd)
SCOTT-LITHGOW LTD	1984-1992	(Offshore Division of Trafalgar House Investments Ltd)

Lithgows Ltd was owned, directed and managed by the direct descendants of the founding Lithgow family, who acquired a number of shipyards in Port Glasgow around the end of the First World War. This independent concern displayed corporate conglomerate tendencies, allied with single-minded resolute management principles towards its comprehensive shipbuilding and associated engineering interests throughout its existence as a private trading company.

Operating two medium-sized shipyards in the town of Port Glasgow, called East and Kingston respectively, these separate establishments employed around a total of 4000 workers between them. The post-war product range from both facilities comprised tramps, cargo-liners, oil tankers and the gradual introduction of specialised ore, coal, and grain ships, later to be classified as 'bulk carriers'. Lithgow built vessels were austere, rugged no-frills ships, designed with the minimum steelwork scantlings. These were competitively priced and rapidly constructed, demonstrating 'father to son' methods of rigidly inflexible working practices, affiliated to payment by results piecework wage rates, that in their day made ship construction programmes, quite definitive in terms of fixed durations. Such consistent production was coupled to meticulous cost control techniques which ensured ongoing monitoring of profitability, generating reasonable earning levels for the top tradesmen whose physical effort and mental aptitude formerly made this system work quite successfully.

Output and productivity from these two traditional shipyards were both prolific and impressive, as well as being remunerative. Marketing the nearest thing to off-the-shelf designs, which could be easily adapted to meet specific ship-owners' requirements, the duo of Port Glasgow shipyards consistently produced a mixed bag of merchant vessels which varied from a low of four small ships of 40,877 g.r.t. in 1960 at the height of yard redevelopment work, to a high of four vessels of 111,326 g.r.t. in 1967, two years before the amalgamation with the adjacent Scotts of Greenock.

Such formidable output from a cooperative and productive labour force established Lithgows Ltd as consistently the most capable volume shipbuilding company in Scotland. When the total of associated group companies like the Fairfield SB & Eng Co Ltd and Wm. Hamilton & Co Ltd were included, the independent Lithgow Group always exceeded 150,000 g.r.t. of annual output, making them among the biggest ship producers in the UK, and sometimes Europe, throughout much of the post-war era. Imbued with inveterate interest and commitment to shipbuilding and marine engineering, the directors of Lithgows Ltd initiated extensive yard modernisation projects, to be completed in between the bread and butter business of on-line ship building.

This need to harness the then infant technology of production engineering and duly apply it to shipbuilding, spurred many British and overseas equipment suppliers to redesign their stock in trade hardware. Travelling crane sizes accelerated from about 10/15 tons to 60 tons capacity within the short time it took respective directors to establish an enquiry, followed up by a firm contract. Machines for steelwork forming, preparation and welding were also affected by the Lithgow Group's need for modernisation.

Costed in units of millions of pounds in the late 1950's, the realisation of this expenditure was the creation of the then state-of-the-art Kingston shipyard. It was totally rebuilt, re-equipped and custom tailored to build the new breed of supertankers and bulk carriers up to 800 ft long which were projected as comprising up to 50% of the then world market for new shipping. East yard was partly modernised with up-to-date welding plant and preparation equipment, but preserved its forest-like skyline of traditional fixed hammerhead cranes and derricks. This retention of customary erection methods did not seem to encumber the output of the older yard. Multiple, ship construction of different types continued there concurrently, on all of the available berths throughout the existence of East yard as a traditional shipbuilding centre.

Greatest annual output under the Lithgow family was achieved at Port Glasgow in 1975 when two large ships of 180,792 g.r.t. were constructed. This statistic was inflated by the respective scantlings of this VLCC (very large crude carrier) and bulk carrier, although the yard regularly built more ships per annum, they aggregated a far lesser g.r.t.

Prolific yearly output figures were common from Lithgows Ltd in the post-war period. With a regular mix of merchant ship types, 1949 saw 11 vessels of 82,952 g.r.t. launched within 12 months. This formidable statistic was not surpassed until 1964 when four oil tankers of 104,540 g.r.t. entered the River Clyde. On a further eight occasions over 100,000 g.r.t. was launched annually by the company from the Kingston and Glen/East shipyards. The largest vessel built by Lithgows was the *s.t. Nordic Clansman* 138,702 g.r.t., a VLCC launched in 1973 and completed a year later; she was also the biggest ship ever built in Scotland. The smaller output statistic of 1949 was nevertheless very significant, in that the unit sizes of the later built ships were much larger, which resulted in higher tonnage outputs being achieved for less complexity. The intricacy of setting-out, erection or outfitting of individual vessels of different ship types, bore witness to the market awareness of the directors, the organised production methodology of the management, and the unique will to work of the labour force. Such productive output from a bygone archaic, labour-intensive industry has long been lost in the subsequent attrition of the River Clyde shipbuilding industry.

Amalgamating with the neighbouring Scotts Shipbuilding & Eng Co Ltd to form Scott-Lithgow Ltd, in 1969, the following decade and a half of shipbuilding on the lower reaches saw a gradual plunge from a euphoric peak of partly profitable, considerable annual new ship output in the late 1960s, to a slough of publicly besmirched loss-making on contracts which were then being absorbed by the UK exchequer, under the umbrella of British Shipbuilders Ltd. The formation of Scott-Lithgow Ltd into a regional, homogenous shipbuilding and marine engineering company was heralded by respective directors, trade unions, politicians and the media as a natural industrial accord, which was bereft of the coercive titular amalgamation enforced on the rump of the upper River Clyde shipbuilding industry in 1968. The initial results of the new group ratified the optimism and well wishes that had surrounded its establishment.

Customer confidence was buoyant with order intake adequate. Output and ship type varied from yard to yard and comprised a truly comprehensive range of marine vessels. The main thrust of the company after amalgamation was the multi-million pound investment and commissioning of the new Glen-East shipbuilding facility for VLCCs which were then in demand throughout the world. The tens of millions spent on this new yard, with some monies in the form of public grants and loans was regrettably compromised by the limited berth length under the 225-ton travelling goliath crane. Such apparently trivial physical constraints were ultimately solved in the Lithgow tradition of innovative engineering. By initiating large tanker construction in two halves, subsequently joined afloat using a submerged cofferdam, which was a dry caisson beneath the hull where tradesman could prepare, and weld the two sections together. This unique solution was necessitated by the fact that no suitable dry dock facilities existed on Clydeside. Transport and rental costs of utilising the nearest European dry docks to effect 'dry' joining together were greater than the home grown underwater solution. In the time honoured Lithgow tradition of working in Scotland, all the VLCCs built at Port Glasgow were joined together using this method, however, it proved more costly and resulted in a longer ship construction building schedule.

The new group wrestled manfully with the combined ills of the 1970s UK industrial scene. Rampant inflation, falling productivity and burgeoning regressive thinking from powerful trade unions overtly hinted of Labour Government coercion towards a state-owned industrial receptacle, where indifferent performance would be underwritten by the taxpayer. This scenario was amazingly unfolding against the concurrent rapid decline, followed by virtual elimination of Lithgow's traditional market, the British Merchant Navy. Throughout the world, predatory competition was further compounded with the emergence of state-of-the-art third world shipbuilding industries, notably that of South Korea, which in less than a decade had gone from an agrarian economy to a smoke-stack super-power, funded by mysterious sources, veiled in subtle subsidies. These combined factors demotivated, destabilised and ultimately denuded what profitability was then remaining in Scott-Lithgow Ltd. New order intakes were sporadically won against cut to the bone competition. Traditional cargo, naval, tanker and bulk carrier contracts were supplemented by orders for dynamically positioned drilling ships which initially taxed the technology of the drawing office and innovative skill of the shop floor. Two such ships were successfully built to proven design of IHC of Holland, and were enthusiastically received by their respective owners. They subsequently performed more than satisfactorily in world wide service, both were launched from the Scott-Lithgow, Cartsdyke facility in Greenock, with considerable assistance from other sections of the group.

The go-ahead board of directors entered the expanding UK North Sea market for semi-submersible craft obtaining an order from British Petroleum, a long standing customer, for the *Iolair* 11,019 g.r.t., an emergency support vessel which proved a technical, practical and commercial minefield, compared with traditional ship orders. This contract was successfully but belatedly completed to the entire satisfaction of her owners and led to a follow-on order for a semi-submersible exploration drilling rig which was built between the Cartsburn and Port Glasgow locations and named *Sea Explorer* 9086 g.r.t.

The Lithgow tradition for enterprise and flair, allied to marine market penetration, proved to be the achilles heel of the company. Possessing a diversely skilled, adaptable labour force, although perhaps not as productive as in previous decades, the new group acquired the most flexible maritime construction portfolio of any UK shipbuilder. Virtually all of this omni-capability had evolved during the brief, successful consort with Scotts of Greenock.

Coercively assimilated into British Shipbuilders Ltd on 1 July 1977, this bureaucratic bouillabaisse of fanciful credo, insidiously directed traditional ship orders away from Scott-Lithgow Ltd. The allocation of new shipbuilding contracts was centralised, firstly in London, along with the marketing department, then in Newcastle, the final location of BSL headquarters. After existing for a few years with a reduced workload, which created an horrendous loss-making profile, Scott-Lithgow Ltd was arbitrarily deemed to be part of the Offshore Division of BSL, along with Cammell-Laird Ltd in Birkenhead. These two individual outfits would now bid, design and construct, offshore structures that *floated*, not fixed, steel platforms which are otherwise known as jackets. Only one further semi-submersible vessel was ordered from Scott-Lithgow Ltd. All of these crafts were completed belatedly in the 1980s and all were delivered to BP.

The last cargo merchant vessel completed at Port Glasgow was the motorship *Oropesa* 9015 g.r.t., launched in 1978, the second of a pair for Furness Withy Line. She was followed four years later by the large oil tanker *British Spirit* 66,024 g.r.t. whose late and controversial completion duration, apparently exceeded her actual contract construction schedule. The penalty clause costs incurred by the UK taxpayer on this ship were seemingly greater than her initial stipulated contract value! This ignominious tanker became the final ship built at the Kingston shipyard. Her protracted construction duration was initially a result of late delivery of technical information from Swan Hunter, the lead contractor on this series of four vessels. Further contributory factors were that the bulk of Lithgows' experienced management had coincidentally retired around the time of nationalisation, and morale in the yard was at an all time low.

The large semi-submersible drilling rig, *Ocean Alliance* 15,517 g.r.t. was ordered by Atlantic Drilling Ltd on behalf of Britoil, placed when there was a worldwide boom and demand for such craft. The management and labour force transitions that had diffused the debacle of BSL left Scott-Lithgow Ltd ill-equipped and non-motivated for the successful completion of this prestigious order. Where the previous Lithgow identity of the shipyard had led by example in the execution of contracts, the initiative in the construction of the new offshore vessel had now been seized by the future owners of the rig. The portents for such a change were ultimately commercial suicide! Progress on the vessel (yard order no. 2002) was replaced with uncharacteristic regress. Thousands of men were unproductively deployed on unit fabrication that bore no cognisance with the vessel erection sequence. In a very short space of time the order was out of control, and the client tried on a number of occasions to cancel the project. Many decades of successful shipbuilding at Port Glasgow were now reduced to a comedy of errors that bode ill for the continuation of the industry on the Lower Clyde.

BSL were divested of Scott-Lithgow Ltd in 1984 when the Trafalgar House Group Ltd acquired the extensive Renfrewshire waterfront, lock stock and barrel bought at a fraction of the replacement value of the shipyard. The Government-sponsored sale included the contentious order for *Ocean Alliance*, completion of which was a precondition of ownership of four working shipyards, a marine engine works, a large dry-dock and various fitting-out quays, all served by extensive craneage. The new owners made meaningful efforts and commitment to finish the then largest semi-submersible-drilling rig in the world, and the hull was launched in the summer of 1987. Recent advancement in new offshore technology during the protracted time-frame of her construction meant that *Ocean Alliance* was far from 'state-of-the-art', when she was finally handed over to her owners over five years late, being ultimately completed by a consortium of offshore specialist contractors called Scottish Rig Repairers Ltd in the Cromarty Firth in 1989.

A new midship section to enlarge the Tyne built Falklands War replacement container ship *m.v. Atlantic Conveyor* 25,301 g.r.t. became the last shipbuilding contract undertaken at the Glen/East site after the launch of yard no. 2002. This jumbo-ising order was successfully performed in the adjacent Inchgreen dry dock, well within her stipulated contract duration. It was significant that the owners of this ship were also by then the owners of the yard, however, the timely completion of this prestigious conversion did not lead to repeat orders.

The loss of the Lithgow name, once synonymous with high volume quality shipbuilding from the town of Port Glasgow, is perhaps less appreciated than those of the more famous former shipbuilders up-river, who tended to achieve their fame from the construction of large passenger liners and warships. Yet this independent private company built more ships of greater aggregate tonnage than any other Scottish shipbuilder! Between 1946 and 1987 the two Lithgow yards at Port Glasgow in its four guises launched 180 ships and rigs of 2,764,628 g.r.t. This was nearly 25% of the total River Clyde output during this era, which comprised 59 oil tankers, 72 cargo liners, 45 bulk carriers, three rigs and one passenger liner—30% of which was for export. The company was consistently among the top five British shipbuilders throughout its existence, building single and repeat orders for virtually every UK shipping company as well as for owners in many foreign countries, notably Norway and India. Employment was given to upwards of 4000 direct workers at the height of post-war ship construction, with as much as two and a half times that number in subcontractors and equipment suppliers throughout Scotland and the UK

The ignominious public profile throughout the '80s that the Port Glasgow yards achieved during their impelled and unsuccessful inclusion in that ill-considered excursion of glib government intervention, 'British Shipbuilders Ltd', was totally out of context with the go-ahead attitude, initiative and meaningful accords with ship-owners that were the hallmark of the Lithgow family and their professional management team. Alas, the misdirected and reckless industrial intrusion by the state in the 1970s is now viewed as the most significant reason for the virtual eradication of shipbuilding in the towns of Port Glasgow and Greenock. It was hoped by those employed in the industry to be the vehicle for collective ownership that would infuse purposeful leadership and significant direction towards the long term existence of shipbuilding. Unfortunately, such optimism proved to be a naive political ruse that achieved the converse of these optimistic anticipations.

In 1996, the innate shipbuilding traditions of the town of Port Glasgow deserved better than 2 km of deserted waterfront, now festooned with for sale signs. A few mangled discarded items of former shipbuilding ironmongery lie strewn between the vast open disused building berths, the largest of which was still straddled by the now redundant goliath crane, its matt green paintwork noticeably bespeckled by the encroachment of rampant rust. What remains of the preparation shop buildings, some of which are partly denuded of of their sheetmetal cladding, now resonate cacophonously with the whistling of the wind…no longer reverberating the clamour and clanging of industrious ironfighters and outfitters regularly creating new ships. Only the prefabrication sheds of what was the Kingston shipyard and part of the former drydock complex see occasional use by itinerant offshore construction firms, employing some local labour on casual contracts for the modification of North Sea rigs and platforms. At this time, the north face of the Kingston fabrication shed still bore the name of Lithgows Ltd, although by then the entire site had been acquired by Clydeport Authority, and future use for continued marine work looked encouraging with the recent lease of part of the site to the up-river firm of UIE (Shipbuilding) Scotland Ltd.

List of ships built by LITHGOWS Ltd, Port Glasgow, and their successors between 1946 and 1987

YEAR	NAME	TYPE	COUNTRY OF REGISTRATION	G.R.T.	TOTAL G.R.T.
1946	TAHSINIA	m. Cargo	Britain	5680	
	CAPE ORTEGAL	m. Cargo	Britain	6907	
	BEAVERLAKE	s.e. Ref/Cargo	Britain	9824	
	SHAHJEHAN	s. Cargo	Britain	5460	
	JALARAJAN	s. Cargo	India	5085	
	SHAHZADA	s. Cargo	Britain	5469	
	CAPE RODNEY	m. Cargo	Britain	6939	
	ARABY	m. Cargo	Britain	5040	
	COULBRECK	s. Cargo	Britain	3654	
	KALEWA	m. Cargo	Britain	4882	58940
1947	RAVNAAS	m. Cargo	Norway	5670	
	MOHAMMEDI	s. Cargo/Pass	India	7026	
	CRAFTSMAN	s. Cargo	Britain	6725	
	LINGUIST	s. Cargo	Britain	6736	
	KATHA	m. Cargo	Britain	4876	
	KVERNAAS	m. Cargo	Norway	5711	
	VIVITA	m. Cargo	Norway	5667	
	MOZAFFARI	s. Cargo/Pass	India	7024	
	KANBE	m. Cargo	Britain	4878	54313
1948	ANDREA BRØVIG	m. Oil Tanker	Norway	8988	
	BRITISH ADVOCATE	m. Oil Tanker	Britain	8573	
	BAHADUR	s. Cargo	Britain	5497	
	BRITISH COUNCILLOR	m. Oil Tanker	Britain	8573	
	MANDEVILLE	m. Ref/Cargo	Norway	6039	
	SCOTTISH TRADER	m. Cargo	Britain	5590	
	SUBADAR	s. Cargo	Britain	5497	
	COULGARVE	s. Cargo	Britain	2946	51703
1949	SOLSTAD	m. Oil Tanker	Norway	9077	
	CAPE GRENVILLE	m. Cargo	Britain	7478	
	BIOGRAPHER	s. Cargo	Britain	6922	
	ALTNES	m. Oil Tanker	Norway	9025	
	RAJAH	s. Cargo	Britain	5791	
	BISCOE	m. Oil Tanker	Britain	9313	
	ISFONN	m. Oil Tanker	Norway	9044	
	GLENVILLE	m. Ref/Cargo	Norway	6320	
	BRITISH PATRIOT	m. Oil Tanker	Britain	8661	
	KINDAT	m. Cargo	Britain	5530	
	RANEE	s. Cargo	Britain	5791	82952
1950	WAZIRISTAN	m. Oil Tanker	Britain	9115	
	BRITISH PEER	m. Oil Tanker	Britain	8661	
	JALVALLABH	s. Ref/Cargo	India	6905	
	POWELL	m. Oil Tanker	Britain	11708	
	KALADAN	m. Cargo	Britain	4915	
	HEKTORIA	m. Oil Tanker	Norway	9027	
	SHERBOURNE	m. Cargo	Britain	4986	
	JALRAJENDRA	s. Ref/Cargo	India	6905	
	BRITISH PREMIER	m. Oil Tanker	Britain	8661	70883
1951	DALMORE	m. Oil Tanker	Britain	10351	
	KONGSFJORD	m. Ref/Cargo	Norway	5934	
	TELNES	m. Oil Tanker	Norway	11006	
	ALAGOAS	m. Oil Tanker	Brazil	11354	
	NEWBURY	m. Oil Tanker	Finland	11199	
	KADEIK	m. Cargo	Britain	7489	
	SYDHAV	m. Oil Tanker	Norway	10946	68279
1952	SILVERDALE	m. Oil Tanker	Britain	11289	
	LARISTAN	m. Oil Tanker	Britain	12446	

YEAR	NAME	TYPE	COUNTRY OF REGISTRATION	G.R.T.	TOTAL G.R.T.
1952	MATO GROSSO	m. Oil Tanker	Brazil	11346	
	KOYAN	m. Cargo	Britain	5537	
	LLANDAFF	m. Oil Tanker	Britain	12501	
	ORMSARY	s. Ore Carrier	Britain	6859	
	GLYNAFON	m. Cargo	Britain	7021	
	TUAREG	m. Oil Tanker	Norway	11480	
	GLEDDOCH	s. Ore Carrier	Britain	6859	
	KOHIMA	m. Cargo	Britain	5597	90935
1953	BEDFORD	m. Oil Tanker	Britain	12578	
	BRITISH GUARDIAN	m. Oil Tanker	Britain	11359	
	RIVER AFTON	m. Ore Carrier	Britain	11558	
	DAVANGER	m. Oil Tanker	Norway	11827	
	OAKWOOD	m. Oil Tanker	Britain	11360	58682
1954	BRITISH HERO	m. Oil Tanker	Britain	11358	
	HYRIA	s. Oil Tanker	Britain	12132	
	TEMPLE LANE	m. Cargo	Britain	7848	
	• SIR JAMES LITHGOW	m. Oil Tanker	Norway	12698	
	ORKANGER	m. Oil Tanker	Norway	11817	
	• HYALA	s. Oil Tanker	Britain	12164	
	KANDAW	m. Cargo	Britain	5599	73616
1955 •	KALDFONN	s. Oil Tanker	Norway	12534	
	CAPE YORK	m. Cargo	Britain	8280	
	BENGUELA	m. Oil Tanker	Norway	13969	
	BORDER LAIRD	m. Oil Tanker	Britain	11366	
	DUNADD	m. Ore Carrier	Britain	10682	
	• SAUDI	s. Cargo/Pass	India	5973	
	HYGROMIA	s. Oil Tanker	Britain	12161	74965
1956 •	KINGSVILLE	s. Ref/Cargo	Norway	7563	
	KADUNA	m. Cargo	Britain	5599	
	• RIPON	m. Ore Carrier	Britain	10731	
	BARON INCHCAPE	s. Cargo	Britain	5490	
	HYDATINA	s. Oil Tanker	Britain	12161	
	DUNCRAIG	m. Ore Carrier	Britain	10687	
	QUEENSVILLE	s. Ref/Cargo	Norway	7586	59817
1957	CAPE HORN	m. Cargo	Britain	8484	
	RIBBLEHEAD	m. Ore Carreir	Britain	10741	
	ARISAIG	m. Ore Carrier	Britain	6872	
	• ATHELCREST	m. Oil Tanker	Britain	7548	
	DUNKYLE	m. Ore Carrier	Britain	10687	
	• BHAMO	m. Cargo	Britain	5932	
	DALHANNA	m. Ore Carrier	Britain	11452	61716
1958	SIR ANDREW DUNCAN	m. Ore Carrier	Britain	10687	
	ORECREST	m. Ore Carrier	Britain	6903	
	• MORAR	gas. turbine Ore Carrier	Britain	6990	
	• AXINA	s. Oil Tanker	Britain	12283	
	KUMBA	m. Cargo	Britain	5439	
	KABALA	m. Cargo	Britain	5445	
	• HARMATAN	m. Cargo	Britain	9236	
	• PRAHSU	m. Cargo	Britain	5445	62428
1959 •	CAPE FRANKLIN	m. Ore Carrier	Britain	11815	
	NURMAHAL	m. Cargo	Britain	8628	
	BRITISH TRUST	m. Oil Tanker	Britain	11211	
	• JAMAICA PLANTER	s. Ref/Cargo	Jamaica	6159	
	• BRITISH ROBIN	m. Oil Tanker	Britain	11211	
	CLARKSPEY	m. Cargo	Britain	7683	56707

YEAR	NAME	TYPE	COUNTRY OF REGISTRATION	G.R.T.	TOTAL G.R.T.
1960 •	BORDER SHEPHERD	m. Oil Tanker	Britain	13600	
	DONGA	m. Cargo	Britain	6565	
	DUMBAIA	m. Cargo	Britain	6558	
•	ORLANDO	m. Oil Tanker	Britain	14154	40877
1961	DALLA	m. Cargo	Britain	6564	
	CAPE NELSON	m. Ore Carrier	Britain	12351	
	PEGU	m. Cargo	Britain	5764	
•	MYLLA	m. Bulk Carrier	Norway	15543	
•	GOTHLAND	m. Ore Carrier	Britain	16664	
	BRUNES	m. Bulk Carrier	Norway	10485	67371
1962 •	BERNES	m. Bulk Carrier	Norway	10485	
•	JAMAICA PRODUCER	m. Ref/Cargo	Jamaica	5781	
•	CAPE HOWE	m. Ore Carrier	Britain	19032	
•	CLARKFORTH	m. Cargo	Britain	7669	
•	BRIMNES	m. Bulk Carrier	Britain	10594	
•	HIGHLAND	m. Cargo	Britain	10035	63596
1963	NURJEHAN	m. Cargo	Britain	8604	
	FORCADOS	m. Cargo	Britain	7689	
•	THORSHAMMER	m. Oil Tanker	Norway	34485	
	FULANI	m. Cargo	Britain	7689	
•	FIAN	m. Cargo	Britain	7689	66156
1964	ORAMA	m. Oil Tanker	Britain	38982	
	BRITISH FERN	m. Oil Tanker	Britain	13252	
	BRITISH HOLLY	m. Oil Tanker	Britain	13271	
•	ORISSA	m. Oil Tanker	Britain	39035	104540
1965 •	CAPE RODNEY	m. Bulk Carrier	Britain	12104	
•	LARISTAN	s. Oil Tanker	Britain	37927	
•	BRITISH IVY	m. Oil Tanker	Britain	13271	
•	WESTMORLAND	m. Ref/Cargo	Britain	11011	
•	JERSEY BRIDGE	m. Bulk Carrier	Britain	22593	96906
1966 •	JALARAJAN	m. Cargo	India	11323	
	JALARASHMI	m. Cargo	India	11323	
•	NAESS TALISMAN	m. Bulk Carrier	Britain	40769	
	JALARATNA	m. Cargo	India	11323	74738
1967	BIRKNES	m. Bulk Carrier	Norway	12456	
	GALLIC BRIDGE	m. Bulk Carrier	Britain	42774	
	SUGAR CRYSTAL	m. Bulk Carrier	Britain	13894	
	WESTMINSTER BRIDGE	m. Bulk Carrier	Britain	42202	111326
1968	SUGAR PRODUCER	m. Bulk Carrier	Britain	13894	
•	BAYNES	m. Bulk Carrier	Britain	12404	
	BORGNES	m. Bulk Carrier	Britain	12404	
	BELLNES	m. Bulk Carrier	Britain	12404	51106
1969†	BRUNES	m. Bulk Carrier	Norway	13124	
	BAUGNES	m. Bulk Carrier	Norway	13124	
	NAESS ENTERPRISE	m. Oil Tanker	Liberia	67443	
	AQUILA	m. Bulk Carrier	Norway	13125	106816
1970	SUGAR TRANSPORTER	m. Bulk Carrier	Britain	13907	
	BROOKNES	m. Bulk Carrier	Norway	13098	
•	GOLD STAR	m. Oil Tanker	South Korea	73201	100206

YEAR	NAME	TYPE	COUNTRY OF REGISTRATION	G.R.T.	TOTAL G.R.T.
1971	BLIDNES	m. Bulk Carrier	Norway	13116	
	SUGAR REFINER	m. Bulk Carrier	Britain	13907	
•	KING STAR	m. Oil Tanker	South Korea	73729	100752
1972	BRIMNES	m. Bulk Carrier	Britain	22908	
	BERNES	m. Bulk Carrier	Britain	22901	
	BRAVENES r/n	m. Bulk Carrier	Britain	22906	68715
•	SILVERDON				
1973	NAESS SCOTSMAN r/n				
•	NORDIC CLANSMAN	s. Oil Tanker	Britain	138702	
	BRITISH SPEY	m. Oil Tanker	Britain	15540	154242
1974 •	JHANSI-KI-RANI	m. Bulk Carrier	India	42141	42141
1975 •	KASTURBA	m. Bulk Carrier	India	42141	
•	NORDIC COMMANDER	s. Oil Tanker	Britain	138651	180792
1976	JALAHIVAR	m. Bulk Carrier	India	42141	
•	WORLD SCHOLAR	m. Oil Tanker	Liberia	126239	168380
1977†	OROYA	m. Cargo	Britain	9015	
•	WORLD SCORE	m. Oil Tanker	Liberia	126260	135275
1978 •	OROPESA	m. Cargo	Britain	9015	9015
1979	*None*	*None*	*None*	–	–
1980	*None*	*None*	*None*	–	–
1981 •	IOLAIR	m.e. Self-prop semi-sub Crane/Diving/ESV	Britain	11019	11019
1982	S.L.B.I.	n.p. Pontoon	Britain	3182	
•	BRITISH SPIRIT	m. Oil Tanker	Britain	66024	69206
1983	*None*	*None*	*None*	–	–
1984†	*None*	*None*	*None*	–	–
1985	*None*	*None*	*None*	–	–
1986	*None*	*None*	*None*	–	–
1987 •	OCEAN ALLIANCE	m.e. Self-prop Semi-sub Drilling Rig	Britain	15517	15517

30% export
70% Britain   180 vessels total = 2,764,628 g.r.t.

Notes
† Became Scott-Lithgow Ltd   1969–77
† Became Scott-Lithgow Ltd (Division of B.S. Ltd)   1977–84
† Became Scott-Lithgow Ltd (Offshore Division of Trafalgar House Investments Ltd)   1984–92

• Indicates vessel depicted in subsequent photographic section.

For explanation of abbreviations see Glossary on page 345.

The following selection of photographs illustrates the locations of the former Kingston, East and Glen shipyards of Lithgows Ltd in Port Glasgow, including some views of the once extensive shipbuilding facility in pre- and post-modernisation modes. Also shown are a significant number of trials photographs depicting the wide spectrum of ship types of varying styles built by these shipyards in their respective guises of post-war ownership.

Previous page, upper. *Lithgows Ltd, East yard at Port Glasgow in the early 1950s looking south. Five of the six berths visible depict merchant ships under construction in the era before prefabrication. An oil tanker is nearest completion on the fourth berth from the left flanked by cargo liners on either side, with keel plates laid out on two other berths. Note the brand new local authority housing on the hillside behind the yard, built to rehouse mainly shipyard workers and their families from sub-standard tenements in the town. The floating boom in the river showed the awareness of this capable company to prevent any flotsam from damaging passing craft.* (Burniston Studios Ltd)

Previous page, lower. *The contrasting scenery of Port Glasgow's tenements, the mouth of the River Clyde, the dormitory town of Helensburgh with the distant hills behind Glen Fruin are shown to good effect in this 1963 view looking north-west. Dominating the recently modernised Kingston shipyard is yard no. 1150, m.t. THORSHAMMER 34,485 g.r.t. a few weeks away from launching. In the fitting-out basin are left to right, m.v. FORCADOS 7689 g.r.t., m.v. NURJEHAN 8604 g.r.t. and m.v. HIGHLAND 10,035 g.r.t., all previously launched by Lithgows Ltd. Note the 'space-age' clock on top of the new fabrication shed.* (Burniston Studios Ltd)

Left. *Yard no. 1076, m.t. SIR JAMES LITHGOW 12,698 g.r.t. prior to launching from the Kingston shipyard of Lithgows Ltd on 3 August 1954. Built for a consortium of Norwegian owners, this tanker bore the name of probably the most visionary and capable Clyde shipbuilder, whose record of achievement stands among the greatest feats of Scottish industrial production. Note the extensive amount of riveting evident on the ship's hull.* (Burniston Studios Ltd)

Left. *Yard no. 1096, m.t. ATHELCREST 7548 g.r.t. prior to launching from Lithgows Ltd, East yard on 12 June 1957. The plethora of rigging and guy strops evident in this picture made for sound communication between cranemen and slingers when lifting sections and travelling with loads. Cellular telephones were not yet invented, and the deafening background shipyard cacophony meant that hand signals were the only effective means of information technology to prevent snagging and clashing of loads and strops.* (Burniston Studios Ltd)

Below, left. *Lithgows Ltd fitting-out basin at Port Glasgow on 15 February 1961. The recently launched motor ore carrier CAPE NELSON 12,351 g.r.t. is manouvered towards the west side quay to share the wet dock with the gas turbine ore carrier MORAR 6990 g.r.t. and m.v. HARMATTAN 9236 g.r.t., both previously completed by Lithgows Ltd, but in dock performing guarantee voyage repairs.* (Burniston Studios Ltd)

Below, right. *Yard no. 1138, motor bulk carrier GOTHLAND 16,664 g.r.t. is towed into the recently modernised fitting-out basin of Lithgows Ltd, Kingston shipyard after her launching on 25 September 1961. In the foreground is part of the new plate stockyard framed by the girders of a magnetic plate handling crane. The three temporary tower cranes on the ship's upper deck were installed by Lithgows to assist with her construction and outfit, a practice the company retained for nearly three decades. GOTHLAND ended her days on the river of her birth. As the DAPO SKY (renamed 77), her engine room caught fire whilst in ballast from General Terminus Quay, Glasgow. On inspection at the tail of the bank she was declared a constructive total loss and was broken up at nearby Faslane.* (Burniston Studios Ltd)

Previous page. *Yard no. 1180, m.t. KING STAR 73,729 g.r.t. enters the River Clyde from the Kingston shipyard of Scott-Lithgow Ltd on 18 November 1971. The second of a pair of large tankers built by Scott-Lithgow Ltd for Sam Yang Navigation Co Ltd of Inchon, South Korea, her contract included extensive training in the art of shipbuilding of many South Koreans by her Scottish builders. Little did her benevolent constructors realise that their skills would be comprehended and improved upon to such an extent that this auspicious occasion of launching the 'largest complete hull' from the town of Port Glasgow would soon never be repeated. KING STAR remained in service until 1983 when she was broken up. Note the aft end of yard no. 1184, later named BRIMNES 22,908 g.r.t., the first in a series of three bulk carriers built at the yard for the Jebsen group who were among Lithgows biggest post-war customers. (Burniston Studios Ltd)*

Right. *Night shift working beneath the 225-ton Goliath crane at Scott-Lithgows Glen shipyard in the 1970s. Longitudinal and transverse bulkheads clearly show the immense amount of welding required to achieve the necessary stiffness and flexibility of a VLCC hull. Note also the extensive framework of scaffolding to allow access for other activities, notably painting and the fitting of internal pipework. (Burniston Studios Ltd)*

Below. *The two halves of m.t. WORLD SCHOLAR 126,239 g.r.t. are brought together for welding shortly after the launching of the tanker's forward section in July 1977. This lengthy and costly operation which entailed underwater working, was conceived and successfully accomplished by Scott-Lithgow Ltd because the shipyard was prevented from extended its large building berth southwards, due to the retention of the old course of the main A8 road until 'money' was available for its necessary realignment. Scott-Lithgow Ltd built four VLCCs using this method. By the time the A8 road was realigned the Glen yard of Scott-Lithgow Ltd, then within the umbrella of British Shipbuilders Ltd, had ceased*
(continued)

building large tankers—and the berth was never extended. This view gives some idea of the scale of the size of shell plates used in this tanker's construction, and the massive diameter of wire strops and rigging hardware used to pull the two halves of the ship together. (Burniston Studios Ltd)

Next page, upper. *The two halves of the s.t. NORDIC COMMANDER 138,651 g.r.t. lie alongside the quay at Inchgreen, Greenock prior to ballasting and trimming, fit-up and welding together in the autumn of 1975. The massive length of this VLCC is shown to good effect due to the proximity of buildings and vehicles. This steam turbine tanker had a very short life, being broken up in 1983. Note the rakes of bogie plate wagons loaded with steel plates in sidings either side of the Glasgow-Gourock railway line waiting unloading by Scott-Lithgow Ltd in the private siding of their nearby yard. (Burniston Studios Ltd)*

Next page, lower. *Virtually the entire huge Port Glasgow shipbuilding complex of Scott-Lithgow Ltd is seen to good effect in this 1976 view looking north-west. Under the Goliath crane in the Glen yard is the stern section of the motor tanker WORLD SCHOLAR 126,239 g.r.t. with many prefabricated units of the forward part of this ship scattered around the yard. To the left of centre, the enlarged Kingston shipyard has the motor bulk carrier JALAVIHAR 42,141 g.r.t. nearing completion. The course of the new A8 road has consumed many old tenements and also given way to some land for additional steel plate storage. (Burniston Studios Ltd)*

s.t. HYALA 12,164 g.r.t. *launched in 1954 for Shell Bermuda (Overseas) Ltd, London. Engined by David Rowan & Co Ltd, she was the second in a four-ship order of 'H' class vessels built by Lithgows Ltd for these owners and remained with Shell Tankers throughout her entire life, being broken up in the Far East in 1975.*

s.t. KALDFONN 12,534 g.r.t. *launched in 1955 for Skibs A/S Ringfonn (Sigval Bergesen), Stavanger, Norway. Engined by David Rowan & Co Ltd, this vessel and many others like her were the largest ships build by Lithgows up until the company embarked on a massive investment scheme in the late 1950s. Sold and renamed CAPETAN MIKES in 1965, she had various other names before being declared a total loss as PERMINA 107 in 1970.*

s.s. SAUDI 5973 g.r.t. *launched in 1955 for the Mogul Line Ltd of Bombay. Engined by Rankin & Blackmore Ltd, Greenock, this unique vessel was built to ferry pilgrims from the Indian sub-continent to Saudi Arabia. She performed this task very successfully for many years until she sank off the coast of Somalia in heavy seas during June 1973 with the loss of 39 lives. This ship was the only true passenger vessel built by Lithgows Ltd in the post-war period.*

s.s. KINGSVILLE 7563 g.r.t. *launched in 1956 for Skibs A/S Mandeville (A.F. Klaveness & Co A/S), Oslo, Norway. Engined by David Rowan & Co Ltd, this dated design of ref/cargo steamship with her detached bridge structure located over a deep tank between Nos 2 and 3 holds, lasted with her original owners until 1977 when she was sold. Renamed SEA UNION, she was broken up with that name in 1978.*

motor ore carrier RIPON 10,731 g.r.t. *launched in 1956 for North Yorkshire Shipping Co Ltd, Middlesbrough. Engined by D. Rowan & Co Ltd, this first generation shallow draft ore carrier plied between the UK iron ore ports of Glasgow, Port Talbot, Workington, Redcar, Immingham and Canada, Sweden and West Africa until she was sold and converted into a non-propelled crane pontoon in Spain in 1972.*

m.v. BHAMO 5932 g.r.t. *launched in 1957 for the British & Burmese SN Co Ltd (Paddy Henderson & Co), Glasgow. Engined by J.G. Kincaid & Co Ltd, she had a long career trading between the UK and Burma. On her final voyage she was renamed* BHAMOT *and as that she was broken up in 1979. She was the eleventh of sixteen ships built by Lithgows Ltd for Paddy Henderson since 1946.*

gas turbine ore carrier MORAR 6990 g.r.t. *launched in 1958 for Scottish Ore Carriers Ltd (J. & J. Denholm Management Ltd), Glasgow. Engined by British Polar Engines Ltd and Rankin & Blackmore Ltd, this ship had novel machinery to allow her owners to assess the economics of gas turbines for merchant ship propulsion. Alas, the high fuel consumption of such engines precluded repeat orders. She was sold and renamed* CLARI *in 1967, later running aground as the* MAHONI *off Taiwan in September 1979, thence broken up as that in the following year.*

s.t. AXINA 12,283 g.r.t. *launched in 1958 for Tanker Finance Ltd, London (Shell Tankers). Engined by David Rowan & Co Ltd, this stylish turbine tanker was the sixth and last ship built by Lithgows Ltd for these owners since 1946. She had a twenty-year life with Shell, going to Far East shipbreakers under her original name in 1978.*

m.v. PRAHSU 5445 g.r.t. *launched in 1958 for Elder Dempster Lines Ltd of Liverpool. Engined by J.G. Kincaid & Co Ltd, this cargo liner had a change of identity within the Elder Dempster Group in 1966 when she was renamed KOHIMA. She was later sold and renamed PAPAGEORGIS in 1973, as which she was broken up in 1980.* (Burniston Studios Ltd)

motor ore carrier CAPE FRANKLIN 11,815 g.r.t. *launched in 1959 for Lyle Shipping Co Ltd, Glasgow. Engined by J.G. Kincaid & Co Ltd, this first generation bulk carrier incorporated the original oil tanker concept of locating officer accommodation two thirds forward. Sold and renamed VITTORIO GARDELLA in 1974, she was broken up in 1988 as the VITO. This was the last vessel built for Lyle Shipping with a black hull, the go-ahead Glasgow ship-owners later specified grey which greatly enhanced the look of their ships.*

s.s. JAMAICA PLANTER 6159 g.r.t. *launched in 1959 for Jamaica Banana Producers SS Co Ltd, Kingston, Jamaica. Engined by David Rowan & Co Ltd, this fast reefer retained a conventional three-island profile, and was among the finest looking Lithgow built ships. Sold and renamed FINE FRUIT in 1974, she was broken up in 1976 under that name. Note the row of stiffened shell doors typical of fruit carrying vessels.*

m.t. BRITISH ROBIN 11,211 g.r.t. *launched in 1959 for the Clyde Charter Co Ltd (BP Tankers). Engined by J.G. Kincaid & Co Ltd, she was sold and renamed LOT in 1977. Later resold she became a constructive total loss after running aground in Pakistan while named FAL XI in July 1986. This ship was the second of a pair of identical products tankers built by Lithgows Ltd for BP in 1959. The other vessel was meant to be called BRITISH THRUSH, however, this was malaproply but nevertheless aptly distorted to become BRITISH TRUST.* (BP Photographic)

Right. m.t. BORDER SHEPHERD 13,600 g.r.t. *launched in 1960 for the Lowland Tanker Co Ltd, Newcastle, a joint venture company formed by BP Tankers Ltd, Common Bros Ltd and Matheson & Co. Engined by J.G. Kincaid & Co Ltd, this distinctive products tanker was the first 'all aft' tanker built by Lithgows Ltd. Her very stylish and unique cross-tree mast also functioned as engine-room ventilators. Sold and renamed MARIVERDA IV in 1981, she was broken up in 1993 as AL NABILA II.*

Below. m.t. ORLANDO 14,154 g.r.t. *launched in 1960 for the Bowring SS Co Ltd, London. Engined by J.G. Kincaid & Co Ltd, this traditional tanker remained within her original owner's fleet until 1966 when she was sold and renamed STOLT FALCON. She was broken up in 1983 under her final name of VARKIZA.*

Below. *motor bulk carrier MYLLA 15,543 g.r.t. launched in 1961 for Simonsen & Astrup of Oslo. Engined by David Rowan & Co Ltd, this vessel was arguably the finest looking bulk carrier built by Lithgows Ltd. Sold and renamed SUNMALKA in 1965 she underwent further changes of name until becoming HONG QI 302 in 1980. She was still in existence in 1996 under that name.* (Burniston Studios Ltd)

motor bulk carrier BERNES 10,485 g.r.t. *launched in 1962 for A/S Kristian Jebsens Rederi, Bergen, Norway. Engined by J.G. Kincaid & Co Ltd, this handsome vessel was the second in a three-ship order built by Lithgows Ltd. Sold and renamed KIAN AN in 1972, she later became a total loss as the AN ANNE in the Red Sea off Jeddah in February 1983 when she ran aground and broke in two.*

m.v. JAMAICA PRODUCER 5781 g.r.t. *launched in 1962 for Jamaica Banana Producers SS Co Ltd, Kingston, Jamaica. Engined by David Rowan & Co Ltd, this distinctive reefer showed the Lithgow flair for producing one-off designs that were successful traders for their owners. Sold and renamed MIRANDA in 1981, she was broken up in 1985 as the CATTLE EXPRESS.*

motor ore carrier CAPE HOWE 19,032 g.r.t. *launched in 1962 for Lyle Shipping Co Ltd, Glasgow. Engined by J.G. Kincaid & Co Ltd, this vessel with distinctive superstructure front side-screens was specifically designed and built to carry the maximum amount of imported iron ore to General Terminus Quay, Glasgow. Sold and renamed AL TAWWAB in 1978, she retained that name until being broken up in 1984. Note the enclosed crow's nest on top of the forward derrick posts, which was something of a Lithgow hallmark on a number of vessels built by the shipyard in the early 1960s.*

m.v. CLARKFORTH 7669 g.r.t. *launched in 1962 for H. Clarkson & Co Ltd (J. & J. Denholm Ltd, Glasgow). Engined by J.G. Kincaid & Co Ltd, this stylish cargo tramp was sold and renamed SALIMIAH in 1965. She was still trading in 1996 as the QING FENG SAN HAO.*

motor bulk carrier BRIMNES 10,594 g.r.t. *launched in 1962 for the Tenax Steamship Co Ltd, London. Engined by J.G. Kincaid & Co Ltd, she was sold and renamed APILIOTIS in 1970, being broken up as the MILOS A in 1986.*

Left. m.v. HIGHLAND 10,035 g.r.t. *launched in 1962 for the Currie Line Ltd, Leith. Engined by J.G. Kincaid & Co Ltd, this cargo-liner was the second vessel built for these owners by Lithgows Ltd since 1946. She was sold and renamed ELYSIA in 1968, then later resold assuming further name changes. After developing a number of cracks in her hull during a typhoon in March 1984, she foundered on rocks and broke up off Kamoda Misaki, Japan, as the* OLYMPUS.

Above, left. m.t. THORSHAMMER 34,485 g.r.t. *launched in 1963 for A/S Thor Dahl of Sandefjord, Norway. Engined by Fairfield-Rowan Ltd, Glasgow, this vessel was the largest motor tanker built in Scotland—a distinction she only held for one year. Sold and renamed* THEODORA *in 1968, she was subsequently resold before being broken up as* VOYAGER *in 1984.*

Above, right. m.v. FIAN 7689 g.r.t. *launched in 1963 for Elder Dempster Lines Ltd, Liverpool. Engined by Fairfield-Rowan Ltd, Glasgow, this vessel was the last ship built for these owners by Lithgows Ltd. She was sold and renamed* MAHAPRIYA *in 1975, being broken up as that in 1985.*

Above. m.t. ORISSA 39,035 g.r.t. *launched in 1964 for Trident Tankers Ltd, London (P & O Group). Engined by J.G. Kincaid & Co Ltd, she is shown 'doing' over 17 knots during loaded speed trials in the Firth of Clyde. Sold and renamed* ANANGEL PRUDENCE *in 1974 she retained that name until being broken up in 1984.* (P & O Archive Library)

Left. motor bulk carrier CAPE RODNEY 12,104 g.r.t. *launched in 1965 for Lyle Shipping Co Ltd, Glasgow. Engined by Fairfield-Rowan Ltd, this small bulk carrier was the ninth and last ship built by Lithgows Ltd for these owners since 1946, being the only one fitted with a bulbous bow. Sold and renamed* OCEAN ENDEAVOUR *in 1971 she retained this name until being broken up in 1984.*

s.t. LARISTAN 37,927 g.r.t. *launched in 1965 for Common Brothers Ltd, Newcastle. Engined by the Westinghouse Electric Corporation, Philadelphia, PA. Plagued by engine commissioning problems, this oil tanker was the last and largest of seventeen ships built by various Clyde shipyards for these owners since 1946. Sold and renamed PYRROS V in 1971, she held a few other identities before being broken up as the YIANNIS PV in 1992.*

m.t. BRITISH IVY 13,271 g.r.t. *launched in 1965 for the BP Tanker Co Ltd, London. Engined by J.G. Kincaid & Co Ltd, this products tanker was the last of three Tree class vessels built by Lithgows Ltd for BP. She was sold and renamed CHARITAS in 1982, and after further change of names she was broken up in 1994 as OHARA. Reflecting the advent of value engineering precepts to naval architecture, this Tree class of ship was every bit as reliable as the large class of Bird tankers she was built to augment.*

m.v. WESTMORLAND 11,011 g.r.t. *launched in 1965 for the Federal Steam Navigation Co Ltd, London. Engined by Sulzer Brothers, Winterthur, Switzerland, this handsome 20 knot ref/cargo liner was the ninth and final vessel built for the P & O Group by Lithgows Ltd since 1946. She was sold and renamed FARES REEFER in 1980, being broken up as HUANGPU in 1985. The ship is photographed performing sea trials in the midst of a dull and lengthy West of Scotland rain storm.*

motor bulk carrier JERSEY BRIDGE 22,593 g.r.t. *launched in 1965 for H. Clarkson Ltd, London (J. & J. Denholm Ltd, Managers). Engined by J.G. Kincaid & Co Ltd, this ship was at her time of completion the largest bulk carrier built by Lithgows Ltd, a distinction she only held for one year. Sold and renamed OINOUSSIAN MOTHER in 1972, she later had further identities before being broken up in 1984 as the PACIFIC.*

m.v. JALARAJAN 11,323 g.r.t. *launched in 1966 for Scindia Steam Navigation Co Ltd, Bombay. Engined by J.G. Kincaid & Co Ltd, this cargo motor ship was the first of a three-ship series built by Lithgows for these long standing customers and gave a long trouble-free career before being sold for scrap in 1989. This ship was the second JALARAJAN built by Lithgows for the same owners since 1946.*

motor bulk carrier NAESS TALISMAN 40,769 g.r.t. *launched in 1966 for the Nile SS Co Ltd, London. Engined by Scotts SB & Eng Co Ltd with the largest Scott-Sulzer diesel built at their Greenock engine works. She was renamed NORDIC TALISMAN in 1974 and had various other names before being declared a constructive total loss after a collision off Taiwan in December 1984 under the name of PANAMAX CENTAURUS.*

motor bulk carrier BAYNES 12,404 g.r.t. *launched in 1968 for the Tenax SS Co Ltd, London. Engined by J.G. Kincaid & Co Ltd, this vessel was similar to a batch of small bulkers built by Lithgows Ltd for the same owners a few years earlier, the major exception being the addition of a bulbous bow. Sold and renamed JING HAI in 1973, she was still in existence in 1996 as the CHANG HAI.*

m.t. GOLD STAR 73,201 g.r.t. *launched in 1970 for the Sam Yang Navigation Co of Inchon, South Korea. Engined by J.G. Kincaid & Co Ltd, she and her sistership, KING STAR, also built by Scott-Lithgow Ltd were the last ship exports from the UK to South Korea. GOLD STAR was broken up in 1986, by which time South Korea was the second major shipbuilding country in the world.*

motor bulk carrier SILVERDON 22,906 g.r.t. *launched in 1972 for the Silver Line Ltd, Glasgow. Engined by J.G. Kincaid & Co Ltd, this ship was in fact launched as the BRAVENES for the Jebsen Group, and would have been the sixteenth vessel built for these owners since 1946. She was sold and renamed whilst fitting-out, and acquired a most attractive and distinctive name and company crest logo. She was resold and renamed FEI CUI HAI in 1978 and was still in existence under that name in 1996.*

s.t. NORDIC CLANSMAN 138,702 g.r.t. *launched in 1973 for Norness (UK) Ltd, London (originally named* NAESS SCOTSMAN*). Engined with Stal-Laval steam turbines supplied by Harland & Wolff Ltd, Belfast, she is seen leaving her Port Glasgow birthplace by a handful of Scott-Lithgow employees who helped to build her. This VLCC which was the first of four such vessels built by Scott-Lithgow Ltd, was the largest ship ever built in Scotland. Her steam turbine propulsion equipment proved expensive to run, and after a very short life she was broken up as* AL JAZIRAH *in 1983.* (Burniston Studios Ltd)

motor bulk carrier JHANSI-KI-RANI 42,141 g.r.t. *launched in 1974 for the Shipping Corporation of India Ltd, Bombay. Engined by J.G. Kincaid & Co Ltd, this large bulk carrier had a brief career under her original ownership. She ran aground off Australia in 1986, was refloated, towed to Singapore, docked and inspected, however, the damage was so bad she was sold for scrap. Under tow to Taiwan she sunk in the South China Sea in February 1987 with the loss of three lives.*

motor bulk carrier KASTURBA 42,141 g.r.t. *launched in 1975 for the Shipping Corporation of India Ltd, Bombay. Engined by J.G. Kincaid & Co Ltd, this large bulk carrier was the second of three similar ships built by Scott-Lithgow Ltd for India, which were the largest bulk carriers ever built in Scotland. Noticeable beyond the ship's port bow is the floating dock and submarine mother ship of the US Navy moored in the Holy Loch, once thought of as a permanent feature of the Clyde estuary, but alas now returned to the USA.* KASTURBA *was still in service with her original owners in 1996.*

m.t. WORLD SCORE 126,260 g.r.t. *launched in 1977 for Dolman Shipping Co of Monrovia (Niarchos Group). Engined by J.G. Kincaid & Co Ltd, this tanker and her sistership,* WORLD SCHOLAR, *became the largest motor tankers ever built in Scotland.* WORLD SCORE *was still in existence in 1996 as the* BERGE FOREST. *Note the impressive Niarchos bow crest and vast width between the midship derrick posts.*

m.v. OROPESA 9015 g.r.t. *launched in 1978 for the Pacific Steam Navigation Co, Liverpool. Engined by Scotts SB & Eng Co Ltd, this vessel (the second of a pair built by Scott-Lithgow Ltd) was the last traditional cargo liner constructed at Port Glasgow. She was sold and renamed* ORDUNA *in 1984, later being resold and renamed again. In 1996 she was still in service possessing the tacky fourth-hand name* MERCHANT PREMIER.

Above, left. self-propelled semi-submersible emergency support vessel IOLAIR 11,019 g.r.t. *launched in 1981 for BP Shipping Ltd, London. Engined by Harland & Wolff Ltd, Belfast, this innovative vessel ably demonstrated Scott-Lithgow's design and build capability. Since her acceptance she has been successfully deployed in the UK sector of the North Sea and was still in existence in 1996 under her original name.* (BP Photographic)

Above, right. m.t. BRITISH SPIRIT 66,024 g.r.t. *launched in 1982 for BP Shipping Ltd, Hamilton, Bermuda. Engined by Harland & Wolff Ltd, Belfast, this segregated ballast tanker was the fourteenth and final oil tanker built by Lithgows Ltd and their successors at Port Glasgow since 1946. Her contentious construction schedule brought unwelcome and bad publicity to Scott-Lithgow Ltd (then within British Shipbuilders Ltd). However, this vessel was still the first delivered from a four-ship order shared between the Clyde, Tyne and Belfast. She has proved in service to be a well-designed, solidly built product. Her further claim to fame is that she became the last ship built at the Kingston shipyard, Port Glasgow and was still in existence in 1996 under her original name. Both tugs in this scene, depicting* BRITISH SPIRIT *leaving for sea trials in the Firth of Clyde, were built by Scott & Sons Ltd at Bowling in the 1960s.* (Burniston Studios Ltd)

Left. self-propelled drilling rig OCEAN ALLIANCE 15,517 g.r.t. *launched in 1987 for Ben-Odeco Ltd, London. Engined by Crossley Peilstick Ltd, Manchester, this vessel was built to the Odeco* OCEAN RANGER II *modified design. She has the unenviable distinction of being the last complete vessel or craft built at the former Port Glasgow shipyard of Scott-Lithgow Ltd. Despite her tardy construction schedule, she has served BP very well in operation and was still in existence under her original name in 1996.* (BP Photographic)

GEORGE BROWN & CO (MARINE) LTD 1900-1983

The Garvel shipyard of Geo Brown & Co (Marine) Ltd was situated at the northern point of an artificial island created between the River Clyde, James Watt Dock and the Great harbour at Greenock. Known disaffectionately as 'Siberia' because of its exposed location to the north easterly winds that blew from that far-off land, the small family-owned and run shipyard, employed between 200 to 300 workers building a mixed range of coastal craft for mainly UK owners, but constructing export orders when tenders were accepted. With such a small facility, restricted on all sides by waterfront, investment in plant and equipment was very much limited to minimal outlay for maximum return. This was ultimately spent on new welding plant, replacement slings, strops and wire ropes for the antiquated lifting derricks in the yard, and the continual replacement of all consumable items used in shipbuilding. Latterly the provision of a fixed tower-type hammerhead crane with a 10-ton lifting capacity greatly improved erection facilities on the berths.

The diminutive shipyard had a contented labour force for most of its existence. Output varied from a single vessel a year, to four small craft in 1955. Supplementary work was routinely accepted in the form of ship repair and marine modifications which were undertaken in the adjacent Garvel dry dock, thus maintaining stability of employment for the yard work force. Maximum annual output was achieved in 1953 with the launching of two coasters, and a small oil tanker totalling 4869 g.r.t. The largest vessel built at Garvel was the coastal oil tanker *Sunny* 3155 g.r.t. launched on 24 November 1953 for Norwegian owners.

The Brown family were innovative naval architects and engineers, aware of the rapacious competition engulfing world shipbuilding, not only for the larger value oil tankers, bulkers, ferries and passenger liners, but also the bread and butter, relatively low value coasters and tugs, which the Garvel yard stylishly designed and built to the satisfaction of a wide spectrum of international ship-owners.

New ship construction ceased in 1963 after the building of the motor tug *Vasabha* 225 g.r.t., for the Government of Ceylon. This situation remained until the launching of the motor trawler *Aramanthes* 130 g.r.t. in 1974. Two trawlers of similar design followed the next year, also for British owners. Much of the workload during this period was taken up with ship repairing and the growing market for the design and fabrication of marine handling equipment. A further gap ensued until 1982 when four small craft were constructed, two of these were a pair of motor bouy tenders for Mexico, and the others were a small ferry and a larger buoy tender for use in the UK, after which shipbuilding finally ended at the Garvel site.

In between this hiatus in new ship construction, the company, developed and successfully sold a range of derricks and ship cranes under the name Cargospeed Ltd. This unique product line was installed in many ships, built both in the UK and overseas, and ensured continuity of employment for their workers in a form of diversification that recognised the marine association of the company. The 'Cargospeed' symbol was extended to include the design and construction of bow and stern doors for mainly car ferries. Market establishment was perhaps greater than expected by a small family concern, with encouraging sales of hardware and designs to various larger shipbuilders. Unfortunately, intensive competition in the marine field for the Cargospeed type of equipment resulted in ever diminishing throughput, thus by the early 1980s the company could not foresee further profitability in this niche.

The firm ceased trading in 1983, having built 46 vessels of 34,462 g.r.t. in the post-war period, 43% of which were for export. The site, still called 'Siberia', bore no alternative attraction for any other company with hardy souls on its payroll. It remains a derelict tract of isolated windswept real estate, showing little identifiable traces of former shipbuilding activity. It is difficult to realise this spartan site was once exploited with impunity by robust stalwarts of Clydeside craftsmanship during the boom era for new ships. Nowadays it displays little appeal for other possible uses by less vigorous and physically adept artisans or risk taking entrepreneurs, however, the adjacent small Garvel drydock was still deployed for infrequent survey and minor ship repair activity in 1996.

List of ships built by GEO BROWN & Co (MARINE) Ltd, Greenock, between 1946 and closure in 1983

YEAR	NAME	TYPE	COUNTRY OF REGISTRATION	G.R.T.	TOTAL G.R.T.
1946	EMPIRE LOLU	s. Tug	Britain (RN)	300	
	THE EMPEROR	s. Cargo[1]	Britain	1058	
	TEDDY	m. Cargo[1]	Denmark	789	2147
1947	HERDUBREID	m. Ref/Cargo[1]	Iceland	366	
	SKJALDBREID	m. Ref/Cargo[1]	Iceland	366	
	JACOB KJØDE	s. Cargo[1]	Norway	1759	2491
1948	KONG DAG	m. Cargo[1]	Norway	1202	
	LENA	Tug (hull only)	Senegal	100	
	BEAULY FIRTH	m. Cargo[1]	Britain	553	1855
1949	MOUNT BLAIR	m. Cargo[1]	Canada	553	
	ATONALITY	m. Oil Tanker	Britain	1221	
	SANDRINGHAM QUEEN	m. Cargo[1]	Britain	1188	2962
1950	LENAHAN	m. Tug	United States	30	
	CHANDLER	m. Tug	United States	30	
	PORTLAND	m. Cargo[1]	Denmark	1098	1158
1951	SECIL NOVO	m. Cargo[1]	Portugal	715	715
1952	BALLYHAFT	s. Cargo[1]	Britain	851	851
1953 •	NETHERLANDS COAST	m. Ref/Cargo[1]	Britain	867	
•	SUNNY	s. Oil Tanker	Norway	3155	
	BALLYHILL	s. Cargo[1]	Britain	847	4869
1954	BAYAD	m. Oil Tanker	Britain	452	
•	FIFE COAST	m. Cargo[1]	Britain	906	1358
1955	ULSTER PIONEER	m. Cargo[1]	Britain	1016	
•	BRENTFIELD	m. Cargo[1]	Britain	1263	
	NORTH LIGHT	s. Tug	Britain	206	
	NORTH ROCK	s. Tug	Britain	206	2691
1956 •	LEMANA	m. Cargo[1]	Australia	946	
	GARNOCK	m. Tug	Britain	78	1024
1957	PARERA	m. Cargo[1]	N. Zealand	823	
•	OTRA	m. Cargo[1]	Britain	1325	2148
1958 •	KINGENNIE	m. Oil Tanker	Britain	1169	
•	CANTICK HEAD	m. Cargo[1]	Britain	1591	
•	SIDDONS	m. Ref/Cargo[1]	Britain	1282	4042
1959 •	YORKSHIRE COAST	m. Cargo[1]	Britain	785	785
1960	BRIGADIER	m. Tug	Britain	223	223
1961	KAKULUWA	m. Hopper D	Ceylon	419	419

YEAR	NAME	TYPE	COUNTRY OF REGISTRATION	G.R.T.	TOTAL G.R.T.
1962 •	N.A. COMEAU	m. Ferry	Canada	1417	
•	KINNAIRD HEAD	m. Cargo[1]	Britain	1985	3402
1963	VASABAH	m. Tug	Ceylon	225	225
1964	None	None	None	–	–
1965	None	None	None	–	–
1966	None	None	None	–	–
1967	None	None	None	–	–
1968	None	None	None	–	–
1969	None	None	None	–	–
1970	None	None	None	–	–
1971	None	None	None	–	–
1972	None	None	None	–	–
1973	None	None	None	–	–
1974	ARAMANTHES	m. Trawler	Britain	130	130
1975	STAR OF HOPE	m. Trawler	Britain	133	
	CORONELLA	m. Trawler	Britain	130	263
1976	None	None	None	–	–
1977	None	None	None	–	–
1978	None	None	None	–	–
1979	None	None	None	–	–
1980	None	None	None	–	–
1981	None	None	None	–	–
1982	WILTON	m. Buoy Tender	Britain	345	
	AIRES	m. Buoy Tender	Mexico	146	
	LEO D.S.M.	m. Buoy Tender	Mexico	146	
	EILAN BHEARNARAIGH	m. Ferry	Britain	67	704

43% export			
57% Britain	46 vessels total = 34,462 g.r.t.		

[1]coaster

• Indicates vessel depicted in subsequent photographic section.

For explanation of abbreviations see Glossary on page 345.

The following batch of photographs depict a few scenes of shipbuilding activity at the former Garvel shipyard of Geo Brown & Co (Marine) Ltd. Also included are some trials pictures of a selection of vessels built by the company during its busiest post-war period.

Above. *This 1950 view looking north of the James Watt Dock, Greenock, depicts the recently launched m.v. AJANA 5627 g.r.t. built by Wm Hamilton & Co Ltd, beneath the giant hammerhead crane in the process of having her engines installed by J.G. Kincaid, part of whose works can be seen in the left centre. Moored on the north side of the dock is the s.s. FLAMENCO 8491 g.r.t., whilst in the Garvel drydock is the s.s. CLAN SINCLAIR 8386 g.r.t., both ships being fitted-out by the Greenock Dockyard Co Ltd. In the centre of Garvel Island the small Geo. Brown & Co (Marine) Ltd shipyard has yard no. 253 the Danish cement carrier m.v. PORTLAND 1098 g.r.t. under construction. Also noticeable in this photograph are many first generation tenements adjoining industrial buildings, a brand new factory for Joy-Sullivan that made mining equipment, and part of Cappielow Park, home of Greenock Morton Football Club.* (Burniston Studios Ltd)

Previous page, lower, left. *Yard no. 268, m.v. OTRA 1325 g.r.t. shortly before launching at the Geo. Brown & Co (Marine) Ltd, Garvel shipyard on 30 July 1957. This coaster was one of five similar vessels built by the smaller Clyde shipyards for the Christian Salvesen Group of companies then trading extensively in the South Atlantic whaling industry. The frames of yard no. 269 the small oil tanker KINGENNIE 1169 g.r.t. are noticeable in the left-hand berth.* (Burniston Studios Ltd)

Previous page, lower, right. *Yard no. 270, m.v. CANTICK HEAD 1591 g.r.t. enters the River Clyde from the Garvel shipyard of Geo. Brown & Co (Marine) Ltd on 22 July 1958. Noticeable in this view is the extensive use of tubular scaffolding, rather than the traditional weighted channel upright grillage that was the norm for external access to ships under construction throughout the UK shipbuilding industry.* (Burniston Studios Ltd)

Above. *Sitting high on the berth at Garvel shipyard, yard no. 275, m.v. N.A. COMEAU 1417 g.r.t. prior to launching on 7 February 1962. The traditional fixed derricks and new fixed hammerhead tower crane are evident in this picture and clearly show the entire length of the small ferry is within the combined lifting radii of these machines.* (Burniston Studios Ltd)

Below, left. *m.v. NETHERLANDS COAST 867 g.r.t. launched in 1953 for the Tyne-Tees SS Co Ltd, Newcastle. Engined by British Polar Engines Ltd, this vessel was the first of three small coasters built by the yard for the same owners during the 1950s. She was sold and renamed BAT HARIM in 1968 then resold and variously renamed, still being in existence in 1996 as the HONG LEONG.* (Burniston Studios Ltd)

Below, right. *s.t. SUNNY 3155 g.r.t. launched in 1953 for A/S Schanches Rederi of Bergen, Norway. Engined by Rankin & Blackmore Ltd of Greenock, this small oil tanker was the largest ship built by Geo. Brown & Co (Marine) Ltd at the Garvel shipyard. Sold and renamed SEASNIPE in 1966 she was broken up under that name in 1976.* (Burniston Studios Ltd)

m.v. FIFE COAST 906 g.r.t. *launched in 1954 for Coast Lines Ltd, Liverpool. Engined by Geo. Clark (1938) Ltd, Sunderland, she was sold and renamed FRUIN in 1958. Converted to the livestock carrier RABUNION VII in 1982, she underwent further name and ownership changes until she was broken up in 1994 as the BARAA Z.* (Burniston Studios Ltd)

m.v. BRENTFIELD 1263 g.r.t. *launched in 1955 for the Zillah Shipping Co Ltd, Liverpool. Engined by Geo. Clark & North East Marine (Sunderland) Ltd, she was transferred and renamed SPANIEL within the Coast Lines Group in 1959. She was broken up in 1981 under the name of CONISTER as which she had been modified to carry containers. Note the precarious stowage of a ladder under the no. 2 derrick and the number of gents dressed in the height of 1950s fashion.* (P & O Library Archive)

m.v. LEMANA 946 g.r.t. *launched in 1956 for W. Holyman & Sons Pty Ltd of Melbourne, Australia. Engined by British Polar Engines Ltd, this vessel was similar to the typical coasters built by Geo. Brown & Co (Marine) Ltd in the post-war years. She sank in a storm in the Macassar Strait in December 1975 under the name INDAH with the loss of 17 souls.* (Burniston Studios Ltd)

m.t. KINGENNIE 1169 g.r.t. *launched in 1958 for the Dundee, Perth & London Shipping Co Ltd, Dundee. Engined by British Polar Engines Ltd, this vessel was the last coastal oil tanker built at the Garvel shipyard, Greenock. Subsequently sold and renamed AMALIA in 1972, she was still in existence in 1996 operating under that name. Note her very low freeboard, very typical of this type of vessel (which necessitated the elevated cat-walk running from her bridge front to the fo'c'sle deck), both are accentuated as she performs loaded speed trials in the Firth of Clyde prior to hand-over.* (Burniston Studios Ltd)

m.v. SIDDONS 1282 g.r.t. *launched in 1958 for Lamport & Holt Line Ltd, Liverpool. Engined by MAN Hamburg, she was sold and renamed* VERAS *in 1962 being broken up in 1984 under her final name* FAYROUZ. *This stylish vessel looked much larger than her coaster dimensions, and also possessed twin derricks to her three holds.* (Burniston Studios Ltd)

m.v. YORKSHIRE COAST 785 g.r.t. *launched in 1959 for the Tyne-Tees SS Co Ltd, Newcastle. Engined by British Polar Engines Ltd, she was the third and last vessel built by Geo. Brown & Co (Marine) Ltd for these owners in the post-war period. She was sold and renamed* SAINT ENOCK *in 1972 and was declared a constructive total loss as the* SAER *in 1986.* (Burniston Studios Ltd)

m.v. N.A. COMEAU 1417 g.r.t. *launched in 1962 for Traverse Matane Godbout Ltd of Quebec, Canada. Engined by British Polar Engines Ltd, this handsome car ferry was built for use in eastern Canada and was the most stylish vessel built by Geo. Brown. Subsequently sold and renamed* NORTHERN CRUISER *in 1978, she was still in service in 1996 as the* XANADU HOLIDAY. *Like a number of other coastal vessels designed and built by the company, her well-proportioned lines suggested she was much larger than her modest dimensions.* (Burniston Studios Ltd)

m.v. KINNAIRD HEAD 1985 g.r.t. *launched in 1962 for A.F. Henry & MacGregor Ltd of Leith. Engined by British Polar Engines Ltd, this functional short sea trader was the last cargo vessel built by Geo. Brown & Co (Marine) Ltd. Sold and renamed* PERELLE *in 1972, she was broken up as* FRANCESA SECONDA *in 1986.* (Burniston Studios Ltd)

THE GREENOCK DOCKYARD CO LTD		**1919–1966**
CARTSDYKE DOCKYARD OF SCOTTS SB & ENG CO		**1966–1969**
CARTSDYKE DOCKYARD OF SCOTT-LITHGOW LTD		**1969–1977**
CARTSDYKE DOCKYARD OF SCOTT-LITHGOW LTD		
(DIVISION OF BRITISH SHIPBUILDERS LTD)		**1977–1984**
CARTSDYKE DOCKYARD (OFFSHORE DIVISION OF		
TRAFALGAR HOUSE OFFSHORE DEVELOPMENTS LTD)		**1984–1988**

The Greenock Dockyard Company Limited was part of the British and Commonwealth Shipping Group, and owned by Clan Line Steamers Ltd, also knows as Cayzer, Irvine & Co Ltd, based in Glasgow. In 1934 the company exchanged Mid Yard premises for Scott's Cartsdyke yard enabling Scotts to enlarge their Cartsburn Dockyard by absorbing the Mid Yard.

The Cartsdyke yard lay between Scotts shipyard to the west and the James Watt Dock to the east. Kincaids engine works and the Glasgow-Gourock railway line provided further restriction to the south. The yard had three berths served by fixed low capacity hammerhead cranes. As the development of welded fabrications progressed it became clear that modernisation of the facilities was long overdue. Such a scheme was approved in the late 1950's and was completed in the early 1960's involving a reduction in the number of berths from three to two. The new slipways were served by four 25-ton electric mono-tower travelling cranes designed and built by Butters Bros Ltd, Kinning Park, Glasgow. New fabrication sheds and plate preparation shops fitted with burning, rolling and flanging equipment supplemented total expenditure in welding techniques, resulting in the Cartsdyke Dockyard being in possession of a modern (if somewhat limited lifting capability) shipyard. This investment cost the yard owners several million pounds. The management now considered the renovated yard was able to undertake the construction of up to four new ships a year, mainly as replacements or additions to their Clan Line fleet. In fact, the Greenock Dockyard built 32 vessels for Clan Line Steamers Ltd and a further eight ships for British & Commonwealth associated companies between 1946 and 1966.

Employing around 800 workers throughout the post-war era, the yard had retained the apposite cognomen of 'Klondyke', apparently bestowed upon it by former grateful, yet industrious employees who valued the weightings applied to the Cartsdyke piecework wage rates, akin to the bounty received by the lucky pan handlers in the Yukon during the last century. Such local folklore transcended many generations, but few, if any Cartsdyke artisans retired prematurely to villas in Monaco, San Remo...or even Dunoon!

Output from the shipyard varied from two to four cargo liners or tankers per annum. Only in 1960 at the height of the modernisation scheme was one vessel, the *m.v. Clan McIlwraith* 7419 g.r.t., launched in a calendar year. This poor statistic was born of the fact that the existing berths were being extensively reworked during this period. Peak output was achieved in 1950 with the launching of four cargo liners aggregating 33,808 g.r.t. The largest ship constructed at the Cartsdyke shipyard was the Indian oil tanker *Jag Priya* 20,416 g.r.t., which was the only ship launched from the yard in 1975.

Ship types constructed by the yard tended to be very traditional cargo motor liners, some with partly automated engine room control systems. Nevertheless, in the early 1960s following modernisation, the style of new fast refrigerated cargo liners on order then reflected the flared marine artistry of that era and the individuality of the firm's naval architect and his team of ship designers. The last batch of 'reefers' built for Clan Line, along with vessels for Safmarine, Geest Line and a West German ship-owner, were elegant examples of the characteristic uniqueness of each ship produced by the shipyard. Although relatively small, at between 7000 and 10,000 g.r.t., all ships saw more than two decades of useful service for their respective owners after completion at Cartsdyke.

In 1966 the Greenock Dockyard Co Ltd was taken over by Scotts SB & Eng Co Ltd, and formed an integral part of the Scotts organisation. The yard then became known as the Cartsdyke Dockyard, remaining so up to and following the formation of Scott-Lithgow Ltd in 1969, a much less acrimonious affair than that of UCS Ltd up-river a year earlier. During the decade that followed, the Cartsdyke yard was utilised in fulfilling Scotts varied programme of sophisticated tonnage, including bulk carriers, reefers, products tankers, cargo liners and dynamically positioned drill ships. This diversity and innovation of vessel type was a reflection of the skill and aptitude of the design staff and shop floor personnel. These latter contracts marked Scotts' entry into the offshore exploration field, with a significant element of high-tech design input from Scotts engineering team. Both drill ships, *Ben Ocean Lancer* 10,823 g.r.t. and *Pacnorse 1* 10,820 g.r.t., launched from Cartsdyke in 1976 and 1977 were perhaps the epitome of the collective skills of the Lower Clyde Group and excellent examples of Cartsdyke workmanship. They were highly rated by their respective owners who deployed them on oil and gas exploration work throughout the world, despite assuming new identities both vessels were still extant in 1996.

New ship construction and volume throughput diminished alarmingly at the yard in the 1970s. The spectre that was now haunting the existence and success of the Scott-Lithgow group, seemed in some part correlated to the inexorable shrinking of the British Merchant Navy in terms of reduction of ships…and also the contraction of traditional shipping companies. Cartsdyke clung precariously to a diet of unprofitable single ship orders, yet was still in existence when swept into the net of nationalised atrophy, called British Shipbuilders Ltd, in July 1977. Throughout its three post-war guises the shipyard built 70 vessels aggregating 649,942 g.r.t., surprisingly only 11% of which were for export.

The final ship launched from the site was the cargo motor liner *Mentor* 16,482 g.r.t. (yard no. 750), handed over in 1980 to Ocean Fleets Ltd, successors to Alfred Holt and Co. She was the sixtieth Blue Funnel Line ship built at the Cartsdyke yard during Scotts association with that company that lasted 115 years! During the early 1980s the fabrication shop became part of the Clark Kincaid Ltd marine engine building concern, and was used for a while to construct a variety of fabricated components and large weldments for use in diesel engine manufacture.

The whole site was acquired by the Trafalgar House Group in 1984 and used for storage space and sub-assembly of equipment for installation in the semi-submersible drilling rig *Ocean Alliance* 15,517 g.r.t., then under construction in the nearby Glen/East yard. However, by the end of the decade the cranes and prefabrication sheds had been dismantled and the berths filled in. Later attempts at low-cost landscaping have succeeded in preventing none but the trained eye from recognising this location as a former once busy shipbuilding yard. In 1996 part of the former stockyard had been acquired by Kværner Kincaid Ltd.

Page 280. *Two views looking north-west of the Cartsdyke shipyard of the Greenock Dockyard Co Ltd taken from the same vantage point only one year apart.*

Top. *Yard no. 500, m.v. CLAN MACGILLIVRAY 9039 g.r.t. nears her date of launching during May 1962. On the adjacent berth, yard no. 501, another cargo liner for Clan Line Ltd, sistership m.v. CLAN MACGREGOR 9039 g.r.t. is under construction. A total of three similar vessels were launched by the yard for the owning British & Commonwealth Group during 1962. Note the profusion of shipping lying at anchor at the 'tail of the bank'. (Burniston Studios Ltd)*

Bottom. *Yard no. 503, m.v. LETABA 6897 g.r.t. is seen being painted shortly before her launching in 1963. Alongside, the forward cargo-holds of sistership, yard no. 504, m.v. DRAKENSTEIN 6837 g.r.t. are clearly seen on the shipyard's west berth. This scene ably demonstrated the Greenock Dockyard company's competence to build a series of ships virtually simultaneously within its compact and reasonably modern shipyard. This philosophy emanated from the policy set out in the previous decade when it was decided to reduce the number of building berths from three to two. (Burniston Studios Ltd)*

Page 281, top. *Launch of yard no. 503, m.v. LETABA 6897 g.r.t. for Safmarine Corporation Ltd at the Greenock Dockyard Co Ltd on 20 August 1963. The first of three fully refrigerated sisterships, they were a different class of cargo liner than the stock-in-trade Clan Line vessels that were regularly built by the shipyard. (Courtesy Safmarine Ltd)*

Bottom. *Part of the hull of yard no. 744, the dynamically positioned drill ship BEN OCEAN LANCER 10,823 g.r.t. under construction at the Cartsdyke dockyard of Scott-Lithgow Ltd in 1975. This unit is a section of the vessel's fore end framing being built upside down in the yard's fabrication shed. The engineer is making a dimension check on one of the apertures that will house the forward pair of variable pitch thrusters, watched by a group of adjacent steel workers. Note the combination of conventional tubular scaffolding and improvised timber baulks laid on welded brackets. (Burniston Studios Ltd)*

List of ships built by the GREENOCK DOCKYARD Co Ltd and its successors between 1946 and closure in 1980

YEAR	NAME	TYPE	COUNTRY OF REGISTRATION	G.R.T.	TOTAL G.R.T.
1946	CLAN CUMMING	s. Cargo	Britain	7812	
	CLAN MACLAREN	m. Cargo	Britain	6021	
	CLAN MACLACHLAN	s. Cargo	Britain	6365	20198
1947	CLAN MACLEAN	m. Cargo	Britain	6017	
	CLAN MACLENNAN	s. Cargo	Britain	6366	12383
1948	CLAN MACLEOD	m. Cargo	Britain	6073	
	CLAN MACLAY	m. Cargo	Britain	6075	
	CLAN MACTAGGART	s. Cargo	Britain	8035	20183
1949	CLAN MACTAVISH	s. Cargo	Britain	8035	
	CLAN SHAW	s. Cargo	Britain	8101	16136
1950	CLAN SINCLAIR	s. Cargo	Britain	8386	
	KENUTA	s. Cargo	Britain	8494	
	FLAMENCO	s. Cargo	Britain	8491	
	CLAN SUTHERLAND	s. Cargo	Britain	8418	33789
1951	THORSKOG	m. Oil Tanker	Norway	11325	
	CORATO	m. Oil Tanker	Britain	11387	22712
1952 •	CLAN MACINNES	m. Cargo	Britain	6517	
	IMPERIAL TRANSPORT	m. Oil Tanker	Britain	11365	17882
1953	ALVA CAPE	m. Oil Tanker	Britain	11252	
	CLAN STEWART	s. Cargo	Britain	8163	19415
1954	CLAN ROBERTSON	s. Cargo	Britain	7878	
	SCOTTISH HAWK	m. Oil Tanker	Britain	11148	19026
1955	POTOSI	s. Cargo	Britain	8564	
	PIZARRO	s. Cargo	Britain	8564	17128
1956	CLAN ROSS	s. Cargo	Britain	7878	
	ARGYLLSHIRE	s. Ref/Cargo	Britain	9359	
•	AYRSHIRE	s. Ref/Cargo	Britain	9360	26597
1957	CLAN MALCOLM	m. Cargo	Britain	7686	
	CLAN MATHESON	m. Cargo	Britain	7685	15371
1958 •	CLAN MENZIES	m. Cargo	Britain	7685	
	CLAN MACIVER	m. Cargo	Britain	7542	
	SWAN RIVER	m. Cargo	Britain	9637	24864
1959 •	ROTHERWICK CASTLE	m. Ref/C/P	Britain	9650	
	ROTHESAY CASTLE	m. Ref/C/P	Britain	9650	19300
1960	CLAN MACILWRAITH	m. Cargo	Britain	7419	7419
1961 •	CLAN MACNAB	m. Cargo	Britain	9428	
	CLAN GRAHAM	m. Cargo	Britain	9308	
	CLAN GRANT	m. Cargo	Britain	9322	28058
1962	CLAN MACGILLIVRAY	m. Cargo	Britain	9039	
	CLAN MACGREGOR	m. Cargo	Britain	9039	
	CLAN MACGOWAN	m. Cargo	Britain	9039	27117
1963 •	LETABA	m. Ref/Cargo	South Africa	6897	
•	DRAKENSTEIN	m. Ref/Cargo	South Africa	6837	13734

YEAR	NAME	TYPE	COUNTRY OF REGISTRATION	G.R.T.	TOTAL G.R.T.
1964	TZANEEN	m. Ref/Cargo	South Africa	6837	
•	CLAN RAMSAY	m. Ref/Cargo	Britain	10542	
	CLAN RANALD	m. Ref/Cargo	Britain	10541	27920
1965	CLAN ROBERTSON	m. Ref/Cargo	Britain	10541	
	CLAN ROSS	m. Ref/Cargo	Britain	10542	21083
1966† •	GEESTCAPE	m. Ref/Cargo	Britain	7679	
	GEESTHAVEN	m. Ref/Cargo	Britain	8042	
•	CLAN ALPINE	m. Cargo	Britain	8713	24434
1967	PARMA	m. Ref/Cargo	W. Germany	7618	
•	PADUA	m. Ref/Cargo	W. Germany	7618	15236
1968	WORLD HONG KONG	m. Bulk Carrier	Britain	12341	12341
1969† •	WORLD PRESIDENT	m. Bulk Carrier	Britain	12340	
•	BAKNES	m. Bulk Carrier	Britain	13241	25581
1970	BULKNES	m. Bulk Carrier	Britain	13325	
	BINSNES	m. Bulk Carrier	Britain	13240	26565
1971	GEESTTIDE	m. Ref/Cargo	Britain	5871	
	GEESTCREST	m. Ref/Cargo	Britain	5871	11742
1972 •	GEESTLAND	m. Ref/Cargo	Britain	5871	
	GEESTSTAR	m. Ref/Cargo	Britain	5871	11742
1973 •	BRITISH TWEED	m. Oil Tanker	Britain	15540	
•	SUGAR CARRIER	m. Bulk Carrier	Britain	17775	33315
1974	SUGAR TRADER	m. Bulk Carrier	Britain	17779	17779
1975 •	JAG PRIYA	m. Oil Tanker	India	20416	20416
1976 •	BEN OCEAN LANCER	m.e. DP Drilling Ship	Britain	10823	10823
1977†	CLYDENES	m. Cargo	Britain	2351	
•	PACNORSE I	m.e. DP Drilling Ship	Liberia	10820	13171
1978	*None*	*None*	*None*	–	–
1979 •	MENTOR	m. Cargo	Britain	16482	16482

11% export
89% Britain

70 vessels total = 649,942 g.r.t.

Notes
† Became Cartsdyke Dockyard of Scotts S.B. & Eng. Co Ltd   1966–69
† Became Cartsdyke Dockyard of Scott-Lithgow Ltd   1969–77
† Became Cartsdyke Dockyard of Scott-Lithgow Ltd
  (Division of British Shipbuilders Ltd)   1977–84
† Became Cartsdyke Dockyard of Scott-Lithgow Ltd
  (Offshore Division of Trafalgar House Investments Ltd)   1984–88

• Indicates vessel depicted in subsequent photographic section.

For explanation of abbreviations see Glossary on page 345.

The group of photographs on the following pages show scenes of shipbuilding activity at the Cartsdyke location of the former Greenock Dockyard Co Ltd. Also included are a number of trials pictures depicting some of the ships built there under its four guises of post-war ownership.

This page depicts four different ships built by the Greenock Dockyard Co Ltd in the 1950s for some of the different shipping companies within the British & Commonwealth Group.

Her foc'sle and poop decks thronging with shipyard workers, m.v. CLAN MACINNES 6517 g.r.t. leaves the James Watt Dock, Greenock in 1952, about to commence trials prior to hand-over to Clan Line Ltd, Glasgow. Engined by John Brown & Co (Clydebank) Ltd, this vessel's two sisterships were also built and engined at Clydebank. Sold and renamed ATHOUB in 1978 she was broken up with that name in 1979. (Burniston Studios Ltd)

s.s. AYRSHIRE 9360 g.r.t. *launched in 1956 for the Scottish Shire Line Ltd, Glasgow, a subsidiary of the British & Commonwealth Group. Engined by Parsons Marine Turbine Coy of Wallsend, she and her sistership, ARGYLLSHIRE, also built at the Cartsdyke yard, were the only two ships built for this line. She ran aground east of Aden and was abandoned as a total wreck in 1965. Note her tasteful mixture of derrick posts, single and bipod masts.*

m.v. CLAN MENZIES 7685 g.r.t. *launched in 1958 for Clan Line Steamers Ltd, Glasgow. Engined by the Wallsend Slipway & Eng Co Ltd, Newcastle, this traditional cargo liner regularly plied the river of her birth whilst trading between the City of Glasgow, East Africa, India and the Persian Gulf. Sold and renamed TRINITY SPLENDOUR in 1979, she later became the XING LONG and remained so into the 1990s.*

m.v. ROTHERWICK CASTLE 9650 g.r.t. *launched in 1959 for the Union-Castle Mail SS Co Ltd, London. Engined by John G. Kincaid & Co Ltd, this passenger/cargo liner with refrigerated spaces was built to augment the B&C Group's shipping trade between the UK and South Africa. Sold and renamed SEA FORTUNE in 1975 she was later broken up in 1983 under the name of SILVER RAYS.*

m.v. CLAN MACNAB 9428 g.r.t. *launched in 1961 for Neptune Shipping Ltd (Clan Line Ltd), Glasgow. Engined by the Wallsend Slipway & Eng Co Ltd of Newcastle, this vessel typified the later class of Clan Line ships built at Greenock, Clydebank and Wallsend, with four holds forward and one aft. Sold and renamed NEW EAGLE in 1980, she still bore that name when broken up in 1984.*

m.v. DRAKENSTEIN 6837 g.r.t. *launched in 1963 for South African Marine Corporation Ltd (Safmarine), Cape Town. Engined by J.G. Kincaid & Co Ltd, this well-proportioned, fully refrigerated vessel was the second of a three-ship order built for this associate company of the shipyard's owners, whose tasteful colour scheme clearly enhanced the looks of all their ships. Renamed S.A. DRAKENSTEIN in 1966, she was later sold and named PAMPERO UNIVERSAL in 1979, being broken up in 1984 as the AEGEAN WAVE. (Courtesy Safmarine Ltd)*

m.v. CLAN RAMSAY 10,542 g.r.t. *launched in 1964 for the Clan Line Steamers Ltd, Glasgow. Engined by J.G. Kincaid & Co Ltd, this large futuristic refrigerated cargo liner was the first of four similar 'R' class vessels built at the Cartsdyke shipyard, and represented a different type of liner for her owners as she and her sisters had no heavy derricks. She was the last Clan Line ship to remain in service and after being renamed WINCHESTER CASTLE in 1977 she was broken up in 1985 as LADY MADONNA. Her superstructure and side screens bear a strong resemblance to the Safmarine vessel pictured above.*

m.v. GEESTCAPE 7679 g.r.t. *launched in 1966 for Geest Line Ltd, Boston, Lincolnshire. Engined by G. Clark/NEM Ltd, Sunderland, this fully refrigerated liner was the first of a pair built by the yard for the fast transportation of bananas from the West Indies to the UK and was the last ship built at Cartsdyke before ownership by Scotts SB & Eng Co Ltd. Sold and renamed NYOMBE in 1975, she became a total loss as the TURTLE after a fire on board off France in October 1983.*

m.v. CLAN ALPINE 8713 g.r.t. *launched in 1966 for Clan Line Steamers Ltd, Glasgow. Engined by J.G. Kincaid & Co Ltd, this traditional cargo liner bore the unfortunate distinction of being the last ship built on the River Clyde for the famous Clan Line. Sold and renamed AFRICAN DIAMOND in 1981 she was broken up in 1984 under the name of PACIFIC AMBER.*

m.v. PADUA 7618 g.r.t. *launched in 1967 for F. Laeisz, Hamburg. Engined by J.G. Kincaid & Co Ltd, this sleek reefer was the second of a pair built for these owners which were the only ships built on the River Clyde for West Germany. Sold and renamed G. WEERTH in 1974 she was broken up in 1993 as the CHERRY BLOSSOM.*

motor bulk carrier WORLD PRESIDENT 12,340 g.r.t. *launched in 1969 for World-Wide (Shipping) Ltd, London. Engined by G. Clark & NEM Ltd, Newcastle, this vessel was the second of a pair built for the above owners at Cartsdyke during the era of Scott-Lithgow Ltd. Sold and renamed ERISORT in 1972, she was broken up in 1994 as the PEARL 3. Note the vessel's protruding anchor recesses necessary to protect her large and flared bulbous bow.*

motor bulk carrier BAKNES 13,241 g.r.t. *launched in 1969 for the Nile SS Co Ltd of London. Engined by Burmeister & Wain of Copenhagen, although the installation was done by J.G. Kincaid & Co Ltd of Greenock. Renamed SILVERCLYDE in 1974 and subsequently resold many times, this well-proportioned bulk carrier with traditional rigging was broken up in 1993 as the TONG LEE.*

m.v. GEESTLAND 5871 g.r.t. *launched in 1972 for Geest Line Ltd, Boston, Lincolnshire. Engined by Scotts SB & Eng Co Ltd, this handsome 'reefer' was the third of a four-ship order built at Cartsdyke by the then owning Scott-Lithgow Ltd. Sold and renamed STARLAND in 1986, she was broken up in 1994 as the VALPARAISO REEFER.*

m.t. BRITISH TWEED 15,540 g.r.t. *launched in 1973 for the BP Tanker Co Ltd, London. Engined by Scotts SB & Eng Co Ltd, this products tanker was one of five similar sisterships built for BP from the shipyards of Scott-Lithgow Ltd. She was renamed BP TWEED in 1984 before being sold and renamed AZNA two years later, and as such she was still in existence in 1996.* (BP Photographic)

motor bulk carrier SUGAR CARRIER 17,775 g.r.t. *launched in 1973 for Sugar Line Ltd, London. Engined by Scotts SB & Eng Co Ltd, this medium-sized bulk carrier transported sugar cane from the West Indies to the UK and was the second last of six ships built by Scott-Lithgow Ltd for these owners in less than a decade. Subsequently sold and renamed PATRICIA in 1979 she was still in existence in 1996 as the EVER GAIN.*

m.t. JAG PRIYA 20,416 g.r.t. *launched in 1975 for the Great Eastern Shipping Corporation of Bombay, India. Engined by Scotts SB & Eng Co Ltd, this products tanker was the largest ship built at the Cartsdyke dockyard and was still in existence under her original name in 1996.*

diesel-electric self-propelled dynamically positioned drilling ship BEN OCEAN LANCER 10,823 g.r.t. *launched in 1976 for Ben Odeco Ltd, London. Engined by Société Alsacienne de Constructions Mécaniques Mulhouse, France, this vessel was the first such craft specifically built by a British shipyard. She was successfully used by her owners throughout the world on exploration drilling work for most major oil companies, and was still in existence in 1996 as S.C. LANCER.*

diesel-electric self-propelled dynamically positioned drilling ship PACNORSE 1 10,820 g.r.t. *launched in 1977 for Pacnorse Drilling of Hamilton, Bermuda. Engined by Pielstick, this vessel was sold and renamed PEREGRINE II in 1996 and was the second of two similar craft built at the Cartsdyke dockyard of Scott-Lithgow Ltd, to the Pelican class of drill ship designed by I.H.C. Gusto Eng of Holland.*

m.v. MENTOR 16,482 g.r.t. *launched in 1979 for Ocean Fleets Ltd of Liverpool. Engined by the Scotts Engine Works Division of Scott-Lithgow Ltd (British Shipbuilders Ltd), this functional cargo liner was the last ship built at the Cartsdyke shipyard. She and her two other Clyde built sisterships bore a Blue Funnel Line name with an Elder Dempster Line funnel. After a short spell with her original owners she was sold and renamed HOEGH NORMANIA in 1985. After further name changes she still existed in 1996 as the TAMATIKI.*

	JOHN G. KINCAID & CO LTD	1868–1977
	JOHN G. KINCAID & CO LTD (BRITISH SHIPBUILDERS LTD)	1977–1978
	CLARK-KINCAID LTD (BRITISH SHIPBUILDERS LTD)	1978–1988
	CLARK-KINCAID LTD (HLD GROUP)	1988–1990
	KVÆRNER-KINCAID LTD	1990–

The Greenock engine works of John G. Kincaid built marine diesel engines to the design of Burmeister & Wain (B & W), under sub-licence from Harland & Wolff Ltd of Belfast. The main works were located between the A8 road through Greenock and the Glasgow-Gourock railway to the south. This plant was dedicated to the manufacture, erection and testing of large bore diesel engines. An additional factory was located in Arthur Street in Greenock which manufactured major fabrications for engines, auxiliaries and other products associated with marine engine outfitting, including funnels, uptakes, piping, engine room flooring and ventilators, etc.

Kincaids had an enlightened management dedicated to the constant improvement of quality and productivity throughout its entire existence as a major builder of marine engines. This fact was evinced by impressive annual reinvestment in machine tools and other plant necessary to keep the company at the forefront of engine building. The firm was founded in Greenock in 1868. It later became partly owned by the Blue Funnel Line of Liverpool in conjunction with a number of wealthy industrialists. The company initially designed and built compound and triple expansion steam engines. When the reduced building costs of marine diesel engines, coupled with their improved operating reliability and cheapness to run, were accepted by many ship-owners, this type of engine then became Kincaid's main product, the first of which was successfully built in 1924.

Employing in the order of 2000 workers at the height of the post-war demand for new ships with diesel engines, the company built and installed machinery for about 20% of the River Clyde shipbuilding industry, as well as for some of the yards on the Scottish east coast, and Rivers Tyne, Wear and Tees. As much as 25% of the Greenock labour force were employed on the installation squads. These travelling men were regularly sent up-river to Glasgow, or to the North-east coast of England, to install and commission new engines, in either ships under construction on the berths or alongside the fitting out quay. From 1946 until the late '70s when the company was nationalised into British Shipbuilders Ltd, output was consistently high, running at approximately an engine completed nearly every month for many years.

The sweeping trend among world ship-owners moved away from steam turbines for large vessels after the oil crisis of the early 1970s, this stimulated the demand for more fuel efficient higher output diesel engines. Kincaids were very fortunate, as sub-licencees to B & W they reaped the benefit of the go ahead Danish company's total commitment to intensive research and development of medium- and slow-speed diesel engines. Two of the four VLCCs and all the large bulk carriers built by Scott-Lithgow Ltd were fitted with Kincaid B & W engines. The B & W 11K90 GF engines installed in both of these motor tankers were the biggest marine diesels ever built in Scotland, and each developed an astonishing 37,500 BHP.

The ongoing rationalisation of British Shipbuilders Ltd resulted in J.G. Kincaid & Co Ltd becoming part of Clark-Kincaid Ltd, an amalgamation with Clark-Hawthorn, one of the North-east of England marine engine builders who manufactured to Sulzer designs. This new company had probably the best chance of survival within the coercive mishmash that was BSL, as the new product range included both types of preferred large bore marine oil engines. Supplying most of what then remained of the gradually contracting total UK shipbuilding industry, Clark-Kincaid Ltd tried to maintain their former high standards of performance within a rapidly diminishing order book. This attrition of base workload quickly reached the point where constant overheads, previously spread over many engine orders, were now being absorbed by a smaller amount of units, a presage for loss making coupled to the uncertainty of supplying whatever remained of mainland UK shipbuilding capacity, which was Kincaids licensed market.

In keeping with the politically-driven philosophy of disbanding BSL and selling-off its many subdivisions, Clark-Kincaid Ltd became part of the Kværner group in 1990. Marine engine building ceased shortly after, as by then the new order intake had dwindled to such levels that this side of the business was no longer viable. The last diesel engine built by the works was a Sulzer 6RTA62 of 15,500 BHP for installation in the Norwegian chemical tanker *Havis* 34,951 g.r.t. built up-river by Kværner-Govan Ltd in 1992. What remains of the once extensive works is now reduced to the manufacture of spare parts for B & W, and now Sulzer large bore marine diesel engines, the other parts of the site having been sold off to industrial asset-strippers.

During the early 1970s, J.G. Kincaid supplied diesel engines to the infant South Korean shipbuilding industry. This 'new market' failed to fill the void created by diminishing UK shipbuilding capacity. The Koreans now have their own formidable marine engine building industry. In 1976 the Greenock works produced 10 engines of 156,200 BHP, their most powerful annual output during the post-war period.

The set of pictures on the following pages illustrates a few scenes of marine engine building and testing at the Greenock works of John G. Kincaid & Co Ltd in the post-war period.

Page 288. *The engine erection shop of John G. Kincaid & Co Ltd, Greenock in 1953 showing numerous B & W diesel engines at various stages of construction. The engine on the left clearly shows the crankcase recess where the crankshaft, bearings and connecting rods will later be located. Other components are also shown waiting subsequent installation. The unfortunate omission of any works personnel from this picture fails to convey any ready impression of scale.*

Page 289, top. *Hidden beneath a tarpaulin the lower half of a Clark-Kincaid built B&W diesel engine is manouvered out of the Greenock works on the back of a specialised low-loader into the busy A8 road. This engine was bound for one of the remaining BSL yards at Sunderland where it was installed in a ship which had recently been launched in 1986. Note some of the hammerhead cranes of Scotts Cartsburn dockyard in the background. (George Young Photographers)*

Page 289, bottom. *The engine test bed of J.G. Kincaid & Co Ltd in 1975 showing a Kincaid-B&W.6K74EF marine diesel engine under test. This six cylinder engine developed 12,500 BHP at 134 r.p.m. and was one of a number built by Kincaids for the infant Hyundia shipbuilding conglomerate of South Korea, to be installed in a Kuwait class cargo liner. Hyundia acquired the design of the Govan conceived vessel for much less than it would have cost to develop such a ship, and duly built a number at a phenomenal rate! Part of the order for the engine depicted in this photograph included an element of training in the finer points of marine engine manufacture by Kincaids towards Hyundia engineers and technicians. The world famous name of J.G. Kincaid & Co Ltd now only has a historic association with marine engine building, whereas Hyundia are among the major engine builders on the planet.*

Above, right. *A Clark-Kincaid 4L70MC B & W diesel engine on the Greenock test bed in 1986. This type of engine with four cylinders each of 700 mm bore was capable of achieving almost 10,000 BHP. The considerable advances made in engine design that allowed far greater output from less (though larger) cylinders greatly reduced the amount of maintenance needed on this new generation of engines. Alas, Clark-Kincaid's success at engine manufacture was at variance with the accelerating demise of UK shipbuilding, their licensed customers, and by 1992 the Greenock works had built their last engine. (George Young Photographers)*

Left. *Installation by a Dutch floating crane ship of a complete Clark-Kincaid built B & W 4L70MC diesel engine of 8782 BHP into the engine casing of m.v. DIETRICH OLDENDORFF 15,987 g.r.t. built at the Southwick shipyard of NE Shipbuilders Ltd, Sunderland in 1986. (George Young Photographers)*

	SCOTTS SHIPBUILDING & ENG CO LTD	**1711-1969**
	CARTSBURN/CARTSDYKE COMPLEX OF SCOTT-LITHGOW LTD	**1969-1977**
	CARTSBURN/CARTSDYKE COMPLEX OF SCOTT-LITHGOW	
	(DIVISION OF BSL)	**1977-1984**
	CARTSBURN/CARTSDYKE COMPLEX OF SCOTT-LITHGOW LTD	
	(OFFSHORE DIVISION OF TRAFALGAR HOUSE DEVELOPMENTS LTD)	**1984-1988**

Scotts of Greenock, founded in 1711, was the oldest family shipbuilding business in the world. It became a private limited company in 1903, following a massive investment programme in new plant and machinery in both the shipyard and engine works, together with the implementation of then state-of-the-art manufacturing systems. Directors and employees jealously boasted of this epithet of industrial longevity for many decades. With such an impressive pedigree, the descendants of the founding Scott family proudly viewed their shipbuilding and engineering establishment, contentedly aware of the firm's invaluable contribution over two centuries to the development of naval architecture and ship propulsion.

The company occupied two sites sufficiently adjacent to each other to be considered a shipbuilding and marine engineering complex, despite being severed by the A8 road. Such minor geographic constraints were considered more of a product of historic development than an encumbrance to integrated ship and marine engine construction. The Cartsburn shipbuilding yard, like that of Lithgows Ltd in nearby Port Glasgow, was seriously limited to the maximum length of vessel that it could launch, without either reclaiming extensive volumes of land from the River Clyde or realigning the adjacent main road. Neither vastly expensive alternatives were ever undertaken. Cartsburn was content to establish maximum ship length at about 250 metres, pursuing orders for vessels up to this size resulting in the existing number of berths being reduced to four. The centre pair of enlarged and realigned concrete slipways, severed by a common crane track, became the main location for future shipbuilding. The preparation shops were totally refurbished and a new fabrication shop was erected. The whole project was considered complete in the early 1960s with the commissioning of two new 60-ton electric travelling hammerhead cranes, designed and built by Sir William Arrol and Co Ltd of Dalmarnock, Glasgow. This integrated project cost the owning family several millions of pounds, which was spread over a few years to minimise the impact both on capital outlay and the serious delay to several new ship contracts then under construction.

The Cartsburn facility possessed its own wet dock, or fitting out basin as well as a small dry dock. This latter item of real estate proved invaluable to the company throughout their lengthy successful construction of diesel-electric submarines, both for the Royal Navy and friendly overseas navies, notably Australia and Chile. In fact, from 1946 until cessation of shipbuilding in 1983, 15 new submarines were built at Greenock, in addition to several modernisations and refits performed on many others. Much of the conversion work was completed in the small dry dock. Other naval work completed during this era comprised two frigates, three large Royal fleet auxiliaries, two trials vessels and probably the most contentious vessel constructed at Greenock (under the aegis of British Shipbuilders Ltd), the diving support vessel *HMS Challenger* 6907 tons displacement. This high-tech vessel, tardy in delivery, suffered much from subcontractor delays and other problems, including massive rewiring and constant 'on the hoof' design modifications, especially to the diving system specified and supplied by the Ministry of Defence.

Ship construction at Cartsburn in the post-war era was consistent for three decades, and always resulted in at least two ships being launched annually. This statistic compared less than favourably with the pure merchant shipbuilding yards on the River Clyde, however, the mixed bag of naval, merchant and naval modification work encompassed different specifications that duly affected throughput. Such emulsifying of standards always meant that Scotts merchant ship owning customers got good vessels…at competitive rates. Some famous, post-war patrons included Blue Funnel Line, British India Steam Navigation Co Ltd, BP Tankers Ltd and Elder Dempster Line, sharing adjacent berths with craft under construction for the Australian, Chilean and Royal Navies, or various overseas owners from Greece, Norway and Liberia.

The merchant ship product range included cargo liners and oil tankers for nearly two decades. The first bulk carriers built by the yard were a brace of two medium-sized ore carriers for Common Bros Ltd of Newcastle, both launched in 1960. Successful completion of these vessels established Scotts as capable builders of medium-sized bulk carriers. With the recent installation of the two 60-ton travelling hammerhead cranes, the construction of such craft with their inherently larger steelwork scantlings became a routine and regular element of the yard's later annual output. A total of 16 such vessels were built at the Cartsburn site up until closure. Greatest yearly post-war tonnage was achieved under the ownership of Scotts SB & Eng Co Ltd in 1950 when the shipyard launched two oil tankers and two cargo liners of 41,551 g.r.t. This annual company output was only surpassed after the 1966 amalgamation with the adjacent Greenock Dockyard Co Ltd, which in effect included the production from another pair of berths. The largest vessel built by the yard was the motor bulk carrier *Clydesdale* 24,024 g.r.t. launched on 7 June 1967. The post-war total from the Cartsburn yard amounted to 93 ships comprising 23 naval vessels of 92,586 tons displacement and 70 other craft of 753,408 g.r.t., of which 24% were for export.

After the commissioning of the pair of heavy hammerhead cranes, most subsequent vessels built at the yard were launched with their main engines and auxiliaries already installed. Scotts' engineering department had been much involved in research and development work pre-war on slow speed diesel engines. As engine builders, Scotts built a greater variety of such machines than any other British competitor. Types built by the firm included the Fiat, Scott-Still, Scott, Werkspoor, NEM, MAN, Doxford and Sulzer designs. Consequently, post-war they found it easy to switch from building geared steam turbine machinery for their naval ships to building the Doxford and latterly the Sulzer slow speed diesels, some of which were exported to Canada, Australia, Hong Kong and Brazil. The considerable engineering involvement in submarines both on board and in the workshops provided Scotts engine works and their installation department with a great deal of high precision activity involving torpedo tubes, periscopes, hydroplanes and escape arrangements which complemented their diesel engine and steam turbine construction programme. Marine engine building ceased after the construction of three Scott-Sulzer units that powered the trio of 'M' class cargo liners built by the company for Ocean Fleets Ltd in the early 1980s. Engineering involvement lingered on for a few more years, rendering assistance with the outfit and commissioning content of the three semi-submersible vessels built by Scott-Lithgow Ltd.

The 1966 acquisition of the adjacent Greenock Dockyard Co Ltd complemented the capacity of the yard. Both facilities continued thereafter as individual shipbuilding centres throughout the remainder of their existence. No major management bickering or labour force squabbling accompanied this amicable takeover. In 1969 the Cartsburn/Cartsdyke complex merged again, this time to become part of Scott-Lithgow Ltd. Despite a low year for launching in 1969, when only three bulk carriers entered the water from the enlarged combine, subsequent output increased then dipped to a disappointing low of two ships per year from 1974 until 1977 prior to the nationalisation of the group. The late '70s, early '80s saw the yard wallowing tediously and unproductively with a greatly reduced throughput, still shackled with the burden of the inherited amalgamated labour force of over 3000 workers. The launch of *m.v. Myrmidon* 16,482 g.r.t. (yard no. 751) for Ocean Fleets in 1980 was viewed as just another event despite the yard's poor order book. Ensuing chicanery within the miasma of BSL deemed this vessel to bear inadvertently the unfortunate distinction of being the last merchant ship built in the town of Greenock.

HMS Challenger 6907 tons displacement was launched for the Royal Navy in 1981, and nothing followed in 1982. Cartsburn dockyard later launched what was to be its last marine product in 1983, the combined pontoons, columns and bracings configuration of the semi-submersible drilling rig *Sea Explorer* for BP. Constructed as two hull sections either side of the 60-ton crane track, the structure was slid conventionally and successfully into the River Clyde, deploying traditional Tail of the Bank shipyard craftsmanship towards a new type of vessel that the labour force hoped would create long term employment. Alas this special craft was the first and last for Greenock. When the Trafalgar House Group acquired Scott-Lithgow Ltd from BSL in 1984, both fabrication facilities at Greenock were used intermittently for selective unit construction of sections for the infamous *Ocean Alliance* (group yard no. 2002). Unfortunately, this stopgap proved no more than a tenuous extension of employment, and on her completion the Cartsburn/Cartsdyke complex was razed in 1988 to make way for a new sunrise industrial estate, served by a partly realigned A8 road. A far from architecturally pleasing edifice now occupies the site of the former building berths, and a hastily designed roundabout with deceptive camber stands in the location of what used to be the plating shop. By 1996, only the small dry dock, its lock gates no longer watertight, attested to a recognisable feature of the former oldest shipbuilding company in the world.

The photograph below and those immediately after the list of ships built by Scotts SB & Eng Co Ltd illustrate the location of that company's former Cartsburn dockyard and Greenock marine engine works. Also included are a batch of trials pictures depicting some of the varied ship types built by the company in its final three decades of operation.

This summer 1961 view of Greenock looking north depicts considerable shipbuilding activity. In the centre drydock of the recently modernised Scotts Cartsburn dockyard, yard no. 687, the diesel-electric Oberon class submarine HMS OTTER 1610 tons displacement is fitting-out. Nearing launching on one of the yard's largest berths is yard no. 689, the first of a pair of motor ships for Elder Dempster Lines Ltd, later to be named FOURAH BAY 7,704 g.r.t., with her sistership yard no. 690 FALABA 7,703 g.r.t. alongside. On the yard's eastern most berth, another Royal Navy submarine, yard no. 688, later named HMS OTUS, is also under construction. In the adjoining Cartsdyke shipyard of Greenock Dockyard Co Ltd, yard no. 498, m.v. CLAN GRAHAM 9,308 g.r.t. is almost ready to enter the River Clyde, barely visible next to her on the adjoining berth is yard no. 499, her sistership m.v. CLAN GRANT 9,322 g.r.t. Most of the large buildings in the left foreground belong to Scotts engine works, with the test-bed and erection shop in the bottom left. Above the Glasgow-Gourock railway line are the machining and outfit shops with the blacksmiths shop to the right. The cluster of light-coloured adjacent buildings in the right centre are the Arthur Street works of J.G. Kincaid & Co Ltd, whose main works are to the right, out of picture. Note the lengthy passenger train hauled by a steam locomotive, the busy goods yard with railway wagons carrying steel, the close proximity of houses to noisy works and the lack of motorcars. (Aerofilms)

List of ships built by SCOTTS SB & ENG Co Ltd, Greenock, and their successors between 1946 and 1983

YEAR	NAME	TYPE	COUNTRY OF REGISTRATION	DISPL/ G.R.T.	TOTAL OUTPUT
1946	SINKIANG	m. Ref/C/P	Britain	3029	
	ARTEMIS	m.e. Submarine	Britain (RN)	1120 displ	
	SHANSI	m. Ref/C/P	Britain	3161	7310
1947	AGAPENOR	m. Ref/Cargo	Britain	7664	
	ARTFUL	m.e. Submarine	Britain (RN)	1120 displ	
	SHONGA	m. Cargo	Britain	4810	
	ASTYANAX	m. Ref/Cargo	Britain	7648	21242
1948	SULIMA	m. Cargo	Britain	4810	
	SWEDRU	m. Cargo	Britain	4809	
	CYCLOPS	m. Ref/Cargo	Britain	7709	
	CHANGSHA	m. Ref/Cargo	Britain	7412	24740
1949	FORT AVALON	s. Ref/Cargo	Britain	3484	
	TAIYUAN	m. Ref/Cargo	Britain	7472	
	ANKING	m. Ref/Cargo	Britain	6119	17075
1950	CHUNGKING	m. Cargo	Britain	9511	
	BUSEN ROLLO	m. Oil Tanker	Britain	11392	
	CHANGCHOW	m. Cargo	Britain	9403	
	LORD CANNING	m. Oil Tanker	Britain	11347	41653
1951	LINDE	m. Oil Tanker	Norway	10347	
	EBOE	m. Ref/Cargo	Britain	9397	19744
1952	EBANI	m. Ref/Cargo	Britain	9396	
•	NIMERTIS	m. Oil Tanker	Liberia	11267	
	BORDER REGIMENT	m. Oil Tanker	Britain	11311	31974
1953	LADY DOROTHY	m. Oil Tanker	Liberia	11261	
	MARIETTA NOMIKOS	m. Oil Tanker	Greece	11577	
	BORDER HUNTER	m. Oil Tanker	Britain	11301	34139
1954	PATANI	m. Cargo	Britain	6183	
	PUMA	s. Frigate	Britain (RN)	2300 displ	
	NOWSHERA	s. Ref/Cargo	Britain	8516	16999
1955 •	CRYSTAL CUBE	m. Bulk Carrier	Britain	8680	
	SPERVIK	m. Oil Tanker	Norway	11356	
•	CALTEX EDINBURGH	s. Oil Tanker	Britain	12492	32528
1956	NYANZA	s. Ref/Cargo	Britain	8513	
	EGORI	m. Cargo	Britain	8586	
•	ANGELOS LUSIS	m. Oil Tanker	Greece	11630	28729
1957 •	LORD BYRON	m. Cargo	Britain	9364	
	LORD CODRINGTON	m. Cargo	Britain	9364	
	CACHALOT	m.e. Submarine	Britain (RN)	1565 displ	20093
1958	N. GEORGIOS	s. Oil Tanker	Greece	13152	
•	DARU	m. Cargo	Britain	6340	
	QUEDA	s. Oil Tanker	Britain	13252	32744
1959	LORD GLADSTONE	m. Cargo	Britain	11299	
•	BRITISH SWIFT	m. Oil Tanker	Britain	11174	
	WALRUS	m.e. Submarine	Britain (RN)	1565 displ	
•	QUILOA	s. Oil Tanker	Britain	13113	37151
1960	DUNKWA	m. Cargo	Britain	6109	
	IRON HORSE	m. Ore Carrier	Britain	11128	
	IRON CROWN	m. Ore Carrier	Britain	11125	28362
1961	DEIDO	m. Cargo	Britain	6109	
	OTTER	m.e. Submarine	Britain (RN)	1610 displ	
•	FOURAH BAY	m. Ref/Cargo	Britain	7704	15423
1962	FALABA	m. Ref/Cargo	Britain	7703	
	OTUS	m.e. Submarine	Britain (RN)	1610 displ	
	KAPETAN GEORGIS	m. Bulk Carrier	Greece	17059	26372
1963	SIMANDOU	m. Bulk Carrier	Guinea	10764	
	EURYALUS	s. Frigate	Britain (RN)	2350 displ	
	RAYLIGHT	m. Cargo[1]	Britain	177	13291
1964	OPPORTUNE	m.e. Submarine	Britain (RN)	1610 displ	
•	GRAIGWERDD	m. Bulk Carrier	Britain	18618	
	BRITISH MONARCH	m. Bulk Carrier	Britain	18616	38844
1965 •	DAWNLIGHT I	m. Cargo[1]	Britain	199	
	OXLEY	m.e. Submarine	Australia	1610 displ	
	BINSNES	m. Bulk Carrier	Britain	10961	12770
1966 •	RESOURCE	m.e. R.F.A. Tanker	Britain (RN)	18029 displ	
	BOLNES	m. Bulk Carrier	Britain	12459	
•	OTWAY	m.e. Submarine	Australia	1610 displ	32098
1967 •	CLYDESDALE	m. Bulk Carrier	Britain	24024	
	OVENS	m.e. Submarine	Australia	1610 displ	25634
1968 •	GAS LION	m. LPG Tanker	Norway	8168	
	GRAIGFFION	m. Bulk Carrier	Britain	18453	
	ONSLOW	m.e. Submarine	Australia	1610 displ	28231
1969† •	ERISKAY	m. Bulk Carrier	Britain	12485	
	GRECIAN LEGEND	m. Bulk Carrier	Liberia	22998	35483
1970	INGEREN	m. Bulk Carrier	Norway	12636	
	WHITEHEAD	m. Expt Trials V	Britain (RN)	3308 displ	
	GRECIAN SPIRIT	m. Bulk Carrier	Liberia	22992	38936
1971 •	CUMBRIA	m. Bulk Carrier	Britain	18570	
	BANBURY r/n	m. Cargo	Britain	11381	29951
•	IRON BANBURY				
1972	BRITISH AVON	m. Oil Tanker	Britain	15540	
•	BRITISH KENNET	m. Oil Tanker	Britain	15540	
	OBRIEN	m.e. Submarine	Chile	1610 displ	32690
1973	BRITISH FORTH	m. Oil Tanker	Britain	15540	
	HYATT	m.e. Submarine	Chile	1610 displ	
•	JAG PRAKASH	m. Oil Tanker	India	15849	32999
1974	ORION	m.e. Submarine	Australia	1610 displ	1610
1975 •	NEWTON	m.e. U/Wat. Res.	Britain (RN)	4510 displ	
	OTAMA	m.e. Submarine	Australia	1610 displ	6120
1976 •	FORT GRANGE	m. RFA Replen	Britain (RN)	16049 displ	16049
1977†	None	None	None	–	–
1978	FORT AUSTIN	m. RFA Replen	Britain (RN)	16053 displ	16053
1979	MARON	m. Cargo	Britain	16482	16482
1980 •	MYRMIDON	m. Cargo	Britain	16482	16482
1981 •	CHALLENGER	m.e. Diving Sup	Britain (RN)	6907 displ	6907
1982	None	None	None	–	–
1983 •	SEA EXPLORER	m.e. Self-prop Semi-submersible Drilling Rig	Britain	9086	9086

24% export	23 vessels total =	92,586 tons displacement
76% Britain	93 vessels total =	845,994 g.r.t.

Notes

† Became Scott-Lithgow Ltd (Cartsburn/Cartsdyke Complex)   1969–77
† Became Scott-Lithgow Ltd (Cartsburn/Cartsdyke Complex)
  Division of British Shipbuilders Ltd   1977–84
† Became Scott-Lithgow Ltd (Cartsburn/Cartsdyke Complex)
  Offshore Division of Trafalgar House Investments Ltd   1984–88

[1]coaster

• Indicates vessel depicted in subsequent photographic section.

For explanation of abbreviations see Glossary on page 345.

Left. *A contrived yet complimentary publicity photograph taken in the autumn of 1961, showing the significant (in its day) lifting capability of Scotts SB & Eng Co Ltd, Cartsburn dockyard. The pair of recently installed 60-ton travelling hammerhead cranes are shown simultaneously lifting the (aluminium) bridge deck fabricated unit for yard no. 689, m.v. FOURAH BAY 7,704 g.r.t., and the steering gear fabricated unit (steel) for yard no. 690, m.v. FALABA 7,703 g.r.t. Both vessels were 'F' class sisterships built by the yard for Elder Dempster Lines Ltd of Liverpool. Note the progress on the launch platform in the left foreground.*

Below. *This 1964 panorama of Scotts SB & Eng Co Ltd, Cartsburn dockyard shows the shipyard to good effect with a varied workload. From left to right, yard no. 691 HMS EURYALUS 2,350 tons displacement, F.15, a Leander class frigate for the Royal Navy is fitting-out. On the pair of large berths, yard no. 696, motor bulk carrier GRAIGWERDD 18,618 g.r.t. is almost ready for launching, and alongside her yard no. 700, motor bulk carrier BRITISH MONARCH 18,616 g.r.t. is at an advanced stage of hull erection. Hidden behind the berth adjacent to the right hand fabrication shed an Oberon class submarine is also under construction. Note the railway sidings in the foreground with large steel plates on a bogie trestle wagon, and four mineral wagons being loaded with steel swarf, such was then the dependency of the shipbuilding and marine engineering industry on this mode of transport.*

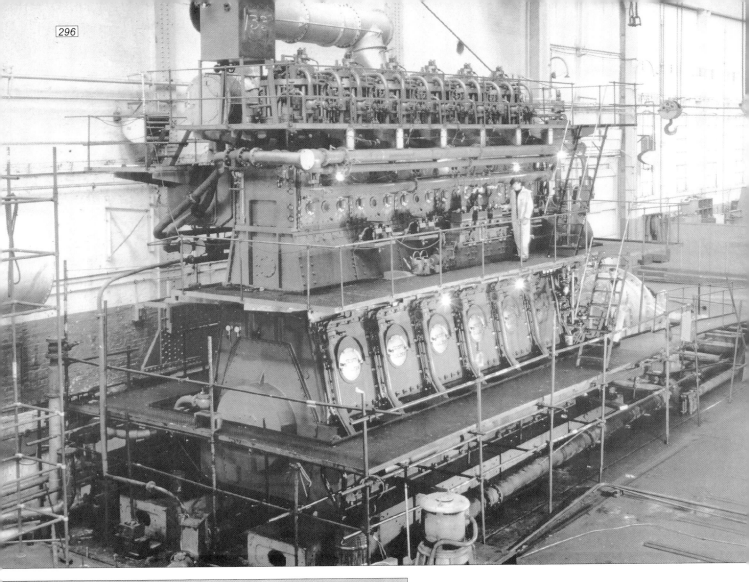

Above. *A six cylinder Scott-Sulzer 6RD-68 diesel engine on the test bed of their Greenock engine works in 1965. This six cylinder engine of 7100 BHP was installed in the* bulk carrier BINSNES 10,961 g.r.t. *which was built at the Cartsburn yard in the same year. The two apprentices give the machinery some idea of scale and the engine is being viewed from the forward direction looking aft.*

Left. *Yard no. 721, m.v. BANBURY 11,381 g.r.t. enters the River Clyde from the Cartsburn dockyard of Scotts SB & Eng Co Ltd on 19 October 1971. Also engined by Scotts, this stylish cargo liner was launched with her machinery already installed. Note the functional sets of deck cranes all mounted on single pedestals, very similar in looks to the BBC's Daleks from Doctor Who! BANBURY was renamed IRON BANBURY whilst fitting-out, in part recognition of her four-year charter to BHP of Australia. Built for the Alexander Shipping Co Ltd of London, she was still in existence in 1996 as MSC ELENA. Note the twin hatches at holds Nos 2, 3, 4 and 5. Divided by a longitudinal centre line bulkhead from the underside of the upper deck to the top of the double bottom, this innovation increased the strength of the ship and also allowed considerable versatility in the types of cargo carried (Burniston Studios Ltd)*

Above. RMAS NEWTON 4510 tons displacement, A367, *launched in 1975 for the MoD. Engined by GEC Rugby, this diesel-electric underwater research vessel was the only surface ship launched at Cartsburn between 1973 and 1976, and was still in existence in 1996 under her original name.* (Burniston Studios Ltd)

Below. *Launch of the twin hull pontoons, legs and diagonal bracing of semi-submersible drilling rig SEA EXPLORER 9086 g.r.t. at Cartsburn dockyard on 16 June 1983. This vessel was constructed on the two berths either side of the 60-ton crane track. The deck section was built at one of the Scott Lithgow Ltd yards in Port Glasgow and both units were mated afloat in the Clyde estuary. This was achieved by floating the deck section on top of a cargo barge over the column legs which were partially submerged, deballasting the pontoons resulting in the location of both sections together for subsequent weld-out, hook-up and completion.* (BP Photographic)

m.t. NIMERTIS 11,267 g.r.t. *launched in 1952 for the Perga SS Co SA of Monrovia, Liberia. Engined by Scotts SB & Eng Co Ltd, this traditional oil tanker was very similar in size to a dozen other vessels built by the yard in the 1950s. Her lengthy career ended in 1985 when she was broken up under her original name.* (Burniston Studios Ltd)

m.v. CRYSTAL CUBE 8680 g.r.t. *launched in 1955 for the Sugar Line Ltd of London. Engined by Scotts SB & Eng Co Ltd, this ship was the first purpose-built bulk sugar carrier (another world's first for Scotts!). Sold and renamed SHAO-AN in 1965 she was broken up as that in 1980. Note the unusual feature of her poop deck extended forward to include the hatch of no. 5 hold.*

s.t. CALTEX EDINBURGH 12,492 g.r.t. *launched in 1955 for Overseas Tankship (UK) Ltd. Engined by Scotts SB & Eng Co Ltd, this steam turbine tanker was the only ship built at the Cartsburn dockyard for these owners. Renamed KOREA EDINBURGH in 1971 she was broken up as that in 1982.* (E.H. Cole)

m.t. ANGELOS LUSIS 11,630 g.r.t. *launched in 1956 for Sociedad Carga Oceanica SA Piræus, Greece. Engined by Scotts SB & Eng Co Ltd, this typical 1950s (pre-war styling) small tanker lasted in service for almost two whole decades, being broken up under her original name in 1975.*

m.v. LORD BYRON 9364 g.r.t. *launched in 1957 for Norships Ocean Carriers Ltd, London. Engined by Scotts SB & Eng Co Ltd, this cargo liner was the first of three vessels built for these owners by Scotts. Sold and renamed MAROUKO in 1983 she was broken up as that in 1984.*

m.v. DARU 6340 g.r.t. *launched in 1958 for Elder-Dempster Lines Ltd of Liverpool. Engined by Scotts SB & Eng Co Ltd, this traditional cargo liner was the first of three 'D' class sisterships built at the Cartsburn dockyard for their owners' UK-West Africa service. Sold and renamed LONE EAGLE in 1979 she was later scrapped in 1982 under the name of ANJO ONE.*

m.t. BRITISH SWIFT 11,174 g.r.t. *launched in 1959 for the Clyde Charter Co Ltd (BP Tankers). Engined by Scotts SB & Eng Co Ltd, this distinctive Bird class tanker was one of nine sisterships built on the Clyde for BP. Sold in 1977 and later renamed NOAH VI, this ship was still trading under that name in 1996.* (BP Photographic)

s.t. QUILOA 13,113 g.r.t. *launched in 1959 for the New Zealand Shipping Co Ltd (although painted in the colours of British India Steam Navigation Co Ltd). Engined by Scotts SB & Eng Co Ltd, this tanker and her sistership QUEDA, also built at Cartsburn, had large tapered funnels that enhanced their appearance. Sold and renamed MICHEL in 1972 she was broken up in 1977 under the name of GREAT JUSTICE.*

m.v. FOURAH BAY 7704 g.r.t. *launched in 1961 for Elder-Dempster Lines Ltd, Liverpool. Engined by Sulzer Bros of Winterthur (although installed by Scotts), this 'modernised' cargo liner with bipod masts was the first of six 'F' class ships built on the Clyde, and had extra accommodation for cadet training. Sold and renamed MAGDA JOSEFINA in 1978 she was broken up in 1984 under the name of LEMINA.*

Right. motor coaster DAWNLIGHT I 199 g.r.t. *launched in 1965 for Ross & Marshall Ltd, Glasgow. Engined by Crossley Bros Ltd of Manchester, this small vessel was the second of a pair of 'puffers' built by Scotts for these owners. Sold to new owners in 1982, the vessel was still extant in 1996 as the AGNES.*

Below. RFA RESOURCE 18,029 tons displacement, A480, *launched in 1966 for the MoD. Engined by AEI Ltd, Manchester, this highly functional fleet auxiliary was still in front line duty with the UK armed forces in 1996 as she approaches her fourth decade, a tribute to her good design, the excellent workmanship of the Cartsburn artisans and subcontractors, as well as first class maintenance by her crew.*

Below, left. *Oberon class diesel-electric submarine OTWAY 1,610 tons displacement running high speed surface trials prior to hand-over to the Australian Navy in 1968. Fitted with British Polar ASR1 diesel engines, eleven Oberon class submarines were built by Scotts: three for the Royal Navy, two for the Chilean Navy and six for the Australian navy. OTWAY and her five sisters were still in existence in 1996.*

Below, right. motor bulk carrier CLYDESDALE 24,024 g.r.t. *launched in 1967 for the Hadley Shipping Co Ltd of London. Engined by Scotts SB & Eng Co Ltd, this vessel bore the distinction of being the largest ship ever constructed at the Cartsburn dockyard. She was renamed CLYDEBRIDGE in 1968 and subsequently resold before being broken up in 1986 under the name of FIVE STAR.*

m.t. GAS LION 8168 g.r.t. *launched in 1968 for Kristian Gerhard Jebsen Skipsrederi of Bergen. Engined by Scotts SB & Eng Co Ltd, this liquified petroleum gas products tanker was the first such vessel built on the Clyde with special low temperature 'Arctic D' carbon steel cargo tanks, designed and installed by Scotts. Sold and renamed GAS PILOT in 1980, this pioneer ship was broken up in 1985.*

motor bulk carrier ERISKAY 12,485 g.r.t. *launched in 1969 for John Swire & Sons Ltd, London. Engined by Scotts SB & Eng Co Ltd, she was sold and renamed SIGANTO AS in 1980. Further various changes of name occurred and she was still in existence in 1996 as the KIMBERLY. This vessel was the last and largest of eight ships built by Scotts for these owners since 1946.*

motor bulk carrier CUMBRIA 18,570 g.r.t. *launched in 1971 for the Hadley Shipping Co Ltd of London. Engined by Scotts SB & Eng Co Ltd, she remained with her initial owners until 1981 when she was sold and renamed DAGOMYS being later broken up in 1996 as the FLAG PAOLA. Note this vessel's distinctive yet squat looking superstructure.*

m.t. BRITISH KENNET 15,540 g.r.t. *launched for the BP Thames Tanker Co in 1972. Engined by Scotts SB & Eng Co Ltd, this tanker was the second of a series of five products tankers built by Scott-Lithgow Ltd for these long standing customers. Sold and renamed MINAB 2 in 1986 this vessel was still trading under that name in 1996.* (BP Photographic)

m.t. JAG PRAKASH 15,849 g.r.t. *launched in 1973 for the Great Eastern Shipping Coy of Bombay. Engined by Scotts SB & Eng Co Ltd, this modern products tanker was still in service with her original owners in 1996. This vessel's 'value-engineered' parallel radiused sheerstrake and almost flat triangular transom stern are shown to good effect in this stern on view.*

RFA FORT GRANGE 16,049 tons displacement, A385, *launched in 1976 for the MoD. Engined by Scotts SB & Eng Co Ltd, this large fleet auxiliary and her sistership* FORT AUSTIN, *also built at the Cartsburn dockyard, were both engaged in the Falklands war and Gulf crisis, and form essential elements of the UK armed forces supply chain in the 1990s.*

m.v. MYRMIDON 16,482 g.r.t. *launched in 1980 for Ocean Transport & Trading Ltd of Liverpool. Engined by Scotts SB & Eng Co Ltd, this distinctive and functional multi-purpose cargo liner became the last merchant ship built at Cartsburn dockyard. Sold and renamed* BELLO FOLAWIYO *in 1986, she was later resold and renamed many times and was still trading in 1996 as* TAMAMONTA.

HMS CHALLENGER 6907 tons displacement, K07, *launched in 1981 for the MoD. Engined by GEC Special Projects Ltd, this twin screw diesel-electric diving support vessel never fulfilled her conceived role. Her brief career was fraught with modifications and redesigns, being decommissioned by the Royal Navy in 1990. She has since been brought by a commercial diving company—Subsea Offshore Ltd of Great Britain—and still existed in 1996.*

▎ ARDROSSAN DOCKYARD LTD   1925–1964

Located within the confines of Ardrossan harbour, the 'old yard' of the Ardrossan Dockyard Ltd existed on a site that had built ships for well over 100 years. The company had previously been called The Ardrossan Drydock and Shipbuilding Co Ltd up until 1925. Called locally the 'old yard', this was a literal description of the yard within the harbour that differentiated it from the 'new yard', which was sited on reclaimed land at The Inches, south of the main harbour, and facing into the waters of the Firth of Clyde. The 'new yard' was constructed during the first world war when the demand for new ships was at an elevated level. This boundless order book was perceived at the time to exist without end, alas the great depression of the 1920s confounded such industrial optimism. The new yard was closed in 1930 under the sponsorship of National Shipbuilding Securities Ltd, an amalgamation of shipbuilding and financial interests that effectively reduced over-capacity in the UK shipbuilding industry in the period between the two world wars. Considered 'new' in terms of plant equipment and facilities of the day, the new yard never produced ships to its designed throughput capacity. After closure, little or nothing of the 'new yards' equipment was transferred to its sister shipbuilding facility, being sold to either other shipbuilders or for scrap.

Concentration of shipbuilding at the older establishment limited the size of vessels that could be built at Ardrossan. The old yard was approximately half the size of its short-lived relative, and could only launch ships about half as big at approximately 3000 g.r.t. After hyper-busy shipbuilding and repairing activity during World War II, the shipyard embarked on a relatively profitable post-war programme of new ship construction, combined with regular ship-repair and conversion work. Employing up to 700 men at the busiest period of the mid 1950s, this workload did not activate extensive investment in replacement of dated plant and equipment. Relying on an adaptable, skilled labour force, kept busy on an influx of steady orders, the yard produced on average two new vessels each year, interspersed with occasional high-profile modification work to small ferries, and coasters. This was regularly supplemented with tank cleaning and repair work to many of the oil tankers that conveyed bitumen to the large Shell refinery in the north side of Ardrossan harbour.

In the post-war period the shipyard built a total of 35 vessels (12 of which were motor barges for use in the Bahamas) totalling 33,202 g.r.t., of which 48% were for export. Greatest annual output was achieved in 1948 with the launching of two passenger vessels totalling 4863 g.r.t. That year included the *m.v. Zambesia* 2625 g.r.t., the largest vessel built at the yard during the post-war period. In 1961, the shipyard also built one of the first ever true container ships, the *m.v. Buffalo* 2163 g.r.t. for Coast Lines Ltd, who were the main owners of the yard by that time and also the most regular customer. This archetypal vessel has subsequently been modified, sold, variously renamed and was still extant in 1996.

Ownership changed to the Greenock entrepreneur, Archie 'Cash-down' Kelly in 1962, after a gradual reduction in new shipbuilding orders over the previous years. Correspondingly the total number of men employed tapered off during this period. The new management team emphasised a future business plan based on repair and conversion work. This influx managed to re-employ some former workers with numbers now up to about 200 from a previous low of just over 100. The last new building, *Affet 6*, a non-propelled oil bunkering barge of 325 g.r.t. for use in Sierra Leone, West Africa (yard no. 432) was launched on 12 February 1964. At this late date, the small yard was still in possession of an array of low capacity fixed swivelling jibs and derricks, which were the only means of lifting steelwork and equipment on the building berths. Ship repair activity lingered on sporadically for a few more years as during that period the port of Ardrossan, in addition to the bitumen traffic mentioned above, still exported sizeable quantities of coal and steel carried in short sea traders, which needed regular maintenance and surveys. The site of the old shipyard was acquired by the Ardrossan Harbour Board in 1969, being later developed as the area for lorry and container parking, as part of a roll-on-roll-off ferry facility between the town, Northern Ireland and the Isle of Arran.

In no way connected with the former Ardrossan Dockyard Company, small ship construction was resurrected in the North Ayrshire town in the 1970's. A former employee, now a businessman in his own right, Bill McCrindle succeeded in creating a small shipbuilding facility on part of the site of what had been the new shipyard at the Inches area. A number of small craft, including the replacement Renfrew Ferry were built there. The rapid decline in much of the small ship construction market, with many ferries at home and overseas now being replaced by new bridges coupled to similar reductions in the fishing and coasting fleets, meant future expansion a decidedly precarious prospect. The hoped-for renaissance of shipbuilding in this Clyde coast town was, alas, optimistically short-lived.

List of ships built by the ADROSSAN DOCKYARD Ltd, between 1946 and closure in 1964

YEAR	NAME	TYPE	COUNTRY OF REGISTRATION	G.R.T.	TOTAL G.R.T.	YEAR	NAME	TYPE	COUNTRY OF REGISTRATION	G.R.T.	TOTAL G.R.T.
1946	ULSTER DUCHESS	m. Cargo[1]	Britain	498		1959 •	DORSET COAST	m. Cargo[1]	Britain	1167	
	OLIVIAN COAST	m. Cargo[1]	Britain	749	1247		COSRAY #1	m. Barge	Bahamas	214	
1947	PACIFIC COAST	m. Cargo[1]	Britain	1188			COSRAY #2	m. Barge	Bahamas	214	
	BALTIC COAST	m. Cargo[1]	Britain	1722	2910		COSRAY #3	m. Barge	Bahamas	214	
1948	ZAMBEZIA	m. Ref/C/P	Portugal	2625			COSRAY #4	m. Barge	Bahamas	214	2023
	EL HALAL	m. Cargo/Pass	Britain	2238	4863	1960	COSRAY #5	m. Barge	Bahamas	214	
1949	LURIO	m. Ref/C/P	Portugal	2639	2639		COSRAY #6	m. Barge	Bahamas	214	
1950 •	EL KERYM	m. Cargo/Pass	Britain	2230			ELIZABETH PATON	m. Trawler	Britain	220	
•	LOCH CARRON	m. Cargo[1]	Britain	683	2913		COSRAY #7	m. Barge	Bahamas	214	
							COSRAY #8	m. Barge	Bahamas	214	
1951	None	None	None	–	–		COSRAY #10	m. Barge	Bahamas	214	1290
1952	THE LADY GWENDOLEN	m. Ref/Cargo[1]	Britain	1166	1166	1961 •	BUFFALO	m. Cargo[2]	Britain	2163	
							COSRAY #26	m. Barge	Bahamas	214	
1953 •	MAID OF CUMBRAE	m. Ferry	Britain	508	508		COSRAY #27	m. Barge	Bahamas	214	2591
1954 •	LAIRDSGLEN	m. Cargo[1]	Britain	1544		1962	None	None	None	–	–
	MARRA	m. Cargo[1]	Australia	1396	2940	1963	None	None	None	–	–
1955	ESSEX COAST	m. Cargo[1]	Britain	892		1964	AFPET 6	n.p. Oil Barge	Sierra Leone	325	325
	TATANA	m. Cargo[1]	Australia	1396	2288						
1956	BIRCHFIELD	m. Cargo[1]	Britain	1265			48% export				
•	OSBORNE QUEEN	m. Cargo[1]	Britain	1424	2689		52% Britain	35 vessels total = 33,202 g.r.t.			
1957 •	ZULU COAST	m. Cargo[1]	South Africa	813							
•	BAY FISHER	m. Cargo[1]	Britain	1289	2102						
1958	LADY ROSLIN	m. Cargo[1]	Britain	708	708						

[1](coaster); [3](container ship)

• Indicates vessel depicted in subsequent photographic section.

For explanation of abbreviations see Glossary on page 345.

The photograph on the next page illustrates the location of the small shipyard of the former Ardrossan Dockyard Co Ltd. Also included on following pages are a limited number of pictures of coastal craft, mostly depicted in revenue earning service, built by the yard during the last years of operation.

The north Ayrshire sea port of Ardrossan looking east in the autumn of 1963. The Ardrossan Dockyard is located in the bottom right-hand corner of the photograph. One of the shipyard's two building berths is being prepared for the future construction of yard no. 432, AFPET 6, 350 g.r.t., an oil bunkering barge for use in Sierra Leone, West Africa. Launched on 12 February 1964, this was the last vessel built by the yard. Ardrossan was then a busy commercial port trading in coal and steel exports, with additional cargoes of bitumen and heavy oil products to and from the Shell refinery, part of which can be seen in the top left corner. Noticeable in this weekend photograph is the considerable reliance on the railway network for the carriage of most of the freight that passed through this once busy port, although a row of stored road trailers on the centre quayside indicate some of this traffic is on the wane. (Aerofilms)

m.v. EL KERYM 2230 g.r.t. *launched in 1950 for the Halal Shipping Co Ltd, London. Engined by J.G. Kincaid & Co Ltd of Greenock, this small passenger/cargo liner was the second of a pair built for the same owners by the Ardrossan Dockyard Ltd in the space of two years. She was sold to the Straits SS Co in 1957 and renamed* KINABALU, *being broken up in 1979 under the name* TUNGFONG. *She is seen off Ardrossan performing sea trials prior to hand-over in 1950. Note her spread of four deck cranes of very basic post-war design.*

m.v. LOCH CARRON 683 g.r.t. *launched in 1950 for David MacBrayne Ltd, Glasgow. Engined by British Polar Engines Ltd, this small coaster was built specifically to trade between the Scottish West coast islands and Greenock and Glasgow. Sold and renamed GIORGIS K in 1977, she has since been resold and was still trading as the RANADA in 1996. She is seen off the Scottish west coast with a deck cargo of sawn timber and a couple of new motor cars. Note her extensive fender typical of coasters that had to moor tightly against stone built quays.* (E.H. Cole)

t.s.m.v. MAID OF CUMBRAE 508 g.r.t. *launched in 1953 for Caledonian Steam Packet Company Ltd, Glasgow. Engined by British Polar Engines Ltd, this twin screw passenger ferry sailed the Firth of Clyde until 1978 when she was sold and renamed HANSEATIC. Subsequently resold and renamed, she was still in service in the Bay of Naples in 1996 as the CAPRI EXPRESS. She is seen departing from Gourock in the 1950s presumably on her maiden voyage.* (E.H. Cole)

t.s.m.v. LAIRDSGLEN 1544 g.r.t. *launched in 1954 for Burns & Laird Lines Ltd, Glasgow. Engined by George Clark (1938) Ltd of Sunderland, this vessel plied the coastal waters of Britain and Ireland for two decades. She was sold and renamed DEVON EXPRESS in 1974 before being broken up in 1984. Her arrangement of five sets of derrick posts is more in keeping with a larger vessel than a coaster.* (P&O Library Archive)

m.v. OSBORNE QUEEN 1424 g.r.t. *launched in 1956 for Queenship Navigation Ltd, London. Engined by G. Clark & NEM (Sunderland) Ltd, this functional coaster remained in service until the 1970s. She was deleted from Lloyds Register in 1973, presumably broken up.* (Courtesy World Ship Society)

m.v. ZULU COAST 813 g.r.t. *launched in 1957 for Thesen's SS Co Ltd, Cape Town, South Africa. Engined by British Polar Engines Ltd, she was sold and renamed ZULU in 1967, and sank off the coast of South Africa in July 1971 after being in a collision.* (Courtesy World Ship Society)

m.v. BAY FISHER 1289 g.r.t. *launched in 1957 for James Fisher & Sons Ltd, Barrow-in-Furness, Lancashire. Engined by British Polar Engines Ltd, this traditional looking coaster was built for navigation through ice. Sold and renamed MOANUI in 1970, she was declared a constructive total loss as the PAHLAWAN when she became stranded at Galle in May 1986. Note the contrast in styles between her shaped and radiused funnel and her adjacent anti-bird's nest galley vent.* (Courtesy James Fisher & Sons)

m.v. DORSET COAST 1167 g.r.t. *launched in 1959 for Coast Lines Ltd, Liverpool. Engined by Geo. Clark & North East Marine (Sunderland) Ltd, this robustly constructed British coaster remained with her original owners until 1979 when she was sold and renamed EL HUSSEIN. After other identities she was broken up in 1985 as ATAMAS.* (P & O Library Archive)

m.v. BUFFALO 2163 g.r.t. *launched in 1961 for Coast Lines Ltd, Liverpool. Engined by British Polar Engines Ltd, this coaster was one of the first ships designed and built to carry containers. She was modified and renamed NORBRAE in 1972 (still remaining within the P & O Group). Later sold in 1977 and becoming NEWFOUNDLAND CONTAINER, she was still in existence in 1996 as the CONTAINER EXPRESS. She is seen in the river mersey during the 1960s with the cranes of the former Birkenhead shipyard of Cammell Laird & Co Ltd just noticeable in the background.* (P & O Library Archive)

	THE AILSA SHIPBUILDING & ENGINEERING CO LTD	1885–1978
	FERGUSON AILSA LTD (DIVISION OF BRITISH SHIPBUILDERS LTD)	1981–1986
	AILSA PERTH SHIPBUILDING CO LTD	1986–1996
	AILSA TROON LIMITED	1996–

The old established Troon shipyard and engine works received the family name of the Marquis of Ailsa when he acquired the company in 1885, becoming the sonorously named Ailsa SB & Eng Co Ltd from that date onwards. Ownership of the company was acquired from the Marquis of Ailsa by a Glasgow family of businessmen called Hutchinson, prior to the start of the Second World War. The firm became the southernmost Firth of Clyde shipbuilder after the cessation of shipbuilding in the county town of Ayr in 1929, where the local yard was latterly owned and run by the Ailsa Company. Ship repairing continued at Ayr throughout World War II finally stopping in 1947. A new shipyard further south was however built by the Lithgow Group at Trench Point, Campbeltown in the 1960s, specialising in the construction of small vessels and trawlers.

The Ailsa shipyard and engine works location, on the south side of Troon harbour was well placed to supplement its staple diet of shipbuilding, with coastal ship repairing and conversion work. Situated approximately seventy nautical miles from Glasgow, the Troon facility attracted custom from many shipping lines who plied their trade between the west coast of Scotland, Northern Ireland and the English ports on the Irish sea. Possessing a small dry dock within the shipyard and marine engineering complex, this investment was used both for performing ongoing voyage repairs to coasters, as well as seasonal repair and upgrading work on the many ferries and passenger pleasure craft that sailed the UK coast in the 1940s and '50s. Employing around 1000 workers between the divisions of shipbuilding, marine engineering and ship repairing in the boom post-war years, the firm was the main employer in the town of Troon, the other being the former British Railways wagon workshops at nearby Barassie. Regularly producing between two to three vessels each year, only some of these ships were engined by Ailsa. The types of propulsion units constructed at Troon were medium speed diesels, up to 3500 BHP built under licence from Wm Doxford of Sunderland, as well as steam turbines and reciprocating engines constructed to the design of the Troon marine engine drawing office, together with those of another proprietary company, notably Christiansen and Mayer of Copenhagen.

Ship types built at Troon varied from run-of-the-mill coasters, through short-sea traders to specialised ferries, dredgers and a pair of small first generation container ships for British Railways. The largest ship built during this period was the *Uskbridge* 3611 g.r.t., a cargo liner launched on 24 February 1959, and later jumbo-ised by Ailsa to 4098 g.r.t. in 1962. In the 1950s, Ailsa were the lead Scottish yard for the building of a series of non-magnetic minesweepers for the Admiralty, building six such vessels. Maximum annual post-war output was achieved in 1949 with the launching of three small cargo liners totalling 9592 g.r.t., all of which were engined with Ailsa designed and built steam turbines. Between 1946 and 1986, a total of 108 ships comprising 21 naval craft of 3667 tons displacement and 87 other vessels of 136,496 g.r.t. were built at Troon, 20% of which were for export.

Engine building became vulnerable as new order intake reduced and duly succumbed to worldwide over capacity in the 1960's. Many Ailsa new shipbuilding contracts were subsequently won on the pre-condition that owner specified engines were installed, not because the Troon engines were inferior, the other propulsion sets were cheaper! Part of the former engine works' premises were taken over by the Weir-Westgarth group who rehired some of the ex-Ailsa engineers, building desalination plants at Troon for over a decade.

Shipbuilding, ship repair and conversion work continued to employ many hundreds on profitable contracts, but the exposed building site facing the south-westerly gales of the Firth of Clyde made the Troon yard a hostile working environment, rivalled only by the equally unsheltered shipyard of George Brown in Greenock. Approval was sanctioned in the late 1960s by the then owning Gilbey family, for a multimillion pound investment in new shipbuilding facilities at Troon. This resulted in the construction of a covered building berth with adjacent new preparation and prefabrication sheds. Completion of these works in 1975 now enabled the company to possess the second covered shipyard in Scotland, the other being at Yarrows in Scotstoun. New order intake in the 1970s was erratic despite the yard recently being modernised. Part of a prestigious order obtained by the Association of Scottish Machine Toolmakers for a number of fishery protection vessels for the Mexican Government kept the Troon yard busy between 1973 and 1975 when 11 craft were built. The other vessels in this order were built by Scotts at Bowling and Lamonts at Port Glasgow. This valuable export order enhanced the River Clyde's worldwide reputation for the design and construction of small specialist craft. Later, sister ships to the Ailsa designs were built by the Mexicans in their own shipyards.

The Ailsa yard was belatedly taken within British Shipbuilders Ltd in June 1978. In 1980, it was formed into a 'forced marriage' with Ferguson Bros of Port Glasgow to form Ferguson–Ailsa Ltd, part of the small shipbuilding division of the nationalised conglomerate. This merger was as illogical as those performed further up–river in the late 1960's. Two small independent shipbuilders whose only commonality was the product range that they designed and built…in healthy competition with each other. Both yards were reasonably modern with skilled labour forces, considered by themselves to be flexible, but far from productive in terms of output measured against new world shipbuilding nations. The geographic separation of the yards, 40 miles by road, over 50 by sea, made their amalgamation a subtle consolidation on the part of British Shipbuilders Ltd, but a hamstrung partnership with Ailsa thereafter being only a production facility of the combination. New order intake during the BSL ownership was never enough to utilise the capacity of the yard, which was by now like most others heavily subsidised under the shipbuilding intervention fund, a grant of monies from the public purse that underwrote the difference between the 'real' cost of building a ship in the Far East and the cost it took to build it in the UK. Further losses incurred due to contract over-runs, etc. were also made up by the UK taxpayer. The rationalisation invoked by British Shipbuilders Ltd at Troon included the elimination of ship repairing and subcontract machine work— shipbuilding became the core function of this once versatile yard.

One ship, the gas tanker *Traquair* 5967 g.r.t., was undertaken as a joint venture between the Troon and Port Glasgow shipyards. The two halves were towed from their respective launch sites, and welded together in the Inchgreen drydock of Scott-Lithgow Ltd. The Ailsa shipyard was the main contract partner for this vessel and after joining together the hull sections, the non-ferrous cargo tanks were installed at Troon, where the ship was completed for the Anchor Line Ltd of Glasgow. The Ferguson-Ailsa association was terminated in 1986 when the Troon yard was closed by British Shipbuilders Ltd. The nationalisation experience was a far from successful period in the history of Troon shipbuilding, as the workload of subsidised orders were nearly all delivered with uncharacteristic tardiness. The pro-active style of management previously associated with the company, had been replaced with a visionless bureaucracy, that directed indifferent output from a disaffected labour force. With little continuity between new orders and the cessation of fill-in work in the shape of ship repairing, losses mounted. Unfortunately, the shipyard never produced the hoped-for continuous shipbuilding output from its new fabrication and outfit facilities.

During the ownership of British Shipbuilders Ltd 16 vessels were completed at Troon. The shipyard was later acquired by an Australian businessman, Mr Greg Copley, who renamed the yard Ailsa Perth SB Co Ltd. Ship repairing, marine subcontract fabrication and maintenance then became the main trading activity of the yard, however, in early 1996 this phoenix organisation plunged into receivership.

It was quickly rescued by the English Midlands Cathelco Group who recognised the untapped potential of the site and immediately divulged their intention to develop the Troon facility. In their brief period of ownership this company have refurbished the shipyard, increased the labour force and successfully won many millions of pounds worth of work for ship repair, marine maintenance and new building contracts, as well as publicly and proudly proclaiming an annual intake of shipbuilding apprentices.

List of ships built by the AILSA SHIPBUILDING Co Ltd, Troon, and its successors between 1946 and 1987

YEAR	NAME	TYPE	COUNTRY OF REGISTRATION	DISPL/ G.R.T.	TOTAL OUTPUT
1946	EMPIRE WARNER r/n				
	USKSIDE	s. Cargo	Britain	2961	
	HUDSON STRAIT	s. Cargo	Britain	3105	
	• HUDSON CAPE	s. Cargo	Britain	2524	8590
1947	DOMINO	s. Cargo/Pass	Britain	2302	
	DAGO	s. Cargo/Pass	Britain	2302	4604
1948	SICILIAN	s. Ref/C/P	Britain	3351	3351
1949	GRECIAN	s. Ref/C/P	Britain	3347	
	HUDSON RIVER	s. Cargo	Britain	3128	
	HUDSON FIRTH	s. Cargo	Britain	3117	9592
1950	• BORODINO	s. Ref/C/P	Britain	3206	
	CAMERTON	s. Suction D	Britain	891	
	HUDSON SOUND	s. Cargo	Britain	2577	6674
1951	CHARNA	m. Yacht	Britain	97	
	FENELLA	m. Cargo[1]	Britain	1019	
	OLIVINE	m. Cargo[1]	Britain	1430	2546
1952	GEM	m. Cargo[1]	Britain	1354	
	THE LADY GRANIA	m. Ref/Cargo[1]	Britain	1152	2506
1953	WHITEWING	m. Ref/Cargo[1]	Britain	1102	
	PEARL	m. Cargo[1]	Britain	1093	
	RINGDOVE	m. Cargo[1]	Britain	1102	
	BOTTISHAM	m. In Mine	Britain (RN)	120 displ	3417
1954	BRANTINGHAM	m. In Mine	Britain (RN)	120 displ	
	COWAL	m. Ferry	Britain	569	
	• MONS CALPE	m. Ferry	Gibraltar	1991	
	BUTE	m. Ferry	Britain	568	3248
1955	ELSENHAM	m. In Mine	Britain (RN)	120 displ	
	IERNE	s. Lt Tender	Britain	995	
	C. 850	n.p. Oil Barge	Britain (RN)	500 displ	
	IRISH ROSE	m. Cargo[1]	Eire	1749	
	C. 851	n.p. Oil Barge	Britain (RN)	361 displ	
	C. 852	n.p. Oil Barge	Britain (RN)	361 displ	4086
1956	AMBER	m. Cargo[1]	Britain	1596	
	IRISH WILLOW	m. Cargo[1]	Eire	1743	
	TYNEWOOD	m. Cargo[1]	Britain	1495	4834
1957	LOCHALSH	m. Ferry	Britain	64	
	• GLEN SANNOX	m. Ferry	Britain	1107	
	• THAMESWOOD	m. Cargo[1]	Britain	1799	2970
1958	• CONTAINER ENTERPRISE	m. Cargo[1]	Britain	982	
	AMETHYST	m. Cargo[1]	Britain	1548	
	CONTAINER VENTURER	m. Cargo[1]	Britain	982	
	ETCHINGHAM	m. In Mine	Britain (RN)	120 displ	3632
1959	USKBRIDGE	s. Cargo	Britain	3611	
	FRESHWATER	m. Ferry	Britain	363	
	SLIEVE DONARD	m. Cargo[1]	Britain	1598	5572
1960	• ST. CLAIR	m. Ferry	Britain	3303	
	KYLEAKIN	m. Ferry	Britain	62	
	EASTWOOD	m. Cargo	Britain	1793	
	OCKHAM	m. In Mine	Britain (RN)	120 displ	
	OTTRINGHAM	m. In Mine	Britain (RN)	120 displ	5398
1961	CERDIC FERRY	m. Ferry	Britain	2563	
	PETERSTON	m. Sand SD	Britain	748	
	DORIC FERRY	m. Ferry	Britain	2573	5884
1962	THEMARA	m. Yacht	Britain	130	
	TOPAZ	m. Cargo[1]	Britain	1597	
	• TOURMALINE	m. Cargo[1]	Britain	1581	
	BOWQUEEN	m. Sand SD	Britain	1317	4625

YEAR	NAME	TYPE	COUNTRY OF REGISTRATION	DISPL/ G.R.T.	TOTAL OUTPUT
1963	PEVERIL	m. Cargo[1]	Britain	1048	1048
1964	BOWBELLE	m. Sand SD	Britain	1486	
	BOWPRINCE	m. Sand SD	Britain	1599	
	RAMSEY	m. Cargo[1]	Britain	446	3531
1965	BOWFLEET	m. Sand SD	Britain	1620	
	• SAPPHIRE	m. Cargo[1]	Britain	1286	2906
1966	• ABERTHAW FISHER	m. Cargo[2]	Britain	2355	
	BOWSPRITE	m. Sand SD	Britain	1503	3858
1967	• TANMERACK	m. Cargo[3]	Britain	1598	
	CLOCH	m. Pilot Launch	Britain	46	1644
1968	–	n.p. Pontoon[4]	Britain (RN)	295 displ	
	GLEN AVON	m. Sludge Car	Britain	859	1154
1969	BOWTRADER	m. Sand SD	Britain	1592	
	GLENACHULISH	m. Ferry	Britain	44	
	CORUISK	m. Ferry	Britain	60	1696
1970	IONA	m. Ferry	Britain	1192	
	SAND WADER	m. Sand SD	Britain	3085	4277
1971	MONA'S QUEEN	m. Ferry	Britain	2998	2998
1972	*None*	*None*	*None*	– –	
1973	BOWHERALD	m. Sand SD	Britain	2965	
	BOWKNIGHT	m. Sand SD	Britain	2965	5930
1974	ANDRES QUINTANA ROO	m. Fish Pr	Mexico	130 displ	
	• MIGUEL RAMOS ARIZPE	m. Fish Pr	Mexico	130 displ	
	JUAN BAUTISTA MORALES	m. Fish Pr	Mexico	130 displ	
	IGNACIO LOPEZ RAYON	m. Fish Pr	Mexico	130 displ	
	MANUEL CRECENCIO REJON	m. Fish Pr	Mexico	130 displ	
	ANTONIO DE LA FUENTE	m. Fish Pr	Mexico	130 displ	780
1975	IGNACIO RAMIREZ	m. Fish Pr	Mexico	130 displ	
	IGNACIO MARISCAL	m. Fish Pr	Mexico	130 displ	
	HERBERTO JARA CORONA	m. Fish Pr	Mexico	130 displ	
	FERNANDO M. LIZARDI	m. Fish Pr	Mexico	130 displ	
	FRANCISCO J. MUJICA	m. Fish Pr	Mexico	130 displ	
	• LADY OF MANN	m. Ferry	Britain	2990	3640
1976	BRIGADIER	m. Tug	Britain	392	
	STRONGBOW	m. Tug	Britain	392	
	NORTHUMBRIAN WATER	m. Sludge Carrier	Britain	1037	
	ISLE OF CUMBRAE	m. Ferry	Britain	201	2022
1977	SATURN	m. Ferry	Britain	860	860
1978	• RELUME	m. Buoy Tender	Britain	1576	1576
1979	LOCHMOR	m. Ferry	Britain	189	
	GOLENIOW	m. Bulk Carrier	Poland	2996	3185
1980	CAMBOURNE	m. Suction HD	Britain	3122	3122
1981†	• TRAQUAIR	m. LPG Carrier	Britain	5967	5967
1982	STAR VEGA	m. Sup. Boat	Britain	1599	1599
1983	• TARIHIKO	m. LPG Carrier	New Zealand	2169	
	SIMBA II	m. Tug	Kenya	362	2531

YEAR	NAME	TYPE	COUNTRY OF REGISTRATION	DISPL/ G.R.T.	TOTAL OUTPUT
1984	NGUVU II	m. Tug	Kenya	362	
	CHUI	m. Tug	Kenya	362	
	DUMA	m. Tug	Kenya	362	1086
1985	FIVLA	m. Ferry	Britain	230	
	SEAFORTH EARL	m. Sup Boat	Britain	857	1087
1986•	SEAFORTH BARONET	m. Sup Boat	Britain	857	
	CORYSTES	m. Fish Pr	Britain (RN)	1280	2137
1987	None	None	None	–	–

20% export	21 vessels total =	3,667 tons displacement
80% Britain	87 vessels total =	136,496 g.r.t.

Notes

† Became Ferguson-Ailsa Ltd (Division of British Shipbuilders Ltd) — 1981–86
† Became Ailsa-Perth Shipbuilding Co — 1986–96
† Became Ailsa Troon Ltd — 1996–

[1]coaster; [2]heavy lift; [3]wood carrier; [4]launcher

• Indicates vessel depicted in subsequent photographic section.

For explanation of abbreviations see Glossary on page 345.

The group of photographs on the following pages illustrates the location of the Troon shipyard of the Ailsa SB & Eng Co Ltd, along with a few scenes of shipbuilding activity. The further batch of pictures depict a selection of some vessels from the diverse range of ships built by the company in the post-war period.

Above. *The Ailsa SB Co Ltd looking west after virtual completion of the yard's modernisation scheme in the winter of 1975. Shown to good effect is the recently erected building that created a covered berth facility. On the company's sole remaining open slipway, yard no. 547, t.s. pass/ro-ro/cargo/ferry LADY OF MANN 2990 g.r.t. nears her launch date. Both drydocks are empty, and the former Troon wet basin, previously used to export coal, is now in use by fishing boats and pleasure craft. In the short period since the preceding photograph was taken all railway lines into Troon harbour and the shipyard have been lifted, however, in the same period most yard workers now own a private car. The unidentified coaster moored alongside the quay is currently in the yard for repair.*

Previous page. *The Ailsa SB Co Ltd and Troon harbour looking north, circa 1968, showing the shipyard in the first phase of a multi-million pound modernisation scheme. Yet to be started was the new covered building berths at the left hand side of the two recently built plating and preparation sheds. Under construction on the left-hand berth, with the yard's only mono-tower travelling crane stooping over her, is yard no. 527, motor sludge carrier GLEN AVON 859 g.r.t., a few weeks away from launching. In the adjacent dry dock an unidentified coaster is under repair, whilst in the right-hand corner of the fitting-out quay a recently launched pontoon, yard no. 526, has just had a derrick structure fitted. On the quayside north of the shipyard a former Royal Navy warship HMS SOLEBAY 3290 tons displacement, D70, a battle class destroyer from World War II is being broken up at the West of Scotland shipbreaking yard. Note the large amount of railway wagons loaded with coal about to be shipped through Troon docks to the left, and a rake of seven plate wagons in a siding outside the shipyard perimeter, recently having delivered several hundred tons of steel to the yard. The buildings south of the yard were the location of the former Ailsa SB Co marine engine works. In the distance can be seen the adjoining town of Barassie recently expanded with a large amount of high amenity private housing. (Aerofilms)*

Above. *Watched admiringly by a bunch of foremen, draughtsmen and managers who helped to build her, yard no. 496, m.v. GLEN SANNOX 1107 g.r.t. is manoeuvred in Troon harbour shortly after her launching from the Ailsa SB Co Ltd on 30 April 1957. Built for the Caledonian Steam Packet Co Ltd, Glasgow, and engined by Sulzer Bros Ltd, Winterthur, this small ferry was built for service in the Clyde estuary. Fitted with a hoist containing a pair of turntables in the transverse well near the aft end, this lowered vehicles to the tween decks where they were turned and driven prior to stowage. She was later modified throughout her career, leaving the Clyde when she was sold and renamed KNOOZ in 1990. She was still in service in 1996 as the AL BASMALAH I. (William McCallum, Photographer, FIIP, FRPS)*

Below. *Two of the open slipways of the Ailsa SB Co Ltd, circa mid 1970s, when the main order being undertaken was the construction of eleven fast fishery patrol craft for the Government of Mexico. The remainder of this large order was shared between the fellow Scottish shipyards of Scott & Son Ltd at Bowling and Jas Lamont & Co Ltd at Port Glasgow. Note the series production of these craft with pairs of ships occupying each slipway, P-03's sister vessel already having been launched from the same berth. P-03 was later named MIGUEL RAMOS ARIZIPE. (William McCallum, Photographer, FIIP, FRPS)*

Left. s.s. HUDSON CAPE 2524 g.r.t. *launched in 1946 for the Hudson SS Co Ltd, London. Engined by the Ailsa SB Co Ltd, this steam coaster remained with her original owners until 1966 when she was sold and renamed EUGENIE, retaining that identity until 1971 when she was broken up. She was the second and smallest of five basically similar small steam ships built by Ailsa for these owners during a four year period.* (E.H. Cole)

Below. s.s. BORODINO 3206 g.r.t. *launched in 1950 for Ellerman's Wilson Line Ltd, Hull. Engined by the Ailsa SB Co Ltd, this well-proportioned traditional passenger cargo liner plied between the UK, Europe and North Africa until being broken up under her original name in 1967. She was the last of five similar vessels built by the yard for these owners since 1946.* (Burniston Studios Ltd)

t.s.m.v. MONS CALPE 1991 g.r.t. *launched in 1954 for the Bland Line Ltd, Gibraltar. Engined by British Polar Engines Ltd, this distinctive ferry, with its large, slightly tapered funnel and extensive coverage of lifeboats, plied between Gibraltar and Tangier for over 30 years before being sold and renamed CITY OF LIMASSOL in 1986. She was still in existence in 1996 as the AFRICA. Note her large side doors above her extensive fender to enable rapid discharge of passengers.* (William McCallum, Photographer, FIIP, FRPS)

This page depicts three vessels designed and built by Ailsa in the 1950s, whose robust construction has enabled them to be modified to achieve extended careers in different roles from those which they were initially intended.

t.s.m.v. GLEN SANNOX 1107 g.r.t. *launched in 1957 for the Caledonian Steam Packet Co Ltd, Glasgow. Engined by Sulzer Bros Ltd, Winterthur, this stylish ferry's looks were compromised by her vertical lift method of car and vehicle transfer. Despite such drawbacks she was a 'weel kent face' for over 20 years on the river of her birth. Sold and renamed* KNOOZ *in 1990, she was still in service in 1996 as* AL BASMALAH I. (Burniston Studios Ltd)

m.v. THAMESWOOD 1799 g.r.t. *launched in 1957 for the Constantine Shipping Co Ltd, Middlesbrough. Engined by H. Widdop & Co Ltd, Keighley, Yorks, this versatile coaster was sold, renamed* SERRA ORRIOS *and converted to a coastal oil tanker in 1968. She has since undergone various name changes and was still in existence in 1996 as the* ANASTASIS. (Burniston Studios Ltd)

m.v. CONTAINER ENTERPRISE 982 g.r.t. *launched in 1958 for British Railways Board, Lancaster. Engined by British Polar Engines Ltd, this vessel and her identical sistership* CONTAINER VENTURER, *also built by Ailsa, were among the world's first true container ships. This statistical maxim was based on the conveyance of the then standard British Railways wooden containers, not the huge stiffened steel boxes that revolutionised sea transport in the late 1960s. Built for service between Heysham and Ireland, she remained under her original name until 1988 when she was sold and renamed* ISACAR I. *In 1996 she was still in existence as the* SEA CONTAINER. *Note the extensive amount of riveting of her hull.* (Burniston Studios Ltd)

m.v. ST CLAIR 3303 g.r.t. *launched in 1960 for the North of Scotland, Orkney & Shetland Shipping Co Ltd, Aberdeen (part of P & O Group). Engined by Sulzer Bros Ltd, Winterthur, Switzerland, this fine looking vessel, with her pronounced Ailsa hallmark of a radiused front to her superstructure, successfully served her original route until 1977. That year she was sold and renamed* AL KHAIRAT, *being effectively displaced because she was too small for the growing trade for which she was built. She retained that second identity until being broken up in 1987.*

m.v. TOURMALINE 1581 g.r.t. *launched in 1962 for the Gem Line Ltd, Glasgow. Engined by Klöckner-Humboldt-Deutz AG, Köln (Cologne), this distinctive short-sea trader remained with her original owners until 1982 when she was sold and renamed* PROBA. *She later underwent further changes of name and ownership and in 1996 was still in existence as* AKRAM V. (Burniston Studios Ltd)

m.v. SAPPHIRE 1286 g.r.t. *launched in 1965 for the Gem Line Ltd, Glasgow. Engined by Klöckner-Humboldt-Deutz AG, Cologne, this coaster was the eighth and last vessel built at Troon for these Scottish shipowners. She was sold and renamed* APOLLONIA VII *in 1981 and was still in existence in 1996 as the* NISSIROS. (William McCallum, Photographer, FIIP, FRPS)

t.s.d.e. heavy lift vessel ABERTHAW FISHER 2355 g.r.t. *launched in 1966 for James Fisher & Sons Ltd, Barrow-in-Furness, Lancashire. Engined by W.H. Allen Sons & Co Ltd, Bedford, this vessel transported high value, bulky items like transformers, boilers, railway locomotives and other types of special equipment throughout the world. She was sold and converted to a mining ship dredger and renamed* MOONSTAR *in 1996.* (Glasgow University Archives)

m.v. TANMERACK 1598 g.r.t. *launched in 1967 for the Charter Shipping Co Ltd, London (P & O Group). Engined by British Polar Engines Ltd, this distinctive vessel was built specifically as a packaged timber carrier. Her profusion of rigging was an attractive if somewhat dated feature that was swept away when she was sold and renamed* QUICKTHORN *in 1973. In 1996 she was still in existence as the* SIBA. *(Courtesy and copyright A. Duncan)*

t.s. motor buoy tender RELUME 1576 g.r.t. *launched in 1978 for the Middle-East Navigation Aids Service, London. Engined by APE-Allen Ltd, Bedford, this very functional vessel built at Troon replaced a ship of the same name built by Fleming & Ferguson Ltd, Paisley in 1952. The replacement* RELUME *was still in existence in 1996 maintaining buoys and lights in the Persian Gulf. (Courtesy Ferguson Shipbuilders Ltd).*

m.t. TRAQUAIR 5967 g.r.t. *launched in 1981 for the Anchor Line Ltd, Glasgow. Engined by Clark-Hawthorn Ltd, Wallsend, this LPG carrying tanker was built in two halves: forward section by Ferguson-Ailsa (Port Glasgow) and the aft section by the Troon yard. Both sections were welded together in Inchgreen drydock, Greenock. This meant she was the largest vessel ever built by both shipyards! She was still in existence under her original name and ownership in 1996. (Courtesy Ferguson Shipbuilders Ltd)*

m.t. TARIHKO 2169 g.r.t. *launched in 1983 for Liquigas Ltd, Wellington, New Zealand. Engined by Krupp Mak GmbH, Keil, this LPG carrying tanker was the second such ship built at Troon. She was still in existence in 1996 under her original name and owners. Note the outline of the top of the vessel's three cylindrical cargo tanks with hemispherical shaped ends. These tanks protrude above the line of the ship's upper deck in order to maximise the volume of LPG carried. (Courtesy Ferguson Shipbuilders Ltd)*

Chapter 7

DEPENDANT INDUSTRIES

The combined 'metal bashing' duo of shipbuilding and marine engine building spanned an immense and diverse spectrum of: 'make-for, fit-on; join-up; add-to; put-in; carry-to; lift-on' etc, etc. industries, all with their own unique products, methods, expertise, sense of identity, and their respective range of subcontractors! In essence, UK shipbuilding was perhaps the ultimate assembly industry, with the combined turnover of a sub-economy. Underwriting national economic growth during its zenith, until it stagnated and festered to be abandoned during its nadir. The total of denuded carcasses of previously successful supply companies ultimately exceeded that of the discarded slipways, wharfs, quays and engine works which once consumed the products and expertise of these dependant industries.

Given that the percentage of bought/made outside cost elements of a ship varied from 30 to 70% of the total price, depending on *that* vessel's type and complexity of specification, the market for sub-contractors and ancillary service industries amounted to a real and tangible component of the West Central Scotland industrial economy.

The most simplistic analogy applied to a ship (any ship), is that in addition to its prime functions of sea-worthiness and propulsion, coupled with whatever commercial, military, utility, leisure or comfort requirements that vessel needs, it also has to provide all the life support services required for its crew, however, large or small. This comprises the supplying of food, water, accommodation, heating, ventilation, communications, workshops and recreation facilities. In short, each ship needed all the services and sometimes more than those bestowed in many small towns! All of these facilities needed complex procurement from the specialist companies throughout Scotland, the UK and abroad who furnished such wares, ultimately depending on a buoyant shipbuilding industry for their existence and future well-being.

By virtue of the fact that some of these industries supplied products with usage other than marine, the consequential demise of shipbuilding did not have the cataclysmic knock-on effect of total market annihilation. Manufacturers of pumps, diesel auxiliaries, boilers, carpets, curtains, sinks, bathrooms, furniture, plastic laminates, windows, valves, paint, pipes, lights, cables, switch-gear, mattresses, tools, cookers and refrigeration to identify the most obvious, merely reduced their respective product output or amended its specifications, then sold their goods in other markets with minimal effect in either their annual turnover or numbers of persons employed.

The totally dependant industries like foundries, forges, heavy machine tool makers, travelling crane makers, suppliers of steering gear, rudders, propellers, anchors, chains, windlasses, hatch covers, ventilators and lifeboats found their future commercial existence fraught with uncertainty. Making unique products these firms were inextricably linked to the River Clyde customer base of 24 shipyards and 18 marine engine builders. When this market insidiously shrank to three shipyards, two offshore construction sites and one ship repair yard, nearly all of these supply companies also closed down. This wholesale contraction meant that not one single large bore marine diesel engine builder exists in Britain. This statistic is an appalling indictment of the sociopolitical interference and economic skulduggery that emerged from the nationalised rump of these once great industries. Manufacture of diesel engines in the small to medium-bore range still continues in the UK, being catered for by the companies whose scope of customers cover the whole spectrum of power application. This range of machines varies from engines used as generators to prime movers of locomotives and heavy vehicles, etc. An *island* trading nation with a purportedly developed economy, retaining a handful of shipyards, yet without one single mainland marine engine builder, is akin to a distillery without a source of water!

The companies who tarried supplying these unique items of nautical hardware, lingered in a state of perpetual uncertainty, catering for an ever-diminishing market. Makers of steering-gear were spared immediate extinction by virtue of the fact that this unique item was invariably an owner specified article in the new ship contract document. Whilst the indigenous shipbuilding industry on Clydeside was in gradual terminal decline by the late 1960s, the British Merchant Navy, formerly the main customer base, was embarking on a multi-billion pound redevelopment of container ships, ferries, products, gas and other types of large tankers. Most of this replacement tonnage was built abroad, with much of the steering gear supplied by John Hastie & Co Ltd of Greenock. Unfortunately, this ship replacement programme was not to last forever. Low cost shipping lines using flags of convenience, with inferior standards and specifications to the British Merchant Navy, were seizing cargoes and established trades routes with remarkable ease. These unscrupulous companies were not as fastidious as their former British competitors, thus the need for Clyde-built steering-gear and its associated captive market disappeared, consigning a major sub-industry to oblivion.

Other 'locked-in' manufacturers of unique components shared varying degrees of longevity. The forges and foundries that made many of the diesel engine components, as well as stern-frames, fairleads, rollers, rudders, cleats, sheaves and bollards, soon found that the extensive overheads of plant, rates, energy and labour became weighty burdens of oncost that could not be spread over contracts now measured in units of tens per year, which had previously been counted in hundreds. Most of these subcontractors depended more on engine building than shipbuilding. This less specialised niche should have made diversification easier, however, the established suppliers to the mechanical engineering industry were already tooled-up with sound customer bases, and fledgling interlopers were to find out that ruthless cut-price tendering only accelerated liquidation.

Heavy machine toolmakers like Hugh Smith Ltd of Possilpark, whose presses, rolls, planers, plate and frame benders were to be found not only in every Clydeside shipyard, but in other yards as far afield as Kobe to Copenhagen and Singapore to Sunderland, managed to wring the 'last orders please' from the amorphous debacle that was British Shipbuilders Ltd, before succumbing to total closure in 1982. This small Scottish company had the unique and enviable reputation of supplying virtually every shipyard in the world with at least one item of shipbuilding machinery throughout its lifetime as the premier designer of heavy plate and section forming machinery. When this world famous company disappeared, the already deprived Glasgow district of Possilpark lost its last tenuous connection with Scotland's industrial past. The two previous steelwork fabricators in the area and long-established subcontractors to the shipbuilding industry, Fleming Brothers Ltd and Lambhill Engineering Ltd closed a decade earlier. The name, auspices, designs, patents and drawings previously owned by Hugh Smith Ltd were acquired by the Kilmarnock locomotive builders, Hunslet-Barclay Ltd, who still act as agents and suppliers of spares to owners of Hugh Smith machine tools throughout the world. Alas, the once regular site of a brand new gleaming Hugh Smith machine tool trundling through the streets of Glasgow, on a low-loader either en route to one of the Clyde yards, or to the docks for export, is now only a memory for those fortunate enough to have witnessed this previously commonplace event.

From the onset of steel shipbuilding in the last century, there emerged the need for lifting appliances and cranes, to facilitate the handling, erection and installation of even the smallest component, frame or plate. The methods deployed in the assembly of the keel, frames, stringers, girders, decks, bulkheads, shell plates, longitudinals and superstructure, were all a product of riveted construction methods that availed in all yards' erection techniques. The draughtsmen and engineers of the day calculated that the largest scantlings for ship types of much less than 5,000 gross registered tons were about 1–3 tons. A 5-ton derrick was therefore considered more than adequate for routine shipbuilding lifting operations. A plethora of these standing poles fixed to slewing jibs, suspended with shackles and sheaves, worked by chain or wire rope driven winches thus became the order of the day throughout the shipyards of Clydeside.

Marine engine builders of steam reciprocating machinery, geared turbines and boilers, were dealing with a quite different product. The component weights of shafts, casings, gears, pistons, cylinders, bedplates and castings in most cases were not much more than 10 tons, but the completed assembly weighed from 50–250 tons! Such engines were built and tested in large erecting halls and test-beds, where the buildings were constructed with built-in roof level crane rail gantries, straddled by travelling cranes capable of lifting these engines, usually using two or more cranes working in tandem. Initially, such cranes were manually operated through massive reduction gear trains. However, as this was a very slow process, this equipment was soon replaced with electric motors, which offered greater increase in hoisting speeds as well as heavier lifting capacities, depending on the strength of the crane rail gantries. Cranes of this latter type remained in use in all of the engine works up until closure of these firms.

The complete engines were then trundled on rail mounted bogies from the test-bed to the outfitting quay, where they were lifted into the engine-room of the awaiting ship, using either initially tripod-mast shear-legs, or latterly fixed hammerhead cranes capable of lifting up to 150 tons. These basic types of cranes were designed, constructed and tested by three famous West of Scotland companies: Sir William Arroll & Co Ltd, Butters Brothers Ltd and the Clyde Crane and Booth Company, as well as a number of other smaller crane makers scattered throughout Scotland and England. The expertise in crane design and manufacture gleaned by these individual firms was a catalyst to the booming post-war shipbuilding industry, intent on modernisation of working practices. Fabrication and erection methods, now in train within the new covered construction sheds, enabled larger pre-assembled hull and superstructure units to be built. From the 5 to 10 tons lifting capacity of pre-war cranes and derricks, lifting range rapidly rose through 20, 25 to 35 tons by the early '50s, culminating in 40 to 60-ton travelling designs of hammerhead, mono-tower and level luffing types by the early '60s. This optimisation of berth craneage was an unfortunate plateau. Such capacity represented a reasonable fabricated unit of the 10,000 g.r.t. vessel that was the bulk of the 'Clyde's' post-war product range. It was, however, not very substantial in terms of the fabricated unit rationale applied to the 30,000 g.r.t. bulk carriers and 50,000 g.r.t. tankers that were now being built by the medium to larger-sized yards. These new cranes were not cheap items of capital expenditure. Once yards purchased cranes…they made them work! There would be no rolling crane replacement projects every five to 10 years to accommodate the ever increasing sizes of prefabricated sections in new ship types.

The one exception to this investment hiatus on the River Clyde was the single 225-ton goliath travelling crane built by Sir William Arroll & Co Ltd to a design of PHB Jucho of Cologne, West Germany. This crane was, and still is, the heaviest travelling crane ever built and operated in mainland Britain. It was installed in the Glen/East shipyard complex of Scott-Lithgow Ltd, and assisted with the construction of all the VLCCs built by that company during the tanker boom of the 1970's. When the Clyde shipbuilding industry began to contract in 1962, crane replacement had passed its turn in the capital expenditure queue. The West of Scotland crane makers diversified their markets into steelworks, ports, docks, quays or other shipyards in the UK and overseas. They continued to design and sell specialised cranes and handling equipment to one-off clients that had less and less likelihood of replacement within working life-spans. Costing more and more for heavier state-of-the-art 'one-off' cranes, the laws of diminishing returns finally caught up with yet another of shipbuilding's dependant industries. Butters Bros Ltd closed in 1979, Sir William Arroll and the Clyde Crane and Booth, by then both part of NEI-Clark-Chapman Ltd, succumbed to closure in the mid-1980s, their last 'footprint on shipbuilding' being the construction of seven, 80-ton electric travelling level-luffing cranes which were built at Mossend, Lanarkshire, for the Govan and Scotstoun shipyards of Govan Shipbuilders Ltd.

Another familiar (though not totally) dependant service industry, was the freight side of British Railways that delivered steel plates, pipes, sections, castings, crankshafts, fabrications, timber and other bulky items to all of the shipyards and engine works along both banks of the River Clyde. From Finnieston and Govan, through Whiteinch, Scotstoun, Renfrew, Clydebank, Dumbarton, Port Glasgow, Greenock to Troon and Ardrossan, branch lines, tramways and sidings from local goods yards, ran between houses, shops and factories along streets and main roads, terminating in the respective stockyards and storage compounds of every shipyard and engine works. Initially all of the larger shipyards had not only a plethora of internal railway lines, but also fleets of privately owned wagons and small tank 'pug' locomotives which were responsible for in-house transport of materials and fabrications. Some of these small engines even had jibs attached, that enabled lifting of components within the yard.

John Brown & Co (Clydebank) Ltd included modernisation of their extensive internal railway system in the yard's post-war refurbishment agenda, and replaced its steam pugs with small diesel shunters designed and built by the Glasgow North British Locomotive Co Ltd. The Fairfield SB & Eng Co Ltd of Govan had the most unique locomotive. An electric tram type shunter with overhead pantograph, it ran along the Glasgow Corporation Tramway system from the yard gates for half a mile to Govan Goods yard, where contact was made with the British Railways network. This system continued for some four years after the closure of the Corporation tramway system which ended in 1962. The tram-lines were lifted either side of the tracks that ran along the Govan Road, until Dr. Richard Beeching's government sponsored edict 'The Reshaping of British Railways' finally caught up with this unique transport system, and the precursors of the juggernauts took over!

Other Clyde yards with their own railway sidings were to be dealt similar involuntary changes to their specialised transport needs, so that by the late '70s all remaining shipyard borne freight would be consigned by road. The thousands of bogie-well 'trestle' wagons specially built by British Railways workshops in the 1950s to convey wide plates in a triangular trestle-frame, and 'boplate' long wheelbase plate wagons for long length narrow plates, were shunted into scrapyards and condemned within less than a quarter of their designed life-spans. Both types of wagons were specifically designed and built to serve the shipbuilding industry, which foresaw maximum plate widths and lengths as creating very significant reductions in the number of welded seams on shell, deck and bulkhead units. Unfortunately neither industry lasted long enough to extract the potential savings in terms of reduction to fabrication or transportation costs! The belated despoiling impact on the environment of road-borne haulage, would regretfully only be appreciated after the insidious dominance of heavy lorries as the prime mode of carrying freight.

Steel products for Clyde shipyards in the shape of plate, angle, column, bulb bar, flat bar and pipe, accounted for over 500,000 tons of annual capacity from British steel-mills between 1945 to the mid 1960s. Not all of these products were supplied directly from Scotland. At that time the then privatised, fragmented United Kingdom steel industry comprised around a dozen independent companies making liquid steel, and a very comprehensive range of specialised and commercial quality finished products from mills in Scotland, Cumberland, Durham, Lincolnshire, Yorkshire, Northamptonshire and South Wales, all of which had customers in the River Clyde shipbuilding industry. This group of steel-makers supplied the fifty or so shipbuilding companies then in existence in the UK. Such competition at source resulted in considerable cost-cutting. Early ordering by shipbuilders to maximise discounts on continuous batch rolling of plates and sections, even if that steel wasn't to be used for months ahead was regularly pursued. In an era of negligible inflation and very low interest rates, cash-flow problems of money up-front palled into insignificance if that investment could allow a shipbuilder to purchase X,000 tons of plate and sections for secured ship orders, without incurring special rolling set-up costs or protracted delivery. Subsequent industrial and commercial development, with their attendant contraction of manufacturing capacity, now belie these tenets of the 1950s as being profligate use of working capital!

The personal-professional contact that existed between shipbuilder and steel-maker spawned continuity of employment, and contributed directly to the stability of prices which then existed during the 1950s. One of the net benefactors of this UK-based spread of work was the infant nationalised British Railways system which, as was outlined above, used their 1955 modernisation plan to invest in larger capacity wagons to assist this considerable foreseeable development of traffic in steel products. The inherent commercial edge that steel companies displayed was manifested in the two established Scottish steel-makers: Colvilles Ltd and Stewarts & Lloyds Ltd. The UK and worldwide customer base that these firms had developed over many decades, concurrent with indigenous shipbuilding, meant that these organisations were not wholly dependant on their considerable clientele on Clydeside.

Having worked almost flat out supplying home and overseas markets since the end of World War II, all of these British steel mills were in dire need of overdue and indispensible modernisation. Colvilles Ltd, the major Scottish steel producer, recognised this immutable necessity and duly embarked on phased upgrading or replacement at their various mills from the mid-1950s. This total commitment to renovation was unanimously advocated by the board of directors of one of Scotland's leading private companies, and predated by almost a decade the nationalisation of the entire UK steel-making industry. The contentious cornerstone of this extensive redevelopment was to have been total re-establishment of their entire steel-making facilities on reclaimed land at Hunterston, a deep water location on the north Ayrshire coast. Stubborn resistance in the combined forces of environmental aversion by local residents, coupled with wholesale reluctance to relocate by the mass of the Central Scotland workforce, resulted in expensive piecemeal modernisation of the various inland steel works.

Provision of a brand new import quay, with attendant cranes and wagon loaders at General Terminus, Tradeston, virtually the farthest point navigable up the River Clyde in the heart of the city of Glasgow, was the other major construction project in this attempt at modernisation. Aimed specifically at replacing the then ancient iron ore discharge facility at Rothesay Dock, Clydebank, built some 50 years earlier, the establishment of the new wharf quickly crippled the long term viability of Lanarkshire steel-making with an inordinate cost burden in iron ore transportation. Limited to ships of less than 30,000 t.d.w. at high tide, the new resource became a liability very shortly after its inauguration in 1958, as the cargo carrying capacity of ocean going bulk carriers soon increased.

Thus Motherwell became the centre of a modern, yet land-locked steel industry that would be limited in the future as much by its geography as its track record, and high operating costs. A notable spin-off from this modernisation project were orders for five of the then extant Clyde shipyards for a total of over 20 medium-sized ore carriers specifically constructed to ship iron ore from Africa, Sweden and Canada to the new import quay. Over two decades later part of the original visionary Colvilles plan for the long-term future of Scottish steel-making was achieved, with the opening of the deep water jetty and stockyard at Hunterston by British Steel in 1980. Immediately after the new facility was commissioned General Terminus Quay was closed.

The insidious demise that was engulfing Clyde Shipbuilding was taking place concurrent with the inauguration, and expansion of the much vaunted 'sunrise' industries of car, tractor and lorry manufacture in the Central Scotland area. If these industries fulfilled their sought after potential, then the required total tonnage of Scottish produced steel would be in excess of that 'lost' from the decaying shipbuilding industry. This hypothetic equation should ensure that the potential vacuum of reduced steel output that might have occurred, would be filled by the needs of these new companies…initially!

Scottish and British steel-making yo-yo'd through a lamentable decade as the industrial pawn in a contest of political ideology, played for real by polemical politicians of assorted hues, whose unaccountable gamesmanship had more effect in the total demotivation of the workforce, than ever it aimed at the needful identity and longevity of the industry. Such interference alternated quite inconsistently from mordant rhetoric, to dilatory actions, resulting in quite detrimental consequences for both steel-making and those thousands of employees, whose livelihoods were affected by this indulgent ineptitude. Discharged haphazardly by a cabal of faceless zealots, inexorably driven by dogma, they displayed apparently very little knowledge or objective about what they were trying to achieve. Policies of *no u-turns* when the direction had changed only resulted in lost customer confidence, loss of markets, stifling of stimulus both of management and employees, creating higher prices leading to massive losses to be borne by the taxpayer, when the industry was still nationalised.

Despite these minor diversions, Scottish steel-making continued. The much vaunted sunrise steel consuming industries barely lasted two decades and never used anything like the quantities of steel espoused at their outset. The first casualties among the group of separate steel mills were the works at Glengarnock in Ayrshire and Clydebridge near Cambuslang, Glasgow. Both of these plants had strong shipbuilding product bases, making bulb flats and plate, respectively. By 1982 each works was denuded of their previous marine client order base, with closure of the pair following the same year.

Material in the form of steel plates, sections and pipes for use in the construction of North Sea oil and gas structures, including piled jackets, topside modules and a few pipelines, filled a niche, only after a lengthy learning curve of investment in new metallurgical, production and quality control processes and procedures. Unfortunately this one-time dependant industry that survived initial market evaporation, nationalisation, denationalisation and re-establishment of new markets, was about to find out that its 'sell-by' date had summarily arrived when its sole 'political benefactor' retired from government office in the early 1990s.

The 'altar' of rigged market forces, intertwined with duplicitous political hyperbole that beckoned the abolition of restrictive practices and inveterate interest in job and industry, conversely inspired and deluded the dwindling labour force in Scotland to 'improve their act'. All mills responded with impeccable quality and timely delivery of each steel product. The reduced and entrusted workforce wholly adopted and implemented this pragmatic attitude throughout the entire Scottish steel industry. Alas, irrefutable compliance with these precepts for bottom line efficiency would not result in either perpetuation of the steel industry, or subsidised job security!

The re-privatisation of Scottish steel-making in the mid-1980s was a poisoned chalice as the former companies who previously controlled the industry now no longer existed. The taxonomic make-up of the reconstituted British Steel would soon be revealed as having imperceptible interest in the retention and development of its Scottish subsidiaries. The much contracted committed skilled labour force accepted with some humility, the criticism bestowed by management lackeys and political toadies. Challenge after challenge was taken on board with improvements regularly achieved. Target after target was bettered resulting in the best ever levels of productivity. Plaudits from satisfied customers rang hollow bells of euphoria with the company's non-Scottish executives. When, finally in the summer of 1992, earlier than planned, the residual rump of the Scottish liquid steel-making industry finally capitulated, with the despised and still inexplicable total closure of the Ravenscraig Steelworks. The contracted, adaptable, commended labour force, by now demoralised, disillusioned and sadly defeated in their quest to retain liquid and finished steel-making in Lanarkshire, were summarily consigned to dubious tenure in a glut of hastily established government sponsored retraining centres in advance of promised employment in future sunrise industries.

Dependant no longer on an industry that did diversify its customer base and modernise its methods of manufacture, they were now reliant on a very inconsistent, incomprehensible political system that appeared to sanction wilful membership of the respect sapping dole queue instead of fecund reward for skilful effort. This baffling handout of moneys by government to the unfortunate souls now without employment, somewhat contradicts the state's aversion to render fiscal assistance to core and strategic industries.

In 1996, plates and pipes were still finished in two remaining isolated mills at Wishaw and Airdrie, employing a combined total of less than 1000 men and women—both these sites now depend totally on plants in England for the supply of raw material. Whether these stumps of Scottish steel-making remain for the future is far from certain.

The selection of photographs on the following pages attempt to illustrate some of the dependant industries that existed to support former volume shipbuilding and marine engineering in the West of Scotland.

Above. *Engineers from the small Scotstoun lifeboat makers Meechans Ltd commission a motor lifeboat on the River Clyde during 1955. In the background the adjoining Scotstoun shipyard of Charles Connell & Co Ltd have yard no. 480, the* motor tanker SCOTSTOUN 12,723 g.r.t. *nearing completion with the keel and stern frame of yard no. 481,* s.s. BENDORAN 10,355 g.r.t. *recently laid down on the right hand berth. Meechans were the main suppliers of lifeboats in the West of Scotland and ceased trading in 1963.*

Below, left. *A compact electro-hydraulic steering-gear unit as designed, manufactured and installed by John Hastie & Co Ltd. This equipment no. HG.6712/3 was installed in yard no. 1609G, m.v. BULIMBA 6796 g.r.t. launched by Harland & Wolff Ltd, Govan in 1958, and was typical of thousands of units built by the Greenock firm. Located at the aft end of the ship in the area known as the steering-gear flat above the rudder, the unit was controlled from the ship's bridge via the lengthy arrangement of shafts and bevel gears shown, which harnessed the high torque from the hydraulic pumps and converted this into usable effort to move the rudder below. The Greenock firm were considered among the world's leaders in the design and manufacture of ships' steering-gear, but are no longer in existence.*

Below, right. *A Coles diesel railway crane shunts a bogie bolster wagon loaded with a prefabricated oil tanker bulkhead section for yard no. 706,* s.t. DERBY 31,791 g.r.t. *on the extensive internal railway system of John Brown & Co (Clydebank) Ltd during 1959. In addition to travelling cranes the company also owned diesel locomotives and many wagons that were used throughout the trackwork of the vast shipyard and engine works complex. The Sunderland firm of Coles Ltd outlived the shipbuilding industry of that famous North-east of England city.*

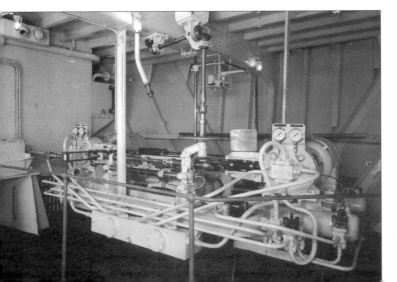

Three photographs that depict the importance and historic reliance of railways to the former shipbuilding industry in the West of Scotland. All views were taken in the Govan area of Glasgow by the eminent railway photographer, W.A.C. Smith.

Above. British Railways Govan goods yard on 7 May 1955. The plethora of fixed hammerhead cranes in the background belong to the former Govan shipyard of Harland & Wolff Ltd. The row of masts running through the yard support the overhead catenary that powered the small Fairfield tram loco which plied between this location and the Govan shipyard until 1966. Note the tenement on Govan Road sandwiched between a church on the left and one of the Harland & Wolff plating sheds on the right. The gantry crane in the centre foreground straddled both railway and roadway and was the erstwhile method for transferring goods from rail to road and vice versa. From this busy yard, railway sidings ran direct to the two shipyards referred to above, as well as the Govan Foundry, British Polar Engines Ltd and the Govan Shafting Co Ltd.

Left. Govan Road, Govan, Glasgow on 26 March 1956 showing the English Electric built 4-wheel tram loco owned and operated by the Fairfield SB & Eng Co Ltd hauling two wagons along the Glasgow Corporation tramway tracks west of Govan Cross. The short train has come from Govan goods yard which lay to the right of this view, and is heading for the Fairfield shipyard about half

a mile away. The rigid flat-bed lorry in the background entering Water Row is most likely crossing the River Clyde by means of the nearby Govan ferry. The ornate building on the left is the Pearce Institute, donated and named after one of the founders of the Fairfield shipyard and engine works. Note the closely packed cobbled roadway and typical Glasgow tenement.

Right. Renfrew Road, Shieldhall, Glasgow on 26 February 1958 showing the small Andrew Barclay 0–4–0 steam pug owned and operated by Alexr Stephen & Sons Ltd, hauling three loaded plate wagons along the Glasgow Corporation tramway tracks. The train has come from the British Railways goods yard at Shieldhall about half way along this road on the left-hand side, and is not far from the Linthouse shipyard which was located on the opposite side of the road. Behind the last wagon an Albion lorry leads a procession of pre-juggernaut road vehicles, whilst in the distance can be seen a Glasgow Corporation tramcar.

Above, left. *Port and starboard single-ended water tube superheated Scotch boilers built under licence by David Rowan & Co Ltd, Finnieston, Glasgow. They are seen painted after testing and prior to installation in the s.s. MATHURA 8782 g.r.t., a ref/cargo liner launched by Wm Hamilton & Co Ltd for the Brocklebank Line on 7 September 1959. These oil-fired boilers raised the steam which drove the double reduction geared turbines, whose energy was transmitted via the engine output shaft coupled to the ship's propeller. Such types of machinery were popular with many ship-owners up until the late 1960s when the combination of very expensive fuel oil and far more efficient and cheaper large bore marine diesel engines combined to consign steam powered ships to relics of a bygone era. Note the works foreman standing in front of the six black furnace doors.*

Above, right. *One of the less notable 'Pride of the Clyde' products! A then state-of-the-art electro-hydraulic horizontal plate rolling machine designed and built by Hugh Smith Ltd of Possilpark, Glasgow. This machine is seen in the Kingston shipyard of Lithgows Ltd where it performed successful plate rolling work for almost three decades. These types of machines can still be found in nearly every country that still builds ships…including the Far East. (Burniston Studios Ltd)*

Below. *Seven fitters are seen hand-burnishing the blades of a batch of bronze alloy propellers in the Yoker works of Stone Manganese Marine Ltd circa 1962. This necessary function was performed to fettle the irregular profile of the cast blades which would result in smooth and efficient propulsion. Note the inconsistent use of filter masks by two of the tradesmen. This operation was performed on a concrete floor where the valuable bronze alloy scrap cuttings could be swept up and deposited in the drums seen in the top right-hand corner. The five different propellers being polished were for various new ships then being built by Scottish and English shipyards.*

Three pictures of different examples of varied designs created and built by the former West of Scotland crane-making industry for customers in Clyde shipbuilding.

Left. A 35-ton mono-tower electric travelling crane designed and built by Butters Bros Ltd, Kinning Park, Glasgow. This crane was one of three identical models supplied to the Linthouse shipyard of Alexr Stephen & Sons Ltd in the 1950s. After closure of the shipyard in 1968, one of these cranes was re-erected on the east quay of UCS Ltd, Govan fitting-out basin, where it saw regular use for another twenty years. By the 1980s, Butters Bros Ltd had disappeared from the industrial map of Scotland.

Below, left. Sir Wm Arroll & Co Ltd, Dalmarnock, Glasgow was probably the most famous structural engineering company in Scotland, a reputation they had built up mainly on their success as bridge builders. Their other less famous products included cranes, and they pioneered fixed position, low-cost hammerhead crane construction which they supplied to many shipyards throughout Britain and the rest of the world. The company conceived, designed and built travelling derivatives of these machines in the late 1950s, and sold nine 60-ton variants to five Clyde shipyards, as well as many more to Harland & Wolff Ltd in Belfast, and some to shipyards on the Rivers Tyne and Wear. This view depicts the higher of the pair installed in the modernised Clydeholm shipyard of Barclay Curle & Co Ltd, at work early in 1960 placing a double bottom unit weighing about 25 tons onto the prepared no. 6 berth for yard no. 745, m.v. HOPECREST 7610 g.r.t. These cranes were state-of-the-art examples of Scottish electro-mechanical-structural engineering, and it is unfortunate that only one example remained on the Clyde in 1996, in the west yard of UIE Ltd, Clydebank. The other examples at Connells (1), Lithgows (2), Scotts (2), UIE Ltd (2) were all dismantled in the 1980s. However, one of the former Clydeholm cranes was still extant at Newcastle in 1996. Alas, the world-renowned Dalmarnock firm ceased to exist shortly after its takeover by the NEI group in the 1970s.

Below, right. A 40-ton mono-tower electric travelling crane designed and built by Sir William Arrol & Co Ltd, Dalmarnock, Glasgow. Of simple yet robust construction this crane was supplied to Yarrows Scotstoun shipyard in 1963. Subsequent operation of the covered building facilities at the company saw less regular use of this crane, however it was still extant in 1996. Despite its lower cost created by functional application of box girders and tubular sections instead of conventional fabricated lattices, this design evolved too late to see any large-scale deployment in the declining shipbuilding industry, although a few other examples were sold, both in the UK and abroad.

Chapter 8

COROLLARY

The factors contributing towards the elimination of volume shipbuilding on the River Clyde make a depressing account of gross under valuation by virtually every facet of the coterie of British commerce, government, the mishmash of inflexible trade unions and traditional employers, who collectively fudged or procrastinated until what remained resembled a cottage industry redolent of a charity sponsored work centre. The ensuing inventory of caveats attempts to identify these deficiencies and shortcomings.

After World War II, the UK public perception of Clyde shipbuilding was on the crest of euphoric admiration. Regrettably, this attitude soon slithered into a trough of abject disgust, imbued with disappointment, following that industry's reluctance, resistance and limited ability to perform the changes needed to meet the new global post-war market place in which it was now competing.

Bolstered by lengthy, profitable order books, yet burdened by the regressive trappings of 'Victoriana', which permeated from board room to building berths, the Clyde shipbuilding industry remarkably completed a consistent and formidable array of ship types during this era, referred to disparagingly, though nevertheless correctly, as the 'strike-strewn '50s'. Impregnated with traditions, strictures, crafts and working practices, whose perpetuation attracted as much criticism from fellow workers in other industries, as their collective retention contributed quite significantly to the ultimate demise of volume shipbuilding. That such dated methods of manufacture were sedulously retained by shipyard labour forces, contradicted the public rhetoric expounded by trade union leaders, who made great politic out of the needs for extensive replacement of plant and equipment. Nevertheless, such hollow intentions never inspired the capital investment necessary which might have replaced many of the labour intensive throwbacks from the industry's inception.

Clyde shipbuilding companies spent around £20 million from their own funds on modernisation of construction facilities, and to a much lesser extent labour force amenities, between the late 1940s until the early 1960's. This varied from the inevitable purchase throughout all of the shipyards, of welding equipment that replaced riveting machines, to completely brand new, fully-equipped fabrication shops, building berths, outfit quays and travelling cranes. More than half of the above sum was spent by Lithgows Ltd on their various establishments on Clydeside. This long overdue commitment to capital expenditure was inextricably linked to the replacement of riveted ship construction, with the substitution of welded prefabrication methods. Unfortunately, the sought after bottom-line savings, in terms of reduced build duration and lower construction costs, then being achieved in Japanese, Scandinavian and West German shipyards, was never fully realised on the River Clyde. This unfortunate comparison did not bode well for the future longevity of the industry, indeed the motionless productivity throughout UK shipbuilding after the replacement of riveting by welding was the augury of incurable decline. Coupled with projects for improved fabrication facilities, some companies embarked on parallel schemes aimed at modernising the workshops currently occupied by the outfit trades of joiners, electricians and plumbers. Again this investment resulted in meagre increases in terms of measured efficiency.

This post-war spending spree was far from pervasive, in terms of magnitude and commitment amongst all of the shipyards and marine engine works. It was non-existent in some yards when it came to provision of basic elements of urbanity, like canteens and wash rooms. Most significantly, it was scheduled and dovetailed to suit the then extensive shipbuilding workload. This overlap proved to be more than a minor encumbrance to the 'bread and butter' every day activities of building ships, as contractors acquired slipways, quays, sheds and stockyards that had to be filled in, piled, dismantled, re-erected...at the same time as ships were being built on fixed price contracts by labour forces indoctrinated into piecework rate-fixing methods of payment.

Such conflicting interventions resulted in some of these refurbishment projects taking a few years to complete. Hardly any of these 'modernised' shipyards managed to complete more vessels in less time than they had previously taken when employing 'manumatic' riveting techniques! A most unfortunate statistic that questioned the ability of the new breed of shipbuilders, and so proclaimed the combined efforts of the previous generation of shipwrights, platers riveters et al., as…'Ironfighters and Outfitters Extraordinaire', nay…supermen! The matrix tables in the Appendix of ships launched on the River Clyde from 1946 until 1987 illustrates this 'record of decline', depicting graphically the failure to surpass previous outputs! A disappointing correlative in that the larger scantlings of these later types of ships, lent themselves to construction, utilising wholesale welding methods which should have meant far greater amounts of new ships built. The boardroom optimism that glibly presaged selective replacement of equipment would result in producing more ships per annum from less berths, summoned the first real questions of confidence aimed at the industry's management. After all, the craft intensive functions of shipbuilding remained very much unaltered. Maybe such dupery was the only way bankers or shareholders would support investment in shipyard modernisation.

By the end of 1960, when most of these schemes had either been completed, or the money had run out, it was interesting to note only two Clyde shipyards launched greater annual tonnage:

- Alexr. Stephen & Sons Ltd, Linthouse – four ships totalling 41,442 g.r.t. plus one warship of 2,150 tons displacement
- Harland & Wolff Ltd, Govan – four ships totalling 43,167 g.r.t.

Both sets of figures were good for their day, however neither yard could be considered as truly 'modern', and Harland & Wolff Ltd was generally deemed the most traditional shipyard on the river. These impressive statistics were derived from a combination of healthy order books, good piecework incentives and motivated (strike-free) labour forces. Furthermore, all nine vessels contained a sizeable amount of riveting. It should be noted that a few years later Lithgows Ltd achieved regular increases in annual output, but this was accomplished by launching a lesser amount of much larger vessels.

Thus an established industry with a then reasonable customer base, having spent considerable amounts of its own money on modernisation or attempted replacement of obsolete equipment and working practices, now found itself embroiled in ruthless international competition, for initially profitable, but latterly break-even contracts that would prevent lay-offs, closures and bankruptcies. The £20 million or so that had been spent during the late 1950s on selective modernisation schemes, reflected the class-based cupidity of the families and individuals who then controlled Clyde shipbuilding and marine engineering. Notwithstanding the fact that this investment was paid for out of these shareholders' personal funds over a number of years, the limited amount of money involved averaged less than 10% of the entire annual turnover of all the shipyards and engine works in the West of Scotland. This niggardly amount, which was boasted about at the time showed how frugal and cheeseparing the ownership of the industry was, it also showed how little capital had been spent over previous decades! Despite the secrecy surrounding annual returns of private firms within the UK shipbuilding industry, collective under-capitalisation was a well known fact. Nevertheless the unyielding resolve of the shareholders and families to control their perceived birthrights discouraged the institutional investment and re-capitalisation that might have transformed the declining performance of what was still a major industry.

Aversion by trade unions to invest in the private shipbuilding industry really summed up the polarised crassitude of both main elements of power. Was it therefore any wonder that UK Governments were coy to financially assist an industry whose ownership and workforce behaved with such disdain towards each other? The obvious area for savings had to be from improvements in productivity. Post-war shipbuilding made concerted efforts with regrettably scanty degrees of success towards recognition and subsequent eradication of its inherited restrictive practices, which were exacerbated by gross overmanning. The protracted, sometimes splenetic transition of replacing riveting by welding, should have been the precursor to the establishment of a steel shipbuilder trade, or at least two, three at the most, capable of performing the fundamental precepts and actions of fabrication, rather than the retention of six 'black trades', supplemented by a further array of labourers and helpers! Identified euphemistically as demarcation, the preservation of this set of trades by the Amalgamated Society of Boilermakers, which by now represented all steelwork trades, was decried as the apogee of union power. In reality it was the nadir of intransigence and crass over-valuation of very limited job parameters, from which shipbuilding would only slither into ignominious decline, thence partial oblivion, no longer to be a major industry in the UK.

Yard owners, directors and managers repeatedly advocated the establishment of such multi-skilled specialists. Concerted efforts were made to converge the job specifications of especially platers and shipwrights, but the Clyde Shipbuilders Association's collective weighting of the incremental increase worthy of such multifarious purveyors of skill, was either not enough to entice acceptance, or the impending burden of responsibility, dexterity, adaptability and improved productivity was beyond the limits of the bulk of the typical ironfighter. Demarcation continued to be a barbed bane yoked to shipbuilding throughout the industry's term as a sizeable employer of labour. Only very infrequently did such disputes surface between specific trades functions, but occurred with depressing regularity between lesser skilled operations, where the interface between jobs was a lamentable identification of gross overmanning, rather than any case for trade union preservation or capricious arbitration. The 'industrial aristocracy' practised between specific crafts, mooted quite inflexibly by loquacious ill-disposed stewards and delegates, soon became perceived as 'industrial antiquity' by other workers in the shipbuilding industry, who were aware that this muscle-flexing posturing was more akin to the actions of fifth columnist supporters of overseas shipbuilding, rather than purported advocates of the indigenous industry. This immutable attitude towards change was a trait steeped in Clydesiders over many generations, and no doubt rooted in the historic distrust with which many workers held nefarious shipyard managements.

The social fluctuations taking place throughout the UK since 1945 required synchronous adaptability from industry, immediately or not too long after the need for such changes had been identified. That such conciliation could not have been achieved with amiable concordance is a regrettable indictment of the cultural impasse, and lack of industrial empathy that transcended management and men.

Inflexible labour forces, selectively oblivious to market inroads being achieved by foreign 'state-of-the-art' shipbuilding competitors, initially assumed perplexed bemusement that anybody other than 'Capable Clydesiders' could build good ships! Not only could these foreigners build vessels purportedly as good as the Scots, but they could design bigger, faster, cheaper bulk carriers and oil tankers which were now accounting for three quarters of the world's market in new merchant shipbuilding orders, with payments for such ships able to be deferred over longer periods at competitive interest rates. This meant ship-owners could order on 'tick', using the profits from voyages to pay off the cost of their new ships, a tactic which greatly stimulated the market domination of shipbuilding by Japan. 'Unfair subsidies!' bellowed the first really concomitant utterances from workers and directors alike. It was no use wailing consonant rhetoric about this new world order of clandestine assistance from supportive overseas governments, they realised the real multi-functional economic value of a buoyant cohesive shipbuilding industry. If the UK industry was not going to respond to this challenge, by enticing ship-owner customers to order in Britain, then shipbuilding would simply wither and rot as a core industry. The considerable multi-economic value of volume shipbuilding was never truly comprehended by post-war British Governments, who were always convinced that most of the industry's problems were either self-perpetuated or self-inflicted.

Unfair competition in the form of subsidies et al., was always closely guarded by foreign shipbuilders, and, for reasons of commercial confidentiality, was neither admitted, denied or divulged. Suffice to say that Japanese, Scandinavian and Western European shipyards had been totally rebuilt since 1945 with invisible fiscal assistance from their respective governments. The main competition identified by these renovated overseas shipbuilders, was the UK, and in particular the 24 shipyards then trading on the River Clyde, at that time world market leader, but which despite its enviable record of unique design and quality, was wallowing in a time warp of antiquated industrialism, riven by class-structured dogma. Collectively full of self-effusive sympathy for its largely congenital state of industrial torpidity, Clyde shipbuilding was ripe to be consigned to the historical statistic books.

Instead of meeting this competition head on, enfeebling contraction enveloped UK shipbuilding. Between 1962 and 1965, nine shipyards and six marine engine works closed, or had their orders and capacities absorbed by takeovers or parent group rationalisation. In three years, capacity had been reduced by about 30% and a total of nearly 10,000 workers lost their jobs. Thus was set in train the initial stage in the reduction of volume shipbuilding on the River Clyde, concurrent with closures of shipyards at Blyth and Hartlepool on the east coast of England. The Conservative Government of the early 1960's showed no more than a perfunctory awareness to the incursions now being made by overseas shipbuilders into what had been considered Britain's established share of the world market. Even less national resistance was offered to the unfeigned contraction of the industry now gathering considerable momentum.

Euphemistically identified as 'minor reductions in available capacity', these were the first tenets of undervaluation of shipbuilding, asseverated by indifferent politicians implicitly more supportive towards free-market competition guilefully underwritten by overseas governments, than affirmative direction, coupled with financial assistance to the UK companies who still had the will, infrastructure, customer confidence and future workload necessary to ensure a reasonable share of the new shipbuilding markets.

A change of government in 1964 with a rubicund hue of political persuasion, was to set in train a more supportive, if somewhat detached and leaderless, role in the next phase of Clyde shipbuilding decline. When the Fairfield SB & Eng Co Ltd announced impending liquidation in December 1965, there emerged a series of events that would further reshape the fast contracting Clyde shipbuilding and marine engineering industries. Spurred on by vociferous public outcry, the then Labour administration emotively reacted to redress the seemingly unjust plight of continuing shipbuilding retrenchment. What made the impending closure of Fairfields incomprehensible and perceptively unpalatable was that this company with over 3000 employees between the shipyard and the recently merged Fairfield-Rowan marine engine works, had a full (but regrettably unprofitable) order book. This situation, unlike those of six out of the seven shipyards which had closed on the Clyde in the preceding three years, because they had either run out of work, or been unable to obtain new profitable contracts, made the imminent closure of the Govan yard much more impassioned, with consequently a far higher public profile. Contraction of the UK shipbuilding industry had now gathered momentum, and the River Clyde was bearing the brunt of this reduction.

All of the old and some new political chestnuts were pulled out of the fire over Fairfields. It was a major employer in a staunch Labour constituency, and was now about to decant many thousands of workers on the dole queue. A group company, ostensibly neglected by its parent Lithgows Ltd; it was criticised as an outmoded shipbuilding and marine engine building facility where, incidentally nearly £4 million had been spent on modernisation projects since the early 1950s. Orders in hand had been taken at below break-even price to prevent closure. Nevertheless these contracts could have been declined, work would have dried up and the firm would have gone down the same ignominious road, as over a quarter of the previous yards on the river. The directors confounded this rationale, and were committed to the retention of the company and the employment of its workers ...even if it was tantamount to commercial suicide! The public outcry, the supportive Labour Government, the poor perception of 1960s shipbuilding management, the vociferous inordinate, inflexible trade union power of that era, comprised the main ingredients of a fudged compromise, along the lines of what could be afforded towards Fairfields...and not what the *whole* UK shipbuilding industry really needed.

The hybrid phoenix that was Fairfields (Glasgow) Ltd in 1966, immediately divested itself of the adjoining marine engine works which were duly closed. It then embarked on a series of superficial efforts at dismantling the trade/craft/practice/management barriers, and commercial ignorance of shipbuilding, which were as formidable in the mid 1960s as they had been previously. Partial success was achieved in creating greater worker awareness of the parlous state of their industry, however the hoped-for improvements in productivity were short-lived and failed to pass the desired benchmark for output per man-hour currently established by Austin and Pigersgill Ltd at Sunderland, the UK market leaders for volume cargo ship construction in the 1960s. The collective emotive discourse propounded by all factions during the 'Fairfield Crisis', conveniently and selectively omitted the single most significant factor that had contributed to that still esteemed company's impending demise…'gross over-capacity in the world market for new ship orders'. This situation had been created by new, or rebuilt overseas shipyards invisibly underwritten by their governments who were supportive towards burgeoning shipbuilding industries, deploying modern equipment and construction methods augmented by attractive credit facilities. This ruthless competition was intent on market domination by the systematic elimination of the established competition. Quoting attractive prices that not only accelerated demand by ship-owners for replacement tonnage, thus distorting shipping rates as well as the value of secondhand ships but also forcing cut-price suicidal tendering that would result in the annihilation of much of the established shipbuilding capability in the UK.

Concurrent with the resuscitation of Fairfields, the Labour Government was perusing the Geddes report on British shipbuilding, an industrial-intellectual-introspective analysis into why this once major industry was now in a state of woe. This document, and indeed the legislation and coercive grouping of regional shipbuilders emanating from it, was at least a decade too late to have any meaningful long-term impact and benefit to the Clyde, and the rest of the UK shipbuilding industry. Fiscal assistance with such a major assembly industry like shipbuilding was needed when the industry was initially rebutting the post-war inroads made by Japan, West Germany and Scandinavia during the 1950s. Morale in the UK shipbuilding industry was then reasonably buoyant (despite wave after wave of strikes), and customer confidence still ensured repeat orders on the strength of long-standing personal contacts between ship-owner and shipbuilder. Unfortunately the inherently polarised structure of private shipbuilding companies, and partial omnipotence wielded by national trade unions, created an ostensibly immiscible technical/commercial miscellany of scattered firms. Each was led by reasonably successful uncompromising owners, directors and managers, whose singular hegemony was complemented by their indubitable loyalty and affiliation to the Shipbuilding Employers Federation, a titular body which aimed to create stability of wage rates throughout most of the industry, but did not interfere with individual company profitability.

The decade that elapsed between the identification by essentially shipyard owners in the late 1950s of the need for some form of UK government financial assistance to combat the disguised subsidies enjoyed by overseas competitors, was a time frame of dilatory vacillation, that merely allowed the worst excesses of British industrial decay to take root, and fester within this undervalued, beleaguered industry. Wholesale resistance to any form of government subsidy for UK shipbuilding was smothered in the crass fair play ideology of a game of cricket. How could shipbuilding be assisted without helping every other manufacturing industry, bellowed the myopic ethically trussed members of the government of the day. Assistance to shipbuilding in the form of capital development grants, or interest free loans offset against achieved measured increases in productivity, coupled with phased attrition of present labour levels, would have been an investment, not only in shipbuilding but also in the myriad of supply industries who existed on the back of its well-being. Reluctance to assist shipbuilding lasted so long that it became clearly inevitable fiscal help was needed in one form or another, or the industry would vanish.

The pro-tem lifeline created by the Shipbuilding Assistance Fund, enacted by the previous Conservative administration in 1963, was a tangible effort by the government of the day at recognition of UK shipbuilding's need for an influx of new contracts via enhanced credit facilities to British ship-owners who ordered replacement tonnage from home shipyards. This stopgap at least prevented a batch of new ship orders from going overseas. It did not accelerate the modernisation of the industry. In fact it prolonged the status quo. It also set the bench mark for state indifference and incomprehension of essentially an assembly industry, whose existence and well-being affected thousands of companies large and small, many located in towns and cities with no marine association other than as subcontractors to supply shipyards and marine engine builders. The intervention fund was a short-term palliative that spread obvious benefits between ship-owners and shipbuilders alike. The former obtaining new vessels, whilst the latter received an influx of work. Meanwhile the remorseless technical and productive advancement of Japanese and European shipbuilders continued. The novel idea of using the public purse to assist shipbuilding at the same time as renovation of the British Merchant Navy surprisingly did not curry favour with subsequent UK Governments. This very sensible form of state intervention could have been used (certainly up until Britain's entry into the EEC) to streamline and modernise the British Merchant Navy, concurrently supporting the UK shipbuilding and marine engineering industries. Had the reactive politicians who sanctioned the assistance fund in 1963 been clairvoyant, ambivalent power brokers, then they could have bartered the longevity of shipbuilding via the support and remodelling of its main customer. This succour could have been bargained in the optimistic return for the abolition of the industry's dispute riven profile, pockmarked strata of craft retention and class structured management, all of which were enmeshed in an order of dated industrial isolation. Such overt subsidy seemingly stimulated the profits of ship-owners at the cut-price continuance of shipbuilders.

Alas, this mollification was quite literally only an intervention fund. Ensuing government ministers would dally with fanciful hybrid panaceas, aimed at the retention of shipbuilding, still underwritten by the public purse. This future assistance remained stupidly isolated from the industry's main customer base, the British Merchant Navy, which later embarked on extensive investment in container ships, ferries and giant oil tankers, only a handful of which were built on the River Clyde or other UK shipyards.

Implementation of the Geddes Report on British Shipbuilding was effected in Scotland, with the formation of Upper Clyde Shipbuilders Ltd in February, 1968 (although set up on St Andrews Day, 1967). It comprised the five shipbuilding companies that remained on the upper reaches of the River Clyde:

- JOHN BROWN & CO (CLYDEBANK) LTD already bereft of its adjacent marine engine works, laboriously and unprofitably trying to complete the prestigious QE2.
- YARROWS LTD, the least parlous of these five most unlikely bed fellows, whose erstwhile success, was directly proportional to the individual competitiveness displayed by its management and labour force, now directed quite specifically at a single profitable element of the shipbuilding market, high-tech warship construction.
- CHARLES CONNELL & CO LTD led by the capable descendants of the founding family, now presiding over existing contracts, whose protracted construction incurred loss of profit.
- FAIRFIELDS (GLASGOW) LTD rescued from oblivion two years earlier, the company flattered to deceive, purporting improvements in every facet of ship construction, yet still hamstrung and gainsayed by non-profitability.
- ALEXANDER STEPHEN & SONS LTD arguably the most enlightened and farsighted shipbuilding family management on the River Clyde, in possession of a comprehensive yet loss-making and diminishing order book, and nowhere near as productive as in previous years.

The consistent, diffused, depressed state of morale and mediocre productivity amongst four of the five press-ganged partners into this arranged marriage was a coincidence that prefaced a far from cohesive or long term amalgamation. The short-lived, ill-harmonious existence of this attempted rescue act, perpetrated by a charitable, yet commercially remiss Labour Government, became an opportunity wasted on the discordant altar of political idealism. The hand picked clique of executives entrusted to run UCS quickly frittered the good chance to revitalise the dwindling performance of shipbuilding on the upper reaches of the River Clyde. Despite the restrictions of limited capital, the hamstrung and fickle foibles of state ownership, the lack of industrial nous and visionary direction displayed by these mostly red brick intellectuals, were the living antithesis of the former directors and executives they had been recruited to replace. The bulk of the shipyard employees had hoped that the formation of the group would be a real endeavour to get what remained of the industry in the Glasgow area on a sound trading basis. Unfortunately, the dubious business plan of the group set about the future dismantling of volume shipbuilding, by systematically alienating some of their past clients and future life blood the ship owning customers, especially the elite, and still successful companies that comprised much of the British Merchant Navy. The new board vicariously dictated the type of low-tech, type of ship that UCS would build, in what was now a highly competitive world market with ever increasing shipbuilding capacity. The heedless contempt shown for decades of Clydeside ship design experience, then engaged on a contract basis by UK ship-owners, to create late 1960's fleet modernisation projects…became a manifestation of market adherence rather than market penetration.

Shipping companies who were household names to yard workers for many years now abandoned the River Clyde, some in very public tirades of rancour over tardy completions. Such bad publicity which was anathema to the former yard-owners, was perceived by this new breed of armchair industrials as 'sour grapes'…no thought or diktat in the UCS boardroom that 'The customer is (maybe) always right!' At least he still retains the right to order from whoever he likes. The burgeoning world markets for large passenger and vehicle ferries, very large crude carriers, products tankers and container ships were considered too volatile and competitive for the complacent leadership of UCS. Although to their credit, the poorly equipped, and under capitalised, shipyards inherited from their previous private owners, were not prepared in terms of fabrication, craneage, or production engineering facilities to implement the successful construction of these much larger and sophisticated ship types with their exorbitant penalty clauses. Yet UCS still received many invitations to tender for some of this replacement tonnage.

Not content with estranging most of the former traditional customer base, the socially enlightened junta that formed the board of directors et al., decided they would buy their way out of the inherited poor productivity legacy by consolidating and enhancing wage rates throughout the group's yards. Long overdue in substance and essence, this act of industrial philanthropy could only be endorsed if it was tied to the obvious prerequisites of increased productivity, flexibility of working practices, and some form of voluntary attrition of the labour force, necessary to combat the inherited chronic overmanning redolent of traditional shipbuilding methods. The spontaneous act of dismantling the antiquated wages totem pole became the opening gambit in a three-year industrial 'tragi-comedy', involuntarily underwritten by the British taxpayer. Performed with depressing regularity on the headlines of Scottish newspapers and television screens, the antics and actions of these 'swinging sixties sentinels' of the upper Clyde shipbuilding industry must have brought snarls of contorted contempt from the former yard owners, and ghosts of their forefathers who were watching from afar the systematic humiliation of a once great industry.

The coincidental drop off in productivity causing late delivery of new ships became regrettably synonymous with UCS. From a total of over 30 ships completed by this short-lived assemblage between 1968 and 1971, not one vessel was handed over to her owners on or ahead of its contracted delivery date! This figure for vessels completed was approximately equal to the respective outputs of the former constituent companies in a similar three-year period, however, the productivity per employee of the new group was now inferior to that of the former firms. This inconspicuous statistic was accounted for by the fact that UCS became a safety net for unfortunate souls who had recently lost their jobs in earlier shipyard closures and was seriously overmanned in each division. All contracts inherited from the previous yard-owners were well behind their construction schedules when vested to UCS Ltd, no doubt due to the uncertainty engulfing the industry at that time. This untoward start to the group's existence was a backlog from which it never recovered.

The high public profile, formerly portrayed by the previous owners and senior managers of the bygone component companies, that presaged the respective divisions of UCS, was now assumed by an inordinate collection of trade union representatives and welfare officials representing the multifarious aspects of the large labour force. Amongst a minority of moderates existed a number of Marxist/Leninist malcontents, whose pseudo-political ideological activist aphorism, 'the right to work', was a subtle misnomer that seemed to substantiate the gross over-manning of the group. Active only in the vociferous rhetorical, usually non-conciliatory sense, their amassed contribution to the synchronous decline of the erstwhile independent trading shipyards reeked of seditious collusion. The collective power base of such multiform representation was aimed at denigrating these former companies, at the same time enhancing the sponsorship of shipbuilding through legislative intervention by the Government of the day, leading to the retention of conventional labour intensive work practices. Publicly resentful of the decline in UK shipbuilding since the early 1960s, but selectively taciturn, and, deliberately oblivious to the contributory parts played by themselves in attracting 'indolent, intransigent, irascible' and other derisory sobriquets. This public defamation culminated in the oft used political euphemism 'Lame Duck' which the British press appended with apposite repletion to the upper Clyde shipbuilding industry. An unfortunate, and glibly used chide that must have made many older shipyard workers cringe with resentful embarrassment, as they recollected the many hours of physical purgatory endured during the 1940s and '50s. Their concerted physical efforts then contributed towards a profitable industry, whose previous managements dismissed regular limb testing arduous toil as no more than 'part of the job'.

The cumulative potency ascribed by the caucus of trade union officials might have been an immeasurable asset to the embryonic UCS, had it not been for the languor of its chairman and board of directors with their aversion to harness the latent energy of such impressive sway. That power base, rapidly and unequivocally acquired by the unions in UCS lacked one essential tenet that was the antithesis of this collective labour force megalomania …responsibility! From the outset of this artificial industrial espousal, trade union officials, labour force and supervision gleaned very rapidly, that this 'cauldron of chaos' which was to be the saviour of Clyde shipbuilding, was no more than an employment agency for many failed armchair managers, and a theoretical anvil for dubious political quasi-economic panaceas. Remarkably, they were recruited with impressive indiscriminate gusto from such diverse concerns as the manufature of ladies' foundation garments, motor cars and domestic appliances to that of crockery, clothing and an assortment of metal bashing concerns. The state sponsors of UCS must have thought some of them could have met their respective job specifications with their knowledge of 'big lifts', 'plates' and 'assemblies'! Alas production of ladies garments with hemispherical shapes, supported in translucent elasticated hammocks, were a wee bit different from that of bulbous bows and shaped stern frames. Steel plate stockyards and the 'outfit' content of a ferry or bulk carrier were far from akin to any other industry that happened to use similar wordspeak. It did not take the 'real' shipyard workers too long to realise that this collection of imported self-aggrandised whiz kids had very constrained capability, which was no match for the street-wise acumen and guile of the yards' stewards and delegates. Depicting less talent than the former owners, who had been discarded and overlooked, this pristine package of administration was charged to manage a subsidised melting pot for this experiment in state intervention, without the definitive mandate necessary for such industrial vision.

That any good ships were successfully completed by UCS, albeit tinged with tardy delivery, is a significant compliment and affirmation to the industry and work ethics of the constituent labour forces. It is in very little way much recognition of the nebulous hands-off attitude assumed by its senior management, or inverted power without responsibility ethos wrenched by its trade unions! The three-year existence of UCS ended in the summer of 1971 with the announcement of receivership. It was a brief epoch, during which the collective reputation of what remained of volume shipbuilding on the upper Clyde, assumed further public pummelling with vitriolic promulgations from customers, politicians and the UK media. An unmitigated failure as a trading company, set up as an employment palliative, administered on the hop, by Micawberism diktats, 'that something would turn up', its inept leadership failed abysmally to understand, let alone try to improve the methods and practices of steel shipbuilding, or enmesh themselves in some sort of partnering arrangement with their employees and customers.

The immutable power and antediluvian attitude of the unions and workforce was shown to belated effect, during the ensuing work-in campaigns that succeeded in retaining conventional, traditional shipbuilding on the upper Clyde, with the formation of another government sponsored phoenix, Govan Shipbuilders Ltd in 1972. Jack-up drilling rig construction would continue at the former Clydebank Division as a sole function under the new ownership of Marathon SB (UK) Ltd. Maybe if the energy and enthusiasm for public awareness, shown by the well intentioned trade union leadership of UCS during the high profile work-in *et al.*, had been previously directed at either assisting or, more likely, removing the sham management regime appointed by the previous government, during the brief but dreadfully unsuccessful existence of the company, then the uphill struggle for the retention of shipbuilding might have had a less protracted duration, more amicable outcome, and not so fudged a solution.

The far from coercive acrimonious affiancing of the lower Clyde shipbuilding and marine engineering interests of Scotts SB Co Ltd and Lithgows Ltd into Scott-Lithgow Ltd in 1969, was a low profile moderately successful event totally eclipsed by the shenanigans and ineptitude of the centre stage industrial theatricals, acted out up-river at UCS. The fusion of yards on the lower Clyde was bereft of the historical enmity that had produced such competitiveness between the former up-river companies, which, as it had created reasonable success in isolation, so it appointed disharmony in attempted group unison. The able, adept and totally convergent talents, traits and attributes of Scotts and Lithgows, were put initially to very good use in the non-confrontational establishment of the then most versatile and proficient shipbuilding group in Scotland, and for a few years the UK. The lower Clyde consortium identified suitable maritime markets, and duly achieved favourable outcome with vociferous public plaudits, where the up-river conglomerate had displayed heedless ineptitude, endorsed with insulting derision.

A diverse range of ship product types was pursued. It was developed to suit what the customer wanted, which could be built to specification on or ahead of time and at a reasonable profit. Not the apparently unsophisticated types chosen as the least hassle-fraught by the visionless board of the bumbling UCS. During its brief nine years existence, the Scott-Lithgow group shipyards of Cartsburn, Cartsdyke, Kingston and the Glen/East complex, plus the small ship divisions of Scott & Sons and Ferguson Brothers, regularly produced around 150,000 g.r.t. of merchant and naval shipping each year, mostly powered by engines built by either J.G. Kincaid or Scotts. This prolific output amounted to 20% of the UK shipbuilding total, and was achieved by less men than were employed at UCS, and much less than 20% of the then total British shipbuilding labour force!

The combined work force from shipyards and engine works within Scott-Lithgow Ltd, stood at around 8000. Output per man compared favourably with the best in Britain and some of the main yards in Europe. Furthermore the ability of Scott-Lithgow Ltd to design, build and engine complete vessels, made them a truly marine manufacturer, and not a selective assembler like UCS. Repeat orders from BP Tankers Ltd, Sugar Line, Geest Line, Ocean Fleets, the Royal Navy and many overseas owners, notably Jebsens of Norway and some Indian ship-owners was the ultimate attestation to the ability of Scott-Lithgow Ltd, to satisfy the international shipping market.

Without the negative impact that the industrially mutant, commercially clumsy interloper 'experts' were having, resuscitating the remnants of shipbuilding further up the Clyde, the directors and management of Scott-Lithgow comprehended their industry very well. They could also inspire and motivate their labour force. They possessed numerous personal contacts with many of the world's ship-owners. They invested in modernisation of techniques for ship design and easier methods of ship construction. The millions of pounds spent on the Kingston and Glen/East shipyards during the brief amalgamation, bore affirmation to this expenditure.

The local authority in Port Glasgow could have helped the 1970 modernisation of Glen/East shipyard by acquiring the land further south of the route of the then existing A8 road. Retention of the course of this main road until the late 1970s prevented the logical, sought after expansion profile desired by the Scott-Lithgow chairman and his directors. The narrow width of the shipyard between the river's edge and the road prevented the company from expanding further to the south. Failure with this compulsory purchase showed an unwillingness on the part of the local authority that seriously affected the shipyard's future efficiency. The innovative but expensive solution accomplished by Scott-Lithgow Ltd to the problems thus imposed by the short length of their new building berth, now straddled by the largest travelling goliath crane in the UK mainland at 225 tons capacity, was to build the 1100 ft long hulls of VLCCs in two halves...and weld them together afloat. The subsequent operation was performed very successfully, but expensively, and in a longer total construction time frame using specially constructed cofferdams, positioned at the splice, under the two halves of the tanker's hull, in which platers, caulkers and welders worked. Four such large VLCCs were built using this method. If only the local authority had had the vision, the funding and will to have realigned the A8 when Scott-Lithgow needed it – not when the public purse allowed – some four years later, maybe the shipyard might still exist today?

The group rapidly achieved industrial uniformity by enmeshing two previously individually structured companies. It also had initial success at obtaining contracts for a diverse range of ship types, subsequently completed and accepted with reasonable compliments bestowed on Scott-Lithgow Ltd by their owners. These measurable milestones of accomplishment were to be the harbingers of Scott-Lithgow's future decline. In addition to a mixed bag of merchant and naval contracts obtained during the early '70s, orders were received by Scott-Lithgow Ltd for three, later reduced to two, mono-hulled dynamically positioned self-propelled drill ships. Built to a Dutch design, the favourable completion of these two vessels, essentially very sophisticated ships, with drilling derricks and a host of computer-controlled condition monitoring equipment, was to lead to a subsequent pigeonhole area of the Scott and Lithgow practices of product flexibility, tailored to suit the customer's operating requirement.

Scott-Lithgow Ltd lasted from 1969 until 1977, the year that the then UK Labour Government nationalised nearly all UK shipyards within the amorphous behemoth called British Shipbuilders Ltd. In this short time frame, rampant inflation, then endemic throughout all manufacturing industries, dealt a far more permanently crippling blow to the financial competitiveness and future longevity of shipbuilding, than all of the internecine trades disputes that had infiltrated the industry in the 1940's and '50s. This out of control money spiral, of increased costs of labour, services and materials, tied in some cases, to ship orders contracted in U.S. dollars, exchanged against a weak inconsistent sterling, meant that the commercial sagacity and business bravado required to tender, finance and underwrite the construction of very expensive new ships, was tantamount to self-inflicted insolvency!

By the time Scott-Lithgow was coercively absorbed into BSL on 1 July 1977, the euphoric performances and pace setting trends of the early '70s had been replaced by a loss prone profile, stagnant productivity, and surprisingly meaningful competition from the third phoenix of the former Fairfield shipyard, now called Govan Shipbuilders Ltd. Extensively modernised in the early '70s after the collapse of UCS, this yard remarkably produced almost 100,000 g.r.t. of merchant shipping in one calendar year! This prolific output in 1976 had never been achieved by the largest shipyard in Glasgow before, nor is it ever likely to be equalled or surpassed!

The late 1970s was an era of transparent complacency for the bulk of the shipbuilding labour force on the River Clyde. It was also a time of fretful foreboding for the senior management who had remained loyal to the industry they had served boy and man. When the entire beleaguered British shipbuilding industry was belatedly recognised as being in need of special care and attention by fiscal intervention, it was perhaps too late to achieve any meaningful assistance and direction. Nationalisation was a retarded, guilt-ridden, knee-jerk reaction to a problem, whose solution needed to eclipse the bigotry of British two party politics. Furthermore, its injudicious creed failed to harness what little commercial dynamism was still extant within the rump of private shipbuilding companies swept into this charitable catch-all.

UK shipbuilding capacity had gradually contracted by about 40% between 1946 and the early 1970s, with token closures of various privately owned shipyards taking place, due to over-capacity or unviable trading on the rivers Tees, Tyne, Wear, Blyth and Clyde. Most of the reduction in Britain was on the River

Clyde. At the investment of British Shipbuilders Ltd, by assent of the Aircraft and Shipbuilding Industries Act of the previous year, the shipbuilding industry on the River Clyde had shrunk to a total of 10 yards and three marine engineering works, with a further three sites then engaged in the fabrication of jack-up rigs or modules for the offshore oil and gas industries. Output had shrunk to around 17 vessels aggregating 268,730 g.r.t. per annum, and employment was approximately 18,000 workers. Over fifty per cent of the West of Scotland shipbuilding and marine engineering industry had disappeared in 15 years. Yet this reduction had taken place against a worldwide increase in demand for new ship products, partly due to continued growth in world trade, but also artificially stimulated by prices quoted by emerging shipbuilding nations, whose new hardware and infrastructure had been publicly created, then surreptitiously amortised by supportive governments, notably in the Far East and mainland Europe.

In the short period it took the republic of South Korea to enter and establish a successful shipbuilding and marine engineering industry, one of the major European shipbuilding nations, Sweden, realised that the previous technical-economic void that once existed between 'West and East', was now identified as a favourable sway. Far Eastern competition was now considerably advantaged, in that they could analyse the market, assess the investment required, project the return, then manipulate and exploit an abundance of cheap labour, coupled with strong work ethics to create a viable, competitive shipbuilding industry. Sweden was the erstwhile free-world, post-war shipbuilding success. Comprising some five large companies, all with new shipyards, boasting high productivity, good designs, strong customer base, the main product range was large oil tankers and bulk carriers. From a high profit profile of the 1950s and '60s, by the mid 1970's new order intake was virtually non-existent. This prompted the country to evacuate from international shipbuilding. A conscious decision taken at the highest level, although opposed and regretted by most shipyard workers, the decision was ameliorated by that country's ability to redirect and reinvest in alternative existing industries. The retraction of Sweden from world shipbuilding weakened European involvement and effectively allowed total world domination by the Orient.

The fusty spontaneous reaction that had created the rudderless state controlled BSL was as ill-conceived and fraught with failure as any other party political palliative germinated by loud-mouthed abstruse activists craving media attention at their annual party conference. Where the once invigorative competition that existed between all of the former independent UK shipbuilders had created standards of excellence in their day, the forced grouping of the handful of remaining shipbuilding and engineering companies into a bureaucratic hotchpotch, brought about an unmanageable slough of mediocrity. The worst combination of excesses and inefficiencies of the outmoded class ridden British industrial system ably enacted Abraham Lincoln's allegorical words, 'The weakening of the strong by the attempted strengthening of the weak'.

Driven onto the statute book by innate Labour Party dogma for state ownership, supported and propelled by the T.U.C. and the Confederation of Shipbuilding and Engineering Unions, this latter-day, artificially inseminated industrial unicorn had as much chance of survival in the modern day international marketplace as a medieval knight had of driving a spaceship!

Nationalisation of industry has always been seen by the Labour Party as a panacea for the failure of private enterprise. In the short life span of British Shipbuilders Ltd, the panacea soon became a panoply of financial disasters! The function of responsible, strategic company direction was adroitly replaced with the comfortable substitution of fuggy collective administration. Attempted to be managed by vague misdirected statute rather than by coordinated motivated direction, the portents were inauspicious from the outset of the company's formation. The former shipbuilding and marine engineering company owners bought out by punitive valuations of their companies, unsuccessfully took the subsequent UK Government to the court of the European Union for greater equity of their former assets. This public experiment at rescuing the fast disappearing remnants of the British shipbuilding industry was to result in a debacle that virtually denigrated the names of all of the remaining once great Scottish and English companies. This brief venture ended up costing the UK tax payer over £2 billion in a combination of loss-making contracts, penalty liens, depreciating asset write-offs and inflated redundancy payments to previous employees.

From its inception, this hybrid, befuddled state corporation was lacking any semblance of concordant strategy, totally destitute of anything like the multi-million pound annual order book such an organisation needed to effect sound trading. Bereft of the former shipbuilding director expertise, with their extensive customer contacts, the whole framework was concocted with such political haste and lack of foresight, that within months of its establishment many of the most rabid, case-hardened socialist work force saw scant chance of any short term, let alone long-term, existence for British Shipbuilders Ltd. Charged at its inception with a political malice, to slay the spectre of nepotistic private enterprise, who had devised, developed and were now wrongly held totally responsible for the demise of shipbuilding, the new company rapidly became a reprehensible statistic for Labour Government meddling. It was not the beseeched enabler anticipated by the bulk of its employees. It failed to inspire customer confidence. The necessary influx of viable new orders never materialised. Meaningful investments in new technology, or the eradication of perpetual overmanning, all to be underwritten by the infusion of solid working capital were either oversights or omissions. Training at all levels was abrogated with transient transition. Bank rolling of underestimated, loss-making contracts was the operating norm. The company was a still born political palliative that simultaneously consigned socialist dogma to the history books, in so doing fuelled the contradictory ideology of Thatcherism.

Subsequent new order intake failed to keep even the smaller yards busy enough to cover overheads, let alone trade profitably or attempt to improve stagnant productivity. For the large Scottish yards, like Scott-Lithgow Ltd, it was the beginning of the end. During its seven year tenure within BSL, the four main shipyards that previously constituted Scott-Lithgow Ltd returned the following abysmal statistics:

- Kingston: No launches on four annual occasions
- Glen-East: No launches on four annual occasions
- Cartsburn: No launches on three annual occasions
- Cartsdyke: No launches on six annual occasions

Govan Shipbuilders Ltd fared slightly better, with a constant yet unprofitable workload. However, the former Connell yard, now called Scotstoun Marine Ltd, became one of the first casualties of whole-sale closure in Scotland, shutting entirely in 1980, despite receiving tens of millions of investment a few years earlier.

Customer confidence was at such a low ebb that an artificial shipping company was set up between the UK and Poland, whereby BSL would build a batch of vessels from coasters and crane ships to medium-sized bulk carriers, to be managed by the Poles, with 'profits' from trading returning to the UK exchequer. This iniquitous contract cost the Poles next to nothing! It cost the British tax payer over several hundred million pounds. The order flew a huge insult in the face of all of the traditional British shipping companies, who at that time were struggling to survive against low cost east European, third world, and flag of convenience operators. Here was the socialist UK Government subsidising its embryo nationalised shipbuilding industry to virtually give away vessels to overseas competition, who didn't operate under the same rules and conditions as those under the Red Ensign! This action, where British Shipbuilders Ltd failed to forge any meaningful long-term trading accord with shipbuilding's UK customer base, was public testimony to the confused ineptitude of the Government of the day, BSL management, the Civil Service and their collective, dubious commitment to UK shipbuilding and, more importantly, lack of support to the UK Merchant Navy.

The two Glasgow shipyards of Govan Shipbuilders Ltd, Fergusons at Port Glasgow and Ailsa at Troon, completed the bulk of the controversial Polish order. Internal labour strife at Swan Hunter on Tyneside ensured transfer of part of the contract to Scotland. At least on this occasion union solidarity and other desultory aphorisms were not used to further inflame the reputation of British Shipbuilders' Scottish shipyards, for even this 'give away contract' carried penalty clauses for the state corporation. Concurrent with this one-sided trading agreement, Ocean Fleets Ltd of Liverpool, one of the most respected and competent UK ship-owners, placed a multi-ship order with Polish State Shipyards.

Less than two years after the investiture of BSL, a Conservative Government was elected, prepossessing scant regard or taste for charitable industrial, or commercial ineptitude. The directors, workforce and, ultimately, the total existence of UK shipbuilding was now threatened, with the legislative realities of far from hollow tub-thumping verbosity propounded by pre-election denunciations, towards the spectre of inefficient socialism. Inculcated with the same inflexible omnipotent dogmatism (albeit of a different political hue), this new government embarked on a hostile anti-industry campaign of 'if it doesn't pay, shut it down' with immediate and astonishing effect. Intellectually denuded of the industrial benignity towards smokestack industries beheld by the previous Labour administration, this new Westminster broom cupboard, full of kerbside philosophers, and still wet with the conjectural mucous of the utterings of ideological economic quacks and other gainsaying industrial voyeurs of the '80s, adopted a savage and ruthless approach to the existence, support and longevity of two well-established industries, whose recent and former owners were in the vanguard of contributions and assistance to the British Tory party! Merchant shipping, its protection by the Royal Navy, their collective construction, continual development and replacement by a vibrant, self-analytical, self-investing, although under-capitalised shipbuilding industry, ensured Britain's position as the major trading island nation on this planet…up until the 1960's.

Propounding a deceitful diatribe of political succour to core industries and customers, the examination of balance sheets written in red ink soon contradicted any appetite for fiscal assistance. Unprovided with the nous of negotiation skills, either collectively or individually, and hamstrung with guilt that mistook inspiration and involvement for interference, the continuation of British Shipbuilders Ltd under a Tory administration would be a short-term excursion, encompassing crisis after crisis, with attrition and closure of capacity, an annual regional exercise in industrial blood-letting. Regrettably, the idiotic formation of BSL and its abject record of woeful productivity since 1977, trading with an order book of bought contracts, meant that virtually each ship completed anywhere within the Group was losing nearly as much as it cost to build, and others lost more! Clearly a state of affairs that no sponsor, be they either Tory or Labour, could expect the UK taxpayers to underwrite indefinitely!

The amazing corollary, synonymous with both UK Governments, who either meddled or inherited the plight of the shipbuilding industry in the late 1970's or early '80s, was that they both executed the wrong game plans for their perceived right reasons. Each was servile to their respective inflexible precepts in the implementation of these plans. The ineptitude of well-intentioned, yet irrational intervention by a Labour Government, was exacerbated by the iniquitous effacement of the nationalised, yet fragmented company by the later Conservative administration.

- Both governments totally undervalued the need, benefit and contribution of shipbuilding towards the total manufacturing industrial base and commercial fabric of the nation.
- Both governments totally overvalued the power base exacted by the trade unions from the labour force of shipyards and marine engine works.
- Both governments lacked the basic humility and political will to solve the problems of over capacity, under-capitalisation, sensible authoritative reductions in manning levels, impelled either by negotiation or as a precondition for fiscal support.
- Both governments failed abysmally to realise that shipbuilding was not a stand-alone labour intensive industry, which either voted for you or against you, but a vital element of the overall industrial process of a developed nation that bartered throughout the world.
- Both governments failed to identify and support the British Merchant Navy, either as an essential element of the free market trading process or, in the case of shipbuilding, the very barometer that ensures the need for ship construction.

- Both governments meddled and dabbled with underwriting of balance sheets, amortisation of loss-making contracts and manipulation of the inimical Redundancy Payments Act. All good political sport, and vote trawling pandering, paid indirectly by the tax paying populace. The active and opposition British political parties ably demonstrated their unique capacities for the substitution of industrial direction and strategy, with the dubious retention of arbitrary, inept administration. Overseen by a surfeit of civil servants, many accountants by profession, they were seemingly accountable to no-one for their abject inertia and aslant beaurocracy.
- Both governments undervalued their own judgements, as evinced by the total lack of ministerial direction exemplified by the wholesale recruitment of toadying executive management and parasitical consultants, whose consonant mediocrity made tiered selectivity virtually impossible.

The consistent infusion of senior personnel of diminished capability was vouchsafed by government intervention, irrespective of its inherent political view. The compliant civil servants entrusted to run BSL were manipulated at the behest of their political masters or replacements. The titular leadership's inability to manage the state corporation, was disappointingly consistent with the parallel collective diminution of shipbuilding output, from the Group's entire labour force, a dreadful statistic that somehow presaged the end for UK volume shipbuilding. Rather than try to retain some semblance of a shipbuilding industry in the UK, with a profuse infusion of Thatcherite whiz kids, the government of the day elected to divest itself and the nation, of its great marine industrial heritage, at arguably greater invisible hereditary costs than the horrendous spontaneous amortisation accrued by immediate closures.

The glib ill-defined categorisation of most of the above issues by detached theorists, as an invocation of abstract economic factors that culminated in the failure of volume shipbuilding on the River Clyde, is a sham attempt at replacing censure with statistics. From its inception until nationalisation, the companies who ran the industry and its entire labour force were totally aware of the basic economics of profit and loss. In fact this simple equation was the main reason why organised labour had to strive for decades to increase their wages. This was clearly exemplified in the shipbuilding industry's long term affair with 'piecework' as its preferred method of payment and major tool of cost-control. Nevertheless, the combined replacement of private ownership with public possession and the substitution of payment by results with guaranteed earnings are causes deliberately enacted by reprehensible individuals that created economic deficit as a wilful act of their gaucheness, not an arcane concocted thesis.

The predicament that enshrouded UK shipbuilding in the 1970s bode ominously for the future. A greatly reduced new order intake was no doubt affected by the impending spectre of nationalisation and whittled customer confidence to a point of pitiable indifference. Contraction or closure of some facilities in the future, an unpleasant yet nevertheless stark reality, was inevitable in a world of increasing over-capacity.

Government intervention in some shape or form was needed! Responsible, ambivalent brokership, that should have recognised the latent expertise within existing yard-owners and work forces. Enforcement of the mandatory changes necessary as a total precondition to state generated financial assistance, to compel yard-owners and trade unions to avow an unflinching commitment to a tripartite accord, whereby the treasury underwrote this investment, as a 'sine qua non' of improved performance rather than the state assuming total control of the industry through the aegis of the civil service. Failure to advocate and achieve this visionary harmony, with perhaps a sizeable investment by the Confederation of Shipbuilding and Engineering Unions, was the opportunity lost, from whence UK shipbuilding slithered into history.

Whilst the Conservative Government ultimately authorised the run-down of shipbuilding and marine engineering to a level and status akin to that of a cottage industry, they adopted a mute and resonating silence at the development, establishment and world dominance of Japan, whose position as leading ship constructor since 1956 has only latterly been challenged. This may some day be eclipsed by South Korea, who went from non-existent obscurity in 1970 to number two shipbuilder in little over a decade. Both these overseas industries were not financed and supported only by visionary industrialists or avaracious overseas investors. The leaders of these countries appreciated the comprehensive benefit to their respective nations industrial economy through the thousands of other industries that vibrant shipbuilding sustains. In the case of South Korea, that country even enlisted the help of Scott-Lithgow Ltd and J.G. Kincaid & Co Ltd, with training and familiarisation of their people in the art of conventional shipbuilding and marine engineering.

Maybe the former UK shipbuilding industry had literally had its day. Like an old prize fighter it stayed on probably too long. Denied retraining, with self-generated reorganisation and fiscal assistance when it was at its peak in the 1950's, its lifeblood was somehow allowed to drain from it as much by its own fear of progress, as its failure to address its stagnating efficiency in unit costs, measured against the yards of the then emerging shipbuilding nations. Steeped in traditional thralldom in virtually every facet of its organisation, this inflexibility was the yoke that petrified progress and became an ostensible excuse, or the reason for the attrition of shipbuilding in Britain. Exposed to the ravages of rampant inflation more so than virtually any other assembly industry, losses sustained in the '70s and '80s were not totally the result of ineptitude with poor estimates or torpid productivity. Keenly won contracts soon became vehicles for financial haemorrhaging even before many ships were launched. Overmanning, trade retention and skill perpetuation were the romantic rhetoric of Red Clydeside in the days of rivets and rigging. Their obdurate continuation by visionless trade union zealots and short-sighted, inflexible artisans was the motionless barometer of 'conservatism' that maybe contradicted the political beliefs of the workforce, but proved an easy bench-mark for foreign competition to gradually eclipse.

Thus between the formation of British Shipbuilders Ltd in 1977 and its catastrophic elimination in less than a decade, the River Clyde emerged with four shipyards, plus one former company engaged in offshore construction work, and not one major marine engine builder! Over 90% of these combined industries had vanished in a quarter of a century. A damning statistic of the ravages of competition and the wholesale failure to adapt or commit to the obvious changes necessary in the workplace.

The comparison between the discriminate contraction of the UK shipbuilding industry during the 1930s and its extensive virtual eradication in the 1980s bears some similarity to the apparently recurrent problem of 'over-capacity'. In 1930, National Shipbuilding Securities Ltd was formed by the vested interests of the main British shipbuilding companies with the banks and financiers who had capital tied up in this core industry, then withering in the torpidity of the great depression. Under the able leadership of Sir James Lithgow, NSS Ltd set about systematic reduction of UK shipbuilding output by selectively buying up, then scrapping or selling-off these surplus facilities. NSS Ltd represented the interests of the bulk of the pre-war British shipbuilding industry, with capital provided by the yard-owners and shareholders. Its formation was an obviously pro-active gesture at self-regulation of a then grossly under-utilised industry. Although the later emergence of World War II questioned the sanity of closures, followed by rapid elimination of the unfortunate shipyards, some of which had been modernised in the early 1920s. Nevertheless, by the end of the NSS Ltd pillage, British shipbuilding capacity had been reduced by about 25%, and what then remained were purportedly the fittest, ablest and most efficient companies. The labour force was reduced by about 40,000 throughout the UK from a total number of 200,000 insured employees. Thus, half a century earlier after a self-inflicted putsch of capacity reduction, shipbuilding was still a vital industry, permeated with a profusion of labour intensive crafts and practices, still latently profitable enough to buy out the competition, but not provide for the thousands of decanted workers!

What now remains of shipbuilding in the City of Glasgow, with only two companies now isolated many miles up-river, in a former port that no longer has any regular commercial shipping, effectively imposes the burden for dredging and establishment of navigation channels as a disparate cost that hopefully will not encumber the future of these shipyards. This minuscule fraction of what the industry used to be, is discerned by a few batches of cranes on the skyline that once was a forest of lattices and jibs. At least the River Clyde can still claim to be the major shipbuilding river in Britain. All of the former yards on the east coast of Scotland have closed, with their previous sites razed. The major English rivers of the Mersey, Wear and Tees are now without any shipbuilding companies, likewise East Anglia. Only the outpost of Belfast in Northern Ireland, a pair of small independent builders on the Humber, North Devon and the exclusive naval shipyards at Barrow and Southampton constitute the extant locations of the British shipbuilding industry.

Swan Hunter, once the largest shipbuilding group in Britain, cut back to two yards on the River Tyne, clings precariously to a tenuous association with ship construction and marine conversion. Sold as a going concern from the remnants of British Shipbuilders Ltd, its new owners made the 'short-term' commitment to pursue lucrative 'cold-war'-stimulated UK naval contracts with initial success in this market. However, failure to win further such work, now greatly reduced as a consequence of British military contraction, exposed the folly of these owners in discarding Swan Hunter's extensive and exemplary merchant shipbuilding capability. This action resulted in the collapse of the company in 1993. The ensuing debacle between the yard receiver, the UK Government, prospective buyers and the restrictions imposed on British shipbuilding capacity by the European Union prevented meaningful continuance or resurrection of merchant or naval shipbuilding by this once fine company. With the most impressive record for VLCC construction among mainland UK shipbuilders, the yard was well placed to build the new type of vessels now needed to support development of deep water oil and gas fields. This record was not lost on the group of Dutch offshore engineers who acquired the major part of the Wallsend site, and may one day revive Tyneside with orders for the building of these giants.

A similar act of industrial regeneration will not befall the moribund Port Glasgow sites of the former Scott-Lithgow group. Now discarded by the Trafalgar House conglomerate, this locus has been acquired by Clydeport Authority and selective non-marine development looks the most likely use of this bygone large tanker building shipyard with the best unimpeded launching facility in the British Isles. In less than four decades, shipbuilding has gone from being the 'keel' of British industry, to a peripheral activity, now so contracted, that its importance has been rendered less than strategic. This is regrettably exemplified by total membership of the European Union, fiefdom to which is illustrated with the recent completion and dependence on the Channel Tunnel as the main corridor for the future transport of high value import and export finished products.

Reliance on the shipyards of Europe or the Far East to provide whatever future merchant shipping the UK needs, clearly shows the ludicrous outcome of the recent demolition policy invoked on the British shipbuilding and marine engineering industries. The wretched surrender of shipbuilding, marine engineering and their myriad of support industries, by a combination of self-inflicted industrial atrophy and oracular political capitulation makes a despicable affirmation to the polarised indifference of the modern British industrial model. If only the *billions* squandered by the UK taxpayer had been invested more wisely between 1977, and the mid 1980s when the last rump of BSL was sold for a song, maybe a broader-based shipbuilding industry would have remained in Britain. Unfortunately most of the management and workforce with either any talent or interest, left the industry when the ineptitude, indirection and death wish of BSL, became apparent.

Even the diminished value downstream function of shipbreaking, a universal source of material and essential commercial component of burgeoning worldwide shipbuilding, has been lost to the Far East and a host of other third world nations. This industry unfortunately became a victim to the long overdue, but restrictive, safety statutes recently enacted within the UK.

Perhaps the final irony in the lamentable debacle of British Government induced eradication of volume shipbuilding and its wholesale surrender to Japan, South Korea and China, is the despicable touting of Far East conglomerates to relocate sunrise high technology manufacturing plants in former British shipbuilding and steel-making towns. Compelled to create vote-winning inward investment, the heedless bureaucrats who butchered industries with sound practical skill fulfilment, seem quite blasé to underwrite the artificial establishment of a selective number of semi-skilled opportunities, provided on the back of ruthless oriental entrepreneurs who, having denuded the UK of heavy engineering prowess, will now set about ensuring it remains at the bottom of the technology ladder.

APPENDIX

GLOSSARY OF TERMS AND ABBREVIATIONS

Compiled by the author, this selective list attempts to explain the colloquialisms, terms and abbreviations used in the narrative, photographic or matrix sections of this book. Further understanding of the more technical aspects of these descriptions, and their applications should be sought from specialised publications on these subjects.

Abbreviations

Types of marine propulsion machinery

codag.	combined diesel engine and gas turbine
codlag.	combined diesel engine, electric motors and gas turbine
cogag.	combined gas turbines (Rolls Royce Olympus and Rolls Royce Tyne)
cosag.	combined steam and gas turbine
m.	motor (diesel engine)
m.e.	motor-electric (diesel engine coupled to electric generator connected to electric motors)
m.e.p.	motor-electric paddle (diesel engine coupled to electric generator connected to electric motors geared to paddle wheels)
m.p.	motor paddle (diesel engine geared to paddle wheels)
n.p.	non-propelled
s.	steam (either geared steam turbine, or steam reciprocating machinery)
s.e.	steam electric (geared steam turbine coupled to electric generator connected to electric motors). Also known as turbo-electric
s.p.	steam paddle (steam reciprocating machinery coupled to paddle wheels)

Types of vessels

m.v.	motor ship
m.t.	motor tanker
s.s.	steam ship
s.t.	steam tanker
t.s.m.v.	twin-screw motor vessel
t.s.s.s.	twin-screw steam ship
HMS.	Her Majesty's Ship (British warships)

General

batten Wooden template used to check the final profile, shape or size of frames, plates, bulkheads, etc.

bulkhead Vertical steel stiffened watertight partition which subdivides and strengthens the hull transversely in cargo vessels and bulk carriers, or transversely and longitudinally in oil tankers.

cushy number An artificially created position of employment, that has come about as a knee jerk response to an obscure criticism of some work function, which usually substitutes activity for performance.

displacement The actual weight of the vessel, expressed by the weight of water it displaces.

d.w.t. Deadweight Tonnage. Expressed in tons, sometimes t.d.w., this measurement is the sum of all cargo, stores and bunkers, etc., that can be loaded on board a vessel to enable her to float at her maximum summer loadline.

flag of convenience Country of registration for merchant shipping that enabled ship-owners to pay low taxes and invoke lax standards of marine capability and safety.

flare Outwards slope of a vessel's hull from the water-line to the upper deck, mostly accentuated at the bow.

frames Transverse or longitudinal rolled steel section members that extend for the entire length of the ship onto which the plating was riveted or welded. Usually made from offset bulb plates (o.b.p.), a flat rolled plate with a triangular-shaped bulb at one end only. These sections replaced bulb angles which were similar in profile but with a right angle flange at the diagonally opposite end from the bulb to enable a strake of rivets to pass through.

g.r.t. Gross Registered Tonnage. Expressed in a measurement of tons per 100 cubic feet, this is the volume of the interior of the vessel including all permanently closed spaces, but excluding double bottom tanks.

hopper tanks Top and bottom triangular-shaped tanks that ran the full length of ore and bulk carriers, and assisted in keeping the centre of gravity of the cargo in the centreline plane of the vessel. The bottom (wing) tanks also helped dockside or shipboard cranes to grab discharge the bulk cargo in port, by deflecting the cargo towards the centre of the hold.

horse power (h.p.) A 'foot per second' unit of power, equal to 550 foot-pounds per second (1 h.p. is equivalent to 745.7 watts). Brake horse power indicates the power at the engine, shaft horse power indicates the power at the propeller.

howf A shelter or den, invariably constructed without yard management approval and disguised by adjacent or adjoining bona fide store, workshop or heap of material.

Isherwood tanker sections Prefabricated stiffened steel panels designed by the eminent naval architect Sir Joseph Isherwood Bt, who pioneered the design of oil tankers.

jimmy The oft iterated moniker bestowed on virtually every Clydeside manual worker, whether his christian name was James or not.

joggle and offset A method whereby plates would be 'bent in plane' for a distance of up to 150 mm at the splice end to enable the abutting plate to lie flush after riveting. Mating frames would have a whole series of joggles and offsets to follow the internal contours of plates thus set.

jumbo-ising The operation of increasing a vessel's size by lengthening, usually by the insertion of a new midship section, or removing the former forebody, and replacing this with a new longer unit.

king of the bing A local lad who aspired to managerial seniority by use of methods fair, foul or favouritism.

mackem North-east of England parlance for a denizen of the Wearside city of Sunderland.

PAMETRADA Parsons and Marine Engineering Turbine Research and Development Association. Formed after World War II by the Department of Scientific and Industrial Research, and most of the then UK marine engine building firms to concentrate on improving the design of steam turbines.

reefer A vessel whose cargo carrying space is wholly refrigerated for the transportation of perishables like fruit, meat and fish, etc.

scantlings Collective sizes of calculated plates and sections pertaining to the steelwork carcass of a vessel.

seeing-eye Clydeside colloquialism for the ability of an individual to visualise a three dimensional finished article, eg. casting, fabrication forging, etc., from 'reading' a two dimensional drawing.

sheer The rise of a ship's deck from midships to the fore and aft ends.

Sicomat A brand name of the West German firm of Messer Sicomat of Griesham, who designed, developed and manufactured accurate, reliable and productive profile steel cutting machines, whose multi-head burning nozzles were directed from one-tenth scale plastic sketches. The name Sicomat later became virtually synonymous with the process of automatic machine burning of steel.

Stülcken derrick Developed by the Hamburg firm of H.C. Stülcken in the 1950's, this device consists of two tapering masts angled outwards from a ship's upper deck, that allows the derrick mounted between them to serve the hatches both forward and aft of it. Its lifting capacity is far greater than conventional single or bipod heavy lift derricks.

supertanker Term loosely applied to the largest oil tankers of the late 1950s, early 1960s with gross registered tonnage in excess of 30,000 g.r.t.

tackity bits Heavy duty protective footwear with steel toe caps and studs in the soles. Later replaced with rubber or composite soles.

upright A vertical column structure, usually fabricated from a pair of channel sections welded or bolted together, from which horizontal brackets were attached. These brackets supported the planks of wood, or staging on which workmen stood, kneeled or lay when working on the hull of a ship under construction.

welder's screen Light weight mask of heat resistant plastic material with toughened dark glass to shield the welders' eyes from the harmful effects of searing white light created by the high temperature melting of metal during the welding process, also called a 'bucket'.

yuppy Young upward professional poseur type of the Thatcher ideaology invariably bereft of the combined commercial/practical pragmatism of yore, and myopically imbued with cupid self-centredness.

Abbreviations used in list of ships tables in Chapter 6

Boom DV	=	Boom Defence Vessel
Bucket D	=	Bucket Dredger
Buoy/LT	=	Buoy/Light Tender
Cargo/B	=	Cargo/Bulk Carrier
Cont Ship	=	Container Ship
Crane Pnt	=	Crane Pontoon
Crane/SB	=	Crane/Salvage Barge
Cutter SD	=	Cutter Suction Dredger
Dipper D	=	Dipper Dredger
Diving Sup V	=	Diving Support Vessel
Drag SHD	=	Drag Suction Hopper Dredger
Drilling B	=	Drilling Barge
DP Drilling Ship	=	Dynamically Positioned Drilling Ship
Expt Trials V	=	Experimental Trials Vessel
Fish Pr V	=	Fishery Protection Vessel
Fish Res V	=	Fishery Research Vessel
Fishing Ves	=	Fishing Vessel
Fl Crane	=	Floating Crane
Gold D	=	Gold Dredger
Grab D	=	Grab Dredger
Grab HD	=	Grab Hopper Dredger
Grab HV	=	Grab Hopper Vessel
Grab SHD	=	Grab Suction Hopper Dredger
H Barge	=	Hopper Barge
Hopper/SD	=	Hopper/Suction Dredger
In Mine	=	Inshore Minesweeper
J Drill Rig	=	Jack-up Drill Rig
LPG Tanker	=	Liquid Petroleum Gas Tanker
L Tender	=	Lighthouse Tender
Ore/Oil C	=	Ore/Oil Carrier
OS	=	Open Screw
Ref/C/P	=	Ref/Cargo/Pass.
Res Vessel	=	Research Vessel
RFA Replen V	=	RFA Replenishment Vessel
Sand SD	=	Sand Suction Dredger
SD	=	Shallow Draft
SD Boat	=	Seaward Defence Boat
Sludge Car	=	Sludge Carrier
Stern FT	=	Stern Factory Trawler
S Trawler	=	Stern Trawler
Suction D	=	Suction Dredger
Suction HD	=	Suction Hopper Dredger
Sup Boat	=	Supply Boat
TS	=	Tunnel Screw
U/Wat Res V	=	Under Water Research Vessel
Whale Cat	=	Whale Catcher
Wreck-LL	=	Wreck-Lifting Lighter

National registration of Clyde-built vessels, 1946–1987

This page illustrates selective national statistical information about post-war River Clyde shipbuilding. The relatively poor overall export profile of the industry is almost totally a result of the size and power of the British merchant and Royal navies, who were between them the shipyards' biggest customers. The combined total of both of these groups accounted for **64%** of all vessels built on the Clyde during the period from 1946 until 1987, which equated to **36%** for export.

Of the 1901 craft built on the River between 1946 and 1987, the main categories of national ownership, depicting total numbers of greater than **10** are tabulated below. Even this table is distorted to provide the above export ratio. Most of the Commonwealth registered vessels were in fact owned by UK groups, likewise were some of the ships registered in Liberia and Panama. Norway was the biggest true export market, taking 6% of the vessels built in the above period. This statistic translated to 10% of g.r.t. indicating that all the Norwegian ordered vessels were relatively large.

COUNTRY OF REGISTRATION	NO. OF VESSELS BUILT ON CLYDE	TYPES OF CRAFT
Britain	1074	Cargo, passenger, ferry, oil tanker, ore/bulk carrier, dredger, tug and other craft
Britain (Royal Navy)	133	Warship, submarine, oil tanker, dredger, tug and other craft
Norway	113	Cargo, oil tanker, ore/bulk carrier, dredger and other craft
Burma	47	Dredger, tug & other craft
India	42	Warship, cargo, passenger, oil tanker, bulk carrier, dredger and other craft
Nigeria	38	Dredger, tug and other craft
Sudan	35	Tug and other craft
New Zealand	31	Warship, cargo, ferry, oil tanker, dredger, tug and other craft
Liberia	26	Cargo, passenger, oil tanker, bulk carrier and other craft
South Africa	25	Warship, cargo, dredger, tug and other craft
Mexico	24	Warship, dredger and other craft
Australia	20	Warship, submarine, cargo, ferry, dredger and other craft
Kuwait	19	Cargo
Canada	18	Cargo, ferry and bulk carrier (great laker)
Poland	17	Bulk carrier
Kenya	15	Ferry, tug and dredger
Panama	14	Oil tanker & other craft
France	14	Cargo, oil tanker, dredger and other craft
Brazil	11	Oil tanker and dredger
Eire	11	Cargo, oil tanker, bulk carrier and other craft
Greece	11	Cargo, oil tanker and bulk carrier
Hong Kong	11	Cargo, ferry, bulk carrier and oil tanker
Turkey	11	Ferry
Venezuela	11	Oil tanker, tug and other craft
Bahamas	11	Other craft
United States of America	10	Tug and other craft
Other nations	109	Cargo, passenger, ferry, oil tanker, bulk carrier, dredger, tug, warship, submarine & other craft
Total	**1901**	

Annual output of ships launched from River Clyde shipyards between 1946–1987

YEAR	TOTAL GROSS REGISTERED TONNAGE*	SHIP TYPES								TOTAL NO. VESSELS LAUNCHED
		CARGO/ REF CARGO	PASSENGER LINER	FERRY	OIL/GAS TANKER	ORE/BULK CARRIER	DREDGER	WARSHIP/ SUBMARINE	OTHER CRAFT & RIGS	
1946	349393	46	1	3	10	0	8	2	34	104
1947	372428	53	2	9	1	0	6	1	14	86
1948	354070	36	2	10	11	0	10	1	13	83
1949	434074	42	2	8	17	0	9	1	20	99
1950	447605	39	2	4	15	0	5	3	27	95
1951	426917	18	1	6	23	1	5	3	19	76
1952	447024	30	1	5	19	3	5	1	17	81
1953	402351	20	3	5	21	1	5	2	20	77
1954	480315	29	2	3	19	2	5	7	23	90
1955	480419	27	5	5	15	2	3	6	23	86
1956	422742	41	1	3	7	4	2	1	20	79
1957	379367	29	0	4	7	7	4	4	15	70
1958	414918	32	0	2	13	4	3	2	22	78
1959	397761	27	0	4	13	2	1	6	14	67
1960	415188	19	0	5	13	4	3	4	13	61
1961	342538	17	1	11	5	5	10	4	6	59
1962	396966	23	0	1	4	8	3	6	11	56
1963	257427	19	0	1	2	1	4	2	9	38
1964	368220	9	0	3	5	6	4	4	6	37
1965	330513	10	1	2	3	6	7	1	6	36
1966	298761	12	0	1	2	5	5	2	9	36
1967	383205	8	1	0	0	8	2	5	10	34
1968	187720	3	0	1	1	8	0	2	10	25
1969	297408	2	0	2	1	11	4	1	5	26
1970	304948	4	1	1	1	11	2	2	4	26
1971	292280	7	0	1	1	8	2	2	6	27
1972	236603	6	0	3	2	7	3	3	3	27
1973	363650	0	0	4	5	8	2	2	5	26
1974	170600	5	0	2	0	3	1	11	4	26
1975	325885	3	0	2	2	4	0	14	10	35
1976	360591	3	0	2	2	7	1	3	10	28
1977	268730	10	0	1	1	1	0	1	2	16
1978	125642	5	0	2	1	5	0	1	7	21
1979	106582	2	0	1	0	12	0	0	7	22
1980	46323	1	0	0	0	1	2	1	2	7
1981	92121	0	0	0	1	2	0	1	5	9
1982	186762	0	0	1	1	3	0	1	10	16
1983	111291	0	0	1	1	4	0	1	5	12
1984	32275	0	0	0	0	1	0	1	5	7
1985	51191	0	0	1	0	3	0	1	3	8
1986	36822	0	0	1	0	0	0	2	3	6
1987	24436	0	0	1	0	0	0	1	1	3
Total	**12224062**	**637**	**26**	**122**	**245**	**168**	**126**	**119**	**458**	**1901**

*These totals include all naval craft constructed whose weight is registered as tons displacement.

League table depicting greatest annual individual output from the top four River Clyde shipyards, 1946–87

YEAR	COMPANY	NO. SHIPS	G.R.T.
1946	Lithgows	10	58940
	John Brown	4	40210
	Chas Connell	5	33359
	Alexr Stephen	4	30591
1947	John Brown	5	74969
	Lithgows	9	54313
	Harland & Wolff	4	39244
	Chas Connell	4	27566
1948	Lithgows	8	51703
	Alexr Stephen	5	38904
	Blythswood	4	30854
	Barclay Curle	4	30478
1949	Lithgows	11	82952
	John Brown	5	65434
	Blythswood	4	33486
	Wm Hamilton	4	32989
1950	Lithgows	9	70883
	John Brown	6	60116 *
	Scotts SB	4	41653
	Wm Hamilton	4	34614
1951	Lithgows	7	68279
	John Brown	6	54344
	Fairfield	4	44843
	Wm Hamilton	4	38675
1952	Lithgows	10	90935
	John Brown	5	66287
	Barclay Curle	4	41835
	Fairfield	3	40053
1953	Lithgows	5	58682
	John Brown	3	46369 *
	Fairfield	3	34142
	Scotts SB	3	34139
1954	John Brown	4	77134
	Lithgows	7	73616
	Fairfield	4	55390
	Wm Hamilton	5	35253
1955	John Brown	6	81838 *
	Lithgows	7	74965
	Fairfield	3	48272 *
	Blythswood	3	42921
1956	John Brown	6	71419
	Lithgows	7	59817
	Fairfield	2	39214
	Blythswood	3	35465
1957	John Brown	5	62050 *
	Lithgows	7	61716
	Fairfield	3	45949
	Blythswood	3	31345
1958	John Brown	3	67950
	Lithgows	8	62428
	Scotts SB	3	32744
	Chas Connell	3	30911
1959	Lithgows	6	56707
	John Brown	3	41976 *
	Fairfield	3	37862 *
	Scotts SB	4	37151 *
1960	John Brown	2	63582
	Alexr. Stephen	5	43592 *
	Harland & Wolff	4	43167
	Lithgows	4	40877

YEAR	COMPANY	NO. SHIPS	G.R.T.
1961	Lithgows	6	67371
	John Brown	3	48235 *
	Harland & Wolff	3	29008
	Greenock Dockyard	3	28058
1962	Lithgows	6	63596
	Fairfield	3	56123
	Alexr. Stephen	4	47979 *
	John Brown	3	44718 *
1963	Lithgows	5	66156
	John Brown	2	51867
	Chas Connell	3	31498
	Barclay Curle	2	17819
1964	Lithgows	4	104540
	Fairfield	4	55013 *
	Barclay Curle	1	38996
	Scotts SB	3	38844 *
1965	Lithgows	5	96906
	John Brown	4	71897
	Fairfield	3	53233
	Chas Connell	2	33591
1966	Lithgows	4	74738
	Chas. Connell	2	39008
	Fairfield	1	38288
	Scotts SB	3	32098 *
1967	Lithgows	4	111326
	John Brown	2	69481
	Fairfield	3	60247 *
	Alexr Stephen	5	36193 *
1968	Lithgows	4	51106
	UCS Scotstoun [1]	2	29751
	Scotts SB	3	28231 *
	UCS Govan [2]	3	23390 *
1969	Lithgows	4	106816
	UCS Govan [2]	4	62668
	UCS Clydebank [3]	3	40849
	Scotts SB	2	35483
1970	Lithgows	3	100206
	UCS Govan [2]	3	46823
	UCS Clydebank [3]	3	40610
	Scotts SB	3	38936
1971	Lithgows	3	100752
	UCS Govan [2]	5	75768
	UCS Clydebank [3]	4	40474
	Scotts SB	2	29951
1972	Lithgows	3	68715
	UCS Govan [2]	4	55091
	Scotts SB	3	32690 *
	UCS Scotstoun [1]	2	28689
1973	Lithgows	2	154242
	Govan Sbdrs [4]	5	83264
	Scotstoun Marine [5]	2	33430
	Scotts Cartsdyke [6]	2	33315
1974	Govan SBDRS [4]	4	63679
	Lithgows	1	42141
	Scotstoun Marine [5]	2	27079
	Scotts Cartsdyke [6]	1	17779
1975	Lithgows	2	180792
	Govan Sbdrs [4]	5	82126
	Scotts Cartsdyke [6]	1	20416
	Marathon SB [7]	3	12017

YEAR	COMPANY	NO. SHIPS	G.R.T.
1976	Lithgows	2	168380
	Govan Sbdrs [4]	6	98868
	Scotstoun Marine [5]	3	46419
	Scotts SB	1	16049 *
1977	Lithgows	2	135275
	Govan Sbdrs [4]	5	77792
	Scotstoun Marine [5]	2	30774
	Scotts Cartsdyke [6]	1	13171
1978	Govan Sbdrs [4]	6	63161
	Scotstoun Marine [5]	3	21378
	Scotts SB	1	16053
	Lithgows	1	9015
1979	Govan Sbdrs [4]	4	35987
	Scotts SB	1	16482
	Scotts Cartsdyke [6]	1	16482
	Scotstoun Marine [5]	5	14973
1980	Scotts S.B.	1	16482
	Govan Sbdrs [4]	1	6421
	UIE SB [8]	1	4426
	Yarrows	1	4100
1981	Govan Sbdrs [4]	2	54829
	Lithgows	1	11019
	UIE SB[8]	2	8852
	Scotts SB	1	6907 *
1982	Govan Sbdrs [4]	3	95464
	Lithgows	2	69206
	UIE SB [8]	2	12183
	Yarrows	2	4815 *
1983	Govan Sbdrs [4]	4	90599
	Scotts SB	1	9086
	Yarrows	2	4815 *
	Ferguson	3	4260
1984	Govan Sbdrs [4]	1	25956
	Yarrows	1	4200 *
	Ailsa	3	1086
	Ferguson	2	1033
1985	Govan Sbdrs [4]	3	43902
	Yarrows	1	4200 *
	Ferguson	2	2002
	Ailsa	2	1087
1986	Govan Sbdrs [4]	1	16793
	UIE SB [9]	1	12460
	Yarrows	1	4200 *
	Ailsa	2	2137
1987	Lithgows	1	15517
	Ferguson	1	4719
	Yarrows	1	4200 *
	–	–	–

* This figure includes displacement tons
[1] UCS Scotstoun (ex Chas. Connell)
[2] UCS Govan (ex Fairfield)
[3] UCS Clydebank (ex John Brown)
[4] Govan Sbdrs (ex Fairfield and UCS Govan)
[5] Scotstoun Marine (ex Chas Connell and UCS Scotstoun)
[6] Scotts Cartsdyke (ex Greenock Dockyard)
[7] Marathon SB (ex John Brown and UCS Clydebank)
[8] UIE SB (ex John Brown, Marathon SB and UCS Clydebank)

Table of major merchant ship-owning customers of the River Clyde shipbuilding industry, 1946–87

NATIONALITY	NO. SHIPS	TYPES	SHIPBUILDERS	
■ P & O GROUP				
comprising...				
BRITISH INDIA STEAM NAV CO LTD				
British	34	Passenger	WM. DENNY	(4)
		Troop-ship	BARCLAY CURLE	(19)
		Ref/Cargo	HARLAND & WOLFF	(5)
		Oil Tanker	ALEXR STEPHEN	(2)
		Cargo	SCOTTS SB	(4)
FEDERAL STEAM NAV CO LTD				
British	17	Ref/Cargo/Pass	JOHN BROWN	(9)
		Oil Tanker	ALEXR STEPHEN	(7)
		Ref/Cargo	LITHGOWS	(1)
UNION SS CO OF NEW ZEALAND LTD.				
New Zealand	16	Ref/Cargo/Pass	WM DENNY	(1)
		Ferry	FAIRFIELD SB	(1)
		Ref/Cargo	ALEXR STEPHEN	(14)
NEW ZEALAND SHIPPING CO LTD				
British	11	Passenger	JOHN BROWN	(8)
		Ref/Cargo	CHAS CONNELL	(1)
		Cargo	ALEXR STEPHEN	(2)
JAMES NOURSE LTD				
British	10	Cargo	CHAS CONNELL	(10)
		Oil Tanker		
HAIN SS COY LTD.				
British	9	Cargo	BARCLAY CURLE	(1)
			WM HAMILTON	(8)

P & O STEAM NAV CO LTD, ASIATIC STEAM NAV CO LTD, COAST LINES LTD, GENERAL STEAM NAV COY LTD, MOSS HUTCHISON LINE LTD, AND OTHER P & O ASSOC^D COYS

British	58	Cargo	WM. DENNY	(4)
New Zealand		Passenger	SCOTT & SONS	(2)
		Ref/Cargo	JOHN BROWN	(5)
		Oil Tanker	BARCLAY CURLE	(5)
		Ferry	A. & J. INGLIS	(1)
		Cargo (coaster)	HARLAND & WOLFF	(1)
		Bulk Carrier	FAIRFIELD SB	(2)
			ALEXR STEPHEN	(7)
			JAS LAMONT	(1)
			WM HAMILTON	(1)
			LITHGOWS	(10)
			GEO BROWN	(5)
			ADROSSAN DOCKYARD	(10)
			AILSA SB	(4)

P & O Total g.r.t. = 1,258,781 (155 ships)

■ BP TANKER CO LTD				
British		Oil Tanker	JOHN BROWN	(10)
Danish		ESV	BLYTHSWOOD SB	(6)
		Drill Rig	HARLAND & WOLFF	(12)
		(excluding	FAIRFIELD SB	(5)
		Tugs)	ALEXR STEPHEN	(3)
			WM HAMILTON	(2)
			LITHGOWS	(16)
			SCOTTS SB (CARTSDYKE)	(1)
			SCOTTS SB (CARTSBURN)	(5)

BP Total g.r.t. = 962,743 (60 ships)

■ BRITISH & COMMONWEALTH GROUP				
comprising...				
CLAN LINE STEAMERS LTD				
British	36	Cargo	JOHN BROWN	(4)
		Ref/Cargo	GREENOCK DOCKYARD	(32)

NATIONALITY	NO. SHIPS	TYPES	SHIPBUILDERS	
British & Commonwealth Group *(cont.)*				
SCOTTISH SHIRE LINE LTD				
British	2	Ref/Cargo	GREENOCK DOCKYARD	(2)
SCOTTISH TANKER CO LTD				
British	2	Oil Tanker	JOHN BROWN	(1)
			GREENOCK DOCKYARD	(1)
UNION-CASTLE MAIL SS COY LTD				
British	3	Passenger	JOHN BROWN	(1)
		Ref/Cargo/Pass	GREENOCK DOCKYARD	(2)
BOWATER SS COY LTD				
British	6	Cargo	WM DENNY	(6)
SAFMARINE LTD				
South African	4	Cargo	FAIRFIELD SB	(1)
		Ref/Cargo	GREENOCK DOCKYARD	(3)

B & C Total g.r.t. = 549,158 (53 ships)

■ OCEAN FLEET GROUP				
comprising...				
PADDY HENDERSON & CO				
British	19	Cargo	WM. DENNY	(3)
			LITHGOWS	(16)
ELDER DEMPSTER LINES LTD				
British	21	Passenger	ALEXR STEPHEN	(2)
		Ref/Cargo	JAS LAMONT	(1)
		Cargo	WM HAMILTON	(1)
			LITHGOWS	(5)
			SCOTTS SB	(12)
BLUE FUNNEL LINE LTD.				
British	7	Ref/Cargo/Pass	JOHN BROWN	(1)
		Ref/Cargo	SCOTTS SB (CARTSBURN)	(5)
		Cargo	SCOTTS SB (CARTSDYKE)	(1)
GLEN LINE LTD.				
British	3	Ref/Cargo	JOHN BROWN	(1)
			FAIRFIELD SB	(2)

Ocean Total g.r.t. = 371,823 (50 ships)

■ FURNESS WITHY GROUP				
comprising...				
FURNESS WITHY & CO LTD.				
British	8	Ref/Cargo	BLYTHSWOOD SB	(3)
		Ore Carrier	HARLAND & WOLFF	(3)
		Bulk Carrier	GOVAN SBDRS	(2)
ROYAL MAIL LINES LTD				
British	7	Ref/Cargo	HARLAND & WOLFF	(6)
		Cargo	LITHGOWS	(1)
PACIFIC STEAM NAV COY				
British	7	Cargo	WM. DENNY	(1)
		Ref/Cargo	LITHGOWS	(2)
			GREENOCK DOCKYARD	(4)
MANCHESTER LINERS LTD.				
British	2	Cargo	BLYTHSWOOD SB	(2)
SHAW SAVILL & ALBION CO LTD				
British	7	Cargo	HARLAND & WOLFF	(1)
		Container	FAIRFIELD SB	(2)
		Ref/Cargo	ALEXR STEPHEN	(4)
HOULDER BROS & CO LTD				
British	3	Oil Tanker	LITHGOWS	(1)
		Cargo	GREENOCK DOCKYARD	(2)

Furness Withy Total g.r.t. = 379,022 (34 ships)

NATIONALITY	NO. SHIPS	TYPES	SHIPBUILDERS	

■ CUNARD LINE GROUP
comprising...

CUNARD SS COY LTD.

British	12	Passenger	JOHN BROWN	(7)
		Ref/Cargo	WM HAMILTON	(5)

THOS & JNO, BROCKLEBANK LTD.

British	15	Cargo	WM HAMILTON	(13)
		Ref/Cargo	ALEXR STEPHEN	(2)

PORT LINE LTD

British	5	Ref/Cargo	JOHN BROWN	(1)
			BARCLAY CURLE	(1)
			HARLAND & WOLFF	(1)
			ALEXR STEPHEN	(2)

Cunard Total g.r.t. = 402,130 (32 ships)

■ J. & J. DENHOLM LTD & ASSOCIATES
including CHAS CONNELL & CO LTD

British	37	Cargo	CHAS. CONNELL	(18)
		Ore Carrier	LITHGOWS	(17)
		Ref/Cargo	UCS (CLYDEBANK)	(2)
		Oil Tanker		
		Bulk Carrier		

Denholm Total g.r.t. = 807,358 (37 ships)

■ BRITISH RAILWAYS BOARD

British	38	Ferry	WM DENNY	(15)
		Cargo (coaster)	JOHN BROWN	(5)
		Cargo	YARROWS	(1)
		(container)	A. & J. INGLIS	(4)
		Train Ferry	ALEXR STEPHEN	(1)
			JAS LAMONT	(2)
			ADROSSAN DOCKYARD	(1)
			AILSA SB	(9)

BR Board Total g.r.t. = 73,344 (38 ships)

■ ELLERMAN LINES LTD

British	23	Cargo	WM. DENNY	(5)
		Ref/Cargo	JOHN BROWN	(2)
		Ref/Cargo/Pass	UCS (SCOTSTOUN)	(1)
			BARCLAY CURLE	(5)
			ALEXR. STEPHEN	(5)
			AILSA SB	(5)

Ellerman Total g.r.t. = 155,954 (23 ships)

■ BEN LINE STEAMERS LTD

British	20	Cargo	CHAS. CONNELL	(17)
		Ref/Cargo	UCS (SCOTSTOUN)	(2)
		Drill Ship	SCOTTS SB (CARTSDYKE)	(1)

Ben Line Total g.r.t. = 212,601 20 (ships)

■ A/S KRISTIAN JEBSEN GROUP

Norwegian	24	Bulk Carrier	GOVAN SBDRS	(2)
& British		Cargo	FERGUSON BROS	(1)
		oil tanker	LITHGOWS	(15)
			SCOTTS SB (CARTSDYKE)	(4)
			SCOTTS SB (CARTSBURN)	(2)

Jebsen Group Total g.r.t. = 319,410 (24 ships)

■ KUWAIT SHIPPING CO LTD

Kuwait	19	Cargo	SCOTSTOUN MARINE	(6)
			GOVAN SBDRS	(13)

Kuwait Total g.r.t. = 295,806 (19 ships)

■ COMMON BROS LTD

British	17	Oil Tanker	BLYTHSWOOD SB	(2)
		Cargo	BARCLAY CURLE	(3)
		Ore Carrier	HARLAND & WOLFF	(3)
			LITHGOWS	(5)
			SCOTTS SB	(4)

Common Bros Total g.r.t. = 207,934 (17 ships)

■ SCOTTISH SHIP MGT. GROUP
comprising...

LYLE SHIPPING CO LTD

British	13	Cargo	WM DENNY	(2)
		Bulk Carrier	JOHN BROWN	(1)
		Ore Carrier	GOVAN SBDRS	(2)
			LITHGOWS	(8)

LAMBERT BROS LTD

British	5	Cargo	UCS (CLYDEBANK)	(1)
		Bulk Carrier	UCS (GOVAN)	(1)
			LITHGOWS	(3)

H. HOGARTH & SONS LTD.

British	3	Cargo	LITHGOWS	(1)
		Bulk Carrier	GOVAN SBDRS	(2)

Scottish Ship Mgt Total g.r.t. = 229,297 (21 ships)

■ REARDON SMITH LINE LTD

British		Cargo	UCS (CLYDEBANK)	(1)
		Bulk Carrier	FAIRFIELD SB	(4)
			UCS (GOVAN)	(8)

Reardon Smith Total g.r.t. = 230,540 (13 ships)

■ SEHIR HATLARI ISLETMESI

Turkish		Ferry	WM DENNY	(2)
			FAIRFIELD SB	(9)

Sehir HI Total g.r.t. = 9,017 (11 ships)

■ SHELL TANKERS GROUP

British		Oil Tanker	BLYTHSWOOD SB	(2)
Argentinian		(excluding Tugs)	HARLAND & WOLFF	(2)
Venezuelan			FAIRFIELD SB	(2)
			LITHGOWS	(5)

Shell Group Total g.r.t. = 137,323 (11 ships)

■ SKIBS A/S ORENOR

Norwegian		Cargo	FAIRFIELD SB	(9)
		Ore/Oil Carrier		

Skibs A/S Orenor Total g.r.t. = 139,465 (9 ships)

■ TEXACO TANKERS GROUP
comprising...

REGENT PETROLEUM TANKSHIP CO LTD, CALTEX O/SEAS TANKSHIP (UK) LTD, TEXACO NORWAY A/S, TEXACO (PANAMA) INC

British		Oil Tanker	BLYTHSWOOD SB	(8)
Norwegian			SCOTTS SB	(1)
Liberian				
Panamanian				

Texaco Group Total g.r.t. = 105,812 (9 ships)

■ BLUE STAR LINE LTD

British		Ref/Cargo	JOHN BROWN	(2)
		Oil Tanker	HARLAND & WOLFF	(2)
			FAIRFIELD SB	(3)
			ALEXR STEPHEN	(1)
			WM HAMILTON	(1)

Blue Star Line Total g.r.t. = 100,503 (9 ships)

NATIONALITY	NO. SHIPS	TYPES	SHIPBUILDERS	

■ IRISH SHIPPING LTD

Eire		Bulk Carrier	FAIRFIELD SB	(2)
		Oil Tanker	GOVAN SBDRS	(4)
		Cargo (coaster)	AILSA SB	(2)

Irish Shipping Total g.r.t. = 94,644 (8 ships)

■ WILH WILHELMSEN GROUP

| Norwegian | | Ref/Cargo | CHAS CONNELL | (8) |
| | | Oil Tanker | LITHGOWS | (1) |

Wilhelmsen Total g.r.t. = 79,311 (9 ships)

■ ELDERS & FYFFES LTD

| British | | Ref/Cargo/Pass | ALEXR STEPHEN | (7) |

Elders & Fyffes Total g.r.t. = 55,646 (7 ships)

■ SUGAR LINE LTD

British		Bulk Carrier	LITHGOWS	(4)
			SCOTTS SB (CARTSDYKE)	(2)
			SCOTTS SB (CARTSBURN)	(1)

Sugar Line Total g.r.t. = 99,836 (7 ships)

■ SCINDIA STEAM NAV CO LTD

Indian		Cargo	LITHGOWS	(7)
		Ref/Cargo		
		Bulk Carrier		

Scindia Total g.r.t. = 95,005 (7 ships)

■ JOHN SWIRE & SONS LTD

British		Cargo	SCOTTS S.B.	(8)
		Ref/Cargo/Pass	A. & J. INGLIS	(1)
		Bulk Carrier		

John Swire Total g.r.t. = 61,746 (9 ships)

■ BIBBY LINE LTD

British		Ref/Cargo	FAIRFIELD SB	(6)
		Troopship		
		Cargo		

Bibby Line Total g.r.t. = 62,097 (6 ships)

■ GEEST LINE LTD

| British | | Ref/Cargo | GREENOCK DOCKYARD | (2) |
| | | | SCOTTS SB (CARTSDYKE) | (4) |

Geest Line Total g.r.t. = 39,205 (6 ships)

■ FEARNLEY & EGER A/S

| Norwegian | | Ref/Cargo | CHAS CONNELL | (4) |
| | | Oil Tanker | ALEXR STEPHEN | (1) |

Fearnley & Eger Total g.r.t. = 43,753 (5 ships)

■ THORVALD BRØVIG A/S

| Norwegian | | Oil Tanker | WM HAMILTON | (4) |
| | | Cargo | LITHGOWS | (1) |

Th. Brøvig Total g.r.t. = 48,219 (5 ships)

■ HARRISON LINE LTD

| British | | Cargo | CHAS CONNELL | (2) |
| | | Ref/Cargo | LITHGOWS | (3) |

Harrison Total g.r.t. = 36,087 (5 ships)

■ FRED OLSEN & CO

Norwegian		Passenger	U.C.S. (CLYDEBANK)	(1)
British		Oil Tanker	HARLAND & WOLFF	(2)
			LITHGOWS	(1)

Fred Olsen Total g.r.t. = 51,924 (4 ships)

■ HARRISONS (CLYDE) LTD.

British		Bulk Carrier	JOHN BROWN	(2)
			SCOTSTOUN MARINE	(1)
			GOVAN SBDRS	(3)
			SCOTTS SB	(1)

Harrisons Total g.r.t. = 127,076 (7 ships)

■ CALEDONIAN-MACBRAYNE LTD
including DAVID MACBRAYNE LTD, CALEDONIAN STEAM PACKET CO LTD

British		Ferry	WM DENNY	(2)
			JAS LAMONT	(10)
			FERGUSON-AILSA (PORT GLASGOW)	(3)
			FERGUSON-AILSA (TROON)	(6)
			ADROSSAN DOCKYARD	(1)

Cal-Mac Total g.r.t. = 16,315 (22 ships)

■ F. BOWLES & SONS LTD

| British | | Dredger | AILSA SB | (8) |

F. Bowles Total g.r.t. = 15,047 (8 ships)

■ CLYDE SHIPPING CO LTD

British		Tug	SCOTT & SONS	(1)
		Ref/Cargo	CHAS CONNELL	(1)
			A. & J. INGLIS	(3)
			JAS LAMONT	(1)
			FERGUSON BROS	(7)

Clyde Shipping Total g.r.t. = 4,427 (13 ships)

■ GEM LINE LTD

| British | | Cargo (coaster) | AILSA SB | (8) |

Gem Line Total g.r.t. = 11,475 (8 ships)

■ PANCONQUISTA CIA NAV SA and associates

| Greek | | Cargo | BLYTHSWOOD SB | (5) |
| Liberian | | Oil Tanker | | |

Panconquista Total g.r.t. = 64,357 (5 ships)

■ UNITED WHALERS (UK) LTD

| British | | Whale Catcher | A. & J. INGLIS | (13) |
| | | Oil Tanker | LITHGOWS | (2) |

United Whalers Total g.r.t. = 29,166 (15 ships)

Number of shipyards, marine engine works and approximate total of workers employed in these industries on the River Clyde between 1946 and 1987

(Source: CBI Statistical Information Office and Glasgow District Archives)

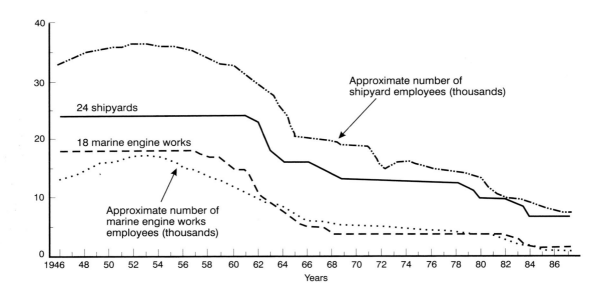

Number of ships including total gross registered tonnage launched from River Clyde shipyards between 1946 and 1987

(Source: Lloyds Register of Shipping)

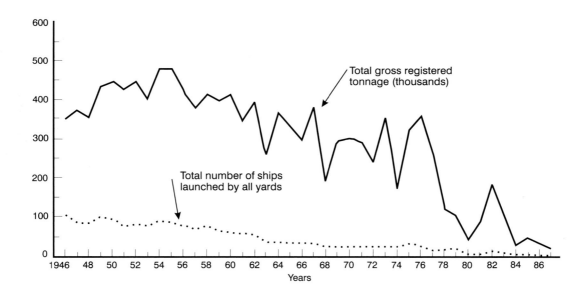

Statistics supporting employment levels and closure dates of post-war River Clyde shipbuilding and marine engineering industries

ORIGINAL NAME AND LOCATION OF SHIPBUILDING COMPANY		APPROX MAXIMUM NO OF EMPLOYEES BETWEEN 1946–1987	YEAR CLOSED
Wm. Denny & Bros Ltd, Leven Shipyard, Dumbarton		1,500	1963
Scott & Sons (Bowling) Ltd, Bowling		200	1980
John Brown & Co (Clydebank) Ltd, Clydebank	*	5,000	(O)
Yarrow & Coy Ltd, Scotstoun, Glasgow	# 5,400	2,000	(O)
Blythswood Shipbuilding Co Ltd, Scotstoun, Glasgow		1,000	1964
Chas Connell & Co Ltd, Scotstoun, Glasgow		1,000	1980
Barclay Curle & Co Ltd, Clydeholm Shipyard, Whiteinch, Glasgow	*	3,000	1967
A. & J. Inglis Ltd, Pointhouse Shipyard, Partick, Glasgow		600	1962
Harland & Wolff Ltd, Govan Shipyard, Glasgow		2,000	1963
Fairfield SB & Eng Co Ltd, Govan, Glasgow	*	4,000	(O)
Alexr. Stephen & Sons Ltd, Linthouse Shipyard, Govan, Glasgow	*	2,400	1968
Wm Simons & Co Ltd, Renfrew } Simons-Lobnitz Ltd from 1959 Lobnitz & Co Ltd, Renfrew		2,000	1963
Fleming & Ferguson Ltd, Phoenix Shipyard, Paisley		400	1969
Jas Lamont & Co Ltd, Castle Shipyard, Port Glasgow	*	400	1979
Ferguson Bros (Port Glasgow) Ltd, Newark Shipyard, Port Glasgow		700	(O)
Lithgows Ltd, East Yard, Port Glasgow		2,000	1992
Wm Hamilton & Co Ltd, Glen Yard, Port Glasgow		1,000	1963
Lithgows Ltd, Kingston Shipyard, Port Glasgow		2,000	1992
Geo Brown & Co (Marine) Ltd, Garvel Shipyard, Greenock		300	1983
Greenock Dockyard Co Ltd, Cartsdyke Shipyard, Greenock		800	1988
Scotts SB & Eng Co Ltd, Cartsburn Dockyard, Greenock	*	2,000	1988
Ardrossan Dockyard Co Ltd, Adrossan	*	700	1964
Ailsa SB & Eng Co Ltd, Troon	*	800	(O)
APPROXIMATE MAXIMUM TOTAL		**35,800**	

(O) Yard still open in 1997
*   These figures include many employed on ship repair and conversion work
#   This number was reached during the mid 1970s and has since drastically been reduced

ORIGINAL NAME AND LOCATION OF MARINE ENGINEERING COMPANY		
Wm Denny & Bros Ltd, Dumbarton Engine Works	800	1963
John Brown & Co (Clydebank) Ltd, Clydebank Engine Works	2,000	(O)
Yarrow Shipbuilders Ltd, Scotstoun Engine Works, Glasgow	800	1963
Barclay Curle & Co Ltd, North British Marine Engine Works, Whiteinch, Glasgow	1,000	1982
A. & J. Inglis Ltd, Anderston Engine Works, Glasgow	300	1958
David Rowan & Co Ltd, Finnieston Engine Works, Glasgow	1,200	1963
Harland & Wolff Ltd, Finnieston Engine Works, Glasgow	1,500	1962
† British Polar Engines Ltd, Govan, Glasgow	1,000	(O) †
Fairfield SB & Eng Co Ltd, Govan Engine Works, Glasgow (became Fairfield-Rowan Ltd after closure of David Rowan & Co Ltd)	2,000	1965
Alexr Stephen & Sons Ltd, Linthouse Engine Works, Glasgow	1,000	1982
Wm Simons & Co Ltd, Renfrew Engine Works } Simons-Lobnitz Ltd from 1959 Lobnitz & Co Ltd, Renfrew Engine Works	200 200	1962 1962
Fleming & Ferguson Ltd, Phoenix Engine Works, Paisley	200	1965
Ferguson Bros (Port Glasgow) Ltd, Newark Engine Works, Port Glasgow	200	1960
Rankin & Blackmore Ltd, Greenock Engine Works	500	1962
Scotts SB & Eng Co Ltd, Greenock Engine Works	1,000	1984
† John G. Kincaid & Co Ltd, Greenock Engine Works	2,000	(O)†
Ailsa SB & Eng Co Ltd, Troon Engine Works	400	1963
APPROXIMATE MAXIMUM TOTAL	**16,300**	

† These companies still operate in 1997, now only making spare parts

Sources: CBI Statistical Information Office, Glasgow City Archives and various former company magazines

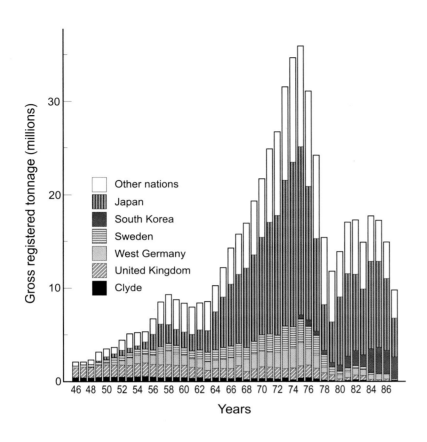

Total gross registered tonnage of ships launched by major shipbuilding nations between 1946 and 1987

1955   United Kingdom and River Clyde shipyards launch greatest post-war total of 276 ships of 1,473, 397 g.r.t.

1956   Japan becomes world's major shipbuilding nation launching 1,746, 429 g.r.t.

1963   West Germany launches greater shipbuilding total than the United Kingdom

1973   Sweden becomes world's second major shipbuilding nation launching 2,517,480 g.r.t.

1975   Japan launches 946 ships totalling 17,987,322 g.r.t.

1975   World's greatest annual total of shipping launched, 35,897,515 g.r.t.

1977   United Kingdom nationalises entire shipbuilding industry when British share of world market is less than 4%

1981   South Korea becomes world's second major shipbuilding nation

Source: Lloyds Register of Shipping

World's major merchant shipping fleets between 1948 and 1992

1948   Combined merchant fleets of the UK and USA represented 59% of the entire world total of 80,291,593 g.r.t.

1960   World total of all merchant shipping fleets was over 36,000 vessels of 129,769,500 g.r.t.

1975   UK merchant navy was over 3,600 vessels totalling 33,157,422 g.r.t.

1979   Liberian registered fleet was over 2,400 vessels totalling 81,528,175 g.r.t.

1990   UK merchant navy was less than 2,000 vessels totalling 6,716,325 g.r.t. This was about 1.5% of the world total

1990   World total of merchant shipping fleets was over 78,000 vessels of 423,627,198 g.r.t.

Source: Lloyds Register of Shipping

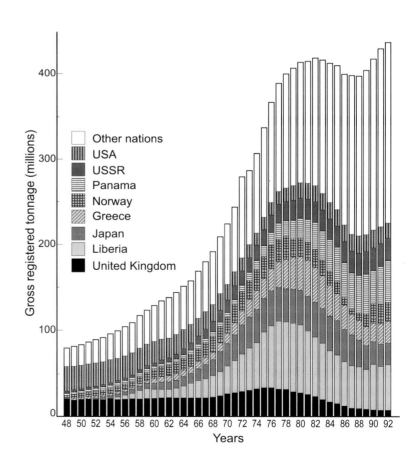

Locations of shipyards and marine engine works on River Clyde circa early 1960s

Key:
1 Wm Denny & Bros Ltd, Dumbarton Engine Works
2 Wm Denny & Bros Ltd, Leven Shipyard, Dumbarton
3 Scott & Sons Ltd, Bowling Shipyard
4 John Brown & Co (Clydebank) Ltd, Shipyard & Engine Works
5 Barclay Curle & Co Ltd, Elderslie Dry Docks
6 Yarrow & Co Ltd, Scotstoun Shipyard & Engine Works
7 Blythswood Shipbuilding Co Ltd, Scotstoun Shipyard
8 Chas Connell & Co Ltd, Scotstoun Shipyard
9 Barclay Curle & Co Ltd, North British Engine Works
10 Barclay Curle & Co Ltd, Clydeholm Shipyard
11 D. & W. Henderson Meadowside Dry Dock & Repair Quay
12 A. & J. Inglis Ltd, Pointhouse Shipyard
13 David Rowan & Co Ltd, Finnieston Engine Works
14 Harland & Wolff Ltd, Finnieston Engine Works
15 British Polar Engines Ltd, Govan Engine Works
16 Harland & Wolff Ltd, Govan Shipyard

17 Fairfield Shipbuilding & Eng Co Ltd, Govan Shipyard & Engine Works
18 Alexr Stephen & Sons Ltd, Linthouse Shipyard & Engine Works
19 Wm Simons & Co Ltd, Renfrew Shipyard & Engine Works
20 Lobnitz & Co Ltd, Renfrew Shipyard & Engine Works
21 Fleming & Ferguson Ltd, Phoenix Shipyard & Engine Works, Paisley
22 Jas Lamont & Co Ltd, Castle Shipyard, Port Glasgow
23 Ferguson Brothers Ltd, Newark Shipyard, Port Glasgow
24 Lithgows Ltd, East Shipyard, Port Glasgow
25 Wm Hamilton & Co Ltd, Glen Shipyard, Port Glasgow
26 Lithgows Ltd, Kingston Shipyard, Port Glasgow
27 Firth of Clyde Drydock Co Ltd, Inchgreen Drydock, Greenock
28 George Brown & Co (Marine) Ltd, Garvel Shipyard, Greenock
29 Greenock Dockyard Co Ltd, Cartsdyke Shipyard, Greenock
30 John G. Kincaid & Co Ltd, Greenock Engine Works
31 Scotts Shipbuilding & Eng Co Ltd, Cartsburn Shipyard, Greenock
32 Scotts Shipbuilding & Eng Co Ltd, Greenock Engine Works
33 Ardrossan Dockyard Co Ltd, Ardrossan Shipyard
34 Ailsa Shipbuilding & Eng Co Ltd, Troon Shipyard & Engine Works

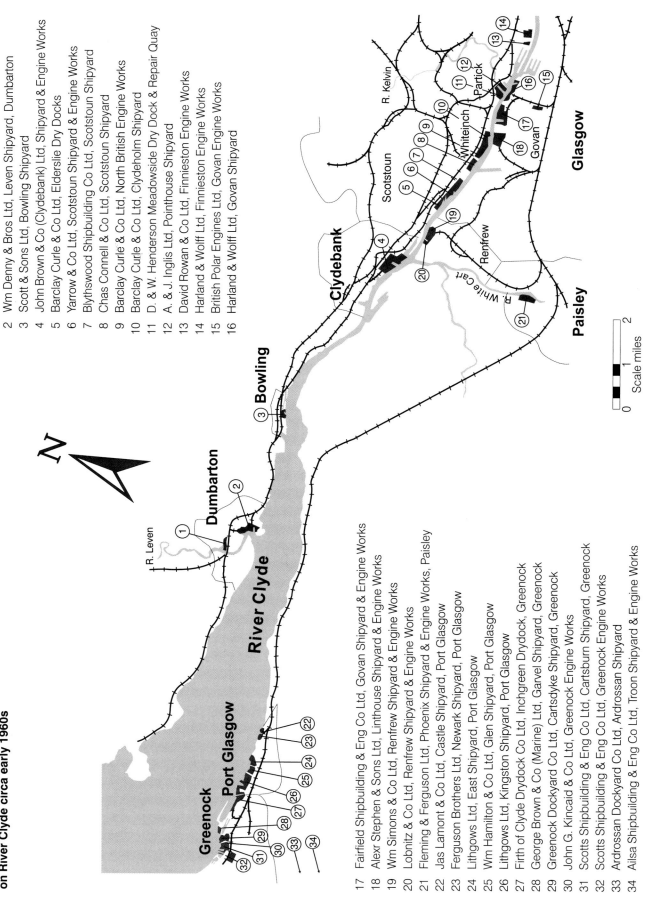

Map of the Clydeholm shipyard and North British Engine Works of Barclay Curle & Co Ltd, 1960

This map of the Clydeholm shipyard of Barclay Curle & Co Ltd is included to illustrate most of the departments of a West of Scotland shipyard. Furthermore, this company has been included because by 1960 it had just completed an extensive modernisation scheme which cost over £3 million. Whilst the facility was considered state-of-the-art in its day, the scope of renovation failed to either improve output from the firm or sustain its long-term future.

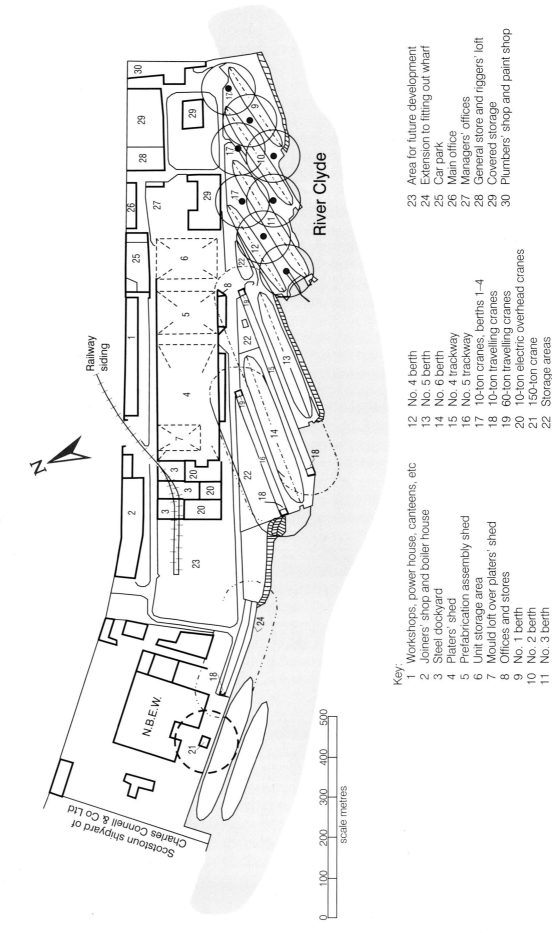

Key:
1   Workshops, power house, canteens, etc
2   Joiners' shop and boiler house
3   Steel dockyard
4   Platers' shed
5   Prefabrication assembly shed
6   Unit storage area
7   Mould loft over platers' shed
8   Offices and stores
9   No. 1 berth
10 No. 2 berth
11 No. 3 berth
12 No. 4 berth
13 No. 5 berth
14 No. 6 berth
15 No. 4 trackway
16 No. 5 trackway
17 10-ton cranes, berths 1–4
18 10-ton travelling cranes
19 60-ton travelling cranes
20 10-ton electric overhead cranes
21 150-ton crane
22 Storage areas
23 Area for future development
24 Extension to fitting out wharf
25 Car park
26 Main office
27 Managers' offices
28 General store and riggers' loft
29 Covered storage
30 Plumbers' shop and paint shop